Gender

Gender

Psychological Perspectives

Linda Brannon
McNeese State University

Allyn and Bacon
Boston • London • Toronto • Sydney • Tokyo • Singapore

Vice President and Publisher: Susan Badger
Editorial Assistant: Erika Stuart
Signing Representative: Norris Harrell
Marketing Manager: Joyce Nilsen
Editorial-Production Service: Trinity Publishers Services
Cover Administrator: Linda Knowles
Composition Buyer: Linda Cox
Manufacturing Buyer: Aloka Rathnam

Library of Congress Cataloging-in-Publication Data

Brannon, Linda, 1948–
    Gender: Psychological Perspectives / Linda Brannon.
        p.   cm.
    Includes bibliographical references and index.
    ISBN 0-205-15460-3 (pbk.)
    1. Sex differences (Psychology). 2. Gender identity. 3. Sex role.
    4. Feminist psychology. 5. Women—Psychology. I. Title.
    BF692.2.B73   1995
    155.3—dc20   95-13299
                                                              CIP

The extract at the beginning of Chapter 6 is from "Sex and Morality" (p. 20) by C. Johmann,
May 1985, *Omni*. Reprinted by permission. Copyright © 1985 Omni Publications International,
Ltd.

Printed in the United States of America
10 9 8 7 6 5 4 3 2   99 98 97 96

Contents

Preface

This book examines the topic of gender—the behaviors and attitudes that relate to (but are not entirely congruent with) biological sex. A large and growing body of research on sex, gender, and gender-related behaviors has come from psychology, sociology, biology, biochemistry, neurology, and anthropology. It is this research that I summarize and critically review to give an overall picture of gender and the behaviors and attitudes related to gender.

The Topic of Gender

A critical review of gender research is important for several reasons. First, gender is currently a "hot" topic, and almost everyone has an opinion about it. These opinions are not usually based on research—most people are not familiar with research findings. Their opinions are strongly influenced not only by their own experience but also by what they have seen in the movies and on television. Whether these programs are news reports or fictional, both types of information make an impact—people create images about how they believe women and men should be on the basis of these portrayals. In *Gender: Psychological Perspectives,* I hope to show what gender researchers have found, complete with the inevitable complexities and even contradictions.

Second, gender research has been subject to extreme biases—researchers have allowed their personal beliefs to influence their work. Although scientific research is supposed to be objective and free of personal bias, this idealistic notion often varies from the actual process of research. Scientists are people, and they carry their biases, including gender biases, with them into their research. This situation makes a critical review especially important.

Despite the bias that can enter into the research process, I believe that research is the most productive way to approach the evaluation of a topic. Others disagree with this view, including some who are interested in gender-related topics. A number of scholars, especially feminist scholars, have rejected scientific research as the best way to learn about gender.

Although I agree that science has not treated women equitably, either as researchers or as participants in research, I still believe that science offers the best chance for a fuller understanding of gender (as well as of many other topics). Some will consider my view biased, but if it is a bias, I am aware of it and want to make my point of view clear. This proscience orientation is the reason I have chosen to concentrate on research throughout the book—to examine what gender researchers have found and how they have interpreted their findings.

The book's emphasis on gender is similar to another approach to gender—the psychology of women—but the gender approach has differences as well as similarities with that approach. The psychology-of-women approach concentrates on women and issues unique to women, whereas the gender approach focuses on the issue of gender as a factor in behavior and in the social context in which behavior occurs. In doing so, gender research and theory draw heavily from the psychology of women, but the outlook differs.

Scholars who take the psychology-of-women approach believe that women have been neglected in the history of psychology research (and other fields), and I agree with them. Until the feminist movement of the 1960s and 1970s, psychology had included relatively few women as professionals and often had neglected to include women as research participants. In attempting to remedy past inequities, some researchers and theorists taking the psychology-of-women approach have gone to the opposite extreme: They have concentrated on women's view and have held that women have innate advantages over men. This view strikes me as a mistake similar to that traditional psychology has been accused of committing—taking one point of view and using it as the standard.

Although feminist scholarship can exclude men, a psychology of gender cannot. Studying both women and men is essential to an understanding of gender. Researchers who are interested in gender issues may concentrate on women or men, but they must consider both, or their research reveals nothing about gender. Therefore, *Gender: Psychological Perspectives* examines the research and theory from psychology and related fields in order to evaluate the behavior, biology, and social context in which women *and* men function.

On a personal level, my interest in gender came from two sources—my research and my experience as a female psychologist. The research that prompted me to examine gender issues more carefully was risk perception related to health problems. I was interested in investigating people's perceptions of the health risks they encountered as a result of their behavior, such as the perceptions of smokers versus nonsmokers about that behavior. In this research, I found that women and men saw their behaviors and risks in similar ways. Indeed, I failed to find gender-related differences in risk perception even for the health risks in which gender differences appear. That is, I found that men and women perceive their health risks in similar ways, even when these perceptions do not reflect the actual level of health risks for men and women. My research showed gender similarities rather than gender differences.

In examining the volume of research on gender-related behaviors, I discovered that many other researchers' findings were similar. Psychology's exploration of gender seemed to show more similarities than differences, and when differences appeared, many were small. I came to doubt the widespread belief that men and women are opposites, and to consider that this view is, at least, overstated—women and men are more similar than different. Gender-related differences exist, but the tendency to concentrate on these differences has obscured the similarities.

As a female psychologist, I was forced to attend to gender issues from the earliest part of my career. Sexism and discrimination were part of the context in which I received my professional training and in which I have pursued my career as a psychologist. Women were a small minority in the field during my early years in psychology, but the numbers have increased, and now women receive over half the doctorates in psychology. This increase and several antidiscrimination laws have produced some improvements in equitable treatment for women in psychology (as well as in other professions and in society in general).

The psychology-of-women approach came from the women in psychology during the feminist movement that began during the 1960s. Most of the women in psychology have not been directly involved in the psychology of women and some are not feminists, but the presence of a growing proportion of women has changed psychology, making a psychology of gender not only possible but, I think, inevitable.

The "Gendered Voices" Narratives

Although I believe that research is a good way to understand behavior, including gender-related behavior, I realize that some people disagree. One group of those who disagree consists of feminist scholars who believe that science is not the best way to approach the study of women—or perhaps anything—and these scholars have proposed a set of alternative methods (discussed in Chapter 2).

At a recent conference, I heard Louise Kidder (1994) speak about not only the advantages but also the dangers of such approaches. One of the drawbacks she mentioned was the vividness of the data generated by accounts of personal experience. Statistical compilations may be more representative, but people are more impressed by personal accounts. These methods of studying people do not lead to a comfortable blurring of the results; each person's account is sharp, with no averaging to blunt the edges of the story.

The text of *Gender: Psychological Perspectives* consists of an evaluation of research findings—exactly the sort of information that people may find difficult to relate to their lives. I decided that I wanted to include personal, narrative accounts of gender-relevant aspects of people's lives, and I wanted these accounts to connect to the research studies. I evaluated the perils of vividness and concluded that the drawbacks were a minor problem compared to the advantages. I believe that people's personal experiences are distilled in research, but I also know that in the process a lot of the interesting details are lost.

These stories replace some of the details lost in statistical summaries, allowing men and women to tell about their experiences. Telling these stories, separated from the text, was an alternative approach to presenting information about gender and highlighting the relevance of research findings with vivid detail. Some of the stories are funny, showing a light-hearted approach to dealing with the frustrations and annoyances of discrimination and gender bias. Some of the stories are sad, revealing experiences of sexual harassment, violence, and abuse. All of the stories are real, not fabricated as good examples. I listened to people talk about gender issues and wrote what they told me, trying to report what they said in their own words. I hope that these stories give a different perspective and add a sense of the reality of personal experience to the volume of research reported here.

Reference Notation

In presenting the research about gender, I used the notations and reference format that psychologists use, with one exception—I mention names. The standard psychology reference style omits professional titles and first names from its references, leaving authors identified by their last names in the text and by last names plus initials in the reference list. This convention omits clues that would allow readers to know the gender of the authors. Perhaps this strategy was intended to remove any basis for sexist assumptions about authorship, since an earlier format used initials for male authors but mentioned women's first names. But omitting gender-related information from the reference format may not be sufficient to eliminate gender-related bias. Having a growing suspicion that readers assume that researchers are usually men, I decided to investigate.

I presented passages taken from introductory level psychology textbooks to students and asked them to rate the passages and authors (Brannon, 1994). I varied the passages to include a variety of areas—body language, dreams, brain organization, child development, and so forth. I took these passages from psychology texts by female authors, but I believed that students would guess that some passages were more likely to have female authors than other passages, depending on the content. My predictions were based on the concept of stereotyping—that certain areas are more likely to be associated with women and others with men. My study revealed a significant difference among the evaluations of the likelihood that the passages had female authors, and the differences were stereotypical: Students rated the passages about children as more likely to have female authors than the passages about physiology.

Since all of the passages were by female authors, these evaluations reflected stereotypical thinking rather than writing style. A number of authors, especially those writing in the area of gender, have come to similar conclusions and made a similar choice in their writing. The finding from my study convinced me that I, too, should use first names to emphasize that both women and men are researchers in the areas of sex and gender. I chose to include first names, both in the text and in the reference list.

Headlines

Long before I thought of writing a book about gender, I noticed the popularity of the topic with the media. Not only are the sexes the topic of many private and public debates, but gender differences are also the topic of many newspaper, magazine, and television stories, ranging from sitcoms to scientific reporting. I had read warnings about the media's tendency to oversimplify research findings and how many reports give an incorrect impression about research. I wanted to examine the research on gender to try to understand what the research says, with all of its complexities, and to present the media version along with an analysis of the research findings.

Of particular concern to me was the tendency of the media and of people who hear about gender research to want to find a biological basis for the behavioral differences between the sexes, as though evidence of biologically based differences would be more "real" than any other type of evidence. As prominent gender researcher John Money (1987a) has discussed, the division of biological from behavioral realms is a false dichotomy. Even genes can be altered by environment, and experiences during a critical period of development can produce changes in behavior as permanent as any produced by physiology. The view that biological differences are real and permanent, whereas experience and culture produce only transient and changeable effects, is widely held yet incorrect.

Unlike several other books about gender, this book spends several chapters examining this biological evidence, because "biology has always been used as a curse against women" (Naomi Weisstein, 1982, p. 41). I wanted to take the opportunity to evaluate and present this research, believing that it is at the basis of popular assumptions about differences between the sexes. I wanted readers to examine the extent to which the curse is justified.

To this purpose I decided to use headlines from newspapers and popular magazines to highlight the issues in gender research, thinking that these popular presentations would be good examples of how findings can be presented accurately or inaccurately. Some of the headlines are examples of responsible journalism, whereas some are examples of sensational or simplified reporting.

My misgivings about the media were dramatically confirmed by a personal experience. As I was beginning to write about chromosomes, hormones, and sex differences in the brain, a student approached me, wanting to interview me for the student newspaper. She was taking a journalism class in which she had to write a story about the differences between men's and women's brains, and a friend had recommended me as a good interview source. I explained to her that the relationship between brain structures and behavior was complex and difficult to establish and that most of the research was based on rat brains rather than human brains, making generalizations tricky. She said she wanted some statistics about differences and she knew such statistics existed. When I explained that statistics on the frequency of occupations or performance differences between men and women do not necessarily reveal brain differences, she said she was not interested in knowing the truth; she just wanted information for her story!

A journalism student's disregard for the truth does not condemn all journalists, but the media sometimes give in to the urge to portray findings in sensational ways, because such stories get attention. Such sensationalism distorts research findings and perpetuates stereotypical thinking about the sexes. At more than one point, I believed that Beryl Lieff Benderly (1989), a science reporter, was correct when she warned about media sensationalism of gender research by writing the headline "Don't believe everything you read..." (p. 67).

Acknowledgments

At the completion of any book, authors have many people to thank, and I am no exception. Without the assistance, support, and encouragement of many people, I never could have completed this book. I thank all of them, but several people deserve special acknowledgment.

My colleagues in the psychology department at McNeese State University were supportive and helpful, offering their assistance and providing information and materials, but several people provided extensive assistance. Jess Feist, my co-author on *Health Psychology: An Introduction to Behavior and Health* (2nd ed.), provided advice and improved my writing on this book, too. Patrick Moreno not only read rough drafts of chapters but also acted as proofreader and librarian.

I feel that I owe a special thanks to my husband, Barry Humphfus. He did a great deal to hold my life together while I was researching and writing—he read chapters, made the computer work, and offered me his support and enthusiasm. I would not have attempted (much less completed) this book without him.

Without the assistance of the staff at McNeese's Frazar Memorial Library, I could not have managed to gather the information I needed. I would like to thank the entire faculty and staff, but especially Joanne Durand, Leslye Quinn, Judith Guzzy, Jan McFarlain, Barbara Royer, Linda Bordelon, Helen Curol, Brantley Cagle, Kenneth Awagain, and Kim Smith. Their patience and skill continue to astound me.

I would like to thank all the people who told me their personal stories for the "Gendered Voices" feature of the book. To allow them their privacy I will not name them, with one exception. Melinda Schaefer deserves special thanks, because her story was so good that hearing it made me realize that others had stories to tell. Without her story I wouldn't have realized how important these accounts are.

The people at Allyn and Bacon have been all that an author might want. Susan Badger deserves special thanks; without her I would not have thought of doing a book on gender, and her continued enthusiasm and confidence have been invaluable. Laura Ellingson has offered reassurance and inspiration in appropriate doses and with the correct timing. Norris Harrell encouraged me, telling me what a good idea it was for me to write this book for Allyn and Bacon. I think he was right.

I would also like to thank reviewers who read parts of the manuscript and offered helpful suggestions, including

Jane Fillmore
Utah Valley State College

Irene Frieze
University of Pittsburg

Grace Galliano
Kennesaw State College

Mykol Hamilton
Lancaster, Kentucky

David Martin
University of Manitoba

Kathlene Preston
Trinidad, California

David Pryzbyla
Denison University

Tanya Renner
Kapiolani Community College and
University of Hawaii

Vicki Ritts
St. Louis Community College—Florissant

Pamela Stewart
Arlington, Virginia

Chapter *1*

The Study of Gender

HEADLINE

Sizing Up the Sexes
—*Time*, January 20, 1992

A story titled "Sizing Up the Sexes," authored by Christine Gorman (1992), included the subtitle "Scientists Are Discovering That Gender Differences Have as Much to Do with the Biology of the Brain as with the Way We Are Raised" (p. 42). As the subtitle suggests, the article's initial emphasis was the biological basis of differences between the sexes, but Gorman did not maintain this acceptance throughout the article. Toward the beginning of the article, she highlighted the role of biology, describing recent research with the summary: "The evidence of innate sexual differences...began to mount" (p. 42).

As the article continued, Gorman became more tentative in her discussion of the biological underpinnings for sex differences and acknowledged that "most of the gender differences that have been uncovered so far are, statistically speaking, quite small" (p. 44). Before the article was half completed, Gorman wrote that the overlap in abilities of men and women and the flexibility of the brains of each reveal "just how complex a puzzle gender actually is, requiring pieces from biology, sociology and culture" (p. 44). Past the halfway point, Gorman acknowledged that "none of the gender scientists have figured out whether nature or nurture is more important" (p. 46) in determining the differences between the sexes. Toward the end of the article, Gorman's emphasis on differences was tempered by her description of research that indicates shrinking differences between women and men in some mental skills. Her conclusions came close to contradicting the strong initial statements about innate biological differences: "Far from strengthening stereotypes about who women and men truly are or how they should behave, research into innate sexual differences only underscores humanity's awesome adaptability" (p. 51).

This popular article about differences between the sexes illustrates the interest in and confusion about the topic. Which is more important in the differences between the sexes, nature (biology) or nurture (culture and society)? What is the extent of these differences? What types of differences exist? And what is the basis for these differences? These questions have answers that are simple and obvious to many people: Men and women are different by nature. They are born with biological differences that dictate the basis for different traits and behaviors. Indeed, they are so different that women are the "opposite sex," suggesting that whatever men are, women are at the other end of the spectrum. Those who hold this view find it obvious that the sexes differ and in important ways. Research in psychology, sociology, biology, and anthropology has complicated these simple answers. Not only is gender a complex puzzle, but there is a good deal of disagreement on deciding the relative sizes of the pieces of the puzzle. That is, research has led to a different and more complex question: How important are the various contributions of genetics, hormones, family, culture, and individual factors in sex differences?

Some people at some times have believed that there are few differences between the sexes, whereas others have believed that the two are virtually different species. These two positions can be described as the **minimalist** and the **maximalist,** or **essentialist, views** (Epstein, 1988). The minimalists perceive few important differences between the sexes, whereas the maximalists believe that the two sexes have fundamental and essential differences. Although these views have varied over time, today both views have supporters who are convinced of the validity of their positions.

This lack of agreement coupled with commitment to the position suggests controversy, and controversy is almost too polite a term for these disagreements. Few areas are as filled with feeling as discussions of the sexes and their capabilities. These arguments occur in places as diverse as playgrounds and scientific laboratories. The questions are similar, regardless of the setting: Who is smarter, faster, healthier, sexier, more capable, more emotional? Who makes better physicians, engineers, typists, managers, politicians, artists, teachers, parents, friends? Who is more likely to go crazy, go to jail, commit suicide, have a traffic accident, tell lies, gossip, commit murder? The full range of human possibilities seems to be grounds for discussion, but the issues are unquestionably important. No matter what the conclusions, at least half of humans (and most probably all of them) will be affected. Therefore, questions about the sexes are not only interesting, but the answers are important to individuals and to society. Future chapters explore the research concerning abilities and behaviors, and an examination of this research will allow an evaluation of these questions.

Answers are not lacking to these important questions about sex differences, but consistency is. Almost everyone has answers, but their answers differ. It is easy to see how people might hold varying opinions about a controversial issue, but some consistency should exist among the findings from researchers who have studied the sexes. Scientists should be able to investigate the sexes and provide evidence concerning these important questions. Researchers have worked on these questions, obtained results, and published thousands of papers. There is no shortage of investigations—or headlines—about the sexes. Unfortunately, these researchers seem subject to the same problems as everyone else: They do not all agree on what the results are and what the results mean.

In addition, research findings on the sexes contradict popular opinion in many instances, indicating that popular opinion is highly subject to stereotypical thinking. Both the past and the present are filled with examples of exaggerations of differences between women and men. Carol Tavris (1992) discussed the tendency for people to think in terms of opposites when only two examples exist, as it does with the sexes. If three sexes existed, people might not have the tendency to draw the comparison in such extremes; they might be able to see the similarities in men and women as well as their differences; they might be able to approach the questions with more flexibility in their thought patterns. But people see only two sexes, and the existence of the two pushes them into thinking of the two as opposites. To maintain oppositional categories, people must exaggerate the differences, resulting in stereotypes that do not correspond to real people. Although these stereotypes are not realistic, they are powerful because they affect the ways women and men think about themselves and how they think about the "opposite" sex.

History of the Study of Sex Differences in Psychology

Speculations about the differences between men and women probably predate history, but these issues were not part of the investigations of early psychology. Wilhelm Wundt is credited with originating modern psychology in 1879 (although there is some debate over the accuracy of this date) at the University of Leipzig (Schultz & Schultz, 1992). Wundt wanted to establish a natural science of the mind to experimentally investigate the nature of human thought processes. Using chemistry as his model, he tried to devise a psychology based on an analytical understanding of the structure of the conscious mind and founded the **structuralist** school of psychology. This structure was based on adult human cognition, and Wundt and his followers believed that psychology could not be applied to children, the feebleminded, or species of nonhuman animals.

Wundt's psychology was concerned with the workings of the mind as unaffected by individual differences among adult humans. The structuralists were interested in investigating the "generalized adult mind" (Shields, 1975a) and therefore any individual differences, including differences between the minds of women and men, were of no concern to the early psychologists who followed Wundt.

This inattention to sex differences did not mean equal treatment of men and women by these early psychologists. Wundt and his followers used a method of investigation called introspection, a type of self-observation of one's mental processes. Wundt described introspection as internal perception (Schultz & Schultz, 1992), and Wundt's students were required to undergo training to learn the type of attention and reporting required in these investigations of thought processes. These students (and thus the subjects in this early psychology research) were men, and the "generalized adult mind" on which the findings were based was a generalization drawn from data collected from and by men.

Wundt's psychology spread from Germany to the United States, where it changed. Although some American psychologists were interested in following Wundt's definition and goals for psychology, many others found Wundt's views too limiting and impractical. As psychology grew in the United States, it developed more of a practical nature. This change is usually described as an evolution to **functionalism,** a school of psychology that emphasized how the mind functions rather than how it is structured (Schultz & Schultz, 1992). Darwin's theory of evolution was a strong influence for the functionalists in American psychology. As these psychologists with a functionalist orientation started to research and theorize, they drew a wider variety of subjects into psychology research and theorizing, including children, women, and nonhuman animals.

The Study of Individual Differences

Among the areas of interest in functionalist psychology were the issues of intelligence and adaptability, and from these interests intelligence testing and the comparison of individuals' mental and personality traits evolved. With these tests and this functionalist orientation came an interest in differences among individuals, including sex differences (Shields, 1975a). The functionalists, due to the influence of the theory of evolution, tended to look for biologically determined differences, including a biological basis for sex differences. Indeed, as Stephanie Shields pointed out, these psychologists were very hesitant to acknowledge any possibility of social influence in the sex differences they found, and their findings usually supported the prevailing cultural roles for women and men.

The studies and writings of functionalists of this era tended to demonstrate that women were less intelligent than men, benefited less from education, had strong maternal instincts, and were unlikely to produce examples of success or eminence. Women were not the only group deemed inferior; nonwhite races were also considered less intelligent and capable. (See Diversity Highlight: "Parallels between Race and Gender.")

These findings of the intellectual deficiencies of women did not go uncriticized. As early as 1910, Helen Thompson Woolley contended that the research on sex differences was full of the researchers' personal bias, prejudice, and sentiment (in Shields, 1975a). However, these studies of sex differences did little to allow women equal opportunities (including the psychologists who were women) for education or careers and tended to relegate women to maternal and domestic roles.

Edward Thorndike was one of the prominent functionalists who believed that women were less intelligent than men. But Leta Stetter Hollingworth, who had been one of Edward Thorndike's students at Columbia University, took a stand against the functionalist view of women (Shields, 1975b). Early in her career, she argued against the prevailing view and criticized the methodology of studies that confirmed women's inferiority. She contended that women's potential would never be known until women had the opportunity to choose the lives they would like—career, maternity, or both.

The functionalist view began to wane in the 1920s, and a new school of psychology, **behaviorism,** gained prominence. The behaviorists emphasized observable behavior as the subject matter of psychology rather than thought processes or instincts. With the change from a functionalist to a behaviorist paradigm in American psycholo-

DIVERSITY HIGHLIGHT
Parallels between Race and Gender

In addition to their poor opinion of women's intellectual, emotional, and physical abilities, white male scientists often have held negative views of the abilities of other races. Indeed, 19th-century thought held that women and men among "more primitive peoples, notably among blacks" were more similar to each other than men and women in Europe (Sherman, 1978, p. 7). Any similarities to these "primitive peoples" were to the inferior European female rather than the superior European male. These openly racist and sexist opinions were part of the intellectual tradition of that time, and the science of that time confirmed the inferiority of women and non-European races.

These similarities of bias highlight the parallels between the research on gender and race. Both women and people of "inferior races" (that is, nonwhite races) were inferior because of their biological endowment, which was the view of biological determinism. According to R. C. Lewontin, Steven Rose, and Leon Kamin (1984), sexism and racism were prominent features of 19th-century biological determinism. They cited Charles Darwin's assertion that the mental traits in which women could excel were similar to the traits that were characteristic of lower races, and they quoted a 19th-century French scientist who maintained that "the Negro resembles the female in his love for children, his family and his cabin....The black man is to the white man what

woman is to man in general, a loving being and a being of pleasure" (p. 143).

As Stephen Jay Gould (1981, p. 103) observed, "'Inferior' groups are interchangeable in the general theory of biological determinism." That is, when making comparisons to the standard set by White men (using themselves as that standard), others often fail to meet this standard (in the assessment of White men). Lewontin, Rose, and Kamin (1984) argued that such biological determinism was directed toward preserving distinctions between the classes in Great Britain and between ethnic groups in America, demonstrating the biological inferiority of the less privileged and thus their inability to attain higher levels of intellectual achievement.

Some basis was needed to preserve the superior position of White men, and science was a respected authority and served to substantiate biological determinism throughout the 19th and into the 20th century. When psychology and sociology began to confirm that the environment and culture are important in determining behavior, biological determinism became a less prominent view. However, the belief that biology is an important influence in determining intelligence, emotion, and other important psychological factors has persisted, and those who wish to argue for the inferiority of women and nonwhite races often propose biological determinism as this basis.

gy, interest in research on sex differences sharply decreased. "The functionalists, because of their emphasis on 'nature,' were predictably indifferent to the study of social sex roles and cultural concepts of masculine and feminine. The behaviorists, despite their emphasis on 'nurture,' were slow to recognize those same social forces" (Shields, 1975a, p. 751). Rather, behaviorists were interested in the areas of learning and memory. Research on these topics ignored social factors, including sex roles and sex differences. In ignoring gender, psychology created what Mary Crawford and Jeanne Marecek (1989) referred to as "womanless" psychology, an approach that either failed to include women as participants or failed to examine gender-related factors when both men and women participated in psychology research.

During the time when behaviorism dominated psychology, the theorists who unquestionably had an interest in sex differences were those with a psychodynamic orientation—the Freudians.

Psychoanalysis

Both Freud's theory of personality development and his psychoanalytic approach to treatment appear in more detail in Chapter 6. However, the history of psychology's involvement in issues of sex and gender necessitates a brief description of Freud's personality theory and his approach to treatment.

Although Sigmund Freud's work did not originate within academic psychology, the two are popularly associated. And unquestionably, Freud's work and Freudian theory concerning personality differences between women and men have influenced both psychology and society in general. These influences have made the work of Freud very important for understanding conceptualizations of sex and gender.

In the United States, Freud's work began to gain popular attention in 1909, when Freud came to the United States to give a series of invited lectures at Clark University (Schultz & Schultz, 1992). Immediately after his visit, newspapers started carrying features about Freud and his theory. By 1920, the interest in Freudian theory and analysis was evidenced both by books and by articles in popular magazines. Psychoanalysis gained popular interest, becoming almost a fad. Indeed, the popular acceptance of Freud's work came before its acceptance by academicians.

Freud emphasized the role of instinct and physiology in personality formation, hypothesizing that instincts provide the basic energy for personality and that the individual child's perception of physical differences between boys and girls was a pivotal event in personality formation. Rather than relying on genetic or hormonal explanations for sex differences in personality, Freud looked to early childhood experiences within the family to explain how physiology interacts with experience to influence personality development.

For Freud, the perception of anatomical differences between boys and girls is critical (Freud, 1925/1989). The knowledge that boys and men have penises and girls and women do not forms the basis for differences between boys and girls in personality development. The results of this perception lead to conflict in the family, including sexual attraction to the other-sex parent and hostility for the same-sex parent. These incestuous desires cannot persist, and Freud hypothesized that the resolution of these conflicts comes through identification with the same-sex parent. However, Freud believed that boys experience more conflict and trauma during this early development, leading to a more complete rejection of their mother and a more complete identification with their father than girls experience. This difference in strength of identification produces enduring differences in personality between men and women. Consequently, Freud (1925/1989) hypothesized that men typically form a stronger conscience and sense of social values than women.

Did Freud mean that girls and women were deficient in moral standards compared to men? Did Freud view women as incomplete (and less admirable) people? It is probably impossible to know what Freud thought and felt, and his writings are sufficiently varied to lead to contradictory interpretations. Thus the question of Freud's view of women has been hotly debated. Some authors have criticized Freud for supporting a male-oriented society and the enslavement of women, whereas others have defended

Freud and his work as applied to women. In defense of Freud, Carol Tavris and Carole Wade (1984) pointed out that his view of women was not sufficiently negative to prevent him from accepting them as colleagues. Freud accepted a number of women into psychoanalytic training and encouraged his daughter, Anna, to pursue a career in psychoanalysis. Freud's writings, however, reveal that he said many negative things about women and seemed to feel that women were inferior to men. As Michael Jacobs (1992) concluded, "It is difficult to avoid the impression that Freud saw women as less developed than men, genitally, emotionally and in their moral thinking" (p. 107).

Regardless of Freud's personal beliefs, his theory's interpretation and popularization represented women as inferior to men, as being less ethical, more concerned with personal appearance, more self-contemptuous, and jealous of men's accomplishments (and also, literally, of their penises). Accepting the feminine role would always mean settling for inferior status and opportunities, and women who were not able to reconcile themselves to this status were candidates for therapy because they had not accepted their femininity.

Freud's theory also held stringent and inflexible standards for the development of masculinity. For boys to develop normally, they must experience severe anxiety during early childhood and develop hatred for their father. This trauma should lead boys to identify with their father and to experience the advantages of the male role through becoming like him. Boys who do not make a sufficiently complete break with their mother were not likely to become fully masculine and to remain somewhat feminine and thus experience the problems that society accords to nonmasculine men.

The psychoanalytic view of femininity and masculinity has been enormously influential in Western society. Although not immediately accepted in academic departments, the psychoanalytic view of personality and psychopathology was gradually integrated into the research and training of psychologists. Although the theory has prompted continuing controversy, interest continues—both in the form of attacks and defenses. This continuing stream of books and articles speaks to the power of Freud's theory to capture attention and imagination. Despite limited research support, Freudian theory has been and remains a force in conceptions of sex and gender.

Development of Women's Studies

The development of interest specifically in the study of women came as a result of the feminist movement of the 1960s (Ferree & Hess, 1985). This movement was not the first to push for changes in women's roles and legal status. Earlier versions of feminism had pressed for the vote for women, availability of birth control, and other legal changes to improve women's social status. The feminist movement of the 1960s grew out of the civil rights movement and brought about some of the changes that earlier feminist movements had sought.

During the 1960s, 1970s, and 1980s, women entered the workforce in record numbers, producing changes in the lives of women, men, and children. Although most of these jobs were in clerical or sales work, women also entered the professions in increasing numbers. The women in psychology began to change the field, bringing an interest in gender-related behaviors that differed from the earlier focus on individual differences (Walsh, 1985).

In 1968, psychologist Naomi Weisstein presented an influential paper, "'Kinde, Küche, Kirche' as Scientific Law: Psychology Constructs the Female," which has influenced a generation of psychologists. In this paper Weisstein (1970) argued that psychology research had revealed almost nothing about women, because the research had been contaminated by the biases, wishes, and fantasies of the male psychologists who conducted the research. Although the criticism was aimed mostly at clinical psychology and the Freudian approach to therapy, Weisstein also charged research psychologists with finding what they wanted and expected to find about women rather than researching women as they were. "Present psychology is less than worthless in contributing to a vision which could truly liberate—men as well as women" (Weisstein, 1970, p. 231).

Weisstein's accusations came at a time when the feminist movement in society and a growing number of women in psychology wanted a more prominent place for women in psychology and sought to create feminist-oriented research. One of Weisstein's points was that psychology research had neglected to take into account the context of behavior, without which psychology could understand neither women nor people in general. Twenty years later, this criticism seems to contain a great deal of foresight (Bem, 1993); psychology's research on gender began to change in the ways that Weisstein advocated.

Psychology held no monopoly on this new orientation to the study of sex and gender. Sociology, anthropology, ethnology, and biology as well as psychology became involved in questions about biological and behavioral differences and similarities between the sexes. Motivated by the feminist movement, women began to assert their view about the inequity of stereotypical views of the abilities and roles of men and women.

Although psychology's history of studying gender is lengthy, its involvement in feminist research is relatively new; the formation of a division of the American Psychological Association (APA) devoted to women's issues and studies did not occur until 1973. Women were admitted as students in doctoral programs from the early years of psychology, but they had to struggle for professional acceptance, having a difficult time finding positions as psychologists. In 1941 a group of women who were psychologists formed an association—the National Council of Women Psychologists—to further the work of female psychologists in the war effort (Walsh, 1985). This group attempted to become a division of the American Psychological Association, but it was rejected repeatedly.

Another group succeeded in gaining division status. Division 35, Psychology of Women, can be directly traced to the Association for Women in Psychology, a group that demonstrated against sex discrimination and for an increase in feminist psychology research at the 1969 and 1970 APA national conventions (Walsh, 1985). Unlike the earlier International Council, Division 35's goals included not only the promotion of women in psychology but also the advancement of research on women and issues related to gender. The great volume of psychology research on sex and gender that has appeared in the past 20 years is consistent with the Division 35 goal of expanding the study of women and encouraging the integration of that research with current psychological knowledge. Indeed, Division 35 members have conducted much of that research, but other disciplines have also contributed substantially. Therefore, not only have psychologists participated in the current plethora of research on sex and gender, but the topic is actively investigated in biology, medicine, sociology, and anthropology.

In summary, psychology research that included women dates back to the early part of the 20th century and the functionalist school of psychology. These psychologists were strongly influenced by Darwin's theory of evolution and viewed the sexes as opposites, with women having inherent biological differences that made them well-suited for motherhood but poorly suited for formal education. This approach emphasized sex differences, searching for the factors that distinguished men and women. After this school's influence faded, the behaviorist school dominated academic psychology. These psychologists were less interested in sex differences, creating a virtually "womanless" psychology. During that same time, Freudian psychoanalysts held strong views on the sexes, and that theory had an impact not only on academic psychology but also on popular opinion. The Freudian view is generally taken to hold that women are physically and morally inferior to men, and this belief in the innate inferiority of women influenced research on women. With the feminist movement of the 1960s, a different type of research arose, producing results that questioned the stereotypes and assumptions about innate differences between the sexes. This research began to examine not only sex differences and similarities, but these researchers also expanded ways to study women and men. This more recent orientation has led to voluminous research in the field of psychology as well as sociology, anthropology, and biology.

The feminist movement questioned the roles and stereotypes for women, and soon the questioning spread to men, who also began to examine how the inflexibility of gender stereotypes might harm them, too.

The Appearance of the Men's Movement

The men's movement appeared in response to the questions and challenges raised by the feminist movement. Women began to question the status quo of legal, social, and personal roles and relationships, and their questions were often aimed at men. Some men failed to see the problem, but other men began to consider that the questions were pertinent to their lives, too.

During the 1970s, these concerned men sometimes became feminists interested in ending the inequalities in power and privilege accorded to men, because they also saw toxic elements connected to the male sex role. Robert Brannon summarized this view by saying, "I have gradually come to realize that I, with every other man I know, have been limited and diverted from whatever our real potential might have been by the prefabricated mold of the male sex role" (Brannon, 1976, pp. 4–5).

Anthony Astrachan (1986) reported on the activities of these feminist men, saying that they formed groups equivalent to the consciousness-raising groups common in the women's movement. Although these group members discussed their common problems and sought support from each other, their activities usually did not progress to the larger organizations that sought political power, as the women's groups had done. Many of these groups tended to remain small, local-level organizations, but a few became national organizations.

The largest of the national organizations for feminist men is the National Organization to Change Men. But another national group within the men's movement is not interested in feminist goals; indeed, these men are interested in restoring the traditional gender roles that they believe have been destroyed by the women's movement. The largest of such groups is the National Organization for Men, a group that wants to "throw off the shackles of female oppression" (Gallagher, 1987, p. 39).

Many of these men's rights groups are organized around specific issues, such as changing divorce laws or promoting joint child custody, but some of the groups offer support to men who feel as though they have experienced discrimination. Rather than feminist groups for men, these groups are closer to antifeminist organizations. Their members feel confused and threatened by the changes that have come about during the past 20 years in women's and men's roles and would like to return to well-defined, separate roles for the sexes. Some of these men would like to see a less sharply gendered society in which both women and men have choices not bounded by their biological sex, whereas other men would like a more sharply gendered society in which the changes brought about by the women's movement would be reversed. Men in both of these types of groups consider themselves part of the men's movement.

Yet another variation of the men's movement comes from men trying to find a masculine identity. Authors such as Robert Bly (1990) and Sam Keen (1991) have contended that modern society has left men with no easy way to form a masculine identity. The culture provides inappropriate models, and fathers are often absent, providing no model at all. This deficit produces men who are inappropriately aggressive and poorly fitted to live in society, to form relationships with women, and to be adequate fathers. Bly proposed explorations of masculinity and ceremonial initiation into manhood as a means of overcoming the failure to establish the missing masculine role. These initiation ceremonies have been the subject of much ridicule (Pittman, 1992), but the need to affirm a masculine identity is a need that many men feel. Unfortunately, Bly's recommendations for achieving masculinity can be characterized as antifeminist, relying on devaluing women and feminine values to help men achieve masculinity.

However, none of the versions of the men's movement has exerted the impact of the women's movement. As Astrachan (1986, p. 289) explained:

> *The women's movement has touched the lives of millions—by its impact on public opinion and social policy. . . . The men's movement has touched the lives of only a few thousands. The men's movement? Most Americans don't know there is a men's movement. Yet there are men who want, like women, to change the boundaries of their lives and reshape sex roles.*

Sex or Gender?

Those researchers who have concentrated on the differences between men and women have usually used the term **sex differences** to describe their work. In some of these studies, these differences were the main emphasis of the study, but for many more studies, such comparisons were of secondary importance (Unger, 1979). By measuring and analyzing differences between male and female subjects, researchers have produced a huge body of information on these differences and similarities. As Rhoda Unger pointed out, this information was not of primary importance to most of these researchers. When the analyses revealed significant differences, the researchers provided a brief discussion; when no significant differences appeared, researchers dismissed their lack of findings with little or no discussion. Thus, the differences between male and female participants' responses have appeared in many studies but have not been the focus of most of these studies.

What have researchers meant by *sex differences?* Maureen McHugh, Randi Koeske, and Irene Frieze (1986) suggested that the term carries implications of the biological basis of such distinctions. Unger (1979) argued that the term has been used too extensively and with too many meanings.

> *A major problem in this area appears to be the too inclusive use of the term* sex. *In various contexts,* sex *can be used to describe the chromosomal composition of individuals, the reproductive apparatus and secondary characteristics that are usually associated with these chromosomal differences, the intrapsychic characteristics presumed to be possessed by males and females, and in the case of sex roles, any and all behaviors differentially expected for and appropriate to people on the basis of membership in these various sexual categories. (pp. 1085–1086)*

Unger proposed an alternative—use of the term **gender.** She explained that this term describes the traits and behaviors that are regarded by the culture as appropriate to women and men. Gender is thus a social label and not a description of biology. This label includes the characteristics that the culture ascribes to each sex and the sex-related characteristics that individuals assign to themselves. Carolyn Sherif (1982) proposed a similar definition of gender as "a scheme for social categorization of individuals" (p. 376). Both Unger and Sherif recognized the socially created differentiations that have arisen from the biological differences associated with sex, and both have proposed that use of the term *gender* should provide a useful distinction.

Unger suggested that use of the term *gender* might serve to reduce the assumed parallels between biological and psychological sex, or at least make explicit those assumptions. If researchers had accepted and used the term consistently, then its use might serve the function Unger proposed. However, no such consistent usage has yet appeared. Some researchers use the two terms interchangeably, whereas others have substituted the term *gender* for the term *sex.* Yet others have created and used the terms *sex-related* or *gender-related behaviors* and *sex-related* or *gender-related differences.* Those who use these terms intend to make the distinctions that Unger proposed—to distinguish between the biological and social components of sex.

Some researchers object to the use of different terms for sex and gender, arguing that attempts to distinguish between the biological and social aspects of sex is not possible. Eleanor Maccoby (1988, p. 755) rejected the distinction, saying that "the two factors interact in any psychological function that we might want to consider. Furthermore, uncovering the biological and social connections to behavior is a major research objective, not something to be assumed at the outset through the choice of terminology." Although the term *gender* has come to be used, it has not replaced *sex differences,* and both terms continue to coexist, sometimes used interchangeably and sometimes used as Unger suggested.

Should Psychologists Study Gender?

Should psychologists study gender? Does past research merit further research? The history of gender research in psychology is filled with examples of bias, and most current studies do not meet stringent requirements for eliminating such bias. Should gender research expand and change to meet these challenges, or should the area be abandoned as too problematic?

Alice Eagly (1987a) and Roy Baumeister (1988) have different answers for resolving the problems of continuing the study of gender. Eagly has suggested that *all* psychology research should become gender research, whereas Baumeister has called for an *end* to gender research.

Eagly's recommendation that all psychology research should report on gender was a response to the suggestions by McHugh et al. (1986), who called for limiting the reporting of gender differences. McHugh et al. argued that gender differences should not be a routine factor in psychology research, but rather that such differences should be the focus of replicable, theoretically grounded research. Eagly argued against this suggestion. She objected to both the criterion of replication and the criterion of theory. She explained that many gender issues have no firm grounding in theory and that requirements for replication would limit the published research to such a degree that many findings would go unreported. Instead, she proposed that researchers "routinely report sex comparisons, regardless of whether these findings are replicated, hypothesized, or theoretically relevant" (Eagly, 1987a, p. 756).

Baumeister (1988) argued that Eagly's strategy would result in virtually all research in psychology becoming gender research. Furthermore, he proposed that psychology should go in the opposite direction—away from reporting on gender comparisons. Baumeister also cited the cautions by McHugh et al. in his discussion of reporting gender differences in psychology research. He pointed out that by reporting and discussing gender differences, psychology research serves to perpetuate the exaggeration of gender differences: Differences that are frequently reported may give the impression of being large and important. Instead, Baumeister would like to see a gender-neutral psychology of people. He proposed that both society and science would be better served by such a strategy than by one that allows the exaggeration of gender differences.

Although their suggestions are completely in opposition, both Eagly and Baumeister have similar concerns—that research on gender may be misunderstood and inappropriately used to perpetuate stereotypes and discrimination. However, neither of their suggestions seems likely to be enacted. Psychologists are not likely to include gender as a variable in every study, nor are they likely to discontinue its study. Psychologists and other researchers, however, may heed some of the suggestions for designing nonsexist research, and these changes would benefit the quality of research and the interpretation of the findings.

Janice Yoder and Arnold Kahn (1993) also expressed concerns over the exaggeration of gender differences in psychology research. They contended that the comparison of women and men places men as the standard, making women appear deficient if the comparison yields differences. They worried that the same disadvantage has occurred in attempting to include women from various ethnic groups. White, privileged women have become the standard for research with women, and when women from other ethnic groups are included, they are compared to White, usually middle-class, college women. Diversity in psychology research is a desirable goal, but Yoder and Kahn (p. 847) warned that "just as there is no singular male experience, there is no one experience or characterization that can be applied indiscriminately to all women."

Psychology and Gender Research

Research on gender has been of interest to psychologists since the early years of the 20th century and, despite the concerns of psychologists like Baumeister, is likely to continue. Indeed, in the past two decades the amount of psychology research on gender and related topics has increased dramatically (Denmark, 1994). However, the current focus of gender research has changed from the traditional viewpoint.

Different Approaches to Gender Research

Psychology's traditional view of gender, which can be traced to the functionalist movement, has been that differences between the sexes were part of the study of individual differences. That is, gender-related differences are among the factors that contribute to differences among people. The emphasis, as in most psychology research, has been on the individual. Thus, researchers have chosen to compare groups of women or girls to groups of men or boys, looking for differences or similarities between the two. In making such choices of design, these researchers have examined gender as a subject variable; that is, as a characteristic of the subjects in the studies.

In 1974 two psychologists, Eleanor Maccoby and Carol Jacklin, published *The Psychology of Sex Differences,* a review of psychology's research-based knowledge about gender-related differences. These authors collected over 2,000 studies in which gender was a subject variable and organized them around different topics, such as aggression and verbal ability. Maccoby and Jacklin then evaluated the topics, determining how many studies failed to find a sex difference, how many studies supported a difference, and the direction of the differences for those topics that showed substantial differences. As Kay Deaux (1984, p. 105) stated, Maccoby and Jacklin's book was the "classic statement of the approach to sex as a subject variable." Their conclusions have not gone unchallenged (Block, 1976; Deaux, 1984), but their encyclopedic work highlighted both areas of gender similarities and gender differences. Deaux summarized the gender-as-subject-variable approach by saying that "approaching sex as a subject variable, although a popular pursuit with a long history, may not be the most productive route for understanding gender" (p. 108). Maccoby and Jacklin's book pointed out gaps in the research and thus prompted additional research within the same framework, but it did not consider a change in the concept of how gender and gender-related behaviors should be studied.

Since Maccoby and Jacklin's review, another type of research has become increasingly common—gender as a social category (Deaux, 1984, 1987). In this view, researchers consider the gender of subjects not as individual differences (within the person) but as a type of information on which people base judgments and individuals choose actions (within the situation). This approach is more likely to incorporate the context of behavior and the complex factors that can influence any situation. Those who take this approach believe that "traditional conceptions of masculinity and femininity have oversimplified that which is not simple, have unidimensionalized that which is multidimensional, and have conveyed a sense of stability and permanence to that which is inherently flexible" (Deaux, 1987, p. 301).

Researchers who take the gender-as-a-social-category approach investigate how people use information about gender as part of their beliefs and expectations about behavior and how people assimilate information about gender into their own behavior. For example, Janet Swim and her colleagues (Swim, Borgida, Maruyama, & Myers, 1989) presented people with background information about two people—John T. McKay or Joan T. McKay. These fictional people supposedly authored a story, and Swim et al. wanted to know if the gender of the writer influenced the evaluation of the writing. Therefore, these researchers manipulated information about the gender of the writer to determine the reaction of participants to this information. According to Deaux's (1984) review of this approach, the results indicated that gender is an important piece of information that people use in forming impressions and interacting with people: "The focus is not on how men and women actually differ, but how people *think* that they differ" (Deaux, 1984, p. 110).

Thus, the view of gender as a social category is an additional way of approaching the study of gender differences, one that has expanded psychology's research. The approach of studying gender as a subject variable may reveal no difference between men and women in a particular behavior, but people may believe that men and women differ and behave according to the differences they imagine.

Psychologists, then, have taken two different approaches to the study of gender—as subject variable and as a social category. These two approaches ask different questions and therefore are destined to give different—but not necessarily incompatible—types of answers concerning gender. The research that considers gender as subject variable has concentrated on differences in gender-related behaviors, whereas that focusing on sex as a social category has examined the social context of gender and how people use this information in constructing views of women and men and react on the basis of these views. Both types of research appear throughout this book.

Gender in the Headlines

This book approaches psychology's study of gender through portrayals in the popular press. Gender has become such a "hot" research topic that news stories appear frequently on television, in newspapers, and in magazines. These stories often present less technical versions of research findings than those appearing in research journals, and these popular versions of research results are easier to understand. However, some important details and limitations of research findings can be lost in the simplification process. Simplistic, unidimensional, and oppositional ways of thinking about women and men are common in our culture, and media portrayals are part of the process. Indeed, they are sometimes part of the problem, as when stories distort research findings and thus promote stereotypical thinking.

These headlines form the unifying theme for this book. Each chapter begins with a headline about the sexes, providing a starting point for an evaluation of the theory and research evidence that contributed to the headline story. This evaluation delves into the research and examines the popular story and the popular stereotypes. By examining how the media presents information about women and men and by contrasting these headlines with the research in psychology, biology, sociology, and anthropology, an evaluation of these popular views of the sexes is possible. Through this evaluation process, readers can develop an understanding of personal and societal beliefs and attitudes as well as a view of what psychology research has revealed about the sexes.

Before continuing to specific topics concerning gender differences and similarities, Chapter 2 more specifically examines how these headlines can misrepresent gender. Although biased reporting is a distinct possibility, biased science can also perpetuate inaccurate views of gender.

Summary

A child's gender is typically the first thing that parents learn about a child, and this situation highlights the importance of gender. Beliefs about gender differences are common, but opinions vary, with some people believing in minimal differences and others holding that the differences are maximal.

Gender research in psychology can be traced to the functionalist school of the late 1800s, which held that men and women differ in ability and personality (a view that received criticism at that time). With the transition to the behaviorist school, interest in gender differences faded from academic psychology but persisted in psychoanalysis. This latter view held that differences in anatomy produce personality differences in women and men, with women being inferior in a number of important ways. The feminist movement of the 1960s produced a resurgence of interest among psychologists concerning questions about gender differences, and research tended to question stereotypes about the sexes.

One issue concerns the traditional terminology— namely, the use of the term *sex differences*. By proposing the use of the term *gender*, psychologists have tried to clarify the difference between socially determined behaviors and biologically determined differences. However, both terms continue in use, and the proposed differentiation between sex differences as biological differences and gender differences as socially determined differences has not yet come into consistent use.

Baumeister and Eagly have taken opposite sides of the argument over the prevalence of gender research, one advocating a decrease and the other an increase in such research. Psychology research on gender reflects two different approaches: gender as a subject variable and gender as a social category. The former approach is historically the most common, and its goal is to investigate gender-related differences and similarities. The latter approach considers gender not as an individual trait but as a type of information that people have and use in making decisions and judgments. This latter approach is a more recent development and promises to be productive.

Research on gender often appears in media reports. These popular reports sometimes reflect complex research findings in a simplified form, and this simplification can perpetuate misconceptions. An evaluation of the headlines and the stories behind them will allow an examination of the media images of women and men, and the research from which the headlines came shows what researchers have investigated and what they have found.

Glossary

Behaviorism   the school of psychology that emphasizes the importance of observable behavior as the subject matter of psychology and discounts the validity of unobservable mental events

Essentialist view   another term for the maximalist view

Functionalism   a school of psychology arising in the United States in the late 1800s that attempted to understand how the mind functions. Functionalists held a practical, applied orientation, including an interest in mental abilities and in gender differences in mental abilities

Gender   the term used by some researchers to describe the traits and behaviors that are regarded by the culture as appropriate to men and women

Maximalist view   the view that many important differences exist between the sexes

Minimalist view   the view that few important differences exist between the sexes

Sex differences   the term used by some researchers (and considered to be inclusive by others) to describe the differences between male and female research participants

Structuralist   a school of psychology arising in Europe in the 1880s that attempted to understand the workings of the conscious mind by dividing the mind into component parts and analyzing the structure of this arrangement

Suggested Readings

Crawford, Mary; & Marecek, Jeanne. (1989). Psychology reconstructs the female: 1968–1988. *Psychology of Women Quarterly, 13,* 147–165. Crawford and Marecek present a historical and philosophical analysis of approaches to studying women in psychology. Although the article is not easy reading, the authors' thoughtful analysis will be interesting to those who want to know more about the different approaches psychology has taken to women in recent history.

Shields, Stephanie A. (1975). Functionalism, Darwinism, and the psychology of women: A study in social myth. *American Psychologist, 30,* 739–754. This lively article details the history of early psychologists' research on gender differences, with all of the biases showing.

Weisstein, Naomi. (1970). "Kinde, küche, kirche" as scientific law: Psychology constructs the female. In Robin Morgan (Ed.), *Sisterhood is powerful: An anthology of writings from the women's liberation movement* (pp. 228–245). New York: Vintage Books. Also reprinted in 1993 in *Feminism & Psychology, 3,* 195–210. Weisstein's article has been reprinted many times and appears in many anthologies, a testimony to its influence. Originally a presentation, this angry criticism details psychology's tendency to distort the view of women and describes its failure to study women in an unbiased way. Psychology research is no longer as inadequate as Weisstein charged, partly because of her charges.

Chapter *2*

Researching Sex and Gender

HEADLINE

Don't Believe Everything You Read...
—*Psychology Today,* November 1989

Journalist Beryl Lieff Benderly's (1989) article cautioned readers "Don't Believe Everything You Read..." Her concern centered around the reporting of research on gender and gender differences, as highlighted in a story that appeared on the front page of the *New York Times* in 1988. Benderly called the resulting publicity a "major media flap" (p. 67), as the front page story contained an error that made the findings appear to be more important than they were (this story is one of the headlines for Chapter 5, with its contents and the error explained there). Although the reporter got the implications of the research wrong, the story appeared in newspapers throughout the country without the background that would have clarified the report. The media seemed more interested in a dramatic story than in an accurate story.

Benderly talked to gender researchers Ruth Hubbard and Anne Fausto-Sterling, who both contended that the story would not have appeared in the newspaper if the findings had not revealed gender differences. That is, stories about *differences* receive prominent coverage, whereas stories that fail to show gender differences receive little coverage in the media. This prejudice in favor of positive results pervades all of science but presents a particular problem for gender research: The public receives information mainly about research that shows differences, but such research may not represent the status of the findings about gender. Therefore, the tendency to report on positive findings may leave a biased picture about gender-related differences.

Biologist Hubbard discussed her misgivings about how journalists cover research on gender, saying "The thing that really disturbs me, is that any time anyone does anything that purports to show sex differences it's front page news. . . . If you set up an experiment and it doesn't show a difference, people think you haven't done it right" (in Benderly, 1989, p. 69).

Gender research findings are "hot" news, often making headlines, but Benderly (1989) and Barbara Beckwith (1984) have both discussed the tendency for the media to emphasize research that proposes biological explanations for gender-related differences. That is, research that seems to confirm gender-related differences makes headline news, especially that research suggesting a biological basis for such differences. On the other hand, research that demonstrates gender-related similarities, fails to confirm a previous finding of differences, or presents a complex pattern of results is not as dramatic and newsworthy. These types of research findings may appear in technical journals, but such results do not make headlines. Thus, the full complexity of research findings does not receive prominent media coverage, and media reports may promote a biased view of the degree of gender differences and the basis for those differences.

The media can bias opinion by selective and oversimplified reporting, presenting only certain results and ignoring other findings. But the process of science too can be biased. The topics that researchers choose for study determine the content and direction of the field. In addition, researchers may bias the findings by allowing their own personal views to influence their work. Therefore, not only the reporting of scientific research but also the research itself may present a biased picture. This possibility sounds incongruous. The popular view of science is that unbiased objectivity is basic to the scientific method.

Does science ensure objectivity? Is science free from bias? These questions have become important to the study of gender because some of the most vocal accusations of scientific bias have come from gender researchers. Gender issues are hotly debated in scientific circles as well as in the media. Understanding the critics requires understanding science—its origins and methods as well as its limitations.

How Science Developed

Researchers who explore issues related to gender may have their training in any of several disciplines, including psychology, sociology, medicine, biochemistry, biology, or anthropology. Their viewpoints may differ, but their methods of investigation usually do not—most researchers adhere to a set of methods that are part of traditional science. However, some researchers have questioned traditional science and proposed alternative methods. These critics of modern science have often been involved with gender research, and the alternatives to traditional science offer different ways to approach gender issues. An understanding of the traditional approach to research is necessary before examining the alternatives.

Modern science arose in the 16th and 17th centuries and brought about radical changes in ways of knowing and understanding the world (Riger, 1992). Instead of looking to religion and the Bible for knowledge and wisdom, the new science looked to knowledge gathered through observation. This view represented a radical departure from ancient and religious thought. This new scientific view assumed that the world works by a set of natural laws and that these laws can be discovered by careful, objective investigation. Humans can understand the laws of nature if they use the correct methods of investigation.

Three related philosophical positions were important to the development of modern science: positivism, materialism, and empiricism (Schultz & Schultz, 1992). **Posi-**

DIVERSITY HIGHLIGHT
Other Ways to Knowledge? Science in Nonwestern Cultures

The activities identified as science arose in 16th- and 17th-century Europe, but all cultures over the world and throughout history have developed some understanding of physical, biological, and social existence. Some of these conceptualizations have been close to the views of modern science, yet many have differed substantially. The cultures that did not develop this type of science took an alternative path due to their view of the world and how it operates. Several prominent cultures have existed within civilizations that have not adopted the positivist, materialist, empiricist traditions essential to European science.

For example, Chinese culture developed some sophisticated technology and engineering but not much science. Colin Ronan (1982) contended that the reason behind this omission was the Chinese outlook, which regarded the entire universe as a vast organism, with humans and the physical world as part of this unity. Their view prompted the Chinese to develop an understanding of some aspects of the world but to ignore others. Their understanding of the world was influenced by those who followed two philosophies—the Confucians and the Taoists. Followers of Confucius tended to make no division between the physical and social world and to concentrate on promoting social justice rather than intellectual understanding about the physical world. Taoists had an interest in nature, but their view was not one of domination of humans over nature, a view basic to Western science. Rather, the Taoists strove to gain knowledge as a path to inner peace. Neither of these views prompted the development of a science comparable to Western science, with its emphasis on objectivity and the separation of the observer to the object observed.

The theme of the unity of nature and humanity was also part of the two religions that dominated India—Hinduism and Buddhism. Ronan (1982) argued that neither of these views was conducive to the development of science, so the science that existed in India largely was borrowed from the West rather than developing independently in India.

Sandra Harding (1986) also discussed the dominance-oriented, objective, rational approach that is basic to Western science, considering how the African view differs from the Western view. She contended that the African conception is one of connection rather than opposition, with a reluctance to divide the world into nonoverlapping categories, including a split between self and nature. Such a split is essential to the type of objectivity required by science, but Harding argued that African philosophy found such divisions impossible. Furthermore, she proposed that the African view is curiously similar to that of Native Americans and many feminist scholars, being one of connection and interrelatedness with an emphasis on relationships to the world rather than an analysis of it.

As Elizabeth Fee (1986) concluded, all of these non-Western views of the world are similar in their conceptualizations of nature as intertwined with humanity rather than as describing the two in dynamic opposition. These views of nature did not prevent these cultures from developing a formal understanding of the world, including engineering, agriculture, medicine, and astronomy. However, none of these cultures developed the kind of science that arose in Europe, and the science that developed in Europe has spread to all countries and dominates modern knowledge, perhaps to the exclusion of other world views.

tivism insists on collecting and describing information obtained through observation and rejects knowledge derived from theology or metaphysics. **Materialism** holds that all things can be described in physical terms and can be understood as physical properties. **Empiricism** emphasizes using direct observation as the way to gain information. The influence of these three philosophical positions resulted in a different way of studying the world and a new set of knowledge.

During the 18th and 19th centuries, science proliferated in Europe and spread throughout the Western world. Research in chemistry, physics, biology, and medicine produced findings that changed the world and the lives of most people. New products, medicines, and industries came into existence because of the research of scientists. The success of science created an enthusiasm that fostered the development of more sciences, including the social sciences of psychology and sociology. These social sciences held to the same assumptions and methods as the natural sciences—that is, the laws of human behavior and society were also subject to discovery by careful, objective investigation.

What constitutes careful and objective investigation? What makes scientific investigation different from other ways of gaining knowledge? What techniques do scientists use to accomplish these goals? The following sections explore these areas.

Methods and What They Reveal

Science is not just a set of methods, it is also a process of gaining information (Ray, 1993); that is, science is an activity. Through this activity, researchers gain information that meets certain criteria, and as such information gathering in science is restricted. One restriction applies to the gathering of information, which must be observable, just as the positivist philosophers insisted. Scientific information must be observable not only to the person doing the observation but also to anyone else; that is, it must be publicly observable. By restricting information in this way, the observer's perceptions and biases can be minimized, and scientific observation can attain some level of objectivity.

Another restriction on the gathering of information in science is that scientific observation must be systematic: Scientists must follow some plan or system to gather information. Everyone makes observations, but most people in most circumstances do so in a nonsystematic, personal way rather than according to a systematic plan. This lack of systematicity can lead people to notice certain things while ignoring others—a selection process that can result in distortion and bias. Scientists strive to be more systematic in their observations in order to gather information that more accurately reflects the situations they have observed. This is not to say that scientists are free of personal biases; as humans, they are subject to the same perceptual distortions (and even biases) as other humans. However, acting as scientists, they strive to recognize and minimize these biases. Working with observable information according to a systematic plan can help overcome the bias of subjectivity.

Thus, science is an activity that is restricted to gathering information through observation and by way of systematic plans. The care such observation requires has led to an erroneous impression about science—namely, that science is precise. The use of numbers for quantification of the observations further contributes to this mistaken impression. People tend to believe that numbers lend precision, when actually numbers are only a way to summarize certain characteristics of a situation. Scientists do work with numbers, and they strive to make exact measurements based on their observations, but neither of these activities makes science precise.

All measurements are subject to error, and researchers need to find ways to eliminate as much measurement error as they can. However, they never succeed in eliminating all measurement error, so the measurements of science are representations rather than exact replications of the observations. That is, scientists collect **data,** which is usually a quantification of the observations they make. These data are not the same as the observed phenomenon but rather are representations of some facet of the phenomenon the researcher considered important.

For example, a researcher who was interested in cross-gender interactions in preschool children might choose to study how many times children approached a child of the other gender in play situations. The researcher would observe children of the appropriate age and count the number of such interactions, perhaps both by girls and by boys. The data would consist of the number of times such interactions were initiated by each gender. These data capture one aspect of the play situation but omit many other factors. Thus, when researchers finish their studies, they usually have a collection of data—in the form of numbers—that they can analyze to determine the results of the studies.

A further narrowing of the observations in science comes from the specification of a **variable** or several variables in research studies. A variable is the factor of interest in a research study. The term comes from the notion that the factor varies, or potentially has more than one value (as opposed to a constant, which has only one value). As most things vary, finding a variable of interest is not nearly as difficult as restricting a study to only a few variables. For example, variables include factors such as time of day, family income, amount of anxiety, number of hours of practice, gender of participants, and so forth. Thousands of variables are of interest to researchers, yet studies typically investigate only a few.

The systematic plans and measurements in science include many different specific techniques or methods, each of which has the power to reveal different types of information. In addition, each method has it own advantages and disadvantages. Rather than consisting of an unorganized assortment of techniques, scientific methods fall (but not neatly) into two types: descriptive and experimental. Different methods exist within each type, but descriptive research techniques have limitations and advantages that experimental techniques do not, and the reverse is also true. Therefore, one approach to understanding research methods is through an examination of these two types of approaches.

Descriptive Methods

Descriptive research methods help investigators answer "what" questions. That is, descriptive research can tell what types of things exist, including great detail about those things and even the extent of relationships among various things. Descriptive methods include naturalistic observation, surveys, and correlational studies. All of these designs allow researchers to gather information about phenomena that already exist, and none of these methods involves manipulation of existing conditions or the introduction of change by the researcher.

Naturalistic observation involves just what the name implies—observation of a naturally occurring situation. Like all scientific observation, this gathering of information must be of publicly observable phenomena and according to a systematic plan. In making these observations, the researchers must not change the situation. If researchers make any change in the situation, it is no longer naturalistic. That is, the phenomenon may change when researchers become part of the situation. Therefore, naturalistic observation is not a particularly easy method. Researchers must find ways to gather their data without influencing the situation.

For example, if a team of researchers wanted to study the gender-stereotypical versus gender-atypical toy choices of 3-year-old children through naturalistic observation, these investigators would have several tasks. First, they would have to define what they considered gender-stereotypical and gender-atypical toy choices so that observers could classify the toy choices the children make. Researchers might choose to specify an **operational definition,** a definition of the concept in terms of operations used to obtain it rather than the concepts underlying it. For the study on toy choices, the researchers would need to specify which choices would count as gender stereotypical and which would count as atypical.

Second, the researchers would have to find a way to observe 3-year-old children playing with toys. In addition, the children could not come in contact with or see the investigators lest their presence change the children's behavior. Barbara Lloyd, Gerard Duveen, and Caroline Smith (1988) conducted such a study. They observed 3- and 4-year-old children playing with gender-stereotyped toys to examine the different toy choices according to situation and play partner. They found that these young children tended to use gender-stereotyped toys, especially in action play and to a lesser extent in pretend play. That is, they found that the situation was an important factor in how gender stereotypical children's toy choices were.

How do researchers become unobtrusive? One common method in situations like this example is observation through one-way mirrors. These devices consist of a mirror on the wall of a room that faces an observation room on the other side. Observers can see through the mirror, but those who are observed see only the mirror. Such observation facilities exist in many laboratory schools to aid researchers in doing naturalistic observations. These observation facilities can be arranged for this type of study, but creating opportunities for naturalistic observation in other situations can require invention as well as flexibility. Researchers may have to hide or use binoculars to gather their information.

What can researchers learn through naturalistic observation? In the example, Lloyd et al. were interested in knowing what types of toys children chose in different play situations. Other similar studies might investigate toys children bring with them to school, how long the children play with each type of toy, which toys children are willing to share and which they are not, or many other such questions. Indeed, many possibilities exist for even this single topic, and other investigators must do as Lloyd et al. did in both choosing a question and finding a way to make their measurements in the naturalistic situation.

The information that researchers can determine from naturalistic observation is limited to descriptions of what occurred. This may be exactly the information that the researchers wanted, and therefore this limitation may not be a disadvantage. An advantage of this method is its lack of artificiality, which is a problem for laboratory research. The specification of the behaviors under observation and the decisions concerning how to collect data narrow the focus of the research to certain aspects of the naturalistic situation. Thus, naturalistic observation is not a recording of a situation but a choice of which data to collect from a complex environment. The complexity of the naturalistic situation results from many factors that make simple interpretations of this type of research nearly impossible. Although researchers may gain some insight into causal relationships through their observations, naturalistic observation lacks the power to allow researchers to determine causal relationships.

Surveys are a second method of descriptive research. In surveys researchers construct questionnaires, choose a group of people to respond to the questionnaire, collect the data, and analyze the data to yield results. This method sounds deceptively simple—almost anyone can think of questions to ask. However, the method is filled with choices. For example, researchers using this method must decide about the wording of questions ("Do you agree…" versus "Do you disagree…"), the answer format (respondents reply versus respondents choose from a set of answers), the appearance of the questionnaire (number of pages, size of type, page layout), the choice of people responding (representative of the entire population versus a select group, such as registered voters), the number of people needed (what number will give a good estimate for accuracy), and the method of administration (face-to-face, telephone, mailed). Unwise choices on any of these decisions may result in a survey that does not allow the researcher to answer the question that prompted the research or, worse, may give the researcher an answer that is misleading.

The main limitation of the survey method is inherent: Surveys pose questions rather than make direct measurements. That is, surveys typically rely on self-reports rather than direct observations of behavior. Researchers ask people to respond to a series of questions either in person or through a mailed questionnaire or telephone survey. In many surveys participants are asked to share their opinions and attitudes, but in some surveys participants try to report on past behavior. The responses that people give may not accurately reflect their beliefs or behaviors. Even if people are honest about their beliefs, they may not always behave in a way that is consistent with reported attitudes. Indeed, people may lie, withhold the truth, or simply not know or remember the information.

Replies to survey questions are open to bias due to participants' beliefs about social standards and their tendency to present themselves in a favorable way. This bias can invalidate a question or even an entire survey, and information obtained through self-reports is generally not considered as strong as information obtained by direct observation. Despite the wide variety of information that can be obtained through the survey method, that information is limited not only by its descriptive nature but also by its potential inaccuracy.

Despite the disadvantages, surveys offer the advantages of allowing researchers to ask people about things that the researchers could not easily (or possibly ethically) observe directly. Thus, the method is flexible and useful in a variety of situations. Surveys are a very common method for measuring people's attitudes. Psychologists, sociologists, market researchers, and political pollsters all use this method to help decide how people feel about a wide variety of issues. For example, Sherry Ahrentzen, Douglas Levine, and William Michelson (1989) surveyed 538 family households to investigate how married couples spent their time during a 24-hour period. They asked about employment, housekeeping, child care, and time spent with other family members. They found that women reported that they spent more time in rooms with other people than men and that fully employed women reported more involvement with housekeeping chores than fully employed men.

If researchers want to know about the relationship between two specific variables rather than information about several variables, researchers will do a **correlational study,** another descriptive method. Correlational studies allow researchers to determine both the existence and the degree of relationships between the variables under study.

To do a correlational study, researchers must choose two variables for study, operationalize and make the measurement, and then analyze the relationship. To perform this analysis, researchers calculate a correlation coefficient, a statistical test that reveals the strength or magnitude of relationship between two variables. The correlation coefficient is described by a formula, and researchers must apply the formula to their data. A number of variations on the correlation coefficient exist, but the most common is the *Pearson product-moment correlation coefficient,* symbolized by the letter r. The results of the analysis yield a number that varies between $r = +1.00$ and $r = -1.00$. Correlations that are close to $r = +1.00$ indicate a strong, positive relationship: As one measurement increases, the other increases. Correlations that are close to $r = -1.00$ indicate a strong, negative relationship: As one measurement increases, the other decreases. Correlations that are close to $r = 0.00$ indicate no relationship between the two variables.

For example, Bernard Whitley, Jr. (1988), conducted a study to investigate the relationship between people's reports of their degree of masculinity or femininity and their masculine and feminine behaviors; that is, he studied the degree of relationship between traits and behaviors. Whitley administered two different tests—one that measured the traits of masculinity and femininity and the other that asked people about their behaviors related to recreational activities, vocational interests, and social activities. These two tests yielded scores, and Whitley then used the correlation coefficient to analyze these scores.

The correlational study by Whitley yielded a number of correlation coefficients indicating relationships between the personality measurement of masculinity or femininity and the participants' reports of behaviors, but few of these correlations indicated strong relationships. For example, the relationship between the trait of masculinity and men's reports of their masculine behaviors was $r = +.32$. This correlation indicates a low relationship between the personality measure of masculinity and the measure of masculine behaviors. For women, the correlation between the feminine personality trait and feminine behavior was $r = +.17$, a low correlation. These correlations indicate a low but positive correlation: As masculine personality score increased, reported masculine behavior also increased, and as feminine personality score increased, feminine behavior also increased. The correlation coefficients of $r = +.32$ and $r = +.17$ indicate a low relationship for two factors that logically should be highly correlated. The magnitude of these correlations would suggest that the personality measures of masculinity and femininity reflect few of the qualities that contribute to masculine and feminine behavior. Indeed, the distance from a perfect correlation of $r = +1.00$ indicates that some other factors omitted from the measures of masculine and feminine personality also contribute to masculine and feminine behaviors.

Correlational studies, like other descriptive methods, do not reveal why the relationship exists. That is, correlations do not indicate causality. However, such a deduction may be very tempting. Indeed, a causal relationship may exist between two variables that have a high correlation, but the method does not allow the conclusion. Even a high correlation would not allow a researcher to know the direction of the causal relationship: Did changes in one variable produce changes in the other, or vice versa? Another possibility is that both highly correlated variables may be causally related to a third variable that has not been part of the study. In any case, a conclusion of causality is not legitimate on the basis of the evidence from a correlational study. Thus, the information that researchers obtain and the conclusions that they may draw from correlational studies exclude causality but include information on the existence and strength of relationships.

Experimental Designs

To obtain information about cause and effect, researchers must do **experiments.** This type of design allows researchers to answer "why" questions—questions with answers that involve explanations rather than descriptions. An experiment is a method that involves the manipulation of one factor, called the **independent variable,** the measurement of another factor, called the **dependent variable,** and the holding constant of all other factors. By manipulating the independent variable, the experimenter tries to create a change. Detecting change requires some basis for comparison, so the simplest version of an experiment requires two conditions to provide this comparison. These two conditions consist of two different levels of the independent variable, with all other factors held constant. The manipulation may be more elaborate, consisting of three, four, or more levels of the independent variable, and experiments may include more than one independent variable.

The dependent variable is the one that the experimenter measures, and the choice and quantification of dependent variables can also be complex. In psychology research, dependent variables are always some type of behavior or response. By choosing such dependent variables, psychology has placed itself among the sciences that require empirical subject matter—behavior and responses that can be observed and measured.

The logic of experimental design holds that the manipulation of the independent variable should produce a change in the value of the dependent variable if the two are causally related. If the experimenter also holds other factors constant, the only source of change in the dependent variable should be the manipulated change in the independent variable. Thus, in a well-designed experiment the changes in the value of the dependent variable can be entirely attributed to the manipulation of the independent variable. That is, the changes in the independent variable caused the changes in the dependent variable.

Although the logic of experimental design is simple, creating conditions of effective manipulation of one factor while holding all other factors constant is far from simple. Such a situation would be almost impossible in a naturalistic setting, because any one change would result in many others. Therefore, almost all experiments take place in laboratories. These settings offer the possibility of the necessary control, but they open experiments to the criticism of artificiality. Despite the validity of that criticism, scientists highly value experiments because of their potential to reveal cause-and-effect relationships, a type of information that other methods cannot show.

Stephanie Shields and Pamela Cooper (1983) conducted an experiment about attitudes toward different childbearing choices, and this factor was the independent variable in their study. Their dependent variable was attitude toward the women. They presented participants with descriptions of women who had made three different choices: They were either pregnant and happy about the pregnancy, pregnant and unhappy about the pregnancy, or childless by choice. The descriptions of these three women were similar except for their childbearing choices: All were the same age, married the same length of time, happy in their marriages, and pursuing careers with flexibility that would allow them to have a child and resume their career later. Therefore, any differences in participants' attitudes should have been due to their different attitudes toward the childbearing choices.

Shields and Cooper found that the happy pregnant woman received significantly more positive evaluations than the unhappy pregnant woman, a finding that indicated an endorsement of a cultural stereotype for motherhood. Surprisingly, they found that the childless woman received evaluations almost as positive as the happy pregnant woman. Shields and Cooper's results allow a conclusion that childbearing choices can cause people to have different attitudes about women.

No other type of scientific method allows conclusions concerning causality, and if the experiment is not done carefully, interpretation of causality can be in error. In addition, the laboratory setting differs from a natural social setting. The participants in Shields and Cooper's study may have behaved differently in the lab than they would have in a more naturalistic situation—evaluating descriptions differs from evaluating people.

The laboratory situation may provide a social setting of its own and may prompt different behavior than would occur in more realistic situations. Because participants are always aware that their behavior is of interest, they may behave differently than they otherwise would. Thus, the laboratory experiment takes place in an artificial situation that may alter behavior, and this possibility limits the extent to which researchers can generalize their results to other situations. The artificiality of the situation and its limitation in generalizing results to other situations are drawbacks of the experimental method. Nonetheless, researchers prize experiments above other methods, and scientists do experiments when they can.

Ex Post Facto Studies

Scientists cannot always do experiments. Some phenomena are beyond possible manipulation, either for practical or ethical reasons. For example, researchers might want to know about the effect of brain damage on memory. To do an experiment, researchers would be required to select a group of people and perform the surgery that would cause brain damage in half of them while leaving the other half with undamaged brains. Obviously, this research is unethical, but the question that prompted it—Does brain damage influence memory?—is still of interest.

Researchers interested in the question about brain damage and memory have at least two choices. They might choose to do the experiment with nonhuman subjects (although some people would object to the ethics of this research, too), but the problems of generalizing the findings to people would be a severe limitation. Another choice would be the **ex post facto study.** In this type of study, researchers might select people who have suffered brain damage in the area of interest and enlist these individuals as research participants, contrasting them with a group of people who have not experienced brain damage of any sort or those who have damage in some other area of the brain. Both groups would participate in the memory study. Therefore, the presence of brain damage would be the subject variable—the characteristic of interest in the subjects—and the scores on the memory test would be the dependent variable.

Such an ex post facto study would not be an experiment, because the researchers did not produce the brain damage, holding all other factors constant. Instead, the researchers entered the picture *after* the manipulation had been performed through accidents (hence the term *ex post facto*—after the fact of the creation of differences). With no opportunity for precision in creating the values of the independent variable or in holding other factors constant, the ex post facto study lacks the controls that would allow researchers to draw conclusion about cause-and-effect relationships (Christensen, 1991).

The ex post facto study seems very much like an experiment, including, as it does, the presence of contrast groups and a dependent variable measurement. These similarities can lead to misinterpretations of these studies and the incorrect attribution of causality. Researchers are usually careful to use the correct language to interpret their findings from ex post facto studies, but people who read the research may not be appropriately cautious, leading to misunderstandings of research findings.

Gender of participants is a subject variable, a characteristic of the subjects that exists prior to their participation in a study but one that can be the basis for division of subjects into contrast groups. The studies that approach gender as a subject variable are ex post facto studies, with all of the limitations of this method. That is, these studies do not and cannot reveal that gender *causes* differences in any behavior. This caution is difficult for many people to keep in mind, and those who are not familiar with research methods have a tendency to believe that gender-related differences in behavior have biological sex as the underlying cause. This reasoning contains two errors: (1) incorrectly attributing causality to a research method that cannot demonstrate cause-and-effect relationships and (2) reducing the many variables that coexist with biological sex

Experimental Design — Gender as a Social Category

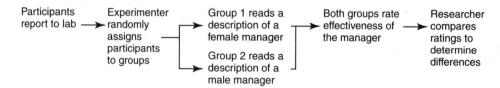

Participants report to lab → Experimenter randomly assigns participants to groups → Group 1 reads a description of a female manager / Group 2 reads a description of a male manager → Both groups rate effectiveness of the manager → Researcher compares ratings to determine differences

Ex Post Facto Design — Gender as a Subject Variable

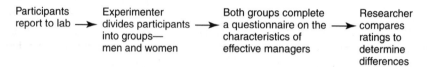

Participants report to lab → Experimenter divides participants into groups— men and women → Both groups complete a questionnaire on the characteristics of effective managers → Researcher compares ratings to determine differences

FIGURE 2.1   Two Designs with Gender as a Variable

to the variable of subject gender. Therefore, an erroneous interpretation of such studies can be dangerous, leading people to conclusions for which there is no research evidence.

Mary Crawford and Diane Gressley (1991) explored gender differences in sense of humor using an ex post facto design in which they contrasted men's and women's senses of humor. Rather than present jokes or cartoons that the experimenters found funny and test gender differences in appreciation of humor, these researchers measured the different dimensions of humor. In contrasting women and men, they found more similarities than differences. However, men scored higher on appreciation of hostile humor, jokes, and slapstick humor, whereas women scored higher on appreciation of anecdotal funny stories.

Figure 2.1 illustrates some of the differences between experimental and ex post facto designs, using gender as an example. In the experimental design, researchers often randomly divide the participants into groups in order to keep individual differences equal in the groups. Therefore, the groups in an experimental design would not consist of one group of men and another group of women, as random assignment would be very unlikely to yield such a configuration. The ex post facto design, on the other hand, assigns participants to groups on the basis of some factor that the participants already possess, such as gender. In this type of design, the researcher might have one group consisting of women and another of men. Indeed, thousands of studies use this design to study gender-related differences and similarities.

An experimental design can use gender as a variable if the researcher manipulates the gender of some target person whom the participants rate, evaluate, or react to, but this approach makes gender a social category, not a subject variable. Also, the subject variable of gender can be included in a study that manipulates an independent variable to study each variable as well as their combination. Therefore, ex post facto designs can examine gender as a subject variable, experimental designs can study gender as a social category to which participants react, and studies can use gender as a subject variable combined with additional manipulated independent variables. These approaches are not equivalent, and each yields information that requires careful interpretation of findings.

In summary, different research methods yield different types of information. Descriptive research methods include naturalistic observation, surveys, and correlational studies. Such studies help to answer questions about *what* occurs; that is, they describe what exists. Experimental research, on the other hand, allows researchers to explain *why* a relationship exists between independent variables and dependent variables. Because it yields information about cause-and-effect relationships, this method is highly prized. A quasi-experimental method, the ex post facto study, is similar to an experiment in the designation of variables (called subject variables) and dependent variables, but these designs differ from true experiments in the choice of the values of the subject variable rather than the creation of the values of the independent variable through manipulation.

Limitations on Gender Research

The type of research design limits the conclusions that researchers can validly draw. The limitations of methodology have to do with the conclusions that are permissible from the various types of designs. The mistakes in interpretation often have to do with the evaluation of research studies, especially the concept of statistical significance. Although researchers tend to be knowledgeable about design and statistics and careful in interpreting their research, such caution may be lost in media reports of scientific research, leading to widespread misunderstanding of a result's meaning and what its practical implications are.

As in the Crawford and Gressley study, gender is often a subject variable in psychology studies. In such studies, gender is part of an ex post facto design rather than an experimental design. Gender of the participants is a variable that cannot be manipulated in an experimental design. Researchers do not choose a group of people who have no gender and make them male and female as part of the study. Instead, researchers select groups of men and women and form two groups in an ex post facto design. Thousands of such studies exist, but none of these studies is an experiment, and none of them allows conclusions about the causal role of gender in the behaviors these studies have measured. However, people who are not very knowledgeable about research design can mistake an ex post facto design for an experiment and may interpret such studies as indicating causality. This error can lead to serious misunderstanding about what gender-related differences mean, with the implication that gender is the cause of differences.

No method that researchers can actually perform will reveal the *cause* of gender differences. Those studies would be experimental, and such experiments are impossible to perform. Any study that uses women and men or even the youngest infant boys and girls is an ex post facto study and has that methodology's limits. This methodological limitation should restrict conclusions about the nature of gender differences, but such discussions still exist. These assertions and discussions are speculation—perhaps with some research finding as a basis, but speculation nonetheless. Both those who speculate and those who read the speculation should be aware of their nature.

Scientists are certainly allowed to speculate. Indeed, the speculations that they can weave into coherent, integrated explanations become theories, and theories guide much scientific research. Such theories are important, powerful, and influential but are not the same as observations or findings. When a discrepancy arises between a theory and a finding, the scientist should discard or revise the theory rather than ignore or question the finding. However, the opposite often happens. According to Thomas Kuhn (1962), scientists tend to cling to theories and find ways to reject their findings rather than the other way around. Although such behavior calls into question the objectivity of scientists, the history of science is filled with examples. Kuhn gave many examples of such bias from the history of science, including the insistence that the earth is the center of the universe despite a growing body of evidence that was inconsistent with this view.

The study of gender is full of examples of situations in which speculations and theories about gender have attained a status in which they are mistaken for results. It is important to keep in mind that the study of gender in ex post facto studies is limited in terms of potential conclusions.

Additional bias in research on gender (and many other topics) comes from the procedures involved in planning studies and evaluating results. Barbara Wallston (1981) argued that researchers' values enter the research process as early as the planning stage of studies, influencing the choice of problem to investigate and the questions to ask. She also contended that research and publication place too much emphasis on results and too little on the conceptualization of the questions underlying the research process. The answers that researchers find depend on the questions they ask, so the planning and questioning part of the process is critically important.

When researchers formulate their studies, they ask questions and choose a method of gathering information that will allow them to answer their questions. As Wallston pointed out, most researchers know what they expect to find when they ask their questions, so research is not free of the values and expectations of the scientists, even at this stage of the research. These expectations lead to the formulation of a **hypothesis,** a statement about the expected outcome of the study. Researchers test hypotheses by gathering data and analyzing it to obtain results. They can then decide if the results support or fail to support their hypothesis.

Table 2.1 shows the stages of research and how bias can enter at various points in the process. The possibilities for gender bias listed in the table are only examples, and the history of gender research is filled with too many other examples.

To evaluate the data collected from studies, researchers often use statistical tests. Many different statistical tests exist, but all of those used to evaluate research data have a common goal—to allow researchers to decide whether or not the results are statistically significant. A **statistically significant result** is one not due to chance alone. If researchers are careful in the design of their studies, then they can attribute significant

TABLE 2.1   Stages of Research and Potential for Bias

Stage	Ways Bias Can Enter	Gender-Related Example
Finding a problem to investigate	Allowing personal and societal values to influence choice of topic	Studying heart disease rather than breast cancer in middle-aged populations
Selecting variables	Using inaccurate, incomplete, or misleading definitions	Defining rape as vaginal penetration accompanied by force or threat of force (excludes other forced sexual acts and excludes men as victims)
Choosing a design	Choosing a design that would not allow for the evaluation of context	Testing participants in a situation that is anxiety provoking for women but not for men
Formulating a hypothesis	Failing to consider the validity of the null hypothesis; following a theory that is biased	Always hypothesizing gender differences rather than similarities; following Freudian theory to hypothesize that women have weak superegos
Collecting data	Permitting personal bias to influence measurement, leading to mistakes in the direction of researchers' prediction	Failing to record some cases of playground aggression in girls because the observer does not believe that girls are as aggressive as boys
Analyzing results	Allowing personal values and expectation to guide the choice of which factors to evaluate	Failing to make a comparison of female and male participants
Interpreting results	Highlighting expected findings while minimizing or ignoring unexpected findings	Failing to discuss a finding of gender similarities

results to the factors they have identified in their studies. The procedure for determining the statistical significance of a result involves choosing the appropriate statistical test and analyzing the data from the study using that statistic. If the analysis indicates significant effects, then the researchers can conclude that their results were not due to chance alone; that is, the study worked as hypothesized. If the analysis does not indicate a significant effect, then the researchers cannot claim that their results are due to anything but chance or that their study worked as hypothesized.

Researchers are constrained from making claims about factors that do not produce significant results, because these results are not considered "real," and researchers have no confidence in the validity of such results. When researchers obtain statistically significant results, they have confidence that their research has revealed effects that are not due to chance. However, the term *significant* can be misleading, because people who are not sophisticated in the logic of statistical evaluation may believe that statistically significant means important.

The concepts of statistical significance and practical significance are not the same. A result is statistically significant when it is unlikely to have occurred solely on the basis of chance. A result has **practical significance** when it is important to the area of research. For example, a low correlation ($r = 0.25$) can indicate a statistically significant relationship if the number of people participating in the study was sufficiently large (what constitutes a large sample varies with the design and statistic), but this magnitude of correlation does not reveal a strong relationship between the two variables in the correlation. That is, this correlation would have little practical significance. People who hear about significant results may believe that the results have practical significance when the researchers have reported only statistical significance. Such misunderstandings can lead people to believe that results mean more than they actually do.

The development of a statistical technique called **meta-analysis** allows researchers to evaluate results from several experimental studies. Janet Hyde (1986, p. 3) explained that meta-analysis allows "the synthesis or integration of numerous studies on a single topic and a quantitative or statistical approach to that synthesis." She contended that meta-analysis offers advantages over evaluations that count the outcomes or combine probabilities from various studies: Meta-analysis allows the combination and statistical evaluation of results from similar studies. This analysis technique allows researchers to simultaneously combine the results from many studies in order to determine the overall size of the effect of a variable of interest. The size of an effect can be an indication of its importance. Thus, meta-analysis gives researchers a technique to evaluate importance.

For example, one common finding of a gender difference is performance in mathematics. Many studies have found that boys score significantly higher than girls in high school and college mathematics courses (Maccoby & Jacklin, 1974). (This difference does not appear before junior high school age, so no general statement is correct about better math performance at all ages.) How much better are boys at math? Do all boys do better than all girls? How much do math scores of boys and girls overlap? Figure 2.2 shows some possibilities for the distributions of math scores for boys and girls. Figure 2.2 A shows two distributions with no overlap. If this figure represented the mathematics performance of boys and girls, then all boys would do better than all girls. Figure 2.2 B shows the performance of boys and girls overlapping slightly. If this figure represented the performance of boys and girls, then most boys would do better than most girls. A few girls would do better than a few boys, but no girls would do better than boys with the highest performance. Figure 2.2 C shows a lot of overlap between the performance of the two. If this figure represented performance, all boys would not do better at math than all girls, and many girls would do better at math than many boys.

Hyde (1981, 1986) contended that the upper range of difference between men and women is no more than 1% in mathematical ability. That is, only a small amount of the distributions of math scores for boys and girls fails to overlap, and most of the scores for the two are in the same range. Figure 2.2 C comes closer to this distribution of math ability than the other parts of Figure 2.2. Gender-related differences in math performance are sufficiently large to show a statistically significant difference, but this difference does not have any practical significance when applied to the performance of most boys and most girls. That is, this magnitude of difference would not lead educators to

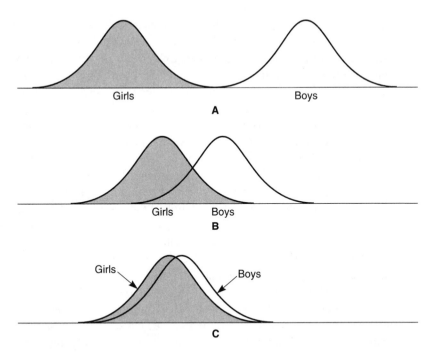

FIGURE 2.2   Distributions with Varying Degrees of Overlap

create different math classes for boys and girls because their abilities are so dissimilar, nor should counselors advise girls to avoid math courses because of lack of ability.

This gender difference in mathematics achievement after junior high school age may be due to many factors other than biological sex. Parents have expectations that their daughters will be less mathematically inclined than their sons and treat each accordingly. Teachers treat boys and girls differently in the classroom. Girls complete fewer math courses during high school and college. (See Chapter 5 for more about mathematics ability of girls and boys and Chapter 12 for more about classroom treatment.) These differences in experience and expectancy make it impossible to conclude that the gender difference in mathematics achievement is due to biological sex.

Finding statistically significant differences is the goal of both experimental and ex post facto designs. When researchers plan studies, they typically look for differences and draw their hypotheses accordingly. Such researchers do not look for similarities. If researchers find the expected differences, they report and discuss these differences. If they fail to find differences, such results do not typically lead to a discussion of the similarity of the groups. Instead, researchers will often dismiss the study (or this part of the study) as a failure and gloss over the lack of statistically significant differences.

Studies that do not find hypothesized differences are less likely to be published than studies that succeed in supporting the hypotheses. As Anthony Greenwald (1975) discussed, a strong prejudice exists in favor of findings that show differences rather than findings that fail to show differences; that is, there is a prejudice against findings that show similarities. This tendency to report and publish findings of significant differences therefore prompts researchers to highlight the differences they find and to dismiss the similarities. Indeed, researchers may omit any mention of failure to find a difference, such as a gender-related difference, but researchers who find statistically significant differences will always mention the differences and the level of statistical significance. Researchers cannot discuss an effect they have failed to find and must discuss effects that they have found. However, the omission of some information and the mention of other information can lead to a distorted view of overall findings by magnifying differences and obscuring similarities.

In summary, the limitations on gender research come from the type of studies that researchers must do and the interpretation of their results, both by the investigators and by others. All studies with gender as a subject variable are ex post facto studies rather than true experiments. Although these studies may appear to be experiments, no manipulation of conditions occurs, and experimenters do not have control over the subject's characteristics. This limitation restricts researchers from drawing conclusions from these studies about cause-and-effect relationships. Therefore, none of the studies with gender as a subject variable reveal the cause of the differences, although differences, not similarities, are the focus of the studies. Researchers look for statistically significant differences in their studies, often considering their studies failures if the results do not reveal such differences. However, studies that show statistically significant differences still may not demonstrate differences of such a magnitude to indicate practical significance. In the case of gender, statistically significant differences may still not reveal much about differences in behavior between women and men.

Debate over Methodology

The philosophers whose work spurred the founding of science were all men, and Evelyn Fox Keller (1985) has argued that they introjected a masculine bias into the very conceptual foundation of science. She has interpreted the emphasis on rationality and objectivity in science as masculine values, and she has contrasted those masculine elements of science with the feminine elements of nature—feeling and subjectivity. Thus, Keller discussed what she interpreted as the gendering of science and nature: masculine for science and feminine for nature. She also analyzed the interaction of the two in the view of one influential philosopher, Francis Bacon, who proposed a metaphor of a marriage between Nature and Science. In his metaphor Nature is the bride and Science is the groom. Keller took Bacon's metaphor as particularly significant in its gender and sexual connotations. She argued that this metaphor has influenced contemporary views of science as a masculine activity striving to bring rationality and to dominate unruly feminine nature. Thus, even at its inception, science carried connotations of maleness, rationality, and dominance. According to Keller, not only have women been discouraged from the pursuit of science as a profession, but the activity of science itself suggests masculinity.

Keller's analysis draws on the symbolic and unconscious images of science in modern culture, and other critics have attempted to replace the gendered terminology of masculine and feminine with the terms *agency* (or *agentic*) and *communion* (or *communal*). Philosopher David Bakan (1966) originated these terms, explaining that "agency manifests itself in self-protection, self-assertion, and self-expansion; communion manifests itself in the sense or being at one with other organisms. Agency manifests itself in the urge to master; communion in noncontractual cooperation" (p. 15). Although Bakan also connected these terms to masculinity and femininity, many gender researchers have adopted his terminology as a less overtly gendered way to describe these two dimensions.

Some feminist scholars have questioned much more than terminology or symbolic issues within science. Indeed, the methodology for investigating sex- and gender-related behaviors is the source of heated controversy. Although the scientific method may seem to be the basis for much modern knowledge, a sizable group of feminist scholars has advocated a rejection of traditional scientific methodology for the study of women, gender, and gender-related behaviors and has proposed alternatives for such investigations. Their dissatisfaction stems from the very nature of the scientific method and can be found in its history.

The traditional view of science holds that by using empirical, objective methods to gather and evaluate data, scientists try to understand the underlying laws of the natural world. As scientists gain more and more information, their view of the world becomes closer and closer to the "truth." However, this picture of the orderly progress of objective science has been the subject of increasing question and criticism.

Thomas Kuhn in *The Structure of Scientific Revolutions* (1962) analyzed the history of science and concluded that science does not proceed in an incremental, orderly way. Instead, Kuhn argued that science, like politics, progresses through a series of upheavals—revolutions—and periods of orderly progress—normal science. During the periods of normal science, the research is organized around a prevailing theory, a paradigm, and this paradigm defines the types and content of investigations. During the times of revolution, very little scientific research takes place, because no ruling paradigm exists to guide and order the work. Thus, Kuhn presented evidence that science is neither orderly nor incremental in its progress.

The objectivity of science has also come into question, especially regarding the study of women. Stephanie Riger (1992) presented the view, originating with feminist scholars, that science cannot distance itself from its subject matter in the ways that would be necessary for true objectivity. Instead, researchers carry their views and prejudices into their investigations, biasing scientific results through the subject matter they choose, through their hypotheses, through the methods chosen for the collection of data, and through their conclusions. Some of these critics take an extreme view, holding that science is inevitably biased and therefore not a legitimate way of knowing about the world, whereas other of these critics argue for trying harder to gain objectivity.

Yet another criticism of the subjectivity in science has come from the **constructionists,** who believe that "we do not discover reality, we invent it" (Hare-Mustin &

Marecek, 1988, p. 455). That is, science does not lead researchers to map a realistic picture of the world but to construct their view of the world in ways that reflect the personal perceptions and biases of these scientists. In this view, science is a process of invention rather than one of discovery. Bias is inevitable, the constructionists argue, because all humans are tied to their perceptions and actively try to organize and interpret all information, including scientific data. To disconnect perception to the point of objectivity would be impossible, and so science will always contain the influence of subjective perceptions.

Although the constructionist position may sound like a minor modification that acknowledges the limitations of human perception, it is a more fundamental criticism of science because it challenges the philosophies that underlie science (Gergen, 1985). According to the philosophy of positivism, one of the philosophies influential in founding science, the only way to legitimately gather information is through observation of objective facts and rejection of information gathered from other sources. Constructionists argue that objective facts do not exist, and anything presented as fact is personal and subjective perception. Therefore, science is not and cannot be free of values, nor can it be socially or politically neutral (Hare-Mustin & Marecek, 1988). The acknowledgment of the constructionist position can lead to either a rejection of science or to the attempt to factor this inevitable bias into science and to become more cautious in research and conclusions. Each of these alternatives has its advocates.

The social and political values of science are a focus for constructionists. Many of those psychologists who follow the constructionists' view have concentrated on presenting information about the oppression of women through manipulation of beliefs about gender. Riger (1992, p. 735) summarized the central question for the constructionists as "not how well our theories fit the facts or how well the facts produced by research fit what is real. Rather, the question is which values and social institutions are favored by each of multiple versions of reality."

Despite the long history and success of science, some modern scholars have questioned its assumptions and procedures. One criticism is that science grew from not only the activities of men but also from a gendered, masculine bias that is part of science. According to this view, this masculine bias affects our modern conception of science, including the men and women who do scientific work. Another more concrete criticism of science has come from the constructionists, who contend that science is incapable of revealing an objective picture of the natural world. This inability stems from the inevitable bias within the perceptions of scientists, who are influenced by their personal and societal prejudices. Scholars who take this view have used the study of gender as a particularly good example of the distortions and misrepresentations of science.

Methodologies for the Study of Gender

Whereas the charges of bias in scientific investigations have led some feminist scholars to call for a more objective study of gender, others have rejected science or called for radical changes in scientific methodology. As Hubbard (1990, p. 9) argued, "Ever since the scientific method became a way of learning about nature, including ourselves, some people have hailed science as the only way to comprehend natural phenomena, while others have questioned whether it is an appropriate road to knowledge."

Riger (1992) identified as *feminist empiricists* those scholars who have called for a more rigorous, objective study of sex and gender. Riger contrasted these empiricists with the view she called *feminist standpoint epistemologies.* Scholars who take this latter view claim that researchers should center their studies on women, because women have a unique point of view and different cognitive processes that have been ignored. These researchers believe that analytical categories that are appropriate for men may not be appropriate for women. They contend that the standards of measurement have come from research on men and thus present inappropriate standards for women. Riger (1992, p. 733) summarized this view by saying, "Although standardized scales might tell us what women have in common with men, they will not reveal the way women would define their own experience if given the opportunity to do so."

As a way of gaining additional information about women and their experience, the feminist standpoint epistemologies may have considerable value. Hope Landrine, Elizabeth Klonoff, and Alice Brown-Collins (1992) called for a revision of the traditional scientific method, arguing that it is inadequate in capturing important factors about women's experience. They demonstrated their point by studying the same problem with two methodologies: one objective and behavioral and the other subjective and relying on personal perceptions. They found that the subjective evaluation allowed participants to express feelings and show differences that the more traditional approach failed to demonstrate. Their study demonstrated that more diverse methods of investigation have the potential to enrich traditional science.

Other feminist researchers have argued that the development of a feminist methodology will not benefit research on women and gender-related behaviors. Letitia Anne Peplau and Eva Conrad (1989) contended that "a distinctive set of feminist methods for psychological research are not only futile but dangerous" and that "any method can be misused in sexist ways" (p. 380). These authors rejected the notion that methodology is gendered or that feminist research must be conducted by women or exclusively on women. Instead, they advocated the use of diverse and appropriate methods for the study of women and gender-related behaviors.

To adequately study gender-related differences and similarities, research must include men (or boys) as well as women (or girls). Without comparisons and contrasts, conclusions about gender-related behaviors will be unfounded. However, the necessary research must differ from much prior research, because so much of the existent research concerning gender is filled with serious bias. In 1986 Maureen McHugh, Randi Koeske, and Irene Frieze presented some suggestions for conducting nonsexist psychological research that were intended to alert researchers to the potential for inadvertently introducing sexist bias and to provide some ways of minimizing those biases. In other words, McHugh and her coauthors have made suggestions to help psychologists become more objective in their research. By taking such an approach, these suggestions fall within what Riger labeled feminist empiricism.

McHugh et al. acknowledged that psychology research has included biases, some of them unintentional, and cautioned that an unwarranted confidence in traditional research assumptions could lead to bias. For example, psychologists have usually acknowledged that self-reports are less objective than observations of behavior. However, observations are not necessarily free of sexist (or other) biases, because the *context* of the observation is rarely included in the analysis of the situation. The gender of the participants may be a factor in the study, but the gender of the experimenter is usually not. Yet, the gender of the experimenter may affect the behavior of participants, and researchers rarely consider this factor. For example, male experimenters may prompt female participants to behave in gender-stereotypical ways, whereas female experimenters might not, and female experimenters may elicit different reactions from male subjects than a male experimenter might.

In addition to excessive confidence in traditional methods, their recommendations included examining explanatory models by exercising care in the terminology employed and considering alternatives to even well-accepted findings. Also, they offered several cautions in interpreting results to avoid claiming more than the results legitimately imply. These suggestions caution researchers to avoid value labeling of behaviors without evidence of the value, to consider the context of the behavior, to include both women and men in research on gender-related behaviors, and to give appropriate emphasis to topics of interest to both men and women. McHugh and her coauthors conceded that following their guidelines would not eliminate gender bias in research, but they contended that such bias could be decreased and that nonsexist psychology research could reveal more about gender.

Thus, McHugh and her colleagues suggested ways to improve the methodology for studying gender rather than proposing a new method. The feminist standpoint epistemologies discussed by Riger (1992) have the disadvantage of departing too radically from accepted methodology to produce studies with well-accepted results and conclusions. Radical departures are accepted too slowly to make an impact on science. The recommendations of McHugh et al. are within traditional science and consist of guidelines for more careful research design. Such careful design might be appropriate for any psychology research but is particularly important for the study of gender.

Summary

Gender often makes the headlines, but the stories tend to concentrate on gender-related differences, especially biological explanations for such differences. These reports may be examples of biased reporting, but some gender researchers have accused science of being biased.

Science as a method of gathering information can be traced back to the 16th century and rests on philosophical traditions that assert the advantages of an objective, observation-based understanding of the world. By using descriptive methods such as naturalistic observation, correlational studies, and surveys, researchers gather and evaluate information that leads them to understand the world. By using the experimental method, researchers can develop an understanding of the cause-and-effect relationship between an independent variable and a dependent variable. Although the ex post facto method resembles experimentation, it differs in procedure and in the type of information it yields: Ex post facto studies do not involve the manipulation of independent variables and do not allow the determination of causality. All studies with gender as a variable are ex post facto designs, and none have the ability to reveal the cause of any differences they might show. In addition, studies that reveal gender-related differences may show a difference that is statistically significant—that is, not due to chance. Yet the difference may not have any practical significance; for instance, it may not reveal important differences between women and men.

Although the scientific method rests on objectivity, the constructionist movement in philosophy has argued that any observation is biased and that researchers can never escape their own personal feelings and beliefs when they do scientific studies. Rather than believing that researchers discover facts, the constructionists believe that all observers invent reality. An extreme version of this belief would demand the abandonment of research, but acknowledging the possibility of bias can

make researchers more careful. Those researchers who advise a greater attention to sexist bias in research can be described as feminist empiricists. On the other hand, some researchers advocate the abandonment of the traditional scientific method and the adoption of alternatives that center on women and different methods of gaining information. These methods can be described as feminist standpoint epistemologies. In psychology research, the former are more numerous than the latter, and some psychologists have considered the problems and proposed solutions for carrying out nonsexist research. Feminist standpoint epistemologies can add new dimensions to the study of both women and men, but abandonment of traditional scientific methods is unlikely. In addition, some feminist scholars have argued against excluding any method and argued for a more objective feminist empiricism.

Glossary

Constructionists   a group of critics of science who have argued that reality is constructed through perception and subject to inevitable bias; included in this bias is all scientific observation, thus excluding science from its claim of objectivity

Correlational study   a descriptive research method that requires researchers to make measurements on two factors from a group of people to determine the degree of relationship between the two factors

Data   representations, usually in numerical form, of some facet of the phenomenon that the researcher observes

Dependent variable   the factor in an experiment that the experimenter measures to determine if the manipulation of the independent variable has an effect

Descriptive research methods   a group of research methods, including naturalistic observation, surveys, and correlational studies, that yield descriptions of the observed phenomena

Empiricism   the philosophy that demands that information be obtained through direct observation

Experiment   a type of study in which a researcher manipulates an independent variable and observes the changes in a dependent variable; only through experiments can researchers learn about cause-and-effect relationships

Ex post facto study   a type of nonexperimental research design that includes a comparison of subjects who are placed in contrast groups on the basis of some preexisting characteristic of the subjects

Hypothesis   a statement about the expected outcome of a study

Independent variable   the factor in an experiment that the experimenter manipulates to create a difference that did not previously exist in the participants

Materialism   the philosophy that holds that all things can be described in physical terms and can be understood as physical properties

Meta-analysis   a statistical analysis that allows the evaluation of many studies simultaneously

Naturalistic observation   a descriptive research method that requires researchers to collect information about a naturally occurring situation without changing the situation in any way

Operational definition   a definition of the concept in terms of operations rather than concepts

Positivism   the philosophy that regards information as facts that are open to objective observation and rejects knowledge derived from theology or metaphysics

Practical significance   an important result with practical implications; different from statistical significance

Statistically significant result   a result obtained by analysis with statistical tests and found unlikely to have been obtained on the basis of chance alone

Subject variable   a characteristic of the subjects, such as gender, that allows researchers to form contrast groups in quasi-experimental studies

Survey   a descriptive research method involving the measurement of attitudes through the administration and interpretation of questionnaires

Variable   a factor of interest to researchers; something that can have more than one value, as opposed to a constant, which has only one constant value

Suggested Readings

McHugh, Maureen C.; Koeske, Randi D.; & Frieze, Irene H. (1986). Issues to consider in conducting nonsexist psychological research: A guide for researchers. *American Psychologist, 41,* 879–890. This thoughtful article carefully outlines the problems and presents solutions that occur in conducting nonsexist research in psychology.

Peplau, Letitia Anne; & Conrad, Eva. (1989). Beyond nonsexist research: The perils of feminist methods in psychology. *Psychology of Women Quarterly, 13,* 379–400. Peplau and Conrad criticize the concept that a feminist methodology is necessary for feminist research in psychology, contending that any method can be sexist or feminist. They instead argue for the use of a variety of methods.

Riger, Stephanie. (1992). Epistemological debates, feminist voices: Science, social values, and the study of women. *American Psychologist, 47,* 730–740. This excellent article outlines the different positions and ongoing debates about the scientific method. Although the article is not easy reading, Riger does a fine job of stating the complex issues in clear terms.

Chapter 3

Hormones and Chromosomes

Aggression in Men: Hormone Levels Are a Key
—*New York Times,* July 17, 1990

Raging Hormones: The Unofficial PMS Survival Guide
—*People Weekly,* May 28, 1990

In 1990 these two stories suggested that hormones affect human behavior in negative ways. Daniel Goleman's (1990b) story in the *New York Times* described the results from several research projects that investigated the relationship between testosterone and aggression. Leah Rozen's story (1990) in *People Weekly* reviewed a humorous book about premenstrual syndrome (PMS). Although the title of Goleman's story suggested that hormone levels are a key to aggression, the story included not only evidence of such a relationship but also some failures to find a relationship between these two factors. Among the skeptics quoted in Goleman's article was Robert Rose, a researcher who cautioned against overemphasizing the role of hormones in human behavior. Rose contended that many other factors influence aggression and that a search for a simple relationship would be unsuccessful.

Rozen's article was a review of a book by the same title, *Raging Hormones: The Unofficial PMS Survival Guide,* by Martha Williamson and Robin Sheets. This book is a humorous examination of the concept of premenstrual syndrome rather than research on PMS. However, all these authors assumed the existence and validity of the PMS concept, which holds that in the days before their periods women experience negative mood, food cravings, increased sexual drive, and difficulty in handling ordinary problems and stress.

Both of these popular articles stressed the role of hormones in a wide variety of behaviors. Are these views correct? If so, what role do hormones play in physical development and ongoing behavior? Are hormones the key to the differences between male and female? Or are chromosomes the key? To answer these questions, this chapter examines development from an individual's conception, exploring the contribution of chromosomes and then tracing the effect of hormones throughout prenatal development and again during puberty. When hormonal or chromosomal abnormalities occur, individuals do not follow the pattern of developing into women or men. Instead, these individuals develop characteristics of each, providing interesting examples of the roles of chromosomes and hormones in the development of sex and gender. Finally, this chapter examines the role of hormones in adult behavior, including the relationships claimed by the headlines between hormone levels and the behaviors associated with premenstrual syndrome and with aggression.

The Endocrine System and Steroid Hormones

Hormones are substances released from **endocrine glands** to circulate throughout the body. Receptors on various organs are sensitive to specific hormones, which produce many different actions in various sites. Although the body contains many endocrine glands that secrete many different hormones, **steroid hormones** relate to the differences between the sexes and reproduction. The reproductive organs are the **gonads,** the ovaries and testes. These organs are obviously among the physical differences between the sexes and are also essential to reproduction, but the ovaries and testes are not the only endocrine glands that are important for sexual development and functioning.

The **pituitary gland** is located within the brain and is often referred to as the master gland because its function controls the production of many other hormones. The pituitary produces many **tropic hormones,** which stimulate the release of other hormones. Thus, the action of the pituitary controls many hormones. Gonadotropins are one type of hormones produced by the pituitary. These hormones circulate through the bloodstream and stimulate the ovaries and testes to release their hormones.

The action of the pituitary is affected by a nearby brain structure, the hypothalamus. The complex action of the hypothalamus results in the production of a type of hormones called **releasing hormones.** The action of releasing hormones is necessary for the pituitary to release its tropic hormones. Therefore, the hypothalamus acts to produce releasing hormones, such as gonadotropin-releasing hormone, which stimulates the pituitary to release its gonadotropins, which in turn stimulate the gonads to produce their hormones. Figure 3.1 summarizes the action of these glands and hormones.

Gonadal hormones are of the steroid type; that is, all these hormones are derived from cholesterol and consist of a structure that includes four carbon rings. The two main classes of gonadal hormones are **androgens** and **estrogens.** Although people tend to think of androgens as "male hormones" and estrogens as "female hormones," that

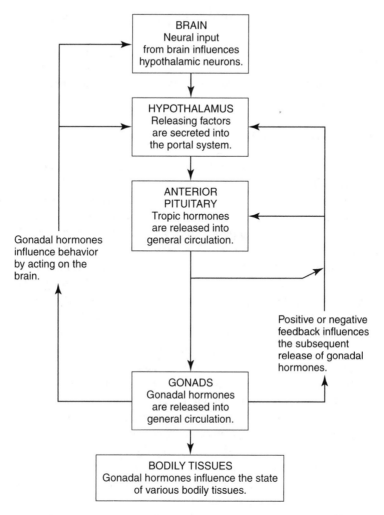

FIGURE 3.1   A Summary Model of the Regulation of Gonadal Hormones

SOURCE: From *Biopsychology* (p. 356) by J.P.J. Pinel, 1993, Boston: Allyn and Bacon. Copyright © 1993 by Allyn and Bacon. Reprinted by permission.

belief is somewhat inaccurate—each sex produces both types of hormones. The most common of the androgens is **testosterone,** and the most common of the estrogens is **estradiol.** Men typically produce a greater proportion of androgens than estrogens, and women typically produce a greater portion of estrogens than androgens.

The gonads also secrete a third type of hormone, the **progestins.** The most common progestin is progesterone, which plays a role in preparing a woman's body for pregnancy. Men also secrete progesterone, but its function for them is unknown (Pinel,

1993). The chemical structure of the androgens, estrogens, and progestins is very similar.

The gonads are not the only glands that produce steroid hormones; the adrenal gland also produces them. Although the amounts of hormones produced by the adrenal glands are smaller than the amounts produced by the gonads, the types are the same.

Stages of Differences between the Sexes

Humans (and most other animals) are sexually dimorphic; that is, they have two different physical versions—female and male. This **sexual dimorphism** is the result of development that begins with conception and ends at puberty, resulting in men and women who are capable of sexual reproduction. Alexandra Kaplan (1980) discussed the process of sexual dimorphism as the product of five stages: genetic, gonadal, hormonal, internal genitalia, and external genitalia. The *genetic stage* refers to the inheritance of the chromosomes related to sex. The *gonadal stage* includes the development of the gonads, the reproductive organs. The *hormonal stage* begins prenatally, when the testes or ovaries start to secrete androgens and estrogens. Hormonal development also occurs at puberty, producing mature, functional gonads. The stage of developing the *internal genitalia,* the internal reproductive organs, occurs prenatally and affects not only the ovaries or testes but also the other internal structures relating to reproductive functioning. Therefore, the **internal genitalia** consist of the internal structures related to reproduction: ovaries, Fallopian tubes, uterus, and upper vagina in women and testes, seminal vesicles, and vas deferens in men. The **external genitalia** are the reproductive structures that can be seen without internal examination: clitoris, labia, and vaginal opening in women and penis and scrotum in men. The stage of developing the *external genitalia* occurs later during the prenatal period than the development of internal genitalia. This last development results in the differences that are apparent at birth.

In producing a woman or a man, prenatal development is critically important. Before a newborn can be pronounced a boy or a girl, a great many prenatal events must occur in a coordinated sequence. These prenatal events usually follow a complex set of stages that result in a girl or a boy, but sometimes things go wrong. When things go wrong, the result is a baby who has some developmental abnormalities as a result of the combination of the female and the male pattern of development. These mistakes are rare, and these cases are not only clinically interesting but also provide a means of understanding the necessary elements of normal development.

Sexual Differentiation

The development of sexual differences is a complex process. The physical differences between men and women start at conception—the fertilization of an ovum by a sperm cell. Most of the cells in the human body contain 23 pairs of chromosomes, but ova and sperm carry half the normal amount of chromosomal material. In the fertilized ovum, the full amount of genetic material is present, with half coming from the mother's ovum and half from the father's sperm.

Of the 23 pairs of human chromosomes, pair number 23 is the one that is critical in determining chromosomal sex. Although most chromosomes are X shaped, only those in pair 23 are called **X chromosomes.** An individual who inherits two of these X chromosomes (one X from their mother and the other X from their father) will have the genetic patterns to develop according to the female pattern. Individuals who inherit one X and one **Y chromosome** (the X from their mother and the Y from their father) will have the genetic information to develop according to the male pattern. Therefore, normal girls and women have the XX pattern of chromosome pair 23, and normal boys and men have the XY pattern.

The presence of the XY chromosome constellation is only the first factor that produces male physiology, and its presence is not sufficient to produce a normal male. Other configurations are possible for pair 23, but those patterns are abnormalities, discussed later in the section titled "When Things Go Wrong."

Development of Male and Female Physiology

After conception the fertilized ovum starts to grow, first by dividing into two cells, then four, and so on. The ball of cells becomes larger and starts to differentiate; that is, to form the basis for different structures and organs. Within the first six weeks of prenatal development, no difference exists between male and female embryos, even in their gonads. Both the embryos with the XX pattern and the XY pattern have the same structures, and this duplication gives both types of individuals the potential to develop into individuals who look like and who have the internal reproductive organs of either boys or girls.

Of the Reproductive Organs

Both male and female embryos have a **Wolffian system,** which has the capacity to develop into the male internal reproductive system, and a **Müllerian system,** which has the capacity to develop into the female internal reproductive system.

During the third month of prenatal development, two things typically happen to fetuses with the XY chromosome pattern that furthers the developing male pattern. The first involves the production of androgens, which begin to be produced by the fetal testes during this period. The presence of androgens stimulates the development of the Wolffian system. The growth of the testes further increases production of testosterone and stimulates development along the lines of the male pattern.

The second event that prompts male development is production of Müllerian-inhibiting substance, which causes the Müllerian system to degenerate. Therefore, one type of secretion prompts the development of the Wolffian system into the male internal reproductive organs, and the other causes the female Müllerian system to degenerate. One action produces a masculinization and the other a defeminization of the developing fetus, and both actions produce male internal reproductive organs in the fetus. Figure 3.2 shows how the male reproductive system develops from the Wolffian system, resulting in testes, vas deferens, and seminal vesicles. This figure also illustrates how both male and female reproductive structures originate from the same prenatal structures.

The development of the female reproductive system requires no surge of fetal hormones. Some estrogen is necessary for normal development but not in amounts similar to the amount of testosterone necessary for development of the male reproductive system. In female embryos the Wolffian system degenerates and the Müllerian system develops, resulting in ovaries, uterus, Fallopian tubes, and the upper part of the vagina. Figure 3.2 also shows how the female reproductive system develops from the Müllerian system.

Six weeks after conception, the external genitalia of male and female fetuses are also identical. That is, the structures that will become the penis and scrotum in males and the clitoris, outer and inner labia, and vaginal opening in females have not yet formed. The fetal structures that exist at this point have the potential to develop into either male or female external genitalia, depending on the presence of androgens, especially testosterone.

Figure 3.3 shows the development of the external genitalia for both the male and female pattern. Notice that the structures are identical at six weeks after conception but start to differentiate into the two different patterns during the third and fourth months of gestation.

Prenatal production of androgens produces the male pattern, and the absence of androgens results in an incomplete version of the female pattern. If little or no hormones of either type are present, a fetus will develop external genitals that appear more like the female than the male structures, but without estrogens the normal female physiology does not fully develop. The presence of some prenatal estrogen results in development of the female pattern. These effects organize developing fetuses around the female or male pattern, resulting in permanent changes in the ability to produce hormones and also in the existence and function of reproductive organs.

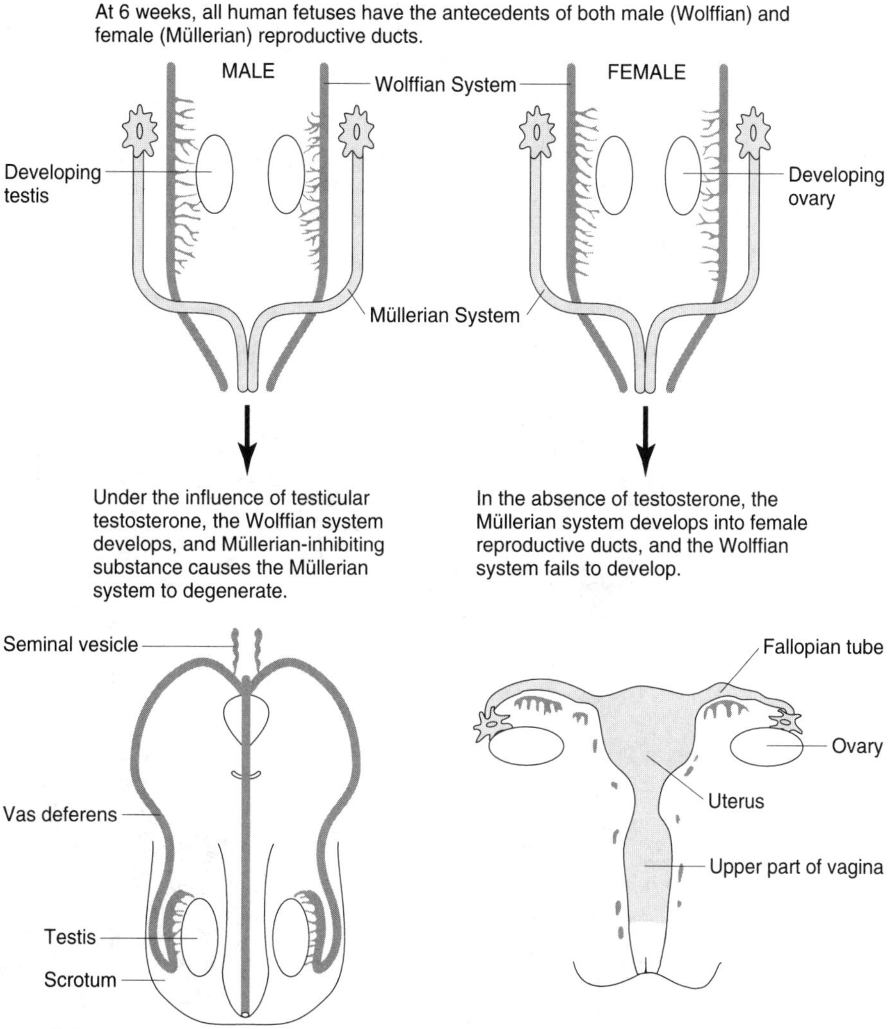
At 6 weeks, all human fetuses have the antecedents of both male (Wolffian) and female (Müllerian) reproductive ducts.
MALE
Wolffian System
FEMALE
Developing testis
Developing ovary
Müllerian System
Under the influence of testicular testosterone, the Wolffian system develops, and Müllerian-inhibiting substance causes the Müllerian system to degenerate.
In the absence of testosterone, the Müllerian system develops into female reproductive ducts, and the Wolffian system fails to develop.
Seminal vesicle
Vas deferens
Testis
Scrotum
Fallopian tube
Ovary
Uterus
Upper part of vagina

FIGURE 3.2 Development of Internal Reproductive System

SOURCE: From *Biopsychology* (p. 360) by J.P.J. Pinel, 1993, Boston: Allyn and Bacon. Copyright © 1993 by Allyn and Bacon. Reprinted with permission.

Of the Brain

Organizing effects influence the development of the brain as well as the organs that relate to reproduction, and the common mechanism determining these differences is the presence of different amounts of androgens and estrogens during prenatal development. With rats, the differences between male and female brains and the course of the developments are easy to investigate, but due to practical and ethical limitations on experimentation with humans, similar investigations are difficult. Thus, many of the find-

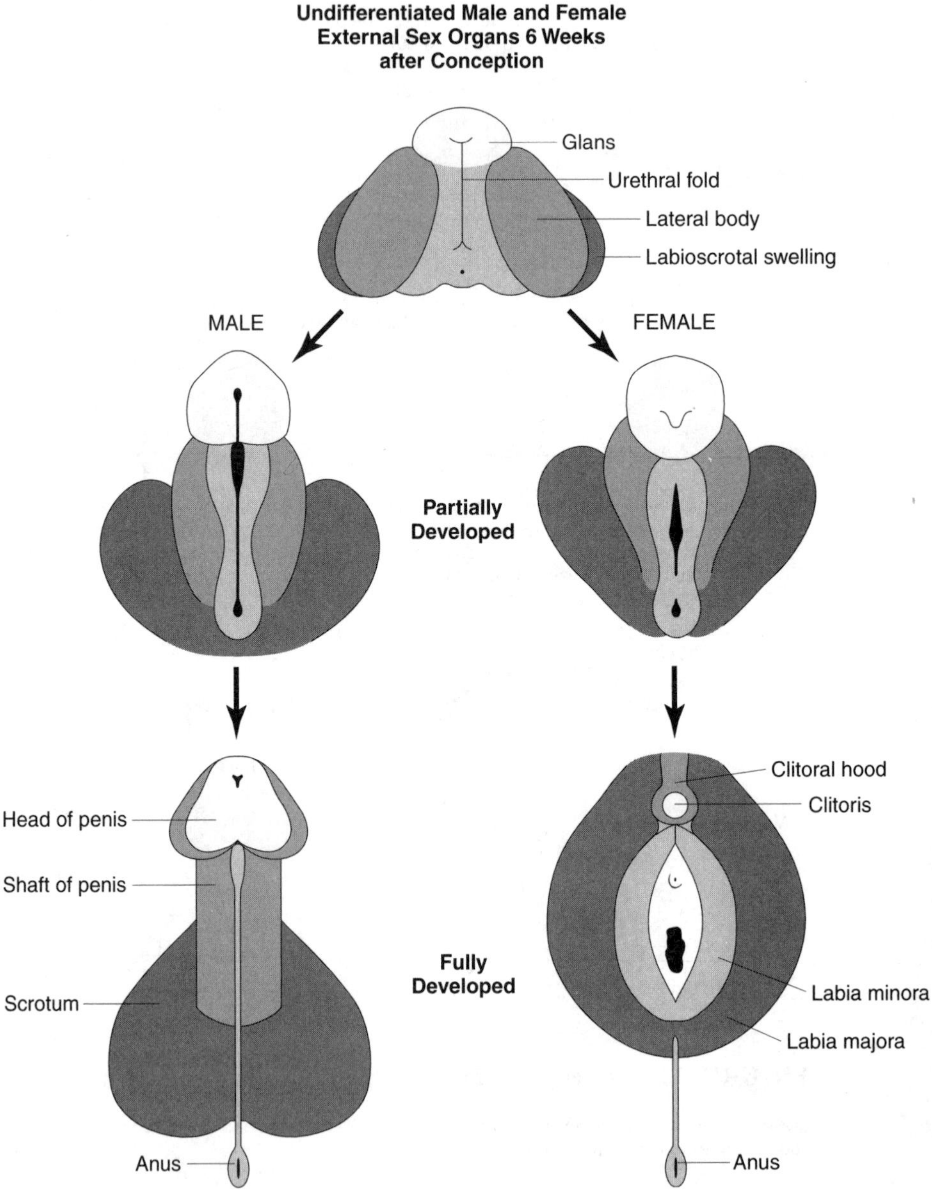

**Undifferentiated Male and Female
External Sex Organs 6 Weeks
after Conception**

**FIGURE 3.3   Development of Male and Female External Reproductive Organs
from the Same Biopotential Precursor**

SOURCE: From *Biopsychology* (p. 361) by J.P.J. Pinel, 1993, Boston: Allyn and Bacon. Copyright © 1993 by Allyn
and Bacon. Reprinted by permission.

ings about brain differences come from studies with rats or other nonhuman subjects, and the generalizations to humans should be done with the proper caution.

The mechanisms for producing the masculine pattern provide one of the most ironic stories in the area of gender differences—how female brains become different from male brains through the action of "female" hormones. The structural similarities of testosterone and estradiol are the basis for this odd occurrence. As Figure 3.4 shows, these two steroid hormones have similar structures. An enzyme found in the brain can transform testosterone (an androgen) into estradiol (an estrogen). Other types of androgens that cannot undergo this transformation are not as effective in masculinizing the brain. Therefore, the main masculinizing agent is the "female" hormone estradiol. Also shown in Figure 3.4 is the mechanism that prevents circulating estrogens from masculinizing a developing female fetus—the presence of alpha-fetoprotein. This protein blocks estrogens from leaving the bloodstream and entering cells. Because the estrogens cannot enter cells and take any action, their presence does not produce masculinization of female fetuses. Testosterone can enter the cells, where it is converted to estradiol, producing masculinization of the brains of male fetuses.

This mechanism operates in rats, and alpha-fetoprotein exists in humans, but its characteristics differ such that its action cannot be equivalent for rats and humans

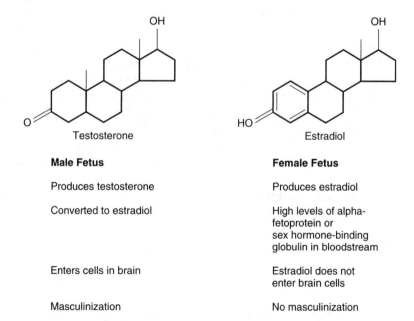

OH   OH

Testosterone   Estradiol

Male Fetus   **Female Fetus**

Produces testosterone   Produces estradiol

Converted to estradiol   High levels of alpha-
                                            fetoprotein or
                                            sex hormone-binding
                                            globulin in bloodstream

Enters cells in brain   Estradiol does not
                                            enter brain cells

Masculinization   No masculinization

**FIGURE 3.4 Mechanisms for Masculinization of the Male
Fetal Brain and Failure to Masculinize the
Female Fetal Brain**

(MacLusky & Naftolin, 1981). Another substance, sex hormone-binding globulin, may perform the same function in humans (Hoyenga & Hoyenga, 1993). This substance also binds to steroid hormones, affecting their function, and sex hormone-binding globulin is more abundant in female fetuses and women than in male fetuses and men. Thus, alpha-fetoprotein and sex hormone-binding globulin may perform equivalent functions, preventing "female" hormones from producing a masculinizing effect.

The organizing effects of hormones take place in human fetuses during critical periods during which the stimulation of these hormones causes permanent changes in structure and function. These changes result in the female or male pattern of gonadal, hormonal, genital, and brain organization. However, these differences are not sufficient to produce sexually interested, active people capable of reproducing. Such changes depend on the activating effects of hormones during puberty.

Changes during Puberty

The levels of circulating hormones are low during infancy and childhood, but these levels increase during puberty, the onset of sexual maturity. The changes that occur during this period include not only fertility but also the adolescent growth spurt and the development of secondary sex characteristics. These characteristics include the differences between male and female bodies other than reproductive ones and are shown in Figure 3.5. Both sexes experience the growth of body and pubic hair and the appearance of acne. Young men experience the growth of facial hair, larynx enlargement, hairline recession, and muscle development, whereas young women experience breast development, rounding of body contours, and menarche—the beginning of menstruation. All of these changes are prompted by changes in the release of hormones.

The adolescent growth spurt is the result of muscle and bone growth in response to increased release of growth hormone by the pituitary. Increased production of tropic hormones by the pituitary acts on the adrenal glands and the gonads to increase their production of gonadal and adrenal hormones. As puberty begins, the pituitary starts to release two gonadotropic hormones into the bloodstream—**follicle-stimulating hormone (FSH)** and **luteinizing hormone (LH).** These hormones stimulate the gonads to increase their production of estrogens and androgens. Increased circulation of these gonadal hormones results in maturation of the genitals; that is, development of fertility, as well as the development of secondary sex characteristics.

In adolescent boys and in men, the production of androgens is proportionately higher than their production of estrogens; in adolescent girls and in women, the production of estrogens is proportionately higher than their production of androgens. Again, it would be inaccurate to think of androgens as "male" hormones and estrogens as "female" hormones. An example of the influence of one hormone on both sexes comes from the growth of pubic and underarm hair: One of the androgens results in the growth of pubic and underarm hair in both boys and girls.

LH and FSH, the hormones that initiate puberty, are also important for reproduction. In girls and women, the production of these two hormones varies cyclically, whereas in boys and men, their production is not cyclic (but neither is it entirely

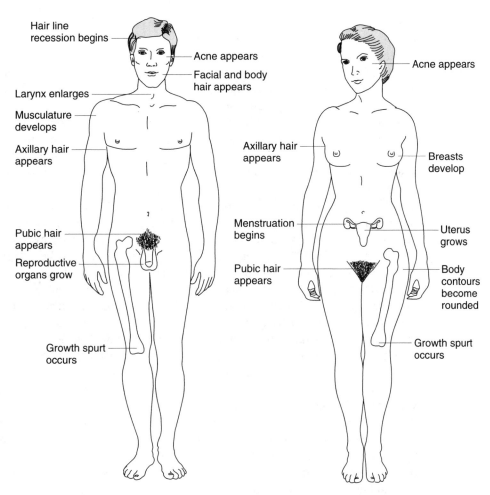

FIGURE 3.5   Changes Occuring in Males and Females during Puberty

Source: From *Biopsychology* (p. 365) by J.P.J. Pinel, 1993, Boston: Allyn and Bacon. Copyright © 1993 by Allyn and Bacon. Reprinted by permission.

steady). The cyclic variation of LH and FSH produces the menstrual cycle, beginning with an increase in the production of luteinizing hormone-releasing factor and follicle-stimulating hormone-releasing factor by the hypothalamus. As with other releasing factors, these two cause the pituitary to produce LH and FSH. Follicle-stimulating hormone stimulates follicles, a group of cells within the ovaries, to mature an ovum. Luteinizing hormone causes the follicle to rupture and release the ovum, which begins to travel down the Fallopian tube toward the uterus. The remainder of the follicle starts to produce the hormone progesterone, which prepares the uterus to receive and implant the ovum, if it happens to be fertilized. Then all of these hormone levels begin to decline. If the ovum is fertilized, pregnancy will produce an increase in estradiol and progesterone, but if the ovum is not fertilized, the prepared lining of the uterus is shed in menstruation, and the cycle starts again.

In boys puberty causes the maturation of internal and external genitalia, including growth of the penis, seminal vesicles, and prostate. The maturation of seminal vesicles and prostate is necessary for ejaculation of seminal fluid, and sperm production is necessary for fertility. Follicle-stimulating hormone and luteinizing hormone are involved in the production and maturation of sperm. FSH is involved in the production of sperm, and LH contributes to the maturation of sperm, but its main function is to stimulate the production of testosterone. Testosterone is controlled by feedback to the hypothalamus that can inhibit or prompt the production of LH and FSH, which can affect the production of sperm.

The role of hormones is essential in the regulation of fertility, and the role of hormones for sexual activity is very clear in some animals. In some animals the cyclic production of hormones by the females relates to sexual receptivity or level of interest in sexual activity. For example, this relationship is very clear in rats: Female rats are receptive during the time of their cycle that they are fertile, and male rats respond to that receptivity. Hormone levels are also important for the development and maintenance of sexual interest. Rats that have their gonads removed before puberty fail to develop any interest in sexual activity. If their gonads are removed after puberty, their sexual interest fades. In humans, the relationship between hormonal levels and sexual interest is far from clear, but some activating effects of hormones on sexual interest exist.

Individuals who do not undergo puberty generally fail to develop much interest in sexual activity (Meyer-Bahlburg, 1980), so hormones seem to be important in the development of sexual interest in humans as well as in other animals. However, the relationship is far from simple, and according to Heino Meyer-Bahlburg (1980, p. 76), "Puberty seems to be a necessary condition for normal psychosexual development but by no means sufficient by itself." No single measure of sexual interest or activity correlates very well with the onset of increased hormone levels in humans during puberty, but conditions that prevent this increase seem to result in a failure to develop sexual interest and activity.

The story is even more complex concerning the maintenance of sexual activity in humans who experience a decline of hormone levels. Such declines can occur for a number of reasons, including removal of the gonads or decreased hormone production associated with aging. For men, removal of the testes tends to produce a decrease in sexual activity, but the extent and rate of decrease vary enormously from person to person. Some men experience a significant and rapid loss of either ability to get an erection, ability to ejaculate, or both, whereas other men experience a slow decrease in interest in sexual activity, followed by difficulty in ejaculating and then followed by loss of ability to achieve erection. Few men remain unaffected by loss of androgens, and replacement testosterone tends to reverse the decline in sexual interest and performance.

On the other hand, women's sexual interest seems less affected by the removal of ovaries. Indeed, some women report increased sexual motivation after such surgery. One possibility is that the hormones that are important for the maintenance of sexual interest in women are androgens, and so a decrease in estrogen is not critical. Adrenal androgens may be sufficient to maintain sexual interest. Another possibility is that humans are so little controlled by their hormones that drastic physical changes in sexually mature adults are mediated by experience and expectation. Additionally, some combination of hormones and expectancy may account for the variations of sexual motivation in men and women without gonadal hormones.

In summary, luteinizing hormone and follicle-stimulating hormone produce the changes in reproductive and secondary sex characteristics associated with puberty. In girls, these changes produce cyclic variations in hormone levels that are associated with the maturation and release of an ovum approximately every month. If this ovum is fertilized by a sperm, the fertilized ovum will implant in the uterus and pregnancy will occur. If no fertilization occurs, the lining of the uterus is shed in menstruation, and the process will reoccur. In boys, the changes during puberty produce growth of the penis and maturation of the internal reproductive system, which will allow them to produce and ejaculate sperm. In addition to the physical changes associated with boys' bodies and reproductive systems, raised levels of gonadal hormones seem to be related to the development of sexual interest. Individuals who do not undergo puberty do not develop motivation to participate in sexual activity. Also, the maintenance of sexual interest in humans is not directly related to the levels of hormones but instead depends on experience and expectancy.

When Things Go Wrong

A number of events relating to the development of the reproductive system can, but usually do not, go wrong during prenatal development. These mistakes can originate even before conception, with the formation of the mother's ovum or the father's sperm. Yet other problems arise when the prenatal hormones are not consistent with the genetic configuration of the developing fetus.

Abnormalities sometimes occur in the assortment of chromosomes carried by the sperm and ova. Instead of the normal 23, sometimes chromosomes are missing or extra chromosomes appear. Several types of chromosomal abnormalities have direct effects on the development of the internal reproductive system, the external genitalia, or both. Beginning with the single cell consisting of fertilized ovum, males differ from females in their chromosomes, but the presence of the normal sex chromosome pattern does not guarantee the development of a normal boy or girl.

Abnormalities in Number of Chromosomes

Turner's syndrome (sometimes identified without the possessive as *Turner syndrome*) occurs when the fertilized ovum has only one chromosome of pair 23—that is, one X. This syndrome is usually described as X0, where the 0 stands for zero, a missing chromosome. Although many embryos with this chromosomal configuration spontaneously abort (Mittwoch, 1973), some do not. Less than 1 in 10,000 individuals are born with this abnormality. Individuals with Turner's syndrome appear to be female at birth, because their external genitals develop according to the female pattern. However, the internal reproductive organs do not develop normally. Their prenatal development begins normally, but their Müllerian system does not continue to develop, and thus their Müllerian system degenerates, producing an individual with no functioning ovaries. At birth they are identified as girls because of the appearance of their external genitalia, but without ovaries, they produce no estrogens, so they do not undergo puberty or produce ova. Without hormone supplementation they do not experience puberty and are not fertile, even with hormone supplements.

Another mistake in chromosome number is the presence of an extra X chromosome—the XXX pattern. Extra chromosomal material typically produces problems in development, often in intelligence. Individuals with the XXX pattern develop prenatally as female, but their development may not be entirely normal. Women with the XXX pattern may be either retarded or of normal intelligence. They may have menstrual irregularities or amenorrhea (absence of menstrual periods) that result in sterility (Mittwoch, 1973), but again they may not, and some women with this chromosomal pattern have had children. According to Ursula Mittwoch, individuals with the XXXX pattern and XXXXX pattern have also been identified, and these individuals tend to have more severe developmental problems and are very likely to be retarded and sterile.

Klinefelter's syndrome is the most common of the sex chromosome abnormalities; these individuals have an XXY pattern. This problem occurs in 2 cases per 1,000 male births (Mittwoch, 1973). Individuals with Klinefelter's syndrome have male internal and external genitalia, but their testes are small and cannot produce sperm, resulting in sterility. They may also develop breasts and a feminized body shape during puberty. Like other people with extra chromosomal material, individuals with Klinefelter's syndrome have an increased chance of mental retardation. Other configurations of chromosomes are similar to Klinefelter's syndrome, including XXXY and XXXXY. These individuals typically have more severe deformities of the reproductive and skeletal systems as well as a higher probability of severe mental retardation.

The XYY chromosome pattern has been the subject of a great deal of publicity. Herman Witkin and his colleagues (1976) reported:

> *Stories about a few men who had or were presumed to have an extra Y chromosome and who had committed serious crimes were given prominent attention in the press, suggesting the intriguing idea that the single Y chromosome normally found in males contributes to "aggressive tendencies" in that sex and that an extra Y carries these tendencies beyond their usual bounds.* (p. 547)

These sensational reports, however, were largely unfounded. Witkin et al. demonstrated that individuals with the XYY pattern of chromosomes were men who tended to be very tall and that these men were more likely than normal men to be in prison. The earlier sensational reports led to great interest and publicity about "supermales" who seemed to show some of the negative behaviors of men—violent aggression and criminal behavior—but in increased amounts. Further examination of XYY men in prison failed to confirm the notion that these individuals are more violent than other criminals (Witkin et al., 1976). Indeed, the XYY inmates were no more likely to be imprisoned for violent crimes than other inmates, although they were significantly taller than other men. Consistent with the general finding that extra chromosomal material has a tendency to produce mental retardation, XYY individuals are more likely than other men to be mildly retarded. Thus, their height and their lower intelligence, or a combination of the two, may be the reason why a disproportionate number of XYY men are in prison: They are not very adept criminals, and witnesses may find a very tall man easy to identify, making their apprehension more likely than other offenders.

In summary, missing or extra sex chromosomes often affect the development of the sexual organs but more often affect other areas of development, especially intelligence. Although some individuals with missing or extra chromosomal material have normal intelligence, there is a tendency for these people to be mildly to severely retarded. Both missing chromosomes (Turner's syndrome) and extra chromosomes (Klinefelter's syndrome) cause sterility, but individuals with the XXX pattern and the XYY pattern may behave sexually and socially as women or men, respectively.

Abnormalities in Prenatal Hormones

The presence of the XY chromosome pattern is not essential for the development of either internal or external genitalia of males; the hormone testosterone is the key to these developments. Therefore, a fetus that is genetically female (XX pattern) can be masculinized by the addition of testosterone during the critical period during the third and fourth months of prenatal development. Normally, female fetuses would not produce testosterone during this critical period of developing the genitalia, but prenatal exposure to androgens can occur, either through the action of tumors in the adrenal gland or through the pregnant woman's inadvertent or intentional exposure to androgens.

The **adrenogenital syndrome** occurs when the adrenal gland decreases its production of the hormone cortisol, which produces an increase in production of adrenal androgens. For a male fetus or for a boy, increased androgen production is not a very serious problem, except that it accelerates the onset of puberty. For a developing female fetus, however, the presence of excessive androgens produces masculinization of the external genitalia. Although their internal genitals are usually normal, because the excess androgens are produced too late to affect this stage of development, these girls are born with a clitoris that may look very much like a penis. If their genitals appear abnormal at birth, their parents and physicians often recommend surgical correction to produce a more normal female appearance. These girls usually receive oral doses of cortisol, which reduces the levels of circulating androgens and allows them normal physical development.

A more serious problem is **androgen insensitivity syndrome.** This disorder occurs in normal XY male fetuses whose body cells are insensitive to androgens; that is, the androgens produced by their fetal testes will not induce masculinization because the androgen receptors in their bodies do not function normally. These fetuses will develop as though no androgens were present, and at birth the XY fetus will appear to be a girl. The internal genitalia are not female, however, as the production of Müllerian-inhibiting substance proceeded normally, causing a degeneration of the Müllerian system. Thus, these individuals do not have the internal genitalia of either males or females but their external genitalia appear female.

These individuals with androgen insensitivity syndrome (and their families) can be completely unaware of the disorder until they reach the age at which puberty should occur. Complicating the diagnosis further, their testes produce sufficient estrogen to prompt breast development, increasing their feminine appearance. As they have no ovaries, Fallopian tubes, or uterus, they will not reach **menarche,** the beginning of menstruation. Nor will they grow pubic hair, a characteristic under the control of the androgens, to which they are insensitive. No amount of added androgens will reverse this problem, because their body cells are insensitive to it. Indeed, they have levels of circulating androgens that are within the normal range for men, but their bodies cannot respond to these hormones.

Individuals with androgen insensitivity syndrome are identified as girls at birth, raised as girls, and have no reason to doubt their gender identification for years. At puberty they grow breasts and begin to look like young women, giving them no reason to imagine they are anything but women. Typically, few suspicions arise concerning any abnormality until they fail to grow pubic hair and fail to reach menarche. Even then these symptoms may be discounted for several years due to the variability of sexual development.

When gynecological examination reveals the abnormality of their internal genitalia, these individuals and their families learn that they are, in some sense, men. This information contradicts years of gender role development, and these individuals often have a difficult adjustment to their new status. No treatments exist to masculinize these individuals, so no attempt is made to change their gender identification. Individuals with androgen insensitivity syndrome continue in the female gender role and most seek sexual relationships with men. Although they cannot have children, surgical alteration can lengthen their vagina so that they can have sexual intercourse. Despite their male chromosomes, these individuals are women in terms of gender identification, physical appearance, and behavior.

Through a variety of mechanisms, a person can be born with characteristics of both sexes. The traditional diagnosis for these individuals is **hermaphroditism,** but a more modern term is **intersexuality,** and both terms continue in use. True hermaphroditism is extremely rare, with no more than 60 cases being identified in Europe and North America within the last century (Money, 1986). Hermaphroditism occurs when an individual has both ovarian and testicular tissue—either an ovary on one side of the body and a testicle on the other side, or both types of tissue combined into a structure called an ovotestis. However, pseudohermaphroditism, in which individuals have some of the structures of both sexes, occurs much more frequently. Those with adrenogenital syndrome would be considered pseudohermaphrodites, as would those with androgen insensitivity syndrome.

These possibilities for variations within development of the reproductive organs led gender researcher John Money (1986) to write:

In my earliest studies of hermaphroditism, I came to the realization that there is no absolute dichotomy of male and female. A person's sex must be specified not on the basis of a single criterion, but of multiple criteria. For example, it is possible to have the genetic sex of a male ... the gonadal sex of a male; the internal morphologic sex of a male; the external genital morphologic sex of a female; the hormonal pubertal sex of a female; the assigned sex of a female; and the gender-role and identity of a female. This is what typically happens in the androgen-insensitivity syndrome—and there are many other syndromes, each with its own story. (p. 239)

A provocative example of pseudohermaphroditism comes from individuals with a genetic enzyme deficiency that prevents chromosomal males from developing male external genitalia during the prenatal period. Like individuals with androgen insensitivity syndrome, these babies appear more female than male at birth and are often identified as girls. The appearance of their external genitals is ambiguous, neither truly female but definitely not male. Unlike people with androgen insensitivity syndrome, these individuals respond to androgens during puberty and undergo masculinization. That is, their voice deepens, their muscles develop, their testes descend into the scrotum, and they grow a penis (Herdt, 1990). If these children had been identified as girls, after puberty they no longer fit into that category.

However, these individuals highlight Money's point: They do not clearly fit into either the category of male or female. Despite an early report of the ease of their transition from female sex role to male sex role (Imperato-McGinley, Guerrero, Gautier, & Peterson, 1974), later research by Robert Rubin and his colleagues (Rubin, Reinisch, & Haskett, 1981) and Gilbert Herdt (1990) has indicated that these individuals may never fit comfortably into either category. Whereas the majority of the pseudohermaphrodites whom Julianne Imperato-McGinley and her colleagues studied made at least fairly successful transitions to the male role, none of those whom Rubin and his colleagues mentioned did so. Indeed, the New Guinea culture that Herdt studied acknowledged the existence of these individuals by devising a third category of sex to describe them. (See Diversity Highlight: "A Culture with Three Sexes.")

Although hermaphrodites and pseudohermaphrodites have genitalia that are ambiguous, these people may identify themselves unambiguously as either male or female and, with hormones or surgery or both, lead lives that fit one pattern or the other. On the other hand, these individuals may not be able to clearly identify with one gender or the other, and they may not conform to the expectations associated with the male or female gender role.

These instances in which chromosomal, hormonal, gonadal, and genital sex are not consistent are not only fascinating cases but also provide tests of what constitute essential elements in sexual and gender development. These cases show that complete consistency is not necessary for personal gender identification: Individuals who are not chromosomally, hormonally, or reproductively normal may still have a clear personal gender identity. For example, individuals with Turner's syndrome are not female in

---

✿ DIVERSITY HIGHLIGHT
A Culture with Three Sexes

Most people develop unambiguously according to the male pattern or the female pattern, and cultures have a word for each classification. Although English includes many words to describe variations in sexual interest and behavior, we have no word for people who do not fit one of the two patterns of sexual development. However, anthropologist Gilbert Herdt (1990) contended that some cultures do; that is, some cultures name a category for a third sex.

These cultures tend to have a factor in common —the relative frequency of the hereditary enzyme disorder that produces pseudohermaphroditism. This disorder is the result of a deficiency in the enzyme 5-alpha reductase, which prevents prenatal testosterone from producing a boy with normal external genitals. These individuals are chromosomally normal males with normal internal genitalia, but they are born with external genitals that more strongly resemble a girl's than a boy's—a clitoris-like penis, an unfused scrotum that resembles labia, and undescended testes. At birth these babies are sometimes identified as boys but are more often identified and reared as girls. At puberty they produce testosterone and become "masculinized": Their penis grows, their testes descend, they grow facial hair, and their musculature increases. That is, they change from individuals who look more like girls to ones who look more like boys.

This disorder is very rare but is more common in the Dominican Republic and New Guinea than in most other parts of the world. Herdt contended that these two cultures have a term for a third sex, one that is neither male nor female but that starts out as female and becomes male. Indeed, the literal translation of the word used by the Sambia of New Guinea, *kwolu-aatmwol,* is "male thing-transforming-into-female thing," but they also use a slang word "which refers to 'turning into a *man'* " (Herdt, 1990, p. 439).

In his evaluation of both cultures Herdt concluded that individuals with this disorder fit into neither the male nor female category and that their cultures acknowledge and respond to these differences. Acknowledgment is not the same as acceptance, however, and neither culture accepts these individuals as normal. Even after they had developed masculine characteristics, the Sambia culture did not grant them full male status.

Herdt argued that the acknowledgment of some other possibility in addition to male and female allowed these individuals an opportunity that our culture does not—a third possibility. "And these poor souls in turn were spared the dualistic ultimate dilemma of having to be what they were not; unambiguously male or female" (Herdt, 1990, p. 441).

---

their chromosomes, hormones, or internal reproductive organs, but they are identified and identify themselves as female. Indeed, they are often stereotypically feminine, preferring to wear dresses rather than jeans and to play with dolls rather than other toys. They are female in their own opinion and in the opinion of society.

Hormones and Behavior Instability

In addition to their role in sexual development and activity, hormones are widely considered to affect other behaviors. The concept of premenstrual syndrome has received wide publicity, and estrogens and progestins may be involved in the mood and physical changes that have come to be known as premenstrual syndrome (PMS). Another of the possible influences of hormones is the effect of testosterone on aggression. If these hormonal effects occur, then hormones may be involved in some undesirable behaviors;

"raging hormones" might be one cause of unstable, problem behaviors in both men and women.

Premenstrual Syndrome

Although Rozen's *People Weekly* article (1990) titled "Raging Hormones: The Unofficial PMS Survival Guide" reviewed the book by the same name by Williamson and Sheets, it did not review or criticize the symptoms that formed the basis for the book's humor. As Rozen wrote:

> *PMS, for those who might have missed either the film in health class or the spate of magazine and newspaper articles about it in recent years, stands for premenstrual syndrome. The idea is that it is not just in women's imaginations that, in the days prior to their periods, they get bloated, feel cranky and moody, will eat anything and make anyone. (p. 29)*

This view reflects the acceptance of the existence of a set of symptoms that relate to hormonal changes involved in the menstrual cycle, but recent, careful research has suggested that the experience of PMS may be more closely associated with expectation than with hormones. That is, PMS may be a way of labeling some behavior rather than explaining the underlying cause of symptoms. The concept's overuse has made it inaccurate as a diagnosis.

The notion that women's reproductive systems affect their lives is ancient, according to Anne Fausto-Sterling (1985), but the concept of the premenstrual syndrome can be traced to the 1960s. During this time, Katharina Dalton published research (reviewed by Parlee, 1973) suggesting that women experience a wide variety of negative emotional, cognitive, and physical effects of the hormonal changes that precede menstruation. These effects became known as a *syndrome,* although the list of symptoms extended to over 150, and some of the symptoms were mutually exclusive (such as *elevated mood* and *depression*).

Elaine Blechman and her colleagues (Blechman, Clay, Kipke, & Bickel, 1988) discussed the symptoms associated with the premenstrual phase of the cycle, including headache; backache; abdominal bloating and discomfort; breast tenderness; tension or irritability; depression; increased analgesic, alcohol, or sedative use; decreased energy; and disruption in eating, sleeping, sexual behavior, work, and interpersonal relationships. The most common among these complaints are tension and irritability. Blechman and her colleagues failed to accept these symptoms as a syndrome, but others have not hesitated to do so.

Until the mid 1970s, researchers tended to find that mood is highest during the ovulatory phase of the cycle and lowest during the premenstrual and menstrual phases of the cycle (McFarlane, Martin, & Williams, 1988). Recall that the cyclic variation of luteinizing hormone and follicle-stimulating hormone produces the menstrual cycle by affecting the release of estrogens and progesterone. In the middle of the cycle, the follicles produce larger amounts of one of the estrogens, estradiol, than during other times of the cycle, and this increase produces a surge of luteinizing hormone and follicle-stimulating hormone. This surge causes the release of the matured ovum, and the remainder of the follicle then starts to produce progesterone. Therefore, during the ovulatory phase of the cycle, estrogen levels are higher 'han progesterone levels. During the premenstrual phase of the cycle, both estradiol and progesterone are falling, and progesterone is at a higher level than estradiol. During the menstrual phase, the levels of both hormones are relatively low. Figure 3.6 shows the levels of hormones during the different phases of the cycle.

All of these hormonal changes have been candidates for the underlying cause of premenstrual syndrome (Rubin, Reinisch, & Haskett, 1981). One possibility is that an excess of estrogens is related to PMS, because the relative levels of estrogens are high during the premenstrual phase in the cycle. Another possibility is that the falling progesterone level is the culprit, and yet another hypothesis has targeted the altered ratio of estrogens to progesterone during this phase of the cycle. However, research has not substantiated that hormonal differences vary according to the experience of PMS (Rubin, Reinisch, & Haskett, 1981). This failure to tie hormonal changes to the experience of PMS is a major problem for the PMS concept.

Other problems come from the changing pattern of research findings on PMS. Jessica McFarlane, Carol Lynn Martin, and Tannis Williams (1988) discussed the change in research findings beginning in the late 1970s, when research failed to find the "classic" pattern. They attributed these failures to methodological problems with menstrual cycle research, problems that Mary Brown Parlee (1973) also noted. Such problems include the bias that expectation can introduce into studies in which the participants know that the research is about the menstrual cycle, a reliance on participants' memories of symptoms, and the failure to use appropriate comparison groups. Indeed, McFarlane et al. pointed out that recent research has indicated that most women do *not* report problems associated with menstrual mood fluctuations.

McFarlane et al. (1988) conducted an elaborate and lengthy study that solved the methodological problems they had criticized in other studies. First, they told their participants that the study was about emotional and behavioral patterns over time (which was true) but not that the menstrual cycle was of special interest. Second, they used a measurement of mood that did not introduce a negative mood bias. Third, they asked participants to keep a daily record of mood, body awareness, and general health. Embedded in the health questions was a question about menstruation. Fourth, they included three groups in the study—women who were cycling normally, women who were taking oral contraceptives and thus not cycling normally, and men. Therefore, the McFarlane study solved the most serious problems that might contaminate research on mood and the menstrual cycle.

The main result of the study by McFarlane and her associates was that no differences in mood stability appeared when comparing the young men and the young women who participated in the study. All participants experienced similar mood changes within a day as well as from day to day. Also, the men and women reported similar variability in mood during the 70 days of the study. Thus, these researchers found no support for the concept of PMS.

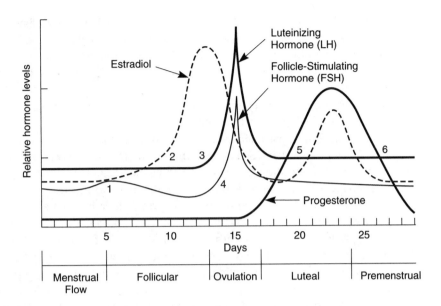

Phases of the human menstrual cycle

1. In response to an increase in FSH, small spheres of cells called ovarian follicles begin to grow around individual egg cells (ova).

2. The follicles begin to release estrogens such as estradiol.

3. The estrogens stimulate the hypothalamus to increase the release of LH and FSH from the anterior pituitary.

4. In response to the LH surge, one of the follicles ruptures and releases its ovum.

5. The ruptured follicle under the influence of LH develops into a corpus luteum (yellow body) and begins to release progesterone, which prepares the lining of the uterus for the implantation of a fertilized ovum.

6. Meanwhile, the ovum is moved into the Fallopian tube by the rowing action of ciliated cells. If the ovum is not fertilized, progesterone and estradiol levels fall and the walls of the uterus are sloughed off as menstrual flow and the cycle begins once again.

FIGURE 3.6 Hormonal Changes during the Menstrual Cycle

SOURCE: From *Biopsychology* (p. 621) by J.P.J. Pinel, 1993, Boston: Allyn and Bacon. Copyright © 1993. Reprinted by permission.

They did find some differences in mood related to the menstrual cycle, but not the expected ones. In comparison to the women taking oral contraceptives and to the men, the women who were cycling normally reported *more pleasant moods* during and immediately after their periods than in the ovulatory or premenstrual periods. That is, one group of women in this study experienced some mood changes associated with menstrual cycle but not changes that support the PMS concept.

In addition to the daily mood and health ratings kept for 70 days, participants in the McFarlane et al. study also completed a questionnaire at the end of the study in which they had to recall their moods. Thus, the researchers obtained not only a daily record of mood (concurrent measurement) but also the participants' memory of their moods (retrospective measurement). These researchers reasoned that if PMS is influenced by biases in memory, then the memory of moods would follow the menstrual cycle, whereas the daily reports would not. Their analysis supported that hypothesis; that is, when the female participants remembered rather than recorded their moods, they reported symptoms of PMS that according to their daily reports they had not experienced. This finding strongly suggests that the mood changes associated with PMS may be a product of expectation and labeling rather than hormones.

This study has not been the only one to fail to substantiate the PMS concept. A study by Pauline Slade (1984) also measured mood and physical symptoms without letting participants know the purpose of the study. She found no evidence that negative emotional symptoms are associated with the premenstrual or menstrual phases of the cycle, but she did find some evidence for physical symptoms, such as premenstrual water retention and menstrual pain. Blechman et al. (1988) suggested that such physical symptoms and the dread of menstruation are the basis for premenstrual complaints rather than a premenstrual syndrome.

Another facet of the study by McFarlane et al. (1988) was an analysis of mood according to two other cycles—weekly and lunar. Although they found no evidence for any mood changes associated with phases of the moon, they did find evidence of strong effects for day of the week—a much stronger effect than any of the menstrual cycle effects. Both men and women experienced more negative moods on Monday and more positive moods on Friday. As McFarlane et al. put it, "The results provide much less support for the stereotype of Monday blues than for Friday-Saturday highs. Both arousal and pleasantness were higher on Friday and Saturday than most other days of the week" (p. 215).

Why do people believe in PMS? The topic is certainly well accepted and even medically treated (Tavris, 1992), yet the research that has supported the concept seems flawed. Better research has failed to either find a hormonal explanation for PMS or to demonstrate the variety of mood and behavioral symptoms associated with it. Research by Randi Koeske and Gary Koeske (1975) suggested a possible explanation: Both women and men seem willing to attribute moody behavior to PMS. That is, when furnished with information about a woman's cycle, both men and women tended to use this information as part of their explanations for the woman's emotional behavior. The more irrational the behavior, the more willing the participants were to attribute it to PMS. Therefore, women who experience problems, stresses, and irritations to which they respond emotionally may explain their reactions by their phase of the menstrual cycle. If they believe that these symptoms are associated with the premenstrual period as well as menstruation, they can apply this explanation about half the time—the week before and the week during menstruation. When they experience the same situations and reactions at other phases of their cycle, they seek other explanations. In this way, premenstrual syndrome can become a self-perpetuating myth for the women who react to problems, stresses, and irritations in their lives as well as for the people who observe the reactions.

In summary, PMS has received wide publicity and wide acceptance, but much of the research supporting this concept suffers from flaws in methodology. The results from more careful studies have indicated that premenstrual syndrome is difficult to define on a biological level and does not appear as emotional symptoms except as a function of expectation. More important to the moods of both women and men are weekly cycles, with more positive moods on Friday and Saturday and less positive moods on Monday.

Testosterone and Aggression

Daniel Goleman's (1990b) *New York Times* article titled "Aggression in Men: Hormone Levels Are a Key" included a summary of several research projects about testosterone and men's behavior. As the title suggests, these research projects all investigated the role of the hormone testosterone in various types of aggression. Testosterone plays an activating role in the fighting behavior of the males of many species (Kalat, 1992), but its effects on humans are less clear. In these various projects the researchers have used different approaches to investigate the actions of testosterone on various behaviors and the reaction of testosterone levels to various experiences. All of the studies found some relationship between testosterone and behavior, but the relationships were very complex. Research on human subjects does not confirm a clear cause-and-effect relationship between hormone levels and aggressive behaviors.

Alan Booth and his colleagues (Booth, Shelley, Mazur, Tharp, & Kittok, 1989) conducted a study on the relationship between testosterone level and winning versus losing in athletic competition. Their participants were the six members of the University of Nebraska varsity tennis team, who agreed to provide saliva samples throughout the season so that the researchers could analyze testosterone levels. Booth and his colleagues measured these players four times in relation to each of the season's six matches—the day before a match, about 15 minutes before each match, immediately after they had finished playing, and one or two days after each match. They wanted to investigate the relationship between winning or losing and testosterone levels, predicting that winning players would experience increased testosterone levels compared to losing players. However, they were also interested in assessing the carryover effects of winning and testosterone level.

One of Booth's colleagues was Allan Mazur, who had earlier formulated a biosocial theory of status, and this study was a test of the theory. According to Mazur (1985), testosterone level is part of a feedback loop in which testosterone and assertiveness are interrelated. When an individual's testosterone level rises, that person is more willing to compete in contests for higher status. Winning such competitions produces a rise in testosterone or helps to maintain a high level of testosterone, which will sustain the willingness to compete. Conversely, losing produces a drop in testosterone, which deters the willingness to compete. Thus, Mazur accounted for "losing streaks" and "winning streaks" in competitions as sustained by the feedback loop's relationship to testosterone level. Mazur also hypothesized that testosterone level and behavior influence each other rather than describe a unidirectional cause-and-effect relationship between the hormone level and behavior.

In the Booth et al. study, the researchers reasoned that the level of testosterone the day before a match would act as a baseline comparison that should be similar to the measurements from the day or so after the matches, and their results confirmed this prediction. They then used this baseline to compare the changes in testosterone level before and after matches. They expected winners to have higher testosterone levels than losers, but their findings were more complex than they had expected. Players showed an increase of testosterone on days when they played, but their hormone levels were highest before the game, complicating the analysis of the effect of winning versus losing. The researchers found that winners showed a rise in testosterone across the match and losers showed a decline but failed to find a significant difference in the average levels of testosterone when comparing winners and losers before and after the matches.

Booth and his colleagues not only measured the tennis players' testosterone but also asked them to rate their feelings about their performance. The researchers found that the players who felt positively about their performance tended to have higher testosterone levels. Therefore, winning and losing did not appear to be simply related to testosterone, but rather, some emotional or mood factor might mediate the hormonal effects. That is, winning might produce a positive mood that in turn might heighten testosterone level. This research was consistent with Mazur's biosocial theory, as the findings demonstrated that testosterone affected and was affected by competition. The study, however, suggested that testosterone's effects and responses follow complex rather than simple patterns related to competition.

Another research project Goleman cited in support of his claim that hormone levels were a key to aggression was one conducted by James Dabbs and his colleagues, who studied several facets of testosterone differences in men. One of these studies (Dabbs, de la Rue, & Williams, 1990) investigated differences in testosterone level for men in various occupations, including physicians, football players, salesmen, actors, ministers, professors, and firemen as well as unemployed men. Although their analysis showed a significant difference among the different occupations, an additional analysis revealed that the source of the difference was that the actors and football players had higher testosterone levels than the ministers. This finding puzzled Dabbs and his colleagues. They had reasoned that salesmen might be high in testosterone due to their need for assertiveness, firemen due to their sensation seeking, and physicians due to their status, but none of these differences appeared.

Nor could these researchers immediately understand what actors and football players have in common (and how they differ from ministers) that would produce elevated testosterone. Two additional studies reported in the same article confirmed the differences between actors and ministers and explored possible reasons for this difference in testosterone levels that might relate to personality differences.

Dabbs et al. argued that despite the similarities between preaching and performing, the factors of competition and antisocial tendencies might differentiate the two groups. Ministers' lives have little competition compared to actors' lives; actors experience a

Effects of Testosterone Poisoning

I think Alan Alda was right," a man in his 40s told me. He referred to Alan Alda's (1975) humorous article, "What Every Woman Should Know About Men," in which he introduced the concept of testosterone poisoning. According to Alda, the higher amount of testosterone in men is not the right amount, it's an overdose. Thus, men suffer from the effects of this problem, which Alda called testosterone poisoning.

The man I spoke to was in the computer business and said, "I see the effects of testosterone poisoning in a number of situations, including computer use, starting early and continuing into adulthood. I was talking to a preschool teacher, and she said that the boys and girls in her classes interacted differently with computers: The boys dominate the computers in her school's lab, and the girls complain about it.

"As adolescents, boys play the most obnoxious, violent games. Actually, the entire computer game market seems oriented toward male adolescents, regardless of the age of the player. Girls either play the available games, or they don't play, and I think that many girls leave the computers to boys because they don't like the games that are available. Of course, the people who develop these games are often young men (very likely testosterone poisoned) who develop games they would like to play themselves.

"Among the computer-user groups, testosterone poisoning is obvious. The men are very competitive and compare the size of their hard drives. These guys are very machine oriented rather than oriented toward what their machines can do, so they ask each other how much RAM they have and how big their hard drives are. It's funny, but these guys are completely serious and very macho about their computers. Alan Alda was right."

constant need to seek employment and win roles. As for antisocial tendencies, Dabbs and his colleagues reasoned that ministers and actors differ in selfishness and that "ministers tend to be self-effacing and actors self-aggrandizing. Ministers praise the glory of God, whereas actors keep the glory for themselves" (Dabbs et al., 1990, p. 1264).

The interpretation that antisocial tendencies are positively related to testosterone level is consistent with other research by Dabbs and his colleagues. A study by James Dabbs, Charles Hopper, and Gregory Jurkovic (1990) examined personality and testosterone in college students and military veterans. They found little relationship between testosterone and personality in the college students, but they found that the veterans showed a relationship between testosterone level and drug and alcohol abuse, antisocial behavior, and affective disorders.

James Dabbs and Robin Morris (1990) completed another study on veterans in which they examined testosterone levels in 4,462 U.S. military veterans to determine if high levels of testosterone related to problem behaviors. They contrasted men whose testosterone levels fell within the upper 10% with the other men in the sample. The relationship was clear:

Individuals higher in testosterone more often reported having trouble with parents, teachers, and classmates; being assaultive toward other adults; going AWOL in the military; and using hard drugs, marijuana, and alcohol. They also reported having more sexual partners. The overall picture is one of delin-

quency, substance abuse, and a general tendency toward excessive behavior.
(Dabbs & Morris, 1990, p. 209)

Therefore, Dabbs and Morris concluded that testosterone level was related to a variety of behavior problems, but not all of these problems were limited to aggression or violence.

Dabbs (1992) explored the relationship between testosterone level and occupational achievement and found that men with higher levels of testosterone have lower-status occupations. He interpreted this finding to indicate that high testosterone levels are related to antisocial behavior, and such behavior "leads away from white-collar occupations" (p. 813).

Testosterone level in men seems to be related to a greater variety of behavior problems, but not consistently over all socioeconomic groups (See Diversity Highlight: "Socioeconomic Status, Testosterone, and Antisocial Behavior.") In addition, as Dabbs and Morris pointed out, the size of their group allowed them to find significant differences when these differences were of a small magnitude That is, with so many participants, even a very small difference will be statistically significant, but as Chapter 2 emphasized, such differences may not be of much practical significance. Although the differences that Dabbs and Morris found were not due to chance, neither would these differences allow precise predictions about antisocial behavior according to testosterone level.

The various research projects attempting to relate testosterone levels to personality factors such as aggression and competition in men have been partly successful. Competition seems to be related to elevations in testosterone levels but not in any simple way. Dabbs and his colleagues have found a difference in testosterone levels between men in different occupational groups and a relationship between hormone levels and antisocial behaviors, but the relationship is complicated by the factor of socioeconomic class.

Women also produce testosterone, and some researchers have studied the relationship between this hormone and women's behavior. Two of these studies have been analogous to the studies done with men: One has measured testosterone's relation to occupation, and the other has related testosterone to antisocial behavior in women. The diversity highlight, "Socioeconomic Status, Testosterone, and Antisocial Behavior," discusses one study—relationship between testosterone and criminal behavior in women. In another study, Frances Purifoy and Lambert H. Koopmans (1979) tested women's levels of androgens to determine if women in different occupations would have higher levels of androgens. These researchers measured several of the androgens, including testosterone, and found some variation in testosterone levels according to occupation. The mean levels of testosterone were significantly higher in women with professional, technical, or managerial jobs compared to women who had clerical jobs or were housewives. Purifoy and Koopmans acknowledged that their study did not demonstrate that high testosterone levels cause women to pursue certain occupations. Rather, the study demonstrated a difference in hormone levels between women in certain occupations and women in other fields. Nor did these researchers interpret their

DIVERSITY HIGHLIGHT
Socioeconomic Status, Testosterone, and Antisocial Behavior

James Dabbs and Robin Morris's (1990) investigation of the role of testosterone in antisocial behavior included the factor of socioeconomic status (SES). These researchers reasoned that SES might interact with hormone levels to produce different behaviors in men from different social classes. They found that men who were both high in education and in income were significantly less likely to be high in testosterone than men who were low in both education and income. For the low SES men, high testosterone levels heightened their risks for problem behavior, including adult delinquency and drug use. In this study socioeconomic status seemed to play a role in the negative consequences of high testosterone: High SES men with high testosterone experienced fewer negative consequences than low SES men with high testosterone. Dabbs and Morris (1990, p. 211) interpreted this finding as evidence that men high in testosterone who are high in both education and income have learned to cope with their antisocial tendencies "to avoid individual confrontations, especially physical ones, and to submit to years of schooling." Thus, their behavior differs from high-testosterone, lower-SES men, who got into more trouble. An alternative possibility is that men who are wealthy and well educated might not get in as much trouble for the same antisocial behaviors as men who are poor and less educated.

Dabbs and his colleagues (Dabbs, Ruback, Frady, Hopper, & Sgoutas, 1988) also studied the relationship between testosterone level and antisocial behavior in women by measuring testosterone levels in inmates of a women's prison and contrasted them with testosterone levels in female college students. Within the prison group, they found some indication that testosterone levels related to violence: Women with the highest levels of testosterone had the highest incidence of unprovoked violence. They found that testosterone levels differed among inmates convicted of unprovoked violence, defensive violence, theft, drugs, and other crimes. The inmates who had committed acts of unprovoked violence had the highest testosterone levels. For these women inmates, testosterone was related to the number of prior charges and to prior parole board decisions about length of time they should serve before being granted parole. Women who had committed violence in protecting themselves, such as those who had murdered an abusive spouse, had the lowest levels of testosterone in the prison group.

Interestingly, the mean levels of testosterone were similar for the inmates and the college students, and the averages fell within the normal range for women. These results provide some support for the notion that testosterone is related to aggression, as the inmates who had committed the most violent crimes—those involving unprovoked violence—also had the highest testosterone levels. However, the failure to find differences between women convicted of crimes and female students indicates that aggression and violence are influenced by more factors than testosterone level, including socioeconomic status, which Dabbs and his colleagues found moderated the relationship of testosterone and problem behavior in men.

findings as evidence of a simple cause-and-effect relationship but instead discussed the possibility that levels of androgens might influence career choice and also that career stresses might influence androgen level. As Booth and his colleagues found a decade later, testosterone levels can not only affect behavior but can be affected by personal experience.

Indeed, the influence of androgens on behavior turns out to be bidirectional and influenced by a multitude of factors. Rather than testosterone producing aggression, the behaviors that the hormone influences are less straightforward. There is some evidence that men *and* women with high testosterone levels are more likely to commit violent crimes than people whose testosterone levels are lower. But socioeconomic status is a moderating factor in men, and possibly research will demonstrate this relationship in women. People with high testosterone levels are also more likely to commit crimes that do not include violence and to exhibit antisocial but legal behaviors, such as heavy drinking. To conceptualize all of these behaviors as aggression would be inaccurate. Furthermore, behavior can influence hormone levels as well as being influenced by hormone levels, as happens as a result of competition.

In his *New York Times* story, Goleman reviewed the evidence concerning the effects of hormones on aggression and cited some provocative evidence. But he also said that "scientists emphasize that the effects of hormones on human behavior are small relative to social and psychological factors, showing up most clearly in studies of large numbers of people" (1990b, p. C1). Therefore, hormone levels probably play a relatively small role in aggression in humans.

Summary

Several steroid hormones are important to sexual development and behavior, including the androgens, the estrogens, and the progestins. All normal individuals produce all of these hormones, but women produce proportionately more estrogens and progestins, whereas men produce more androgens. The prenatal production of these hormones affects the brains of fetuses to organize along the male or the female pattern. During puberty these hormones activate the internal genitalia to develop fertility and prompt the development of secondary sex characteristics, such as beards for men and breasts for women.

The role of hormones in the activation and maintenance of sexual interest and activity is less clear in humans than in other species, but humans who do not experience the pubertal surge of hormones tend not to develop much interest in sex. Testosterone, one of the androgens, plays a role in maintaining sexual activity in men and possibly in women as well.

There are five stages of sexual development—genetic, gonadal, hormonal, internal genitalia, and external genitalia—all of which usually proceed according to either the male or female pattern. The first stage in sexual development is genetic, the inheritance of either XX or XY chromosomes of pair 23. Although the inheritance of chromosomes is the beginning of the pattern, embryos are not sexually dimorphic until around six weeks into gestation. Those with the XY pattern start to produce androgens and Müllerian-inhibiting substance during the third month of gestation. These hormones masculinize the fetus, prompting not only the further

development of the testes but also degeneration of the Müllerian structures and development of the Wolffian structures that form the other internal genitalia. Shortly thereafter, external genitalia develop, and this development also depends on androgens.

The female pattern is not as dependent on the presence of estrogens as the male pattern is on androgens, but some estrogen is necessary for the development of normal ovaries, other internal genitalia, and external genitalia. During the third month of pregnancy, those individuals with the XX pattern of chromosomes start to develop the Müllerian structures, which become the ovaries, Fallopian tubes, uterus, and upper vagina. In addition, their Wolffian structures start to degenerate. An absence of all steroid hormones will allow the feminization of external genitalia, but some estrogens are necessary for normal development of internal and external genitalia.

Things can go wrong at any stage, beginning with the inheritance of the chromosomes that determine sex, the X and Y chromosomes. A number of disorders exist that create individuals with too few or too many sex chromosomes, and some of these configurations produce problems with the development of internal or external genitalia. In addition, several of these disorders produce individuals with developmental disorders, especially lowered intelligence. Individuals with Turner's syndrome (X0) appear to be female but lack ovaries; individuals with Klinefelter's syndrome (XXY) appear to be male, often with feminized body contours, but have nonfunctional testes; XXX individuals are female and may be otherwise normal; XYY individuals are tall males who may be reproductively normal but are often mentally retarded.

Even normal chromosomes do not guarantee normal development in subsequent stages, and several types of hermaphroditism and pseudohermaphroditism exist. These cases of individuals with physiology of both males and females suggest the inadequacy of two categories of sex and provide examples of the complexities of sexual development.

The headlines have contained stories that indicate a role for hormones in two areas of problem behavior—premenstrual syndrome (PMS) and aggression. Careful research has indicated that the premenstrual phase of the cycle may include some physical symptoms, but it also suggests that expectation, nor hormones, is the major cause of the emotional symptoms associated with PMS.

Research on the role of testosterone in aggression has revealed that the relationship is not a simple cause-and-effect one. Testosterone affects and is affected by competition in complex ways. Men in different occupations differ as to testosterone level, with actors having higher levels than ministers. Men with higher-than-average testosterone levels tend to engage in a wide variety of antisocial behaviors that include (but are not restricted to) violence. The complexities of testosterone activity also extend to women, whose testosterone levels vary according to several occupations. For women as well as for men, testosterone levels differ in people who have committed violent crimes, with higher testosterone levels in the criminally violent. However, testosterone is not a very accurate predictor of criminal violence, as both male and female inmates do not differ in testosterone levels from male and female college students. Such findings highlight the inadequacy of testosterone level alone as an index of aggression.

Glossary

Adrenogenital syndrome   a disorder that results in masculinization, producing premature puberty in boys and masculinization of the external genitalia in girls

Androgen insensitivity syndrome   a disorder in which body cells are unable to respond to androgens, resulting in the feminization of chromosomal males

Androgens   a class of hormones that includes testosterone and other steroid hormones; men typically produce a greater proportion of androgens than estrogens

Endocrine glands   glands that secrete hormones into the circulatory system

Estradiol   the most common of the estrogen hormones

Estrogens   a class of hormones that includes estradiol and other steroid hormones; women typically produce a greater proportion of estrogens than androgens

External genitalia   the reproductive structures that can be seen without internal examination: clitoris, labia, and vaginal opening in women and penis and scrotum in men

Follicle-stimulating hormone (FSH)   the gonadotropic hormone that stimulates development of gonads during puberty and development of ova during the years of women's fertility

Gonads   reproductive organs

Hermaphroditism   a disorder in which individuals have characteristics of both sexes

Hormones   chemical substances released from endocrine glands that circulate throughout the body and affect target organs that have receptors sensitive to the specific hormones

Internal genitalia   internal reproductive organs, consisting of the ovaries, Fallopian tubes, uterus, and upper vagina in women and testes, seminal vesicles, and prostate gland in men

Intersexuality   a more modern term for hermaphroditism

Klinefelter's syndrome   the disorder that occurs when a chromosomal male has an extra X chromosome, resulting in the XXY pattern of chromosome pair 23; these individuals have the appearance of males, including external genitalia, but they may also develop breasts and a feminized body shape; their testes are not capable of producing sperm, so they are sterile

Luteinizing hormone (LH)   the gonadotropic hormone that prompts sexual development during puberty and also causes a maturing ovum to be released

Menarche   the beginning of menstruation

Müllerian system a system of ducts occurring in both male and female embryos that form the basis for the development of the female internal reproductive system—ovaries, Fallopian tubes, uterus, and upper vagina

Pituitary gland an endocrine gland within the brain that produces tropic hormones that stimulate other glands to produce yet other hormones

Progestins a group of steroid hormones that have the function of preparing female bodies for pregnancy and have a unknown function for male bodies

Releasing hormones hormones produced by the hypothalamus that act on the pituitary to release tropic hormones

Sexual dimorphism the existence of male and female bodies, including differences in genetics, gonads, hormones, internal genitalia, and external genitalia

Steroid hormones hormones related to sexual dimorphism and sexual reproduction that are derived from cholesterol and consist of a structure that includes four carbon rings

Testosterone the most common of the androgen hormones

Tropic hormones hormones produced by the pituitary gland that influence the release of other hormones by other glands, such as the gonads

Turner's syndrome the disorder that occurs when an individual has only one of chromosome pair 23, one X chromosome; these individuals appear to be female (have the external genitalia of females) but do not have fully developed internal genitalia; they do not produce estrogens, do not undergo puberty, and are not fertile

Wolffian system a system of ducts occurring in both male and female embryos that form the basis for the development of the male internal reproductive system—testes, seminal vesicles, and vas deferens

X chromosomes one of the possible alternatives for chromosome pair 23; two X chromosomes make a genetic female, whereas genetic males have only one X chromosome in pair 23

Y chromosome one of the possible alternatives for chromosome pair 23; one X and one Y chromosome make a genetic male, whereas genetic females have two X chromosomes in pair 23

Suggested Readings

Fausto-Sterling, Anne. (1985). *Myths of gender: Biological theories about women and men.* New York: Basic Books. Although this book does not have the most recent research, the chapter titled "Hormonal Hurricanes" contains a readable, critical review of the role of hormones in women's behavior.

Money, John. (1986). *Venuses penuses: Sexology, sexosophy, and exigency theory.* Buffalo, NY: Prometheus Books. This volume is a collection of Money's extensive works on problems concerning sex and gender development.

Pinel, John P. J. (1993). *Biopsychology* (2nd ed.). Boston: Allyn and Bacon. For more details about the action of the endocrine system, the brain's involvement in endocrine function, sexual development, and some of the things that can go wrong, see Chapter 11 of this biological psychology textbook.

Chapter 4

The Brain

The Brain as a "Sexual Organ"

—*Science,* August 30, 1991

In 1991, *Science* offered a story with the intriguing headline, "The Brain as a 'Sexual Organ'" (Gibbons, 1991), summarizing recent research about the differences between male and female brains. In the 1960s most researchers believed that no differences existed between the brains of men and women (or between the brains of male and female rats, for that matter). However, Geoffrey Raisman and Pauline Field began to investigate the differences in the brains of male and female rats and found structural differences (Raisman & Field, 1971). Their research prompted others to search for differences, and the developing technology of brain research allowed not only autopsy studies but also studies involving imaging techniques on intact brains in living humans.

Ann Gibbons's story asserted that brain research has progressed to the point that "there is now a solid body of data indicating sex differences in the brains of almost every mammalian family examined so far" (p. 957). In humans sexual dimorphism (differences between the sexes) in the brain exists in several structures, including the hypothalamus, the anterior commissure, the corpus callosum, and the massa intermedia of the thalamus. These anatomical differences may have implications for behavior, but "their functional significance is far from clear" (p. 958). That is, the relationship between anatomy and behavior is difficult to determine.

In addition, the research on the behavioral implications of brain anatomy is very controversial. If male and female brains differ, then perhaps women and men have different mental abilities; that is, different kinds of or levels of intelligence. This possibility may seem to threaten equality of opportunity, because different abilities imply both advantages and disadvantages. However, the step omitted from this reasoning involves the assumption that women are the ones at a disadvantage. Women have historically made different choices concerning their lives and have worked toward different goals than men, resulting in women being underrepresented in many areas of achievement. Although many may be willing to follow the logic that brain differences equal disadvantages for women, thus explaining the inevitability of their lower achievement, this logic is flawed in several places.

Differences do not necessarily imply advantages and disadvantages. In addition, if advantages and disadvantages exist, women may not be the ones at a disadvantage. The convenience of explaining discrimination by brain structure may be appealing to those who want to rationalize discrimination, but brain research does not support such a position. Indeed, the majority of the research on sexual dimorphism of the brain has not been based on human brains; rats have been more common as subjects. What, then, have the studies revealed about differences in male and female brains, and what implications might differences have for behavior?

The Brain and Sex

Before examining the differences in structure between male and female brains, a brief introduction to the brain and nervous system is explored in the following subsection.

The Brain and the Nervous System

The brain and nervous system provide internal communication within our bodies and also furnish a link to the outside world. This internal communication allows the rapid relay of messages from one area of the body to another. The link to the outside world comes through the sensory and motor systems. The sensory systems allow our bodies to receive stimulation from the outside world of light, sound, taste, smell, pressure, heat, cold, and pain; the motor system provides for the possibility of physical reactions and movement.

The brain and nervous system are comprised of billions (there is some argument over just how many billions) of **neurons,** or nerve cells. These neurons function by way of a complex electrochemical action, and the action of neurons provides the basis for internal communication as well as for the sensory and motor functions of the nervous system. When neurons are stimulated, a neural impulse forms, and if the impulse is sufficiently strong, this electrochemical message will continue through a chain of neurons to the brain, where it will be processed through additional interconnections of neurons.

The brain itself contains an estimated 100 billion neurons (Pinel, 1993), most of which have dozens to hundreds of synapses; that is, interconnections with other neurons. The enormous number of connections makes an almost incomprehensibly complex system. Indeed, the brain is such a complex structure that neuroscience is far from a complete understanding of its function and the relationship between its structures and functions. However, a great deal is known about the structure of the brain, including the outermost part, the cerebral cortex.

The Cerebral Hemispheres and Lateralization

Much of the research concerning sexual dimorphism of the brain has concentrated on the forebrain, the anterior (toward the front) part of the brain. The forebrain contains several structures, including the cerebral cortex, the outermost part of the brain. Figure 4.1 shows the exterior of the brain as it would appear with the skull and protective membranes removed. The folds, or fissures, are quite regular from person to person and divide the cortex into different sections, called lobes. Although many of the cerebral cortex's functions are not completely understood, knowledge about areas in the different lobes that receive the sensory input from the body is well established.

The occipital lobe at the back of the brain contains the sensory area that receives visual input. To be able to see, an animal not only needs eyes but also must have intact pathways of nerves that relay neural stimulation about visual information to the occipital lobe, and the occipital lobe must process and interpret the visual input information. The temporal lobe lies under the temples and receives auditory information. The parietal lobe contains a map of the skin's surface, receiving information about touch, pressure, heat, cold, and pain from the neurons in skin covering the entire body. The frontal lobe contains the motor cortex, the origin of neural impulses that result in voluntary movement of muscles. Therefore, part of the function of the cerebral cortex is to receive and interpret sensory information from the outside world and to originate neural impulses that result in motor movement for the body.

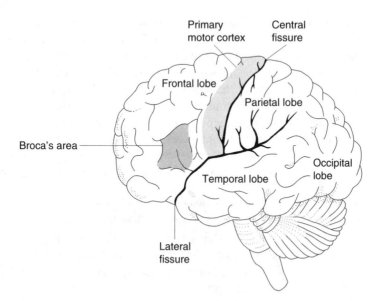

**FIGURE 4.1   Location of Broca's Area in the Inferior Left
            Prefrontal Cortex**

SOURCE: From *Biopsychology* (p. 497) by J.P.J. Pinel, 1990, Boston: Allyn and Bacon. Reprinted by permission.

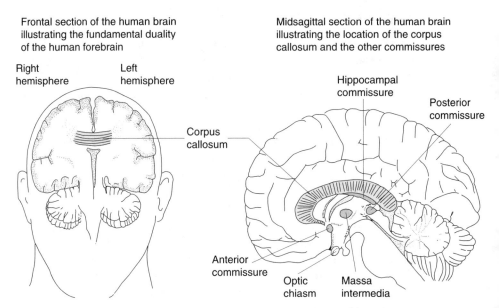

Frontal section of the human brain
illustrating the fundamental duality
of the human forebrain

Midsagittal section of the human brain
illustrating the location of the corpus
callosum and the other commissures

Right
hemisphere

Left
hemisphere

Hippocampal
commissure

Posterior
commissure

Corpus
callosum

Anterior
commissure

Optic
chiasm

Massa
intermedia

FIGURE 4.2   Cerebral Commissures and the Hemispheres of the Human Brain

Source: From *Biopsychology* (p. 537) by J.P.J. Pinel, 1993, Boston: Allyn and Bacon. Reprinted by permission.

Figure 4.2 shows two views of the brain, one view as seen from above and another of a brain cut down the middle. The view from above the brain shows that the cerebral cortex is divided down the middle into two halves, or hemispheres. This division forms a left cerebral hemisphere and a right cerebral hemisphere. The view through the midsection shows some of the structures in the brain beneath the cerebral cortex. These structures—the anterior commissure, the massa intermedia, and the corpus callosum—are all structures that, according to some researchers, are sexually dimorphic. In addition, the left and right cerebral hemispheres may also differ in men and women. However, a more prominent difference in the two cerebral hemispheres is the one between the left and right hemisphere, which differ from each other in almost all humans.

Discovery of Differences between the Hemispheres

The differences between the two cerebral hemispheres were not known until the middle of the 1800s (Springer & Deutsch, 1989), and in many ways the two hemispheres appear to be symmetrical mirror images of each other. Two French physicians, Marc Dax and Paul Broca, discovered the difference (perhaps independently) by observing their patients who had suffered strokes. A stroke results in damage to the brain, and people who have experienced strokes may lose some abilities they had before the stroke. One of the possibilities for a loss of function is the loss of the ability to speak, and it was this type of loss that prompted investigation into differing hemispheric capabilities.

The person generally credited with discovering one asymmetry (lack of mirror-image symmetry) in the cerebral hemispheres is Paul Broca, who in 1861 made a connection between left hemisphere stroke damage and loss of the ability to speak. His autopsies revealed that these patients' strokes had damaged an area in the left frontal lobe (see Figure 4.1). Although his proposal about the localization of speech in the left frontal lobe was initially controversial (Springer & Deutsch, 1989), his hypothesis was correct, at least for the majority of people, and that area is now called **Broca's area.** Damage to Broca's area results in loss or impairment of the ability to speak, and such a loss is called **aphasia.**

Prior to Broca's research, the predominant view was that the two hemispheres duplicated each other in function, but soon an alternative view arose—that of **cerebral**

DIVERSITY HIGHLIGHT
Brain Capacity and Race

The discoveries of the 19th century concerning lateralization of brain functions came about during a period of intense interest in the capabilities of the brain. As information about the brain accumulated, researchers held firmly to their assumptions about sexual and racial differences in the brain's capacity. According to Stephen Jay Gould (1981), these scientists provide a good example of the influence that culture can have on research findings. These 19th-century neurology researchers believed that the male European brain was superior to all others: "The white leaders of Western nations did not question the propriety of racial ranking during the eighteenth and nineteenth centuries" (Gould, 1981, p. 35).

During the 19th century, the main technique for measuring the capacity of the brain was craniometry, measurement of the capacity of the skull (Gould, 1981). These researchers believed that the skull's capacity was a direct reflection of the size of the brain and that the size of the brain was a measure of intelligence. From the 1820s until 1851, Samuel George Morton collected skulls from many parts of the world so that he could measure their capacity and rank the different races according to their relative intelligence. Of course, he found the evidence he sought, matching "every good Yankee's prejudice—whites on top, Indians in the middle, and blacks on the bottom; and, among whites, Teutons and Anglo-Saxons on top, Jews in the middle, and Hindus on the bottom" (Gould, 1981, pp. 53–54). White women's brains were more like the brains of these "primitive" races than like white men's.

Gould (1981) reanalyzed the data from Morton's skull collection and found no differences among the cranial capacity of different races. He concluded that "Morton's summaries are a patchwork of fudging and finagling in the clear interest of controlling a priori convictions" (p. 54). However, Gould noted that he believed that Morton had not consciously cheated but had been so influenced by his prejudice that he had misread and misinterpreted his own data.

The last half of the 19th century saw no decrease in racism or sexism connected with assessing the brain. During this time measurements changed from cranial capacity to the configuration of the skull. One measurement of skull configuration was based on the facial angle, the jutting forward of face and jaws, and another popular measurement was the cranial index, the ratio of maximum width to maximum length of the skull. Jaws that did not jut forward too much and relatively shorter skulls indicated intelligence (Gould, 1981). Of course, non-European races had skulls that indicated less intelligence. Indeed, these races were considered ape-like and not as fully evolved as the white races.

Gould's (1981) analyses indicated that body size and age influence the estimates of the size of the brain more strongly than race or sex. With these factors taken into account, no differences in brain capacity exist. However, the racism and sexism in neurology only began to fade during this century, and Gould argued that remnants of these biases still exist in science.

dominance (Springer & Deutsch, 1989). This hypothesis holds that the left hemisphere dominates the right by virtue of its superior abilities and that the left hemisphere is more important in directing behavior than is the right hemisphere. Further research in the late 1800s seemed to confirm the notion that many types of language disorders can result from damage to the left hemisphere. That is, aphasia can result from damage to areas of the left cerebral cortex other than Broca's area. Loss of abilities can include not only difficulties in speaking but also difficulties in understanding the speech of others. Therefore, interest in the left hemisphere and in its capabilities was intense, and the right hemisphere was referred to as the "minor hemisphere."

In the 1930s research on the right hemisphere began to reveal its special abilities (Springer & Deutsch, 1989). Patients with damage to the right hemisphere showed different patterns of function that were lost or changed when compared to patients with left hemisphere damage. Those with damage to their left hemisphere tended to have various types of aphasia, whereas those with right hemisphere damage tended to perform poorly on nonverbal tests that involved manipulating geometric figures, assembling puzzles, completing patterns and figures, and doing other tasks that involve form, distance, and spatial relationships among objects. Growing research evidence about the different abilities that seemed to be directed by the two hemispheres led to the concept of **lateralization**; that is, that the left and right hemispheres are each specialized for different functions.

Additional explorations of hemispheric differences came from research on patients who had undergone brain surgery to control seizures. Although surgical treatment has never been a usual choice for the control of seizure activity, during the 1950s and 1960s several hundred patients in the United States and Canada received such surgical treatment (Springer & Deutsch, 1989). Many variations existed, but the preferred type of surgery involved cutting the **corpus callosum,** a band of nerve fibers that connects the right and left cerebral hemispheres. Figure 4.2 shows the corpus callosum, the major connection between the two hemispheres.

After these patients had recovered from the surgery, they provided researchers with the unique opportunity to study the capabilities of the two cerebral hemispheres functioning independently of each other, yet without damage to either. The research on these patients (sometimes referred to as "split-brain" patients) has elaborated what the research from brain damage studies suggested: The two hemispheres have different capabilities.

By devising experimental procedures that allowed information to enter either the right hemisphere or the left hemisphere (but not both), researchers confirmed that the left hemisphere is fluent in language-related tasks, whereas the right hemisphere has less verbal fluency. On the other hand, the right hemisphere is much more capable than the left at tasks requiring perception of objects and their spatial relationships to each other—tasks such as reproducing geometric figures and putting together jigsaw puzzles. In addition, the right hemisphere seemed to be involved in the interpretation and expression of emotion (Tucker, 1981). Cerebral function appeared to be lateralized, with specific abilities for each hemisphere.

Researchers developed experimental procedures that allowed the investigation of lateralization in people with intact brains (Springer & Deutsch, 1989). This step was necessary, because the few patients who had experienced split-brain surgery did not have completely normal brains; they had experienced such severe seizures that surgery was necessary. Thus, researchers were hesitant to generalize the results obtained from these patients to normal people. In general, the research on people who have intact brains has supported the findings about split-brain patients: Cerebral lateralization exists in normal people.

Speculations about the implications of lateralization have captured the attention of people in many fields. Psychologist Robert Ornstein (1972) proposed that the different functions of the hemispheres are associated with different modes of thought: The left hemisphere is capable of logical and analytical thought, but the right hemisphere is capable of more intuitive, holistic thought processes. Ornstein also proposed that education in Western societies fosters left hemisphere function, whereas the abilities of the right hemisphere are fostered by Eastern societies but may remain undeveloped in Western culture. In extending the dichotomy of the two hemispheres to the East-West contrast, Ornstein laid the foundation for hemispheric differences to be extended to other dichotomies, such as rational-metaphorical, intellectual-intuitive, abstract-concrete, realistic-impulsive, objective-subjective, and analytical-holistic (Springer & Deutsch, 1989).

Included in many lists of such dichotomies is the labeling of the left hemisphere as "masculine" and the right as "feminine." Thus, this formulation would describe the left hemisphere as masculine, rational, intellectual, abstract, objective, and analytical, whereas the right hemisphere would be seen as feminine, metaphorical, intuitive, concrete, subjective, and holistic. These associations are not unique to the brain research on lateralization but represent stereotypical descriptions of masculine and feminine traits that have appeared throughout history (Keller, 1985). Do differences exist between the cerebral hemispheres of men and women, and is this stereotypical dichotomy the result of differences between the two cerebral hemispheres?

Gender-Related Differences in Lateralization

According to Sally Springer and Georg Deutsch (1989), almost 100 years of investigation of cerebral lateralization had passed before anyone noted gender-related differences. From the 1860s to the 1960s, no one had noticed any differences in the effects of stroke between women and men. When researchers began looking, they found that women were much less likely to experience loss of speech abilities after left hemisphere damage than were men. That is, similar brain damage did not seem to cause similar impairment in men and women.

Additional research on normal women and men suggested differences in lateralization: Men had more lateralized language and spatial functions, whereas women seemed to have these functions represented in both hemispheres. However, not all studies have found these gender differences in lateralization. As Springer and Deutsch (1989) pointed out, the magnitude of difference is typically small; many studies have failed to find any differences, and very few studies have found that women are more lateralized. They concluded that gender differences in lateralization are real but small.

After reviewing the research on cerebral lateralization in children, William Hahn (1987) reached a different conclusion: No gender differences exist in cerebral lateralization in children. In addition, Hahn argued that his view was not restricted to children, as cerebral lateralization is constant over development. Therefore, lateralization in childhood persists into adulthood, and the similarities in cerebral lateralization in boys and girls predict the brain organization of men and women.

Gender-related differences in lateralization may or may not exist; expert opinion is divided on the question. But if such differences exist, why do they? What are the mechanisms and reasons for gender-related differences in brain organization? A number of theorists have speculated on the source and reason for gender differences in brain lateralization. Norman Geschwind and Albert Galaburda (1987) proposed a complex theory that explains lateralization as well as many other neurological and physiological individual differences. This theory relies on prenatal events, especially the existence of prenatal hormones, to explain gender differences in lateralization. They hypothesized that testosterone is the most important factor, acting during critical periods of fetal development to control the rate of development of the right and left cerebral hemispheres. As Chapter 3 discussed, male and female fetuses are exposed prenatally to estrogens and androgens, and these hormones influence the development of internal reproductive organs and external genitalia.

Geschwind and Galaburda proposed that this prenatal influence extends to brain development and makes a permanent difference for the organization of the cerebral hemispheres and thus for mental abilities. Part of their theory hypothesized that testosterone slows the growth of the left hemisphere, allowing a more rapid development of the right hemisphere. They proposed that these different growth rates produce different abilities, giving the larger hemisphere an advantage. Even if the two hemispheres eventually grow to equal size, they postulated that the different rates of growth will have permanent effects on brain function and mental abilities.

These theorists hypothesized gender differences in mental abilities. (Chapter 5 examines these abilities and the existence and magnitude of gender-related differences.) Geschwind and Galaburda conjectured that girls and women are more likely to have greater verbal abilities because their prenatal testosterone levels would not have depressed growth in the left hemisphere. Girls and women would, however, have poorer spatial ability, because their right hemispheres experienced no compensatory growth spurt from depressed left hemisphere growth, leaving girls and women more verbally fluent but less capable at tasks involving spatial functions. On the other hand, boys and men would excel at spatial tasks because prenatal testosterone had depressed left hemisphere growth and prompted right hemisphere development, boosting its function. Boys and men, however, would tend to be poorer at verbal tasks than girls and women.

Geschwind and Galaburda's theory extends to factors other than lateralization and is sufficiently complex to be difficult to test (McManus & Bryden, 1991). In addition, their theory assumes a straightforward division of verbal and spatial tasks lateralized

GENDERED VOICES
Cerebral Chauvinism

I asked a number of people if they believed that men's and women's brains were different. Most people said no, and some people qualified their answers, saying that they believed in no structural differences in the brains of women and men but that hormonal differences might exist. Several told me that they believed in functional differences in thought but not structural differences in the brain itself.

A substantial minority said that they believed in differences at the level of the structure of the brain, and one young woman said, "I think that the differences are much deeper than that. I think that it's not just brains or hormones or chromosomes, but deeper. I think that there are differences way down there in the DNA. It's almost like women and men are two different species."

The men and women who expressed beliefs about differences in the brain tended to show a prejudice in favor of their own gender or against the other, or both. The women said things like, "Yes, I believe there are differences—women's brains are better," or "Yes, I believe in differences—men don't use as much of their brains as women." One man said it very simply, "Yes—men are smarter." Another man reported that he jokes about differences in women's and men's brains, telling the couples he counsels, "Yes, men's and women's brains are different. Men have a small penis as one of the structures in their brains; this accounts for many of their differences in behavior."

into the left and right hemispheres, and this division may be too simplified (see Kimura, 1992).

Deborah Waber's (1976) view of gender differences in lateralization also involved differential growth rates. She emphasized the influence of puberty, hypothesizing that children who mature early would perform better on verbal tasks, and those who mature late would perform better on spatial tasks. As girls tend to mature earlier than boys, she predicted that gender differences would exist in verbal and spatial abilities but that gender would be incidental rather than essential in these different abilities. A test of this hypothesis on children with different levels and rates of maturation supported her view. Thus maturational rate rather than gender may play a role in differences in hemispheric specialization.

Jerre Levy (1969) and Doreen Kimura (1992) emphasized the role of evolution in gender differences in lateralization. Each of these researchers argued that the different role demands of men and women in the hunter-gatherer societies of prehistory posed different demands and resulted in different brain organization. Although the logic of these stories may be appealing, these speculations are impossible to confirm or disconfirm through systematic testing. Also, alternative stories make as much sense. For example, Beryl Lieff Benderly (1987) looked to more remote periods in prehistory, when prehumans were tree dwellers, to argue against differential selection pressures for spatial abilities. She argued that such abilities should have been very important for both sexes. For example, falling out of trees would not be conducive to survival and reproduction. Despite the potential validity of the evolutionary view, the explanation of differential cognitive abilities tied to different evolutionary pressures is a theory with many possible versions and no way to provide confirmation.

All of these theories about brain lateralization have tried to explain why and how women develop brains that are less lateralized than the brains of men. More recently, Kimura (1992) has questioned the notion that women are less lateralized than men. She proposed an alternative type of gender difference—that men and women have differences in the cerebral organization of language abilities but that these differences have to do with front and back part of the hemispheres rather than left and right hemispheres. Kimura suggested that women are more likely to suffer from loss of language abilities when the anterior (front part) of their left hemisphere is damaged, whereas men are more likely to experience deficits when the posterior (back part) of their left hemisphere is damaged. She also explained that damage to the posterior is more frequent than damage to the anterior, resulting in more men than women with language loss. Although Kimura questioned the concept of different lateralization for men and women, she hypothesized other gender differences in the hemispheres. Her theory replaces the differences in lateralization with the possibility of other differently organized abilities within the cerebral hemispheres of women and men and constitutes a major revision of views on gender differences in lateralization.

In summary, a great deal of research and theory has explored gender differences in the lateralization of the cerebral hemispheres. Early studies neither sought nor found differences between men and women. When researchers started looking, they concluded that women are less lateralized than men; that is, women tend to have both language and spatial function more equally represented in both hemispheres, whereas men tend to have language represented in the left and spatial abilities represented in the right hemisphere. Several theories have attempted to explain why the brains of women and men might differ. Some theories emphasize prenatal hormones, another postulates that growth rates produce gender differences, and other theories use differential social demands during evolutionary prehistory to explain the brain organization of women and men. One recent proposal holds that gender-related differences exist in the organization of the cerebral hemispheres but that differences between men and women in lateralization do not exist.

However, a common view from the research on brain organization is that the brains of men and women differ at the level of the cerebral hemispheres. In addition, other brain structures beneath the cerebral cortex show sexual dimorphism, and some research has suggested that the corpus callosum may also differ in women and men.

Other Gender-Related Differences in Brain Structure

In addition to gender differences in cerebral hemispheres, differences between the brains of men and women may exist in the hypothalamus, the thalamus, and the corpus callosum. Figure 4.3 shows the brain as it would appear if cut down the middle. The massa intermedia and the area of the hypothalamus near the optic chiasm, structures shown in this figure, are two of the brain structures that differ in women and men.

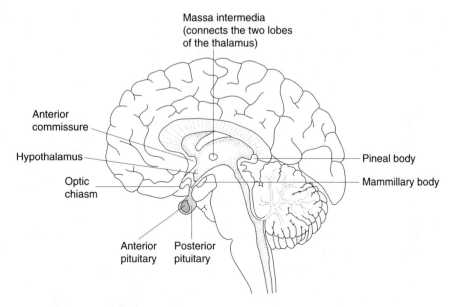

FIGURE 4.3   Midsection of the Brain

SOURCE: From *Biopsychology* (p. 273) by J.P.J. Pinel, 1993, Boston: Allyn and Bacon. Reprinted by permission.

In the late 1970s, a research team from UCLA discovered that a small area of the hypothalamus called the **sexually dimorphic nucleus** (SDN) is much larger in male rats than it is in female rats (Gorski, 1987). This brain structure consists of about a cubic millimeter of tissue in the area of the hypothalamus near the optic chiasm. This nucleus is very sensitive to testosterone and estrogen, so the presence or absence of these hormones influences its development. Furthermore, hormonal manipulation of baby rats can alter the size of the sexually dimorphic nucleus, decreasing its size in male rats or increasing its size in female rats. A search for the equivalent structure and the equivalent difference in humans succeeded (Swaab & Fliers, 1985), showing that men have a sexually dimorphic nucleus that is 2.5 times larger than the same structure in women.

In the rat this area of the brain is involved with sexual response and mating behavior, and Dick Swaab (in Gibbons, 1991) has speculated that this structure plays a role in the development of male gender identity. This speculation represents a considerable leap, as male gender identity is a complex concept relating to feelings about gender identity that are not limited to or necessarily congruent with sexual behavior or sexual orientation. Although studies have documented the structural differences of the sexually dimorphic nucleus, Swaab's speculation concerning implications of the size of the SDN is unconfirmed, and the function of this structure in humans remains unknown.

An even more intriguing finding concerning the hypothalamus has come from Simon LeVay (1991), who claimed that he had found brain-level differences between heterosexual and homosexual individuals. (Note that his claim is not the same as Swaab's; LeVay made no claims about a brain basis for gender identity but instead for sexual orientation.) LeVay autopsied the brains of homosexual men, men whom he presumed to be heterosexual, and women (whose sexual orientation he did not know). He found that the interstitial nuclei of the hypothalamus was twice as large in the heterosexual men compared to the homosexual men and the women. LeVay interpreted this finding as a biological basis for sexual orientation, but obviously, this interpretation is questionable. In addition to the presumption of sexual orientation for the group labeled heterosexual, all of the homosexual men had died of AIDS, but less than half of the group labeled heterosexual had died of AIDS complications and only one of the women had died of AIDS. Thus, different causes of death and a doubtful method of determining sexual orientation cast doubt on the validity of LeVay's results. His finding, however, is intriguing, demonstrating that some individual variability exists with respect to this area of the hypothalamus and suggesting that this variability may relate to sexual orientation.

Several of the other structures in the brain that Gibbons (1991) reported as showing gender differences are the fibers that connect the left and right sides of the brain. The anterior commissure, massa intermedia of the thalamus, and corpus callosum all provide such connections. As Gibbons reported, evidence for sexual dimorphism of the anterior commissure and the massa intermedia of the thalamus are sketchy, but the massa intermedia is sometimes completely absent in men but not in women. According to Gibbons, these differences are difficult to quantify, so both the existence and importance of such differences remain to be seen.

Research on differences of the corpus callosum in women and men is more plentiful. Interest in the corpus callosum as a sexually dimorphic structure began with a report by Christine de Lacoste-Utamsing and Ralph Holloway (1982). These researchers autopsied 14 brains and found that the brains of the women showed relative size differences in the posterior (back part) of the corpus callosum, called the **splenium**. They found that the splenium was larger and more bulbous in women relative to its size in men. Sandra Witelson (1985) performed another autopsy study (on 42 brains) that failed to confirm these differences, as did a study of living humans (Byne, Bleier, & Houston, 1988).

Another of Witelson's studies (1991) found a difference in the corpus callosum of men and women, but the difference was related to age. She found that the size of the callosum decreased in aging men but remained constant in size in aging women. Thus, differences in the corpus callosum that relate to gender may interact with age, and the corpus callosum may not be one of the brain structures that shows clear sexual dimorphism.

Other than the differences in the cerebral hemispheres, the evidence for sexual dimorphism in the brain is strongest for the sexually dimorphic nucleus of the hypothalamus. This structure is larger in male rats and men than in female rats and women. Its function is not understood but may be related to sexual behavior or gender identity. Differences in the structures of the anterior commissure, massa intermedia of the thalamus, and corpus callosum are not as well established, although the corpus callosum

TABLE 4.1 Summary of Brain Differences between Men and Women

Structure	Difference
Cerebral hemispheres	Men may be more lateralized than women for language and spatial functions
Sexually dimorphic nucleus of hypothalamus	SDN in men is 2.5 times larger than in women
Splenium of corpus callosum	Early studies indicated larger and more bulbous splenium in women; later studies found an interaction with age and gender
Anterior commissure	Evidence for sexual dimorphism is sketchy
Massa intermedia of the thalamus	Evidence for sexual dimorphism is sketchy

varies in size for men but not women over the life span. Table 4.1 summarizes the results of studies on brain differences between women and men.

Implications of Structural Differences

The structural differences in the brains of women and men are important for biology, but their importance to psychology exists only insofar as structure and function are related. For psychology, the important issue in determining differences between the brains of men and women is the relationship between brain structure and behavior. If the brains of women and men differ in structure, function, or the ways in which neural inputs are processed, then the relative abilities and behavior of men and women might reflect those differences. Such differences might have implications not only for educational and professional opportunities but also for many aspects of everyday behavior.

The argument that brain differences produce differences in mental abilities or behavior borders on biological determinism. Although a great prejudice exists in favor of biological determinism, Katharine Hoyenga and Kermit Hoyenga (1993) argued against this fallacy. They explained how people tend to believe that biological differences are not subject to change—that labeling a difference "biological" is the same as saying it is permanent or unchangeable. They pointed out that this belief is incorrect; factors with a biological basis are as subject to change as psychologically based differences. Furthermore, Hoyenga and Hoyenga asserted that it is impossible to pinpoint the source of a complex behavior as biological because so many different biological and experiential factors interact to produce any behavior. Thus, Hoyenga and Hoyenga argued that the quest for a biological explanation for behavior cannot be successful.

Other researchers, such as Kimura (1992), believe that establishing a biological basis for behavior is possible. Through careful research, a connection between sexual dimorphism in the brain and gender differences in behavior can be established. However, several types of evidence must exist. First, structural differences between the brains of women and men must occur. Second, gender differences in performance on mental tasks must occur. And third, gender differences in task performance must be linked to the structural differences. This chapter has examined the evidence about sexual dimorphism in the brain, and this evidence indicates that some differences in brain structure exist between women and men. Chapter 5 will examine and evaluate the research about gender differences on several types of mental tasks. If these differences exist, then the argument depends on evidence about the link between the two. Although not all researchers believe that it is possible to establish such connections, many do, and their research has influenced popular beliefs about the nature of gender differences in intelligence.

Summary

Many people believe that the differences in male and female intellectual and occupational achievement must be linked to differences in male and female brains. This chapter began with an article that claimed that the brain is "a sexual organ" and that many differences exist between the brains of men and women. The basic unit of the nervous system, the neuron, shows no such differences, but the uppermost part of the brain, the cerebral cortex, may.

The cerebral cortex is divided into left and right hemispheres, and the hemispheres are lateralized, with the left and right hemispheres controlling different abilities. The left hemisphere is more capable in verbal tasks, such as speech recognition and language production. The right hemisphere is more involved in emotion and more capable of perceiving spatial relationships. Many (but not all) researchers have concluded that gender differences exist in lateralization, with men being more lateralized than women. However, not all experts agree on the existence of these differences.

Other brain structures show sexual dimorphism, especially the sexually dimorphic nucleus, a part of the hypothalamus that is 2.5 times larger in men than in women. The results of these differences are not known. Some research has indicated that the corpus callosum, the brain structure that connects the two hemispheres, is larger in women than in men, but further research has failed to confirm this difference. Other possible differences are not well confirmed.

Some researchers have argued that it is not possible to separate the influences of biology and experience, but others believe that establishing a biological basis for behavior is possible. For those who believe in biological determinism, the implications for structural differences in the brain are that such differences produce functional differences in cognitive abilities and behavior. To establish this link, evidence of cognitive differences in women and men must be strong, and such evidence is not strong.

Glossary

Aphasia   loss of the ability to speak or use language

Broca's area   the area in the left frontal lobe of most human brains that controls the ability to speak

Cerebral dominance   the concept that the left cerebral hemisphere is more important in brain function than the right cerebral hemisphere and controls or dominates the right

Corpus callosum   a band of nerve fibers that connects the right and left cerebral hemispheres

Lateralization   the concept that the two cerebral hemispheres are not functionally equal but rather that the left hemisphere has different abilities than does the right hemisphere

Neurons   nerve cells

Sexually dimorphic nucleus   a brain structure in the hypothalamus, near the optic chiasm, that is larger in male than female rats and larger in men than women

Splenium   the back (posterior) part of the corpus callosum

Suggested Readings

Benderly, Beryl Lieff. (1987). *The myth of two minds.* New York: Doubleday. Chapter 10 of this nontechnical book—"Different Brains?"—presents some of the research on brain differences in a readable way.

Kimura, Doreen. (1992, September). Sex differences in the brain. *Scientific American,* pp. 119–125. Kimura's research has been controversial, partly due to misinterpretation and partly due to her belief in differences between the brains of women and men. In this presentation in a popular magazine, Kimura summarizes her research and her position in this controversy.

Springer, Sally P.; & Deutsch, Georg. (1989). *Left brain, right brain* (3rd ed.). New York: Freeman. This book details the history and status of the research on cerebral dominance, including a chapter titled "Sex and Asymmetry." Although the authors summarize a great deal of technical research, their presentation is easy to follow, and their review is critical without being biased.

Tavris, Carol. (1992). *The mismeasure of woman.* New York: Simon & Schuster. The first chapter of Tavris's excellent book contains several subsections, the last of which is titled "Brain: Dissecting the Differences." This section provides a good, current, easy-to-read (and critical) examination of the research on gender-related differences in the brain.

Chapter 5

Intelligence and Mental Abilities

Female Sex Hormone Is Tied to Ability to Perform Tasks
—*New York Times,* November 18, 1988

Men's Test Scores Linked to Hormone
—*New York Times,* November 14, 1991

On November 18, 1988, the *New York Times* carried a story on its front page that described research on the relationship between estrogen levels and the performance of verbal and spatial tasks (Blakeslee, 1988). The article, which described research by Doreen Kimura and Elizabeth Hampson, claimed that this research was the first to demonstrate the relationship between fluctuations in estrogen and ability to perform verbal and spatial tasks. However, Beryl Lieff Benderly (1989) contended that the report was incorrect; the relationship between estrogen levels and performance on various tasks had been established years earlier. What Kimura and Hampson's research had found was a reciprocal change in women's performance on a verbal task and a spatial orientation task with different estrogen levels. That is, when women's level of estrogen was high, they did better on a "feminine" task—a verbal fluency task—but poorer on a "masculine" task—a spatial orientation task. That is, their verbal fluency fell and their spatial orientation performance rose when their estrogen level was lower. Although interesting, this finding is not the scientific breakthrough that the front page story proclaimed. However, the reported finding does indicate an interesting relationship: Performance on some mental abilities is associated with changes in levels of estrogen.

The November 14, 1991, *New York Times* headline proclaiming "Men's Test Scores Linked to Hormone" (Blakeslee, 1991) was followed by a story about more research by Kimura. This research involved testing men and women on verbal and spatial tasks at different times during the year. During the fall men's testosterone levels are higher than during the spring, and Kimura was interested in assessing the relationship between hormone level and performance on verbal and spatial tasks. She found that men performed better on spatial tasks in the spring, when their testosterone levels were lower.

Kimura's result is interesting because it suggests that no straightforward relationship exists between testosterone and spatial abilities. If testosterone boosts spatial abilities, men should be better at these tasks when their hormone levels are highest, yet Kimura's research indicated that *lower* testosterone levels were associated with higher performance on spatial tasks. This result suggests a complex relationship between hormone levels and task performance. Men's verbal performance did not differ by season, and women showed no significant seasonal variations in verbal or spatial performance.

These two reports have described an extensive program of research that has attempted to determine the relationship between hormonal fluctuations and performance on mental tasks. In both reports, Kimura emphasized that the size of the fluctuation effects were small and "would not affect daily life" (in Blakeslee, 1991, p. B14). However, Kimura's research and many other findings have reported some overall differences in women's and men's performance on verbal and spatial tasks. Do these overall differences reflect different types of mental abilities in men and women? Do differences in the ability to perform different tasks mean that specific mental abilities or overall intelligence varies by gender? Or do these differences represent insignificant differences in how women and men think?

Mental Abilities

Other than defining intelligence as "how smart a person is" (a trivial and circular definition), an acceptable definition of this concept has been difficult to formulate. Indeed, heated debate over the nature of intelligence has occurred throughout the history of psychology, and this controversy has not been confined to psychology. The prominence of such concern highlights the importance of the issue: Understanding intelligence and the types of abilities that contribute to intelligence is a basic question for understanding humans.

Psychologists have been concerned with the concept of intelligence since the early years of psychology, during the 1890s (Schultz & Schultz, 1992). However, the most influential development for the current conceptualization of intelligence was the creation of the intelligence test in 1905. This test, formulated by Alfred Binet, Victor Henri, and Théodore Simon, measured a variety of mental abilities related to school performance, including memory, attention, comprehension, vocabulary, and imagination. A version of this test, the Stanford-Binet, appeared in the United States in 1916, and the mental testing movement became an important part of psychology, especially in the United States.

The prevailing view of intelligence during the 19th and early 20th centuries was that women's intellect was inferior to men's (Lewin, 1984a; Shields, 1975a). Lewis Terman, who adapted the Binet-Simon test into the Stanford-Binet test, did not believe in the intellectual inferiority of women, so he had no trouble accepting the results of his test, which revealed no average differences between the intelligence of men and women. Indeed, the scores on the early versions of the Stanford-Binet showed that women scored slightly higher than men, but eliminating some of the items that showed differences yielded a test on which the average scores for women and girls were equal to those of men and boys (Terman & Merrill, 1937).

With the development of the mental testing movement came increased attention to the different abilities that might be included within the tests of intelligence. The test devised by Binet and his colleagues and adapted by Terman into the Stanford-Binet included mostly items classified as verbal; that is, questions that require the understanding and use of language.

Psychologist David Wechsler created an alternative intelligence test that made a division between abilities he labeled verbal and performance skills. The verbal subtests required that those being tested provide verbal answers by supplying factual knowledge (information), defining vocabulary items (vocabulary), performing basic arithmetic computation (arithmetic), repeating a series of digits (digit span), understanding similarities between objects (similarities), and properly interpreting social conventions (comprehension). The performance subtests of Wechsler's test required no verbal responses, but instead people responded by performing some action. The performance subtests included arranging pictures into a sensible story (picture arrangement), duplicating designs with blocks (block design), completing pictures that have some missing part (picture completion), assembling cut-up figures of common objects (object assembly), and learning and rapidly applying a digit symbol code (digit symbol) (Gregory, 1987). Figure 5.1 shows samples of the type of items on the Wechsler tests.

Unlike the Stanford-Binet test, Wechsler's test showed differences between the scores of men and women, with women scoring higher on the verbal subtests and men scoring higher on the performance subtests. Wechsler performed no item adjustment to equate average performance of women and men on the subtests. Although the combined scores on the Wechsler tests do not show gender differences, the subtest scores always have.

Nor are the Wechsler tests the only assessments that have revealed different abilities between male and female participants. Eleanor Maccoby and Carol Jacklin's (1974) review of gender differences in intellectual performance confirmed the findings of differences in performance on verbal, mathematical, and spatial tasks. More recent research, however, has revealed that the patterns of gender differences in these mental abilities are more complex than the early reviews suggested. In addition, these differences have changed, and gender-related differences seem to be decreasing or disappearing.

Verbal Subtests	Sample Items
Information	How many wings does a bird have? Who wrote *Paradise Lost*?
Digit span	Repeat from memory a series of digits, such as 3 1 0 6 7 4 2 5, after hearing it once.
General comprehension	What is the advantage of keeping money in a bank? Why is copper often used in electrical wires?
Arithmetic	Three men divided 18 golf balls equally among themselves. How many golf balls did each man receive? If 2 apples cost 15¢, what will be the cost of a dozen apples?
Similarities	In what way are a lion and a tiger alike? In what way are a saw and a hammer alike?
Vocabulary	This test consists simply of asking, "What is a _____?" or "What does _____ mean?" The words cover a wide range of difficulty or familiarity.

Performance Subtests	Description of Item
Picture arrangement	Arrange a series of cartoon panels to make a meaningful story.
Picture completion	What is missing from these pictures?
Block design	Copy designs with blocks (as shown at right).
Object assembly	Put together a jigsaw puzzle.
Digit symbol	

1	2	3	4
X	III	I	O

Fill in the symbols:

3	4	1	3	4	2	1	2

FIGURE 5.1   Sample Test Items Similar to Items on Wechsler's Tests of Intelligence

Verbal Abilities

The tasks that researchers have used to study verbal ability include not only the verbal subtests of the Wechsler tests but also verbal fluency, anagram tests, reading comprehension tests, synonym and antonym tasks, sentence structure assessments, and reading readiness tests as well as the spelling, punctuation, vocabulary, and reading subtests from various achievement tests. Researchers have defined all of these tasks as verbal, despite the wide variation in the tasks themselves.

Maccoby and Jacklin (1974) reviewed dozens of studies that had compared the verbal abilities of girls and women to boys and men. Although these studies had used many different measures of verbal ability and some of the studies had failed to find gender differences, Maccoby and Jacklin concluded that girls and women have an advantage in verbal abilities, but they also concluded that these advantages are small.

Diane Halpern (1992) also reviewed studies in the area of verbal abilities, confirming that verbal abilities consist of various skills and that girls and women generally have the advantage. Halpern also noted that boys and men are more likely than girls and women to have language-related problems, such as stuttering and reading problems. Despite the preponderance of boys diagnosed with these problems, recent research has suggested that the number of boys and girls with such problems may be closer to equal, as boys receive referrals for these problems more often than girls (Karlen, Hagin, & Beecher, 1985; Shaywitz, Shaywitz, Fletcher, & Escobar, 1990). Halpern also pointed out that girls acquire language with greater speed and proficiency than boys and that gender-related differences in verbal abilities appear as early as children begin to talk. Girls maintain this advantage throughout elementary school, but during middle and high school, the pattern becomes more complex.

That complexity is reflected in results from the Differential Aptitude Tests (DAT), a battery of eight scales appropriate for pupils in grades 8 through 12. The DAT battery includes three tests of verbal ability. Two of these subtests, spelling and language, show advantages for girls, but the verbal reasoning subtest shows no gender-related difference (Feingold, 1988). Therefore, the female advantage in verbal abilities is both small and fails to appear in all measures of verbal ability.

Meta-analysis, a statistical technique that allows the evaluation of results from many studies and the estimation of the size of the effect, was not available 1974 when Maccoby and Jacklin completed their review of gender-related similarities and differences. But Janet Hyde (1981) completed such a meta-analysis of the studies from Maccoby and Jacklin's review and concluded that the gender-related differences in verbal ability are small. About 1% of the difference in verbal ability relates to gender, leaving the other 99% of the differences related to other factors.

A later meta-analysis by Janet Hyde and Marcia Linn (1988) examined 165 studies that had reported gender differences in verbal abilities. Their analysis indicated that women have the advantage in some verbal abilities, but men have the advantage in others. Based on the 1985 administration of the Scholastic Aptitude Test, men, not women, showed slightly superior scores on the verbal section. In addition, Hyde and Linn's analysis indicated that earlier studies showed gender-related differences, whereas more recent studies have not. Overall, women have a small advantage, but Hyde and Linn argued that the difference was too small to be of any practical importance. Indeed, they maintained that gender differences in verbal abilities no longer exist.

Mathematical and Quantitative Abilities

Most studies with children as participants show either no gender differences or advantages for girls in mathematical ability, which is defined as proficiency in arithmetic computation (Fennema, 1980; Hyde, Fennema, & Lamon, 1990). Around age 13 years, gender differences favoring boys begin to appear in many of the assessments of mathematical ability, and these differences persist throughout adulthood.

Girls who are good at arithmetic computation do not become women who are poor at such tasks. The DAT numerical ability subtest shows no gender differences for students in grades 8 through 12 (Feingold, 1988). Instead, the measurements of what constitutes mathematical and quantitative abilities change between the middle school and the high school years. Rather than consisting of arithmetic computation, the tests of quantitative ability begin to include tasks that are more abstract and perhaps more dependent on spatial ability, another cognitive ability for which boys and men have an advantage. (This is explored further in the next section.) Therefore, the measurement of some mathematical abilities may not be independent of spatial ability, and the widely observed disadvantage for women in the two areas may be connected (Eccles, 1987). On the other hand, the disadvantage for women may not be as large as general belief indicates. As Hyde's (1981) meta-analysis of quantitative abilities showed, only 1% of the difference in performance was related to gender, which indicates a very small overall gender-related difference in mathematical ability.

A later meta-analysis by Janet Hyde, Elizabeth Fennema, and Susan Lamon (1990) revealed additional complexities concerning mathematical abilities. These researchers analyzed 100 studies and found that in the general population, women, not men, have a small advantage in quantitative ability. Although this advantage is too small to be important, their analysis suggests that the pattern of mathematical and quantitative abilities is complex and different from the stereotype.

The meta-analysis by Hyde and her colleagues divided quantitative abilities into different skills, and this division showed that women have a small advantage in computation and an even smaller advantage in understanding mathematical concepts. During elementary and middle school, no gender difference appears in mathematics problem solving, but boys begin to do better at solving math problems during high school, and this advantage continues during college. The gender-related differences in problem solving that begin to appear during high school show a larger discrepancy in selected groups of students than in the general population. This selection factor shows its influence in high school and college as well as in groups of gifted students.

Two tests that have consistently revealed gender-related differences in math performance are the mathematics subtests of the Preliminary Scholastic Aptitude Test (PSAT) and the Scholastic Aptitude Tests (SAT) (Feingold, 1988). The gender-related differences in performance on these two tests demonstrate the influence of a progressively selected group of students. The PSAT, as the name suggests, is a preliminary form of the SAT, a test used as a college entrance examination. Students who take the SAT are typically a self-selected group taking the test as a college entrance exam, not a representative sample of the general population or even of high school students.

Performance on the PSAT reflects the scores of a more representative sample of high school juniors and seniors. Although the PSAT and the SAT are equivalent in content, the test score averages differ due to the selection of students who take each test. Both tests show advantages for boys on the mathematics subtests, but the SAT mathematics subtest shows a larger advantage than the PSAT mathematics subtest. This difference indicates that male college-bound students have a larger advantage over female college-bound students in math than male high school students have over female high school students. This comparison also suggests that the male advantage in mathematics is greater at higher levels of mathematics performance.

Studies by Camilla Benbow and Julian C. Stanley (1980, 1983) have shown a large gender difference in higher-level mathematics, with boys having the advantage. They found these differences by administering the SAT to intellectually gifted children under 13 years old, before these students had formally studied higher mathematics. Their results indicated that "by age 13 a large sex difference in mathematical reasoning ability exists and that it is especially pronounced at the high end of the distribution" (Benbow & Stanley, 1983, p. 1029). That is, as the scores indicated higher levels of mathematics performance, comparatively fewer girls than boys scored in this range.

Benbow and Stanley (1983) argued that the difference in mathematics ability they observed was the expression of innate, biological abilities and thus reflected innate differences between boys and girls. They collected no biological data, which makes this conclusion unfounded (Jacklin, 1989). Although boys and girls at this age have taken an equal number of math courses, their experience with mathematics might differ according to parental attention and encouragement, computer experience, and peer acceptance. All of these experiences might influence gifted boys to develop higher levels of math skills than equally gifted girls. On the other hand, these differences in math performance might reflect different levels of math ability in gifted children. Although Benbow and Stanley's conclusion concerning an innate basis for differences in mathematics performance was unfounded, they were properly cautious about generalizing their results to other, nongifted children. They acknowledged that their results do not show that boys and girls generally differ in math ability.

To examine the possibility that math performance is influenced by problem-solving strategies, James Byrnes and Sayuri Takahira (1993) studied high school students' performance on SAT math problems. Consistent with other studies, they found that the male students outperformed the female students, but their results indicated that gender per se was not related to math performance. Instead, prior knowledge and the appropriate use of problem-solving strategies differentiated the male and female students. That is, preparation and not gender formed the basis of the difference in math problem solving.

The differential preparation of female and male students provides a complication for assessing the underlying mathematical abilities of women and men. Starting during high school, girls take fewer math courses than boys (Fennema, 1980). Because of this difference, any assessment of ability will be inseparable from the influence of differential experience. However, this situation reflects an important and unquestionable gender-related difference: Girls make different choices than boys in their curricula. Regardless of any possible differences in ability, choices made by girls and boys can have far-reaching implications in their lives as men and women.

Jacquelynne Eccles (1989) reported that beginning at age 12 years, girls start to feel less confident about their ability to do mathematics. As students age, the amount of gender-related difference in confidence grows, continuing into adulthood. Girls also begin to believe that math is not important to them at the same age that they begin to lose confidence in their ability to do math. Boys, on the other hand, have greater confidence in their mathematical ability and evaluate math as more important to their future. Eccles (1987) proposed that girls' choice to avoid math courses stems from their beliefs concerning the likelihood of success and the perceived lack of value of the coursework. Their combined lack of confidence and the belief that math is not important to their future form a powerful disincentive for girls when they have the option to choose elective math courses.

The choice to avoid math courses can have lifelong repercussions, according to Lucy Sells (1980). She argued that the selection of high school mathematics courses can act as a filter, effectively barring female and ethnic minority students from many professions. For example, if a student has only two years of high school math, that stu-

---

DIVERSITY HIGHLIGHT
Cultural and Ethnic Differences in Mathematical and Spatial Ability

Lucy Sells (1980) studied the effects of choices of curricula during high school on career options, with an interest not only in gender but also in ethnic background. She found that young women tend to take fewer math courses than young men during high school and that ethnic differences are even more pronounced than gender differences in high school mathematics achievement. Her examination of enrollment in California high schools indicated that only 25% of Hispanic-American and 20% of African-American students were enrolled in math courses that would allow them to pursue scientific and technical majors in college, compared to 79% of Asian-American and 72% of European-American students.

The difference in choices also appeared in college students in Sells's study: Asian-American women chose physical science, life science, and mathematics majors not only more often than European-American women but also more often than European-American men. Overall, the ethnic differences were as large as the gender differences in choice of college major.

Marjorie Schratz (1978) also found an interaction among ethnic background, gender, and mathematical ability. She tested Hispanic-American, African-American, and European-American adolescents enrolled in New York schools. Unlike much previous research, she found that Hispanic-Ameri-

can girls showed better mathematical performance than Hispanic-American boys, and African-American girls showed the same trend. The scores for European-American adolescents showed the same pattern as much previous research—the boys scored higher than the girls.

Schratz also investigated gender and ethnic differences in spatial ability as measured by performance on an embedded figures task. She found no difference for preadolescent participants, but she found an interaction between gender and ethnic group for adolescents, which results were comparable to those she found for mathematics performance. That is, for adolescent Hispanic Americans and African Americans, the girls did better than the boys, whereas the European-American boys did better than the European-American girls. However on this measure of spatial ability, the Hispanic-American girls did better than *any other group*.

Schratz's findings support the possibility that the traditional conclusions of a male advantage in some mathematical and spatial abilities may be a result based on inadequate comparisons rather than universal advantage. Her study highlights the importance of considering ethnic differences before making sweeping conclusions about gender differences and casts doubt on the validity of any biological theory of gender differences in mathematical and spatial performance.

dent cannot take calculus as a freshman in college, which thereby eliminates some college majors and filters some students from those majors and from careers requiring those majors.

In examining the mathematics preparation of first-year university students, Sells found a large difference between women and men. Only 8% of the women compared to 57% of the men had completed more than three years of high school math. These differences in preparation were reflected in their choice of majors, with men choosing majors in physical science, life science, or mathematics more often than women.

Another intriguing finding from Sells (1980) was the strong relationship between reported social support from peers, parents, or teachers and the choice by high school girls to take advanced mathematics courses. Not only did social support increase the likelihood of these girls' enrolling in advanced math, but social support also was significantly related to their grades. Girls who reported support for their enrollment were much more likely to earn A's or B's, whereas those who reported no social support were more likely to get C's and D's. These findings demonstrate the power of social support for academic choices and success and also challenge the idea of innate factors in mathematics achievement.

Support from parents and teachers might also influence feelings about math achievement, and Eccles and her colleagues (Eccles & Jacobs, 1986; Jacobs & Eccles, 1992; Jussim & Eccles, 1992; Yee & Eccles, 1988) have investigated this relationship. Doris Yee and Eccles found that parental attitudes influenced children's math achievement and varied according to children's gender: Parents perceived that their daughters put more effort into math, whereas they saw their sons as having more talent for the subject. Janis Jacobs and Eccles (1992) found that mothers' gender stereotypical beliefs combined with their children's gender to influence the mothers' perception of their children's math ability. That is, mothers with gender stereotypical beliefs saw sons as more capable than daughters at math.

Eccles and Jacobs (1986) found that beliefs of both parents and teachers affected math achievement and related to children's beliefs concerning their ability at math. Lee Jussim and Eccles (1992) found that teachers' attitudes act as self-fulfilling prophecies, with teacher expectations playing a role in student achievement. Therefore, parent and teacher expectations influence not only children's beliefs about their own capability but also how children perform in mathematics.

A meta-analysis of attitudes toward mathematics showed surprisingly few gender-related differences (Hyde, Fennema, Ryan, Frost, & Hopp, 1990). Contrary to the stereotype, girls and women do not dislike and fear math, but when differences exist, women have more negative attitudes than men toward math. Similar to the findings concerning math performance, the results concerning math attitudes showed no gender difference during elementary school but some differences during high school. The only dramatic difference revealed by this meta-analysis was in gender stereotyping, with men being likely to perceive math as a male domain.

Gilah Leder (1990) has proposed that mathematics achievement is influenced by a combination of learner and environmental variables, and her model appears in Figure 5.2. In this view, cognitive abilities are only one of the personal factors in achievement, and beliefs concerning personal ability and the usefulness of math achievement also contribute. Environmental variables also provide a host of factors that can result in differential achievement for boys and girls, including social, home, and school factors.

Social factors in Leder's model include cultural expectations, such as the stereotyping of math as a male domain (Hyde, Fennema, et al., 1990), media emphasis of differences, and peer encouragement for math-related activities. Home factors include family socioeconomic status as well as parental encouragement (or lack of such encouragement) and sibling behavior related to math. School-related factors include teachers' attitudes and behavior, organization of instruction, methods of assessment, and acceptance by peers. Although Leder constructed this model to explain mathematics achievement, the combination of factors could apply to all achievement situations.

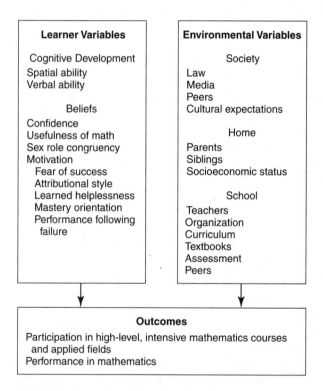

**FIGURE 5.2 Variables Studied in Relation
to Gender Differences
in Mathematics**

Chapter 12 discusses the gender bias that occurs in schools and classrooms. Teachers interact with female and male students in different ways, giving boys more instruction and encouragement than they give girls. Mary Schatz Koehler (1990, p. 145) summarized these differences and marveled that this treatment has not resulted in greater gender differences in math achievement:

> *When one considers that females endure remarks from teachers or texts indicating that mathematics is not a female domain, are involved in far fewer interactions with their teachers involving mathematics, are rarely asked high-cognitive-level questions in mathematics, are encouraged to be dependent rather than independent thinkers, spend more time helping their peers and not getting helped in return, and are often not placed in groups that are appropriate to their level, it is amazing that the gap [in mathematics achievement] is not considerably larger.*

In summary, gender-related differences in mathematics performance do not exist in the general population, but differences appear in selected groups. Among students, girls and boys do not differ in mathematics performance until junior high school. At this time, boys begin to show higher average levels of math performance and confidence, and these differences persist throughout adulthood, at least for European-American students in the United States. Studies of gifted children have shown that extraordinary mathematics performance is much more common among boys than girls, although this level of ability is rare even in boys. Such math talent may be the result of innate ability but may also be influenced by cultural expectation and parental encouragement.

For nongifted adolescents, differences exist in the number of math courses completed, with boys choosing to enroll in and complete more math courses than girls. Sells's research has found ethnic as well as gender differences in course enrollment, with African Americans and Hispanic Americans choosing to take fewer math courses than European Americans and Asian Americans. Such choices may limit the career options for members of these ethnic groups, just as it may for women or men who make similar choices.

Differences in mathematics performance and attitudes toward mathematics show small gender differences, despite the stereotype that girls and women dislike math and do poorly in the subject. This stereotype may be the underlying basis for the biased treatment regarding their mathematical ability that girls and women experience from their peer, parents, and teachers.

Spatial Abilities

The definition of what constitutes spatial ability has varied, as Paula Caplan and her colleagues (Caplan, MacPherson, & Tobin, 1985) have pointed out. This variation has not hindered acceptance of the notion that men are better at these tasks than women. Yet this gender-related difference remains controversial, partly due to the difficulties involved in defining the term *spatial ability*.

Although some variation has existed in the definitions of the other two cognitive abilities that show gender differences—verbal ability and quantitative ability—researchers have defined spatial ability in a wide variety of ways (Caplan et al., 1985). These definitions have included the ability to visualize objects, to mentally manipulate objects, to perceive spatial patterns, to locate objects in space, to recognize shapes, to locate a figure embedded in a larger figure, to succeed at putting together block designs or jigsaw puzzles, and to estimate the time of arrival of a moving object. These various definitions have existed, as Caplan et al. suggested, because various researchers have been forced to define the concept of spatial ability in precise, specific terms in order to conduct their research. Thus, a researcher interested in studying spatial ability might choose any of these tasks as a reasonable way to measure the concept.

Once any researcher has chosen a measurement technique and found a difference, the researcher might generalize the results to conclude that "gender differences exist in spatial ability," without any further consideration for the validity of the connection between the concept of spatial ability and the specific task chosen to assess the concept. This process has allowed the existence of many measures of spatial ability and has created the situation in which spatial ability is not a unitary construct; thus, the term should be pluralized—*spatial abilities.*

Indeed, Heinrich Stumpf (1993) contended that hundreds of tests of spatial ability exist and that these tests can be classified into 16 groups. This variety of tests

---

✤ GENDERED VOICES
I Was Good at Math and Science

A female chemical engineer said, "I was good at math and science, so my high school counselor suggested engineering. I looked into the various kinds of engineering. I didn't really like physics that much, so I decided that electrical engineering would not be a good choice. I didn't consider myself very mechanical, so I ruled out mechanical engineering. I liked chemistry, so I thought chemical engineering would be a good choice, but I didn't really know what chemical engineers did. My high school had a cooperative arrangement so I could work for an engineer, but that experience didn't really let me know what the work of a chemical engineer was like. In fact, I didn't really understand the work of chemical engineers until I was a junior in college, and I learned that I didn't find the work all that interesting.

"I went to a technical college that specialized in engineering, and it was definitely male dominated; only about 25% of the students were women. But I never felt any favoritism either for or against the women. Everybody was treated fairly. The courses

during the first two years were designed to weed out students, so everybody felt that the curriculum was difficult, but the women did as well as the men, and I never felt that the professors or students showed any bias.

"What was missing on campus were ethnic minorities. The campus was very White. There just weren't any Black students, and there was one Hispanic girl. The geographic area had lots of minorities, but they didn't go into engineering at this school. I noticed the absence or minority students more than the small number of women.

"I didn't feel that being a woman was a factor in school, but it sure was on the job. I didn't necessarily feel discriminated against, but the women were very visible. There were few women, and whatever a woman did stood out. If I did a great job, I got noticed more than a man who did a great job. If I screwed up, I got noticed more than a man who made a mistake. Whatever a women did—good or bad—came to the attention of everyone."

confirms the many ways that researchers have defined and measured spatial ability and substantiates the claim that spatial ability is far from unitary. As Halpern (1992) suggested:

> *Given the large variety of tests that have been used to measure visual-spatial ability, it is not surprising that sex differences seem to depend on the type of test used. Not coincidentally, this is an area replete with contradictory findings because of the multidimensional complexity of visual-spatial abilities. (p. 70)*

Marcia Linn and Anne Petersen (1986) reviewed the research on spatial abilities and summarized these abilities into three categories—spatial perception, mental rotation, and spatial visualization. **Spatial perception** includes the ability to identify and locate the horizontal or vertical in the presence of distracting information. Examples of measures of spatial perception are the rod-and-frame task and Piaget's water-level task, both shown in Figure 5.3. These tasks usually show gender-related differences, with boys and men outperforming girls and women. The magnitude of this difference is small during childhood and adolescence but fairly large for adults.

Mental rotation includes the ability to visualize objects as they would appear if rotated in space. An example of a measure of this type of ability also appears in Figure 5.3. The gender-related difference for this spatial ability is large, with boys and men scoring substantially higher than girls and women on speed and accuracy of mentally rotating objects (Halpern, 1992).

Spatial visualization refers to the ability to process spatial information so as to understand the relationship between objects in space, such as the ability to see a figure embedded in other figures (also shown in Figure 5.3), find hidden figures in a drawing or picture, or imagine the shape produced when a folded piece of paper is cut and then unfolded. Gender differences do not always appear on measures of these tasks. When such differences appear, they are small, and men have this small advantage.

Halpern (1992) added a fourth category of spatial ability, which she called **spatiotemporal ability.** This ability involves judgments about moving objects in space, such as making a judgment about when a moving object will arrive at target. Her evaluation of the limited research on this ability indicated that men do better than women on such tasks, but a more recent study by David Law and his colleagues (Law, Pellegrino, & Hunt, 1993) has shown that prior experience was a factor in performance on this type of task, and feedback concerning performance improved the performance of both men and women. Thus, any advantage that boys or men show might be due to their experience with such tasks.

An additional complication in assessing gender differences in spatial ability comes from the possibility that tasks labeled "spatial" may not all constitute clear measures of spatial abilities. Instead, some of these tasks or the situations of their measurement may include other factors. For example, Julia Sherman (1978) has criticized the rod-and-frame task, arguing that its measurement may include factors other than spatial ability. This testing typically occurs in a darkened room, with a male experimenter testing participants. Sherman proposed that the testing situation may contribute to the

Mental rotation
Which figure on the right is identical to the figure in the box?

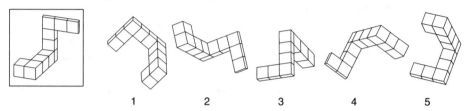

Piaget's water-level problem
This glass is half filled with water. Draw a line across the glass to indicate the top of the water line.

Rod-and-frame test
Ignore the orientation of the frame and adjust the position of the rod so that it is vertical.

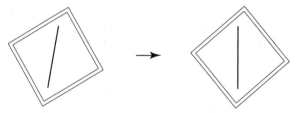

Disembedding
Find the simple figure on the left embedded in one of the four more complex figures on the right.

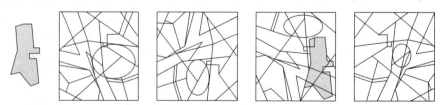

FIGURE 5.3   Spatial Tasks Favoring Men

gender differences—female participants may feel uncomfortable in this situation and be less likely to persist in asking the male experimenter to continue to adjust the rod. Thus, lack of assertiveness and uneasiness with the testing situation may contribute to the gender differences that often appear on this measure of spatial ability.

Naditch (cited in Caplan et al., 1985) used a testing procedure that eliminated the male advantage on the rod-and-frame task. By using a human figure rather than a rod and by explaining that the task was a measure of empathy, women outperformed men. This result is interesting, as the task still involved the same spatial factors as the original task—namely, judging relative position in space.

Matthew Sharps and his colleagues (Sharps, Welton, & Price, 1993) also found that the instructions influenced men's and women's performance on a spatial memory and a mental rotation task. When these researchers emphasized the spatial nature of a task, women's performance decreased compared to their performance when instructions deemphasized the spatial nature of the tasks. Women's (but not men's) performance changed in relation to the instructions. Both this study and Naditch's study demonstrate the importance of expectation and context: Although the tasks remained the same, performance varied in stereotypical ways with different instructions.

Other research has suggested that the gender differences that exist in performance on Piaget's water-level task might be due to factors other than gender. Lynn Liben and Susan Golbeck (1984) found that college women performed more poorly than men on this task. However, they also found that these gender-related differences disappeared when both women and men received specific instructions about the principles underlying performance on the task. That is, this gender difference changed with experience, suggesting that such differences might be due to the different experiences of men and women.

A meta-analysis on the role of experience in spatial test performance confirmed the advantages of experience in such tasks (Baenninger & Newcombe, 1989). This analysis revealed that a relationship exists between spatial activity participation and test performance in spatial tasks and that performance improves with training. Both findings applied to women and men, which means that both men and women are influenced by their experiences with spatial tasks and both improve with specific practice on such tasks.

To further complicate a simple conclusion for male advantage on spatial tasks, women show an advantage on some spatial tasks (Kimura, 1992). Women tend to do better on tasks of perceptual speed in which people must rapidly identify matching items. Women also outperform men on tasks in which people must remember the placement of a series of objects. Examples of these tasks appear in Figure 5.4.

These various findings raise the question Do gender differences in spatial abilities really exist? The tasks that researchers have used to measure spatial ability are varied, leading to the conclusion that it would be more accurate to think of *spatial abilities* rather than *a spatial ability factor.* Of the many spatial abilities, men show an advantage in some, and women show an advantage in others. Men do better than women in spatial perception, such as Piaget's water-level task, and in mental rotation, but training decreases this difference. The rod-and-frame task, often used as a measure of spatial perception, has been criticized for including factors in addition to spatial ability.

The embedded figures task has also yielded complex results for gender and ethnic background, suggesting that no clear male advantage exists for this measure of spatial ability. The female advantage in spatial abilities appears on measures of perceptual speed and memory for the placement of objects. Therefore, gender differences in spatial abilities exist, a number of which favor men, a few of which favor women, and some of which may vary with combinations of gender, context, and expectation.

Study the objects in group **A** for one minute and cover it up. Then look at group **B** and put an X through the figures not in the original array. Score one point for each item correctly crossed out and subtract one point for each item incorrectly crossed out.

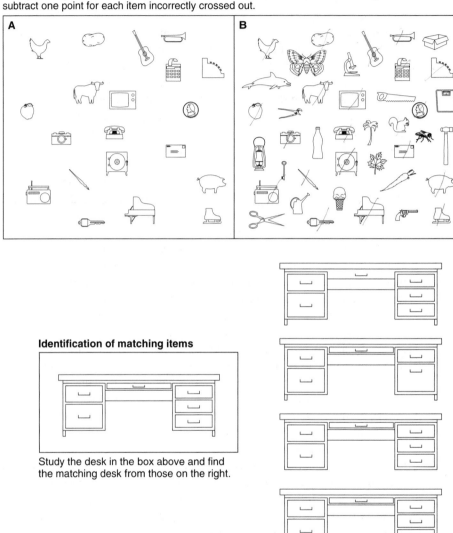

Identification of matching items

Study the desk in the box above and find the matching desk from those on the right.

FIGURE 5.4   Spatial Tasks Favoring Women

Other Mental Abilities

Verbal, mathematical, and spatial abilities are important but not the only mental abilities. These other abilities have not been investigated for gender-related differences as intensely as have verbal, mathematical, and spatial abilities. Memory, creativity, musical ability, and nonverbal communication are all abilities that have been the focus of research, but within this research, gender has not been the emphasis, or the research has failed to show gender-related differences.

A consideration of these other mental abilities is important for putting comparisons concerning gender-related mental abilities in perspective, as these other abilities have shown that such differences are in the minority. As Halpern (1992, p. 96) pointed out, "It is important to note that the number of areas in which sex differences are even moderate in size is small. Males and females are overwhelmingly alike in their cognitive abilities."

Memory can reflect either verbal or spatial abilities, depending on the material learned and remembered. The majority of tasks that psychologists have studied fall into the category of verbal learning and memory. According to Maccoby and Jacklin's (1974) review of research in this area, few gender-related differences exist in the various types of learning and memory. When studies show differences, girls and women have a small advantage. Subsequent research has indicated similar findings: no gender-related differences (Savage & Gouvier, 1992) or a small female advantage for learning verbal material (McGuiness, Olson, & Chapman, 1990).

Women's small advantage in verbal abilities and men's small advantage in spatial abilities lead to the prediction of differential memory performance in these areas. To some extent, the research confirms these predictions. In a study on learning routes, Li-isa Galea and Doreen Kimura (1993) explored gender differences in learning a route on a map. Women remembered more landmarks, but men made fewer errors in learning the route. Thomas Crook and his colleagues (Crook, Youngjohn, & Larrabee, 1993) also investigated route learning, and they too found gender differences, but "the effect size was so small it made this difference trivial" (p. 41). That is, men's advantage in memorizing spatial information gives them little advantage over women in getting around in the world.

Some of the gender-related differences in memory seem more strongly related to the gender-stereotypical nature of the task than to the gender of the learner. For example, Douglas Herrmann and his colleagues (Herrmann, Crawford, & Holdsworth, 1992) asked women and men to memorize a shopping list and directions to a particular place. They found the predicted results: Women were better than men at memorizing the shopping list, and men were better than women at memorizing the directions.

Furthermore, Herrmann et al. found that the labeling of the task influenced women's and men's memorization. When they told people that the shopping list pertained to groceries, they found an advantage for women, but when they described the same list as pertaining to hardware, men's memory was better. Halpern (1985) obtained similar results from a memory test using high school students. Halpern varied the name of the protagonist that she presented to her participants, and then she tested their memory of the story. She found that the participants remembered more about the same-gender than the other-gender protagonist. Furthermore, participants tended to remember the other-gender protagonist in stereotypical terms, whereas their memory for the same-gender protagonist was more accurate. Thus, memory may depend on factors other than ability, with men and women performing according to their attention, interests, and stereotypes.

Creativity is a term that researchers have defined in a variety of ways, leading to a great diversity of findings. Studies of kindergarten and the 1st grade children (Lewis & Houtz, 1986), children in the 4th through 8th grade (Rejskind, Rapagna, & Gold, 1992), and college students (Goldsmith & Matherly, 1988) have failed to find gender-related differences in creative thinking.

When researchers have defined creativity in terms of achievement, men show higher levels. This advantage, however, may not be due to greater creative ability but rather to access to training, parental and societal encouragement, and nonacceptance of women in creative fields. Halpern (1992) concluded that the greater number of prominent musicians who are men is not due to the greater musical ability of boys and men: "Sex differences in most tests of musical ability are small enough to disregard" (p. 77).

Jane Piirto (1991) discussed the discrepancy between the numbers of male and female visual artists and musicians. The title of her article concerning creative women asked "Why Are There So Few?" Her answer to this question proposed that creatively gifted boys and girls are very similar in personality but differ in commitment to their field. Piirto argued that the differences in creative accomplishments come from this lesser commitment on the part of girls and women and that gifted girls should be encouraged to devote themselves to their talents in the same ways that boys are.

Nonverbal communication includes a variety of behaviors related to conveying and receiving information through gestures, body position, and facial expression. According to stereotype, women are supposed to be able to decipher nonverbal cues better than men. Indeed, women are supposed to have "intuition"—the ability to understand social situations, people's motives, feelings, and wishes, all without being told. Sara Snodgrass (1985, 1992) has investigated this facet of gender-related behavior and has found that no gender differences exist in the ability to read such cues. Snodgrass found, instead, that people in subordinate positions are better at reading the nonverbal behaviors of those in dominant positions. That is, women's intuition is really subordinate's intuition and is shared by those whose advantage rests in understanding small nuances in the behavior of those in charge.

Although the gender differences are small in verbal, mathematical, and spatial abilities, differences do not exist in other mental abilities, such as memory, creativity, musical ability, and nonverbal communication. The studies that have revealed gender-related differences in performance in these areas have shown that the differences come from social stereotypes and expectations rather than from ability differences. In addition, research has indicated that the performance differences are trivial, making little or no difference in people's lives.

Implications of Gender-Related Differences

Research has shown that gender-related differences in mental abilities are small, even in the areas in which they do exist, and this finding does not seem consistent with the large differences in choices that men and women make concerning careers and in their confidence in their abilities. That is, the small differences in mental abilities seem to

---

<table>
<tr><td>✿ **GENDERED VOICES**
It's Not Something on the Y Chromosome</td></tr>
</table>

"I don't think that it's something on the Y chromosome," a 13-year-old girl said, referring to the ability to play percussion. "But some boys act like it is. The boys in the school band are used to me because I've played percussion all through junior high school with them, but when I go to competitions, the boys act like I shouldn't be playing percussion. Almost like it's an insult that a girl should be playing."

She explained that lots of girls play in the school band. There is generally no prejudice against girls who are musicians, but the band is gender segregated by musical instrument. The instruments toward the front of the band are more "feminine," such

as violins, clarinets, and cellos. The instruments toward the back are more "masculine," such as tubas and the percussion instruments. "There are lots more girls toward the front of the band, and the boys dominate the back."

"At the all-city band competition, it was especially bad. The boys who played percussion were especially obnoxious, acting like I shouldn't be trying. They acted like it was their right as boys to be able to play drums or other percussion—like there was something on the Y chromosome that gave them the gift. Well, I guess they were really surprised when I won."

---

have larger implications for the lives of women and men. These choices may be mediated through stereotypical beliefs about the abilities of men and women: People's behavior may be more closely related to their images of what men and women can do than to what women and men can actually do.

Hyde (1981) has discussed the ways in which research on gender-related cognitive differences has led to erroneous beliefs about these abilities. Her meta-analyses have been important in demonstrating that the magnitude of these differences is small. These small differences mean that a factor, such as gender, that accounts for 1% of the variance in an ability leaves 99% of the difference in that ability varying according to other factors. Figure 5.5 shows two distributions of scores that have a 99% overlap and a 1% difference. This figure reveals how similar the two distributions are. If 1% of the variance in verbal ability is due to gender, we would not know much about any specific person's verbal ability by knowing that person's gender, because too much variation in verbal ability would be due to other factors.

Assumptions about the person's verbal ability would be unfounded if based on the knowledge that the person was a woman, because many men have verbal abilities that equal or exceed most women's verbal abilities. Stereotypes based on gender differences in these cognitive abilities will lead to incorrect conclusions about the abilities of men and women, because women and men vary more from one person to another than from one gender to another. With only a small percentage of the variance attributable to gender, individual differences overwhelm the gender difference.

Hyde (1981) also contended that the term *well-established* should be distinguished from *large*. She suggested that people tend to consider the two terms similarly, but in this case they are not the same. When researchers conclude that a difference is well-established, that conclusion does not mean that the difference is also large, merely that it is not due to chance factors. Hyde criticized the inclusion in many psychology text-

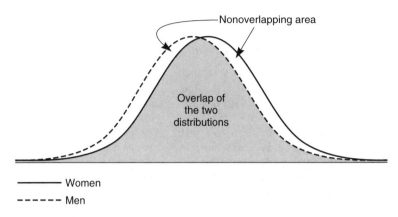

FIGURE 5.5 An Example of Two Distributions with 99% Overlap

NOTE: This distribution represents differences similar to those for verbal ability in men and women.

books of information about women's advantage in verbal abilities and men's advantages in quantitative and spatial abilities. Although her analysis confirmed that gender differences in verbal, quantitative, and spatial abilities might be well-established, such differences were by no means large. Describing the differences as well-established in texts tends to imply that the magnitude is large, and this incorrect implication can mislead students about their own abilities as well as the abilities of others.

Hyde did not argue that these differences should be ignored, and she acknowledged that small differences in average ability can produce larger differences in curricula or occupations that require high levels of some specific ability. For example, if engineering requires a very high level of the spatial abilities in which men excel, such as spatial visualization or mental rotation, then fewer women than men might be qualified to be engineers. Hyde's analysis indicated that a job such as engineering that requires a very high level of spatial skills might result in twice as many male as female engineers. However, the gender gap in engineering has been much larger than the difference in these abilities would predict. Until the 1970s, about 1% of students receiving engineering degrees were women, and that percentage rose to around 10% in the 1980s (Vetter, 1992). Hyde's analysis indicated that this huge discrepancy is due to factors other than cognitive ability.

The size of the difference in gender-related cognitive ability is sufficiently small to have limited implications for men's and women's lives, yet people's beliefs allow these small differences to have a large impact. In accepting that cognitive abilities vary by gender, cognitive abilities become gender stereotyped. For example, when parents, teachers, and children come to accept that boys are better at math than girls, this acceptance of a gender-related difference leads to differential expectations for math achievement. These expectations influence the level of encouragement that teachers and parents give children, thus affecting how girls and boys feel about their own abilities. These feelings affect the choices that girls and boys make concerning their elective math courses, and these choices have lifelong consequences for careers as well as attitudes toward the subject. Although the gender-related differences in cognitive abilities are small, society's acceptance of these differences creates additional divergence.

In summary, meta-analysis has shown that the magnitude of gender differences is small for verbal, quantitative, and spatial abilities. Gender differences in these three areas account for between 1% and 5% of the differences in these abilities, too small a difference to explain or predict most variation from person to person. The gender stereotyping of cognitive domains has magnified small differences, thus perpetuating the belief that gender-related differences exist and make a large difference in the abilities of women and men.

Source of the Differences

The previous chapter mentioned the controversy over the source of cognitive gender differences: Some researchers believe that these differences have biological origins, whereas others hold that social factors account for any differences. These two views are in opposition. Halpern's (1992) examination of the evidence for each resulted in clear support for neither, with evidence supporting and contradicting each view.

Anne Fausto-Sterling (1985) contended that biologically based theories of gender differences are very popular, as though people want to be persuaded that any observed gender difference is due to biological factors. Before any conclusion can be made that gender differences in mental abilities are based on structural differences in the brain, those who propose biological determinism of behavior must present several types of evidence: (1) the existence of structural differences in the brains of men and women, (2) the existence of gender differences in mental abilities, and (3) a link between the two. Is the evidence for sexually dimorphic brains and gender differences in behavior sufficiently strong to attempt to link the two?

On the contrary, the evidence is weak for such a link. Researchers have found evidence for sexually dimorphic structures in the brain, but the strongest evidence of difference concerns the sexually dimorphic nucleus, a structure that no research to date has connected to mental abilities. Evidence for sexual dimorphism of the cerebral hemispheres, the corpus callosum, and other structures is less clear. For all of these brain structures, some research has indicated differences, but other researchers have disputed or failed to replicate these findings. What research has concluded is that none of the differences in these structures between women and men are large.

On first consideration, the evidence about brain lateralization might seem to fit nicely with the differences in mental abilities: The left hemisphere is specialized for verbal skills, and the right hemisphere is more expert in spatial abilities. In addition, many (but not all) researchers have contended that gender differences exist in lateralization. Women are less lateralized than men; that is, women have verbal and spatial abilities spread more evenly throughout the brain, whereas men have their verbal abilities in the left hemisphere and spatial abilities in the right hemisphere. However, on further examination, no coherent explanation covers all the evidence about brain lateralization and gender differences. The argument that lateralization is an advantage for mental abilities is not supported by the evidence: Men have an advantage in some spatial abilities but are at some disadvantage in other spatial abilities and in some verbal tasks. If strong lateralization were an advantage, then it should be an advantage for both types of abilities (Springer & Deutsch, 1989). Likewise, if less lateralization is an advantage, it should extend to spatial as well as verbal abilities. Thus, the evidence shows that differences in brain organization at the level of the cerebral hemispheres do not coincide with gender differences in mental abilities.

Neither does the characterization of the right hemisphere as "feminine" and the left hemisphere as "masculine" fit with the evidence about the function of the two hemispheres. If any gender distinction must be applied to the hemispheres, "feminine" would seem to apply to the left hemisphere, with its specialization that leads to advantages in several of the verbal skills, at which women tend to have a small advantage. Likewise, "masculine" would seem to apply to the right hemisphere, with its specialization for spatial abilities, at which men tend to have some advantages. Instead, the descriptions have been the opposite, with the right hemisphere labeled feminine and the left masculine. Only in gender-stereotypical descriptions would "feminine" be associated with the other descriptions applied to the right hemisphere—"metaphorical," "intuitive," "concrete," "impulsive," "subjective," and "holistic." The descriptions associated with the left hemisphere are equally gender stereotypical—"rational," "intellectual," "abstract," "realistic," "objective," and "analytical." Obviously, the extension of gender to the hemispheres is not warranted. This characterization arose as part of what Sally Springer and Georg Deutsch called "dichotomania," the tendency to see all contrasts in the world reflected in the two cerebral hemispheres. Thus, for every pair of oppositional adjectives, the attempt has been made to fit these opposites to the left and right cerebral hemispheres. This tendency has resulted in a great deal of overinterpretation, and the masculine-feminine contrast is such an error.

The hypothesis that sex hormones affect brain function and thus mental abilities is a more viable possibility. As Chapter 3 explained, prenatal hormones influence brain development, producing permanent changes in the brain's organization. These organizational differences might continue to exert effects throughout people's lives, resulting in differences in mental abilities. Kimura (1989, p. 66) stated that "it seems reasonable that, whatever hormonal mechanism originally establishes these individual variations, it may simply continue to be sensitive to changes in the critical hormones throughout life." However, she admitted that these findings explain more about how patterns of cognitive abilities might be formed than about how men and women think, because the performance differences attributable to hormonal effects are very small. "We need a great deal more information about the basic action of sex hormones before we can work out their specific contributions to cognitive patterns" (Kimura, 1989, p. 66). Therefore, the relationship between hormones and cognitive abilities remains an intriguing possibility, one that will require more information before it becomes an explanation for gender differences in cognitive abilities.

Findings on gender differences in mental abilities seemed strong at one time, but later research showed how small these differences are. In addition, some research suggests that cognitive gender differences have changed over the past 25 years. Alan Feingold (1988) examined performance on two tests of cognitive ability to determine changes in gender differences on these tests. He examined the performance of girls and boys on testings of the Differential Aptitude Tests (DAT) from 1947 to 1980 and the Preliminary Scholastic Aptitude Test (PSAT) and the Scholastic Aptitude Test from 1960 to 1983.

Feingold found that the gender differences that appeared on several subtests of these tests have changed over the years, with the gender differences declining significantly from 1947 to 1980 for the DAT and by 1980 disappearing completely on the PSAT verbal subtest. That is, Feingold found evidence that gender-related cognitive difference in verbal ability is disappearing. On the DAT subtests of mechanical reasoning and spatial visualization, Feingold found that boys showed higher performance but that these advantages were smaller in 1980 than in 1947. These gender-related cognitive differences also seem to be disappearing.

Proponents of biological determinism argue that biologically based differences tend not to change over short periods of time, to vary from culture to culture, or to disappear with training. Research on gender-related cognitive differences has shown that all of these things have occurred, indicating that the evidence fails to support a biological basis for gender-related cognitive differences. The research on different ethnic backgrounds has supported the contention that the male advantage on mathematical and spatial tasks may be more typical of European-American, middle-class U.S. students than of other social classes, countries, or age groups, and thus this pattern of abilities represents socially structured more than biologically determined differences.

Eccles (1987) proposed an explanation of gender differences in math achievement, and an extension of this model might also explain other gender differences in cognitive performance. Eccles's model attempts to explain gender differences in achievement according to motivational rather than ability differences. Her model of achievement focused on choices and their link to expectancies for success and to the values an individual places on the available options. She attempted to anchor the choices an individual makes in the cultural setting, examining gender roles and different parental and social pressures on boys and girls when they decide to take a course or choose a college major. Therefore, Eccles's model emphasized the social factors that influence achievement rather than the biological factors that might influence cognitive abilities.

Eccles stressed the importance of choices for educational and vocational achievement and how women and men make different choices. She reviewed research that found that women and men have different expectancies for success as well as different evaluations of difficulty and of personal relevance regarding mathematics. Eccles argued that women's lower math achievement fits into this framework. Women choose to take fewer math courses because they believe that they may not succeed in the courses, that they will have to work hard to do well, and that math achievement is not as important for them. Eccles thus presented a theory and evidence that could explain why men and women differ in achievement.

Are gender differences in verbal, mathematics, and spatial performance caused by biological or social factors? Some theorists have argued for differences that are due to biological factors, and others have maintained that any difference is due to the different environments that females and males experience. That is, the differences that exist in cognitive abilities might be due to nature (biology) or nurture (environment). This dichotomy is false in this case (as it is in so many others), because separating biological from environmental influences is virtually impossible. As Halpern (1992) pointed out, not only do biological factors influence behavior, but behavior influences biology, forming a complex interaction of these factors. No resolution of the nature-nurture controversy is possible in the case of cognitive gender differences because it is impossible to disentangle these factors.

Concentrating on the source of gender differences in cognitive abilities obscures the more important consideration: Such differences are small and may have few practical consequences, whereas the choices that women and men make differ a great deal and have enormous practical consequences. Halpern (1989) questioned the approach of dwelling on the average differences and hoping for a decrease in gender differences. She advised that "our efforts are best spent encouraging all individuals to develop their cognitive talents and let group norms fall where they may" (p. 1157).

Summary

The assessment of mental abilities has a long history in psychology, dating from the development of the intelligence test. The Stanford-Binet, an early intelligence test, showed no gender differences, but the Wechsler tests revealed advantages on verbal tasks for women and girls and advantages in performance tasks for men and boys. In addition, mathematics ability tests have shown an advantage for boys and men starting at junior high school age and persisting into adulthood. These gender differences have become well accepted, and many studies have confirmed these differences in mental abilities, though all of these differences are small.

However, the verbal advantage that was once associated with women is not only small but disappearing. Differences in mathematical performance continue, but these differences are not clearly due to differences in innate ability and may be attributable to different experiences with math, especially the number of math courses completed.

Examining the gender differences in spatial ability is more complex than for either verbal or mathematical abilities because researchers have defined and measured spatial ability in many ways. Men show an advantage on spatial visualization and mental rotation tasks and an occasional advantage on spatial perception tasks, but women show advantages on tasks of perceptual speed and memory for placement of objects. Therefore, any conclusion about a male advantage in spatial ability is overly simplistic. Meta-analysis has shown that the size of cognitive gender differences is small, and analyses of verbal and mathematical tests have shown that the differences are decreasing in size.

Other cognitive abilities show no gender-related differences. These abilities include learning and memory, creativity, musical ability, and the ability to read nonverbal cues. Some studies have shown gender differences in these abilities, but these studies have fallen along gender-stereotypical lines: Women tend to have better memory for grocery lists, whereas men can better remember how to get to a particular place. The differential achievement for men and women in creative arts and music reflects variance in social support and access to these careers rather than differences in ability.

Although there is evidence for sexual dimorphism in the brain, any theory linking dimorphism with cognitive gender differences should be considered tentative. However, even without strong evidence, such theories exist. One biological theory for cognitive differences relies on gender differences in hemispheric lateralization to explain cognitive differences. This view is not consistent, hypothesizing that stronger lateralization produces an advantage on spatial tasks and a disadvantage on verbal tasks for men even though women, who are less lateralized, have an advantage in verbal tasks and a disadvantage on spatial tasks. The view that hormones influence brain development is well established, and hormonal influences may relate to brain function, producing small differences in performance of verbal and spatial tasks. Although the details of this theory remain to be completed, it seems likely that hormones may influence cognitive functioning.

Theories that emphasize the social aspects of gender-related cognitive differences hypothesize that ethnic and cultural variations should exist in cognitive performance, and research confirms this hypothesis.

Such variations should not occur if these abilities were biologically determined.

Although gender-related differences in cognitive ability may be relatively small, the choices that men and women make in taking courses, choosing college majors, and pursuing occupations differ enormously. Differences in occupational achievement are influenced by a large number of social and personal factors, producing gender and ethnic differences in achievement. Biological and social factors are intertwined and impossible to separate in understanding gender-related differences in cognitive abilities, making acceptance of either the nature theory or the nurture theory unwarranted. In any case, the differences are small, and individuals vary from one to another a great deal more than men differ from women.

Glossary

Mental rotation one of the subtypes of spatial abilities that includes the ability to visualize objects as they would appear if rotated in space

Spatial perception one of the subtypes of spatial abilities that includes the ability to identify and locate the horizontal or vertical in the presence of distracting information

Spatial visualization one of the subtypes of spatial abilities that refers to the ability to process spatial information so as to understand the relationship between objects in space, such as the ability to see a figure embedded in other figures, find hidden figures in a drawing or picture, or imagine the shape that folding will produce on a sheet of paper

Spatiotemporal ability one of the subtypes of spatial abilities that involves judgments about moving objects in space, such as making a judgment about when a moving object will arrive at target

Suggested Readings

Benderly, Beryl Lieff. (1987). *The myth of two minds.* New York: Doubleday. Chapter 9, "Different Intellects?" of this nontechnical book discusses evidence about the issue of differences in mental abilities in an entertaining, readable way.

Halpern, Diane. (1992). *Sex differences in cognitive abilities* (2nd ed.). Hillsdale, NJ: Erlbaum. Halpern reviews the extensive research and theory on cognitive differences. Her thorough examination of the literature includes the complications and contradictions in this work, which make it difficult to accept either a social or a biological basis for the gender-related differences.

Hyde, Janet Shibley; & Linn, Marcia C. (Eds.). (1986). *The psychology of gender: Advances through meta-analysis.* Baltimore: Johns Hopkins University Press. This edited book is a collection of articles about the statistical technique of meta-analysis and what those analyses have shown about gender. Hyde's introductory chapter is especially informative, but other chapters focus on various abilities.

Jacklin, Carol Nagy. (1989). Female and male: Issues of gender. *American Psychologist, 44,* 127–133. Jacklin critically reviews research on gender differences from a developmental perspective and includes sections on mental abilities and the brain and hormonal differences that might underlie these differences.

Chapter *6*

Gender Development I

The Psychoanalytic Approach

HEADLINE

Sex and Morality

—*Omni*, May 1985

> Do you think a man should steal an expensive drug to save his dying wife if he is too poor to pay for it?
>
> *Take a moment to ponder the problem. How you respond, says Harvard psychologist Carol Gilligan, may have a lot to do with your sex.*
>
> *Like other researchers interested in studying the moral development of human beings, Gilligan asked her subjects to respond to hypothetical moral dilemmas like the one above.... But unlike other researchers, including Harvard colleague Lawrence Kohlberg, who pioneered the field and formulated the above dilemma, Gilligan included women in her study.... Previous studies had either dismissed women as morally inferior beings or dropped them when their answers didn't fit the data obtained from males.*
>
> *What Gilligan found is that women differ from men in the way they approach moral decisions.... When faced with a moral conflict, men focus on a set of abstract principles, whereas women tend to weight the impact a decision would have on the people involved. (Johmann, 1985, p. 20)*

Carol Johmann's article, "Sex and Morality," like many about Carol Gilligan's research, discussed findings of differences in moral reasoning between men and women, emphasizing the advantages of women's style of moral reasoning. Although later research showed that neither women nor men use an exclusive, gender-specific way of moral reasoning, this emphasis on women (especially the suggestion that women's

113

moral judgments may have advantages) diverged from previous research and conceptualizations. Many theories of personality development have included different patterns of development for men and women, but the most influential of the traditional theories, Freud's psychoanalytic theory of personality, viewed the development of women's personalities as problematic. This theory postulated that the course of female personality development is likely to produce individuals whose moral judgment is inferior to men's.

Do the personalities of women and men differ? Do these differences produce a different set of moral values for men and women? If so, is one set of values superior, or do the two present valid variations of ways to make judgments?

The Traditional Approach to Personality

Ironically, psychology's traditional approach to personality theory has come from outside psychology—from Sigmund Freud, a Viennese neurologist who devised a theory of personality development and a method of treatment for psychological problems. Freud developed his theory during the late 19th and early 20th centuries, a time when psychology did not include the study of personality. Only later did theories of personality development and functioning become part of psychology.

Differences between the personality development and functioning of men and women were an essential part of Freud's theory, and those differences became a point of contention that led other theorists, including Karen Horney, to propose alternatives. The traditional approach to personality has emphasized not only gender differences but also sex and sexuality, hypothesizing that sex is a basic factor in personality. Therefore, issues of gender and sex have always been factors in traditional personality theories.

Freud's Theory of Personality

Although Freud's theory of personality has been the most influential of the traditional approaches, its popularity and acceptance in psychology have varied over the years. During the early years of Freud's theorizing, in the late 1800s and early 1900s, academic psychology did not include theories of personality or treatment for people with mental problems, the subject matter of Freud's theory and the recipients of his treatment. Freud's background was in neurology, not psychology, an area that was not well accepted either as part of medicine or of psychology (Schultz & Schultz, 1992).

As Freud's work gained prominence, his treatment became the accepted approach for dealing with people with mental problems. Also, the field of psychology underwent changes: Theories of personality came to occupy a central role, as did practical applications, such as treatment for mental problems. The Freudian approach became associated with psychology, and many psychologists were strongly influenced by Freudian theory during the 1930s, 1940s, and 1950s.

As psychologists evolved other theories of personality and other psychotherapies, Freud's theory dwindled in popularity among psychologists. The decades of interest in and association with Freud's work, however, have led to the popular belief that psychology is Freudian, when actually Freudian concepts are of greater interest in other fields, such as psychiatry and sociology, than in psychology. As Julia Sherman observed in 1971, "While Freud's theory is passé in some circles, psychoanalytic theory continues to be influential and important in the helping professions and in the thinking of the literate public" (p. 43). During the 1980s, Freud's theory once again became a topic of academic interest and, as always, the subject of continuing controversy.

Basic Concepts in Freud's Theory

Freud's theory hypothesizes the existence of the **unconscious,** a region of the mind that functions beyond conscious personal awareness. Freud was not the first to consider the existence of something like the unconscious (Ellenberger, 1970), but he was the first to place a great deal of emphasis on the influence of this region of the mind. He described the basic energy for personality development and functioning with a word that is most often translated as "instinct" but might also be translated as "drive" or "impulse" (Feist, 1994). Freud hypothesized that the life, or sexual, instinct and the death, or aggressive, instinct furnish the dynamic energy for personality development and functioning; that is, these **instincts** are the forces that underlie thought and action.

Freud's medical background influenced his theory in that he considered these instinctive forces to be biologically determined. The role of biology was also of essential importance in personality development, which Freud described in terms of **psychosexual stages.** These stages occurred from birth and continued through adulthood in a sequence named according to the regions of the body that were most important for sexual gratification. The early stages were the most important for personality development, emphasizing the importance of early childhood for personality development.

By hypothesizing that the first psychosexual stage began at birth, Freud described infants as sexual beings and explained many of their actions as sexually oriented. Freud termed the first psychosexual stage the *oral stage,* during which babies receive sexual gratification from putting things into their mouth. Although this interpretation can be difficult to accept, his description of infants' behavior is easy to verify: Babies have a strong tendency to put things into their mouths.

During the *anal stage,* the child receives pleasure from excretory functions. The main frustrations at this stage come from toilet training, and problems in this psychosexual stage appear in adult behavior as concerns with neatness, stubbornness, and retaining possessions.

The *phallic stage* begins in children around 3 or 4 years of age and is the first of Freud's psychosexual stages that describes a different course of personality development for boys and girls (Freud, 1933/1964). During this stage, sexual pleasure shifts from the anal region to the genitals; children begin to focus on their genitals, and they gain pleasure from masturbation. Parents are often disturbed by their children's masturbation and try to discourage or prevent this activity, furnishing one source of frustration during this stage.

Freud believed that the focus on genital activity resulted in a sexual attraction to the parent of the other sex and an increasing desire to have sex with this parent. These dynamics occur on an unconscious level, outside of children's awareness, and set the stage for the **Oedipus complex.** Freud used the Greek tragedy as an analogy for the interactions that occur within families during the phallic stage. According to the story, the oracle prophesied that Oedipus would kill his father and marry his mother, and this prophecy came true. Freud hypothesized that all boys feel jealousy, hatred, and aggression directed toward their fathers and sexual longing for their mothers.

In boys, these family interactions result in competition with their fathers for their mothers' affections and growing hostility of the fathers toward their sons. Boys in the phallic stage concentrate on their genitals and prize their penis, and they also notice the anatomical differences between girls and boys, which leads them to realize that everyone does not have a penis (Freud, 1925/1989). The realization that girls do not have a penis is shocking, disturbing, and threatening because, boys reason, penises must be removable. Indeed, boys come to fear that their fathers will remove their penis because of the boys' hostility toward their fathers and affection for their mothers. Thus, boys experience the **castration complex,** the belief that castration will be their punishment. Boys believe that girls have suffered this punishment and are thus mutilated, inferior creatures.

These feelings of anxiety, hostility, and sexual longing are all intense and produce great turmoil for boys. All possibilities seem terrible—to lose their penis, to be the recipient of their fathers' hatred, to be denied sex with their mothers. To resolve these feelings, boys must end the competition with their fathers and deny their sexual wishes for their mothers. Both of these goals can be met through identification with their fathers. This identification accomplishes several goals. First, boys no longer feel castration anxiety, as they have given up the sexual competition that originated such feelings. Second, boys no longer feel hostility toward their fathers; they now strive to be like their fathers rather than competing with them. Third, boys no longer want their mothers sexually, but instead they receive some sexual gratification from the identification with their fathers, who have a sexual relationship with the mothers. By identifying with their fathers and becoming masculine, boys develop a sexual identity that includes sexual attraction to women. Therefore, identification with their fathers is the mechanism through which boys resolve the Oedipus complex and develop a masculine identity.

Freud hypothesized a slightly different resolution to the Oedipus complex in girls. During the phallic stage, girls too notice the anatomical differences between the sexes. Noticing that they do not have a penis, girls become envious of boys—that is, girls experience *penis envy* (Freud, 1925/1989). Freud hypothesized that penis envy is the female version of the castration complex and that girls experience feelings of inferiority concerning their genitals. They notice that their clitoris is so much smaller than a penis, and they perceive their vagina as the wound that results from their castration. Furthermore, girls hold their mothers responsible for their lack of a penis and develop feelings of hostility for their mothers. Fathers become the object of their affection, and girls wish to have sex with their fathers and to have a baby. Freud saw both the desire for sex and the wish for a baby as substitutes for a penis and as expressions of penis envy.

The feelings that accompany the male Oedipus complex—hostility and competition—are also present in the female version. Girls, however, cannot experience the castration complex in the same way that boys do, as girls have no penis to lose. Thus, girls do not experience the frustrations and difficulties of the phallic stage as strongly as boys. Girls must still surrender their sexual desires for their fathers and identify with their mothers, but the process is not as quick or as complete as for boys (Freud, 1933/1964).

After the resolution of the Oedipus complex, children enter the *latency stage,* during which little overt sexual activity occurs. This stage lasts until puberty, when physiological changes bring about a reawakening of sexuality and the *genital stage.* During the genital stage, individuals should desire a genital relationship with people of the other sex. The regions of the body that have furnished sexual pleasure during childhood are now secondary to genital pleasure obtained through intercourse.

Table 6.1 shows Freud's psychosexual stages and the types of gender-related differences that he hypothesized for these stages. Development is similar for girls and boys in several stages but differs drastically in the phallic stage. Freud also believed that women have a more difficult time achieving a mature sexual relationship than men. He described the sexuality of the phallic stage, with its emphasis on masturbation, as immature sexuality that should be replaced in the genital stage with mature, heterosexual intercourse. For men such activity involves their penis, but women must redirect their sexual impulses away from their clitoris toward their vagina.

Freud believed that girls have little awareness of their vagina until puberty and that the redirection of their sexual energy is another difficult hurdle for women. Freud saw masturbation as an immature form of sexuality for both men and women, but he also believed that women who failed to achieve pleasure from vaginal intercourse had not achieved the mature, genital type of sexuality that signaled adequate personality development.

TABLE 6.1   Freud's Psychosexual Stages and Gender-Related Differences in Each Stage

Stage	Gender-Related Differences
Oral	None
Anal	None
Phallic	Boys notice that they have a penis and that girls do not.
	Girls notice that boys have a penis and that girls do not.
	Oedipus complex
	Boys experience extreme trauma connected with the Oedipus complex, undergo stronger identification with their fathers, and develop stronger sense of morality.
	Girls experience less Oedipal trauma, undergo weaker identification with their mother, and develop a weaker sense of morality.
Latency	None
Genital	Women must transfer their sexual pleasure from their clitoris to vagina, making mature sexuality more difficult for them.
	Men's penis remains the center of their sexuality, making mature sexuality easier for them.

Moral Development

Until the resolution of the Oedipus complex, Freud saw children as ruled by seeking pleasure and gratification—as controlled by a component of personality he called the **id.** This component is part of the unconscious and is ruled by the instincts, even to the point of irrationality. Through development of the **ego,** children learn to moderate their behavior and seek pleasure and gratification in ways that are not irrational or harmful. Nonetheless, Freud believed that the ego was practical, not moral, and that initially children, having only an id and ego, were without morals or conscience.

Freud hypothesized that children develop a conscience by developing a third structure, the **superego,** that incorporates the rules of society. The superego acts to control sexual and aggressive impulses. Freud believed that the superego develops during the resolution of the Oedipus complex. But he imagined that this process happened differently in boys and girls, with unequal results (Freud, 1933/1964).

Identifying with fathers prompts the development of the superego and thus of morality in boys. Through identification with fathers, boys develop a conscience, morals, and a way to incorporate the rules of society into their behavior. Freud believed that such development is essential to the maintenance of society and is dependent on the proper resolution of the Oedipus complex. As the male Oedipus complex is resolved more completely and more swiftly than the female Oedipus complex, boys and men have stronger superegos than girls and women. The difficulty of resolving the female Oedipus complex results in weaker superegos and thus weaker morals in girls and women. Therefore, Freud contended that women are morally inferior to men, lacking a mature sense of justice and incapable of reaching full psychological maturity:

> *The fact that women must be regarded as having little sense of justice is no doubt related to the predominance of envy in their mental life; for the demand for justice is a modification of envy and lays down the condition subject to which one can put envy aside.... There are no paths open to further*

GENDERED VOICES
Big Guns

"I just joined a gun club," a man told me, "and the men in the club do appear to have a relationship with their guns that seems symbolic to me. Of course, guys who own guns are pretty macho, but I have noticed two distinct styles, one of which seems more Freudian than the other.

"One style concentrates on shooting, and those men seem to like weapons that allow accuracy. Those types of guns tend to be rifles and are pretty lightweight. Maybe that's symbolic, but the other style concentrates on the size of the weapon. With some of these guns, it's just not possible to shoot accurately, but they are big guns with lots of firepower. That's all that some of these guys go for, that's all they talk about—how many guns they have and how big they are. They don't really want to shoot targets, but they want to shoot, and they seem to love their big guns. It's pretty embarrassing, in a symbolic sense."

development; it is as though the whole process had already run its course and remains thenceforward insusceptible to influence—as though, indeed, the difficult development to femininity had exhausted the possibilities of the person concerned. (Freud, 1933/1964, pp. 134–135)

Freud and Women

Freud knew that his theory was uncomplimentary to women, because his female associates, such as Karen Horney, told him so (Gay, 1988). He gave the matter a great deal of thought and heard many criticisms but never changed his mind about women being essentially failed men. Although Freud may have thought women were inferior in some ways, intelligence was not among them. Freud considered that an intelligent, independent women deserved credit and praise and might be "virtually as good as a man" (Gay, 1988, p. 507).

As Jess Feist (1994) pointed out, Freud seemed to have held contradictory attitudes about women. On the one hand, Freud was a proper Victorian gentleman who wanted women to be sweet, pleasant, and subservient. On the other hand, he admired women who were intelligent and "masculine" in their pursuit of scientific careers. Freud acted on both beliefs. His wife, Martha, held the role of wife and mother and shared none of his professional life. And he disparaged the efforts of feminists who argued for the equality of men and women, holding that the sexes could never be equal. But Freud also admitted women into the ranks of psychoanalytic training at a time when women were admitted to few professions (Tavris & Wade, 1984), providing himself with female colleagues whom he respected and valued. And the person who carried on his work was his daughter, Anna, whom he encouraged to become an analyst. However, his most intimate personal friends were all men.

Therefore, Freud's attitudes about women and their personalities showed some inconsistency. Freud undoubtedly held negative attitudes about women, and he expressed his lack of understanding and lack of certainty about women in several of his papers. One of Freud's last statements about women was his 1933 paper, "Femininity," which he concluded with a tentative statement about women, acknowledging his awareness of the criticisms and also his own far-from-complete understanding:

That is all I had to say to you about femininity. It is certainly incomplete and fragmentary and does not always sound friendly. But do not forget that I have only been describing women in so far as their nature is determined by their sexual function. It is true that influence extends very far; but we do not overlook the fact that an individual woman may be a human being in other respects as well. If you want to know more about femininity, inquire from your own experiences of life, or turn to the poets, or wait until science can give you deeper and more coherent information. (Freud, 1933/1964, p. 135)

Other researchers and theorists have attempted the last alternative rather than the first two and have sought other information about personality and gender. One of those theorists was Karen Horney, one of Freud's colleagues.

Horney's Theory of Personality

Like Freud, Horney was also a physician and psychoanalyst, but the two were a generation apart in age, and this difference contributed to their different views of the world and their different theories (Williams, 1983). Horney was one of the first German women to enter medical school, where she specialized in psychiatry. In 1910, Horney began psychoanalysis with one of Freud's close associates, and after her analysis was completed, she began to attend seminars on psychoanalysis (Feist, 1994). By 1917, Horney had written her first paper on psychoanalysis, which reflected the orthodox Freudian view. Her orthodoxy did not last, however, and Horney became a vocal critic of Freud's theory of personality, especially concerning gender differences in personality development. Horney reexamined Freud's concepts of penis envy, inferiority feelings in women, and the masculinity complex. In addition, Horney's interpretation of feminine masochism differed from the Freudian version.

Between 1922 and 1935, Horney wrote a series of papers in which she reexamined some of the concepts of Freud's theory and argued for a course of female personality development much different from the one Freud hypothesized (Quinn, 1987). Horney began to write about the masculine bias in psychoanalysis, and she reinterpreted psychoanalytic theory, "turning the usual arguments upside down" (Quinn, 1987, p. 223). However, Horney stayed within the framework of psychoanalysis, with her acceptance of the unconscious as a motivating force in personality, her emphasis on sexual feelings and events in personality development, and her belief in the importance of early childhood experiences for personality formation. She differed from Freud in her interpretation of the significance of the events of early childhood and her growing belief in the importance of social rather than instinctual, biological forces in personality development.

Part of Horney's reinterpretation of psychoanalysis was an alternative view of the notion of penis envy, the feelings of envy that girls have when they discover that boys' penis is larger than their own clitoris. Horney argued that penis envy was a longing for the social prestige and position that men experience, rather than a literal physical desire for a penis. Indeed, she hypothesized that men envy women's capability to reproduce and proposed the concept of *womb envy*. She interpreted the male strivings for achievement as overcompensation for their lack of ability to create by giving birth.

Freud argued that for women, penis envy is such a strong and threatening feeling that it must be rejected by the conscious mind and pushed into the unconscious. Horney suggested that for men, envy of women's breasts and reproductive abilities is equally strong and must also be repressed into the unconscious. Thus, both women and men have unconscious envy and fear concerning each other, and these unconscious feelings can be manifested in attempts to portray the other as inferior. Horney believed that men fear and attribute evil to women because men feel inadequate when comparing themselves to women. To feel more adequate, men must see women as inferior.

Horney postulated that men's assertion of women's inferiority exists to keep men from contending with their own feelings of inferiority. Horney explained that men still retain the feelings of inferiority that originated with the perception of the small size of their penis during childhood, when they initially noticed it. Therefore, men go through life needing to prove their masculinity, and they do so by having sexual intercourse. Any failure in erection will be perceived as a lack of masculinity, making men constantly vulnerable to feelings of inferiority. Women have no similar problem and do not suffer feelings of inferiority for reasons related to sexual performance. Horney (1932/ 1967, p. 145) summarized this conflict, writing:

> *Now one of the exigencies of the biological differences between the sexes is this: that the man is actually obliged to go on proving his manhood to the woman. There is no analogous necessity for her. Even if she is frigid, she can engage in sexual intercourse and conceive and bear a child. She performs her part by merely being, without any doing—a fact that has always filled men with admiration and resentment.*

This resentment can lead men to attempt to diminish women, and these attempts can succeed, leaving women with feelings of inferiority. Therefore, female inferiority originates with male insecurities rather than, as Freud hypothesized, with the female perceptions of inferior genitals. These female feelings of inferiority are perpetuated by men's behavior toward women and by the masculine bias in society.

Horney agreed with Freud's concept of a *masculinity complex,* a manifestation of the wish to be male by behavior that is achieving, active, and independent (Horney, 1926/1967). Horney saw such behavior as a retreat from femininity through an identification with the father and through behaviors that are masculine. Horney believed that the masculinity complex is a result of girls' avoidance of the realization of their sexual wishes for their fathers. Girls identify with their fathers due to their unacceptable sexual attraction to their fathers. Identification is a more acceptable way to resolve the attraction than is incest. On a more practical level, Horney also considered the social reasons for women's choosing behavior that is masculine—men have social and professional advantages. Therefore, Horney accepted the concept but reinterpreted the reasons for the masculinity complex in women.

Horney also revised the psychoanalytic concept of **masochism**—feelings of sexual gratification from the experience of pain or humiliation. Freudian theory hypothesizes that masochism is an inevitable, biologically determined factor in the personality development of women. Thus women are *normally* masochistic, accepting and receiving pleasure from the pain of menstruation, first intercourse, and childbirth, and this masochism tends to spread to other nonsexual areas of their lives. Masochistic men, those who show enjoyment from pain or humiliation, are exhibiting "feminine" characteristics.

Horney did not question the existence of masochism, but she did question its biological origin and its inevitability in women (Quinn, 1987). Her critique of the Freudian position included the method of data collection and observation. These analysts had concluded that the masochism they observed in their patients was present in all women in all cultures, clearly a generalization far beyond their data. Horney called for a cross-cultural examination of women and men to determine the pervasiveness of masochism,

TABLE 6.2   Points of Agreement and Disagreement in Horney's and Freud's Psychoanalytic Theories

Concept	Horney's Theory	Freud's Theory
Existence of unconscious	Yes	Yes
Importance of early childhood experiences	Yes	Yes
Gender differences in personality	Yes	Yes
Source of differences	Social	Biological
Feelings of envy for other gender	Men envy women's ability to give birth.	Women envy men's penis.
Feelings of inferiority	Constant need to perform sexually leads men to feel inferior.	Lacking a penis leads women to feel inferior.
Masculinity complex	Driven by girls' lack of acceptance of femininity and identification with their father	Driven by girls' feelings of inferiority
Masochism	Socially determined part of development that is abnormal for women as well as men	Biologically determined, inevitable part of feminine development; abnormal in men

and she described the cultural and social factors that would contribute to masochism in a society. By specifying such factors, Horney argued for the social rather than the biological determination of masochism.

Horney thus argued against several Freudian concepts that posit a different course of personality development for women and men. She disputed the biological basis of penis envy, hypothesizing that women's envy was for men's power and social position. She also argued against the view that women see themselves as inferior because of their genitals, pointing out that men also envy women's ability to give birth and that men have feelings of inferiority about their genitals. Horney again relied on social and cultural factors to explain why women might exhibit the active, achieving behavior associated with masculinity and why both men and women might exhibit masochism.

Table 6.2 shows the points of agreement and disagreement between Freud's and Horney's psychoanalytic theories. As this table shows, both theories are psychoanalytic, in that they accept the importance of unconscious forces and early childhood experiences. However, the difference in their interpretation of the importance and source of other events makes the two theories unique.

Feminine psychology was of lesser interest to Horney later in her career, but the issues that she raised and her theoretical and therapeutic endeavors contributed to her development of a general theory of personality that retained the emphasis on dynamic, unconscious forces in personality and the importance of early childhood experiences. Unlike Freud, she emphasized social and cultural forces rather than biological factors in shaping and maintaining personality. Her theory applied equally to men and women, but she also saw that society and culture treat women and men differently.

Women, Men, and Psychoanalytic Theory

Freud's theory of personality appeared during the late 19th and early 20th centuries in a Victorian culture that viewed women as passive, dependent, and intellectually inferior to men. This view of women was easy for Freud to accept, not only because it was the view of his culture but also because his female patients reflected these characteristics. Freud built his theory on the basis of observing his patients, many of whom were upper-class, bored, unhappy, mentally unhealthy women who lived in a society that held women to be inferior. The extent to which their experience reflects that of women in general is questionable, but these women and the culture in which they lived influenced Freud's view of women.

During the time that Freud built his theory, a feminist movement was active in Europe and the United States. Many of these feminists, both women and men, objected to Freud's theory as insulting to women, with its proposal that women experience penis envy, feelings of inferiority, and inadequate superego development. Freud (1933/1964) prefaced his remarks about personality development in women as tentative and speculative, but he ridiculed the feminists of his time who argued for equality between men and women. Thus, Freud's theory was never popular among feminists, those women and men who believed in and worked for fair treatment for women, both by society and in personal relationships.

Among Freud's colleagues, opinions differed on the question of gender differences in personality development (as well as on many other issues). Some psychoanalysts, such as Horney, disagreed with Freud on the issue of gender differences in the personality development of girls and boys. Other psychoanalysts, such as Helene Deutsch, agreed with Freud's view of the difficulties and generally poorer outcome of personality development in women. Those analysts who disagreed strongly with Freud's position tended to break with him and work on alternatives to his theory. The result of these breaks was an inner circle of analysts whose beliefs were similar to Freud's views. After Freud's death in 1939, the orthodox position solidified, and changes were, for most purposes, impossible on the issues of personality related to gender differences. Thus, psychoanalytic theory gained and lost popularity but failed to change in any substantial way throughout the 1940s, 1950s, and 1960s.

During the 1970s and 1980s, heated controversy erupted within psychoanalytic circles. These controversies involved an event in the history of psychoanalysis—Freud's abandonment of the seduction theory—and the appearance of an alternative psychoanalytic theory of personality development—feminist psychoanalytic theory. Freud rejected the seduction theory early in the history of psychoanalysis, and this revision had important implications for the credibility of psychiatric patients and for society's beliefs about early childhood sexuality. Feminist psychoanalytic theories provide modern alternatives to orthodox Freudian psychoanalytic theory, complete with a reinterpretation of the processes and effects of early family dynamics. These two events in psychoanalytic theory help account for its ongoing popularity and influence.

Effects of Freud's Abandonment of the Seduction Theory

Much criticism of traditional Freudian theory has appeared, ranging from the inherent difficulty in testing any of the theory's hypotheses in a scientific way to its male-centered point of view. However, beginning in the 1970s, several psychoanalytically trained theorists have attacked Freud for his rejection of the **seduction theory,** the view that sexual activity between parent and child is the basis for psychological problems when the child grows to adulthood. These attacks differed from the previous criticisms in their intensity and in their personal nature; not only his theory but Freud personally was the object of these criticisms.

Although the seduction theory was part of Freud's early thinking about the source of psychological problems, he rejected this concept and postulated that attraction between children and their opposite-sex parent is part of the children's *fantasy,* having no basis in reality. The finished version of psychoanalytic theory did not include the seduction theory but rather hypothesized that children become attracted to their other-sex parent during the phallic stage. This attraction forms the basis for the Oedipus complex, the unconscious sexual attraction to the other-sex parent combined with feelings of rivalry and hostility for the same-sex parent. Children wish to be initiated into sexual activity with their other-sex parent, but this incest never occurs except in the children's fantasies. Indeed, Freud came to believe that societies must develop strong prohibitions against actual incest, making incestuous relationships rare.

Both Marie Balmary (1979/1982) and Jeffrey Masson (1984) have analyzed Freud's rejection of the seduction theory, and both have concluded that Freud probably made a mistake in doing so. Balmary took the approach of applying the psychoanalytic method to Freud's own life, whereas Masson examined unpublished letters in the Freud Archives. However, their concerns were similar, as were their conclusions.

Balmary concluded that Freud misinterpreted the Oedipus legend on which he based his entire metaphor for childhood sexuality and personality development, contending that Freud overlooked the actions of the father in the Oedipus legend and how those actions set the tragedy into motion. According to Balmary, Freud's inability to see the fault of the father in the Oedipus legend came from Freud's difficulty in dealing with his relationship with his own father; he could not consciously acknowledge that his father contributed to the psychological problems exhibited by his children, including Sigmund himself. The result of this failure to acknowledge his own father's faults produced a distortion of the entire direction of psychoanalysis, including the notion that childhood seduction is a fantasy. Balmary argued that Freud incorrectly emphasized the fantasy aspect of children's seduction by a parent.

Masson held the position of projects director of the Freud Archives, which allowed him access to unpublished documents. In examining letters written by Freud, Masson came to believe that the official version of Freud's rejection of the seduction theory differed from what had really happened. Freud did not quickly and easily reject the notion of childhood seduction. Instead, it was the notion of parental seduction that he relinquished slowly and reluctantly. Masson concluded that Freud rejected the seduction theory because his colleagues found the notion so unacceptable. Freud believed that he would never find acceptance for his theories if he maintained that many children were molested by their parents and that these incestuous relationships produced permanent psychological damage in the children.

Masson argued that Freud had been aware of the rape and murder of children by parents, especially on the part of fathers, from the time of his early interest in "nervous disorders." This knowledge led Freud to believe his patients' stories about childhood seductions. Masson interpreted Freud's rejection of the seduction theory as an act of cowardice; Freud was not willing to endure the poor opinion of his colleagues, so he chose to disbelieve his patients and began interpreting their stories of childhood seduction as fantasy rather than reality.

Both Balmary and Masson have argued that psychoanalysis might have been more useful and closer to the truth if Freud had kept his original notion that adult emotional problems can occur as a result of childhood seduction by a parent. By rejecting the notion of parental seduction, Freud portrayed his patients in several negative ways. First, patients cannot distinguish fantasy from reality. Although they believe the stories of their childhood seduction, these seductions are fantasy rather than reality, and therefore the stories are not credible. By his rejection of the seduction theory, Freud cast doubt on information furnished by patients, especially information about incest, thus diminishing their credibility.

Second, by asserting that childhood seduction was a fantasy, Freud suggested that children are the ones who wish this seduction. Children want to commit incest with their parents and during the phallic stage may behave seductively toward the other-sex parent. Therefore, if any incest occurs, children are at fault and not parents.

Balmary and Masson contended that Freud's influence has been great but that some of that influence has been negative. Freud created a pattern of thinking about people with psychological problems by attacking the credibility of patients and by blaming children for any sexual activity in which they had been involved. As the majority of Freud's patients were women, his rejection of the truth of their stories led to the general belief that women have fantasies about sexual abuse during childhood or rape during adulthood but that these fantasies are not based on reality and should not be believed. According to this view, any story that a child tells about incest is probably not true, but if evidence exists, then the incest was initiated by the child.

Those critics who accused Freud of incorrectly abandoning the seduction theory blame Freud for some contemporary problems. Freudian theory has so influenced our society that its claims about the fantasy nature of childhood sexuality and the prevalence of fantasies of rape are not only popularly accepted but incorporated into our legal systems. This lack of credibility of children and women who claim to have been sexually abused poses a problem for successful legal action against those who commit rape or childhood sexual abuse. If Freud had not changed his mind about the seduction theory, society might have different views about these problems.

Contemporary Psychoanalytic Theories of Personality Development

Horney worked toward reinterpreting psychoanalytic theory into a more positive view of women's personality while retaining the psychoanalytic emphasis on the unconscious and early childhood sexuality. Although her desire to remain within the psychoanalytic framework was strong enough to prevent Horney from formulating a radically different theory of personality development, other theorists have rejected not only Freud's view of women but also his basic framework for describing personality. However, the urge to retain the basic tenets of psychoanalytic theory has led some theorists to either remove the objectionable elements of Freud's theory or to create revisions of his theory that emphasize women and their personality.

Psychoanalyst Shahla Chehrazi represents one group of thinkers within the psychoanalytic movement that promotes a psychoanalytic position believed to be compatible with feminism. Chehrazi (1986) argued that research findings about female personality development can be integrated into the psychoanalytic framework but that Freud's followers have been unwilling to change from the traditional psychoanalytic position, and have taken Freud's remarks, no matter how tentative, as undisputed fact. She described psychoanalysis as lagging behind research due to the unwillingness of the traditional Freudians to deviate from Freud's words.

Although she acknowledged that some of Freud's hypotheses have been disconfirmed by research, Chehrazi saw few problems with the integration of modern research into traditional psychoanalytic theory. She described a system in which the Oedipus complex is of primary importance for personality formation and in which psychoanalysis is still the treatment of choice for both women and men. The resulting view is an update, with only minor modifications, of psychoanalytic theory.

Other theorists have departed from the Freudian tradition in more radical ways. Sociologist Nancy Chodorow (1978, 1979) and psychologist Ellyn Kaschak (1992) have formulated psychoanalytic theories that are significant departures from Freud's view. Chodorow's theory proposes a progression of development that gives women advantages, and Kaschak's theory replaces the emphasis on male psychological development with a woman-centered view of personality. Both of these theories are examples of feminist psychoanalytic theory.

Chodorow's Emphasis on Mothering.   Like Freud, Chodorow (1979) expressed pessimism about any potential equality between men and women. Unlike Freud (who concentrated on the perception of anatomical differences), Chodorow's reasons for believing in the continuation of inequality focused on the early experiences of children in relation to their mother. Chodorow described a psychoanalytic theory of development that concentrates on the **pre-Oedipal period** during early childhood, before the Oedipus complex, and centers on the process of being mothered by a woman.

Although Chodorow (1978) acknowledged that women are not uniquely capable of caring for infants, she also granted that most nurturing is done by mothers (or other women) and not by fathers (or other men). Chodorow explained how this early relationship between mothers and infants makes a permanent imprint on personality development—an imprint that differs for boys and girls.

Chodorow (1978) described early infant development in terms similar to traditional psychoanalytic theory. Babies have no sense of self versus other people or the world; infants are one with the world, and most of their world is their mother. The early mother-daughter relationship is closer than the mother-son relationship, because mothers and daughters are of the same sex. Infants have no initial perception of their gender, but mothers always know about the gender of their infants and treat girls differently than they treat boys.

Chodorow (1978) hypothesized that when children start to develop a sense of self and to separate from their mother, events differ for girls and boys. Girls have an easier task in developing a sense of self because they have already identified with a female mother. This identification gives them an advantage in developing a separate identity, as this identity will likely be feminine and much like their mother's. Boys, on the other hand, have a more difficult time in developing a separate identity, as they have already identified with a female mother. To become masculine, boys must reject the femininity of their mothers and develop an identity that is different as well as separate. Thus, boys have a more difficult task than girls in accomplishing these developmental goals of separation and identity.

But according to Chodorow, girls never become as separate from their mothers as boys do. The gender similarity is something that both mothers and daughters know, and this similarity between the two influences each. Boys must work to accomplish their separation, even with the aid of their mother. This effort extracts a price. Chodorow (1978) described the aftermath of boys' separation in terms of their rejection of all femininity and the development of fear and mistrust of the feminine. Chodorow thus explained the almost worldwide denigration of women by men as a by-product of boys' efforts to distinguish and separate themselves from their mother. On the other hand, girls have no such need, and they accept their mothers and the feminine role without the turbulence that boys experience. Girls grow into women and reproduce their early relationship with their mother in their own mothering.

Figure 6.1 shows the differences between traditional psychoanalytic theory and Chodorow's feminist psychoanalytic theory. Notice that the differences lie not only in the outcomes but also in the stage of development that each theory hypothesizes to be important in personality development and in gender-related differences.

	Stages	Gender-Related Outcome
Chodorow's Theory	Pre-Oedipal stages	Boys work toward separation from mother, rejecting femininity. Girls retain connectedness with mother, becoming feminine.
	Oedipus conflict	Gender differences have already emerged.
Freud's Theory	Pre-Oedipal stages	No gender-related differences emerge.
	Oedipus conflict	Family dynamics and perception of differences in genitals prompt personality differences.

FIGURE 6.1   Differences between Chodorow's Feminist Psychoanalytic Theory and Traditional Freudian Theory

Thus, Chodorow's psychoanalytic theory is an alternative to Freud's theory, and the two theories differ in several ways. Although retaining the emphasis on early childhood, Chodorow concentrated on the pre-Oedipal period and on the early infant-mother relationship. She hypothesized a different course of personality development for boys and girls, with girls having an easier time than boys of accomplishing the goal of separation from their mothers. In their incomplete separation from their mother, girls develop a feminine identity and the ability to mother. In the more complete separation from their mother, boys reject femininity to develop masculinity. The difficulty of this separation leads them to reject and denigrate the feminine. In this way Chodorow explained the personality development of women and men, plus men's common tendency to believe that women are inferior.

Kaschak's Antigone Phase.   Kaschak (1992) revised psychoanalytic theory by making an analogy in personality development to Antigone, who like Oedipus is a character from the plays of Sophocles. Kaschak argued that the Oedipus legend was useful in Freud's theory of male personality development but that the minor changes Freud made to accommodate women in his female Oedipus complex were inadequate. Instead, Kaschak casts female personality development in terms of Antigone, Oedipus's daughter (and half sister).

In Sophocles' plays, Antigone was the daughter of Oedipus and Jocasta (who was Oedipus's mother). After Oedipus learned of his incest with Jocasta, he put out his eyes, and Antigone then became her blinded father's guide and caretaker. Antigone sacrificed an independent life to care for her blind father, and he considered it his right to have this devotion. Kaschak interpreted personality development of men and women in similar terms: "As Oedipus' dilemma became a symbol for the dilemma of the son, so might that of Antigone be considered representative of the inevitable fate of the good daughter in the patriarchal family" (p. 60).

Men grow and develop in societies that allow them power in those societies and in their families, and in taking this power, men come to consider women their possessions. "For a boy or a man in patriarchal culture, women are often not experienced as individuals separate from himself. First his mother, then his wife, and finally his daughters are experienced as extensions of himself and his own needs" (Kaschak, 1992, pp. 61–62). Women grow and develop in positions of subservience in which they are possessions of men, and women's lives and personalities reflect this status.

Kaschak hypothesized that many men and women never resolve these complexes because the social structure perpetuates differential power for women and men, encouraging both to adhere to these different roles. For men, an unresolved Oedipus complex results in them treating women as extensions of themselves rather than as independent people. With this sense of entitlement, men tend to seek power and sex in self-centered ways that may be destructive to others, such as incest and rape. For example, Kaschak explained father-daughter incest in terms of fathers' feelings of owning their daughters (and, to some extent, all women) and being able to do as they wish. She cited the disproportionate number of father-daughter incest compared to mother-son incest as evidence for this interpretation.

Kaschak considered the resolution of the Oedipus complex unlikely in a patriarchal society. Those men who do resolve these feelings relinquish their grandiosity and drive for power, see women as whole persons rather than possessions, and come to see themselves as individuals with boundaries and limits rather than as kings.

When women fail to resolve the Antigone phase, they allow themselves to be extensions of others rather than striving for independence. "A daughter, in what can be considered the early Antigone phase, learns that men are central and that her function is to please them. She learns her own limits" (Kaschak, 1992, p. 76). Among those limits are restrictions on what women may do in the world and a limited sexuality, all defined and controlled by men. In addition, women learn to deny their physicality, trying to make their bodies invisible, and this denial can be expressed in terms of eating disorders. These limits can lead to feelings self-hatred and shame and the need to form relationships with others to feel self-worth.

Women who successfully resolve the Antigone phase separate from their fathers and other men to become independent people. This independence allows them to form relationships with women, which Kaschak believes to be a problem for women who have not resolved the Antigone phase. In their relationships with men, women who have resolved these issues are able to stop making men central to their lives and form interdependent, flexible relationships. Figure 6.2 shows the four possibilities in Kaschak's view of personality development—men and women who have and have not resolved major developmental issues.

Is feminist psychoanalytic theory an improvement over traditional psychoanalytic theory? Any theory that relies heavily on unconscious mental processes will rely on events that are not directly observable, which is a problem for scientific testability. All

	Not Resolved	Resolved
Men (Oedipal phase)	Patriarchical	Nonpatriarchical
	Gaining power a major goal	Gaining power not a major issue
	See women as extensions of self— they have the right to have women serve them	See women as independent
	Sexually self-centered	Sexually unselfish
Women (Antigone phase)	Accept subservience	Reject subservient role
	Passive and dependent	Assertive and independent
	Accept male-defined sexuality	Define their own sexuality
	Deny their own needs, including physical needs	Accept and express their own needs
	Cannot form friendships with other women	Form friendships with other women

FIGURE 6.2   Possible Outcomes of Personality Development According to Kaschak

versions of psychoanalytic theory have this shortcoming. Proponents of these psycho-analytic theories tend to accept the evidence of patients and their own interpretations of what patients say, evidence that some researchers would not accept as objective. Therefore, any psychoanalytic theory shares the problem of providing adequately objective, observable evidence in its research.

Unfortunately, feminist psychoanalytic theory shares all of the drawbacks of traditional psychoanalytic theory. The feminist revisions offer a more favorable view of women, but these advantages occur at the expense of their views about men. Chodorow's theory hypothesizes that women have an easier course of personality development than men, whereas Freud's theory holds the opposite view. Kaschak's theory views men as proprietary and demanding, as ignoring women except as extensions of themselves. Some women have found that these feminist theories validate their personal experiences and as such these theories are attractive. Understandably, fewer men than women consider these feminist theories relevant to them.

Therefore, both traditional and modern psychoanalytic theory emphasize the importance and inevitability of gender differences. Whereas Freud's psychoanalytic theory has a masculine bias, newer psychoanalytic theories, like the ones proposed by Chodorow and Kaschak, are part of a view of personality from a feminist standpoint, a view that emphasizes and values the unique qualities and special experiences of women.

Feminist Standpoint Theory: A Different Voice

Chodorow's (1978, 1979) and Kaschak's feminist psychoanalytic theories are only two of several theories that have concentrated on women. These theorists justify their interest in women as an attempt to remedy their past exclusion, as women have often not been included as participants in many studies. This exclusion has led to theories that explain men's personality development and behavior and assume that women's should be similar. Feminist theories have attempted to consider women and their unique experiences in an attempt to enlarge personality theory to include women. "Giving voice to women's perspective means identifying the ways in which women create meaning and experience life from their particular position in the social hierarchy" (Riger, 1992, p. 734).

In their attempts to include women, feminist standpoint theorists often exclude or denigrate men. Their reasoning is that men have been the center of existing theories and that women need special consideration or else their exclusion will continue. However, feminist standpoint theory is as exclusionary as traditional personality theory, the difference lying only in who is excluded. Although both approaches can make contributions to research and theory, neither the exclusion of men nor of women will lead to a theory of personality that captures gender development; studying gender requires the inclusion of both sexes. Although feminist standpoint theory will not lead to a complete investigation of gender, this approach might provide a different and valuable point of view.

Gilligan (1982, p. 1) found that, when she questioned women and men about moral judgments, she "began to hear a distinction in these voices, two ways of speaking about moral problems, two models of describing the relationship between other and self" and that these two voices belonged distinctively to men and women. Her observation led to the publication of her research in the book *In a Different Voice: Psychological Theory and Women's Development,* which detailed the characteristics of the different voice Gilligan heard from women.

Gilligan's Theory of Moral Development

Gilligan began her research because of an interest in moral development and a belief about how women's moral development had been neglected and slighted by psychology. Two important influences on her work were Chodorow's (1978) feminist psychoanalytic personality theory and Lawrence Kohlberg's (1981) cognitive developmental theory of moral development. Chodorow's theory explained how girls develop a personality that is influenced by similarities to their mother, thus promoting a feeling of interpersonal connection, whereas boys must work hard to separate themselves from their mothers, thereby promoting a feeling of personal separation. In Gilligan's theory, these two orientations form the psychological basis for a difference in moral reasoning.

Kohlberg's theory of moral development took a cognitive developmental rather than a psychoanalytic approach to moral development, explaining that children go through a series of stages in understanding and making moral decisions. These stages relate to cognitive capabilities, with younger children unable to make moral decisions based on abstract, rule-governed principles. Instead, young children make moral choices based first on their own needs and later on their relationships with others. Only as they cognitively mature do adolescents and adults make moral choices based on their knowledge of abstract principles of justice.

Much of Kohlberg's theory came from information from a longitudinal study, a project in which he repeatedly tested a group of boys from their years in late elementary school through young adulthood. These boys answered questions about moral dilemmas, hypothetical situations involving a moral problem like the one from Johmann's (1985) story that opened this chapter—"Do you think a man should steal an expensive drug to save his dying wife if he is too poor to pay for it?" On the basis of the responses, Kohlberg formulated a theory of moral development with three levels: preconventional, conventional, and postconventional. The preconventional level involves responses based on fear of getting caught, the conventional level involves a respect for the existence of rules and laws, and the postconventional level involves an acknowledgment that moral rules should be sufficiently flexible to put human life over any other values.

Kohlberg's stages of moral development came from research on boys and men, and their answers formed the basis for his theory. But does his theory apply to girls and women? Of course, the stages can be applied to the responses of girls or women and analyzed in the same terms as responses from boys and men. However, girls and women tend to score lower than boys and men, on the average. Kohlberg's cognitive developmental theory of moral development, like the psychoanalytic theories, seems to indicate a female moral inferiority.

Gilligan (1982) maintained that girls and women develop a different moral sense than boys and men. Whereas the male moral sense is based on abstract principles of justice, the female moral sense is based on the value of human relationships. Men are oriented toward "separateness," whereas women are oriented toward "connectedness." In Kohlberg's system of classification, the emphasis on human relationships results in a score indicating a lower level of moral development than does reasoning based on abstract principles of justice. Therefore, Kohlberg's system is biased against the type of moral reasoning that girls and women tend to use and leads to the misclassification of girls and women as morally less developed than boys and men.

Gilligan contended that women were capable of the type of abstract reasoning that would lead them to make moral judgments like men; thus, the differences were not due to cognitive deficiencies. But women value human relationships and feelings and make their moral judgments on the basis of damage to those relationships. This means that women have different priorities than men in making moral decisions, not that they are inferior in their moral reasoning.

Indeed, valuing human relationships over abstract principles might be considered superior. Women's orientation to care for others could be considered a better value system than the abstract and impersonal one that men tend to use, as Johmann's (1985) story suggested. The variation in possible approaches to moral decision making also brings up the possibility that, contrary to Kohlberg's position, no one universal set of moral principles exists. (For further discussion of this possibility, see Diversity Highlight: "Relativism and Universality in Moral Judgments.")

Gilligan's theory qualifies as a feminist standpoint theory in that it makes a traditional female "deficit" into a female advantage, taking the position that women have a unique contribution to make and that society should acknowledge and value this contribution. Johmann's (1985) article discussed how this moral orientation might make women better suited to jobs in which personal relationships and dealing with people are an important part.

Although Gilligan's theory spurred a great deal of excitement and enthusiasm, some psychologists expressed misgivings. Anne Colby and William Damon (1983) criticized Gilligan's methodology and her conclusions, claiming that Gilligan's data collection resembled clinical case studies more than objective data gathering. That is, she questioned participants and scored their responses rather than asking for choices to moral dilemmas as Kohlberg had done. Also, Colby and Damon pointed out that Gilligan reported no systematic evaluation of the participants' responses, so her conclusions seem to be based on some informal evaluation rather than on systematic data analysis. Furthermore, Gilligan's selective citation of illustrative examples could differ from characteristics that might appear in a more representative analysis. That is, Gilligan's methods of data collection and analysis differ from the usual research procedures, making her conclusions more difficult for research psychologists to accept.

Catherine Greeno and Eleanor Maccoby (1986) also questioned Gilligan's conclusions, contesting her original contention that studies of moral development slight

---

✼ GENDERED VOICES
It Seems Wrong to Me

A woman and a man each told me about judgments about right and wrong made by men and women and how odd these judgments seemed to them, as though each was using a different moral sense to make their judgments. These stories are consistent with the orientation toward personal caring that Gilligan found to be a prominent feature of women's moral judgments. However, the man found this orientation disturbing, and the woman found it disturbing that men fail to use this standard.

The man was a retired supervisor and said that he found working with women difficult because they seemed to take everything personally. "I couldn't tell a woman she had made a mistake and hope to have her let it go. They always seemed to take any criticism personally—and to hold a grudge. It was like nothing could be just business; everything was personal. I think that's wrong, and I

found it very difficult to work with and especially to supervise women who took everything personally. It seemed wrong to me, and it made me uncomfortable."

The woman talked about her husband's business dealings in much the same terms; he considered things business that she considered personal. "I don't see how a man can do business with someone he considers a sleaze. That just seems wrong to me. How can a person fail to take personal factors into account? In a sense, everything is personal—how you treat people—what can be more personal? I would find it very difficult to do business with someone I considered a bad person, and I don't think I could hurt someone I liked in the name of a business deal. My husband will try to hurt people in business deals that he likes on a personal level. It's like a game. That seems wrong."

---

women. Greeno and Maccoby contended that the issue of gender bias in studies of moral development had been resolved before Gilligan's work appeared; that is, no gender differences exist in standard tests of moral reasoning. When differences appear, they relate to differences in educational level and not to gender. Greeno and Maccoby questioned how different the "different voice" is, saying, "We need to know whether what is being said is distinctively *female,* or simply human" (p. 315).

Further research by Gilligan and her colleagues (Gilligan, Ward, Taylor, & Bardige, 1988) has spoken to some of these questions. Studies by Nona Plessner Lyons (1988) and D. Kay Johnson (1988) tested the Gilligan hypothesis that two types of moral reasoning exist. Both Lyons and Johnson found evidence for the justice orientation and the care orientation in moral reasoning. However, both researchers found that neither orientation was uniquely associated with men or women. Women more frequently expressed the care orientation, and men more frequently expressed the justice orientation, but both were capable of using either orientation. These researchers concluded that studies of moral reasoning would be incomplete without considering both orientations. Carol Gilligan and Jane Attanucci (1988) summarized the necessity for including both orientations:

> *Our analysis of care and justice as distinct moral orientations that address different moral concerns leads us to consider both perspectives as constitutive of mature moral thinking. The tension between these perspectives is suggested by*

❈ DIVERSITY HIGHLIGHT
Relativism and Universality in Moral Judgments

Do people take circumstances and cultural values into account when they judge the actions of others, or do people develop toward a universally accepted set of moral principles? Lawrence Kohlberg's position was that people work toward an abstract set of moral principles that hold justice and human life as the highest values. On the way to understanding and accepting these principles, children, adolescents, and even adults use moral reasoning that is relativistic rather than universal. The gender-related differences in moral reasoning found by Carol Gilligan and her colleagues suggest a deviation from universality in moral reasoning. Which principle governs—relativism or universality?

Cecilia Wainryb (1993) studied children, adolescents, and young adults to answer the question of cultural relativity or universality. She presented scenarios to people in these three age groups and asked them to make a judgment about the action that one participant had taken. First, Wainryb presented the scenario, then she added information about the different beliefs of people in that culture. Wainryb's prior research indicated that people are better able to vary their judgments when a culture holds different beliefs about how the world works compared to a different set of moral values, so Wainryb varied both types of information.

For example, one scenario asked if it was acceptable to fail to hire a pilot because he was getting old. The information that Wainryb provided about the culture was that this is "a country where people believe that God helps old pilots fly their planes safely" (p. 928). One of Wainryb's scenarios that provided information about a different culture's moral beliefs involved gender bias in hiring women. Wainryb provided information that this person lives "in a country where it is believed that women exist to serve men and therefore it is right to order them around and tell them where they can and cannot work" (p. 928).

Wainryb found that people of all ages were able to assimilate information about another culture's set of moral values in judging the actions of people in that culture, and she found no gender differences in these judgments. In the situations in which the information concerning the moral beliefs of another

culture varied (like the aging pilots), two-thirds of participants took this information into account in making their judgment; they said that it was all right to take such action in this context. In a culture in which people believe that God helps old pilots, U.S. residents said that it is fine to hire them.

Participants were not so relativistic in their judgments concerning other cultures' moral values: Only 13% of judgments were relativistic, and 60% made the same judgment, with or without information about that culture's values. That is, a majority of U.S. children, adolescents, and young adults believe that it is not acceptable to discriminate against women in hiring, even in a culture that believes women are made to serve men.

Are people in the United States different from those in other countries? Research by Jonathan Haidt and his colleagues (Haidt, Koller, & Dias, 1993) suggested that they are not but that educational or socioeconomic level may be a factor in moral judgments. These researchers asked U.S. and Brazilian children and adults from high and low economic levels to make moral judgments about harmless but distasteful actions, such as washing the toilet with the country's flag or eating the family dog. They found that college students from high economic levels tended to say that such actions were a matter of social convention or personal preference, but other participants were less willing to see disgusting actions as acceptable.

Therefore, a complex picture emerges concerning relativistic versus universal standards for moral judgments. Under some circumstances, people are willing to take a culture's standards into account when making a judgment about the action of someone in that culture. Those circumstances include the culture's beliefs about how the world works, but people are reluctant to say that an action is acceptable when it violates their beliefs about justice and fairness. Many people have difficulty in separating the disgusting from the morally unacceptable, but unlike Gilligan's research, these studies on cultural relativism indicate that men and women are similar in their tendencies to be relativistic in their moral judgments.

the fact that detachment, which is the mark of mature moral judgment in the justice perspective, become the moral problem in the care perspective—the failure to attend to need. Conversely, attention to the particular needs and circumstances of individuals, the mark of mature moral judgment in the care perspective, becomes the moral problem in the justice perspective—failure to treat others fairly, as equals. (p. 82)

Therefore, Gilligan's original contention that women have a unique moral orientation is not a position she continued to support. Instead, Gilligan and her colleagues have provided evidence that the different voice, the moral orientation characterized by concern for people and relationships, is not unique to women but is more likely to be held by women than men. Furthermore, both the care and the justice orientations are types of reasoning that both men and women can use, and both are desirable for mature moral reasoning. The different voice is different but not unique to women.

Gilligan's altered position has not received the publicity that her original work did. As is often the case in media coverage of gender issues, the findings of a complex relationship between gender and morality failed to gain the media attention that the simpler, more sensational findings generated. No stories equivalent to Johmann's (1985) have appeared to publicize the advantages that both men and women derive from their ability to make moral judgments from either a care or a justice perspective. This lack of attention is a factor in perpetuating the belief that women and men are different in many essential ways, and many people want to continue to hold this position.

The Maximalist Approach and Its Implications

Gilligan's *In a Different Voice* (1982) represents an approach to gender differences that highlights the essential differences between men and women. This concentration on differences typifies the **maximalist,** or essentialist, view—the view that the differences between the sexes are more important than the similarities. Although Gilligan later modified her position about the different voice of women in making moral judgments (Gilligan & Attanucci, 1988), her early work inspired others and promoted the view that women and men operate on a different moral basis. Thus, her view has been maximalist, concentrating on the differences between women and men.

The maximalist view highlights differences, searching for the points of divergence rather than commonality. Concentrating on differences has several implications for the study of gender, including a perpetuation of the notion that men and women are at opposite ends of a continuum, a tendency to ignore individual differences, and a concentration on one gender or the other rather than the study of both. Although many contemporary theorists take a feminist orientation to the maximalist view, this position can also reflect the opposite stance—that the essential differences between men and women give men the advantage and put women at a disadvantage. The maximalist view, regardless of position, therefore perpetuates polarities.

Feminist researchers and theorists who promote the maximalist view (Belenky, Clinchy, Goldberger, & Tarule, 1986; Chodorow, 1978, 1979; Gilligan, 1982) believe that emphasizing differences between women and men will allow researchers to concentrate on the strengths of the overlooked point of view and bring it attention and acknowledgment. "In this view, women are intrinsically better than men and their virtues are not available to men" (Chodorow, 1979, p. 43). For example, in researching the care orientation to moral judgments, Gilligan hoped to validate women's special perspective. Those researchers and theorists who object to the maximalist view (Crawford, 1989; Epstein, 1988) believe that highlighting differences perpetuates stereotyping based on overgeneralization. For example, if the care orientation is unique to women, then women should be well suited to certain jobs (like elementary school teachers, who must care) and poorly suited to other jobs (like judges, who must be detached and objective).

In addition to encouraging stereotyping, the maximalist view tends to overlook individual differences. Dividing people into oppositional categories obscures the differences of individuals within these categories. Therefore, the individual differences among women and among men are of less interest to the maximalists than differences between the two groups. By ignoring individual differences, this view also minimizes the important influences of factors such as age, ethnicity, and social class. These factors have a long research history; hundreds of studies have shown that each can contribute to many facets of behavior. In overlooking these factors or assuming the influences to be small, the maximalists endanger the credibility of their research (Crawford, 1989).

The maximalists have tended to concentrate on either men or women, but not both. The traditional maximalist theories, like Freud's psychoanalytic theory of personality, detailed the development of men to the neglect of women. The modern maximalist theories from feminist scholars like Gilligan have concentrated on the unique aspects of women's experience to the neglect of men. These feminist scholars argue that women deserve special attention to compensate for the long history of neglect, but they cannot claim that their research and theories reveal anything about gender unless they study both men and women. Neither can these researchers rely on existing research using only male subjects to furnish valid comparisons for the female subjects they have studied, as both Gilligan (1982) and Belenky et al. (1986) did. As Crawford (1989) pointed out, men who participated in research during the 1950s would not be an appropriate comparison for women who participated in research during the 1980s. Therefore, singling out either women or men as subjects tends to endanger the scientific validity of a study.

As Crawford (1989, p. 128) commented, "If masculinist values have undermined the validity of past sex difference research, do feminist values lead to more valid research or merely substitute a different set of biases?" Some scholars believe that the substitution of feminist values would bring about desirable changes in research. Like Crawford, other scholars believe that substituting one set of biases for another offers no improvement. This issue is a philosophical point of contention: Some people hold one point of view and others disagree. Both opinions have produced valuable research and have raised important questions. This controversy is presently a part of gender research and shows no sign of disappearing.

Summary

Psychoanalytic theory, originated by Freud, is the traditional approach to personality theory and relies on the concepts of unconscious forces and biologically determined instincts to explain personality development and functioning. Freud's theory hypothesized a series of psychosexual stages—oral, anal, phallic, latency, and genital—to account for the influence of childhood experiences on adult personality. Gender differences appear in the phallic stage, with its Oedipus complex in which children are attracted to their other-sex parent and feel fear and hostility toward their same-sex parent. Boys experience a more traumatic and a more complete resolution of the Oedipus complex than girls, resulting in a stronger superego for boys. Freud believed that this difference in superego strength produces a stronger morality in men than in women.

Horney disputed Freud's view that women inevitably experience inferiority, penis envy, and masochism by arguing that social, not biological, forces form the basis for personality differences between the sexes. Her analysis of the differences in personality development between men and women showed how men have feelings of inferiority compared to women, especially regarding women's ability to give birth, and Horney hypothesized that men try to feel more adequate by disparaging women.

Although the popularity of psychoanalytic theory has declined over the years, its influence has never disappeared. During the 1970s and 1980s, Freudian theory was once again brought to prominence and controversy by accusations that Freud acted improperly in abandoning the seduction theory and by the appearance of feminist psychoanalytic theory.

The seduction theory held that adults experience psychological problems because of childhood seductions by an adult, usually a parent. Freud formulated the seduction theory as an explanation for adult emotional problems but abandoned that explanation in favor of the view that these seductions were the children's fantasies rather than realities. Two psychoanalytic scholars, Balmary and Masson, accused Freud of acting improperly in rejecting the seduction theory and proposed that psychoanalysis would have been more accurate and more useful if Freud had retained this element of the theory.

Feminist psychoanalytic theory, such as the one originated by Chodorow, hypothesizes differences in the personality development of girls and boys, with girls having the advantage. Chodorow explained how gender differences begin when children strive to separate themselves from their mother and form a separate identity. This separation is easier but never as complete in girls as it is in boys, as girls are the same sex as their mothers. This similarity forms the basis for girls' identification with their mothers and causes mothers to treat daughters in different ways than they treat sons. This different treatment and perceived difference between boys and mothers produces a more difficult separation process, which forces boys to work harder to form a separate identity. Men's success in forming a masculine identity results in a denial of all that is feminine, including a rejection of female values.

Kaschak also devised a feminist psychoanalytic theory, hypothesizing that Oedipus personifies men's drives for power and feelings of entitlement, whereas Antigone, the faithful daughter, personifies women's self-sacrifice. She maintained that patriarchal culture perpetuates these roles and makes resolving these complexes difficult for men and women.

These feminist psychoanalytic theories are among feminist standpoint theories that approach personality from the point of view of women and their unique experiences. Gilligan's research on moral development is a feminist standpoint theory that originated in Gilligan's hearing a "different voice" in women's moral decisions. She studied moral development and, influenced by Chodorow's theory, decided that women are more likely to make moral decisions based on care for relationships than on abstract principles of justice. Criticisms of her method of study and conclusions resulted in additional research, indicating that the types of moral reasoning Gilligan heard from women are not unique to women. Although women are more likely to use the care orientation in their moral reasoning than are men, both men and women can take the care orientation and the justice orientation in their moral reasoning.

Traditional psychoanalytic theory and feminist standpoint theories both take a maximalist approach to personality, holding that men and women are essentially different. Such theories tend to encourage stereotyping, obscure individual differences, and exclude one sex or the other from research. Although maximalist theories may provide interesting and valuable information about women or men, this approach does not work toward a study of gender, as both men and women must be included in such studies.

Glossary

Castration complex   in Freudian theory, the unconscious fear that the father will castrate his son as a punishment for the son's sexual longings for his mother

Ego   in Freudian theory, the structure of personality that is rational and practical

Id   in Freudian theory, the structure of personality that is the repository for instincts and urges to seek pleasure and avoid pain at any cost

Instincts   in Freudian theory, the drives or impulses that underlie action, thought, and other aspects of personality functioning, which include the sexual, or life, instinct and the aggressive, or death, instinct

Masochism   feelings of pleasure as a result of painful or humiliating experiences

Maximalist   a person who holds the view that many important differences exist between the sexes and that women and men are more different than similar

Neurotic personality   in Horney's theory, a pattern of interacting with the world limited by unrealistic goals and beliefs

Oedipus complex   in Freudian theory, the situation that exists during the phallic stage in which the child feels unconscious hostility toward the same-sex parent and unconscious sexual feelings for the opposite-sex parent; Freud used the story of Oedipus as an analogy for the family dynamics that occur during personality development

Pre-Oedipal period   events that occur during early childhood, before the phallic stage and the Oedipus complex; some feminist psychoanalytic theorists, including Chodorow, have emphasized the importance of this period for personality development

Psychosexual stages   in Freudian theory, the series of stages ranging from birth to maturity through which the individual's personality develops; these stages include the oral, anal, phallic, latency, and genital

Seduction theory   in Freudian theory, the view that sexual activity between parent and child is the basis for psychological problems when the child grows to adulthood; Freud held this view for only a short time, replacing it with the notion that the seduction was fantasized rather than real

Superego   in Freudian theory, the structure of the personality that incorporates the moral rules of parents and society

Unconscious   in Freudian theory, a region of the mind functioning beyond a person's awareness

Suggested Readings

Chodorow, Nancy. (1978). *The reproduction of mothering: Psychoanalysis and the sociology of gender.* Berkeley: University of California Press. Chodorow's book is difficult reading, with its psychoanalytic terminology, but it offers a compelling alternative to Freud's theory and has influenced many of the scholars who take the feminist standpoint on personality.

Crawford, Mary. (1989). Agreeing to differ: Feminist epistemologies and women's ways of knowing. In Mary Crawford & Margaret Gentry (Eds.), *Gender and thought: Psychological perspectives* (pp. 128–145). New York: Springer-Verlag. Although Crawford is critical of the feminist standpoint approach, her article summarizes both the advantages and disadvantages of this viewpoint.

Freud, Sigmund. (1933/1964). Femininity. In James Strachey (Ed. and Trans.), *New introductory lectures on psychoanalysis* (pp. 112–135). New York: Norton. Freud's last lengthy statement about the psychology of women is interesting to read rather than read about, because Freud seems much more tentative on some issues but completely convinced on other issues of gender differences.

Kaschak, Ellyn. (1992). *Engendered lives.* New York: Basic Books. Kaschak's book is not easy reading, but she offers an interesting, radical alternative to traditional psychoanalytic theory. Chapter 3, "Oedipus and Antigone Revisited: The Family Drama," presents her revision of Freudian theory, but the entire book is worth reading for its different view of gender and the impact of gender on all facets of psychology and culture.

Segal, Naomi. (1988). Freud and the question of women. In Edward Timms and Naomi Segal (Eds.), *Freud in exile: Psychoanalysis and its vicissitudes* (pp. 241–253). New Haven, CT: Yale University Press. This article is difficult but interesting reading. Segal manages to summarize a great deal of the modern criticisms of Freudian psychoanalysis, including the feminists' criticisms and Freud's failure to acknowledge the reality of reports of childhood sexual abuse.

$$Chapter \quad 7$$

Gender Development II

Social Theories

What Are Little Boys (and Girls) Made Of?

—*Parents Magazine,* February 1987

Five-year-old Bobby didn't have much experience with babies, and he was fascinated with my six-month-old daughter, Heidi. "She's a girl, right?" he asked. "That's right," I answered. "And she has brown hair just like me," he said. "So she does," I replied. There was a pause, and his next question caught me by surprise. "Does that mean that she'll be a boy when she grows up?" I told him no, and he quickly said, "Oh, I know that. I was just kidding." (Bjorklund, 1987, p. 88)

David Bjorklund knew that Bobby was not kidding. Children younger than around 5 years old have difficulty understanding the critical elements of gender, and they do not grasp that being a boy or a girl is a permanent characteristic. Bjorklund described the difficulties that children have with forming **gender identity,** the process of coming to identify oneself as female or male, and **gender constancy,** the knowledge that gender is a permanent characteristic.

Bjorklund wrote that, contrary to Freudian theory, knowledge of genitals is not critical information in gender identity formation. Bjorklund described a 4-year-old boy who had forgotten that boys have penises and that he had one, too. He also cited evidence showing that being able to see a doll's genitals did not help preschool children identify the sex of the doll; children use clothing and hairstyles rather than genitals as identifying information.

Coming to understand which activities go with being male or female is also a challenge for young children. This task is especially difficult in technological societies, because women and men often behave in similar ways and perform many of the same tasks. Children observe their parents, other children, television, and books, which bombard them with messages about femininity and masculinity. These messages do not form a coherent whole, and sometimes children pick some behavior as critical that is irrelevant, such as the 4-year-old who had been anxious to share his father's pizza but unwilling to share his mother's lasagna at a restaurant. His parents understood why he had made these choices when "on the way home, after some unusually quiet moments, he announced that he'd figured it out. 'Men eat pizza and women don't'" (Bjorklund, 1987, p. 91).

Chapter 6 examined the psychoanalytic personality theory's view of the development of gender differences, a view that unconscious forces and early childhood experiences form personality. The psychoanalytic view is not the only explanation for the development of personality, including gender differences. Bjorklund's story about the development of gender concepts during childhood concentrated on the social and cognitive views of gender development, drawing from the research on social learning theory, cognitive developmental theory, and gender schema theory.

Social Learning Theory

Social learning theory explains gender development in the same way that it explains other types of learned behaviors, placing gender development with behaviors that are learned rather than biologically determined. This theory takes a stand on the nature-nurture controversy, for the influence of nurture, the social environment. Albert Bandura, a prominent social learning theorist, described the relative weight of biology and psychology in gender role development: "Although biological characteristics form a basis for gender differentiation, many of the social roles that get tied to gender are not ordained by biological differences. . . . Gender-role development is, therefore, largely a psychosocial phenomenon" (1986, p. 92).

The social learning approach is a variation of traditional learning theory. Of the many advocates of traditional learning theory, the person who has been most closely associated with this approach has been B. F. Skinner. He extensively researched an approach to learning called **operant conditioning,** a form of learning based on the occurrence of **reinforcement** and **punishment.** Before understanding the social learning variation, consideration of traditional learning theory and the concept of operant conditioning is in order.

In this traditional view, learning is defined as a change in behavior that is the result of experience or practice, and operant conditioning is one type of learning. In operant conditioning, a person (or other animal) changes behavior as a result of the experience of receiving reinforcement or punishment. The behavior is more likely to be repeated in the future if that person (or animal) has received a reinforcement after performing the behavior in the past. That is, reinforcement increases the probability that a behavior will recur. On the other hand, a person is less likely to repeat a behavior in the future if that person has been punished after performing the behavior in the past. That is, punishment decreases the probability that a behavior will recur. The previous consequences of a behavior are important to its repetition, with reinforcement making the behavior more likely and punishment making it less likely. Patterns of reinforcements or punishments are the experiences that produce the change in behavior that is defined as learning.

For example, a 3-year-old girl whose mother praises her when she plays with dolls is being reinforced with attention and approval for this activity. If the girl's mother scolds her when she chooses a toy truck, then the child is being punished for that choice. If both situations occur, then the child is being reinforced for one choice and punished for another. Reinforcement tends to be more effective than punishment in changing behavior, but the situation in which one behavior is punished and another incompatible behavior is reinforced can be a very effective combination (Hergenhahn, 1988).

Traditional learning theorists attempted to avoid mentalistic concepts and terminology in their explanations of behavior. They rejected all concepts of internal mental processes that might underlie learning and concentrated on objectively observable behaviors. This approach emphasized the importance of the conditions under which learning occurs and the factors that affect performance, especially reinforcement and punishment, rather than the internal cognitive factors within the learner.

The experiences of reinforcement and punishment furnish each individual with a unique learning history—no other person has exactly the same experiences. The reinforcements and punishments in each individual's history contribute to present and future behavior. Thus, future behavior can be predicted from past experience.

Social learning theory also includes the concepts of reinforcement and punishment, but in addition, it accepts the importance of cognitive processes in learning. Social learning theory is a variation and extension of traditional learning theory, having a cognitive component that changes its emphasis. This difference revolves around the importance of observation, which social learning theorists consider more important than reinforcement to learning. To these theorists, learning is cognitive, whereas performance is behavioral. The social learning approach thus separates learning from the performance of learned behaviors and investigates factors that affect both.

According to social learning theory, the basis of learning is observation rather than the direct experience of reinforcement or punishment (Mischel, 1966, 1993). Observation provides many opportunities for learning, including children's learning of gender-related behaviors. The social environment provides examples of male and female models who perform different behaviors, including some that are gender-related. These models include mothers and fathers but also many others, both real people and media portrayals of boys, girls, men, and women. In observing these many male and female models, children have abundant opportunities to learn. However, not all models have the same influence for all children, and not all behaviors are equally likely to be imitated.

The differential influence of models relates to their power or prestige as well as to the observer's attention and perception of the similarity between model and observer. Children tend to be more influenced by powerful models than by models with less power (Bussey & Bandura, 1984). But children are also more influenced by models who are similar to them, and this similarity extends to gender. Therefore, children are more likely to imitate same-sex models than other-sex models, especially when the same-sex models also have demonstrated power.

Imitation of powerful models may not be the same for girls and boys. Kay Bussey and Albert Bandura (1984) found imitation of a powerful model especially likely in 3- to 5-year-old boys, who imitated powerful female models, whereas girls in the same age range were less likely to imitate powerful male models. Karen Nicholas and Hugh McGinley (1985) found similar results with 3- and 4-year-olds, but they considered the possibility that girls may face the dilemma of choosing a similar female model or a powerful male model. Although gender and power of models may not exert the same effects for girls and boys, both factors play a role in modeling.

Another important factor in performing a learned behavior is the consequences of the observed behavior. If a person observes a behavior that is rewarded, then the observer is more likely to perform that behavior than if the observer sees the same behavior punished or unrewarded. Social learning theorists believe that reinforcement and punishment are not critical for learning, which occurs through observation. Instead, reinforcement and punishment are more important to performance, affecting the likelihood that a learned behavior will be performed in circumstances similar to those observed.

Bandura (1986) explained that children develop in an atmosphere in which they are exposed to models of gender-stereotypic behaviors "in the home, in schools, on playgrounds, in readers and storybooks, and in representations of society on the television screens of every household" (p. 93). These presentations do two things. First, all children learn the gender-related behaviors associated with *both* genders; all children are exposed to both female and male models. Second, children learn which behaviors

GENDERED VOICES
I Didn't Like Dolls

"When I was a girl, my mother had this lovely collection of dolls," a woman in her 50s said. "I just wasn't interested. I never wanted to play with dolls. They were pretty, but I never had any interest in dolls. She saved them for my daughter, and now she's not interested, either—even less than I was. She would play dolls with other girls, but she complained, saying, 'They're playing dolls, so I have to bring one, but I wish they would do something else. It's such a dumb game—putting clothes on them, and then taking the clothes off again. Dumb.' Poor Mom, she was disappointed twice over her doll collection.

"My son was more interested in my mother's doll collection than either my daughter or I ever was. He liked the He-Man and GI Joe dolls. I guess you're not supposed to call them dolls when they are the things boys play with, but that's what they are. Anyway, he was more interested in dolls than my daughter ever was, but that was when he was younger. He doesn't play with dolls anymore, and I don't think he wants the doll collection.

"It can't be genetic, because I was adopted and so are both my children. It can't be modeling, at least on my part. My mother was the one with the collection, so apparently she liked dolls, but I didn't. For me and my daughter, it's probably my influence, but how do you explain my son's playing with dolls?"

they should perform; models' behaviors are specific to one gender and not the other. Children learn that certain behaviors are rewarded for girls but not for boys; for other behaviors, the opposite is true.

For example, children see girls rewarded for playing with dolls, whereas they see boys discouraged from this same behavior. Children see boys rewarded for playing with toy trucks, but they may see girls discouraged from that behavior. Both boys and girls learn how to play with dolls and trucks, but they are not equally likely to do so due to the differential rewards they have seen others receive. Their learning is not based on observation of a few models; the world is filled with examples of men and women who are rewarded and punished for gender-related behaviors. Therefore, children may behave in ways different from their parents, including expressing sexist views that their parents do not share. The vast number of same-sex models on TV and the stereotypical roles that women and men portray in the media provide ample opportunity for children to learn sexist behavior, even if they have families in which they do not learn such behaviors.

Not all of these observed consequences are consistent with each other; some people are rewarded and others punished for the same behavior. According to Bandura (1986), consistency is not necessary for children to learn gender-related behaviors. As children observe many models, they notice the consistencies among the behavior of some models and start to overlook the exceptions. The more same-sex models exhibit a behavior, the more likely children are to connect that behavior with one or the other sex. Through this process behaviors come to be gender related, although these behaviors may have no direct relationship to sex. "Young children thus learn to use gender as an important characteristic for classifying persons and activities and to use gender features as a guide for selective modeling" (Bandura, 1986, p. 96).

Hilary Lips (1989) reviewed the many sources of modeling and reinforcement that children experience and discussed how these sources might influence their gender-related behaviors. Beginning when their children are infants, parents interact differently with their sons and daughters. Children accept and show enthusiasm for toys typically considered girls' and boys' toys (Idle, Wood, & Desmarais, 1993), but *parents* show some gender-typical preferences for activities and toys for their children.

Parents' behavior differs with their male and female children. Beverly Fagot, Mary Leinbach, and Cherie O'Boyle (1992) tested 2- to 3-year-old children and found that children who understood the labels for boys and girls had mothers who endorsed more traditional gender roles and reinforced more gender-typed toy play with their children than less traditional parents.

Fagot and Richard Hagan (1991) found that mothers gave more instructions and directions than fathers while playing with their children, but fathers spent more time playing with their 18-month-olds. Their different treatment of the toddlers appeared in fathers giving fewer positive responses to sons who chose playing with girls' toys and mothers giving more instructions to daughters who tried to communicate. Thus, the fathers failed to reinforce their sons for choosing a feminine activity, whereas mothers reinforced their daughters for attempting verbalization, a "feminine" activity.

These forces affect gender-related thoughts, and social learning theory hypothesizes that children come to develop gender knowledge and gender standards for their own behavior. Bussey and Bandura (1992) studied the development of gender self-concept in 2- to 4-year-olds, finding that "all children engaged in more same-sex than cross-sex typed behavior" (p. 1236). The younger children in their study reacted to their peers in gender-stereotypical ways but did not regulate their own behavior by these same standards, whereas the older children did both. These results indicate that these 4-year-olds had begun to develop a coherent set of cognitive strategies for controlling their gender-related behaviors.

When children start interacting with peers outside the home, these other children become a major source of both modeling and approval. Children's play groups are gender segregated, and children put a great deal of effort into maintaining this division, including insults and severe prohibitions toward those attempting to join an other-sex group. This gender segregation and the formation of relationships are covered in Chapter 10.

Thalma Lobel and her colleagues (Lobel, Bempechat, Gewritz, Shoken-Topaz, & Bashe, 1993) studied grade school children's evaluation of gender-related behaviors. These researchers showed preadolescents films containing other children in activities either typical or atypical for their gender. The researchers asked the participants to make judgments about these filmed peers, such as how popular the filmed children were and how the participants would accept the filmed children as playmates. Lobel et al. found that all children were affected by the targets' gender-related behaviors, including children who were not themselves strongly gender typed. That is, these preadolescents were willing to apply criteria for gender-related behavior to others that they did not apply to themselves. This study demonstrated that gender-related behaviors are important for children's judgments of their peers, including popularity and acceptance as a playmate.

The differential treatment of boys and girls includes parents' and teachers' expectations and encouragement during the school years. Both parents and teaches urge boys to persist in solving problems more than they urge girls. By the time children reach adolescence, their models and reinforcements tend to encourage boys toward careers and sexual expression and girls toward domesticity and physical attractiveness (Lips, 1989). Therefore, children develop in an environment that contains many sources of social learning that should lead to differences in the gender-related behaviors of boys and girls.

In summary, social learning theory views the development of gender-related behavior as part of the many behaviors that children learn through observation and modeling. This theory emphasizes the contribution of the social environment to learning and behavior. In this view learning, which occurs through observation, is cognitive and separate from performance, which is behavioral. Whether a learned behavior is performed or not depends on the observed consequences of the behavior and beliefs about the appropriateness of the behavior. Thus, children have many opportunities to observe gender-related behaviors and to develop beliefs about the consequences of those behaviors. Children observe many gender-related behaviors from a wide variety of models and come to exhibit appropriate gender-related behaviors as a result of their observation and modeling.

Sandra Bem (1985) criticized social learning theory, arguing that the theory casts children as too passive. Bem pointed out that children's behavior shows signs of more active involvement than social learning theory hypothesizes. Children do not exhibit a gradual increase in gender-related behaviors but rather seem to form cognitive categories for gender and acquire their gender-related knowledge around these categories. In addition, research evidence suggests that children may develop stronger gender stereotypes than their parents convey, implying that children actively participate in organizing information about gender. Other social theories of gender development place a stronger emphasis on cognitive organization than does social learning theory.

Cognitive Developmental Theory

The cognitive developmental theorist Lawrence Kohlberg (1966, p. 82) described this theory by saying, "Our approach to the problems of sexual development starts directly with neither biology nor culture, but with cognition." Cognitive developmental theory views the acquisition of gender-related behaviors as part of children's general cognitive development. This development occurs as children mature and interact with the world, forming an increasingly complex and more accurate understanding of their bodies and the world.

This approach follows Jean Piaget's theory of cognitive development, which fits the development of gender-related concepts into the growth of cognitive abilities and emphasizes the active organization of children's thoughts (see Ginsburg & Opper, 1969). Piaget described four stages of cognitive development, beginning at birth and ending during preadolescence, when children achieve cognitive maturity. During infancy, Piaget hypothesized that children have no concept of themselves as individuals separate from the world or even any idea of the permanence of objects separate from their perception of those objects. For example, children below age 6 months behave as though an object no longer exists when that object is hidden from sight.

Even after children have developed a sense of self and a concept of object permanence during their preschool years, they still systematically misunderstand the physical world. For example, 3-year-olds are usually not able to classify objects according to any given physical characteristic such as size or color. When asked to divide objects into groups, they make choices that appear to be inconsistent. During their elementary school years, children gain in cognitive abilities but may still have difficulty in dealing with abstractions, such as the ability to imagine "what if." In addition to the limitations on children's ability to deal with abstraction, they lack the ability to solve problems in a systematic way. These phenomena result in limitations on children's thoughts, beliefs, and problem-solving ability. For example, 6-year-old children can describe what they see, but they have great difficulty describing a scene from the point of view of anyone else, because they lack the abstract cognitive ability to visualize a scene from another's point of view.

Piaget believed that once children reach cognitive maturity, at around age 11 or 12 years, they no longer have any cognitive limitations on their understanding. (Although lack of information may be a limitation at this or any age, this problem is different from the limits on cognitive ability that appear during childhood.) Thus, Piaget explained cognitive development in a series of stages leading to an increasing ability to understand physical reality and deal with abstract, complex problems. Infants are capable of almost no abstract thought, but by preadolescence, children have fewer limitations on their cognitive abilities.

Cognitive developmental theorists see the development of gender-related behaviors as part of the task of cognitive development. Very young children, lacking a concept of self, can have no concept of their gender. Most 2 1/2-year-olds are unable to consistently apply the words *boy* or *girl* to self or others, thus failing at **gender labeling.** Kohlberg (1966) hypothesized that children acquire some preliminary category information about gender during early childhood, but gender constancy, the belief that their gender will remain the same throughout life, is a cognitively more complex concept that may not appear until between ages 4 and 7 years.

By age 3 years, children are more often successful at gender self-labeling; over half of children at this age are able to correctly use the words *boy* or *girl* to describe themselves. This word usage does not signal development of gender identity, as 3-year-olds apply these words incorrectly in many cases. For example, a child may label all people she likes or all members of her family as "girls" and all others as "boys."

When children can consistently apply gender labels, they may still do so on the basis of some external and irrelevant physical characteristic, such as clothing or hairstyle, like Bobby in Bjorklund's (1987) story—the boy who thought that having brown hair might be important for determining gender. In addition, children of this age do not see gender as a permanent feature, believing that a boy can become a girl if he wishes or that a girl might become a boy if she dressed in boys' clothing (Kohlberg, 1966). Between ages 5 and 6 years, most children develop a gender identity that is based on a classification of self and others as irreversibly belonging to one gender or the other. This gender constancy is part of children's growing ability to classify objects based on physical criteria. Thus, in the development of gender identity, children below age 5 or 6 years make mistakes in understanding gender and using gender-related words, but by age 6 years, children have a sense of gender identity that includes correct gender labeling of self and others and gender constancy.

These cognitive developments in conceptualizing gender parallel other cognitive changes that children undergo. Kohlberg discussed how children below age 5 or 6 years have an incomplete understanding of the qualities of physical objects, and he conceptualized gender identity as based on the physical differences between the sexes. By around age 6 years, children have developed correct, if concrete, understandings of physical reality, including gender identity. Cognitive developmental theory sees changes that occur in gender identity as part of cognitive development, and the mistakes that children make concerning gender identity are part of their general cognitive limitations during the course of development.

The cognitive developmental approach is similar to the social learning approach in its emphasis on the role of cognition. However, the two approaches differ in several ways. Cognitive developmental theory hypothesizes development through a series of stages, whereas social learning theory does not rely on the concept of stages in development. That is, cognitive developmental theory sees gender role development as proceeding through discrete stages, with internal consistency within a stage and differences among stages. Social learning theory sees development as more continuous and not bounded by stages. Figure 7.1 shows the difference between development as a continuous process and as a series of stages.

Cognitive developmental theory views the acquisition of gender-related behaviors as occurring due to the cognitive development of gender identity. Children begin to adopt and exhibit gender-related behaviors because they adopt a gender identity. On the other hand, social learning theory hypothesizes that children come to have a gender identity because they model gender-related behaviors. Through the performance of these behaviors, children conform to either the masculine or feminine social roles of their culture. In summary, social learning theory sees gender identity as coming from performance of gender-related behaviors, whereas cognitive developmental theory sees gender-related behaviors as coming from the cognitive adoption of a gender identity.

When children develop an understanding of categories, including gender categories, they tend to concentrate on the classification rules and show a great reluctance to make exceptions. Applied to gender, this strategy would lead to the classification of all women and all men by invariant physical or behavioral characteristics according to gender. That is, cognitive developmental theory predicts that children will develop gender stereotypes as part of their process of developing gender identity. A great deal of research evidence substantiates the notion that children form stereotypical gender concepts beginning early in their lives.

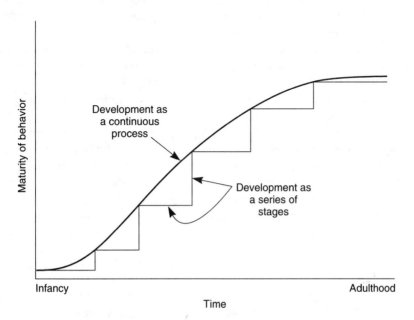

FIGURE 7.1   Two Views of Development

"I never thought of myself as very feminine, but I wouldn't begin to know how to be a man," said a woman in her 30s. "There are thousands of things about being a man or being a woman that the other doesn't know. It takes years to learn all those things. I have been struck several times by the differences in women's and men's experience, by small things.

"During college one of my roommate's boyfriends decided to paint one of his fingernails. It was an odd thing to do, but he said that it was an experience he hadn't had, and he just wanted to try it. What was interesting was that he didn't know how to go about it—didn't know how to hold the brush, which direction to apply the polish. It was interesting to watch him. That was the first time that I really thought, 'Men and women have some unique experiences that the other does not know.' I've had that thought several times since then, usually about small experiences or skills that women have and men don't.

"I'm sure that it works the other way, too. There's a world of little experiences that are part of men's lives that women don't have a clue about. For example, I wouldn't know how to go about shaving my face. In some sense, these experiences are trivial, but they made me think about the differences between the worlds of women and men."

Deanna Kuhn and her colleagues (Kuhn, Nash, & Brucken, 1978) found that children as young as 2 years old had stereotypical gender-related knowledge, and this level of knowledge related to their comprehension of gender identity and gender constancy. The process of acquiring gender stereotypes, however, is complex, and Chapter 8 explores this process more fully.

One problem with cognitive developmental theory comes from its emphasis on gender constancy as the primary force underlying the development of gender identity. Although Kohlberg's predictions are not completely clear on this point (Stangor & Ruble, 1987), his formulation of cognitive developmental theory hypothesizes that gender constancy is the most important component of the theory and that all other facets of gender identity stem from the development of gender constancy. Research by Carol Lynn Martin and Jane Little (1990) has failed to substantiate this contention, leaving a major component of this theory in doubt.

Another problem with cognitive developmental theory comes from its treating gender the same as any other cognitive category. As Sandra Bem (1985, p. 184) put it, "The theory fails to explicate why sex has primacy over other potential categories of the self such as race, religion, or even eye color." This theory fails to explain why children choose gender as a primary domain around which to organize information. This problem is addressed by the extension of cognitive developmental theory known as gender schema theory.

Gender Schema Theory

Gender schema theory is an extension of the cognitive developmental theory of gender development. A **schema** is "a cognitive structure, a network of associations that organizes and guides an individual's perceptions" (Bem, 1981, p. 355). Piaget used the term *schema* (plural, *schemata* or *schemas*) to describe the internalization of cognitions organized around various topics, and gender schema theory hypothesizes that children develop gender-related behaviors because they develop a schema that guides them to adopt such behaviors. In this view gender-related behaviors appear not only as a result of general cognitive development but also due to the adoption of special schemata related to gender.

According to gender schema theory, the culture also plays a role in gender development, providing the reference for the formation of gender schemata. Bem (1985, p. 186) described this complex of factors:

> *Gender schema theory proposes that sex typing derives in large measure from gender-schematic processing, from a generalized readiness on the part of the child to encode and to organize information—including information about the self—according to the culture's definitions of maleness and femaleness. Like cognitive-developmental theory, then, gender schema theory proposes that sex typing is mediated by the child's own cognitive processing. However, gender schema theory further proposes that gender-schematic processing is itself derived from the sex-differentiated practices of the social community.*

As children develop, they acquire schemata that guide their cognitions related to gender. Schemata can "guide information processing by structuring experiences, regulating behavior, and providing bases for making inferences and interpretations" (Martin & Halverson, 1981, p. 1120). Gender schema theorists believe that children use these schemata to develop a concept of self versus others and that each child's gender schema becomes part of that child's self-schema or self-concept.

Ronnie Janoff-Bulman and Irene Frieze (1987) discussed the influence of gender schema in formulating self-concept, pointing out the ways that schemata can guide concepts of personal masculinity and femininity, including personal judgments about how people personally fit or fail to fit these schemata. Janoff-Bulman and Frieze (1987, p. 169) wrote that "our gender schemas represent deeply embedded assumptions that we hold about maleness and femaleness in our society, and that we use to evaluate ourselves as well as others." Gender schema theory provides an explanation for the concepts of masculinity and femininity and how people apply these concepts to themselves.

Bem (1985) emphasized the process rather than the content of gender schemata. The information in the schemata is not as important as the process of forming schemata and acting in ways that are consistent with them. Gender schema theory predicts that the cognitive changes that accompany schema formation lead to the ways that children process gender-related information, resulting in better accuracy and memory for gender-consistent information compared to inconsistent information.

Bem (1981) demonstrated this information-processing effect by presenting college students with a list of words to memorize. The words included proper names, verbs, animals, and articles of clothing, some of which had been judged as masculine, some feminine, and some neutral. She divided the participants into four groups according to how strongly gender-schematic they were—masculine, feminine, androgynous (sharing characteristics of both), or undifferentiated (having few characteristics of either). She found that the gender-typed participants tended to remember the words in clusters related to gender—for example, the women's proper names in a cluster and the men's names in another. Although there was no overall difference in the number of words recalled by any group, the organization of their memory differed according to their gender schema.

Bem (1981) also found that gender-schematic participants were faster at making gender-related judgments that were consistent with their gender schema compared to judging characteristics that were inconsistent with their schema. Results from both of Bem's studies show that acquiring a gender schema changes how people process information related to gender, facilitating gender-consistent processing while hindering gender-inconsistent information from being processed.

The type of differences that Bem found among gender-schematic college students prompted a body of research using a similar approach with participants of various ages. Charles Stangor and Diane Ruble (1987) reviewed the research on gender schema and information processing. Their review indicated that children with well-defined gender schemata tend to remember gender-consistent information better than gender-inconsistent information. For example, when children see a series of drawings, photos, or a videotape in which men and women perform activities such as cooking and sewing as well as driving a truck and repairing appliances, gender-schematic children remember the gender-typical pairings (women cooking and sewing and men driving a truck and repairing appliances) better than the gender-atypical pairings (women driving a truck and repairing appliances and men cooking and sewing). In addition, children tend to change their memory to fit the gender-typical activities, such as remembering a man driving a truck when he was pictured as cooking. This tendency to distort memory in ways consistent with gender schemata suggests that the development of gender schemata influences the way that people interpret information.

According to Deborrah Frable (1989), adoption of a personal gender schema should influence attitudes and behavior related to gender as well as information processing. That is, gender schema should affect behavior other than memory-related processes. Frable tested college students to find individuals who were strongly masculine, others who were strongly feminine, and others who did not show such strong gender self-schemata. She compared the willingness of individuals in these groups to endorse gender-related rules of behavior for men and women and to make discriminatory evaluations of job and graduate school applicants. She found that those participants who had adopted strong self-schemata for gender were more likely than those who had not to endorse gender rules and to discriminate against female applicants. This study demonstrated that gender schemata are not only a developmental phenomenon but such schemata affect young adults in making judgments and decisions. Frable interpreted these findings as evidence that people who have adopted a strong gender schema tend to use it in making a variety of gender-related judgments about self and others.

The validity of the gender schema approach was investigated by Marguerite Lavallee and Rene Pelletier (1992), who studied women in traditional and nontraditional jobs. Lavallee and Pelletier assessed these women's gender self-schemata to determine if women in nontraditional jobs differed from those in more traditional occupations. They found that the women who were pursuing nontraditional jobs had different gender self-schemata, just as Bem's theory would predict.

In developing gender schemata, children become increasingly ready to interpret information in terms of gender. A tendency to interpret information in gender schematic terms may lead to gender stereotyping—exaggerated and narrow concepts of what is appropriate and acceptable for each gender. According to Carol Lynn Martin and Charles Halverson, Jr. (1981), the formation of gender stereotypes is a natural reflection of the use of gender schemata. Many of the effects of gender stereotyping are positive, such as increased ease in classifying behaviors and objects, which can give children the feeling that the environment is manageable and predictable. But stereotyping can also have negative effects, leading to inaccurate perceptions and failures to accept information that does not fit the stereotype. Thus, the existence of gender schemata prompt the formation of gender stereotypes, with both positive and negative consequences.

DIVERSITY HIGHLIGHT
A Schema for Race

Gender schema theory holds that schemata arise from the culture's differential treatment of women and men. Other dimensions exist on which schemata can be based, and race is one such dimension. In many ways racial and ethnic information is similar to gender in that many cultures hold differential expectancies for people from various ethnic groups and treat members of these groups differently. According to Sandra Bem (1985, p. 211), a category will become a schema if

> *(a) the social context makes it the nucleus of a large associative network, that is, if the ideology and/or the practices of the culture construct an association between that category and a wide range of other attributes, behaviors, concepts, and categories; and (b) the social context assigns the category broad functional significance—that is, if a broad array of social institutions, norms, and taboos distinguishes between persons, behaviors, and attributes on the basis of this category.*

Rebecca Bigler and Lynn Liben (1993) investigated cognitive factors in racial stereotyping by using an approach similar to that used to investigate memory and information-processing effects of gender schemata. These researchers presented European-American children with stories featuring European-American and African-American characters. In the course of the stories, the European-American primary character encountered a secondary character who was either European-American or African-American. In some versions of the stories, the secondary character had a negative trait that either fit or failed to fit the cultural racial stereotypes. Other stories involved a European-American child who encountered a social situation in which he or she interacted with either other people of the same race or with African Americans.

Bigler and Liben hypothesized that children who had formed a schema around racial characteristics would remember the stereotypical information from the stories better than the counterstereotypical information. As studies have found with gender-related information processing, Bigler and Liben believed that children who have formed a schema for race would remember information consistent with that schema. Their results confirmed these predictions, showing that lower degrees of racial stereotyping were associated with better memory of counterstereotypical information from the stories.

Thus, schema can be formed around characteristics that societies distinguish and emphasize. As gender schema theory predicts, other schemata are possible and lead children to make similar types of judgments, which can lead to changes and distortions in the information they encounter and process.

What should parents do if they prefer that their children avoid the culture's prevailing gender schema and the resulting gender stereotyping? Bem (1985, 1987) addressed this question of raising "gender-aschematic children in a gender-schematic world" (Bem, 1985, p. 213). The answer is not to ignore gender, because society does not. Rather, parents can attempt to eliminate gender differentiation that has nothing to do with gender; that is, the multitude of cultural messages concerning gender that have no relation with sex except by association. For example, occupations, household chores, leisure activities, and even color preferences are gender typed by their association with either men or women, and none of these needs to be so. Bem advised parents to remove gender-related differences from parents' activities and to teach their children about the bias in the culture's message.

In addition, Bem recommended that parents emphasize the biological rather than social correlates of sex. By teaching children about anatomy and reproduction, Bem argued that parents can limit gender-related association to the biological, thus minimizing the pervasive associations of gender with many aspects of life. Although she acknowledged that parents usually do not use this strategy, she believes that this approach offers advantages. "In the American context, children do not typically learn to define sex in terms of anatomy and reproduction until quite late, and as a result they...mistakenly treat many of the cultural correlates of sex as definitional" (Bem, 1985, p. 216).

Instead, Bem (1985) suggested that parents substitute alternative schemata, and she proposed several. One alternative is the individual differences schema, the view that gender-related differences are minor in comparison with the variability among people. Another alternative is the cultural relativism schema, the view that different groups of people have different beliefs regarding gender. By adopting this view, parents can teach their children that others have different beliefs and that all these different sets of beliefs can coexist. Bem also suggested that parents teach their children about the sexism schema, letting them know that people hold such beliefs and proposing that children need to know about them. Bem contended that ignoring the culture's gender roles would not produce aschematic children, and she advised parents to give their children ways to achieve flexibility in the application of their gender schema.

Bem (1989) also demonstrated that genital knowledge was an important element of gender understanding by testing 3- to 5-year-olds on gender constancy. She found that the children who could identify individuals by gender had the specific knowledge that genitalia are the critical elements for determining female or male sex. Therefore, Bem recommended that parents emphasize the importance of the genitals in understanding gender and in averting some of the sexist elements of gender knowledge.

Other researchers have investigated the difficulties in raising nonsexist children. Mary Sedney (1987) discussed the limits on parental behavior for children in the wider culture, with its pervasive sexism. Thomas Weisner and Jane Wilson-Mitchell (1990) found that some family patterns were more likely to produce nonsexist children than others. Traditional families, of course, were likely to have children with strong gender schema, but some nonconventional families also produced schematic children. The families that followed Bem's suggestions—egalitarian behavior patterns combined

TABLE 7.1   Factors in the Development of Gender-Related Attitudes in Children

Children Who Exhibit Inflexible Attitudes about Gender	Children Who Exhibit More Flexible Attitudes about Gender
Have parents who exhibit traditional attitudes concerning gender-related behaviors	Have parents who question traditional attitudes concerning gender-related behaviors
(Weisner & Wilson-Mitchell, 1990)	
Have parents who concentrate on the social correlates of gender	Have parents who concentrate on the physical determinants of sex
(Bem, 1989)	
Interact more with parents	Interact less with parents
(Levy, 1989)	
Have more siblings	Have fewer siblings
(Levy, 1989)	
Have mothers who are homemakers	Have mothers who work outside the home
(Levy, 1989)	

with questioning of societal norms—produced children with less gender-typed knowledge than other family patterns. Table 7.1 summarizes the factors that relate to children with and without strong gender schemata, showing the combination of factors that tends to make children sexist. Regardless of family attitudes and behavior, all children displayed gender-related information that went far beyond the knowledge that genitals determine a person's sex. That is, no family attitudes or behavior can completely counteract the influence of society's pervasive gender associations.

In summary, gender schema theory extends the cognitive developmental theory of gender development by hypothesizing the existence of gender schemata, cognitive structures that internally represent gender-related information and guide perception and behavior. Children internalize their schema for masculinity or femininity, forming a self-concept, or self-schema, for gender-related behaviors. Research has indicated that gender schemata can affect the processing of gender-related information and can lead to gender stereotyping. Parents can attempt to circumvent gender-related messages by concentrating on the biological rather than the social correlates of gender, but all children come to understand their culture's messages about gender.

Social learning theory, cognitive developmental theory, and gender schema theory all attempt to explain how children come to exhibit gender-related behaviors and have personal concepts of masculinity and femininity. These theories all share an emphasis on children's surroundings in the family and in society, but each theory has a different view of children's role in coming to understand gender. Table 7.2 presents and compares each of these theories. Each of these theories hypothesizes a course of development of gender-related knowledge and behavior, but what does the research on this topic indicate? How do children come to understand gender and develop gender typing, and which theory best explains the data?

TABLE 7.2   Comparison of Social Theories of Gender Development

	Social Learning Theory	Cognitive Developmental Theory	Gender Schema Theory
Gender differences develop through	Reinforcement and observation of models	General cognitive development, especially gender constancy	Development of gender-specific schemata
Children's participation involves	Choosing which models to imitate	Organizing information about physical world	Developing schemata specific to gender
Gender development begins	As soon as the culture emphasizes it, usually during infancy	During preschool years	During preschool years
Gender development proceeds	Gradually becoming more like adult knowledge	Through a series of stages	Through development of schemata
Gender development finishes	During adulthood, if at all	During late childhood or preadolescence	During late childhood
Girls and boys	May develop different gender knowledge as well as different gender-related behaviors	Develop similar cognitive understanding of gender	May develop different structures and schemata, depending on parents and family pattern

Developing Gender Identity

A child's sex is announced at birth; at that point (and often thereafter) girls usually are dressed in pink, boys in blue. This type of differential treatment is the sort that all the social theories of gender development rate as important in leading children to attend to and adopt the appropriate gender role. Thus, the process of developing gender identity can start early in infancy.

Some research indicates that infants possess the ability to begin gender typing—that they can tell the difference between male and female faces. Although studying infants' thoughts is a difficult task, one approach involves showing the infant objects, in this case, photos of faces, and measuring how long these objects hold the infant's attention. When infants see something new, they tend to look at the novel object, attending to it; when they grow bored, they begin looking around rather than at the object. The process of becoming accustomed to an object is called habituation, and by using this procedure researchers can determine which objects or features of objects infants can distinguish and which they cannot. By noting when infants attend and when they grow bored, researchers can deduce which stimuli infants can distinguish and which they cannot.

By using such a procedure, Mary Leinbach and Beverly Fagot (1993) found that 12-month-old infants responded differently to photos of male and female faces. These researchers tested 5-, 7-, 9-, and 12-month-old infants and found that both the 9- and 12-month-olds could recognize both male and female faces. Even when they altered the photos with clothing or hairstyle changes, the 12-month-olds still made the distinction between male and female faces, but altering both features changed the category for the infants. This study showed that infants can distinguish between women and men, the basic distinction necessary for forming gender identity.

Factors in the development of gender identity include not only the ability to distinguish between the sexes but also the ability to label each, knowledge of gender roles, adoption of gender roles, gender constancy, and the ability to be flexible in applying gender roles to self and others. Research indicates that these elements of gender identity are separable and develop at different times.

During Childhood

Fagot and Leinbach (1993) contended that the ability to make the categorical distinction between men and women is far from having a gender concept or identity, arguing that the gender-related knowledge of 1-year-olds is beyond conscious awareness. A missing factor is the ability to use appropriate gender labels—correctly referring to women (or girls) and men (or boys). In an earlier study, Fagot and Leinbach (1989) found that none of the toddlers they studied had passed the gender-labeling task before age 18 months, and these children also displayed no differences in gender-typed behaviors. By age 27 months, half could apply gender labels, and the children who succeeded in this task had parents who showed more traditional gender role behavior and provided their toddlers with positive and negative feedback for playing with gender-typed toys. This study showed not only that children start to develop the ability to label gender at around age 2 years but also—as social learning theory predicts—that parents' attention to gender is a factor in this development.

Children as young as age 2 years possess considerable gender knowledge, according to a study by Deanna Kuhn and her colleagues (Kuhn, Nash, & Brucken, 1978). Their study indicated that 2- and 3-year-olds know quite a bit about their culture's gender stereotypes. Some children in this age group knew that their gender was a permanent feature; that is, they had developed gender constancy. This facet of gender identity, however, is not typically part of early gender knowledge—other aspects evolve earlier.

Research by Martin and Little (1990) revealed that children's gender knowledge has several different dimensions and develops in a pattern. They tested 3- to 5-year-olds on several aspects of gender knowledge and found a relationship between age and gender knowledge: The older children had more complete and complex knowledge concerning gender roles and stereotypes.

The youngest of Martin and Little's participants were able to label the sexes, form groupings based on gender, and exhibit some knowledge of gender stereotypes. They did not show evidence of gender constancy at age 3, nor did they show extensive knowledge of gender-typical clothing or toy choices. Around age 4 years, the majority of these children passed the tests of gender discrimination and gender stability, and their understanding of gender-typical clothes and toys was closer to the stereotypes.

Martin and Little examined the patterns of gender knowledge for the children in their study, proposing a sequence of gender-related knowledge. Young children may fail to exhibit all gender-related knowledge, even the ability to label and show preferences for gender-typical toys. Those children who have accomplished gender labeling may not have acquired gender knowledge or preferences, but children will not have gender knowledge or preferences without the ability to label. Those children whose gender knowledge is complete should be able to succeed on all the tasks. Table 7.3 shows these stages. An analysis of the responses from their participants showed that 98% of the children fell into one of these categories. Their findings revealed that, contrary to Kohlberg's conceptualization, gender constancy was not a critical component in the development of gender knowledge.

Gender constancy may not be an all-or-nothing development. Martin and Little separated *gender stability,* the knowledge that gender is a stable personal characteristic, from *gender consistency,* the belief that people retain their gender even when they adopt behaviors or superficial physical features associated with the other gender. For example, a child who shows gender stability will say that she was a girl when she was a baby and will be a woman when she grows up. A child who shows gender consistency will say that a boy will remain a boy even if he grows long hair or wears a dress. Martin and Little's analysis revealed that some children showed gender stability without gender consistency, but never the other way around. Thus, gender constancy might consist of two separable cognitive components, explaining why researchers have found age variation in its development.

Preschoolers, 1st graders, 2nd graders, and even some 4th graders can be misled into mistakes about gender consistency, the more advanced of the components of gender constancy. According to a study by Carole Beal and Maria Lockhart (1989), changes in appearance and proper name can produce this confusion. Beal and Lockhart changed the appearance of a target child, making the target look more like the other sex, and in some cases also changed the name and pronoun used to refer to this target child. They found that the children were more likely to say that the target kept

TABLE 7.3   Stages of Developing Gender-Related Knowledge

	Gender Labeling	Gender Preferences or Knowledge	Gender Constancy
Stage 1	No	No	No
Stage 2	Yes	No	No
Stage 3	Yes	Yes	Possibly
Stage 4	Yes	Yes	Yes

SOURCE: Based on The relation of gender understanding to children's sex-typed preferences and gender stereotypes (pp. 1434–1435) by C.L. Martin & J. Little, 1990, *Child Development, 61.*

"When my daughter was 2 or 3 years old, she clearly had no concept of gender or the permanence of gender," a man told me. "She would say that she was a girl or a boy pretty much randomly, as far as I could tell. One day, she would say one, and maybe even later the same day, the other—for both herself and others. You could be a boy one day and a girl the next. This lack of permanence also extended to skin color. She would say that your skin was the color of your clothes, so that changed from day to day, too.

One day, you were blue, the next day, your skin was red. I thought that was very odd, even more odd than being a boy one day and being a girl the next.

"She's 5 years old now, and gender is a very salient characteristic for her. She seems to realize that she is a girl, and I think that she knows that she will always be a girl, but she is very concerned with gender and gender-related things—as though she is working on sorting out all this information and making sense of it."

the same sex, even if they changed the target's appearance, when the target kept the same proper name throughout the transformations. They concluded that children whose understanding of gender constancy was not solid could be misled by changes in superficial characteristics, such as appearance or proper names. The age of their participants and their difficulty in demonstrating this facet of gender constancy show how difficult this concept is for children and how long children take to develop gender constancy.

There is some indication that the course of gender development varies between girls and boys. The boys and girls in the Kuhn et al. (1978) study had different notions about gender-related concepts, with girls attributing positive characteristics to girls and negative characteristics to boys, and boys doing the reverse. Martin and her colleagues (Martin, Wood, & Little, 1990) found that children first learned about characteristics relevant to their gender and only later about the other gender. Gary Levy and Robyn Fivush (1993) concluded that young children have better organized knowledge of events and behaviors stereotypically associated with their own rather than the other gender.

During middle childhood children have well-formed concepts of gender, and their gender stereotyping becomes stronger as their tolerance for flexibility in applying gender roles becomes weaker. In their study of children between 3 and 10 years old, Martin et al. (1990) found that the older children made more extreme stereotype judgments than the younger children. The family environment is important in developing gender stereotyping or gender role flexibility, as Levy's (1989) research demonstrated. Levy found that children who interacted more with their parents showed less gender role flexibility than children who spent less time with their parents, and children with fewer siblings showed more gender role flexibility than those with more brothers and sisters. Girls whose mothers worked outside the home and girls who expressed a preference for educational television showed more gender role flexibility than other girls.

In summary, children begin to acquire knowledge concerning gender at an early age. Although infants show some signs of being able to differentiate between women and men, this ability does not constitute cognitive knowledge about gender. Between ages 2 and 3 years, children succeed at gender labeling but usually not at other aspects of gender knowledge, such as gender preferences, gender stability, gender consistency, or knowledge of gender stereotypes. These aspects of gender knowledge develop between the ages of 3 and 6 years for most children, and do so in a regular pattern consisting of gender labeling, gender stereotype knowledge and gender preferences, and then the two components of gender constancy—gender stability and gender consistency. Even during the first few grades of elementary school, children can be misled into making mistakes of gender consistency by the transformation in physical appearance or proper name, indicating how difficult this aspect of gender knowledge is for children to acquire.

When children have developed the components of gender identity, they tend to become very rigid in their application of gender-related behaviors and characteristics, tolerating limited exceptions. Additional development during preadolescence or adolescence can allow individuals to become more flexible in their acceptance of gender-related behaviors and characteristics.

Levy's (1989) study demonstrated the range of influences that families exert on children in their development of gender stereotypes versus tolerance of gender role flexibility. This theme of gender stereotyping versus flexibility is a major focus of the development of gender-related knowledge and behavior during adolescence.

During Adolescence and Adulthood

Research on gender development during adolescence is more sparse than research on gender development during childhood. The reason for this deficit lies in the widespread belief that gender development is complete by the end of childhood and that adolescence and adulthood hold no further developments. Some researchers, however, have held different assumptions, and these investigators have examined continuing changes in gender identity and attitudes during adolescence and adulthood.

Katheryn Urberg (1979) studied gender role development in 7th graders, 12th graders, and adults to consider changes in stereotyping at various ages and to compare these participants to an earlier study she had completed. She found that the 12th graders showed the most and the adults the least gender-related stereotyping. This result indicates that stereotyping does not increase with gender knowledge. Rather, the relationship between age and gender stereotyping shows a curvilinear relationship: low at early ages, before gender becomes an important factor for dealing with people; then higher, when dating and career choices become important; and finally, lower, when young adults accept greater flexibility for gender-related behavior.

In addition to her findings concerning the pattern of gender stereotyping, Urberg also found that the male and female participants in her study gave similar self-descriptions but described the other in more stereotypical terms. That is, Urberg found no significant differences in ratings that male and female participants assigned to themselves: Both saw themselves similarly in terms of characteristics such as affiliation, personal effectiveness, control, and impulsivity. The only exception was that 12th-grade girls saw themselves as more dependent than 12th-grade boys rated themselves.

The conceptualizations of men and women, however, differed in the opinion of both the female and male participants, who tended to see the other gender in more stereotypical terms than they saw their own. These results suggest a tendency to evaluate self in terms that people are reluctant to apply to others—to see oneself in personal and others in stereotypical terms, especially during adolescence.

A more recent study by Phyllis Katz and Keith Ksansnak (1994) confirmed the tendency to apply different gender standards to others than to self in age groups ranging from elementary to high school. These investigators also found that people showed a greater tolerance and flexibility of gender-related behaviors for self than for others. This study revealed a complex pattern of gender role flexibility, but with a general increase in tolerance for gender-atypical activities for self and others with increasing age. That is, this study suggests a linear increase from childhood to adulthood in gender flexibility and tolerance for deviations from the traditional gender role.

Although the patterns of gender role development do not seem the same in these two studies, the findings may not be dissimilar. The age groupings for the participants in the Katz and Ksansnak study were not the same as in Urberg's study, making direct comparisons unwarranted. Katz and Ksansnak failed to include adults in their study, and Urberg failed to include elementary-aged children. The inclusion of these groups in both studies may have revealed similar patterns. The discrepancy in the findings for high-school-aged adolescents may be due to the time difference in the two studies. Perhaps adolescents have become less rigid in the enforcement of gender roles in the 15 years between the publication of the two studies.

In investigating the correlates of gender flexibility, Katz and Ksansnak searched for the social factors that related to flexibility of gender roles. They found that gender flexibility was more influenced by siblings and peers than by parents. Indeed, same-sex siblings were an especially important force in the development of gender flexibility. Consistent with the findings from other studies, Katz and Ksansnak found that girls were more flexible than boys in both their preferences for other-gender activities and tolerance for such activities in others.

It is apparent that gender identity continues to develop during adolescence and even in adulthood. When children have developed the cognitive and motivational components of gender identity, they tend to be inflexible in the application of their understanding of these rules; they are intolerant of gender-atypical behavior in themselves and in others. Some research indicates that this inflexibility peaks late in the high school years and is lower during adulthood, whereas other research indicates increasing flexibility throughout junior high and high school. In either case, young children and adults both exhibit gender flexibility—young children due to a lack of understanding of gender-typed behaviors, and the adults due to flexibility in their application of gender-related rules of behavior. Gender inflexibility occurs during childhood and adolescence,

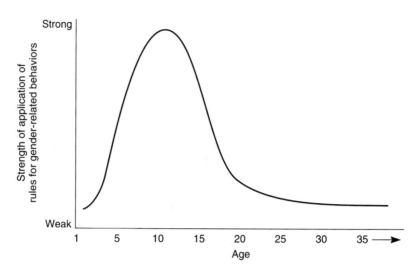

FIGURE 7.2 **Course of Application of Gender-Related Rules Throughout the Life Span**

when the rules of gender-typed behaviors are applied with little flexibility. Figure 7.2 shows this course of development for gender flexibility over the life span.

Which Theory Best Explains the Data?

Each of these theories of gender development presents an orderly pattern of development, but the research shows a complex pattern with many components that do not necessarily correlate with each other. That is, none of the theories is able to explain all the data from research on gender development.

Social learning theory predicts a process of learning gender roles that results in a gradual matching of gender-related behaviors to the cultural prescription through modeling and reinforcement of gender-appropriate behaviors. Although the research shows that children begin learning information consistent with gender stereotypes at an early age, gender knowledge consists of several different concepts that do not appear incrementally. The finding that children learn gender labeling before gender-typical toy and clothing preferences indicates a pattern of gender knowledge development that social learning theory does not predict.

Research has substantiated the influence of parents, siblings, and peers in directing gender-related behavior. Social learning theory predicts that family, peers, teachers, and media images of men and women affect children in their learning and performance of gender-appropriate behaviors. Studies by Bussey and Bandura (1984, 1992) showed the power of modeling in prompting the performance of gender-related behaviors, and studies such as the one by Katz and Ksansnak (1994) demonstrated that same-sex siblings, parents, peers, and teachers were all important in the development of gender flexibility. These findings are consistent with the predictions of social learning theory.

Social learning theory allows that girls and boys might differ not only in their gender-related behaviors but also in cross-gender behaviors. The male gender role carries more power, and power is one of the factors that affects children's modeling. Boys are discouraged from performing feminine behaviors, whereas girls may not be discouraged from performing behaviors typical of boys. These differences lead to the prediction that boys should be more strongly gender typed than girls, and research supports this difference. Cognitive developmental theory does not allow for a different pattern of development for boys and girls. Gender schema theory hypothesizes that parental attitudes and family patterns may produce variations in individual schemata, but this theory does not specifically address differences in schemata between girls and boys.

Cognitive developmental theory hypothesizes that gender development comes about through cognitive changes that occur by way of general cognitive development. Research has indicated that gender development produces cognitive changes in accuracy and memory for gender-related information, but gender schema theory also predicts that cognitive changes come with the development of gender schema, making findings that support these cognitive changes applicable to either theory.

The prediction that gender constancy is the basis for developing all other gender knowledge has not been substantiated. Indeed, research has shown that gender constancy develops late, with many other components of gender knowledge appearing earlier. This failure is a serious problem for cognitive developmental theory. Another problem for this theory is the continuation of gender development during adolescence. According to this theory, children undergo no additional cognitive changes after early adolescence, but research has shown that late adolescence is a time during which individuals gain flexibility of gender beliefs.

Gender schema theory predicts that children develop a cognitive organization for gender, a schema, that forms the basis for their understanding of gender and directs their gender-related behaviors. The types of cognitive changes that this theory predicts have been found in information processing, such as accuracy of judgments and memory effects. In addition, Lavallee and Pelletier (1992) found that women in traditional versus nontraditional jobs have different conceptualizations of gender-appropriate behavior, a finding consistent with gender schema theory.

As Martin and Little's (1990) study suggests, gender development may consist of several different cognitive abilities. Barbara Hort and her colleagues (Hort, Leinbach, & Fagot, 1991) proposed that the cognitive components of gender development do not have a great deal of coherence, postulating that such knowledge varies among individual children of the same age and stage of cognitive development. That is, they suggested that gender knowledge does not fall into a pattern sufficiently coherent to be called a schema.

It is evident from this discussion that all of the social theories of gender development make predictions that research has supported, and all make predictions that research has failed to confirm. The picture from the research is that gender development presents a more complex process than any of the theories can fully explain. Gender development consists of separate components—gender labeling, preferences for gender-typed activities, gender stereotyping, and gender constancy. These components appear to develop in a pattern, but the pattern is not exactly the one predicted by any of the theories. Thus, all of the social theories of personality development have been useful and have been partially confirmed, but none is without weaknesses.

Summary

The social theories of gender development provide three alternatives to psychoanalytic theory to explain how infants come to identify themselves as masculine or feminine, to understand gender, and to behave in gender-appropriate ways. The social learning approach is a variation on traditional learning theory and relies on the concepts of observational learning and modeling to explain how children learn and perform gender-related behaviors. Families and then the broader culture provide models and reinforcements for adopting certain gender-related behaviors while discouraging the adoption of others. Research has supported the power of children's family and social surroundings in the development of gender-related behaviors, but the orderly pattern of gender development is not consistent with this theory.

Cognitive developmental theory holds that gender identity is a cognitive concept that children learn as part of the process of learning about the physical world and their own bodies. Children younger than 2 years of age have no concept of gender and cannot consistently label themselves or others as male or female. When children learn to classify according to gender, they develop gender constancy, the understanding that gender is a permanent personal characteristic that will not change with any other physical transformation. According to cognitive developmental theory, other facets of gender development spring from gender constancy, but research has indicated that gender constancy is among the last types of gender knowledge to be acquired. These findings present a problem for this theory.

Gender schema theory is an extension of cognitive developmental theory and explains gender identity in terms of schemata, cognitive structures that underlie complex concepts. When children acquire a gender schema, they change the way that they deal with information concerning gender and also change their behavior to conform to their gender. This theory suggests that gender stereotyping is an natural extension of the process of developing gender schema and that children become stereotypical in their gender behavior and judgments. Parents who wish to raise nonsexist children can attempt to substitute an alternative schema that is less sexist than the one predominant in their culture, but avoiding the formation of gender schema is not possible.

The process of gender development may begin during infancy. Twelve-month-olds can distinguish between male and female faces, but knowledge concerning gender seems absent until around age 2 years. During the time between ages 2 and 3 years, most children learn to apply gender labels and understand some behaviors and features stereotypically associated with gender. Their understanding of gender is far from complete, however, and children may be 7 or 8 years old before they have a complete understanding of gender constancy.

When children develop an understanding of gender, they tend to be rigid and inflexible in their application of gender rules to themselves and others. Gender stereotyping is not as strong during adulthood as during adolescence, indicating that additional gender development occurs during adolescence and adulthood.

Evaluating the social theories of gender development leads to the conclusion that each has supporting research, yet research fails to support any theory to the exclusion of the others.

Glossary

Gender constancy   the knowledge that gender is a permanent characteristic and will not change with superficial alterations

Gender identity   individual identification of self as female or a male

Gender labeling   the ability to label self and others as male or female

Operant conditioning   a type of learning based on the administration of reinforcement; receiving reinforcement forms an association between the reinforcement and the behavior that preceded it, making the behavior more likely to be repeated

Punishment   any stimulus that decreases the probability that a behavior will be repeated

Reinforcement   any stimulus that increases the probability that a behavior will be repeated

Schema (plural, **schemata** or **schemas**)   an internal cognitive structure that organizes information and guides perception

Suggested Readings

Bem, Sandra Lipsitz. (1985). Androgyny and gender schema theory: A conceptual and empirical integration. In Theo B. Sonderegger (Ed.), *Nebraska symposium on motivation, 1984: Psychology and gender* (pp. 179–226). Lincoln: University of Nebraska Press. Bem evaluates the other theories of gender development and presents gender schema theory, the research supporting her theory, and advice about raising nonsexist children.

Lips, Hilary M. (1989). Gender-role socialization: Lessons in femininity. In Jo Freeman (Ed.), *Women: A feminist perspective* (pp. 197–216). Mountain View, CA: Mayfield. Lips reviews the many sources of socialization pressure that tend to encourage the adoption of the appropriate gender roles.

Martin, Carol Lynn; & Little, Jane K. (1990). The relation of gender understanding to children's sex-typed preferences and gender stereotypes. *Child Development, 61,* 1427–1439. Martin and Little's complex study examines many facets of children's gender knowledge and the relationships among these components. The article is not easy reading, but it is interesting to understand the basis for the pattern of development for gender-related knowledge they propose.

Chapter 8

Gender Stereotypes

Masculinity and Femininity

HEADLINE

Sexist Piglets: Studies Show That Sex-Stereotyping Is Part of Childhood

—*Parents' Magazine,* December 1983

> *I'm battling with my girls all the time. At seven and nine their values are archaic. They believe that girls are dopey in math and boys should not play with dolls. Worse, one day I heard Joanne tell her younger sister that women shouldn't work! Those are the values I grew up with and it's taken me years to straighten myself out. Did I come this far just to watch my own children backslide two generations? (in Pickhardt, 1983, p. 32)*

This mother told Irene Pickhardt (1983) of her surprise and frustration at the sexism her daughters expressed. The woman was very concerned; she had tried to give her daughters positive messages about women's capabilities, beliefs that she herself had striven to demonstrate. Now her daughters seemed to be rejecting her values and accepting outdated opinions about women and men; they had become miniature sexist "pigs."

Pickhardt presented the view of sociologist Judy Corder Bolz, who specializes in gender role development. Corder Bolz suggested to Pickhardt that, no matter how liberal or egalitarian the parents, children will still show sexist stereotypes during the early elementary school years: "Starting at the age of five, children go through a fascinating stage that I call 'developmental sexism'.... For a few years they are enormously sexist in their sex-role perception and choice of play activities" (in Pickhardt, 1983, p. 34).

Corder Bolz told Pickhardt that between ages 5 and 10 years children have very little tolerance for exceptions to rules they have come to understand concerning gender. Children tend to conceptualize the world in terms of male or female, and variations on this dichotomy are unwelcome. This thinking leads children to have stereotypical pictures of men, women, boys, and girls. Children may even be upset by adults whose behavior goes beyond these narrow boundaries of acceptability, and may even berate their fathers for washing dishes or their mothers for fixing things around the house.

Pickhardt's story contended that gender stereotyping is an almost inevitable part of children's learning gender roles, but gender stereotyping is not necessarily a part of adults' gender understanding. Throughout their lives some people continue to hold stereotypical views of women and men, whereas others develop more flexible attitudes about gender-related behaviors.

From Gender Roles to Gender Stereotypes

A **gender role** consists of activities that men and women engage in with different frequencies (see Williams & Best, 1990). Robert Brannon (1976) discussed the origin of the concept of role, tracing its adoption by social science back to the terminology of the theater. The word *role* was French for "roll," referring to the roll of paper on which an actor's part was printed. Brannon considered this usage particularly meaningful, as the role, the part a person plays, differs from the person. Therefore, the male gender role or the female gender role is like a script that men and women follow to fulfill their appropriate parts in acting masculine or feminine. Brannon defined the social science usage of *role* in terms of expected, socially encouraged patterns of behavior exhibited by individuals in specific situations. Thus, a person acts to fulfill a role by behaving in the expected way in the appropriate situation.

In many cultures men perform some activities more often than women, and women perform some activities more often than men. Activities such as repairing cars and repairing clothing are associated predominantly with men and women, respectively. These gender-related behaviors thus become part of a pattern accepted as masculine or feminine, not because of any innate reason for these differences but because they are associated with women and men.

A **gender stereotype** consists of beliefs about the psychological traits and characteristics as well as the activities appropriate to men or women. Gender roles are defined by behaviors, but gender stereotypes are beliefs and attitudes about masculinity and femininity. The concepts of gender role and gender stereotype tend to be related. When people associate a pattern of behavior with either women or men, they may overlook the individual variations and exceptions and come to believe that the behavior is inevitably associated with one, and not the other, gender. Therefore, gender roles can become gender stereotypes, as happened with the children in Pickhardt's story.

Gender stereotypes are very influential, affecting conceptualizations of women and men and establishing social categories for gender. These categories represent what people think, and even when beliefs vary from reality, beliefs can be very powerful forces in judgments of self and others. Therefore, the history, structure, and function of stereotypes are important topics in understanding the impact of gender on people's lives.

Stereotypes of Women and Men

The rigid formulation of what is acceptable for women and men is not unique to children such as the ones in Pickhardt's story or even to contemporary society. Rather, current gender stereotypes can be traced to the past century. Many of the elements of current stereotypes can be found in Victorian conceptualizations of femininity and masculinity.

According to Miriam Lewin (1984c), the current gender stereotypes, especially those about women, reflect beliefs that appeared during the 19th century, the Victorian era. She discussed how the Industrial Revolution changed the lives of a majority of people in Europe, the United States, and Canada by moving men outside the home to earn money and leaving women at home to manage households and children. This separation was unprecedented in history, forcing men and women to adapt by creating new behavior patterns. As men coped with the harsh business and industrial world, women were left in the relatively unvarying and sheltered environments of their homes. These changes produced two beliefs: the Doctrine of Two Spheres and the Cult of True Womanhood.

The Doctrine of Two Spheres is the belief that women's and men's interests diverge—that women and men have their separate areas of influence (Lewin, 1984a). For women, the influence is home and children, whereas men's sphere includes work and the outside world. These two spheres are different, with little overlap, forming opposites ends of one dimension. Lewin contended that this conceptualization of opposition forms the basis not only for social views of gender but also for psychology's formulation of its measurement of masculinity and femininity.

The Cult of True Womanhood

According to Barbara Welter (1978), who discussed the rise of the Cult of True Womanhood between 1820 and 1860, "The attributes of True Womanhood, by which a woman judged herself and was judged by her husband, her neighbors, and society could be divided into four cardinal virtues—piety, purity, submissiveness, and domesticity" (p. 313). Welter quoted extensively from women's magazines and religious literature of the 19th century to furnish evidence of that society's emphasis on these four areas. The Cult of True Womanhood held that the combination of these characteristics provided the promise of happiness and power to the Victorian woman, and without these no woman's life could have real meaning.

Religion formed the basis for the Cult of True Womanhood (Welter, 1978). During this time society saw women as more naturally religious than men. This tendency toward religion was part of women's natural moral superiority, and the belief in the moral superiority of women was stronger in America than in Europe and England (Lewin, 1984c). Woman's natural superiority also appeared in her refinement, delicacy, and tender sensibilities. Religious studies were seen as compatible with femininity and deemed appropriate for women, whereas other types of education were thought to detract from a woman's femininity. Included in these other types of education were not only formal studies but also the reading of romantic novels, which might lead women to ignore religion, become overly romantic, and lose their virtue (that is, their virginity) to some man.

The loss of purity was a "fate worse than death"; having lost her virtue, a woman was without value or hope. "Purity was as essential as piety to a young woman, its absence as unnatural and unfeminine. Without it she was, in fact no woman at all, but a member of some lower order" (Welter, 1978, p. 315).

Men, on the other hand, were not as naturally religious and thus not as naturally virtuous as women. According to this view of True Womanhood, men were, at best, prone to sin and seduce, and at worst, brutes. A True Woman would withstand the advances of men, dazzling and shaming them with her virtue. Men also were supposed to be both religious and pure, although not to the same extent as women, and through association with a True Woman, a man could increase his own virtue. True Women could elevate men.

The third virtue of Cult of True Womanhood was submissiveness, a characteristic not true of and not desirable in men (Welter, 1978). Women were supposed to be weak, dependent, and timid, whereas men were supposed to be strong, wise, and forceful. Dependent women wanted strong men, not sensitive ones. These couples formed families in which the husbands were unquestionably superior and the wives would not consider questioning this authority.

The last of the four virtues, domesticity, was connected to both submissiveness and to the Doctrine of the Two Spheres. True Women were wives whose concern was with domestic affairs—making a home and having children. "The true woman's place was unquestionably by her own fireside—as daughter, sister, but most of all as wife and mother" (Welter, 1978, p. 320). These domestic duties included cooking and nursing the sick, especially a sick husband or children.

Women who personified these virtues passed the test of True Womanhood. Of course, the test was so demanding that few, if any, women met the criteria. However, beginning in the early 1800s women's magazines as well as social and religious leaders held these virtues as attainable and urged women to work toward these qualities, and women tried to match these ideals. Although the Cult of True Womanhood was dominant during the 19th century, remnants have remained in our present-day culture and have influenced current views of femininity.

Male Sex Role Identity

The 19th-century idealization of women had implications for men as well. Men were seen as the opposite of women in a number of ways. Women were passive, dependent, pure, refined, and delicate; men were active, independent, coarse, and strong. These divisions between male and female domains, the Doctrine of the Two Spheres, formed the basis for the polarization of male and female interests and activities. The Cult of True Womanhood reached its height in the late Victorian period, toward the end of the 19th century. The Victorian ideal of manhood was the basis for what Joseph Pleck (1981a, b; 1984) referred to as the Male Sex Role Identity. Pleck discussed the Male

GENDERED VOICES
Raising a Sissy

"Being twins, my brother and I were closer than most brothers and sisters. We didn't look alike, but we were together a lot," a college student told me. "We had different interests. I was the one who went outside and helped my dad, while my brother stayed inside with my mother. Everybody always said I should have been the boy and he should have been the girl.

"He didn't want to play alone, so he played with me and my friends—dolls, or whatever we played. He never got to choose. And when we played dolls, he got the one that was left after me and my friend chose the ones we wanted. My mom said, 'Let him play with the Ken doll—you have two Ken dolls—don't make him play with a Barbie,' but we didn't. So he got the Barbie with one arm missing or something.

"I always liked the outdoor activities, and my brother didn't. I was so upset that I couldn't join the Cub Scouts. My dad was a troop leader, and I just couldn't understand why I couldn't join; I had always done outdoor things with my dad. Besides, the Brownies did wimpy things, and the Cub Scouts did neat stuff. I was so ticked off.

"When we were in about the 7th grade, I told my mother 'Mom you're raising a sissy,' and I told her that my brother should stop hanging around with her and start doing things more typical of boys. She was really angry with me for saying so.

"Did we change as we grew up? I don't consider myself very feminine—I don't take anything off anybody. My mom can't believe that her daughter acts like I do. I still like outdoor activities—camping, hiking, bicycling. I don't think I've changed as much as my brother has. I wouldn't consider him a sissy now. In high school he played football, and he started being more in line with what everyone would consider masculine. As an adult, he's not a sissy at all, but I'm still kind of an adult tomboy."

Sex Role Identity as the dominant conceptualization of masculinity in our society and as a source of problems, both for society and for individual men.

Pleck (1984) explored the historical origins of the Male Sex Role Identity by reviewing the social climate of late 19th century, citing examples from the late 1800s of the increasing perception that men were not as manly as they once had been. Growing industrialization pressured men to seek employment in order to be good providers for their families, a role that became increasingly difficult for men to fulfill (Bernard, 1981), thus endangering their masculinity. In addition, education became a factor in employment, and men often held better jobs (and were thus better providers) if they were educated. Pleck discussed how education during early childhood became the province of women and how these elementary school teachers tried to make boys into well-behaved pupils—in other words, "sissies."

The prohibition against being a sissy is a strong element of the Male Sex Role Identity. According to Brannon (1976, p. 12), it is one of the four themes he saw as the essence of the Male Sex Role. The entire list included:

1. **No Sissy Stuff**: The stigma of all stereotyped feminine characteristics and qualities, including openness and vulnerability.
2. **The Big Wheel**: Success, status, and the need to be looked up to.
3. **The Sturdy Oak**: A manly air of toughness, confidence, and self-reliance.
4. **Give 'Em Hell**: The aura of aggression, violence, and daring.

The more closely that a man conforms to these characteristics, the closer he is to being a "real man." As Brannon pointed out, the pressure is strong to live up to this idealization of masculinity, which is as ideal and unrealistic as the True Woman of the Cult of True Womanhood. However, even men who are fairly successful in adopting the Male Sex Role Identity may be poorly adjusted, unhappy people, as this role prohibits close personal relationships, even with wives or children, and requires competition and achievement at work.

Pleck (1981a) suggested that rather than adhering to the Male Sex Role, men have started to make significant departures from that role's requirements; they have begun to question the desirability of the Male Sex Role Identity. He proposed a new model, which he called Sex Role Strain, that departs in many ways from the Male Sex Role Identity concept. Pleck argued that during the 1960s and 1970s, both men and women started to make significant departures from their traditional roles. Men began to behave in ways that violate the Male Sex Role, but he also acknowledged that the features of the Male Sex Role Identity remain a powerful influence over what both men and women believe men should be. Although many men deviate from the role and some even believe that the role is harmful to them personally and to society, the Male Sex Role Identity has retained its power to shape beliefs and to make men worry that they are not living up to this role's requirements.

Development of Stereotypes

In examining the research on social theories of gender development, Chapter 7 reviewed the process of gender development, including some information about the development of gender stereotypes. This body of research indicates that gender learning consists of several components, which children begin to acquire around age 2 years and may not complete until they are 7 or 8 years old. The first of these components to be learned is the ability to label the sexes, and this initial gender information may be adequate to allow children to begin to develop gender stereotypes. "Once children can accurately label the sexes, they begin to form gender stereotypes and their behavior is influenced by these gender-associated expectations" (Martin & Little, 1990, p. 1438). Thus, children as young as 3 years old start to show signs of gender stereotyping.

Research by Carol Lynn Martin, Carolyn Wood, and Jane Little (1990) revealed a pattern in the course of gender stereotype development. These researchers presented 4- to 6-year-olds with information about a child's toy interests and asked about what other toys this child might like. The children demonstrated selective stereotyping, making gender-stereotypical judgments about children whose toy interests were similar to their own but failing to make stereotypical judgments for children whose interests were different from their own. This finding demonstrated not only the complexity of stereotypes but also the tendency for children to develop an understanding of their own gender before the other.

Greater gender stereotyping also appeared in a second study with 6- to 10-year-olds (Martin et al.,1990). The 6-year-olds made the same stereotypical judgments as the children in the first study; that is, their judgments were stereotypical for children

---

❈ GENDERED VOICES
You Don't Hit Girls

"She's a girl—I can't hit her. You don't hit girls," a 16-year-old boy said, when his mother asked him why didn't he hit his sister rather than throw a chair. Their mother thought it was probably appropriate for him to hit her, because his sister had spent about 16 years of their lives beating on him, and he'd never retaliated. Mom thought it was about time.

The two siblings had always been very competitive, and the girl had dominated her brother, both physically and verbally. She remembers fighting with her brother throughout their childhood and always winning. "I remember lying in our playpen when we were about 18 months old, kicking him. He acted like a baby, even though he was older than I was. I never held back and I beat him. I always won. I remember one incident that was particularly bad. We were in junior high school, and for some reason, I got mad at him while we were at school. My father had warned us not to fight at school, so I waited until we had gotten off the school bus and jumped him in the front yard. It was pretty bad, because all the kids

on the bus saw us. They were taking bets the next day on our next fight, with me as the favorite. That incident really embarrassed my brother. I realize now that it was a terrible thing to do, but I felt completely justified then.

"I could always make him really angry with my sarcastic comments, and when we were 16 I said something about his girlfriend. He really got mad. He was shaking all over he was so mad, and I could see that he was furious and wanted to hit me, but he didn't. My mom always took his side, and she asked him why he didn't just let me have it. After all those years, she thought I deserved it, and that was when he said, 'She's a girl—I can't hit her. You don't hit girls.' I'm probably lucky he felt that way, because he was bigger than me by that time. He never hit me, and now I feel bad about how terrible I was to him. I didn't see how competitive we were and how that made me try to win at everything we did, usually at his expense."

---

for their own gender but not for the other. The older children, however, made stereotypical judgments for both genders, demonstrating that stereotype development is not complete until middle childhood.

After considering their results and reviewing research by others, Martin et al. proposed a pattern of stereotype development, which appears in Table 8.1. Children in the first stage have learned characteristics and behaviors associated directly with each gender, such as the toy preferences of each. In this stage they have not learned the many secondary associations with gender, and these associations are essential to the formation of stereotypes. In the second stage, "children begin to develop the more indirect and complex associations for information relevant to their own sex but have yet to learn these associations for information relevant to the opposite sex" (Martin et al., 1990, p. 1901). In the third stage, children have learned these indirect and complex associations for the other gender as well as their own, giving them the capability of forming stereotypes for both women and men.

Anita Meehan and Leann Janik (1990) investigated a cognitive process that allows children (and adults) to maintain stereotypes once they have formed. This process is called illusory correlation; that is, "the erroneous perception of covariation between two events when no correlation exists or the perception of a correlation as stronger than it actually is" (Meehan & Janik, p. 84). These researchers maintained that people per-

TABLE 8.1   Stages of Gender Stereotype Development

Stage	Gender Knowledge	Status of Gender Stereotypes
1	Behaviors and characteristics directly associated with gender	Undeveloped
2	Beginnings of indirect associations with gender for own sex but not other	Self-stereotype but none for other sex
3	Complex, indirect gender-related associations for same and other sex	Stereotypes for self and other sex

SOURCE: Based on The development of gender stereotype components (pp. 1891–1904) by C. L. Martin, C. H. Wood, & J.K. Little, 1990, *Child Development, 61.*

ceive that relationships exists between gender and various behaviors when no relationship exists or the relationship is not as strong as their perception indicates.

In a study with 2nd- and 4th-grade children, Meehan and Janik presented pictures of women and men engaged in gender-stereotypical, gender-counterstereotypical, or gender-neutral activities and asked the children to remember who did what. Although there was actually no relationship between the pictured activities and gender, the children remembered more stereotypical than counterstereotypical or neutral activities. Meehan and Janik argued that the perception of correlations can be an important factor in maintaining stereotypes for both children and adults.

With increased gender stereotype knowledge comes both the acceptance of such stereotypes as well as the ability to make individual exceptions to those stereotypes. This latter ability allows for gender flexibility rather than the rigid acceptance of gender stereotypes. Anne Locksley and her colleagues (Locksley, Borgida, Brekke, & Hepburn, 1980) found that college students deviated from gender stereotypes in evaluating men and women, relying more on information about the individual than on gender-stereotypical information. This study showed that college students can be flexible in their evaluations.

By studying gender stereotyping in individuals ranging from kindergarten children to college students, Monica Biernat (1991) found that the flexible application of gender stereotypes increases with age. She found that younger children relied more on gender information than on information about individuals when making judgments about people, whereas older individuals took into account information about deviations from gender stereotypes. This pattern of development indicates that the acquisition of full information concerning gender stereotypes is accompanied by greater flexibility in the use of stereotypes but that the tendency to rely on the stereotype is always present.

Therefore, the development of gender stereotypes begins early, with 3-year-olds knowing about gender-related differences in behavior. As children acquire information about gender, they become capable of forming and maintaining elaborate stereotypes for men and women, but they also become more willing to make exceptions to the gender rules they have learned. Older children and adults are more willing to allow for deviations from stereotypes when they consider people's characteristics and past behavior. Nevertheless, gender stereotypes provide a system for classifying people that operates as a standard throughout people's lives, influencing their expectations for self and others, as well as in making judgments about people based on their gender-related characteristics and behaviors.

Perceptions of Women and Men

How have these stereotypes influenced people's perceptions of men and women? Do people measure women by the feminine stereotype of the Cult of True Womanhood? Will men experience problems if they do not adopt all of the characteristics of the Male Sex Role Identity? Or have the changes in women's and men's behaviors produced changes in the stereotypes, broadening the boundaries of acceptable behaviors for men and women?

Michael Cicone and Diane Ruble (1978) investigated beliefs about the "typical male" and found that both children and adults describe men in ways that match some parts of the Male Sex Role Identity. Those descriptions were a close match for Brannon's (1976) categories—No Sissy Stuff, the Big Wheel, the Sturdy Oak, and Give 'Em Hell. In reviewing studies on both children's and adults' beliefs, Cicone and Ruble concluded that they could summarize findings from the various studies into three dimensions—activity and achievement orientation, dominance, and level-headedness.

The dimension of activity and achievement orientation includes characteristics that would make a man "the Big Wheel"—ambitious, competitive, independent, and a leader. The characteristics that Cicone and Ruble listed in the dominance category described men as aggressive, powerful, assertive, and boastful; that is, "Give 'Em Hell." The characteristic that they called level-headedness matches the "the Sturdy Oak," a logical, self-controlled, and unemotional way of dealing with other people and the world. However, this last dimension was present only in studies with adults, whereas Cicone and Ruble found evidence for the first two in both children's and adults' views of males. Martin (1989) found evidence for "No Sissy Stuff" when she investigated children's use of gender-related information in making judgments about personal acceptance. She found that both 4- and 10-year-olds said that they disliked children described as "sissies." Therefore, elements of the Male Sex Role, including its requirements and prohibitions, are part of how people think about men.

Paul Rosenkrantz and his colleagues (Rosenkrantz, Vogel, Bee, Broverman, & Broverman, 1968) studied stereotypes of gender roles by investigating the beliefs held by college students in the 1960s and found strong evidence for acceptance of gender stereotypes by both college men and women. They asked students to list items that would differentiate women and men and obtained a list of traits and behaviors that both men and women accepted as making such a differentiation. Table 8.2 shows their findings, which contain many of the characteristics of the Cult of True Womanhood and of the Male Sex Role Identity.

Rosenkrantz and his colleagues also found that these college students clearly evaluated themselves as masculine or feminine. That is, male and female college students held personal self-concepts that reflected stereotypical gender differences. Another of

TABLE 8.2 Stereotypic Traits of Men and Women

Male-Valued Traits

Aggressive	Knows the way of the world
Independent	Feelings not easily hurt
Unemotional	Adventurous
Hides emotions	Makes decisions easily
Objective	Never cries
Easily influenced	Acts as a leader
Dominant	Self-confident
Likes math and science	Not uncomfortable about being aggressive
Not excitable in a minor crisis	Ambitious
Active	Able to separate feelings from ideas
Competitive	Not dependent
Logical	Not conceited about appearance
Worldly	Thinks men are superior to women
Skilled in business	Talks freely about sex with men
Direct	

Female-Valued Traits

Does not use harsh language	Interested in own appearance
Talkative	Neat in habits
Tactful	Quiet
Gentle	Strong need for security
Aware of feelings of others	Expresses tender feelings
Religious	

SOURCE: From Sex-role stereotypes and self-concepts in college students (p. 291) by P. Rosenkrantz, S. Vogel, H. Bee, I. Broverman, and D.M. Broverman, 1968, *Journal of Consulting and Clinical Psychology, 32.* Copyright 1968 by American Psychological Association. Reprinted by permission.

their findings was that both the women and the men in the study positively rated more masculine than feminine traits. Rosenkrantz et al. expressed some surprise at the negative evaluations that women gave to the stereotypically feminine characteristics; that is, to characteristics they acknowledged that they possessed. This more positive evaluation of masculine over feminine characteristics showed some prejudice against stereotypically feminine and for stereotypically masculine characteristics by both men and women.

Inge Broverman and her colleagues (Broverman, Vogel, Broverman, Clarkson, & Rosenkrantz, 1972) examined gender role stereotypes and concluded that a bias exists in favor of characteristics associated with men. Although people perceive both positive and negative aspects of stereotypically masculine and feminine characteristics, "stereotypically masculine traits are more often perceived to be desirable than are stereotypically feminine characteristics" (Broverman et al., 1972, p. 75).

Other researchers have also found prejudice against or problems with the feminine stereotype relating to mental health. Jacob Orlofsky and Connie O'Heron (1987) found differences in self-esteem and adjustment that related to gender role characteristics, with masculine traits having the advantage. They used two tests that distinguished masculine and feminine traits in terms of the instrumental-expressive distinction. Their findings showed that men and women whose scores revealed more instrumental characteristics were also better adjusted and had higher self-esteem than people whose scores revealed higher expressive qualities. These researchers interpreted these results as evidence that positive instrumental characteristics, such as independence, self-reliance, ability to deal calmly with stress, and willingness to take risks, are positively related to self-esteem and adjustment, regardless of the person's gender. Positive expressive characteristics, such as compassion, affection, sensitivity to the needs of others, and sympathy did not relate to adjustment or self-esteem as the positive instrumental characteristics did. Although both types of characteristics have positive social value, the masculine-instrumental characteristics were the ones related to positive mental health.

Not all research has found negative implications for the characteristics stereotypically associated with femininity. Alice Eagly and her colleagues (Eagly, Mladinic, & Otto, 1991) asked people to evaluate the general category of women or men and found that women received more favorable evaluations than men. These researchers acknowledged that women may be poorly evaluated in some situations, but their results indicated that people have positive feelings about the characteristics stereotypically associated with women: People believe that these characteristics provide fine examples of human beings. Indeed, these participants evaluated women more favorably than men. (See Diversity Highlight: "Do Stereotypes of Nationalities Apply to Women?" for an examination of how these positive evaluations can transcend other negative stereotyping and yet still have negative implications.)

Rosenkrantz et al. (1968) speculated that male and female stereotypes might change rapidly, as the social roles of men and women have been changing. Later research by Lloyd Lueptow (1985) indicated that these changes in gender role stereotypes had not occurred by the 1980s. At three-year intervals from 1974 to 1983,

---

✥ GENDERED VOICES
The Problem Disappeared

"Our car was having some problem, and my wife took it to be repaired," a man said. "She called me from the auto repair place, furious with the treatment she had received. The men there were stonewalling her—failing to listen to what she was telling them and treating her as though she couldn't possibly be capable of relating problems concerning an automobile. She was steamed.

"I went down there, and the problem disappeared. I was a man and apparently privy to the innermost secrets of automobiles. They treated me as though I would understand everything perfectly. Both my wife and I thought it was really absurd."

"One of my friends was upset that it cost $3.20 to get a shirt dry cleaned," a woman told me. "She asked them why it was so much—the shirt was a tailored, plain shirt. They told her that women's blouses cost more than men's shirts, regardless of the style, because women's clothes don't fit on the standard machine for pressing and must be hand pressed. She wondered if that was really true, and she gave the shirt to a male friend to take to the same dry cleaners. The problem apparently disappeared, because they charged him $1.25 for the very same garment. Isn't that beyond stereotyping?"

❈ **DIVERSITY HIGHLIGHT**
Do Stereotypes of Nationalities Apply to Women?

In addition to gender stereotypes, people also have stereotypes of people of different nationalities; that is, people in one nation tend to agree about the attributes they believe people of different nationalities possess. Alice Eagly and Mary Kite (1987) discussed how most people do not have sufficient face-to-face interaction with people of different nationalities to supply a basis for nationality stereotypes as they do for gender stereotypes.

Eagly and Kite hypothesized that people form stereotypes of nationalities on the basis of exposure to newsworthy events involving those nationalities. For many nations this information is largely negative, being based on reports of international competition or hostilities. In addition, the people who are most visible in these international situations are most often men, so Eagly and Kite reasoned that people's stereotypes of different nationalities may be based more on information associated with men than women. If so, the stereotypes of nationalities might not extend to women as they do to men, and women of different nationalities might be perceived in terms of their gender stereotype.

On the basis of U.S. college students' ratings of men and women from 28 different countries, Eagly and Kite (1987, p. 459) found that the "stereotypes of nationalities are more similar to stereotypes of the men than of the women of these nationalities." But the differences between countries was also large, and these researchers found some patterns of response they had not anticipated. In some positively evaluated countries, the predicted relationship—namely, that the national stereotype would match men more than women—did not occur. The participants perceived both men and women from these nations as having qualities often associated with women—that is, of being warm and concerned with the welfare of others. For the nationalities with negative ratings, Eagly and Kite's participants tended to see the men as having more negative and the women as having more positive qualities. Therefore, people tend to perceive women more positively than men when the women are from negatively evaluated nationalities, but they perceive both men and women similarly when they come from positively evaluated nations.

This research demonstrated the strength of gender stereotypes and how gender and people's nationality stereotypes interact with their gender stereotypes. The gender stereotypes seem to overrule the nationality stereotypes to form positive views of women of many nationalities. This positive view of women does not include power or competence. Women of many nationalities are seen in ways that are consistent with the feminine stereotype—as kind, caring, and nonthreatening.

Lueptow asked college students to rate themselves and either the typical woman (for women) or man (for men). He found evidence of *stronger* gender stereotypes in 1983 than in 1974. Therefore, gender stereotypes did not weaken during a time when gender-related behaviors changed. However, Eagly et al. (1991) found that participants in their study rated women more positively than men, and these results may provide evidence that the prejudice against feminine characteristics may have shown some of the predicted positive changes.

Men may be the victims of more stringent stereotyping than women, according to a study by Barbara Hort and her colleagues (Hort, Fagot, & Leinbach, 1990). After asking college students to describe their views of women and men, the results indicated that the participants described men in more stereotypical terms than women. For both physical and social characteristics, the masculine stereotype was more extreme than the feminine. The women in the study tended to describe men's physical appearance in stereotypical terms, and the men tended to stereotype men in terms of their social characteristics. Although both women and men can be misrepresented through stereotypes, men may be seen in more stereotypical terms than women—by both men and women.

In addition to being the victims of more stringent stereotyping, men are the perpetrators of more stringent stereotyping than women. Thomas Parish and Merton Powell (1980) found that men were more negative than women about both men and women. The men in their study gave negative evaluations to descriptions of both men and women, confirming men's tendency to be stringent in their views. Mary Hudak (1993) found that some men were more likely to stereotype than other men. Men who scored high in stereotypical masculinity viewed women in more stereotypical terms than men who were not so strongly stereotypical.

Some evidence suggests that men and women may not apply the stereotypes to themselves as strictly as they apply these stereotypes to others. John Williams and Deborah Best (1990) studied U.S. college students to understand their beliefs about gender stereotypes and how the students matched those stereotypes. Like other researchers, Williams and Best found evidence for differing male and female stereotypes. However, they also found that these college students rated themselves as varying from the stereotype. Although people hold stereotypical views of men and women, they may make exceptions for themselves, allowing a wider variety of behavior than the stereotype would permit. By allowing such routine, personal exceptions, people decrease the power of stereotypes to control and restrict their lives.

Kay Deaux and Laurie Lewis (1984) investigated the content of gender stereotypes and identified four separate components that people use to differentiate male from female—traits, behaviors, physical characteristics, and occupations. All of these components are relatively independent, but people associate a set of features from each of these with women and a different set with men. On the basis of knowledge of one of these dimensions, people extend judgments to the other three. Figure 8.1 shows the components of this model; the arrows indicate the associations among components. Given a gender label for a target person, people will make inferences concerning the person's appearance, traits, gender role behaviors, and occupation. Information about one component can affect the others, with people attempting to maintain consistency among the components.

Deaux and Lewis found that people viewed men and women as more different in terms of physical features than psychological characteristics and also that people relied more on physical information than on trait, behavioral, or occupational information in making gender-related judgments. As Figure 8.1 shows, Deaux and Lewis found that physical appearance was the most influential of these components, affecting the other components more strongly than information about traits, behaviors, or occupations affected judgments about appearance. Given information about behaviors, people make inferences about traits, and information about occupations can affect judgments about behaviors. In addition, specific personal information can outweigh gender as a factor in subsequent judgments about a person. For example, men who were described as managing the house or taking care of children also were judged as likely to be emotional and gentle. Such counterstereotypical information about men also increased the likelihood that such men would be judged as likely to be homosexual.

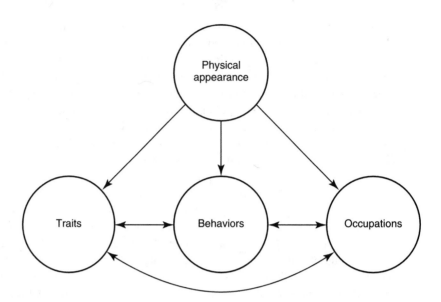

FIGURE 8.1 Components of Deaux and Lewis's Model of Gender Stereotyping

Although the participants in Deaux and Lewis's study saw differences in the traits, behaviors, physical characteristics, and occupations of women and men, their ratings of the two categories reflected the possibility that a woman may have some characteristics more typical of men or a man may have some characteristic more typical of women. That is, people do not view the stereotypes for women and men as separate and dichotomous but as probabilistic and overlapping categories. For example, Deaux and Lewis asked people to judge the probability of a man and woman having certain characteristics. On a scale of 0 (no chance) to 1.00 (certainty), their participants judged the

---

✣— GENDERED VOICES
If You Had Been a Woman

A male college student went to the dormitory basement to check on his laundry, only to find his clothes gone. He soon noticed that all the laundry was gone and recalled that the two men he had passed in the hall were carrying mesh laundry bags full of clothes. He had been robbed.

He ran after the men, but they had disappeared, so he reported the theft to the campus police. They asked him for a description of the men he had seen, but he wasn't able to give a very detailed descrip-

tion. When they asked, "What were they wearing," he couldn't give more detail than "Clothes." The police officers said, "If you had been a woman, you would be able to do much better. Women notice clothes."

The young man wondered, "Is that right? Would a woman really have attended to the clothing of two men she passed in the hall?" He wasn't sure that the police officers were right, but he thought that the comment was very stereotypical on their part.

probability that a man would be strong as .66, a high probability but not a certainty. However, they also judged the chances that a woman would be strong as .44. Although these judgments reflected stereotypical views of the relative strength of men and women, being male was not perfectly associated with strength nor was being female associated with complete lack of strength.

Research has tended to confirm not only the existence of gender stereotypes but also their similarity to the ideal woman according to the Cult of True Womanhood and the male-identified man of the Male Sex Role Identity model. Over the past 30 years of research on gender stereotypes, many studies have found prejudice in favor of the male role, but recent studies have found more favorable ratings for the female role. Research also has indicated that people may be willing to make exceptions for themselves in deviating from stereotypical gender-related behaviors, decreasing the power of these stereotypes to control behavior. As for the structure of gender stereotypes, research by Deaux and Lewis has suggested that gender stereotypes are complex, with multiple components and inferences about one component based on information about others.

Stereotypes across Cultures

Gender stereotypes still exist and affect how women and men think of themselves and how they evaluate their own behavior as well as the behavior of others. But how do the participants in such studies (mostly European-American college students in the United States) compare to people from other ethnic groups? Do cultures around the world and ethnic groups in North America make similar distinctions between what is considered masculine and feminine? Do other cultures stereotype gender-related behaviors?

The gender stereotypes for African Americans differ from those of European Americans, and Donna Davenport and John Yurich (1991) looked to history to explain these differences. They wrote that slavery disrupted the patriarchal family patterns that existed in Africa, rendering the men powerless and imposing a type of equality between women and men: Both were slaves. After slavery had ended, racism restricted earning power, keeping African-American men from attaining the type of power associated with the breadwinner role in patriarchal families. Instead, women not only worked at caring for their children, but they also worked outside their homes to support their families.

African-American women's employment has led to the view that African-American families are matriarchies, but this stereotype is not completely accurate (Davenport & Yurich, 1991). African-American families fit several different patterns, depending on economic level and geographical location. Middle-class African-American families (regardless of ethnicity) tend to be similar to other middle-class families, having a couple and children. Poor families are more likely to consist of a single woman and her children.

Stereotypes exist for African Americans in each of these patterns. Poor African Americans are stereotyped as lazy and dangerous, with the women having many children and the men being unemployed and possibly criminal. Media portrayals and news stories perpetuate these stereotypes despite their lack of validity for the majority of poor African Americans.

For middle-class African Americans, gender stereotypes vary from those of European Americans. African-American men have trouble in attaining the power associated with the male stereotype, but African-American women, with their greater likelihood of attaining a college education, can be successful, independent professionals. This lifestyle can put them in a position of not needing a man to provide for them, and the self-reliance of such African-American women has added both to the tension between the sexes and to the stereotype of African-American women as strong, resourceful women who value both motherhood and employment.

The different gender stereotypes for African-American women and men might mean that they also differ from European Americans in their beliefs about self and others. William Bailey and his colleagues (Bailey, Silver, & Oliver, 1990) studied the attitudes toward women's roles of European-American compared to African-American students in the United States. They found no differences between the two different ethnic groups, but they found that men and women held different attitudes. Both European-American and African-American women held more positive attitudes toward women than European-American and African-American men. Thus, these researchers found a stronger effect for gender than for ethnic background for U.S. college students' views.

Hispanic-American women have also been the topic of research on gender stereotypes related to their ethnic background. Ena Vazquez-Nuttall and her colleagues (Vazquez-Nuttall, Romero-Garcia, & De Leon, 1987) reviewed studies that measured the perceptions of masculinity and femininity of Hispanic-American (mostly Mexican-American) women in North America. Davenport and Yurich (1991, p. 67) described the stereotypes of Hispanic Americans: "The men were depicted as clearly oppressive and the women as passive and compliant." Both Davenport and Yurich and Vazquez-Nuttall et al. questioned the traditional concept that Hispanic culture is one of male dominance and female submissiveness, conceding that the dynamics of the relationships were often more complex than the stereotypes. This complexity is especially true for the women who have come into contact with European-American culture by pursuing education and careers.

Several of the studies reviewed by Vazquez-Nuttall et al. showed that Hispanic-American women held a more feminine stereotype of the ideal woman than African-American or European-American women. They also discussed evidence suggesting that Hispanic-American women see themselves as more masculine than their ideal. Therefore, the stereotype of Hispanic-American women may be feminine, but these women feel that they might not fit these stereotypes, just as studies on European-American college students have found (Williams & Best, 1990).

Attempting to understand the development of gender differences across many cultures, Beatrice Whiting and Carolyn Edwards (1988) conducted a large cross-cultural study on the development of social behaviors. They tested children from 12 different communities in Kenya, Liberia, India, the Philippines, Okinawa, Mexico, and the United States. Rather than limiting their investigation to different treatment of children by gender, they wanted to look at the experiences and personal interactions of children and

GENDERED VOICES
Some Things Are Different There

"I think of femininity more in terms of what a woman wears than anything else," a young man told me. He had grown up on an island in the Mediterranean, lived in Paris for two years, and now lives in the United States. He sees some differences in what is considered feminine and masculine in the three cultures he has known. "Where I grew up, there was very little sexual activity among teenagers; it was a very conservative culture, and adolescent sexuality was strictly discouraged. The girls didn't dress in any way that was sexual, so they didn't seem very feminine to me. I guess I would consider some of them more feminine than others, probably in the same way that a person in the U.S. would: Small and dainty girls were more feminine. So I don't see any differences there.

"In Paris, nothing was hidden—things were openly sexual. The United States is very sexualized culture, but there are differences. For example, kinds of clothing that people wore in Paris were different from the United States, and those differences related to femininity. Wearing jeans and tennis shoes would be considered very unfeminine rather than just another way to dress. I remember one girl in my student group who often wore tennis shoes, jeans, and a big sweater, and she was considered very unfeminine. Not that her way of dressing kept her from being pretty or attractive, but she didn't seem feminine. I guess I would say that Paris was less casual, and the women seemed more feminine than in the United States or in the Mediterranean.

"There were also some differences in what was considered masculine. At home, men tend to be small, so masculinity is not determined by size but more by behavior. Even men who are 5'4" or 5'6" can be macho, depending on what they do. Gangsters are very masculine, and so are those who are involved in politics, especially radical politics. The communists are considered the most masculine—lots of testosterone there. Men can demonstrate their masculinity by drinking—it has to be liquor and straight, without ice—and smoke unfiltered cigarettes. Also, women who drink or smoke are considered masculine. So masculinity is a matter of what you do in the Mediterranean, not how you look, except the gangsters always have a three-day growth of beard.

"One of the differences in what is considered masculine involves bodybuilding and weight lifting. Men in the Mediterranean and in Paris just didn't do anything like that. They wouldn't consider bodybuilding masculine; it would be considered odd rather than a way to demonstrate masculinity. If they exercise, it's oriented more toward fitness than bodybuilding, so that seems very American to me.

"Political activism is masculine where I come from, whether men or women are involved. As I said, the communist radicals are considered very macho, and women who become involved in politics or become lawyers are considered masculine. As career opportunities increase for women, this may change, but now, women lose their femininity when they gain power through legal or political careers—even more than in the United States.

"Also, on the island where I grew up, there was a status for women that I haven't seen anywhere else. Postmenopausal women lose their sexuality, but they gain power and can become very influential in the community. They are considered almost neuter in terms of sexuality, so they are not feminine at all, but these women can have a lot of power, whereas younger women do not. As long as a women is young and unmarried or married, she has almost no voice in the community, but these older women made a transition to a position of respect and power.

"The only men who lose their sexuality in a similar way are artists, who are not considered feminine but almost neutral. Being an artist is well accepted and doesn't really carry any connotations of feminity, unlike homosexuality, which is strongly prohibited. It is a conservative culture, and homosexual activity is not tolerated at all, unlike Paris, where gay men and lesbians are very open about their sexuality. The United States seems to be the worst of both cultures in that respect; homosexuality is fairly open but poorly tolerated. That seems like a bad combination to me. As far as masculinity and femininity and homosexuality are concerned, I can't see any relationship. I know I can't tell who is homosexual by how masculine the men seem or how feminine the women seem. So sexual orientation does not seem to coincide with these characteristics to me."

the settings in which they developed. Whiting and Edwards (1988, pp. 5–6) explain their approach:

Rather than analyzing the age, sex, and cultural differences in children's activities and companions as simply the result of developmental changes of socialization pressure by parents, other caregivers, and teachers, we are analyzing these differences as a cause in the process of socialization.

Whiting and Edwards found some differences in the treatment of and subsequent behavior of boys and girls, but they also found many similarities in the types of interactions children experienced. Their analysis showed that age was more important than gender in predicting the experiences of children in these various cultures.

This is not to say that these cultures failed to make distinctions between the behaviors and traits related to gender—all did, but these differences in gender roles often made little difference in the lives of young children. Older children tended to be treated differently according to their gender, including having different assigned chores. For example, in most of the cultures both girls and boys performed chores similar to work done by adult women, but girls were more likely to participate in the care of younger children than boys.

Whiting and Edwards found that during infancy and early childhood, children spend much of their time in their homes, surrounded primarily by their family, especially their mother and other female family members. After middle childhood children were more likely to participate in same-sex groups, with boys beginning to avoid girls and women, especially in some strongly male-dominated cultures. In most of the cultures they studied, girls experienced more pressure than boys to behave in socially acceptable ways, and girls showed more nurturant behaviors. Whiting and Edwards attributed the greater female nurturance to their greater involvement in child care.

Despite some differences among cultures, Whiting and Edwards found situations and behaviors that they interpreted as suggesting pancultural similarities—similarities across many cultures. Williams and Best (1990) also investigated cross-cultural gender stereotypes, studying 30 different countries in North America, South America, Europe, Asia, Africa, and Oceania. Their study included children, but the emphasis was on gender stereotypes held by young adults. They asked college students in these countries to rate a list of 300 adjectives as to whether each description was more frequently associated with men or women. Their goal was to study the associations that people in different cultures make about women and men and look for female and male stereotypes.

Like Whiting and Edwards's cross-cultural study, Williams and Best's research also revealed more similarities than differences in the gender stereotypes of many cultures. They identified six adjectives that were male associated in all of the cultures—adventurous, dominant, forceful, independent, masculine, and strong—and three adjectives that were female identified in all cultures—sentimental, submissive, and superstitious. In addition, a wide list of adjectives appeared as male associated or female associated in a large majority of the cultures, and only a few adjectives were male associated by one culture and female associated in another, or vice versa. Williams and

Best interpreted these findings as evidence for pancultural similarities in gender stereotypes.

Some of the cultures in Williams and Best's study evaluated the male stereotype more favorably than the female stereotype, but this pattern did not appear with consistency. Considering the entire group of countries, they found no tendency to evaluate one stereotype more favorably than the other. In addition, the young adults in some of the cultures made sharp differentiations between the characteristics they attributed to male and female stereotypes, whereas others made relatively few such distinctions. For example, the male stereotype was much more positive than the female stereotype in Nigeria, with views that males are much more active and much stronger than females. In Italy, the differences were reversed or minimized: The female stereotype was the more positive, and beliefs about activity and strength showed small differences.

Despite similarities in many aspects of gender stereotypes, not all cultures hold the same views of what traits, characteristics, and patterns of behavior men and women should exhibit. However, the researchers who have studied gender stereotypes in many cultures (Whiting & Edwards, 1988; Williams & Best, 1990) have argued that behavior is not infinitely variable: Human behavior tends to fall into patterns, with some similarities in all cultures. These patterns may be limited by the biological underpinnings of the human species or by the similar problems that all social groups must solve. For example, women give birth, and young children require nursing and care. An efficient social arrangement would involve women not only in bearing and nursing children but also in other child-care activities. Men are larger and stronger than women, equipping them for tasks that require these characteristics, such as hunting. But even jobs that have few physical hazards, such as working in an office, force men from home and family. Such divisions of activities form the basis for gender roles and furnish the potential for gender stereotyping.

Function of Stereotyping

The term *stereotyping* has negative connotations, but some theorists have considered the positive as well as the negative effects of stereotyping. Other researchers have demonstrated that stereotyping produces such distortions and incorrect generalizations that its disadvantages are overwhelming.

Carol Lynn Martin and Charles Halverson, Jr. (1981), contended that gender stereotyping is a normal cognitive process. They explained gender stereotyping as an especially useful type of information processing that allows children to form categories based on gender and to understand this important attribute, if in a simplified and distorted way. Martin and Halverson acknowledged that the simplification and distortion inherent in stereotyping can have negative effects, but they argued that the positive benefits to children of forming gender stereotypes outweigh the negative effects of making some mistakes and thinking too narrowly about gender-related behaviors. Therefore, the function of gender stereotyping can be understood in developmental terms as a useful way to approach the complexities of gender.

However, Eagly (1987b) pointed out that understanding the development of behavior does not necessarily lead to an understanding of the factors that maintain behavior in adults. That is, the existence of gender stereotypes in children does not necessitate the maintenance of gender stereotypes in adults. Research has indicated that older children, adolescents, and adults are willing to make exceptions to the dictates of their gender stereotypes, both for themselves and for others. The tendency to see gender stereotypes as inflexible prescriptions for behavior lessens with age. So what is the point of keeping a rule with so many exceptions?

One view of the maintenance of gender stereotypes is the "kernel of truth" position—that stereotypes have some validity as well as some inaccuracy (Martin, 1987). The existence of gender roles, the behaviors performed more often by men or women, forms the basis for gender stereotypes. That is, the social roles that women and men fulfill allow people to perceive differences between men and women and to extend these differences to areas where none exists. Martin (1987) assessed the accuracy of gender stereotypes and found that gender stereotypes are accurate in encompassing actual differences between men's and women's behavior and reported characteristics and that the inaccuracy comes from the exaggeration of stereotypes, making them much more inclusive than reported gender differences.

Janet Swim (1994) also evaluated the accuracy of gender stereotypes and found that people do not consistently overestimate gender differences. Her results, however, indicate that both overestimation and underestimation of gender-related behavior occur. Perceptions of women and men deviate from accuracy in some ways but not necessarily in a stereotypical direction, and Swim found that gender perceptions are often accurate. That is, the participants in her study tended to underestimate rather than overestimate gender differences, and they were often accurate in matching their descriptions to the magnitude of actual gender differences. Swim acknowledged that her college student participants may have underestimated gender differences out of a desire to appear unbiased and that these participants may have less stereotypical views of men and women than other groups of people. Her study showed that gender stereotyping is not inevitable.

Curt Hoffman and Nancy Hurst (1990) investigated the discrepancy between observed gender differences and exaggerated gender stereotypes and concluded that gender stereotypes are not based primarily on observed gender differences. Observation cannot form the basis for stereotyping, as many gender differences are statistically too small for personal observation to form the basis for these differences. Rather, they argued that gender stereotypes are rationalizations for the distribution of men and women into different social roles.

Hoffman and Hurst tested their view in two clever experiments in which they provided descriptions of members of two fictional categories, the majority of each differing in their activities. Hoffman and Hurst did not specify a total division of labor in their scenarios; in one study they described one group as 80% "child-raisers" and 80% of another group as "city-workers." The researchers wanted to see if their participants would explain the differing activities by rationalizing different personalities that suited each for the activity most common in its group. They found strong evidence of stereotyping, including differences in personality traits. When they specified a habitual activity, they found that people deduce an underlying personality trait that would explain why this difference exists. Hoffman and Hurst (1990) concluded that

> *objective sex differences in personality are not necessary to the formation of gender stereotypes; the fact of an unequal role distribution is sufficient.... This result strongly supports the idea that stereotypes such as those based on gender constitute, in part, beliefs about intrinsic, category-wide tendencies or predispositions. (p. 206)*

Therefore, Hoffman and Hurst explained that people feel better, for example, about women being child-care workers or homemakers if they believe that some element of women's personalities suits them to do such work. Additionally, this view holds that if women have the personal qualities that are necessary for such jobs, then men should not hold these jobs. Such rationalizations would also extend to racial or ethnic stereotyping as well as stereotyping based on gender roles. This view of stereotyping proposes that such cognitive processing offers rationalizations for existing situations and allows people to avoid thinking about the complexities of gender.

Power rather than cognitive processing was the explanation that Susan Fiske (1993) offered for stereotyping. She proposed that power encourages stereotyping through differential attention of the powerless and powerful. The powerless attend carefully to the powerful to help understand their motives and predict their behavior. This attention promotes the formation of complex perceptions rather than stereotypes. The powerful, on the other hand, do not have the need to attend to the powerless, who do not exert control over the powerful. This lack of close attention is conducive to stereotyping.

In addition, Fiske contended that the powerful are often attentionally overloaded, making superficial attention common for them, and they may also have a high need for dominance, making them willing to control others. Furthermore, "stereotyping and power are mutually reinforcing because stereotyping itself exerts control, maintaining and justifying the status quo" (Fiske, 1993, p. 621).

Fiske's view highlights the negative aspects of stereotyping, pointing out that stereotyping has more impact than convenience of cognitive processing. The function of gender (or any other type of) stereotyping may be ease of cognitive processing: Stereotypes omit some individual details. This neglect of details allows people to think in simplified ways about a class of individuals rather than about each person on an individual basis. For children, such simplification may be a necessary part of dealing with a complex world. Adolescents and adults are capable of considering information about individuals and allowing violations of stereotypical prescriptions for behavior. However, adolescents and adults still have access to strong stereotypes, and these views influence their expectations about gender-related behavior. For adults, such simplification may be a convenient rationalization for relegating women and men to stereotypical activities or a consequence of the power differentials that exist between men and women in many societies.

Masculinity, Femininity, and Androgyny

As Eleanor Maccoby (1988) pointed out, the concepts of *male* and *female* are relatively easy for people to understand, as these words relate to biological differences understood by everyone except young children. But the concepts of masculine and feminine are much less closely related to biology and thus much more difficult to separate into two nonoverlapping categories: "One can be more or less feminine. One cannot be more or less female" (Maccoby, 1988, p. 762). Nonetheless, these dimensions seem important—perhaps essentially important—and psychologists have attempted to conceptualize and measure masculinity and femininity as part of their attempts to measure other important personality traits. After many years of difficulty with such measurements, the concept of **androgyny**—having the characteristic of both male and female—appeared as an addition to the conceptual framework and several techniques exist for measuring this attribute.

Psychology's attempts to understand and measure masculinity and femininity has had a long history but not a great deal of success (Constantinople, 1973; Lewin, 1984a, b). The problems began with the first effort, and no measurement technique has escaped serious criticism.

After Lewis Terman adapted the Binet intelligence test into the Stanford Binet, he became interested in measuring masculinity and femininity (Lewin, 1984a). Terman believed that masculinity and femininity (MF) were essential components of personality, and he wanted to construct a test to measure these concepts. He and Catherine Cox Miles produced the Attitude Interest Analysis Survey, a 456-item test that appeared in 1936. Terman and Miles chose items for inclusion by determining which ones men and women answered differently, producing items labeled masculine (M), feminine (F), and neutral. They scored the test by awarding one point for each answer to M or F questions and then subtracting F scores from M scores. The resulting MF scores were increasingly positive in the masculine direction and increasingly negative in the feminine direction. Therefore, this early test conceptualized masculinity and femininity as a single dimension, with strong masculinity lying at one extreme and strong femininity at the other.

Both Anne Constantinople (1973) and later Lewin (1984a) criticized the Attitude Interest Analysis Survey for taking a unidimensional, overly simplistic approach to the measurement of masculinity and femininity. Constantinople rejected both the attempt to put both masculinity and femininity on one scale and the decision to place them at opposite ends of a single continuum. She argued that neither unidimensionality nor bipolarity helps in clarifying these concepts. Lewin (1984a) also pointed out other difficulties with the Attitude Interest Analysis Survey, including Terman and Miles's failure to validate the test in any way other than to distinguish men from women and for their acceptance of MF as invariable over different ages. Indeed, children showed stronger masculinity and femininity on the test than mature adults, a finding that Lewin considered unlikely for a valid test. Lewin argued that the Terman and Miles Attitude Interest Analysis Survey actually measured Victorian concepts of masculinity and femininity rather than the masculinity and femininity of individuals.

Although Terman and Miles's test is no longer used, it influenced other measures of masculinity and femininity. The Mf scale of the Minnesota Multiphasic Personality Inventory (MMPI) appeared in 1940 and soon became the most common measure of masculinity and femininity, largely because of its inclusion in this personality test developed to measure psychological disorders (Lewin, 1984b). This scale was also unidimensional and bipolar, with masculinity and femininity at opposite ends of the scale.

However, the psychologists who developed the MMPI were more interested in their Mf scale measuring homosexual tendencies in men than masculinity and femininity in heterosexual men and women. As a result of this interest, their **validation** procedure included a comparison of the Mf responses of 13 homosexual men to the responses of 54 heterosexual male soldiers. They used the responses of the 13 homosexual men as a standard for femininity, thus defining femininity as the responses of these men. The test makers knew that the scale should not be used as a valid measure of femininity, and they were initially tentative in describing its use for a nonhomosexual population. But the test was soon extended to thousands of people, and the reservations disappeared. As Lewin (1984b, p. 181) exclaimed, "It is rather staggering to realize that the *femininity dimension of this popular test was "validated" on a criterion group of 13 male homosexuals!"* (emphasis in original). However, the scale was not even very successful in diagnosing homosexuality in men.

Harrison Gough also constructed a personality test that contained a measure of femininity (Lewin, 1984b). Gough's California Personality Inventory includes a femininity (Fe) scale, but in creating this scale Gough also tried to construct a single scale that would distinguish among more and less feminine women and identify male homosexuals. Lewin (1984b) criticized this test and the approach Gough took, saying that the combination of these two goals was inappropriate. Indeed, the confusion of masculinity-femininity and sexual orientation posed a problem for the understanding of both concepts.

Despite the problems with a unidimensional measure of masculinity-femininity and the poor success with identification of homosexuals with these scales, this approach to the measure of masculinity and femininity was the most common until the 1970s. When theorists realized that masculinity and femininity were separate dimensions from sexual orientation, the measurements of both changed, bringing clarity to both areas.

During the time of unidimensional, bipolar measurements of masculinity and femininity, sociologist Talcott Parsons and social psychologist R. Freed Bales originated an alternative conceptualization to the study of masculinity and femininity (Lewin, 1984b). They formulated the instrumental-expressive distinction, interpreting women's behaviors as expressive and men's behaviors as instrumental. Parsons and Bales made this distinction based on their views of families around the world, contending that men occupy the role of leader, with an autonomy and achievement orientation, whereas women occupy roles of support and nurturance. Although this distinction grew out of their studies of family roles, they neither made systematic observations nor constructed a test to measure their conceptualization. Anthropologists attempted to validate the instrumental-expressive distinction, but according to Lewin (1984b), what these researchers found was biased by their own views of the masculine-feminine d tinction. Parsons and Bales's instrumental-expressive distinction later became imp tant to those who have attempted to conceptualize and measure psychologi masculinity and femininity.

In 1974, Sandra Bem published a different approach to the measurement of m culinity and femininity, adding the concept of androgyny. She proposed that some pe ple have characteristics associated with both masculinity and femininity; that is, sor people are androgynous. The androgyny concept requires both masculinity and fen ninity in combination, so it is incompatible with a unidimensional view of MF. Inste. Bem constructed two scales to capture her concept of androgyny. Her test, the Bem S Role Inventory (BSRI), measured masculinity and femininity with two scales, one tl measured masculinity and one that measured femininity. Figure 8.2 shows the diff ence between the traditional unidimensional approach to personality measurement a Bem's two-dimensional approach.

People who take the BSRI respond to 60 characteristics by rating how well ea of these characteristics applies to them on a 7-point scale. Of the 60 items, 20 repres cultural stereotypes of masculinity (ambitious, independent, competitive), 20 repres femininity (gentle, warm, understanding), and 20 are filler items. The 7-point sc: ranges from *always or almost always true* to *never or almost never true*. Scores on t masculinity and femininity scales yield four different possibilities: masculine, fer nine, androgynous, and undifferentiated. People who score high on the masculin scale and low on the femininity scale would be considered *masculine,* whereas peo who score high on the femininity scale and low on the masculinity scale would be co sidered *feminine.* These people not only accept cultural stereotypes of masculinity femininity, they also reject the other role. Thus, such individuals fit the stereotypi

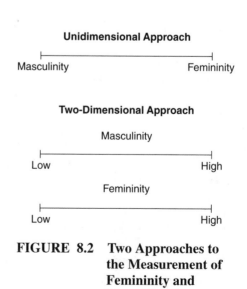

**FIGURE 8.2   Two Approaches to
the Measurement of
Femininity and
Masculinity**

notions of masculinity or femininity, classifications similar to those obtained on other MF tests.

Bem labeled those people who score high on both scales *androgynous* and those who score low on both scales *undifferentiated,* classifications that do not appear in traditional MF tests. Androgynous people evaluate themselves as having many of the characteristics that our culture associates with men and women, whereas those people who are undifferentiated report few traits of either.

The concept of androgyny rapidly grew in popularity. Janet Spence, Robert Helmreich, and Joy Stapp (1974) soon published another test, the Personal Attribute Questionnaire (PAQ), to overcome what they saw as problems with the BSRI (see Spence & Helmreich, 1978). The PAQ also identified people as masculine, feminine, androgynous, and undifferentiated. Both tests continue in use, with some researchers preferring one and some the other. Although the MMPI Mf scale is still widely administered as part of that personality test, researchers interested in measuring masculinity or femininity often use the BSRI and the PAQ rather than any of the older scales that measure masculinity and femininity.

Not all researchers accept the concept of androgyny. Lewin (1984b) also criticized the tests that include measures of androgyny, saying that they provide no revolutionary reconceptualization of the measurement of masculinity and femininity. She contended that the masculinity scales of these tests measure instrumentality and the femininity scales measure expressiveness, the distinction that Parsons and Bales made in the mid 1950s. Lewin's criticism seems well placed, as many researchers now refer to scores on these two scales in terms of instrumentality and expressiveness rather than masculinity and femininity. Indeed, Spence (1985) has acknowledged the inadequacy of even her own measurement of masculinity and femininity (the PAQ) and has adopted the terms *instrumental* and *expressive* to describe the traits that such tests measure. She discussed the conceptual inadequacies of psychology's measurements of masculinity and femininity, proposing that these concepts are even more complex than any existent tests.

Some researchers have adopted David Bakan's (1966) terminology, using the term *agentic* to refer to the assertive, controlling tendencies that are associated with men and *communal* to refer to the concern with the welfare of others associated with women. Although these terms are associated with men and women, the association is weak and includes so much overlap that other terms are a better choice than *masculine* and *feminine.* The choice of these other terms suggests the inadequacy and inaccuracy of the terms *masculinity* and *femininity* in measuring personality.

Although the terms *masculinity* and *femininity* are meaningful to most people, psychologists have not managed to measure them in theoretically meaningful ways. Constantinople (1973, p. 405) went so far as to suggest that "while it is clear that something is being measured by the tests...one is left with the question of whether or not M-F is a useful dimension in studying a normal population." She suggested that a great deal more research and test development are necessary before any valid and useful measurements of these concepts will exist. Lewin (1984b) failed to find the addition of the concept of androgyny adequate to solve the problems she and Constantinople found with the measurement of masculinity and femininity. Lewin (1984b, p. 198) concluded by asking, "Are MF tests satisfactory?" Her answer was: "No. There is no evidence that the MF tests of the last sixty years provide a valid measure of the relative femininity of women or the relative masculinity of men." Instead, Lewin contended that these tests measure our society's conceptualization of what women and men should be using values that date from the Victorian era. The tests purport to measure masculinity and femininity, but measure gender stereotypes rather than personality characteristics.

Summary

The term *gender roles* refers to the activities or behaviors typically associated with women or men, whereas the term *gender stereotypes* refers to the beliefs associated with the characteristics and personalities appropriate to men and women. Current stereotypes of women and men have been influenced by historical views of women and men. The Cult of True Womanhood arose during Victorian times and held that women should be pious, pure, submissive, and domestic. The Male Sex Role Identity proposed that to be successful as men, identification with the elements of that role is necessary. These elements include avoidance of all feminine activities and interests, an achievement orientation, suppression of emotions, and aggression and assertiveness.

Gender stereotyping begins early in development and results in children holding rigid rules for gender-related behavior. Stereotyping is maintained by the illusion that more activities and characteristics are associated with gender than they are. As children approach adolescence, they become more flexible in applying the rules, allowing more exception for individual variation. Research indicates that children and adults accept elements of these stereotypes and use the stereotypes in making decisions and judgments, but adults apply the rules less strictly than children do, having the ability to make many personal exceptions.

Gender stereotypes have four different aspects—physical characteristics, traits, behaviors, and occupations. Each may vary independently, but people make judgments about one based on information about another, forming an interdependent network that people use in making deductions based on limited information about gender-related characteristics.

Cross-cultural research on gender roles and gender stereotyping indicates that all cultures delegate different roles to men and women. The stereotypes of the gender have more similarities than differences across cultures, with the male stereotype fitting the instrumental, or agentic, model and the female stereotype fitting the expressive, or communal, model. However, not all cultures make sharp divisions between the characteristics and behaviors of men and women.

During childhood, stereotyping may serve to simplify cognitive processing and allow children to make easier decisions and judgments. During adulthood, such simplification is not required but still exists. Its function may be convenience, rationalization of the gender-related divisions that exist, or maintenance of power differences between men and women.

The concepts of masculinity and femininity have a long history in psychology as personality traits measured by various psychological tests. The Attitude Interest Analysis Survey appeared in 1936, conceptualizing masculinity and femininity as opposite poles of one continuum. This test is no longer used, but the approach of a unidimensional scale for measuring masculinity-femininity still exists in some personality tests, most notably the Minnesota Multiphasic Personality Inventory (MMPI). In addition to its unidimensional approach to masculinity and femininity, the MMPI also attempted to measure homosexual tendencies in men, going so far as to define femininity in terms of the responses of homosexual men.

A more modern approach to the measurement of masculinity and femininity includes the concept of androgyny. Several tests have adopted this strategy, and such tests include separate scales for masculinity and femininity. People who score high on one but not on the other are considered masculine or feminine, but those who score high on both scales are considered to be androgynous. However, some critics have argued that none of the personality tests that purport to measure masculinity and femininity do so; rather, these tests measure characteristics that would be better labeled as instrumental-expressive or agentic-communal dimensions of personality; the underlying concepts of masculinity and femininity remain elusive.

Glossary

Androgyny a blending of masculinity and femininity in which the desirable characteristics of each combine, resulting in individuals who show many socially desirable characteristics associated with men and women

Gender role a set of socially significant activities associated with men or women

Gender stereotype the beliefs about the characteristics associated with or activities appropriate to men or women

Validation the process of demonstrating that a psychological test measures what it claims to measure; the procedure that demonstrates the accuracy of a test

Suggested Readings

Deaux, Kay. (1987). Psychological constructions of masculinity and femininity. In June Machover Reinisch, Leonard A. Rosenblum, & Stephanie A. Sanders (Eds.), *Masculinity/femininity: Basic perspectives* (pp. 289–303). New York: Oxford University Press. Deaux reviews not only the leading theories of gender role development but also the efforts to measure masculinity and femininity.

Lewin, Miriam. (1984a). "Rather worse than folly?" Psychology measures femininity and masculinity: 1. From Terman and Miles to the Guilfords. In Miriam Lewin (Ed.), *In the shadow of the past: Psychology portrays the sexes* (pp. 155–178); and Lewin, Miriam. (1984b). Psychology measures femininity and masculinity: 2. From "13 gay men"

to the instrumental-expressive distinction. In Miriam Lewin (Ed.), *In the shadow of the past: Psychology portrays the sexes* (pp. 179–204). New York: Columbia University Press. Lewin's two articles critically review psychology's attempts to measure masculinity and femininity. She points out the difficulties and the mistakes, including conceptualizing femininity as the responses of 13 gay men.

Pleck, Joseph H. (1981, September). Prisoners of manliness. *Psychology Today,* pp. 68–79. This popular article presents the elements of Pleck's concept of Male Sex Role Identity, which he sees as unrealistic and constraining for men, women, and society.

Chapter 9

Emotion

HEADLINE

Sex Roles Reign Powerful as Ever in the Emotions
—New York Times, August 23, 1988

The headline from Daniel Goleman's (1988) story suggested that gender roles and gender stereotypes remain important in the experience and expression of emotions. Goleman presented information from various researchers indicating that women and men report different emotions in similar circumstances, and these differences fall along stereotypical lines. Men tend to suppress or deny their emotions, whereas women are more likely to express their feelings. Furthermore, the types of emotions that each expresses and that each suppresses tend to adhere to stereotypes: Men are likely to suppress emotions like sadness and sympathy, whereas women are more likely to suppress anger and sexuality.

Although women and men differ in their willingness to express and suppress different emotions, Goleman reported on research that has indicated gender similarity in the experience of emotion. That is, when measuring the physiological responses that accompany emotion, men and women seem to experience similar reactions. Therefore, the interpretation of the situation and the appropriateness of the emotion are factors that lead men and women to report differences in emotion. Indeed, women and men may have very similar experiences of emotion on a physiological level. As psychologist Leslie Brody told Goleman (1988, p. C13): "Although women don't admit to feeling angry as much as do men, they may feel just as angry inside. It's their early training that tells women not to be as open about their anger. And the same is true for men with emotions like sympathy."

This tendency toward the expression of anger by men versus inhibition of anger by women may have important consequences. First, men's expression of anger may be a problem for those around them: Men are about four times more likely to commit acts of violence than women. However, women are more likely to experience problems with depression, being twice as likely to become seriously depressed as men. These different expressions of emotion may have a similar underlying cause—difficulty in managing emotions.

Goleman also considered the sources of gender differences in emotion, emphasizing parents' treatment of girls and boys with regard to the expression of emotion. Even as toddlers children receive different treatment from parents, with more inquiries about feelings and discussions of feelings with girls than with boys. In addition, Goleman reported that parents emphasize emotional *control* with their sons and emotional *closeness* with their daughters. As Goleman concluded, "The patterns of emotional inhibition among adult men and women seem in large part attributable to how parents treat their children" (p. C13).

This article about gender differences in emotion highlighted several important issues in the area of emotion—namely, gender differences in the expression of emotion and the similarities in the experience of emotion, the problems that can occur in connection with emotions, and the strength and perpetuation of the traditional gender stereotypes of emotionality. This chapter explores all of these issues, beginning with the physiological and cognitive aspects of emotion.

Physiological, Cognitive, and Behavioral Aspects

Emotion has been a subject of interest for psychology since its early years as a discipline. Emotion has also been a topic of interest for philosophy, even before psychology began experimental investigations of behavior. From the start, philosophers tended to conceptualize emotions as irrational and to place emotion in opposition to the rational thought processes (Averill, 1982). This attitude shaped the rational-emotional dichotomy that persists today.

Psychologists have devised several theories to explain the various components of emotion and their relative contribution to the experience. Early theories (McDougall, 1923) emphasized the physiology of emotional reactions and proposed the instinctive nature of emotions. Other theories attempted to integrate the contribution of cognition to the physiological reactions that accompany emotion (Cannon, 1927; James, 1890). All approaches held that both the physiology and the cognitive components were important to the experience of emotion.

A clever experiment by Stanley Schachter and Jerome Singer (1962) demonstrated that similar levels of physical arousal could result in different emotions, depending on the setting and the expectation of the participants. This study showed that both physiological arousal and cognitive labeling are important components in the individual experience of emotion. Despite the results from Schachter and Singer's study, the relative contribution of physiology and cognition has been the source of continued controversy in psychology, with some taking the position that the physiological component is more important (Zajonc, 1984), and others arguing that cognitions are more critical to the experience of emotion (Lazarus, 1984).

The primacy of either physiology or cognition would have important implications for understanding emotion. If cognition were the primary factor in emotion, then emotional experience should be dependent on setting and expectation, and the physiology underlying emotion should be the same, regardless of the emotion. If physiology were the primary factor, then emotional experience should vary with bodily states, with each emotion having a pattern of physical responses.

Paul Ekman and his colleagues (Ekman, 1984; Ekman, Levenson, & Friesen, 1983) studied the different facial movements that accompany the experience of emotion and contended that facial expressions are characteristic of emotions across societies. That is, people experience a standard set of emotions regardless of differences in culture. Ekman argued that this consistency exists because emotions have evolved to help people deal with tasks that arise in life.

This evolutionary view can be traced to Charles Darwin (1872), who believed that both humans and animals innately experience emotions. Although Ekman's view of emotion does not exclude cognition as a factor in emotion, his evolutionary explanation emphasizes the role of physiology and the consistency of emotional experience for people in all cultures. Other researchers' investigations have tended to confirm Ekman's view, but James Russell (1994) argued that these studies have been limited by the techniques these investigators used, which relied primarily on identification of facial expressions. When researchers use other the methods of investigation, such as examining languages for emotion-related words or investigating the social context of emotion, the results no longer support universality of emotional experience.

Regardless of the consistency of emotional experience, people do not show similar consistency in emotional expression. That is, the behaviors associated with emotion show some variation from culture to culture and from individual to individual. (See Diversity Highlight: "Cultural Consistency or Cultural Diversity in the Emotions?") Associations exist between emotion and expression in terms of behavior—for example, between anger and aggression. However, the experience of emotion requires no behavioral manifestation: People do not have to *do* anything when they feel an emotion. The emotional experience is internal, and behavior is not an inevitable consequence of that experience.

The lack of correspondence between emotion and behavior results in the ability to disguise or conceal emotion. People can experience an emotion and yet manifest no overt behavior that signals their experience. Those who believe that emotions are inherent must explain the discrepancy between emotion and behavior. Ekman (1984) discussed the concept of **display rules,** "overlearned habits about who can show what emotion to whom and when they can show it" (p. 320). These display rules provide the possibility for the experience of one emotion and the display of another, or even for the display of no emotional reaction at all despite the internal experience of strong emotion. In addition, the learning of display rules provides an explanation for the variability of emotion from person to person and from culture to culture. Learning of display rules, or some other similar process, is necessary to explain the variability of expressions of emotion in behavior.

✿ DIVERSITY HIGHLIGHT
Cultural Consistency or Cultural Diversity in the Emotions?

Researchers who have conducted cross-cultural studies of emotion and others who have reviewed the cross-cultural and anthropological evidence have concluded that emotions show both consistency and diversity across cultures. One such cross-cultural study by Klaus Scherer and colleagues (Scherer, Wallbott, & Summerfield, 1986) surveyed students in Belgium, France, Great Britain, Israel, Italy, Spain, Switzerland, and West Germany to investigate similarities and differences of emotion in these cultures. These researchers found more similarities than differences, including the tendency for everyday situations to be the main sources of strong emotion. Of the emotions, anger was the most commonly reported, followed by joy. Close relationships were the main source of both positive and negative emotion. This survey revealed the expected stereotypical gender differences—women reported more expression of emotion than men—but the study found a smaller magnitude of gender difference than the researchers had hypothesized.

Scherer et al. were surprised to find some evidence against the emotional stereotypes associated with these countries: The English were very talkative rather than reticent; the Italians were very concerned with achievement rather than personal relationships; and the Swiss were very emotional rather than very reserved. Overall, this study showed fewer differences in emotion than the researchers had expected. Perhaps these similarities are not too surprising, considering how similar European cultures have become.

Other cross-cultural studies have included a wider geographical variety of cultures and have found more variation in the situations that prompt emotional responses as well as in the emotional responses. James Russell (1991) reviewed the cross-cultural work on the categorization of emotion by the use of emotion words and facial expressions and concluded that "people of different cultures and speaking different languages categorize the emotions somewhat differently" (p. 444). However, Russell concluded that more similarities than differences exist in the categories of emotion in different cultures and languages.

Batja Mesquita and Nico Frijda (1992) analyzed the cross-cultural evidence on emotion by examining the components rather than only the categorization of emotions. By doing this type of analysis, they also found similarities and differences across cultures. They concluded that "there exists some evidence that, by and large, certain kinds of events elicit emotions in widely different cultures and that they tend to elicit the same emotions in these different cultures" (p. 181). These similar emotions include anger, disgust, joy, fear, sadness, and surprise. For example, loss of a loved one was associated with sadness in all cultures. Interaction with strangers was a source of anger in many cultures. Within these broad similarities lie specific differences. For example, interaction with strangers was a source of anger for 52% of Japanese compared with 15% of Americans and 20% of Europeans—a substantial cultural difference.

The experience of shame is common to all cultures as a response to being observed doing bad things, but what constitutes "bad things" varies enormously among cultures. For example, among the Bedouins a loss of honor is cause for shame, and their culture is very sensitive to the many causes of a loss of honor. Signs of dependency or weakness cause a loss of honor, and the Bedouins believe that women are at constant peril because they are weak and dependent by nature. Women in Bedouin society must be very careful when they are in the presence of men lest they do something that will dishonor them and their families. On the other hand, the Japanese are shamed by displays of emotion, because their modesty code demands that the self and true feelings remain hidden. Not all emotions bring shame to the Utku Eskimos, but anger does; it is considered dangerous and its display is completely unacceptable for adults.

At an abstract level of analysis, across cultures emotions have many similarities—the types, the antecedent situations, the labels used, and the physical reactions and facial responses people exhibit. However, cultural differences exist in the specifics of each component, especially in the regulation processes concerning emotion (Mesquita & Frijda,

Continued

DIVERSITY HIGHLIGHT *Continued*

1992). Cultures vary both in restricting and in prescribing the display of emotion—who should express what emotion under what circumstances. That is, although many similarities exist across cultures, the rules that govern the display of emotion and the rules that govern what emotion should be experienced vary enormously among cultures. As Mesquita and Frijda (1992, p. 199) concluded, "Although there are universal patterns of expressive behavior, there also are culture-specific behavior modes, deriving from culture-specific models and from culturally based expectations regarding behavior that is appropriate under particular circumstances." Although people may all feel the same emotions, they do not express them in the same ways or under the same circumstances.

Does learning provide an explanation for the gender differences in emotion? Do men and women learn different display rules and show different emotions, or do they experience differing types and intensities of emotions?

Gender and the Experience of Emotion

"From the 19th century onwards, rationality and emotionality have largely become associated with the supposedly different natures of men and women, the former fitted for productive labor and the latter for household and emotional labor" (Fischer, 1993, p. 303). This emotional double standard holds that women are more emotional than men, but only for a restricted range of emotions—happiness, sadness, disgust, fear, and surprise. Anger is notably absent from the list of emotions stereotypically associated with women. The emotions associated with boys and men are, likewise, restricted, with sadness and fear notably absent.

To test the stereotype of female emotionality, Stephanie Shields (1987) asked college students to think of the most emotional person they knew. She found a difference between the number of women and men her participants named, with significantly more women named in this category. And she found that her participants tended to think of women displaying a negative emotion, such as sadness, depression, or anger. In analyzing the justifications for their judgment, Shields found that her participants considered a person emotional when the reactions were extreme and exaggerated in proportion to the stimulus that provoked it. Shields's study confirmed that people think of women in stereotypical terms—as "emotional females" who overreact.

Shields's study measured people's beliefs and not women's emotional responses, confirming that people tend to think of women in stereotypical terms but leaving untested any possible gender differences in emotional responses. Such assessments can be difficult. Unfortunately, expectancy can bias the measurement of emotional responses, leading observers to see what they expect to see. For example, John and Sandra Condry (1976) asked participants to rate infants' emotional responses to four different situations. They told half of their participants that they would be rating a girl and told the other half that they would see a boy, when in fact the child was a girl in both cases. The researchers expected that this gender information would lead participants to "see" different emotions in the infants, although the infants and the reactions were always the same. They found that not only did the emotions vary but also the level of emotionality changed according to what gender the raters believed the child to be. The participants' attributions varied the most in an ambiguous situation, when the babies reacted to a jack-in-the-box. Participants were especially likely to describe the "boy's" reaction as anger and the "girl's" reaction as fear. These results demonstrated that the gender stereotypes associated with emotion bias observers in their attributions of emotion, leading them to believe that girls experience greater and different emotions to the same situations than boys. Nor is this study an isolated finding. Eleanor Maccoby and Carol Jacklin's (1974) review of gender differences supplied many examples of parents and teachers who evaluated girls as showing more fear and timidity. With such expectations, raters cannot make judgments of emotional responses that would allow the unbiased evaluation of gender and emotion.

Women may experience more intense emotions than men, and social expectation may be a factor in the difference. Frank Fujita and his colleagues (Fujita, Diener, & Sandvik, 1991) found that women reported a greater emotional intensity than men. This greater variation in emotion resulted in women experiencing more negative but also more positive emotions. Overall, men and women reported equal happiness, suggesting that women's heightened experience of negative and positive emotion balances out for them. Michele Grossman and Wendy Wood (1993) found that women who endorsed stereotypical gender roles reported greater emotional intensity than men. These researchers found that they could eliminate gender differences in the report of emotion by manipulating the social expectation of a response. By telling participants that previous research had shown either a positive or a negative relationship with emotionality, the gender-related differences in emotional reactions disappeared. Thus, women's greater emotional intensity may be attributable to their expectation of such experiences.

Rather than detailing the gender differences and similarities in a list of emotions, this chapter concentrates on two types of emotional experience that have figured prominently in the stereotypes of emotion: the concepts of maternal instinct and aggression (one "feminine" and the other "masculine" expressions of emotion). In addition, the concept of instinct, with its note of biological determinism, is often associated with both maternal behaviors and aggression. These two concepts provide a good contrast for considerations of gender and emotion. Psychologists have considered both as primary instincts basic to human and animal behavior (Hilgard, 1987). Those who consider these two instincts as primary believe that large gender differences exist, with nurturing and caregiving behaviors being the province of the female of many species, and anger and aggression being a male specialty.

The Myth of Maternal Instinct

The concept of maternal instinct holds that nurturing behaviors of mothers toward their children are determined by biological factors and are largely insensitive to environmental or experiential effects. Shields (1984) discussed the influence of the concept of maternal instinct on the study of caregiving, contending that Darwin and the late 19th-century scientists who accepted maternal instinct have shaped subsequent research on the topic. Notions of instinctive nurturing can be traced to assumptions of the 19th century, an acceptance of both women's intellectual inferiority and their emotional reactivity to the young. Scientific thinking of that time held that women could not be as intellectually developed as men because their energies were required to go toward reproduction and caregiving. Nature had suited them to focus on the immediate rather than the abstract (hence their intellectual inferiority) and to be more perceptive and emotional (hence their attraction to the small and helpless).

Instinct explanations of behavior fell into disfavor in psychology with the rise of behaviorism and its emphasis on learning and the environmental factors that shape behavior. Furthermore, the notion of fixed behavior patterns seemed deterministic and incompatible with the democratic ideal. As Ernest Hilgard (1987) pointed out, science takes place in a social context, and the United States was more receptive to the behavioral flexibility promoted by the behaviorists than the biological determinism promoted by instinct theory.

Despite the decline of instinct as a general explanation for behavior, the concept of maternal instinct did not fade from psychological explanations of behavior: "Even with the decline of the Victorian model of gender roles, social scientists continued to comment on the innate bases of caretaking behavior" (Shields, 1984, p. 264). Louise Silverstein (1993) examined fields as different as primate biology and social policy to evaluate the impact of the assumptions concerning motherhood and fatherhood. She contended that scientists and social policymakers have accepted the views of early primatologists, whose work emphasized male aggression and sexuality and female passivity and nurturance.

Silverstein pointed out that later work with various primate species has changed the view of mothers as primary caregivers and fathers as only marginally involved with babies or children. Considering a variety of species, male primates' involvement with infants varies from primary caretaker to benign disinterest. In addition, individual differences concerning male involvement with infants exist within species; some males form numerous relationships with infants and young primates, even those they did not father, whereas other males of the same species are less involved. Silverstein argued that the evidence from studies of other primate species shows the behavioral flexibility of caregiving rather than supports the concept of maternal instinct (and paternal disinterest). That is, the behavior of primates offers no evidence for biological invariability of nurturance among females and lack of nurturance among males.

Despite the growing unpopularity of the concept of instinct during the 1940s and 1950s, many scientists selected the evidence they considered, continuing to believe in maternal instinct. One of these scientists was psychologist Harry Harlow, whose research ironically provided evidence against the validity of this concept.

Maternal Deprivation and Its Consequences for Nurturing

During the 1950s, Harlow and his colleagues (including his wife, Margaret) conducted a series of experiments concerning affection and attachment. Harlow (1971) had many questions about the nature of attachment—of mothers for their babies, of babies for their mothers, of fathers for their babies, of children for each other, and so forth. One of Harlow's questions concerned the effects of maternal deprivation, but ethics prevented him from using human subjects. Therefore, he chose to experiment on monkeys.

Harlow described the origins of the studies on the results of maternal deprivation:

Our investigations of the emotional development of our subjects grew out of the effort to produce and maintain a colony of sturdy, disease-free young animals for use in various research programs. By separating them from their mothers a few hours after birth and placing them in a more fully controlled regimen of nurture and physical care we were able both to achieve a higher rate of survival and to remove the animals for testing without maternal protest. Only later did we realize that our monkeys were emotionally disturbed as well as sturdy and disease-free. (Harlow & Harlow, 1962, p. 138)

The infant monkeys raised in isolation behaved abnormally, staring into space for hours, circling their cages or rocking repetitively for long periods of time, and repeatedly injuring themselves, especially when a human approached. Not only did these young monkeys behave oddly when alone, they also exhibited abnormal behavior when placed in a social group of other monkeys. They failed to fit into the social group, fighting more and interacting less than normally raised monkeys. They were also sexually abnormal, appearing interested but unable to mate. Thus, the experience of maternal deprivation seemed to have permanent effects on the social and sexual behavior of monkeys.

Isolation also affected the monkey's maternal behavior. When the isolated female monkeys became mothers themselves, they made spectacularly poor ones. These monkey mothers were negligent and abusive, refusing to allow their infants to nurse and sometimes beating them for trying to establish physical contact. Such negligent and abusive behavior does not support the concept of maternal instinct but rather suggests that the isolation experience affected nurturing behavior. That is, Harlow's research suggests that caregiving is dependent on an experience and not on inherent biological factors.

Harlow (1959) initially believed that being mothered was the critical experience that allows a monkey to be an adequate mother. To explore what constitutes adequate mothering, he conducted a series of experiments that became his most famous. Harlow had observed the negative effects of complete isolation and wanted to know how much "mothering" was necessary for normal development. He and his research team constructed surrogate mothers of two types, wire or cloth-covered wire. Neither type of surrogate was very much like a real monkey mother; they did not move, hold the infants, or respond to them in any way. In some of Harlow's studies, both types of surrogates provided milk for nursing, whereas in some conditions, only the wire surrogate provided milk.

Although the surrogate mothers were unresponsive, the infants were not. Harlow found that the infants strongly preferred the cloth-covered surrogates to the wire surrogates, even if the wire surrogate was the only source of food. Infants nursed from the wire "mother" but clung to the cloth-covered surrogate for hours and ran to it when frightened. Harlow concluded that the cloth-covered surrogates provided some factor that the wire surrogates could not, and he called this factor *contact comfort,* the security provided by physical contact with a comforting object. However, these monkeys did not become socially, sexually, or maternally normal, indicating that the cloth surrogate failed to provide the experiences that are necessary for normal monkey development.

An additional series of experiments showed that the experiences that promote normal nurturing and caregiving in monkeys involve contact with other monkeys. Despite the logic of modeling and imitation, such contact does not have to include the experience of being mothered. That is, being a good mother does not require being adequately mothered. Harlow and Harlow (1962) reported on studies indicating that age mates can provide the social experiences necessary for normal development. The study involved separating infant monkeys from their mothers and raising them together. Although the monkeys showed some abnormal behavior as infants—clinging together practically all the time they were together in their cage—they developed into normal adolescent monkeys. In addition, another study in which infants were raised with their mothers but without peer contact showed that mothering alone is not adequate for normal development; some contact with peers is a necessary component for development.

Therefore, the studies by Harlow and his colleagues demonstrated (at least in monkeys) that maternal behavior does not conform to the definition of instinct. As Table 9.1 shows, nurturing and caregiving are not behaviors that appear in all females regardless of experience. Instead, Harlow's research showed that specific social experiences are necessary for the development of adequate maternal (and other social) behavior. Without these experiences, adequate maternal behaviors fail to appear.

Attachment

Although research has demonstrated no innate, fixed pattern of caregiving, the contention that nurturing behavior has innate components has not disappeared from psychological theory. Instead, that notion has been transformed into the concept of attachment, or **bonding,** an emotional attachment that develops between infant and caregiver within a few days after birth (Shields, 1984). Bonding, however, is not

TABLE 9.1   Types of Deprivation and Effects on Nurturing in Monkeys

Type of Deprivation	Adequacy of Nurturing
No deprivation—contact with mother and peers	Normal
Complete isolation	Inadequate and abusive
Wire or cloth "mother"	Inadequate
Contact with mother only	Inadequate
Contact with peers but not mother	Normal

restricted to mother-infant attachment but can also occur with fathers and infants or with any others who happen to be present during the critical time period.

The concept of **critical periods** in development comes from ethnology, the study of animal behavior in natural settings, and the work of Konrad Lorenz, who discovered a type of attachment in geese (Schwartz, 1986). Lorenz researched the factors that are important for baby geese developing an attachment to their mothers. He found a critical period in the lives of young geese, a time during which they learn to follow their mother. During this critical period, goslings learn to follow their mother with only one exposure to her walking past, so critical period learning is not like typical learning, which requires repetition or practice.

In addition to the timing, the mother's behavior is also important; she must walk past the goslings within two days after they hatch. If the timing and the mother's behavior coordinate, then the goslings *imprint* on their mother and follow her, thus helping them to stay out of trouble and to learn things important for being a goose. If the critical period passes without the mother walking past, then the goslings do not imprint on her, leaving them without attachment to a caretaker and at increased risk for the many dangers that may befall small fowl. Although the mother's behavior is important, the attachment may occur to animals other than geese, as Lorenz himself demonstrated. By timing his behavior to the critical period, groups of goslings were imprinted to follow Lorenz as though he were their mother.

The concept of imprinting may apply to the attachment that forms between babies and their caregivers, but it does not explain the attachment between mothers and their infants. That is, Lorenz's work should not resurrect the concept of maternal instinct. His work demonstrated the existence of critical periods in development, but those critical periods relate to *infant* attachment to a caregiver and not to maternal (or paternal) behavior toward a child. And of course, geese and humans are very different, and one should be hesitant about applying Lorenz's findings to humans.

The popular concept of bonding is very similar to imprinting, but bonding is a reciprocal process that applies to mother-infant as well as infant-mother attachment. This concept is a variation on maternal instinct in that bonding also depends on innate components that are triggered by the early interaction of infant and caregiver. However, bonding is not restricted to mothers, so it is definitely a variation on the maternal part of maternal instinct.

The concept of bonding was popularized with the publication of research by Marshall Klaus and John Kennell (1976), who reported that the first few hours after a child's birth are critically important to attachment. Not only do infants form a bond with their mother, but mothers bond with their babies, forming an attachment that is important for the duration of the relationship. Klaus and Kennell's studies showed that mothers who were allowed to cuddle their babies felt a stronger attachment to the infants and showed more interaction with them during the children's infancy than mothers who were not allowed this physical contact. However, other researchers have failed to confirm these results and have criticized the concept of bonding (Chess & Thomas, 1982). As a result, the concept of bonding remains more favored by the popular press than by developmental researchers. Shields (1984) attributed the popularity of the concept to the desire to explain caregiving in biological terms—the latest version of maternal instinct.

Gender and Caring for Children

Although research has failed to find a biological basis that prompts women to mother, at least two possible explanations exist for gender-related differences in nurturing behavior: responsiveness to children and pleasure in taking care of children (Shields, 1984). That is, perhaps girls and women respond more quickly and strongly to children or derive greater pleasure out of caring for children than men do, or both.

Gail Melson and Alan Fogel (1988a, b) have questioned gender differences in nurturance, but they acknowledged that gender difference in responsiveness to babies shows a developmental increase during childhood. These researchers studied preschoolers' interest in babies and found that before age 4 years, boys and girls showed similar levels of interest, but older girls increased and older boys decreased their involvement with an infant in a play situation (Melson & Fogel, 1988a). Boys tend to care for and nurture pets during the time that they are becoming less interested in babies, and Melson and Fogel (1988b) argued that boys at this age are becoming aware of the gender role they should follow. This awareness prompts a decrease in their responsiveness to babies, but boys still have the capacity to be nurturant caregivers, as expressed by their feelings for and behavior toward pets. Melson and Fogel contended that boys are as nurturant as girls, although this nurturance may be expressed in different ways.

Phyllis Berman (1980) reviewed studies that had investigated gender differences in responsiveness to infants, and found that researchers have used many different representations of infants, such as real babies, photographs of infants, and the young of nonhuman animals, to investigate responsiveness to infants. In addition, the measurements of responsiveness have included self-reports, such as ratings of liking; behavioral measures, such as speed of response to crying; and physiological measures, such as changes in heart rate or respiratory rate. These different measures have revealed different results.

According to Berman's review, the strongest gender differences have come from studies using self-report measures of responsiveness to children. Girls and women are more likely than boys and men to report that they find infants more appealing and attractive and to respond more positively to pictures of infants. As many of these studies have not used real babies, the self-reports of liking or attraction could be responses to the situation rather than to infants. That is, the girls and women who have participated in such studies may have responded to the situation of being asked about their feelings about babies, and they may have been more willing to say that they find babies appealing. Girls and women may be more willing to express (or believe that they should express) positive feelings about babies than boys and men. Such behavior would conform to the stereotype of what these female participants should say: Girls and women are supposed to like babies, and boys and men are supposed to be more restrained in their enthusiasm for infants. Therefore, the significant gender differences in self-reports of responsiveness to infants may reflect conformity to social roles.

GENDERED VOICES
If Men Mothered

"I think that men could do as good as women at taking care of children," two college students told me. Both the young man and the young woman said that they believed that women have no instinctive advantage in nurturing children. Both of them said that the differences were due to experience rather than inherent biological factors. Indeed, both said that they believed there were few differences in ability to care for children.

"Well, men can't breast-feed," the young man said, "but I think that is about the only advantage women have except for experience. They have a lot more experience in caring for children. Girls babysit, and boys don't." He knew how difficult it is for men to get experience caring for young children because he attempted to get such experience. He had volunteered to care for the young children in his church while their parents attended the service and had answered advertisements for babysitters. Neither of these efforts had met with enthusiasm from others; he had gotten the impression that wanting to care for children was considered odd for a man. He considered the possibility that people might think he was a pedophile, when all he really wanted was to learn to be more nurturant.

"I think if men were responsible for caring for children, there would be more changes in men than in children. If they had to learn to care for children, then men would. It wouldn't be automatic, because they don't have the experience, but they could learn. I don't believe in maternal instinct—that women have some innate advantage over men in caring. But women do have more experience, and men would have to learn the skills they lack.

"Men would learn to care for children if they had to, and they would become more nurturant in other aspects of their lives, maybe even in their careers. They might not care so much about competition and high-status careers."

The young woman had a slightly different view: "I think that the children would be different. This opinion is based on my own family and the differences between my mother and my father. My father was more willing to let us be on our own, but my mother was more involved. My mother took care of us, but my father let us make our own decisions. Maybe that wouldn't be good for young children, but I think I would have learned to be more self-reliant with my father's style of caretaking. But maybe if he had been the one who had to look out for us, he would have been as protective as my mother was."

In examining the studies that have used physiological measurements of responsiveness, Berman found little evidence for gender differences. The studies that have used behavioral measurements of responsiveness have revealed complex findings; many show no simple gender-related differences but rather interactions between gender and situational factors. For example, the gender of the experimenter and the gender of the participant might interact, producing different behaviors in male experimenter–male participant than in male experimenter–female participant or some other combination of testing situations. The lack of clear gender-related differences in behavioral and physiological measures of responsiveness confirms the view that social roles may be the most important factor in the gender-related differences in responsiveness to infants.

The differences in patterns of child care—namely, that women perform the vast majority of child care—complicate comparisons of the pleasure that women and men derive from these activities. Although some fathers are involved in all aspects of child care, the accepted role for fathers is helper, and the role for mothers is primary caregiver. Linda Thompson and Alexis Walker (1989, p. 861) described the gender roles in parenting, saying that "mothers provide the 'continuous coverage' that babies require" and "fathers are novel, unpredictable, physical, exciting, engaging, and preferred playmates for young children." Therefore, any comparison of the pleasure of nurturing is not based on a direct comparison of the satisfaction of specific caregiving activities but on a comparison of the role of mother and father and the types of caregiving each provides.

Thompson and Walker (1989) concluded that the time and effort mothers spend in child care lead to feelings of both satisfaction and dissatisfaction. The experience of involvement and their feelings of the social value of nurturing children produce satisfaction, but the loss of freedom and the irritation of attending to the demands of small children lead mothers to feel dissatisfaction. Indeed, many mothers feel disappointment over mothering because they had expected the experience to be both easier and more fulfilling.

Mothers tend to find more pleasure in taking care of their children than fathers do, unless the fathers are as involved with child care as mothers typically are. Fewer fathers are primary caregivers of young children, but Barbara Risman's (1989) study of such fathers indicated that their feelings and behavior toward their young children were similar to women who provide such care. Therefore, the greater pleasure that women derive from caring for children seems to be a function of their greater involvement with their children, and men who have similar levels of involvement experience similar feelings.

Summary of Evidence Concerning Maternal Instinct

Maternal instinct continues to be a popular concept and has taken several forms. According to the Victorian version of maternal instinct, women supposedly possess greater emotionality and lesser intellect, making them well suited to caring for children and poorly suited for other careers. A more modern version of maternal instinct holds that women inherit a predisposition to mother. Both the Victorian and modern version of maternal instinct can be traced to evolutionary theory, which points to the adaptive value of maternal care of infants, giving them a better chance of survival.

Sociologist Alice Rossi (1977) proposed a variation on the concept of maternal instinct, asserting that women have a biologically based predisposition to mother that men lack. The concept of predisposition differs from instinct in that a predisposition makes it easier or more likely that an individual will learn a behavior or behavior pattern, whereas an instinct produces a behavior or behavior pattern without any learning. Rossi traced the predisposition for women to mother to human prehistory and the different roles occupied by women and men in hunter-gatherer societies. Other than describing the gender differences in these prehistoric societies, however, Rossi presented no evidence of a biological gender difference for nurturing.

Despite its long history of acceptance, the concept of maternal instinct has little in the way of research support. Indeed, the work of Harry Harlow and his colleagues, which showed that infant monkeys that are deprived of all social relationships grow up to be neglectful and abusive mothers, provided evidence that adequate mothering is dependent on social experiences during childhood. Harlow's work also showed that the experience of mothering is not critical for the performance of nurturing; other social experiences with age mates can substitute for a mother's care to produce a normal monkey. Although monkeys and humans differ, few people imagine that humans would be more controlled by instinct than monkeys, so Harlow's research demonstrated the importance of experience in maternal caregiving.

Another version of maternal instinct can be found in the concept of maternal bonding, the hypothesized emotional attachment that forms between mothers and their newborn babies in the first few hours after birth. Although this concept is very popular, the research support for it is mixed, and the influence of the idea exceeds its credibility.

Nor does evidence exist to support the notion that girls and women are more responsive to babies and children, although they are more willing to report their attraction to babies than men are. When the measures of responsiveness are behavioral or physiological rather than self-reports, no differences in this area appear between men and women. Likewise, the greater pleasure that women derive from caring for children is related to their greater degree of involvement rather than to their biological inheritance. In addition, research with children has indicated that both boys and girls are equally interested in babies, but boys decrease their involvement with babies after age 4 years.

Prominence of Male Aggression

Aggression is another candidate for the status of instinct, again with explanations of evolutionary advantage (Cairns, 1986). The standard version says that during human prehistory while the women were at home taking care of the children, the men were out stalking large game and defending the group against various threats. In both the hunting and the defending, aggressive action could be adaptive and even essential. Thus, women became passive homebodies and men became aggressive conquerors.

This view of human prehistory may be a fiction based more on the theorists' personal views than on prehuman behavior. There have been questions both about the idea of female passivity and the adaptive advantage of aggression (Benderly, 1987; Weisstein, 1982). Women in the hunter-gatherer societies of prehistory probably not only gathered plants for food but participated in small game hunting, making them essential to the groups' food supply and far from passive. As for aggression, it can offer advantages if directed at the proper targets, but it can also be disruptive and dangerous within a group. Therefore, the men in these societies must have been selectively rather than pervasively aggressive.

Despite the widespread acceptance of an instinct for aggression, a definition has been difficult to formulate. Although most people would agree that aggression is active and behavioral and that the result (or at least the intent) is harm to another, not all people would easily agree on what behaviors should be included and what consequences constitute harm. Actions like hitting, kicking, biting, and even yelling seem obviously aggressive, but sulking might also be considered aggressive (Tavris, 1982). Aggression can produce not only physical but also psychological harm. An additional problem in defining aggression comes from determining what counts as aggression; intent as well as action are important considerations. For instance, doing harm to someone accidentally may not count as aggression.

Psychologist Leonard Eron (1987) discussed how he had solved the dilemma of defining aggression in his 30-year history of aggression research. He chose a behavioral, objective definition of aggression as "an act that injures or irritates another person" (p. 435). Eron contended that intentionality is very difficult to measure, especially in children, and his definition avoided that problem by ignoring aggressive intent and sticking to harm or irritation as the outcome. Eron acknowledged that some accidents would be included in his definition, but he argued that assertive acts would largely, and in his opinion correctly, be excluded. Therefore, Eron opted for a completely behavioral definition of aggression, with no qualifiers. His approach avoided not only the issue of intent but also the relationship between anger and aggression.

Anger and Aggression

Anger and aggression seem intimately related, with anger as the internal emotion and aggression as the behavioral reaction (Plutchik, 1984). However, the two are not inevitably connected: A person can experience anger and take no action, aggressive or otherwise, and a person can act aggressively without feeling anger, such as the violence of a hired killer.

Psychological and popular explanations of aggression have accepted that aggression is the outcome of some prior circumstance, either in the emotions or in the environment. Psychologist William McDougall and psychoanalyst Sigmund Freud believed that aggression was the result of instinctive expressions of frustrated wishes. Based on this premise, the frustration-aggression hypothesis (Dollard, Doob, Miller, Mowrer, & Sears, 1939) holds that aggression is the inevitable result of frustration, and research on the frustration-aggression hypothesis has attempted to understand the relationship between the two. In this formulation, anger is not an important concept (Averill, 1982).

The frustration-aggression hypothesis prompted a great deal of research, mostly in laboratory settings, with experimenters measuring aggression as the response to a frustrating stimulus. James Averill (1982) criticized the limitations of such laboratory experiments, discussing how these investigations tended to use standard and limited frustration stimuli and aggression measures, often involving the administration of electric shock. These experiments yielded information about one facet of aggression but failed to explore aggression prompted by everyday events in more natural settings. However, several investigations have surveyed people about their experience of anger and subsequent aggression. Although these surveys rely on self-reports and do not directly measure either anger or aggression, the survey method provides a way to investigate a wider range of topics than are possible through laboratory experiments.

In a survey of university students in eight European countries, Klaus Scherer and his associates (Scherer, Wallbott, & Summerfield, 1986) found that anger occurred more frequently than other emotions, with about 75% of participants reporting anger within the four weeks prior to the survey. Averill (1982) surveyed community residents and college students in the United States about their experience of anger and subsequent aggression by administering an extensive questionnaire. Averill wanted to investigate the angry person's experience of the emotion, the consequences of anger, and gender differences in anger and aggression. He found that anger was very common—85% of the people surveyed reported at least one experience of anger within the week. However, Averill also found that physical aggression was rare during anger and even that the impulse to use physical aggression is not all that common. Although aggression may be a visible manifestation of anger, Averill concluded that anger could be expressed in a great variety of ways.

Averill's survey yielded surprisingly few gender differences in the experience of anger. Averill did find gender differences in the targets of anger, with men being somewhat more frequent targets of anger than women. However, he also found that the relationship between the two people was an important factor. For people who were not well-known to each other, men were more likely than women to be the targets of anger. For loved ones, men and women were equally likely targets. For friends, male-male and female-female anger was the most common pattern. Averill also found that women reported more intense experiences of anger than did men and that women's responses were more varied, especially in their tendency to cry when they were angry.

June Crawford and her colleagues (Crawford, Kippax, Onxy, Gault, & Benton, 1992) also discussed the tendency for women to cry when they feel angry, a behavior that they contended is often misinterpreted as sadness or grief. Crawford and her research group conducted their study by exploring their own memories of emotional experiences, including anger. They found a common experience of crying in response to anger and explained this response as an acceptable expression of female anger, whereas physical aggression is less acceptable. Their work indicated that women have a tendency to restrain their impulses toward physical violence due to the possibility that their violence might anger and thus prompt violence in others, escalating the angry confrontation to a dangerous level. "Since becoming angry with someone else often makes them angry, this fear provides a powerful sanction against anger on the part of women (especially towards the physically more powerful)" (Crawford et al., 1992, p. 171).

Crawford et al. attributed both women's tendency to cry and their restraint of physical aggression when angry to their lack of power. Their analysis of anger revealed anger as a response to situations involving an imbalance of power, such as when a person has experienced an injustice, and they interpreted anger as the feeling of being victimized: "Anger is the expression of our frustration and powerlessness. A person with power does not need to be angry" (Crawford et al., 1992, p. 182). These researchers concluded that power is an essential difference in the experience of anger for men and women.

Carol Tavris (1982) also discussed how inequities of power can produce the sense of injustice that prompts anger, both on an individual level and at the level of a social group. Her analysis of the anger present in several social movements, including the feminist movement, focused on perceived powerlessness. She saw few gender differences in the experience of anger: Both men and women feel angry in response to the same categories of provocations, including actions that lead to violations of their plans or expectations, personal insults, and someone breaking social rules. However, Tavris acknowledged that what counts as a personal insult may differ for women and men, producing some apparent differences in the circumstances that prompt anger. Tavris also expressed limited enthusiasm for the power of developing and expressing anger, emphasizing anger's limited effectiveness in bringing about change. Furthermore, expressions of anger tend be more destructive than constructive.

In summary, the relationship between anger and aggression is far from automatic, with far more feelings of anger existing than acts of aggression. Of the studies that have explored gender differences in the experience of anger, few have found differences between men and women. Instead, these studies have shown that men and women not only feel anger but that both experience anger from similar provocations. Crawford and her colleagues (1992) contended that power was one difference between men and women in the experience of anger, with women having less power than men and suppressing their anger because of this power inequity. This analysis explains why women might be less likely to express their anger in terms of physical aggression than would men.

Developmental Gender Differences in Aggression

Observing gender differences in aggression during the early months and even early years of life is very difficult, because what counts as aggression in an infant is virtually impossible to define. Rather than attempting to assess aggression in young children, researchers have used other behaviors, beginning with activity level during infancy. Maccoby and Jacklin (1974) reviewed studies that measured activity level in infants and children and concluded that boys showed higher activity levels than girls, although many studies failed to find such gender differences.

The existence of gender differences in aggression among preschool children is controversial, but gender differences in aggression among elementary school children are clear: Boys are more aggressive than girls. Janet Hyde (1984) used meta-analysis to investigate the developmental nature of these differences and their magnitude. Her analysis indicated that gender differences decrease with age; that is, boys and girls show greater differences in aggression during elementary school than during college. In addition, Hyde's results showed a decrease in the magnitude of aggression over the course of development, with both boys and girls becoming less aggressive as they develop into adults.

Another way to approach the question of the stability of aggression over the course of development is through longitudinal research—studies that test the same group of children over many years. Eron and his colleagues (Eron, 1987; Huesmann, Eron, Lefkowitz, & Walder, 1984; Lefkowitz, Eron, Walder, & Huesmann, 1977) conducted one such longitudinal study of aggression, which tested 600 children, beginning when the children were in the 3rd grade (approximately 8 years old) and continuing for 22 years. By using this longitudinal approach, the researchers hoped to determine the stability of aggressive behavior from middle childhood into adolescence and adulthood.

Eron and his colleagues measured aggression among the 3rd graders by asking them questions about who acts aggressively, such as "Who in the class pushes other children?" The children could name as many of their peers as they wanted, providing a score representing peer-defined aggression for each child. As the initial phase of their study, the researchers compared this aggression score to parenting styles and found that parents who were less nurturant and acceptant at home tended to have children who behaved more aggressively at school than the children of more nurturant and acceptant parents.

In the second phase of the study, Eron and his colleagues located the children 10 years later to determine if their aggression had changed. They found that

> *children, both boys and girls, who were rated as aggressive by their peers when they were 8 years old tended to be rated as aggressive by their peers 10 years later. Furthermore, those who were rated as aggressive by their peers tended to rate themselves as aggressive, to rate others as aggressive, and to see the world about them as an aggressive place. (Eron, 1987, p. 438)*

That is, the results at the 10-year follow-up showed that aggressive children tended to grow up to be aggressive adolescents, recognized as such by not only peers but by the aggressive adolescents themselves.

This longitudinal study also investigated the influence of watching violent television programs and found that the violence on television acted as an effective model for aggressive children. Indeed, the preference for violent television programs at age 8 years was a good predictor of how aggressive male adolescents would be at age 19 years. However, this study failed to find a relationship between viewing habits and aggression in girls. Another longitudinal study by Eron's group (Eron, Huesmann, Brice, Fischer, & Mermelstein, 1983) tested both boys and girls in grades 1 through 5 using the same peer-nominee method of assessing aggression. The results showed that violent television viewing was significantly related to aggression in both boys and girls. In addition, the relationship between violent viewing and aggression increased until age 10 to 11 years. Eron and his colleagues interpreted these findings as indicative of a cumulative effect of observing violence on television, and they saw evidence of a developmental period during which children may be especially sensitive to the effects of televised violence.

Although the girls were not as aggressive as the boys at any grade level, the patterns were similar, showing an increase in aggression through the 5th grade. Interestingly, the correlations between violence viewing and aggression were higher for the girls than for the boys for all five grades, and Eron and his colleagues hypothesized that the effect of viewing television violence may be stronger for girls than for boys.

In the third phase of their 22-year longitudinal study, Eron and his colleagues (Eron, 1987; Huesmann et al., 1984) again contacted the participants, who were then around 30 years old. Table 9.2 shows the stability of aggression for the participants in the studies conducted by Eron and his colleagues. They found that aggression during elementary school predicted a number of aggressive behaviors during adulthood, including criminal behavior, traffic violations, convictions for driving while intoxicated, aggressiveness toward spouses, and severity of punishment of children. The stability

TABLE 9.2   Aggression over the Life Span

Children identified at age 8 years by their peers as aggressive toward other children.

At age 8 years	At age 18 years	At age 30 years
had less nurturant and acceptant parents	were still rated by peers as aggressive	were more likely to have criminal record
also	*also*	*also*
preferred violent TV programs	rated themselves as aggressive	were more likely to abuse spouse
	also	*also*
	rated others as aggressive	were more likely to have DWI (DUI) conviction
	also	*also*
	saw the world as a dangerous place	were more likely to have traffic violations
		also
		were more likely to use severe punishment with children

of aggression over this 22-year time span was higher for the men than for the women, and as had been the case when they were boys, the men showed more aggressive behavior than the women.

The results of this longitudinal study demonstrated that adult aggression can be predicted to some degree from childhood aggression, indicating that the two are related on a conceptual level. However, the specific behaviors that constitute adolescent and adult aggression differ substantially from the behaviors measured in studies of children. Although children may fight and get into trouble at home and at school, physical maturity and access to weapons make adolescents and adults much more capable of doing harm.

Robert Cairns and his colleagues (Cairns, Cairns, Neckerman, Ferguson, & Gariépy, 1989) explored the development of aggression by conducting a longitudinal study that concentrated on the developmental differences in aggression between boys and girls. These researchers tested a group of children annually, starting when they were in the 4th grade and continuing for the next six years; that is, from middle childhood until early adolescence.

Cairns et al. found that the 4th grade boys were much more likely to have a confrontation that involved physical aggression with another boy than with a girl, and this pattern became stronger over the 6-year time span. As adolescents, boys were much more likely to engage in a physical confrontation than were girls, and the chance of a physical confrontation between a boy and a girl was unlikely. Indeed, these researchers found an age-related trend for denial of cross-sex aggression. However, they found that the girls were increasingly likely to engage in a type of "social aggression" that involved attempts to alienate or ostracize a girl from a social group or to defame her character. This

---

DIVERSITY HIGHLIGHT
When Children See the World as a Violent Place

The longitudinal research on aggression conducted by Leonard Eron (1987) suggests that aggressive children see the world as a violent place, making their own aggression justifiable. Eron omitted the factor of intent from his research, as he found intent difficult to measure. However, Sandra Graham, Cynthia Hudley, and Estella Williams (1992) concentrated on the factor of intention in studying aggression in minority children, investigating the link between perception of intention and aggressive retaliation.

Graham and her colleagues chose a sample of Latino and African-American preadolescents identified as aggressive by teachers and peers and compared them to a similar group whose behavior was nonaggressive. They chose to study minority children, owing to the prevalence of violence among minority adolescents, and were particularly interested in the links between intention, anger, and aggression. They reasoned that children who perceive more hostile intent in the actions of others might feel more anger toward those people and be prompted to take more aggressive action, which they would view as justified because of the hostile intent of others.

Graham et al. presented these African-American and Latino children with situations in which the outcome clearly involved harm but the intent was not clear, and they asked the participants to judge the intent of the person who caused the harm. The aggressive children attributed greater hostile intent than the nonaggressive children, confirming Eron's notion that aggressive children see the world as a hostile place. Compared with nonaggressive children, the aggressive children reported that they would feel greater anger in the situations they saw as intentionally harmful and that they would choose to "have it out then and there'" and "get even," confirming the link between anger and aggression.

These findings prompted Hudley and Graham (1993) to devise and evaluate a program to decrease aggression among African-American boys. Their program was a cognitive intervention designed to teach these children to interpret the actions of others as nonaggressive when the intent was not clearly hostile, and they found that this program was effective in helping these boys to think differently about the actions of others. Even more important, those boys who participated in the cognitive intervention were less likely than boys in a no-treatment control to use verbal aggression in a laboratory task, to receive disciplinary referrals at school, and to be rated as aggressive by their teachers. That is, changing the way these boys interpreted the actions of others tended to change their behavior, decreasing aggression and helping them to see the world as a less dangerous place.

---

type of social aggression increased from the 4th grade, when about 10% of the girls reported it, to over 33% by the 7th grade. Boys very rarely reported this type of conflict. Teacher and counselor ratings of aggression showed a gender difference, with far fewer girls than boys receiving the ratings "gets into fights" and "has trouble at school," the most serious categories of aggression. Despite the mean difference in aggression between boys and girls, these researchers found that teachers and counselors rated both girls and boys at the high extreme of the aggression ratings. That is, when considering the most aggressive of the participants, no gender differences appeared. This finding suggests that on the average, girls may exhibit less aggressive behavior than boys but that very aggressive children are similar to each other, regardless of gender.

This study showed that the adolescent girls and boys gave themselves similar ratings of aggression, but their behaviors varied greatly. The boys were more likely to be involved in physical confrontations with other boys, whereas the girls showed a developmental decrease of physical violence but an increase in behaviors intended to foster ostracism and alienation of other girls from the social group. Developmentally, aggression decreased over the six years of the study, both in self-ratings and in teacher and counselor ratings.

Therefore, these two longitudinal studies of aggression have confirmed the developmental trend toward a decrease in aggression from middle childhood to young adulthood, confirming the results of Hyde's (1984) meta-analysis. These studies also confirm a gender-related difference in aggression. Although the difference is not large, it exists, with boys and girls using different strategies and behaviors in their displays of aggression. Cairns and his colleagues pointed out that adolescent aggression is much more dangerous than childhood aggression, especially the physical confrontations that are more typical of adolescent boys. With their size, strength, and greater likelihood of owning a weapon, adolescent boys become more likely to be involved in aggression that causes serious damage and violates the law than adolescent girls.

Gender Differences in Aggression during Adulthood

If gender-related differences in aggression decrease during development, then few differences should exist between adult men and women, but differences might exist in the styles of expression. Two reviews of the experimental research on aggression have confirmed these predictions, finding that the differences between men's and women's aggression are not large and that some differences in circumstances and style do exist.

Before the development of meta-analysis, Ann Frodi, Jacqueline Macaulay, and Pauline Thome (1977) conducted a review of gender differences in psychological experiments on aggression. Later, Alice Eagly and Valerie Steffen (1986) used meta-analysis to evaluate gender differences in aggression. Both reviews evaluated experimental studies in psychology, omitting surveys and crime statistics and concentrating on laboratory studies. As previously mentioned, such laboratory studies typically measure aggression as the willingness to deliver a punishment to another participant, who is typically a stranger. Both reviews found that women are not always less aggressive than men in these laboratory situations. In situations in which participants believe that their aggression is justified, women and men are equally aggressive toward the offender.

These reviews did find gender differences related to type of aggression, with men likely to be more aggressive when aggression was defined as physically harmful actions, and few differences when aggression was defined as actions designed to inflict psychological or social harm. Also, women seem to restrain themselves from performing physical aggression when they believe that their actions will produce harm and that their aggression may prompt counteraggression.

Women may restrain their aggression due to the potential for reprisal, because aggression, like anger, is related to power (Crawford et al., 1992). As Cairns (1986) pointed out, aggression can be a very effective way of exerting power, of forcing another to behave according to one's wishes. When considering aggression as a method of exerting power, women may be reasonably concerned about the potential for reprisal; the size and strength difference between men and women makes women more vulnerable to the effects of aggression.

Although the reviews of gender differences in aggression among adults have shown that men are, on the average, more aggressive than women, Frodi et al. concluded that the difference was one of degree rather than pattern. Women are more restrained in engaging in physical aggression than men, but under circumstances of perceived justification, gender differences disappear.

Gender and Crime.   Given the relatively small gender difference in aggression found in laboratory studies, the statistics on societal aggression reveal large gender differences. That is, men commit many more criminal acts than women do, and their arrest and incarceration rate is much higher than women's. According to the U.S. Department of Justice (1990), men are over four times more likely than women to be arrested for various types of offenses, such as murder, robbery, vandalism, fraud, drunkenness, and so forth. Although not all of these violations involve violence, many do, and as Table 9.3 shows, those offenses are more likely to be committed by men than women.

Not all crimes result in arrest, and the possibility exists that the rate of crimes committed by men and women is more equal than the arrest rates suggest. Surveys have indicated that although the reported rates of crime exceed the arrest rates, men still outnumber women in committing crimes (Feyerherm, 1981; Osgood, O'Malley, Bachman, & Johnston, 1989).

Crime has been so strongly associated with men that before the 1970s, most criminologists and officials in the criminal justice system assumed that crime was almost exclusively a male problem (Warren, 1981). During the 1970s research interest in female offenders increased, prompted by the increase of criminal activity among women. Although one hypothesis about this increase is that it resulted from the women's movement—a type of equal opportunity applied to crime—research has indicated that female offenders tend to be traditional rather than feminist in their beliefs. Even considering the increase in crime rates for female offenders, the rate of offenses remained lower and the offenses less serious for women than for men (Tjaden & Tjaden, 1981). That is, the increase in crimes committed by women was in nonviolent rather than violent crimes. Therefore, the gender difference in violent crime persists, with men being several times more likely than women to commit and be arrested for such crimes.

Men are also more likely to be the victims of crime than are women, particularly for crimes of violence (U.S. Department of Justice, 1990). Not only are men more likely to commit acts of violence, they are also more likely to be the victims of this violence. This pattern of male-male violence substantiates the findings of Cairns and his colleagues (Cairns et al., 1989), who investigated aggression longitudinally and found that adolescent boys were much more likely than adolescent girls to use confrontation and aggression as a strategy of managing conflict. In addition, Cairns et al. found that exchanges involving physical aggression between boys and girls decreased during adolescence, making male-female violence less common than physical aggression among

TABLE 9.3   **Percent of Male and Female Offenders Arrested for Various Offenses**

Offense	Men	Women
All violent crimes	89	11
All property crimes	75	25
Murder	90	10
Rape	99	1
Robbery	92	8
Aggravated assault	87	13
Burglary	91	9
Larceny/theft	68	32
Arson	87	13
Forgery	65	35
Fraud	58	42
Embezzlement	61	39
Prostitution	35	65
Drunkenness	90	10
Disorderly conduct	80	20
Curfew violation/loitering	73	27
Runaway	44	56

SOURCE: Based on information from "Bureau of Justice statistics sourcebook of criminal justice statistics—1992," 1993, U.S. Department of Justice, Washington, DC: U.S. Government Printing Office.

boys. The physical violence among boys also decreased, but their size, strength, and likelihood of owning weapons made young men more likely to both commit and to be the victims of physical aggression.

Despite their lower rate of victimization, women fear being the victims of crime more than men do. Mark Warr (1985) found that women's perceived risk of crime victimization followed two principles—perceived severity of the crime and feelings of personal vulnerability. In general, the more severe the crime, the less at risk women felt, following the principle of optimistic bias—the belief that very bad things are less likely to happen to you than to other people. But he also found one exception—rape. Women of all ages reported a fear of rape, and among women aged 35 and younger, it was the most feared crime, more than assault, robbery, or murder.

Sexual Violence.   Women's fears of sexual violence are not misplaced—rape is a common crime. In addition, rape often goes unreported, making the official estimates lower than actual occurrences (Koss, 1992). The U.S. Department of Justice (1993) reported that rape—defined as some form of forced sexual intercourse (vaginal, oral, or anal) by the use of force or threats of force—occurs at a rate of 4.3 per 1,000 people. This estimate is based on the number of reports of rape, but the reluctance to report rape has led to the belief that the actual rate may be several times larger.

Mary Koss and her colleagues (Koss, Gidycz, & Wisniewski, 1987) sampled U.S. college students to try to determine the rate of sexual violence. They asked both men and women about their sexual behavior and found that 27.5% of the women reported being raped since the age of 14 years and that 7.7% of the men reported behavior that met the legal definition of rape, including attempted rape. These rates yielded estimates for rape that were 10 to 15 times greater than the arrest rates for this crime, confirming the magnitude of the problem and the enormous number of rapes that go unreported.

Not only does rape go unreported to legal authorities, many women are reluctant to tell anyone about being raped. Although this reluctance is common, Gail Wyatt (1992) found that African-American women were significantly less likely to tell anyone about being raped than European-American women. Her study revealed no significant difference in the attempted or completed rapes for the women in the two ethnic groups, and women from both ethnic groups had difficulties in identifying attacks by acquaintances as "real" rape. Wyatt acknowledged the similarities of rape for all women but emphasized the unique history of rape for African-American women and the impact of that history on attitudes toward rape of this ethnic group.

Asian Americans hold more negative attitudes toward rape victims than European Americans (Mori, Selle, Zarate, & Bernat, 1994). Both Asian-American men and women were more likely than European Americans to endorse rape myths, such as that rape is the woman's fault and that women secretly enjoy rape, and Asian-American men had more negative attitudes about women than any other group. Asian-American women's acceptance of blame for rape may make them particularly unlikely to report this crime.

The stigma of rape involves the sexual nature of the crime and the tendency to blame the victim. Blaming and stigmatization are particularly common in rape—for perpetrators, victims, and those who hear about the rape. According to research by Colleen Dreyfus (1994), the stigma is even more severe when men are the victims. Dreyfus contended that male rape victims have been largely ignored by both authorities and researchers, leading to underestimation of the extent of their victimization and a lack of services for male rape victims. Her research showed that male rape victims were more socially rejected than robbery victims and that men stigmatized male victims more than women. Such attitudes do not help victims report and seek services to help cope with being raped.

Although rape has been considered a rare form of deviation, Diana Scully (1990) contended that rapists were not "sick" or unusual but rather that they enact social attitudes condoning violence toward women. Scully studied convicted rapists by conducting extensive interviews, and her results revealed unexpected similarities between the attitudes and behaviors of rapists and those of other men. In many ways the rapists were ordinary; they had not experienced an unusually high level of treatment for psychopathology or experienced an unusually high rate of childhood physical or sexual abuse. Although their family histories were filled with instability and violence, so were the backgrounds of other felons in Scully's study. The rapists were able to form relationships with women, and most had wives or girlfriends at the time they committed rape. As Scully summarized, "The background profile of convicted rapists does not suggest a unique category of criminal offender. Instead, it reveals a typical felon with no remarkable history to suggest a greater likelihood of rape" (p. 91).

Scully found that convicted rapists held attitudes that made their behavior predictable. Their attitudes toward women were a combination of the beliefs that women belong "on a pedestal" and that men have the right to treat women with violence. The largest subgroup of the rapists admitted their crime and found it reprehensible. These men justified their actions by blaming alcohol, drugs, the victim's character, or the victim's behavior. A smaller subgroup of the rapists denied that a rape had occurred, viewing their behavior as acceptable if a bit extreme. These men tended to minimize the severity of their actions and to find excuses for their behavior. Amazingly, the rapists believed that their victims had enjoyed the sexual experience, even when they had been beaten or murdered.

Some of the rapists in Scully's study conformed to the classic pattern of an attack on a stranger and the use of force or weapons to accomplish the rape. Many of these rapists told Scully that they planned their action because they were angry with their wives or girlfriends and wanted to do violence to a woman. These men reported that the common characteristic of these women was their vulnerability: They were in the right place at the wrong time—usually alone somewhere at night. Their appearance made no difference, and many of the rapists had trouble describing their victims.

The proportion of rapists who were acquainted with their victims was underrepresented in Scully's sample because this pattern is less likely to result in complaint, prosecution, or conviction than stranger rapes. The violent attack by a stranger is the vision of rape that women fear, but the most common experience of rape is an attack by an acquaintance, sometimes called date rape. The Koss et al. (1987) survey included questions about various types of sexual activities, and these researchers were able to estimate the rate of sexual coercion as well as behaviors that met the definition of rape. A total of 54% of the women in the survey reported that they had been sexually victimized in some way, and 25% of the men in the survey admitted to some level of sexual aggression. Koss et al. argued that the discrepancy in the rates for men and women was not due to a few sexually predatory men but rather to some degree of denial of sexual aggression by many men. This failure to recognize sexual aggression was similar to the denial expressed by the convicted rapists in Scully's study.

Rather than conceptualizing rape as the action of pathological men, more recent views of sexual violence hold that it is the action of men behaving in ways that their culture allows and perhaps even encourages under some circumstances (Brownmiller, 1975; Herman, 1989). William Walker and his colleagues (Walker, Rowe, & Quinsey, 1993) confirmed the relationship between acceptance of traditional social beliefs and sexual aggression in men. Karol Dean and Neil Malamuth (1994) constructed a model to conceptualize the appeal of sexual aggression based on individual, psychological factors. Acceptance of rape myths, acceptance of interpersonal violence, desire for dominance, and hostility toward women were all factors related to the appeal of sexual aggression. Although all men who find sexual aggression appealing may not act, this factor is a predictor of sexually aggressive behavior.

Social explanations of rape include social, political, and economic inequality between men and women; high levels of acceptable violence within a culture; high levels of general social disorganization—the breakdown of authority and control in a society's institutions; and widespread circulation of pornᶜ ʒraphy. Each of these hypotheses arose separately as potential explanations for rape, but Larry Baron and Murray Straus (1989) combined and evaluated these four hypotheses, attempting to build an integrated theory of rape.

Baron and Straus used the different rates of rape in the different states of the United States to test these four hypotheses. They found evidence to confirm three of the four hypotheses—a direct, positive link between social disorganization and the rape rate. As the level of instability and disorganization increase, so does rape rate. Sex magazine circulation and rape rate also showed a positive relationship. Baron and Straus found a direct, negative relationship between gender equality and rape: The less equal women and men were in the communities, the higher the rape rate. Although they failed to find a direct relationship between the amount of acceptable violence and rape, they concluded that indirect relationships exist between acceptable violence and social disorganization. Indeed, their analysis indicated complex relationships among the variables specified in their four hypotheses, such as unemployment, economic inequality, and urbanization in relation to rape rates. Table 9.4 shows the factors that have a direct and an indirect relationship with rape rates. A combination of these factors predicted 89% of the variation in rape rates within the United States, demonstrating the power of sociological factors in the occurrence of rape.

In summary, women also commit sexual violence but at very low rates, making sexual violence men's problem and women's fear. This fear is not without some basis:

TABLE 9.4   Sociological Factors Showing Direct and Indirect Relationships with Rape Rates

Factor	Type of Relationship
Sex magazine circulation	Positive and direct
Social disorganization	Positive and direct as well as indirect (related through gender equality and sex magazine circulation)
Gender equality	Negative and direct
Urbanization	Positive and direct
Percent unemployment	Positive and direct
Ratio of men to women	Positive and indirect (related through sex magazine circulation and gender equality)
Economic inequality	Negative and indirect (related through gender equality and sex magazine circulation)
Percent African American	Positive and indirect (related through level of violence)

SOURCE: Based on *Four theories of rape in American society: A state-level analysis,* by L. Baron & M.A. Straus, 1989, New Haven: Yale University Press.

The arrest records indicate that about 8% of women will be victims of rape. Other methods of estimated rape rates have revealed a much higher rate—27.5% of women reported being raped and 54% reported some type of sexual victimization. Convicted rapists differ surprisingly little from other men, but their attitudes toward women are extreme, in that they believe that "good" women should be placed on a pedestal but that men have the right to use violence with women. Although rape is an individual action, social factors contribute to its prevalence, including social disorganization, pornography, and gender inequality.

Situations Prompting Gender-Related Differences in Aggression

Although men commit more crimes than women, especially violent crimes, women and men are similar in their feelings of anger, and laboratory studies have indicated that men are not always more aggressive than women. The feelings that restrain people from using physical aggression include a reluctance to harm others and a fear of counteraggression, both more common among women. However, both women and men are likely to use physical aggression when they feel justified.

The studies that have investigated the development of aggression have found that gender differences exist but that these differences are small. In addition, children commit more aggressive acts than adolescents or adults. That is, aggression decreases with development. The greater prominence of aggression during adolescence and adulthood is a reflection of the greater damage done by adolescent and adult aggression, not its frequency.

Beginning during adolescence, boys and girls tend to use different strategies to handle conflict. Adolescent boys are much more likely than adolescent girls to use direct confrontation and physical violence, whereas girls are more likely to use social ostracism and group exclusion to express their anger toward other girls. Therefore, gender differences in aggression may appear to be large but these differences exist in style of expression rather than in quantity. Controlling for style, the gender differences in aggression are quite small. Indeed, gender role may be more important than gender in the experience of anger. According to research by Beverly Kopper and Douglas Epperson (1991), gender role, not gender, showed a consistent relationship to anger and the expression of anger.

Chapter 3 examined the connection between the hormone testosterone and aggression. The research on the connection between these two factors has revealed a complex interaction rather than a simple cause-and-effect relationship. Men who have high testosterone levels are more likely to have committed socially inappropriate acts, including criminal violence (Dabbs & Morris, 1990), but educational background and social class are also important factors in antisocial violence. Also, some evidence has indicated that aggression boosts testosterone level rather than the other way around (Booth, Shelley, Mazur, Tharp, & Kittok, 1989), making any simple, causal relationship between hormones and aggression implausible. Therefore, the presence of testosterone is probably not the underlying cause of male aggression.

Researchers like Todd Tieger (1980) have pointed to the different standards of behavior for boys and men compared to girls and women.

At a very early age, children come into increasing contact with a highly sex-role-stereotyped society. Television, parents, peers, and the educational system continue to present to the child the standardized version of male-female gender stereotyping that is reflected throughout the structure of the society. Children, as we have seen, come to observe that a highly salient behavior such as aggression is typically the "proper" activity of males only. (p. 958)

Furthermore, Tieger discussed how girls experience socialization that leads them to restrain their aggressive impulses, as physical aggression is not "ladylike."

Social standards for the expression of anger in the form of physical aggression may differ for men and women, but both boys and girls are discouraged from being physically aggressive by parents and teachers. However, by middle childhood both boys and girls have developed different expectations about expressing aggression. Boys expected less parental disapproval for their aggression, and both expected less parental disapproval for aggression against a boy than against a girl (Perry, Perry, & Weiss, 1989). Even with general parental disapproval for aggression, children learn about circumstances under which their aggression is at least somewhat acceptable, and boys learn different rules for displaying aggression than girls.

So are men more aggressive than women? Under some circumstances they are. Those circumstances involve the use of physical aggression against other men as a strategy of conflict resolution. Some men also hold attitudes that make them likely to be sexually violent with women, which include the beliefs that women should be held to higher standards of behavior than men (be put on a pedestal) and that men have the right to use violence against women.

Under some circumstances women and men are equally likely to be aggressive. When they feel justified, both men and women are willing to use physical aggression. Research indicates that women may restrain their aggression because they are less

---

GENDERED VOICES
They Put a Lot of Effort into Showing Nothing

I talked to a psychologist who had been employed as a therapist in a prison, and he told me that the prisoners exhibited what he considered to be an inappropriate level of emotion—none. He said, "I thought they put a lot of effort into showing no emotion. Their goal seemed to be to show no sign of any emotion. For example, even if they were hurt, their faces didn't change expressions. Every once in a while, I would see a slip, and a prisoner would show some sign of pain when he got hurt. I assume that they had feelings that were similar to anyone's, but their expression of emotion was very abnormal.

"Showing no emotion didn't mean that they let things go. They would retaliate against another prisoner who had hurt them, even if it was mostly an accident and he hadn't meant to hurt anyone. But they didn't show any emotion when they were hurt or when they hurt the other guy. It was part of the prison society to keep their faces like masks, showing nothing about what they felt, closing themselves off from the others."

willing than men to inflict harm or pain on others and they fear retaliation for their violence. However, none of the research has indicated that women and men feel different amounts or levels of anger. Therefore, the gender differences in aggression are examples of display rules, the rules that govern the expression of emotions.

Expressivity and Emotion

The similarities in the feelings that men and women experience and the differences in their behavior suggest that the gender difference in emotion may be in the expression of their emotions. Indeed, women have been described as the expressive gender, whereas men fail to express their emotions (Fischer, 1993). As Shields (1994) pointed out, this interpretation is only possible with a selective definition of what counts as emotion. Only by concentrating on fear and sadness in women and by overlooking aggression in men could women be considered more expressive than men. The evidence indicates that both women and men feel similar emotions under similar circumstances but that women express the emotions of sadness, anxiety, and fear more than men, whereas men express their anger more than women. This difference in expressivity can be explained by differences in display rules: Men and women are supposed to restrain displays of certain emotions yet are free to show others.

In his discussion of the requirements for the Male Sex Role, Robert Brannon (1976) listed four criteria, two of which relate to the gender differences in emotionality: (1) No Sissy Stuff, meaning the avoidance of anything vaguely feminine, and (2) Give 'Em Hell, meaning the display of anger and aggression. (See Chapter 8 for a discussion of all four components.) The stereotype holds that women are emotional, so the prohibition of anything feminine would include displays of most emotions. Anger is acceptable, however, because it is the essence of "giving 'em hell." These two components are essential elements of the display rules for men, but women may express more of what they feel, with the exception of anger.

The discrepancies among the three types of measures of emotionality (self-reports, observed behavior, and physical arousal) support the gender difference in display rules. When researchers have used participants' self-reports as their measure of emotion, they often find that women are more emotional than men. For example, Maccoby and Jacklin (1974) reviewed evaluations of self-reports of emotionality and found that girls and women were more likely than boys and men to admit to feelings of fear and anxiety. When researchers have used observations of participants' behavior in public, they measure the enactment of display rules and the potential bias of observers, who may be influenced by the stereotypes of emotion. Such studies tend to find gender differences (Eagly & Steffen, 1986), although the differences are not large, on the average. When researchers unobtrusively measure behavior in private, participants are more likely to display their emotions, and such studies often fail to find gender differences (Eisenberg & Lennon, 1983).

The measurement of the physiological component of emotion provides a method of comparing the emotional responses of women and men, and some studies have used physiological measures of emotionality, often in combination with self-report or behavioral measures. Ann Frodi and Michael Lamb (1978) conducted one such study in which they measured behavioral and physiological responses of children who were interacting with babies. They found a behavioral difference between girls and boys—the girls responded to and interacted with the babies more than the boys—but they found no difference in the physiological measures.

Women learn a slightly different set of display rules for emotion than men do, and the behavior of both men and women tends to conform to the display rules for each. According to these display rules, women should behave more nurturantly than men, and in self-reports and in public behavior they do. Boys and men should not be interested in babies or responsive to them, and under some circumstances they are not. However, boys tend to nurture pets, and men who care for children are as nurturant and responsive as women who perform these tasks. According to these display rules, men should be more physically aggressive than women, and in self-reports and in public behavior (including criminal violence) they are. However, women experience anger as strongly as men, and when they feel justified (and anonymous), women are as likely to show as much physical aggression as men. Therefore, the gender differences in emotion are more a function of circumstances and social learning of display rules than biologically determined differences due to instinct.

Summary

The stereotype of gender and emotion presents women as emotional and men as rational, but research on the different components of emotion has revealed that there may be few gender differences in the inner experience of emotion but substantial gender differences in the display of emotion. Included in the components of emotion are physiological and cognitive components. A classic experiment by Schachter and Singer demonstrated that expectations and setting can exert dramatic effects on the experience of emotion. Although psychologists continue to debate the relative contributions of physiology and cognition to the experience of emotion, most psychologists acknowledge that both are important.

The notion that some emotions are the result of instincts can be traced to Charles Darwin's theory of evolution. In psychology the explanation that emotion is instinctive has faded, with the exception of maternal instinct and an instinct toward aggression. Scientists have continued to believe in maternal instinct, although research by Harlow and his colleagues demonstrated that monkeys deprived of contact with other monkeys during the first six months of their lives failed to show adequate nurturing and caregiving. Other versions of

maternal instinct include the concept of bonding, an attachment formed between adult and infant during the first hours of the infant's life, and the concept of biological predisposition toward mothering. Neither of these concepts has much research support.

Research on gender differences in responsiveness to babies has shown differences in self-reports but not in behavioral observations of young children or in physiological measures of older children and adults. These findings indicate that girls and women show more responsiveness to babies because they believe they should and that boys and men show less responsiveness for the same reason. Women usually have a great deal more involvement in child care than men, and the greater pleasure that women derive from caring for children is coupled with their greater irritation in caring for children; men who are very involved in child care tend to report similar feelings. Therefore, the concept of maternal instinct has no support as a biologically based explanation for caregiving, and both men and women have similar emotions related to nurturing.

Aggression has also been nominated as an instinct, with the belief that men have more innate tendencies toward showing aggressive behavior than women. When considering the link between anger and aggression; that is, between emotion and behavior, few gender differences appear. Women and men experience anger similarly, but there are gender differences in the expression of this emotion. Boys and men tend to be more likely to use direct, physical confrontation when they are angry, whereas girls and women are more likely to avoid physical confrontation. There is no difference in the use of verbal aggression, but girls and women are more likely to cry when angry, an expression that is often misunderstood.

Developmental gender differences in aggression exist, with boys more likely than girls to use physical aggression at all ages. Longitudinal studies have revealed that aggression is moderately stable over time, and aggressive children are more likely to be violent adults than are less aggressive children. However, both boys and girls tend to become less aggressive as they develop, and by adulthood, the gender difference in aggression is small.

Despite small gender differences in aggression in laboratory studies and the overall decrease in aggression during adolescence and adulthood, very large gender differences exist in crime rate, with men about four times more likely than women to commit a violent crime. The victims of these violent crimes are more likely to be other men, but women fear crime victimization more than men, especially sexual violence. Nor is their fear unfounded: Official reports indicate that about 8% of women will be raped, and surveys indicate a rape rate as high as 28%. Explanations of rape have changed from the view that a few pathological men commit sexual violence to a view that cultural factors support violence against women. A study of convicted rapists indicated that they are like other men in many ways but that their attitudes differ in the extent to which they want to put women "on a pedestal" and in the extent to which they find violence against women acceptable.

Although men are more violent and less nurturant than women, these differences may relate to the expression rather than the subjective experience of emotion. The cultural display rules that govern the behaviors associated with emotion differ somewhat for men and women, allowing women more expression and restraining men from expressing many emotions. Therefore, gender differences in emotion may reflect differences in expressivity.

Glossary

Bonding   an emotional attachment that develops between mother or primary caregiver and infant within a few days after birth

Critical period   a time period in development during which animals are capable of rapid learning when presented with the necessary stimulus; once the critical period has passed, no amount of exposure will produce the learning

Display rules   the learned social rules that govern who may display which emotion and in what situation each emotion may be displayed

Suggested Readings

Eron, Leonard D. (1987). The development of aggressive behavior from the perspective of a developing behaviorism. *American Psychologist, 42,* 435–442. Eron describes his involvement in a longitudinal study of the development of aggression. This fascinating study confirmed the stability of aggression from childhood to adulthood as well as its relationship to parenting techniques and television viewing.

Fischer, Agneta H. (1993). Sex differences in emotionality: Fact or stereotype? *Feminism & Psychology,* *3,* 303–318. This article from Fischer is a good place to start in considering the issue of gender and emotion. She critically reviews the stereotypes, the research, and simplistic thinking concerning emotionality.

Risman, Barbara J. (1989). Can men "mother"? Life as a single father. In Barbara J. Risman & Pepper Schwartz (Eds.), *Gender in intimate relationships: A microstructural approach* (pp. 155–164). Belmont, CA: Wadsworth. Risman explores the responses of men who are called on to nurture children and how they respond to the situational demands by "mothering."

Tavris, Carol. (1982). *Anger: The misunderstood emotion.* New York: Simon & Schuster. This popular book is not recent, but Tavris provides a readable review of research on the subject. She contends that the benefits of getting in touch with and expressing anger have been overrated, and she argues that the benefits of control outweigh the advantages of expression.

C h a p t e r **10**

Relationships

HEADLINE

When a Fellow Needs a Friend, Not Just a Buddy
—*New York Times,* August 14, 1991

Author Sam Keen told journalist Jon Nordheimer (1991, p. C1) that "there is much about our experience as men that can only be shared with, and understood by, other men." Keen's opinion was of interest because his book, *A Fire in the Belly: On Being a Man* (1991), has become one of the major books of the men's movement. The book detailed the difficulties of being a man and provided suggestions about how men might make changes in their lives, including building better relationships with other men as well as with women.

The stereotype holds that men have difficulties in forming intimate relationships, whereas women are experts at intimacy; men have buddies or chums, whereas women have friends with whom they can share intimate feelings and emotions. Keen (1991) argued that men have a difficult time in forming friendships due to the competition that often exists among men. Homophobia is an additional barrier to intimate friendship among American men; when a man begins to feel close to another man, he pulls away for fear that his behavior may be interpreted as sexual rather than friendly. Keen explained that men tend to seek women as intimate friends rather than cultivate the friendship of other men in any intimate way.

Nordheimer's story told about groups of men who had sought intimate friendships with other men for the first time. Although these men were successful and most had many friends, they all felt the need for a different type of friendship—one that allowed for more emotional intimacy. Such intimacy is not typical of men's friendships, which often revolve around activities rather than around talk or self-disclosure. Some of these men had been able to develop this type of emotion-oriented intimacy with women but not with men, and others had never experienced such relationships. All had come to feel isolated and constrained by the style of friendships men typically form.

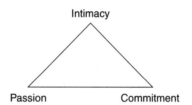

Liking = Intimacy without Passion or Commitment
Companionate love = Intimacy + Commitment without Passion
Romantic love = Intimacy + Passion without Commitment
Empty love = Commitment without Passion or Intimacy
Fatuous love = Passion + Commitment without Intimacy
Infatuated love = Passion without Commitment or Intimacy
Consummate love = Passion + Commitment + Intimacy

**FIGURE 10.1 Sternberg's Triangular Theory
of Love**

SOURCE: Adapted from A triangular theory of love (pp. 123, 128) by R.J.
Sternberg, 1986, *Psychological Review, 93.*

Keen has hypothesized that men who pursue success in corporations are especially
at risk of being restricted from entering intimate friendships, as these men are bound to
what Joseph Pleck (1981a) has called the myth of masculinity, beliefs about what a
man must do to achieve true masculinity. These rules do not include emotional sharing,
especially with other men. The friendships that are typical of men follow the pattern
reflected in the title of Nordheimer's story: Men are buddies but not intimate friends.

Robert Sternberg (1986) proposed a model for understanding all relationships, including friendship and romantic love. He called this model the triangular theory of love
because he hypothesized love's three points: intimacy, passion, and commitment. In his
conception, intimacy encompasses feelings of closeness, passion includes romantic
and sexual attraction, and commitment involves the decision that love exists and the
relationship should continue. Figure 10.1 shows Sternberg's model and the different
types of relationships that result from the combinations of these elements.

Sternberg argued that if none of these components exists, there is no relationship.
Sternberg's model distinguishes between two types of friendships—liking and companionate love. Liking occurs when people share intimacy but not passion or commitment. Sternberg (1987) included both sharing feelings and sharing activities as
intimacy. The combination of intimacy and commitment without passion results in
companionate love, a definition that would come close to what most people regard as
close but platonic friendship.

Friendships

Although Sternberg's triangular theory of love makes no distinction between intimacy
developed through sharing feelings or through sharing activities, the men in

Nordheimer's article felt that their activity-based "buddy" relationships with other men were not "real" friendships, and some had attempted to break this pattern and form friendships based on emotional intimacy. The feelings of deficiency that these men had about their friendships fit with Francesca Cancian's (1987) argument that the current definition of love, including close friendship, has been feminized: Love means emotional sharing and self-disclosure, not sharing activities or providing help.

The view that men are deficient at friendship has not always existed, nor do all cultures discourage intimate, emotional friendships between men (Nardi, 1992a). The Greeks believed that true friendship could exist only between free and equal individuals, omitting all women, slaves, and men of lesser social standing from the experience.

The nature of men's friendships has changed over the past 100 years (Nardi, 1992a). During the 19th century, intimate friendships were common for both men and women. Courage and loyalty were seen as the basis for a special type of friendship that men could share, and men were considered capable of experiencing closeness and feelings for other men that women could not feel for other women nor women and men for each other. However, contemporary men do not often form intimate friendships with other men, and men like those in Nordheimer's article sometimes feel that they are missing an important experience. Currently, women are seen as more capable of intimate friendship, and women's style of friendship is viewed as more intimate than the relationships formed by men.

Development of Styles

As Eleanor Maccoby (1988) pointed out, children segregate themselves according to gender starting at preschool age and continuing throughout elementary and middle school. This segregation is noticeable during preschool, becoming much more pronounced during the elementary school years, and may be imposed by parents or teachers. If not, children will segregate themselves, with girls associating with girls, boys associating with boys, and very little association between girls and boys. When the two are put into situations in which they must interact, they do, but the tendency to group into same-gender associations is a persistent pattern for children. Furthermore, the interactions of boys and girls differ, beginning very early in development.

Carol Jacklin and Eleanor Maccoby (1978) arranged interactions between pairs of 33-month-old children to observe their reactions to each other. The pairs consisted of all possible combinations—boys with boys, girls with girls, and boys with girls. These children interacted more with children of the same than of the other gender, for both positive and negative behaviors. That is, children in a boy-boy or girl-girl pair were more likely to offer a toy to their partner or try to take a toy from their partner than the children in a girl-boy pair. Indeed, children in mixed-gender pairs behaved differently from those in same-gender pairs, with the girls being more passive and the boys more unresponsive when each interacted with the other. Girls in such pairs tended to stand by and watch the boys play or to withdraw and seek their mothers. The boys in such pairs tended to ignore what the girls said to them, but they paid attention to other boys.

Jacklin and Maccoby found these behaviors interesting because their appearance seemed to be part of the situation rather than characteristics of the children. Girls and boys behaved similarly when they interacted with children of the same gender: The girls were active in their exchanges, and the boys were responsive to their partners' messages. However, when put in mixed-gender pairs, these children's behaviors changed. Jacklin and Maccoby speculated that, even before age 3 years, children understand that there are differences between the genders, and their reactions fall along stereotypical lines. Furthermore, the unequal interactions in mixed-gender pairs may relate to the gender segregation that is typical of children's play and friendships. Playing would not be much fun if your partner failed to react and listen. Therefore, the types of interactions exhibited by boys and girls would tend to make each more eager to seek the company of someone of the same gender.

Children as young as 2nd grade have a concept of friendship and expect friends to behave differently toward them than other children who are only acquaintances (Furman & Bierman, 1984). At this age their notion of friendship centers mostly around what friends should do for each other, such as helping each other and sharing secrets. As they develop, children add to their notion of friendship so that personal characteristics such as loyalty become important. Children also begin to rely on friends for emotional and tangible support during the elementary and junior high school years, and they consider these types of support important to friendship (Berndt & Perry, 1986). During preadolescence, children become increasingly able to integrate the notion that conflict is an acceptable part of friendship, forming an increasingly complex concept of friendship during the years of middle childhood and preadolescence. This concept includes the types of things that friends should do for each other and the type of characteristics that friends should share; children start to acknowledge that friends may disagree and still be friends.

During elementary school, children begin to rely on peers for companionship and intimacy, shifting from a reliance on siblings and parents (Buhrmester & Furman, 1987). These relationships more closely resemble the sharing and mutual concern for each other that typify the closeness and intimacy component of Sternberg's triangular model of relationships. The research on elementary school children demonstrated that same-gender friends were important sources of companionship for the 2nd, 5th, and 8th graders who participated in the study. The study also revealed gender differences in the development of intimate friendship, with girls both seeking and valuing intimacy at younger ages than boys. Like other investigations, this study showed that children exhibit a resistance to cross-gender friendships; only the 8th graders valued the company of the other gender.

One possible basis for the gender differences in friendships during middle childhood comes from the different activities that girls and boys enjoy during these years. For example, boys are more fond of rough-and-tumble play than girls. Such play involves play-fighting and chasing and is very common among preschool children, especially boys (Humphreys & Smith, 1987). The persistence of rough-and-tumble play throughout middle childhood and into preadolescence might seem to escalate into aggression, but such play is actually done in a spirit of fun. Boys also tend to play in somewhat larger groups, to spend more time outside (Maccoby, 1990), and to be more fond of activities that involve **gross motor skills,** such as running, jumping, and throwing a ball.

William Bukowski and his colleagues (Bukowski, Gauze, Hoza, & Newcomb, 1993) investigated the basis for gender segregation during childhood and found that activity preference might be one factor in gender segregation. Boys who preferred high levels of motor activity preferred the company of other boys, and girls who disliked such activities preferred the company of other girls. Thus, activity preference is one of the factors relating to girls and boys forming separate groups.

The conception of girls playing quietly with their dolls is stereotypical rather than typical: Girls engage in active and even athletic play, but their preferred partners are other girls rather than boys. Maccoby (1990) explained that a large part of children's play time is occupied by gender-neutral activities, but the decision to play with children of the same gender persists. Maccoby (1988) also reported that the more active, assertive girls—the "tomboys"—were the ones who tended to have the strongest preference for the companionship of other girls. Also, the play groupings of girls tended to be smaller than those of boys, with girls forming more intimate but fewer relationships.

Evidence also indicates that girls tend to evolve a different style of group interaction than boys (Maccoby, 1988, 1990). Girls make more polite requests and use persuasion to get their way, whereas boys make more direct demands and attempt to get their way through becoming dominant in their group. Girls try to involve other girls in the ongoing activities of the group, whereas boys tell other boys what to do. Girls do not lack assertiveness, but their style of assertion and influence differs from that of boys. Furthermore, during middle childhood the style of persuasion typical of girls begins to be less effective with boys than with other girls, providing an additional basis for restricted association.

Barrie Thorne (1986) investigated the gender segregation that occurs during the elementary school years and also the areas and conditions of interactions between girls and boys. Thorne's observations in elementary schools revealed that the organization of the schools and the teachers contributes to gender segregation. For example, teachers often organize classroom competitions in which the girls form one team and the boys the other, and situations in which teachers' aides considered one section of the playground to be the girls' area and another to be the boys' area also occurred. Thus, schools and adults may perpetuate the tendency for girls and boys to form separate work and play groups.

Thorne's investigation of the areas and conditions of cross-gender interactions revealed the animosity that often accompanies such interactions. Thorne observed that the adult-organized contests and playground games of chasing do not ease interactions between boys and girls, but rather make them more difficult. Thorne did observe some situations of comfortable interaction between girls and boys, and these tended to be either very absorbing activities, such as group projects or interesting games, or activities organized by an adult so as to include both girls and boys, such as games involving assigned rather than chosen teams. Thorne found few children who traveled between the worlds of girls and boys, and she saw the beginnings of heterosexual awareness in the gender segregation of elementary school children.

❊ DIVERSITY HIGHLIGHT
Friendships in a Desegregated School

Gender is not the only basis for self-segregation during the early school years. Ethnic and racial background are also characteristics that children notice and use as a basis for forming groups. Janet Ward Schofield (1981) studied preadolescent children in a desegregated junior high school (containing grades 6 through 8) to examine the influence of both gender and race on children's interactions. The school was located in a large, industrial northeastern city in the United States, and the racial composition was approximate 50% African American and 50% European American. The staff of the school was also biracial and dedicated to operating a racially desegregated school. Teachers did not view race as an appropriate characteristic for grouping and tried to encourage children of both ethnic groups to work together and to get along with each other.

The teachers' efforts to promote equal and harmonious interactions were not entirely successful. Although the teachers did not group the children according to race, the children still tended to group themselves. Even when the arrangements of classes ensured an equal balance of African Americans and Whites as well as boys and girls, the students "often resegregate themselves along racial and gender lines to a remarkable extent, avoiding even surface contact when possible" (Schofield, p. 62). In classrooms the children divided themselves into four groups according to race and gender and seated themselves accordingly, unless the teachers arranged them into a different pattern.

Schofield studied seating patterns in the school's cafeteria, where children could sit where they wished, analyzing these seating patterns according to who sat by whom. She found that, on a typical day, less than 10 of 200 students were involved in cross-race seating arrangements, and even fewer were involved in cross-gender seating. Schofield concluded that "sex is generally a more potent grouping factor than race" (p. 62). When children had to choose whether to interact with someone of their own gender or someone of their own ethnic group, they chose the child of the same gender, crossing ethnic lines. The prohibition against crossing gender lines was so strong that Schofield saw children accept a punishment rather than interact with a child of the other gender.

David DuBois and Barton Hirsch (1990) conducted a similar study and obtained similar results; they also found that junior high school students were reluctant to cross ethnic lines to form friendships. They found more evidence of interracial friendships than Schofield had, but these friendships tended to be restricted to school and did not carry over to activities outside the school environment. The African-American and European-American students who were most likely to be friends were those who lived in integrated neighborhoods and attended integrated schools.

Thus, children in integrated schools behave like other children in avoiding the opposite gender, but in addition, they also tend to avoid peers from other ethnic groups. DuBois and Hirsch's more recent study found more evidence of interracial friendships, but these friendships tended to be limited to school rather than extending to the full range of preadolescents' friendship activities. Even with these restrictions, friendships between children of different ethnic groups are more common than cross-gender friendships, revealing the most salient type of segregation for children.

L. Alan Sroufe and his colleagues (Sroufe, Bennett, Englund, & Urban, 1993) considered the dilemma that gender segregation poses for preadolescents: They must avoid members of the other gender except under certain sanctioned circumstances, yet each gender must have sufficient contact to learn about the other. These researchers found evidence of the importance of gender segregation. Preadolescents who maintained gender segregation were both more popular with their peers and rated as more socially competent by adults than children who violated the boundaries between the genders. Sroufe et al. proposed that same-gender friendships during childhood allow individuals to learn how to form relationships without the pressure of sexual contact. Referring back to Sternberg's model of relationships, these relationships allow children and pre-adolescents to develop intimacy and commitment without passion. Childhood friendships, then, might be a type of practice for adolescent and adult romantic relationships.

Although preadolescent children avoid friendships with children of the other gender, they are acutely aware of their future roles as romantic partners. Maccoby (1988) discussed how gender segregation seems forced during preadolescence and how children of both genders use threats of contact and proposed romantic feelings—threats to kiss, teasing about who "likes" whom, and avoidance of physical contact for fear of catching "cooties"—as ways to harass each other. This active avoidance changes to active interest during adolescence; contact between girls and boys becomes more common, but friendships between girls and boys remain uncommon.

Friendship over the Life Span

Friendships during adolescence are similar to those of preadolescence, but adolescents find intimacy increasingly important and form relationships with a greater degree of personal sharing and self-disclosure than those of younger children. The gender differences in the value and attainment of intimacy persist, with girls more likely to be interested in forming emotionally intimate friendships with a smaller set of girls and boys more likely to form activity-based friendships with a more extensive set of boys. Thomas Berndt's (1982) review of research on adolescent friendships indicated that adolescent girls use talk as a way to develop intimacy, revealing and learning intimate knowledge about each other. Such self-disclosure is not as characteristic of boys' friendships, and research has indicated that boys might think of friendship in different terms than girls: Boys are less likely than girls to say that they would treat friends differently than other classmates. However, the research Berndt reviewed was not consistent in showing gender differences in self-disclosures to friends. Perhaps girls and boys are not so different in their behavior with their friends but differ in what they think is important to friendship.

Berndt speculated that boys might be discouraged from forming the same type of intimate friendships that girls form out of fear that such closeness might lead to homosexuality. As Peter Nardi (1992a) emphasized, the current prohibitions against same-gender sexual activity make men hesitant about emotional closeness in friendships, and the activity-based relationships of adolescent boys and adult men illustrate one strategy for avoiding the emotional intimacy that could suggest homosexuality.

Intimacy becomes an increasingly important facet of friendship during the transition from preadolescence to adolescence for Israeli youngsters. Ruth Sharabany and her colleagues (Sharabany, Gershoni, & Hofman, 1981) confirmed that girls are more advanced than boys in valuing and creating emotionally intimate friendships with other girls, but they also found that adolescents began to form intimate friendships with individuals of the other gender. However, adolescent girls increased their intimacy with boys more rapidly than boys with girls, and this difference was maintained for the oldest adolescents in the study, the 11th graders. These results suggest that a gender asymmetry may exist in attainment of intimate friendships during late adolescence.

Research by Ladd Wheeler, Harry Reis, and John Nezlek (1983) also showed some gender asymmetry in relationships, revealing that men may find their relationships with women more emotionally fulfilling than their relationships with men. These researchers investigated the social interactions and loneliness of college students and found that the time spent with men had no relationship to feelings of loneliness for men. That is, spending time with other men did not decrease feelings of loneliness in men, but meaningful interactions with men did. Spending time with women, however, decreased loneliness, regardless of the meaningfulness of the interaction. Indeed, for both women and men, spending time with women seemed to protect against feelings of loneliness. These researchers concluded that both men and women need the same qualities in their relationships, but they speculated that women are better at providing these qualities to both their male and female friends.

A study of friendship among college students by Mayta Caldwell and Letitia Anne Peplau (1982) confirmed suggestions from previous studies—that gender differences exist in what each considers the basis for friendship and that young men and women differ in their conceptualizations of friendship. Caldwell and Peplau questioned college students about their friendships as well as observing them in a role-playing exercise. They found no differences in the number of friends or the amount of time spent with friends for young men and young women, but they confirmed that men were more likely than women to choose an activity to do with a friend rather than "just talk" and to choose their friends on the basis of shared activities rather than shared attitudes.

The women in Caldwell and Peplau's study were more likely than the men to mention talk as an important factor in their friendships and to concentrate on personal sharing with their friends. These researchers found that both men and women *said* that they valued intimacy in their friendships, but women created friendships with more emotional intimacy than did men. "Men and women may be equally likely to define friends as intimate; however, men and women may have different standards for assessing the intimacy of friendship" (Caldwell & Peplau, 1982, p. 731). In addition to confirming the persistence of different patterns of friendship that start in childhood, this study suggested that men and women might have different standards for intimacy in relationships, with men defining their activities with other men as intimate and women defining their talk and self-disclosure as intimate.

Unmarried, childless college students may have the most time to devote to friends. In addition, the demands of friendships for men and women may be most similar among college students (Caldwell & Peplau, 1982). As individuals become involved with romantic relationships, existing friendships often change, occupying less time and possibly becoming less intimate.

With marriage comes a different pattern of friendship as relationships with other couples are added to relationships with individual friends. Barry Wellman (1992) analyzed the relationships of married couples by conducting extensive interviews, investigating the factors that relate to the formation and maintenance of these people's social networks. Traditionally, men have formed friendships as a result of their work and public lives, whereas women have formed a network of friends and family relationships centered around the home. Wellman contended that the home had become the base for friendships for both the male and female working-class participants in his study. Furthermore, the women were the monitors of social activity, arranging most social gatherings as well as get-togethers with other couples. The associations with other couples did not require both members of a couple to be equally close friends, and the most typical pattern was for either the husbands or the wives to be friends and the other member of the couple to tolerate his or her counterpart. This pattern of friendship does not promote intimate sharing for both members of any couple, as neither are likely to feel close to the other couple.

The men whom Wellman interviewed also had buddies whom they saw separate from couple-oriented activities. These buddies were likely to be companions for activities such as going to a ball game together, but these buddies also helped with small services (fixing a car) or large services (roofing a house). The men in this sample got less emotional support from their friends than their wives received from their friends, but then the men did not necessarily feel that their friends should provide emotional support. Husbands tended to look to their wives rather than to their friends for emotional support. These married couples demonstrated that some patterns of friendship change with marriage, but the greater emotional intimacy of women's friendships persist after marriage.

During the early years of marriage, both spouses may relinquish other relationships to develop their marriage, seeking emotional intimacy and support from each other. In addition, when couples have children, the children take up time that might have been devoted to friends or to spouses. Thus, young marrieds, especially those with children, tend to devote less time to other friendships than people who are unmarried or childless. Theodore Cohen (1992) found that the men in his study had restricted their friendships both when they were married and again after the birth of a child. Some of that restriction was due to time limitations and the obligation to fulfill the husband and father role, but some withdrawal from friendship was due to friends' perception of the married friends' roles. That is, unmarried men perceived that married men were not supposed to spend as much time with their friends, so they restricted their attempts to stay in contact when a friend married. Married men reported that they felt they should restrict their other relationships so as to maintain greater intimacy with their wives than with other male or female friends. This process may also apply to women. Thus, each member of a married couple may undergo a restriction of outside friendships.

As their children mature, couples once again have more time for each other and for friendships. Joseph Veroff, David Reuman, and Sheila Feld (1984) investigated motives across the life span and found that women experienced a decline in motivation to seek the company of peers, whereas men did not. Indeed, men's motivation to seek the company of similar others remained quite stable across their adult years. Veroff et al. interpreted the difference in men's and women's motives to affiliate as indicative of their different life experiences and roles: Women are more likely to occupy roles within the family that satisfy their needs to be with others, whereas men are not.

When children become adults, both the adult children and their parents can become friends. Due to the wide difference in power and authority, this possibility is not likely during childhood or adolescence, but adult children and their parents sometimes form relationships that have the characteristic emotional sharing and self-disclosure that typifies friendships. However, many people cannot abandon the roles of parent and child, preventing friendship from forming.

Flexibility of Styles

Men may find emotional intimacy easier with women than with other men. As Cancian (1987) proposed, love has come to be defined in feminine terms, as the expression of feelings and self-disclosure. These characteristics are commonly associated with women and are actually more common in women's than men's friendships. Some evidence exists that men also can use this style of relationship and tend to do so when they relate to women. That is, men may be able to use different styles of relating to different friends. Helen Reid and Gary Alan Fine (1992) studied self-disclosure in same-gender and cross-gender friendships and found evidence of flexibility in style of relating for both men and women. One of the important factors in self-disclosure was the type of relationship between the two people. For instance, lovers and spouses reported more intimate self-disclosure than platonic friends.

Reid and Fine hypothesized that both men and women conform to a role in maintaining different types of relationships and that the rules of relating differ both for type of relationship and for the gender of the target person in the relationship. Women's emphasis on talk and sharing feelings is part of the pattern people accept for women's friendships, and a different pattern exists for friendship among men. "For men, the homophobia of our society requires carefully choreographed behaviors when with other men—togetherness is acceptable if in the context of sports, business, or family groups, but getting together just to talk raises discomfiting feelings on the part of the man or questions from others" (Reid & Fine, 1992, p. 149).

According to Reid and Fine, yet another pattern exists for cross-gender friendships, with even more constrained rules. In his study of cross-gender friendships, which explored these constraints, Scott Swain (1992) contended that such friendships are a recent development, "a social anomaly that is overshadowed by cultural emphasis on same-sex friendships, and heterosexual love and sexual relationships" (p. 153). These cross-gender friendships did not exist 100 years ago, when Western societies were strongly gender segregated and women governed the home and men occupied the world of work, politics, and business. Although gender segregation still exists in many situations, school and work offer opportunities for cross-gender relationships.

Swain concluded that cross-gender friendships are not only more rare but also more difficult to sustain than same-gender friendships. His participants found satisfactions in such friendships, claiming that they derived pleasure from their cross-gender friendships that they missed in their same-gender relationships. All were aware of the boundaries they had to maintain so that their friendships would not become sexual relationships. In addition, the men were aware that they must adopt a different style when relating to a female friend, a style similar to the one used by women. Likewise, the women interacted differently with their male friends than with their female friends, using a more "masculine" style of interaction with men. These young adults saw limitations and drawbacks to the style typical of their own gender and enjoyed the different type of friendships they experienced with members of the other gender.

The ability to adapt to the situation by using a more "feminine" or "masculine" style of interaction indicates that styles of friendship are indeed roles that men and women learn. Although not all men may learn the intimate sharing and self-disclosure that is typical of women's friendships, some do, and these men use this style when they form friendships with women. More likely, men learn the behaviors but feel uncomfortable in enacting this friendship style. As several researchers have pointed out, **homophobia**—the unreasonable fear and hatred of homosexuality—restrains men from seeking emotional intimacy with other men. Even when men know the style, they may be reluctant to use it. When they use it, they may feel more comfortable in this type of relationship with a woman rather than another man.

The constraints on women's behavior are not as strong; their typical style of emotional intimacy with other women has no homosexual connotations. However, emotional intimacy between women and men often has an element of a sexual relationship, so women who seek friendships with men also must be vigilant in maintaining a non-sexual friendship. Women who adopt an activity-based style of relationship with men, being "one of the boys," can participate in the same activities that men enjoy with each other—playing baseball, poker, or other recreational activities. This choice creates a style of relationship typical of men and not necessarily infused with emotional intimacy. Some men and women have chosen to break the boundaries established during preschool and form friendships with members of the other gender. The research indicates that men and women know about both friendship styles, suggesting that any limitations in creating cross-gender friendships come from reluctance to apply these styles.

Cancian (1987) argued that the restriction of one style of relationship to women and the other to men has forced each into a way of relating that fails to allow the development of full potential for anyone. Cancian contended that the feminized definition of love as intimate sharing and self-disclosure has made women into the experts in relationships and has left many men feeling incompetent at relationships, as they may have problems with the emotional, intimate style of relating. She asserted that these restrictions have affected love relationships even more strongly than friendships. Cancian advocated an acceptance of the benefits of both styles of relationship and criticized the equation of emotional intimacy with love, both romantic love and friendship. Her analysis of the history of love relationships led her to the conclusion that the male and female roles present restrictions on the development of both men and women.

Love Relationships

Taking love relationships between men and women as her main emphasis, Cancian (1987) contended that the roles that men and women play encourage emotion and intimacy for women and independence and self-development for men. However, this pattern has not always existed, and Cancian described several different patterns of love relationships that have existed over the past several centuries. Before the 19th century, few differences existed between masculine and feminine love. Agriculture was the basis for most people's livelihood, and both men and women worked together on family farms, making the family the center of both men's and women's lives. Although men were the head of households, both men and women believed that they had the duty to love and help one another. "Men owned almost all the property and monopolized positions of power in the community, while women were responsible for the care of infants and of the sick and disabled, but the activities and personality traits associated with love were not highly differentiated by gender" (Cancian, 1987, p. 16).

In Sternberg's (1986) triangular model of love, this Family Duty blueprint ensured an equal relationship between the partners. Such marriages had commitment, and the sharing of home life made intimacy very likely, but the component of passion might be missing from such duty-bound relationships. Indeed, in arranged marriages, this component might never be part of the relationship of a married couple.

By the end of the 18th century, the Industrial Revolution had changed the pattern of many people's lives. Work and family had been separated, with men working in jobs in factories and offices rather than around the home. Women, too, might work in factories, but the ideal pattern of family relationship was for men to fulfill the Good Provider role (Bernard, 1981) and for women to be mothers and wives. This division led to the Doctrine of the Two Spheres (Welter, 1978), the division that resulted in women's preeminence in family life and men's dominance in the outside world.

Cancian credited the Companionship blueprint for love relationships with the feminization of love. Women became responsible for the maintenance of the home and family, a sanctuary from the hostility of the outside world of business and factory. This responsibility made women the experts in love: They were the ones who had the tender feelings and experienced the emotions; they were the ones who needed love and depended on men and children for it; they were the ones most capable of providing love to others.

Through this family arrangement, women became dependent on men for financial security, and maintaining the love of a husband was essential to women's financial security. During the 1920s, women started to invade the male world of work, taking paid jobs outside the home. With increasing economic power, women were less dependent on men for financial security, and the blueprint for marriage changed to the Companionship model (Cancian, 1987). This model focused on affection and support for each other, but women were still the experts on love and held the responsibility for the relationship: "Marriage was to be all of a women's life but only part of a man's" (Cancian, 1987, p. 34).

The Companionship model for marriage emphasized the similarity of the partners, and personal characteristics in the selection of marriage partners became important as this model of marriage became more well accepted. Spouses were supposed to love each other before they married and to choose their partners rather than relying on partners chosen by parents. Using Sternberg's model to analyze these relationships, consummate love was the ideal, with an equal mixture of intimacy, passion, and commitment. However, romantic love was also a possibility, with its combination of passion and intimacy but lack of commitment. As evidence for the rising lack of commitment under the Companionship blueprint, the divorce rate increased (Cancian, 1987).

The emphasis on personal compatibility and romance in marriage prompted a different method of selecting marriage partners. Rather than relying on the family to choose a partner or making a decision on an economic basis, individuals started to choose their own mates. Dating arose as a way of finding suitable marriage partners for Companionship-style marriages.

Dating

Although dating began during the 1920s as a form of courtship, it has expanded to fulfill other functions—recreation, status and achievement, socialization, learning about intimacy, sexual exploration, companionship, and identity formation (Santrock, 1993). Since the 1940s, dating has become less formal and structured than during the preceding decades (Miller & Gordon, 1986). Rather than following the traditional pattern in which boys ask, plan, and pay for dates, current dating patterns include girls taking the initiative in asking, planning, and paying for dates in addition to a pattern of mixed-gender group dating.

Dating has become an important part of adolescent life, and most young people in the United States have their first date between the ages of 12 and 16 years, with girls dating slightly earlier than boys. By age 16 years, more than 90% of adolescents have had a date (Santrock, 1993). Dating becomes more frequent for older teenagers, with about 50% of adolescents in high school having at least one date per week.

Changes in the reasons for dating occur throughout adolescence. A study by Bruce Roscoe, Mark Diana, and Richard Brooks (1987) revealed that younger adolescents (6th graders) tended to date as a recreational activity or as a way to achieve status. These adolescents were self-focused in their dating patterns, showing concern for status, acceptance, and physical appearance rather than concern for their dating partner or for developing a relationship. Older teenagers showed more concern for the social and companionship aspects of dating and less concern for superficial characteristics, such as a fashionably dressed date. Personal characteristics, such as kindness and confidence, were more important to adolescents of all ages than prestige factors, such as money or ethnic group membership.

Boys and girls in the Roscoe et al. study showed some differences in the characteristics they valued in a date, with boys being more concerned with physical appearance and more interested in dating a sexually active partner than were girls. Adolescent boys who hold traditional attitudes toward masculinity have reported more sexual partners, less intimacy with their sexual partners, and a greater belief that relationships with girls are adversarial than have adolescent boys who have less traditional views of masculinity (Pleck, Sonenstein, & Ku, 1993).

For girls in the Roscoe et al. study, confidence, kindness, dependability, parental approval, and not drinking alcohol were more important characteristics in a date than

GENDERED VOICES
I Was Terrible at Being a Girl

"I was fairly bad at being a girl when I was a child," a middle-aged woman told me. "I did tomboy-type things. But I was really terrible at it when I was a teenager and trying to date and attract boys. Dating seemed like a game, and the rules were so silly. And I was bad at the game. Flirting was a disaster—I felt so silly and incompetent.

"My mother practically despaired of my ever behaving in ways that would lead to dates. She would give me advice, such as 'Hide how smart you are, because boys don't like to date girls who are smarter than they are' and 'Wait for him to open the door for you.' I thought both those things were pretty pointless. Why should I hide how smart I was? I had gone to school with most of the guys in my high school since we were all in elementary school, so they knew how smart I was. Besides, if I could have fooled one, I didn't think that I could have kept up the charade. I wasn't smart enough to play dumb for

all that long. Also, why would I want to date a guy who wanted a dumb girl? Sounded like a poor prospect to me.

"I know that opening doors became an issue in the 1970s feminist movement, but my objections were about 10 years earlier. It just seemed silly to me that a perfectly capable person, me, should inconvenience a guy to open a door. I was more than capable of doing so, and I never saw why I shouldn't—still don't for that matter. I now see having doors opened as a courtesy, which is O.K. I open doors for both men and women. There's probably too much made of that particular issue, but when I was a teenager, it was something my mother warned me about on numerous occasions. I just had a hard time getting the rules of the game, and I was terrible at the girl stuff. I am much better at being a women than I was at being a girl."

they were for boys. In general, Roscoe and his colleagues found that younger adolescents looked for self-centered and superficial characteristics in dating partners, perhaps indicating unrealistic standards for dating choices. Older adolescents, on the other hand, showed that they had developed more flexible and personal standards for dating.

Traditional gender role behavior is evident in the dating behavior of both genders. Suzanna Rose and Irene Frieze (1993) found that young men's and women's behavior on dates follows a script, a model that people use to guide their behavior. They investigated how closely college students adhere to this script in describing an actual and a hypothetical first date. They found a great deal of agreement between the two, but they also found a difference for gender role behaviors: Following the script would lead men to act and women to react. The man's active role includes initiating the date, controlling the activities, and initiating sexual activity. The woman's reactive role includes being concerned about her appearance, participating in the activities her partner planned, and reacting to his sexual advances. Both the hypothetical and actual dates reflected this script, which follows traditional gender stereotypes.

Although dating is the method through which most people now choose mates, only around 7% of the college students, and even fewer of the younger adolescents in the Roscoe et al. study, said that mate selection was the reason for dating. Interestingly, the characteristics preferred by late adolescents in dating partners and the list of characteristics that young married adults find desirable in a mate were very similar (Buss & Barnes, 1986). People seek both dates and mates who are kind, intelligent, physically attractive, and socially exciting. In this study of mate selection as in the selection of dating partners, men valued physical attractiveness more than women.

Few differences in partner preference appeared when Judith Howard and her colleagues (Howard, Blumstein, & Schwartz, 1987) asked male-male, female-female as well as male-female couples to describe the characteristics they wanted in a partner. Both said they wanted romantic partners who were kind, considerate, and physically attractive. The partners in same-gender couples expressed a preference for partners who were more athletic and expressive about their feelings than the mates described by partners in male-female couples, but these differences were small. Regardless of sexual orientation, people seek similar qualities in romantic partners. The results of this study raised questions about the belief that reproductive fitness is a factor in mate selection.

Other characteristics that attract people to romantic partners include similarity of personal values. As John Antill (1983) phrased it, mate selection is more a matter of "birds of a feather flock together" than "opposites attract." That is, people are romantically attracted to others more like them than different from them. These similarities include not only personal values but also social class, religion, and gender role acceptance. The notion that opposites attract may relate to the concepts of masculinity and femininity and the belief that the two lie on opposite ends of a continuum. (See Chapter 8 for a discussion of this conceptualization.) According to this view, masculine men should be attracted to their "opposite"—feminine women—and vice versa.

An alternative interpretation of compatibility and gender roles holds that men and women who have traditional beliefs about gender roles are not opposite, but similar to each other in accepting stereotypical gender roles. This match might make people more compatible, but William Ickes (1993) argued that such relationships have problems. Women and men may be attracted to those with traditional gender roles, but they have trouble getting along with these partners in a long-term relationship.

In studying gender roles and relationship stability, Peplau and her colleagues (Peplau, Hill, & Rubin, 1993) studied dating couples in the 1970s and followed these relationships over 15 years. They found evidence for a great deal of variability in gender role attitudes during the 1970s; some couples held traditional attitudes and some believed in egalitarian relationships. Both members of a couple tended to be similar in their beliefs, but the men were more conservative than the women. No relationship emerged between satisfaction and gender role attitudes, with both traditional and egalitarian couples forming equally satisfactory relationships. Gender role traditionalism was more strongly related to relationship stability for the women than for the men. College women with traditional gender role attitudes were more likely to marry their boyfriends and to be married to them 15 years later than more liberal women.

Despite the opinion of adolescents that their dating is not oriented toward mate selection, dating is the process through which most men and women find partners. The patterns of relating to each other established during dating carry over into marriage, but marriage is a major life transition. When people marry, they assume the new roles of husband and wife.

Marriage and Committed Relationships

Marriage is not the only form of committed romantic relationship. Both heterosexual as well as gay and lesbian couples cohabit without marrying. Whereas gay and lesbian couples cannot legally marry in most places, heterosexual couples sometimes choose to live together without marrying. For some heterosexual couples, cohabitation can be a type of trial for marriage, whereas others cohabit as a form of very steady dating. The number of cohabiting heterosexual couples has dramatically increased since 1970 to about 4% of all heterosexual couples (Blumstein & Schwartz, 1983). However, the number of marriages far outnumber other types of committed love relationships, and the majority of research on gender and committed relationships has focused on marriage.

Several styles of marriage now exist, following the patterns Cancian (1987) called the Companionship, the Independence, and the Interdependence blueprints. The Companionship blueprint, discussed earlier, was the model for most marriages in the United States from the 1920s until the 1960s. Partners who follow this pattern tend to have well-defined and separate gender roles, and women are responsible for maintaining the love relationship. This type of marriage is now considered traditional, as adherents oppose self-development for women, a major tenet of the Independence blueprint.

The Independence blueprint arose during the 1960s, a period of personal freedom and change. Increases in paid employment for women and the women's movement led to an examination of the ground rules for relationships, and both men and women started to believe that marriage should be a partnership of equals. This model emphasizes self-development over commitment and obligations, holding that relationships are the meeting of two independent individuals. The emphasis on self-development resulted in less well-defined gender roles, and the concept of androgynous marriage arose. Cancian criticized this blueprint for encouraging empty relationships without sufficient commitment.

Interdependence is an alternative to the Independence blueprint. The Interdependence model also includes flexible gender roles but calls for commitment based on mutual dependence. Cancian argued that self-development and interdependence were compatible goals for relationships and that men and women are always dependent on each other in marriage. Both the Companionship and Independence blueprints ignore this inevitable interdependence. Table 10.1 shows the three blueprints and the important characteristics of each. The Companionship blueprint proposes that women depend on men but ignores men's dependence on women, whereas the Independence blueprint discourages dependence. "Interdependent couples try to strike a balance between opposing forces—to have a relationship of equality unconstrained by traditional gender roles and still depend on each other for emotional and material support" (Cancian, 1987, p. 131).

Sternberg's (1986) triangular model of love explains these different blueprints for marriage as differing in the three components of intimacy, passion, and commitment. Companionship-style marriages would have all three components but not in equal proportion for men and women. Under this blueprint women seek more intimacy than

TABLE 10.1   **Cancian's Blueprints for Love Relationships**

	Companionship (devotion to each other)	Independence (self-development)	Interdependence (mutual dependence)
Are traditional gender roles maintained?	Yes	No	No
Is the relationship stable?	Yes	No	Yes
Who is responsible for maintaining relationship?	Women	Neither partner	Both partners
Who develops personal interests?	Men	Both partners	Both partners

men, producing an unequal balance between such partners. As Cancian contended, the Independent blueprint lacks the component of commitment, but Interdependent marriages should fit what Sternberg called consummate love, the equal balance of all three components.

Marriages and other committed relationships may follow any of the blueprints, and contemporary couples may build any of these various types of relationships. Researchers interested in love have investigated gender and relationships, including men's and women's concept of romantic love and marriage, communication between partners, division of labor in households, power and conflict in marriage, and the stability of love relationships.

Concepts of Love and Marriage
Contrary to popular expectation, men have more traditional concepts of love and marriage and are more romantic than women. Although men and women tend to choose partners who have similarly traditional or nontraditional beliefs about gender roles, according to Letitia Anne Peplau and Steven Gordon (1985), the man of any given couple is likely to be more traditional than the woman. Men are more likely than women to endorse statements like "Women's activities should be confined to the home." More recent research (Mirowsky & Ross, 1987) has confirmed the discrepancy between husbands' and wives' beliefs in innate gender role differences, but this research has also indicated that these discrepancies become smaller through the years of marriage. The continued association of marriage partners does not produce identical beliefs, and the majority of the differences remain. Thus, even after years of marriage, husbands are more likely than wives to hold traditional, conservative beliefs about gender roles.

Despite the stereotypical view that women are the romantics, research reviewed by Peplau and Gordon (1985) indicates that men are more romantic than women. Men report that they are in love earlier in relationships than women. Also, while women say that they would be more likely to marry someone they did not love than men, a majority of men say they would not marry without love. Men are also more likely to have romantic beliefs such as "Love lasts forever" and "There is one perfect love in the world for everyone." Women, however, are more likely to report physical symptoms of being in love, such as feeling like they are "floating on a cloud." This willingness to report physical symptoms of love is the only sign of romanticism on which women exceed men. In most ways, men are more romantic than women.

Romanticism does not necessarily make men feel more favorably toward marriage. Men are supposed to elude marriage, considering it a "trap," while women plan and scheme to "land a husband." Jessie Bernard (1972) pointed out that this characterization is unfair, as men tend to profit from marriage more than women. Bernard contended that in any marriage there are actually two marriages—his and hers. She further argued that "his" is more of an advantage to him than "hers" is to her. That is, marriage offers benefits to men that do not accrue to married women. Married men are physically and mentally healthier than unmarried men, but married women are less healthy than their unmarried counterparts. (Chapters 13 and 14 include a consideration of the impact of marriage on the physical and mental health of men and women.)

Married men report higher levels of life satisfaction and happiness than unmarried men, and studies have found few gender-related differences in marital satisfaction (Peplau & Gordon, 1985). Richard Ball and Lynn Robbins (1986) contended that most of these studies of marital satisfaction had questioned only white participants and that this choice limited the conclusions about attitudes toward marriage. These researchers investigated marital satisfaction among African Americans, and their findings for African-American women paralleled other research: Married women were more satisfied with their lives than single women. However, this difference in satisfaction disappeared when these researchers controlled for demographic factors such as age and health. That is, the positive attitudes about marriage may be attributable to factors associated with marriage, such as a stable life and financial security, rather than to positive feelings about marriage itself. The life satisfaction of African-American men, on the other hand, was lower among married than single men, and these differences did not disappear when controlling for demographic factors. These results suggests that African-American men may differ from African-American women and European-American couples in their feelings of satisfaction in marriage.

Communication between Partners

The issue of communication in marriage has also been a topic for gender researchers. The same gender differences that researchers have found in friendship styles also influence communication in marriage: Women create emotional intimacy through talk and self-disclosure, whereas men do so through activity. In marriage, sex is often the activity that men use to create intimacy. Cancian (1987) argued that in most contemporary couples, wives do not count sex as communication or as a method for establishing intimacy. This difference can produce a discrepancy in what each thinks is the level of communication in their relationship. Her survey of couples revealed that wives value talking about feelings more than husbands, but husbands may feel threatened when their wives want to talk. "Talking about the relationship as she wants to do will feel to him like taking a test that she has made up and he will fail" (Cancian, 1987, p. 93).

Communication is a major task for couples, and the differences between men's and women's typical styles of communication provide one potential source of conflict in marriage. Deborah Tannen (1990) examined the barriers to communication for men and women, citing different strategies even when the goals are similar. Tannen argued that men and women find communication "a continual balancing act, juggling the conflicting needs for intimacy and independence" (p. 27). She contended that women's communication is oriented toward intimacy, focusing on forming communal connections with others, whereas men's communication is oriented toward hierarchy, focusing on attaining and demonstrating status.

The differences in communication styles make it difficult for women and men to talk to each other. Both interpret the underlying messages as well as the words, and the differences in styles may lead men and women to understand messages that their partners did not intend to send. For example, Tannen cited an example of a husband who had failed to tell his wife about a pain he had been feeling in his arm. When his wife found out, she was very upset with him for withholding this information, which she believed was important to her. She felt excluded from his life. He had not intended to exclude her from anything important but instead had wanted to protect her from worrying about his health. Tannen contended that such miscommunication is common for women and men and constitutes a persistent problem for couples.

According to Tannen, learning the conversational style of the other is not the answer to all communication problems. She described sensitivity training as an attempt to teach the conversational style of women to men and assertiveness training as a method for teaching the conversational style of men to women. Although flexibility of styles has benefits, Tannen expressed pessimism concerning changes in communication that would blend these divergent styles—both women and men like their way of communicating.

In addition to differences in styles of communication, influenceability is another factor in communication in intimate relationships. Research has indicated that men and women differ in ability to be influenced and styles of influence. Alice Eagly and Wendy Wood (1985) discussed their findings about gender differences in influenceability in terms of power. In laboratory experiments, few gender differences appear in influenceability, but outside the lab, women are more easily influenced than men. Eagly and Wood discussed these findings as a reflection of the subordinate roles that women typically occupy in relationships with men. Subordinates are supposed to be easily influenced; it is part of the role. Their subordinate role is also a factor in patterns of communication in love relationships.

Thus, men and women emphasize different activities to establish intimate communication—self-disclosure for women and sex for men. These different strategies for establishing intimacy are not the only gender differences in communication. Women and men tend to use different verbal styles, with women adopting a communal, empathic style and men adopting a competitive, hierarchical style. These differences can cause misunderstanding rather than foster communication. No influence strategy is associated uniquely with men or women, but rather, the association occurs relative to the power in a relationship. As women are more likely to have the subordinate role in marriage, their subordinate status has an impact on their communication and influence strategies.

Division of Household Labor

The division of household labor has become an area of interest to gender researchers, and their results have revealed another potential source of conflict for couples. Traditional gender roles include a division of labor in households, with men working outside the home for wages and women working in the home providing housekeeping and child care. This division arose during the Industrial Revolution, when men started working for wages rather than working in agricultural or home-based trades and the association of household chores with women began. The separation of labor occurred when women did not work for wages outside the home, but this pattern has changed throughout the 20th century, with an increasing number of women joining the paid work force. Now, a majority of women, even those with young children, work for wages outside the home.

The changes in paid labor for women might have prompted a concomitant change in the division of housework, but instead, few changes have occurred in the division of household work. Sociologist Arlie Hochschild (1989) called this arrangement the Second Shift, an arrangement in which women work for wages outside the home plus perform the majority of housework and child care chores at home. This arrangement can result in a situation in which women work the equivalent number of hours of two full-time jobs. According to Linda Thompson and Alexis Walker's (1989) review, wives do two to three times more housework and child care than husbands. Looking at the division of labor in a different way, only 10% of husbands do as much work at home as their wives.

One factor that changes the balance of labor around the house is the status of wives' careers (Bernardo, Shehan, & Leslie, 1987). Wives who hold professional or managerial jobs spend less time on household chores than women in less prestigious careers or wives who do not hold paying jobs outside their homes. Husbands of dual-career couples spend proportionally more time on household chores than other husbands, but they do not spend more hours doing housework. This situation possibly occurs because the wives of dual-career families spend less time doing housework than other wives, making the husbands' contribution proportionally more but not more in terms of absolute time. This finding suggests that wives who have professional or managerial careers do less housework; their husbands do not compensate by doing more chores, so the housework either does not get done or is done by hired workers.

The types of household chores that men and women perform tend to be divided along gender-stereotypical lines: Women clean, cook, shop, care for children, do laundry, and straighten; men take out the trash, mow the lawn, garden, work in the yard, and make household repairs. This division is not only stereotypical but also allots women repetitive, routine, time-locked tasks while allowing men irregular chores that they can arrange to their convenience (Thompson & Walker, 1989). In addition, the timing of these chores differs during the day, with women's chores occurring both in the morning and during the early and late evening, whereas men often have leisure time during the evening. Men can often arrange their chores so that they can do them on the weekend, but women have daily housework as well as larger chores they do on weekends.

Sampson Lee Blair and Daniel Lichter (1991) devised a method to measure the division of household labor, and their measurement confirmed the gender segregation of housework and the stereotypical nature of the division. Their analysis indicated that employment was not a significant factor in bringing about a more equitable division of household labor but that earning power was. Blair and Lichter argued that employment and earnings alter the power within marriages and thus alter the balance of housework—as women's wages increase, they perform less housework and their husbands perform more. These researchers did not ignore the influence of gender role stereotypes in perpetuating the division of labor in housework, but their analysis supported the importance of power within marriage as a factor in who does the dishes.

Married couples allot tasks primarily on the basis of gender, but gay and lesbian couples cannot use this strategy. Lawrence Kurdek's (1993) research indicated that these couples use different methods to determine who does what. Both gay and lesbian couples tended to share household work more equitably than heterosexual married couples, but the patterns of sharing differed. Gay couples were more likely to split tasks, with each partner performing a set of chores. Lesbian couples were more likely to share tasks, taking turns in performing the same chores.

The division of household chores may be a source of conflict in marriage (Thompson & Walker, 1989). Between 25 and 33% of wives believe that their husbands are not doing a fair share of housework and want them to do more. These figures do not reflect the discrepancy between the contributions of husbands and wives, indicating that some wives are satisfied with the housework their husbands do even if the division is not fair. Thompson and Walker concluded that if wives do a disproportionate share of chores, husbands tend to be happier with the marriage. Perhaps some wives find the extra housework an acceptable price to pay for a happier husband.

On the other hand, some wives resent the disproportionate amount of housework they do. Susan McHale and Ann Crouter (1992) identified wives who held views of equal participation in housework for men and women and who were doing more chores than their husbands. Such beliefs should put the stability of the marriage at risk, because these wives should feel overburdened. Husbands who hold traditional beliefs about segregation of household chores yet who are doing an equal share should also feel overburdened, and their relationships should also be at risk. McHale and Crouter found that these wives and husbands rated their marriages less favorably than other spouses who felt less burdened, and for the wives, the feelings persisted over the time span of a year. The persistence of resentment may be a factor in the stability of marital relationships.

Mary Holland Benin and Joan Angostinelli's (1988) study confirmed that division of chores may be a major source of marital conflict. Their participants expressed the greatest satisfaction when the division of chores was almost equal (with wives doing more than husbands), and both husbands and wives were dissatisfied with inequitable divisions of household labor. However, husbands wanted both an equitable division and a low number of hours spent doing housework, whereas wives wanted an equitable division and their husbands' help. These shared goals of equitable sharing of chores may not be compatible with the secondary goals for husbands and wives. Therefore, even a mutual desire to share household work may not allow husbands and wives to negotiate this problem.

The division of household labor may fall into traditional "masculine" and "feminine" tasks, or the division may be one of necessity dictated by the time constraints of women's work schedules. For example. women who work the evening shift may have to go to work immediately after an early dinner, leaving their husbands and families with the night-time chores. Shift work is more common in working-class than middle-class or upper-middle-class families, making working-class couples somewhat more likely to share equally in housework than more affluent couples (Thompson & Walker, 1989). Although working-class men do not have more egalitarian attitudes than other men, their family situation may result in greater sharing of household work. Therefore, social class is relevant to patterns of family work.

The differences in division of household labor by social class and gender role attitudes may relate to the differences of power in these couples. Working-class wives' economic contributions are more essential to their families' subsistence than middle-class wives' salaries. By making essential contributions, these women may gain power in their marriages, and their husbands may respond to the more equal balance of power by sharing housework. Scott Coltrane and Elsa Valdez (1993) found some evidence that more equal contribution to family income related to shared household chores. For middle-class Hispanic-American couples, wives whose income made them coproviders were more likely to get their husbands' help than women who contributed less to family income. Even the husbands who acknowledged the importance of their wives' income were often reluctant to do household chores and child care, using their own job demands as an excuse for doing little at home.

Wives who have high-status, highly paid employment (such as professional or managerial jobs) may also experience increased power in their marriages, and this increased power may give these wives the freedom to do less housework, as Donna Bernardo et al. (1987) found. When husbands and wives experience discrepancies in their attitudes about household labor, conflict may arise in the marriage. Therefore, the issue of household work may be related to both power and conflict within marriages.

Power and Conflict

Most dating couples believe that marriages should be an equal sharing of power and decision making, but the members of these couples acknowledged that their own relationships have failed to show an equal balance of power (Peplau & Campbell, 1989). Although 95% of the women and 87% of the men said that they believed each partner should have an equal voice about the relationship, only 49% of the women and 42% of the men reported a relationship with equal power. This finding suggests that, even before couples marry, the balance of power is not equal.

For those couples whose relationships are not equal in power, either the men or the women could have more power, but traditional gender roles dictate that the man will be the leader and head of the household. These traditional gender roles shape current relationships, and men are likely to have more power in marriages than women. According to an extensive survey of couples by Philip Blumstein and Pepper Schwartz (1983), almost 64% reported an equal balance of power. The remaining 37% reported an unequal balance of power in their marriage—28% of husbands and 9% of wives said they had more power. Thus, for couples who do not equally share power, husbands are likely to have more power in the family than wives. Table 10.2 shows the ideal and actual power structure in couples.

One drawback about Blumstein and Schwartz's survey was the educational and ethnic composition of their sample: Many couples were college-educated and most were white. In contrast, Letitia Anne Peplau and Susan Miller Campbell (1989) reviewed studies on the balance of power in African-American and Mexican-American families. They examined the myths of black **matriarchy** and Latino **machismo** and found that both patterns of unequal power were more myth than a description of the balance of power in these families. Although African-American families are more likely to be headed by a woman than white families, black couples do not have significantly different power relationships than white couples. The sharing of power that was the most common pattern in Blumstein and Schwartz's study also appeared as the most common pattern in African-American couples. For couples with an unequal balance of power, male dominance was more common than female dominance. The same patterns appeared in Mexican-American families, with the most common pattern being one of shared power. Therefore, some equal balance of power seems to be the rule for most couples.

Saying that couples exhibit an equal balance of power does not mean that both partners have an equal say in all decisions. Decision-making power may be divided along traditional lines, with men making financial decisions and women making household decisions (see Peplau & Gordon, 1985). What couples report as an equal balance of power may actually be a division of decision making into husbands' or wives' domains.

TABLE 10.2 Ideal and Actual Power Structure in Couples

| | Peplau and Campbell Study (1989) | | Blumstein and Schwartz Study (1983) |
	Men	Women	Couples
Believe in equal power	87%	95%	
Have equal power	42	49	64%
Husband has more power			28
Wife has more power			9

This division may reflect wives' lack of real power; wives may be put into the position of making decisions that their husbands consider too trivial for their own attention. For example, wives may decide what to have for dinner and what brand of cleaning products to use, and husbands may decide which house to buy and where to live.

Paid employment is a factor in the balance of power in marriage. Women who do not have paid employment tend to have less power in their marriages than women who earn money (Blumstein & Schwartz, 1983; Peplau & Campbell, 1989; Peplau & Gordon, 1985; Steil, 1989). The amount of earnings is also a factor: Husbands who earn more money have more power, but wives' earnings show a complex relationship to their power. In working-class couples, wives who earn more money have more power, but middle-class wives may not gain power by making money (Thompson & Walker, 1989). These differences may have to do with the relative necessity of wives' earning income in the two social classes. Working-class wives' salaries are more likely to provide essential incomes, whereas middle-class wives' salaries may not be as necessary to their families. When husbands know the importance of their wives' salaries, this knowledge may give wives more or less power. In the rare families in which wives earn more than their husbands, however, the balance of power does not tip in the wife's favor. These couples tend to follow the male dominant tradition in their gender roles (Thompson & Walker, 1989), perhaps because wives abdicate the power that their incomes could give them. Therefore, wives' income has a curvilinear relationship to power in marriage. Wives who earn no income have low power, wives who earn more money have increasing power to the point of equal incomes, but wives who earn more than their husbands have (or exercise) less power than their spouses.

Consistent with the income and power interpretation, Blumstein and Schwartz (1983) found that money was an important factor in the power equation for couples other than married couples. Blumstein and Schwartz studied not only married couples but also cohabiting couples—heterosexual as well as gay and lesbian. They found that money was an important factor in determining which partner had more power for all except the lesbian couples, who tried to maintain an equal monetary contribution in their relationships so as to avoid unequal power. The failure to do so was a source of problems for these women.

Janet Saltzman Chafetz (1989) considered the balance of power as it relates to conflict between partners in a couple. She argued that equal power in love relationships has a tendency to increase conflict, whereas inequality in marriages fosters little conflict. With one partner clearly dominant and the other clearly subordinate, the dominant partner gets his or her way, and no conflict ensues. Equal partners, on the other hand, may have prolonged conflicts and less stable relationships than partners with unequal roles. Chafetz considered conflict one of the costs of equality in relationships.

Some evidence suggests that men and women experience some differences in the sources of conflict and use different tactics to resolve conflict. David Buss (1991) tested recently married couples to determine the sources of conflict in their relationships. Wives' most frequent complaint was that their husbands were inconsiderate, and husbands' most frequent complaint was of their wives' moodiness. Not surprisingly, both husbands and wives who were low in emotional warmth, high in selfishness, low in security, and high in temper behaved in many ways that angered their spouses and caused conflict in the relationship.

Conflict management in couples was the topic of Thomas Lavin's (1987) investigation, and he found gender differences in the ways that wives and husbands seek to understand each other's behavior. The husbands tended to take personal credit for both their positive and negative behaviors, attributing them to internal stable traits, but husbands saw their wives' behavior as determined by unstable internal forces. Wives did not explain their husbands' behavior in different terms than they described their own. In this conceptualization, husbands can resist their wives' requests to change because men's behavior reflects unchanging personality traits, whereas wives should change in response husbands' requests because women's behavior is not only changeable but also under personal control. Lavin argued that the husbands' beliefs about conflict management gave them more power in the relationship; they could rightfully demand changes but could not reasonably be asked to change.

Cancian (1987) asserted that women are more eager than men to avoid conflict and preserve their relationship, as they see themselves as responsible for maintaining the relationship. However, women are more likely to bring up problems (Blumstein & Schwartz, 1983), perhaps in an attempt to correct them. In explaining women's tendency to use emotional appeals to win arguments, Thompson and Walker (1989) contended that women use the same style of conflict management as other subordinates. That is, gender differences in resolving conflicts may be a reflection of the differential power within marriage relationships.

GENDERED VOICES
When I Got Sober

"The balance of power in my marriage didn't change when I went to work but when I got sober," a woman in her 40s told me. She had been a homemaker for a number of years before she started a career, and she said that earning money didn't make much of a change in her marriage. By the time she began her job, she had already started drinking heavily, and she continued to do so.

"Everybody took care of me, so I could drink and take drugs and get away with it. So I did. My daughter took care of me for most of her childhood. My husband also let me get away with being drunk most of the time. I was dependent on them, but then I got sober, and things changed.

"When I got sober, I started being able to take care of myself, and my family wasn't used to it. The balance of power changed in my marriage, and we eventually split up. I was sober and involved in AA, and my husband was still drinking, but that wasn't the main problem. I started to become independent, and he couldn't adjust. I realize that it was quite an adjustment: I had never taken care of myself—never in my life—and then I started.

"I remembered one incident in particular. I was trying to change the batteries in my small tape recorder, and my husband came over and took the recorder out of my hands and did it for me. I thought, 'I can do that for myself.' I started thinking that about a lot of things. As I started to become more independent, our marriage changed. In fact, our entire family changed, and most of those changes were good. The kids could come to me rather than go to their father for everything. I became a responsible person. With that responsibility came a growing desire to be independent, and now I am. The marriage became an emotional power struggle, with my growing self-reliance and my husband still trying to be in control."

Wife battering is an example of both power and conflict in marriage. Richard Gelles and Claire Cornell (1990) discussed domestic violence in historical context, pointing out that women have been considered the appropriate targets of marital (and even premarital) violence in many societies and throughout many time periods. Even though physical abuse is not the most common method of resolving conflicts in contemporary relationships, violence is not unusual between married and cohabiting partners. Both men and women are violent toward each other, but Gelles (1979) contended that women are at a disadvantage in physical conflicts with men. The rate of violence may be close to equal, but injury is not: Women are much more likely to sustain serious injury as a result of domestic violence.

Based on a national survey conducted in 1986, 16% of homes reported some kind of violence between spouses within the previous year. This figure represents a decrease from a similar survey in 1975 (Straus & Gelles, 1986) and includes minor violence, but 1 in 22 women in the United States were victims of abusive violence within the year preceding the survey. Scott Feld and Murray Straus (1989) warned against discounting the acts of minor violence in domestic conflict; their study indicated that minor violence predicted more serious violence between spouses. Furthermore, they found that women who fought back were likely to escalate rather than halt the violence directed toward them.

Unfortunately, many people find violence between partners acceptable. A survey by Murray Straus, Richard Gelles, and Suzanne Steinmetz (1980) revealed that about 25% of wives and over 30% of husbands found violence toward each other acceptable under some circumstances. Given these attitudes, the escalation of minor violence to abuse is not surprising, nor is it likely to change.

Contrary to Chafetz's (1989) contention that equality fosters conflict, marriages in which the partners have an equal balance of power are less likely to involve physical violence than marriages in which one partner is dominant (Thompson & Walker, 1989). Regardless of which partner has more power, both partners are more likely to be the targets of violence in couples with a dominant and a subordinate partner (Gelles & Cornell, 1990). That is, women are more likely to be battered in both female-dominant and male-dominant marriages, and men are more likely to be the targets of violence in not only female-dominant but also male-dominant relationships. Inequalities of power promote violent conflict in couples, putting both partners at increased risk.

Therefore, a connection exists between the issues of power and conflict in committed relationships. The majority of couples endorse equal power within their love relationships, but most also acknowledge that their relationships have not attained an equal balance of power. Men are more likely to be dominant than women, as they traditionally occupy the provider role and they typically earn more money. Both gender roles and money affect the balance of power in relationships. Power also affects conflict and conflict management. Women tend to either avoid conflict or use emotional appeals to resolve conflict—tactics associated with subordinate status. When conflict results in violence, women are more likely than men to be injured in the confrontation. Both women and men find physical violence acceptable as a conflict resolution strategy under some circumstances, an attitude that perpetuates domestic violence.

Stability of Relationships

Relationships that involve physical violence are less stable than those with no violence, but some of these violent relationships endure. Many people find it difficult to imagine why a woman would stay with a man who repeatedly abuses her, but some women do. Abusive men often work to isolate their wives from family and friends, depriving them of social support and alternative residences (Gelles & Cornell, 1990). If abused women are unemployed, with few marketable skills, and have young children who need the financial support the husband gives, these women may feel as though they have no options except to stay in the relationship, no matter how abusive. With the rise of shelters for women to escape abusive homes, abused women have an option, and thousands take this option each year.

Abusive relationships are an extreme case of conflict in love relationships, but all couples experience some level of conflict. These conflicts tend to decrease the stability of a relationships and increase the chances of the relationship dissolving. Blumstein and Schwartz (1983) found that couples who experienced conflict over money, wives' employment, power, division of household labor, or sex were more likely to split up than couples who experienced fewer conflicts. They found that couples who were married were less likely to break up than cohabiting heterosexual, gay, or lesbian couples, but married couples also tended to have a lower level of conflict except in the early years of marriage. Blumstein and Schwartz speculated that the institution of marriage holds couples together when they might otherwise dissolve their relationship. Couples who do not have the force of the institution are thus more likely to part.

Similarity is not only a factor in attraction, it is also a factor in the stability of relationships. Dating couples are more likely to stay together if their attitudes match rather than conflict (Hendrick, Hendrick, & Adler, 1988). Members of the couple are not the only ones whose opinions should match; parents of dating couples can also contribute to the stability and progress of a dating relationship (Leslie, Huston, & Johnson, 1986). Mothers' opinions are most important, and young adults try to influence their mothers to think well of their partners. The more serious the relationship, the more frequent the attempt to convince parents of the partner's merits.

Congruence of partners' attitudes and values is also important in marriage (Blumstein & Schwartz, 1983). The similarity also extends to gender roles, and married couples are happier if both partners have expressive ("feminine") rather than instrumental ("masculine") characteristics. That is, partners who are cheerful, warm, gentle, and understanding have happier marriages than those who are assertive, dominant, decisive, individualistic, and ambitious.

Conflict, even heated conflict, is not necessarily threatening to the stability of marriages. Indeed, some elements of conflict relate to the strengthening of relationships over the long run, whereas other factors are destructive, predicting separation or divorce. John Gottman and Robert Levenson (in Gottman, 1991) investigated the stability of marriages and found factors that predicted separation. Surprisingly, their research indicated that marital satisfaction was not a strong predictor of separation, but the level of physical arousal during conflicts was. That is, couples in their study who had higher heart rates, blood pressure, sweating, and physical movement during an argument were more likely to separate within the next three years than couples with lower levels of arousal. Couples whose physiological reactions were calmer tended to have marriages that improved over a three-year span.

Gottman also reported that behavioral factors predicted divorce, including wives' tendency to be overly agreeable and compliant and husbands' tendency to "stonewall," by withdrawing emotionally, avoiding eye contact, holding the neck rigid, and being unresponsive to their wives during an argument. In their conversations, both members of couples who would separate were more defensive; additionally, the wives complained and criticized more and the husbands disagreed more than did couples who remained together. The couples who were headed toward separation also showed different facial expressions during their conversations, the most important of which was wives' expressions of disgust. Husbands' fear also related to later separation, as did a facial expression Gottman called the "miserable smile," a smile that affected only the mouth, as when people try to "put on a happy face." Gottman concluded that the couples who would later separate were in the process of dissolving their relationship emotionally, and their physiological reactions, conflict tactics, and facial expressions signaled their impending separation. Table 10.3 summarizes these factors.

According to Sternberg's (1986, 1987) triangular theory of love, relationships that have only one of the components should be more stable than those that lack one. Two-component relationships should be less stable than those that have all three. Friendships should be less enduring if only intimacy is present, rather than intimacy plus commitment. Furthermore, love relationships that have two components should be more stable than those with only one. For example, romances that have only the passion component should not last as long as those with both passion and commitment. Indeed, passion alone is the classic "one night stand," whereas passion plus commitment is a "whirlwind

TABLE 10.3   Factors Relating to Marital Separation

Factor	Prediction
Marital satisfaction	No strong relationship to separation
Physical arousal during conflict—heart rate, blood pressure, sweating, moving	Higher levels predict increased likelihood of separation; calmer reactions predict strengthening of relationship
Wives being overly agreeable	Increased likelihood of separation
Husbands participate in housework	Increased satisfaction for husbands and wives; increased health in husbands
Husbands "stonewall"	Increased likelihood of separation
Wives criticize and complain	Increased likelihood of separation
Husbands disagree with wives	Increased likelihood of separation
Couples are defensive	Increased likelihood of separation
Facial expressions during conflict—"miserable" smile, wives' disgust, husbands' fear	Increased likelihood of separation

courtship." The most stable of all relationships should be Sternberg's consummate love, a combination of all three components in equal proportion.

The commitment component of Sternberg's model is the most important for relationship stability. Commitment "can be essential for getting through hard times and for returning to better ones. In ignoring it or separating it from love, one may be missing exactly that component of loving relationships that enables one to get through the hard times as well as the easy ones" (Sternberg, 1986, p. 123).

Dissolving Relationships

Relationships go through phrases of attraction, development, and sometimes dissolution (Duck, 1991). All relationships are subject to these stages, but people expect the dissolution of casual relationships and believe that such breakups pose no problems for the people involved. Unfortunately, even relationships with commitment sometimes fail to endure. When close friendships or love relationships dissolve, the end of such relationships poses problems for both people involved as well as for their social network of friends and family, who must make adjustments in their relationships with the members of the separated couple.

Love relationships without institutional support, such as cohabitation, are more likely to break up than are marriages. In their study of couples, Blumstein and Schwartz (1983) found that married couples were more likely to remain together than couples who were cohabiting. In a follow-up 18 months after the initial interview, they found that the lesbian couples were most likely to have broken up and that married couples were least likely to have done so. Figure 10.2 shows the separation rates for the four types of couples in Blumstein and Schwartz's survey.

The institutional support for marriage is no guarantee of stability for such relationships. Although marriages have never been permanent, divorce has increased over the past 80 years (Hendrick & Hendrick, 1992). The rising divorce rate has resulted in approximately 50% of marriages ending in divorce. This divorce rate is not necessarily a condemnation of marriage as much as the failure of women and men to fulfill their vision of what they believe marriage should be.

In her extensive interviews with divorced men and women, Catherine Riessman (1990) found that both held an ideal of marriage as the fulfillment of three components: emotional intimacy, companionship and primacy (the belief that the relationship with the spouse constitutes the primary relationship), and sexuality. That is, these people's vision of marriage matches what Cancian called the Companionship blueprint for marriage. When they separated and divorced, women and men did not question the blueprint. Rather, they found fault in their own marriage, blaming either their former spouses or themselves for failing to fulfill some component of their ideal for marriage. Riessman's interviews showed the ways in which men and women found fault in their marriages and how they coped with separation and divorce.

Although divorced men and women both described failures to live up to their ideals, their descriptions showed some variation according to gender and social class. Both

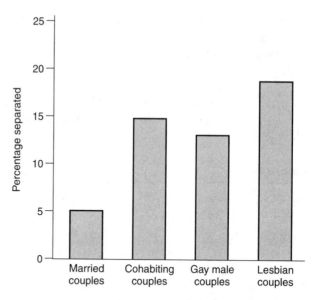

FIGURE 10.2   Separation Rates for Couples over an 18-month Period

SOURCE: Based on *American couples* by Philip Blumstein & Pepper Schwartz, 1983, New York: Pocket Books.

women and men saw failures in achieving emotional intimacy, but each attributed the failures to different reasons. Two-thirds of the women said that they did not get the emotional intimacy they expected from their husbands, defining such intimacy as talking and sharing feelings. They claimed their husbands just didn't communicate with them.

Divorced men largely agreed with this assessment, blaming themselves for not communicating with their former wives and maintaining that they had difficulties in talking about their feelings and sharing the important elements of their work. One-third of the divorced men also believed that their wives had failed to give them emotional support, which they tended to define as physical affection. The working-class men repeatedly said that their wives were not waiting "with their arms open and a kiss" when the men came home from work. Such physical manifestations of intimacy were lacking, resulting in their feelings that their marriages lacked emotional intimacy. These gender-related differences reflect the talk-based versus action-based styles of showing support that are typical of women and men and highlight the importance of these differences in the dissolution of relationships.

The divorced men and women also believed that their marriages had fallen short of the ideal in the second component of companionate marriage—companionship and primacy. Both the women and men in Riessman's study described differences in interests that prevented each from being primary companions for the other, and both reported that they felt slighted by this lack of shared interests. The discrepancy of leisure interests was a factor in this problem, especially for working-class women whose husbands' involvement with sports was a common complaint. The men reported that their wives' devotion to friends, family, and children was a problem; these other relationships made the husbands feel that they did not come first. The women did not resent such other relationships of their husbands, but some described their husbands' work as an intrusion, especially middle-class women whose husbands had prestigious, time-consuming careers.

Sex is the third component of the companionship model of marriage, and the divorced people in Riessman's study mentioned problems with sex in connection with their divorce. The men mentioned dissatisfaction with the frequency of sex and resentment over their wives' refusal to have sex as often as the husbands wanted. Sexual affairs were a factor in 34% of the divorced people in this study, and both women and men believed that affairs had been the impetus for the dissolution of their marriage. The women took their own as well as their husbands' affairs as a sign of emotional betrayal, signaling that their marriage was over. The men did not necessarily share that attitude, but they also acknowledged that affairs had been a factor in their divorce. Wives found it difficult to forgive husbands' affairs, and wives who had affairs tended to leave their husbands for their lovers.

These feelings suggest that women might be the ones to initiate breakups, and Steve Duck (1991) confirmed this finding, stating that women initiate 80% of the breakups of heterosexual couples. He explained that this gender difference may be due to women's tendency to be more vigilant about monitoring their relationships so that they know when something is going wrong more quickly than men. This finding highlights a substantial asymmetry in love relationships: Women fall out of love more quickly and fall in love more slowly than men.

Women and men both experience different lives after the dissolution of a love relationship. For couples who have been married or have cohabited, the dissolution of the relationship is usually financially as well as emotionally difficult. Women's lower

GENDERED VOICES
I Wasn't Any of His Business Anymore

A woman talking with her friend about her ex-husband said, "I saw Ed at a country western club last Friday night. He was there with some of his friends, drinking. I went there because I wanted to get out and have some fun. He didn't see me at first, and then he kept looking in my direction, trying to make sure he was seeing right.

"Finally, he came over to me and said, 'What are you doing in a place like this? You shouldn't be here.' I told him that what I did wasn't any of his business anymore. We were divorced, and I could do what I wanted. I didn't need his permission to go to a bar, and he didn't have any right to say anything to me. He said some pretty ugly things, calling me a bitch and a whore, and I just walked away from him. I had enough of his ordering me around when we were married."

"Although we were divorced three years ago, my ex-wife acts like we're still married," a man in his mid 30s said. "I understand why she calls me when something involves the kids, but she calls me when she needs things done to the house." He considered these requests inappropriate because he and his ex-wife had both remarried. "I can't help it if she married a wuss who can't fix the toilet. I don't think she should be calling me to do the chores. We're not married anymore, and taking care of her house is not part of my job now."

earning power coupled with their custody of children tend to create financial hardship, whereas men's financial position tends to improve after divorce. Lenore Weitzman (1985) found that divorced women experienced a 73% decline, whereas men experienced a 42% increase in their standard of living a year after their divorce.

Riessman's study indicated that both men and women find positive as well as negative consequences as a result of the divorce experience. Both women and men enjoyed the freedom that came with divorce, but their feelings had different sources: Women liked being free from their husbands' dominance, whereas the men liked being free of their wives' expectations. The women in Riessman's study experienced more positive as well as more negative emotions in connection with their divorce than the men. All of the women found something positive in the experience, whereas 15% of the men found nothing positive about their divorce. The women experienced more symptoms of depression, but they also discovered heightened self-esteem and feelings of competence through performing activities their husbands had done when they were married.

Dissolution of marriage often deprives men not only of companionship and emotional support from their wives but also of their children and of their network of friends and family (a network typically maintained by women). Women tend to use these support networks after divorce, but men do not. The men in Riessman's study were surprised at the difficulties of being alone, but they also described feelings of satisfaction from their developing competencies in domestic chores.

As Riessman's interviews suggest, divorced men and women are likely to feel displeased with their ex-spouses rather than with marriage itself, and most showed their endorsement of marriage by remarrying. With the growing acceptability of cohabitation, some divorced people choose to live with a new partner rather than marry, but cohabitation is a form of trial marriage for some of these couples, who married after living together for one or two years (Blumstein & Schwartz, 1983). Some evidence exists that the second marriage is less traditional than the first, with a more equal balance of power and a more equal sharing of decision making and household chores (Furstenberg & Spanier, 1984). Second marriages are even more likely to end in divorce than first marriages, which Riessman interpreted as an increased unwillingness to endure an unhappy relationship combined with the knowledge that divorce offers positive as well as negative experiences.

Summary

Some men have begun to attempt emotionally intimate friendships with men, but this pattern is not typical of men's "buddy" relationships. Women's friendships are more likely to be based on emotional intimacy and sharing, whereas men are likely to develop a style of friendships based on activities. These gender differences in friendship styles appear early in development. Children voluntarily segregate themselves according to gender and resist attempts at interaction before age 5 years, possibly because girls are fond of talking and sharing secrets and boys tend to enjoy active games. Even the girls and boys who do not like their gender-typical activities are not welcome in cross-gender groups.

Adolescents are more concerned with developing emotional intimacy in their relationships, but girls emphasize this aspect of relationships more than boys. Although young men say that they value intimacy in relationships, they often find it difficult to develop such relationships, especially with other men. Some men develop emotionally intimate love relationships with women, and such relationships often decrease the amount of time and emotional energy men have to devote to male friends. Friendships tend to be tied to developmental stage of life, and marriage and the birth of children tend to restrict friendships.

Cancian has argued that love has become feminized. The current concept of love is emotional intimacy—a pattern closer to the typical relationship for women than for men. This definition slights the style of intimacy men tend to adopt—the activities of providing help and doing things together. Some research has indicated that both men and women have a flexibility of friendship styles and that they use different styles to relate to male and female friends. Cross-gender nonsexual friendships are a recent phenomenon, and both men and women acknowledge that such relationships require special rules.

Love relationships currently form through dating, an activity that arose during the 1920s as a response to changing patterns of mate selection. Dating has become not only a method of courting but also a forum for recreation, socialization, and sexual exploration. Adolescents tend to choose dates similar to future mates, preferring dates who are kind, considerate, socially exciting, intelligent, and physically attractive. People with either heterosexual or homosexual orientation describe their preferred partners in similar ways, but men emphasize the importance of physical attractiveness more than women.

Currently, marriage and other committed relationships can follow several different blueprints—Companionship, Independence, and Interdependence. The Companionship blueprint involves separate gender roles and emphasizes the woman's role in maintaining a love relationship. Both the Independence and Interdependence blueprints emphasize self-development for both men and women, but the two differ in the importance of commitment.

Gender researchers have explored several issues in love relationships, including conceptualizations of love, communication, division of household labor, power and conflict, and relationship stability. Men are more romantic in their conceptualization of love than women, and marriage tends to benefit them more, but they are not necessarily happier with their marriages. Men and women may have trouble communicating in love relationships, partly because their styles and goals of communication differ, with men trying to establish independence and dominance and women trying to share feelings and make connections.

The division of household labor is usually unequal in marriage: Women perform far more of this work than men, even when women have paid employment. The ideal pattern of household work for both partners is closer to an equal distribution than exists in most marriages, but both women and men feel satisfied with women performing a disproportionate share. When women do most household work and hold outside jobs, their disproportionate work load may be a source of conflict. Although paid employment is a source of power, both partners do not usually have equal power in a marriage. Couples experience conflict from many sources, but some marital conflict results in violence. Over 25% of women and men find violence acceptable in their personal relationship under some circumstances, but women are more likely to be injured as a result of relationship violence.

Violence decreases the stability of relationships but does not necessarily end them. Stable love relationships tend to occur in couples with similar attitudes and values, and the commitment factor in marriage produces greater stability than in other love relationships. Even marriages dissolve, and divorce has increased in the past several decades. People who have divorced tend to see the fault in their ex-spouses rather than in the institution of marriage. Although divorce brings financial and emotional problems, most women and men also find positive factors in divorce. Most remarry, and some evidence suggests that both women and men form more equitable second than first marriages.

Glossary

Companionate love   a combination of commitment and intimacy without passion

Gross motor skills   skills involving activity of large muscles of the body, producing large movements, such as throwing, kicking, running, and jumping

Homophobia   the unreasonable fear and hatred of homosexuality

Machismo   a Spanish word meaning strong and assertive masculinity and implying complete male authority

Matriarchy   a family pattern in which women are dominant or a pattern in which women are the head of the household due to the father's absence

Suggested Readings

Blumstein, Philip; & Schwartz, Pepper. (1983). *American couples*. New York: Pocket Books. Although not recent, this book examines the relationships of all types of couples—married and cohabiting heterosexual partners as well as gay and lesbian couples. Through interviews with couples, Blumstein and Schwartz explore attitudes toward power, money, and sex, and their impact on happiness and stability.

Cancian, Francesca M. (1987). *Love in America: Gender and self-development*. Cambridge, England: Cambridge University Press. Cancian analyzes the history of love relationships, including the historical changes in what spouses expect from their marriage. She also explains the drawbacks of too much independence and the increasingly feminine definition of what constitutes love.

Maccoby, Eleanor. (1990). Gender and relationships: A developmental account. *American Psychologist, 45,* 513–520. Maccoby summarizes and reviews the volume of research on gender differences and similarities in social interactions and relationships. Her developmental approach includes children, adolescents, and adults, and this brief review is easy to read.

Peplau, Letitia Anne; Hill, Charles T.; & Rubin, Zick. (1993). Sex role attitudes in dating and marriage: A 15-year follow-up of the Boston Couples Study. *Journal of Social Issues, 49*(3), 31–52. This report describes a longitudinal study of gender role attitudes, including the complexities of gender roles and behavior for dating, careers, marriage, and choosing to be parents.

Chapter *11*

Sexuality

HEADLINE

Why We Want Sex: The Difference Between Men and Women

—*Psychology Today,* December 1989

Men want sex for physical pleasure and women for love and intimacy, right?" asked Lydia Denworth (1989, p. 12), but she reported that the answer to this question is "Wrong." The motivation for sex is much more complex, depending not only on gender but also on age. Denworth wrote that gender differences in sexual motivation exist, but the differences do not always match the stereotypes.

Denworth's article summarized research by Joey Sprague and David Quadagno (1989), who surveyed men and women about their motivations for engaging in sex and questioned them about what they saw as the most important benefits of sexual intercourse. These researchers found that the motivations for sex change with age. For 61% of the women between ages 22 and 35 years, love was the most important reason for having sex, but this was true for only 38% of the women aged 36 to 57 years. Love became a less important reason for having intercourse for these women, and the physical pleasure of sex became a more frequently mentioned reason—43% listed it as their most important reason for having sex.

A substantial number of the younger men in Sprague and Quadagno's study—44%—matched the stereotype of wanting sex for physical pleasure, but only 36% of the men over age 36 reported physical pleasure as their most important reason for having sex. Half of these older men said that their main reason for sex was love and emotional intimacy.

The motivation for having sex differs for women and men at any age but also over the life span. The stereotype of men wanting sex for physical pleasure and women wanting sex for love may come from the age group of participants in sex surveys; college students have been the most common source of information for many researchers.

According to Sprague and Quadagno, only the younger participants demonstrated these stereotypical motivations for sex, and the older participants showed a reversal.

It should be noted that the percentages of reported preferences represent a far-from-unanimous endorsement of any reason for having sex from any of the age groups, reflecting a great deal of diversity in reasons for having sex. Sprague and Quadagno found gender and age interactions in response to the question concerning the usual reason for having sex, but they found no gender difference in response to the question about the ideal reason for having sex.

In another study by Valerie Hoffman and Ralph Bolton (1994), college-aged women and men described their sexual motivation, and the gender-related differences that appeared matched the stereotypes in some ways but diverged in other ways. The men in this study were more likely to report that they had sex for fun, but this reason was also the most common among the women; no significant differences appeared in the motivation to have sex to feel emotionally close. Consistent with stereotypes, the quest for new experiences, avoiding boredom, and making a conquest were more common motivations among the men, and the women reported that they had sex when they did not want to more often than the men. Although several of the motivations differed significantly, the differences were small. The men and women were also similar in many ways, such as having sex to feel loved, to express love, to reduce tension, to demonstrate power or domination, or because one's partner wants to have sex. Consistent with Sprague and Quadagno's contentions, these college students showed some (but not all) of the differences typical of others of their age group.

College students are a convenient group to test because many researchers are professors who have access to large groups of college students who are willing to participate in research. Despite the convenience, researchers know that college students are not a representative sample of the general population. That is, college students both have and lack characteristics that make them like the general population; thus, studies using only students do not reflect the characteristics of the general population. As Sprague and Quadagno's survey indicated, a more diverse group of participants revealed information about sexual motivation that a college-aged sample could not show—how sexual motivation changes with age.

Other researchers who have studied sexuality have had to contend with the problem of obtaining a representative sample. In addition, sexuality is a sensitive and personal topic for many people, and these feelings influence their willingness to discuss sex with researchers or to have sex so that researchers may observe their sexual behavior.

The Study of Sexuality

Researchers who want to know about sexual behavior and attitudes have several options in choosing a method of investigation. They may question people about their sexual behavior, or they may directly observe people's sexual behavior and responses. Both of these approaches present scientific, practical, and ethical problems.

Those researchers who choose to question people about their sexual behavior or attitudes may survey a group of people to determine characteristics, attitudes, opinions, or reports of behavior. Chapter 2 described surveys and the advantages and disadvantages of this method of investigation. One limitation is especially relevant to sexuality research: Some people feel that sex is a private, personal issue and not a subject for research. These people refuse to participate in sex surveys, and they very likely differ from people who are willing to answer questions about their sexual attitudes and behavior. Potential subjects who refuse to participate can bias results, because the opinion of this group is of necessity systematically excluded.

Another possibility for investigating sexual behavior is through direct observation of sexual activity. Most people are even less cooperative with this type of research than with a survey, but nonhuman animals have (or at least voice) no such objections. The problems with generalizing results from studies on nonhuman sexual behavior to humans are even more serious than with generalizing from one group of humans to another. Nevertheless, this strategy has been useful, adding breadth to the study of sexual behavior. A prominent example of this type of research appears in *Patterns of Sexual Behavior* (1951) by anthropologist Clellan Ford and psychologist Frank Beach. These two researchers presented not only a cross-cultural study of human sexual behavior but a cross-species comparison as well.

Only a small percentage of people have been willing to have sex in a research laboratory. Such participants allowed William Masters and Virginia Johnson (1966) to study human sexual behavior in ways that no other researchers had managed. Not only were Masters and Johnson's participants willing to answer questions about sex, they were willing to have sex in the lab and to have their physical responses measured during the activity. Although the results of Masters and Johnson's research have become widely accepted, their participants were less typical of the general population than those of any of the other sex researchers, a situation that Masters and Johnson considered unimportant—their interest was in the physiology of sexual response.

Thus, although researchers who want to study sexual attitudes and behavior have several options; most researchers have surveyed people about their attitudes or behavior or both, by asking questions and recording the responses. The problems with survey research include finding a **representative sample**—a group of people that reflects the characteristics of the general population—as well as securing truthful and accurate responses. Despite the problems connected with surveying people about sex, this approach has been the most common one.

Sex Surveys

Before Alfred Kinsey's ground breaking survey of men's and women's sexual behavior in the 1930s and 1940s, several earlier investigators reported on sexuality (Brecher, 1969). Henry Havelock Ellis, a British physician, wrote a series of books between 1896 and 1928 in which he detailed the differences in sexual customs of various cultures and collected sexual case studies of women and men. These studies led him to the conclusion that the Victorian social norms of repression and denial of sexuality that he saw around him were not reflected in behavior. Ellis came to believe that sexual behavior was varied and complex: "Everybody is not like you and your friends and neighbors," and even, "Your friends and neighbors may not be as much like you as you suppose" (in Brecher, 1969, p. 39). Ellis was one of several sex researchers in the 1800s who was important in making sex an acceptable topic for scientific research, and this research helped to end the sexual repression that was the standard of that time.

Historian Carl Degler (1974) discovered an unpublished sex survey conducted by Dr. Clelia Duel Mosher, a physician who began questioning American women about their sexual behavior and enjoyment in 1892. Although Mosher's sample size was small—only 45 women—and far from representative—all were college students—the responses indicate that sexual repression might not have been as common as Victorian standards held. About half of the women reported that they had no knowledge of sex before their marriages, but 35 of the 45 women reported sexual desires, and 34 of the 45 said they experienced orgasm. This small, unrepresentative sample might not reveal the average woman's attitudes for that time, but the existence of women who enjoyed sex seems to contradict the prevalent view of the Victorian period. The marriage manuals of the day portrayed women as lacking in sexual feelings, and after examining Mosher's data, Degler warned against relying on the marriage manuals of the Victorian era to understand female sexuality during that time.

Several other researchers completed small-scale sex surveys during the early 1900s, but the most famous of the surveys on sexual behavior were those completed by Kinsey and his colleagues.

The Kinsey Surveys

In 1920, biologist Alfred Kinsey took a position as instructor at Indiana University (Brecher, 1969). In 1937, he began to teach a newly created course in sex education, which at that time was a controversial topic. One of the factors in the university's choice of Kinsey was his respectability: He was middle-aged, happily married, a father of four, and a respected biologist. Kinsey took the assignment seriously, and because he knew little about the research on sexuality, he went to the library to learn.

Kinsey found that little systematic research existed on sexuality, and this gap prompted him to begin such research. He started collecting data in 1938 with a preliminary interview, that he later expanded to include extensive information about nine areas: social and economic background information, marital history, sex education, physical and physiological information, nocturnal sex dreams, masturbation, heterosexual history, history of same-gender sexual activity, and sexual contact with animals. Each of these areas included subdivisions, making the interview extensive and time consuming. Amazingly, Kinsey completed more than 7,000 such interviews himself. His associates, Wardell Pomeroy, Clyde Martin, and Paul Gebhard, conducted other interviews, for a total sample of 17,500.

Although the interviews were extensive and numerous, the sampling procedure did not yield a representative sample of the people in the United States. He started with interviews of students and staff at Indiana University, and some of his interviews led him to other participants. He was fond of interviewing entire organizations, such as fraternities, sororities, and civic groups. Kinsey did not necessarily strive to obtain a representative sample; his goal was to test as great a variety of people as possible. He accomplished that goal, but his sample did not allow generalizations to all U.S. residents. Kinsey questioned African Americans, but he excluded these data from his analysis because he knew that the individuals he had questioned were too selected a group. This choice further biased his results. His final groups of 5,300 men and 5,940 women were therefore White, well educated, mostly from Indiana, and largely Protestant.

Kinsey was skilled at getting a wide variety of people to talk with him candidly about their sexual histories (Brecher, 1969; Hyde, 1990). His technique included asking questions that required participants to deny rather than admit a practice, such as "At what age did you first experience full intercourse?" This approach assumed that everyone had done everything. Perhaps this strategy helped to make people more comfortable and encourage them to tell the truth. Reinterviewing some participants 18 months after their first interview revealed that people supplied consistent information about their sexual behavior, indicating to Kinsey that they were telling the truth. Some inconsistencies appeared, but of the type primarily due to memory problems rather than intentional deception. Thus, Kinsey's surveys managed to overcome some problems associated with survey research.

The results from Kinsey's surveys appeared in two parts, *Sexual Behavior in the Human Male* (Kinsey, Pomeroy, & Martin, 1948) and *Sexual Behavior in the Human Female* (Kinsey, Pomeroy, Martin, & Gebhard, 1953). The results surprised (and even shocked) many people, because the participants reported such a wide variety of sexual behavior, including some that was socially unacceptable and even illegal. Kinsey's reports appeared during a time when sex was not a topic of polite conversation; when women were supposed to be reluctant to have sex; and when same-gender, premarital, and extramarital sexual activities were illegal in many places.

Kinsey's results indicated that women enjoyed sex; that many men had participated in male-male sexual behavior; that children experienced sexual excitement and activity, and that masturbation, premarital, and extramarital sex were common for both women and men. Around 90% of the women in the study had experienced orgasm by age 35 years. Of the 10% who had not, another 8% reported experiencing sexual arousal, leaving only 2% of women who had failed to enjoy sexual activity, a figure much lower than most people imagined.

A total of 37% of the men in Kinsey's survey reported at least one sexual experience with another man; that is, an experience with another man that led to orgasm. This figure included men who had sexual experiences with other men only as young adolescents and men who only had one such experience. Some of these men reported that they no longer felt sexual attraction toward other men or had no subsequent sexual experiences with other men. When considering the men who have had sexual experiences with only other men (4%), with only men for a period of three years or longer (4%), and predominantly with men (5%), the total reached 13%. Both the percentage of men who had some type of sexual experience with men—37%—and the percentage of men who were primarily or exclusively had sex with other men—13%—were higher than previous estimates (Brecher, 1969) and may have been overestimates (Hyde, 1990).

Kinsey's figures on female sexual activity with other women were similar to the figures for men, but the percentages were smaller. That is, few women reported exclusively lesbian (3%) or primarily lesbian (4%) sexuality, but more (28%) had at least some sexual experience with other women. Table 11.1 shows these figures.

Some of the people with sexual partners of their own gender object to the term *homosexual,* a term that Kinsey used to describe male-male and female-female sexual behavior. The term has become stigmatized and highlights the sexual aspect of these individuals' lifestyle. Choosing a relationship with a same-gender partner is much more than sexual (Blumstein & Schwartz, 1983), and other terms have replaced *homosexual.* The term **gay** is an alternative that many find preferable, and may apply to both men and women, but more often to men. The term ***lesbian*** refers to women who have sexual relationships with other women.

The relatively high percentage of men and women who reported some same-gender experience but who did not have an exclusive same-gender orientation suggested to Kinsey that sexuality should not be considered in terms of independent categories. He believed that sexual activity could be placed on a continuum from exclusive heterosexuality to exclusive homosexuality, with gradations in between representing people who have both types of sexual relationships in varying proportions.

Many participants in the Kinsey survey reported that as children they had sexual feelings and sometimes acted on those feelings. The most common type of childhood sexuality was **masturbation**, manipulation of the genitals to produce sexual pleasure. Infants and young children masturbate, some to orgasm. A total of 14% of the women and 45% of the men in Kinsey's survey said that they had masturbated before the age of 13 years. They also remembered other-gender and same-gender exploratory play with peers as well as sexual contact with adults. Men recalled preadolescent intercourse more frequently than women. Almost one-fourth of the women recalled incidents during which adult men had shown their genitals, touched them, or attempted intercourse. Over half of these incidents involved acquaintances or family members. The recollections of adults of their childhood sexual activities are most likely not completely accurate, but Kinsey's results suggested that children experience sexual curiosity and exploration as well as sexual abuse by adults.

Kinsey's survey revealed that masturbation was a common sexual activity. Although the percentages of people who reported preadolescent masturbation were not large, the activity increases during adolescence, and by the time they were adults, almost all of the men and about two-thirds of the women had reached orgasm by masturbating. Married women and men told Kinsey that they continued to masturbate, although they also had sex with their spouses. Around 30% of married women and 40% of married men reported that they masturbated. These figures contradicted the popular notion that masturbation was primarily a practice of adolescence and that people with a sexual partner no longer masturbated.

Kinsey surveyed people who lived in a society that accepted different sexual standards for men and women. Although both were supposed to be sexually inexperienced before marriage and to have sex only with their spouses, men were not held to this standard and women were. That is, men were allowed a greater range of heterosexual activity than women (although neither were allowed same-gender sexual activity without severe social and even legal censure). This **double standard for sexual behavior** had a history that stretched back at least a century, and Kinsey found evidence for it in the different rates for both premarital and extramarital sex. By the age of 25, 83% of unmarried men but only 33% of unmarried women said that they had participated in intercourse. A similar discrepancy occurred in the reports of extramarital affairs—that is, about half of the men but only 26% of the women admitted extramarital affairs.

In summary, Kinsey and his associates interviewed thousands of men and women during the 1930s and 1940s to determine the sexual behavior of Americans. They questioned a variety of people but not a representative sample, so the results have limitations. Kinsey's results suggested that people engage in a wide variety of sexual activities, beginning during childhood. He found that most women experience orgasm and that masturbation and extramarital sex are common. In addition, Kinsey's results showed that more than one-third of men have had some type of sexual experience with another man but that few were exclusively gay. The reports of female-female sexual activities were less common but with parallel findings; few women were exclusively lesbian, but more had past or occasional sexual experiences with other women. After the Kinsey reports, many other sex researchers have chosen the survey method of investigation.

Hunt's Playboy Foundation Survey

In the 1970s, the Playboy Foundation commissioned a survey of sexual behavior in the United States, and Morton Hunt reported the results in 1974 in his book *Sexual Behavior in the 1970s.* The researchers involved in this survey wanted to update the Kinsey findings and attempted to obtain a more representative sample than Kinsey managed.

The survey began with a sample of people randomly drawn from the telephone books of 24 U.S. cities. Although most people had telephones, not everyone did, which posed some problems for constituting a representative sample. In addition, 80% of those contacted declined to participate, raising further doubts about the sample. Despite the problems with the sampling procedure, Hunt contended that the sample matched characteristics of the U.S. population in terms of ethnic background, education, age, and marital status. The 2,026 participants filled out a lengthy questionnaire about their background (including sex education), attitude toward sex, and sexual history. A total of 200 also participated in an even more lengthy interview similar to the Kinsey interviews.

As Table 11.1 shows, this survey confirmed the prevalence of masturbation, finding a higher rate of preadolescent masturbation and similar high rates of masturbation. Hunt found a lower percentage and a different pattern of same-gender sexual activity than Kinsey. He concluded that most such activity occurs as a form of adolescent experimentation, given that most of the women and men who had same-gender sexual experiences discontinued this form of sexuality by age 16 years. Hunt estimated that 2% of men and 1% of women were exclusively gay or lesbian in their sexual orientation.

Hunt found some evidence for a sexual revolution in the form of increases in some sexual activities. More unmarried people had engaged in intercourse than reported in

TABLE 11.1   Sexual Activities Reported by Participants in Three Sex Surveys

Sexual Activity	Kinsey Surveys (1948, 1953)		Playboy Foundation Survey (1974)		Janus Report (1993)	
	Percentage Reporting Each Behavior					
	Men	Women	Men	Women	Men	Women
Masturbation to orgasm	92%	58%	94%	63%	93%	75%
Masturbation before age 13	45	14	63	33	72	44
Masturbation during marriage	40	30	72	68	66	67
At least one homosexual experience	37	28	—	—	22	17
Primarily homosexual orientation	13	7	2	1	4	2
Premarital intercourse	71	33	97	67	85	69
Extramarital sex	50	26	41	18	35	26
Molestation during childhood	10	25	—	—	11	24

the Kinsey surveys. A total of 97% of the unmarried men and 67% of the unmarried women reported having intercourse by age 25 years, representing an increase in intercourse and a decrease in the double standard. According to Hunt, by the 1970s extramarital sex was more common, especially among younger women.

The Playboy Foundation survey also found evidence that more people were engaging in a wider variety of sexual activities than Kinsey reported. For example, a higher percentage of respondents in the Playboy Foundation survey reported oral-genital sexuality than in Kinsey's surveys. **Fellatio** is oral stimulation of the male genitals, and **cunnilingus** is oral stimulation of the female genitals. Kinsey found a difference in popularity of oral-genital sexuality according to educational background, with such activity more likely among college-educated people (60%) as compared to those with a high school education (20%) and a grade school education (10%). Hunt reported that 90% of the young married couples in his survey said they had engaged in oral-genital stimulation, revealing a dramatic increase in prevalence and a leveling of social class differences.

In summary, Hunt's Playboy Foundation survey attempted to obtain a representative sample of U.S. residents and question them about their sexual attitudes and behavior. One of the goals was to complete an interview similar to Kinsey's technique so as to furnish updated comparisons. This survey showed that Kinsey was correct in concluding that people's sexual behavior is more varied than the social norms suggest, and confirmed the prevalence of masturbation and childhood sexuality. Hunt's estimates for same-gender sexuality were much lower than Kinsey's figures, but Hunt found evidence for an increase in premarital, extramarital, and oral-genital sexual activity.

The Janus Report

The Janus Report on Sexual Behavior (1993) took its name from its authors, Samuel and Cynthia Janus, as well as the subject matter of the report—sexual behavior. The Januses enlisted the cooperation of a network of researchers in an attempt to obtain a representative sample of U.S. residents. Since the Playboy Foundation survey in the 1970s, a number of other sex surveys had been completed. The large surveys were accomplished through polling magazine readers, a procedure that yields a less representative sample than either Kinsey or Hunt obtained. The smaller surveys were mostly college or community studies that sampled from special populations rather than a representative sample. The Januses argued that their sample, consisting of 1,347 men and 1,418 women, reflected the characteristics of the U.S. population and furnished the first sex survey that could reveal the sexual attitudes and behavior of the country.

This survey found evidence for an even greater variety of sexual behavior and more liberal attitudes toward sex than did the Kinsey and Playboy Foundation surveys. Table 11.1 shows the frequency of different sexual activities reported by participants in Kinsey's surveys, the Playboy Foundation survey, and the Janus report. The comparison of these three surveys reveals an increase in masturbation. About two-thirds of the respondents in the Janus survey accepted masturbation as a normal part of life and as continuing during marriage.

The Janus survey also asked about same-gender sexual experiences and found that 17% of women and 22% of men responded affirmatively; however, only about 2% of the women and 4% of the men identified themselves as gay or lesbian, a percentage similar to Hunt's estimates.

The Janus report also confirmed the Kinsey findings concerning adult sexual activity with children. A total of 24% of the women and 11% of the men recalled at least one episode of childhood molestation by an adult. Unlike Kinsey, the Januses found that these adults were more likely to be relatives or acquaintances and not strangers. In addition, an overwhelming majority of the participants failed to report these incidents, and if they did, most reports did not result in arrest or conviction. These figures highlight the frequency of sexual abuse of children and the low probability of retribution for the adults who perpetuate this abuse.

This survey confirmed the continuation of the double standard of sexual behavior for men and women but also showed that there was some decrease, especially when comparing the Janus survey to the Kinsey reports. The Janus survey included a question specifically about the existence of a double standard of sexual behavior for men and women, and 91% of women and 79% of men agreed that it still exists.

The Januses included questions about changes in sexual behavior over the past few years in an attempt to assess the impact of concern over **sexually transmitted diseases** on sexual behavior. Sexually transmitted diseases are by no means new, but the threat from herpes and AIDS, coupled with wide publicity about the dangers, may have prompted changes in sexual behavior. Although sexually transmitted diseases were an area of concern for participants, this concern had not prompted them to decrease their sexual activities or number of partners. Indeed, almost half of the single women and men in the Janus survey reported an *increase* in their sexual activity over the three years prior to the survey.

In summary, the Januses attempted to survey a representative sample of U.S. residents about their sexual attitudes and behavior. Their results extended and updated the findings of previous sex surveys, indicating that people find a variety of sexual behaviors acceptable. An increasing number of men and women reported that masturbation as well as oral-genital, premarital, and extramarital sexual activity are acceptable, and their behavior reflects this acceptance.

The higher percentages of many sexual behaviors in the three successive surveys probably represent changes in sexual behavior over the decades of the surveys (see Table 11.1). Even Kinsey's surveys, completed in the 1930s and 1940s, showed that people's behavior failed to reflect the social standards of sexuality; that is, a wider variety of people engaged in a wider variety of sexual activities than the social standards or the laws allowed.

Gender Differences (and Similarities) in Sexual Attitudes and Behavior

The three major sex surveys have shown gender differences in several sexual behaviors and in some attitudes toward sexuality. Although the more recent surveys have indicated a smaller difference in sexuality of men and women, even the Januses' report indicated that men are more sexually active at a younger age than women. To analyze the magnitude of gender differences in sexuality, Mary Beth Oliver and Janet Hyde (1993) conducted a meta-analysis of the studies that have tested sexual attitudes and behaviors. Their results indicated that gender differences exist in some aspects of sexuality but not in others.

Two large gender-related differences emerged from the Oliver and Hyde meta-analysis: incidence of masturbation and attitudes toward casual premarital sex. Studies of male adolescents and adults have indicated a higher rate of masturbation and a greater acceptance of casual premarital sex than for female adolescents and adults. These researchers pointed out that the magnitude of the differences for these comparisons surpasses other gender-related differences, such as those in mathematics or verbal abilities. (See Chapter 5 for a discussion of these cognitive differences.)

Gender-related differences in other aspects of sexuality were smaller, and some comparisons in Oliver and Hyde's meta-analysis failed to show such differences. Of the differences that appeared, men reported and were more acceptant of sexual behaviors than women. Small differences also appeared in the acceptance of premarital and extramarital intercourse, sexual permissiveness, number of sexual partners, and frequency of intercourse. In addition, men reported less sexual guilt or anxiety than women. Analysis of acceptance of the double standard for sexual behavior indicated, ironically, that women believed in the double standard more than men. No gender differences appeared in attitudes toward same-gender sexuality, rights for gays or

**TABLE 11.2   Sexual Attitudes and Behaviors Showing
and Failing to Show Gender-Related Differences**

Sexual Behaviors/Attitudes	Direction of Difference
Large Differences	
Incidence of masturbation	Higher for men
Acceptability of casual sex	Higher for men
Moderate to Small Differences	
Acceptability of sexual permissiveness	Higher for men
Incidence of sex in committed relationship	Higher for men
Incidence of intercourse by engaged couples	Higher for men
Acceptability of premarital sex	Higher for men
Age at first intercourse	Lower for men
Frequency of intercourse	Higher for men
Incidence of same-gender sexual experiences	Higher for men
Anxiety, fear, and guilt associated with sex	Higher for women
Acceptability of double standard of sexual behavior	Higher for women
Acceptability of extramarital sex	Higher for men
Number of sexual partners	Higher for men
No Differences	
Incidence of oral sex	
Incidence of kissing	
Incidence of petting	
Acceptability of masturbation	
Acceptability of same-gender sexuality	
Belief that gays and lesbians should be given civil rights	
Sexual satisfaction	

lesbians, attitudes toward masturbation, incidence of oral sex, or sexual satisfaction. Table 11.2 shows some of the behaviors and attitudes from Oliver and Hyde's meta-analysis, along with the magnitude of gender-related differences.

Oliver and Hyde (1993) also attempted to assess changes over time, reporting that "almost all of the significant effects showed gender differences becoming smaller over time" (p. 45). Thus, this analysis confirms the trends that appeared in the comparison of the three major surveys, as shown in Table 11.1—that is, a decrease of differences between men's and women's sexual attitudes and behavior, along with some persistent differences.

Masters and Johnson's Approach

As noted earlier, researchers who want to directly observe sexual behavior can conduct their studies on nonhuman animals, or they can attempt to enlist the cooperation of people who are willing to engage in sex in a research laboratory. Although such participants are far from average, they might furnish important information about the physiology of sex. Other researchers have taken this approach, but the most famous have been William Masters and Virginia Johnson.

Masters began his study of the physiology of sexual response in the 1950s by interviewing prostitutes (Brecher, 1969), but he was interested in making measurements during sexual activity and considered prostitutes unsuitable participants. He sought volunteers from the medical community in St. Louis and found people who were willing to masturbate or have intercourse while being observed in the laboratory. During the time Masters was recruiting participants for the laboratory studies, he also recruited Virginia Johnson to assist him with the interviewing, and she became an essential part of the research.

Masters and Johnson chose a total of 694 people, including 276 married couples as well as 106 single women and 36 single men to serve as research participants. These participants not only had to be willing to have sex in the lab, but the researchers selected women who regularly experienced orgasm, a criterion that has raised questions about how representative the group was (Tavris, 1992). All participants received payment for their participation, resulting in an overrepresentation of medical school students, who were interested in contributing to scientific research and also needed the money. These criteria and procedures were reasonable but resulted in a sample that was far from representative. Masters and Johnson were not as concerned with drawing a representative sample as other sex researchers. They believed that the physiological sexual responses they were studying varied little from person to person; thus, any sample should contain the characteristics of interest to them. This assumption remains untested.

In these laboratory studies, the married couples had intercourse, masturbated each other, or engaged in oral-genital stimulation. The unmarried participants did not have sex with a partner; the men masturbated, and the women either masturbated or were stimulated by an artificial penis designed to measure vaginal responses during sexual arousal and orgasm. In addition to collecting information by measuring genital activity during sex, both the women and men cooperated by providing Masters and Johnson with physiological measurements such as heart rate, muscle contraction, and dilation of the blood vessels.

Masters and Johnson measured physiological responses during more than 10,000 orgasms and presented their findings in *Human Sexual Response* (1966). Their findings suggested that four phases of sexual excitement exist—excitement, plateau, orgasm, and resolution. As with other physiological processes, individual variations exist, and Carol Tavris (1992) criticized Masters and Johnson for ignoring these individual differences. However, Masters and Johnson contended that these four phases describe the sequence and experience of sexual arousal and orgasm for both women and men. Figures 11.1 and 11.2 show the four phases and the affected organs for both women and men.

The *excitement phase* includes the initial physiological responses for sexual excitement—erection of the penis in men and the clitoris in women. These responses are both produced by vasocongestion, the swelling of tissues due to engorgement of the area with blood. The penis and clitoris are not the only affected areas; the testes, nipples, vaginal opening, and labia also swell, and the skin may become flushed. The vaginal walls secrete lubrication, and heart rate, blood pressure, and muscle tension increase.

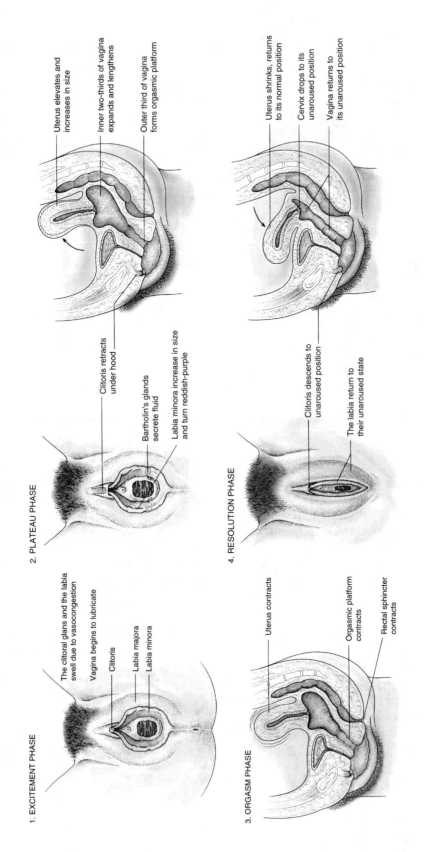

FIGURE 11.1 Female Genitals during the Phases of the Sexual Response Cycle

1. EXCITEMENT PHASE

The clitoral glans and the labia swell due to vasocongestion

Vagina begins to lubricate

Clitoris

Labia majora

Labia minora

2. PLATEAU PHASE

Uterus elevates and increases in size

Inner two-thirds of vagina expands and lengthens

Outer third of vagina forms orgasmic platform

Clitoris retracts under hood

Bartholin's glands secrete fluid

Labia minora increase in size and turn reddish-purple

3. ORGASM PHASE

Uterus contracts

Orgasmic platform contracts

Rectal sphincter contracts

4. RESOLUTION PHASE

Uterus shrinks, returns to its normal position

Cervix drops to its unaroused position

Vagina returns to its unaroused position

Clitoris descends to unaroused position

The labia return to their unaroused state

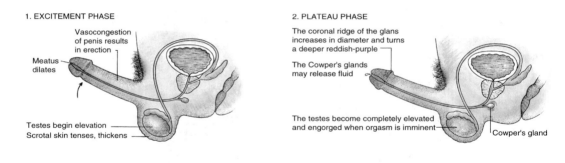

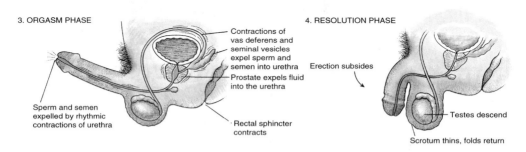

FIGURE 11.2 **Male Genitals during the Phases of the Sexual Response Cycle**

A leveling of sexual arousal occurs during the *plateau phase,* with less dramatic changes than those during the excitement phase. In women, the outer third of the vagina swells while the inner part expands. The clitoris withdraws beneath its hood, becoming shorter, and secretions from Bartholin's gland appear. The labia minora deepen in color. In men, the penis may enlarge slightly more than in the excitement phase and turns a deep purple color. The testes elevate further, and the Cowper's gland secretes a small amount of fluid that appears at the tip of the penis. Heart rate, blood pressure, and muscle tension increase slightly. Flushing of the skin is even more likely to occur in this phase than in the excitement phase.

The *orgasm phase* for both women and men consists of muscle contractions at 0.8-second intervals, releasing the tension that has built up during the first two phases. In women, between 3 and 15 contractions occur in the muscles that surround the vagina, and an additional three to six contractions may also occur, although these are weaker and slower. In men, orgasm occurs in two stages. The first stage results in a collection of seminal fluid in the urethral bulb due to muscle contractions of the vas deferens, seminal vesicles, and ejaculatory duct. The second stage results in ejaculation of semen from the body through the urethra due to a series of three or four muscle contractions at 0.8-second intervals, possibly followed by several additional slower contractions. For both women and men, other spasmodic muscle movements occur for muscles in the abdominal region and throughout the body. Heart rate and blood pressure reach their peak in this phase.

In the *resolution phase,* the body returns to its normal prearousal level. In women, the clitoris, vagina, labia, nipples, and uterus all return to their normal sizes. In men, the penis loses its erection over a period of about a minute, and the testes and scrotum return to normal size. Both women's and men's skin returns to its normal low level of flush. All of these responses are part of the decreased vasocongestion that occurs in this phase. The muscle tension has been dissipated during the orgasmic phase, and the decrease of vasocongestion returns to prearousal levels. This process may take as long as five minutes after experiencing orgasm, but for those who do not experience orgasm, return to prearousal functioning may take as long as an hour.

Not only did Masters and Johnson's research suggest that both women and men are similar in their experience of the four stages of sexual response, it showed that women experience one type of orgasm. Freud hypothesized that women experience two types—clitoral or vaginal orgasm. He believed that girls begin to experience clitoral orgasm during masturbation, beginning during early childhood, and that women are immature if they continue to require clitoral stimulation for orgasm. Freudian theory described women who experience orgasm through intercourse as healthier and more mature than women who have only clitoral orgasms. Masters and Johnson's results showed that women experience only one type of orgasm—a clitoral orgasm—and their data provided no evidence for different types of orgasms, thus refuting Freud's contention that two types of orgasm exist. Some women have clitoral orgasms during intercourse, and some do not; intercourse may not provide sufficient clitoral stimulation to produce orgasm in some women.

Masters and Johnson's research has been controversial but influential. Their goal of measuring human sexual response by physiological measurements during sex made headlines, but their research also established the similarities in sexual response for women and men. According to their findings, all people experience four phases of sexual response—excitement, plateau, orgasm, and resolution. Muscle tension and vasocongestion increase during the first two phases, reach their peak during orgasm, and return to prearousal levels during resolution. In addition, the findings about the physiology of sexual response showed that women have one type of orgasm produced by clitoral stimulation. For both men and women, orgasm is probably a similar experience.

Childhood Sexuality: Exploration and Abuse

As the Kinsey, Playboy Foundation, and Janus surveys indicated, sexuality begins before puberty. Even as infants children take part in sexual exploration and are sometimes the victims of sexual abuse.

Even babies are capable of sexual response. Before birth, male fetuses have erections; infant boys have erections and infant girls experience erection of the clitoris as well as vaginal lubrication (Masters, Johnson, & Kolodny, 1992). Infants touch their genitals as they explore their bodies, and this exploration gives children the knowledge that their bodies can produce pleasurable sensations. Preschool-aged children masturbate, sometimes several times a day.

Parents who notice their children's masturbation may accept it, or they may be surprised or shocked. Their attitude and their method of dealing with their children's masturbation can convey positive or negative messages about sexuality, and these messages can have a permanent impact (Masters et al., 1992). Parents who say, "That's not nice" or "Nice boys and girls don't do that" or who move their children's hands away from their genitals send negative messages about sexuality.

Other aspects of childhood sexuality that may make parents uncomfortable include questions about sexuality, pregnancy, and birth as well as their children's sexual explorations with other children. By age four years, most children have begun to form a concept of gender and the roles that women and men occupy. Part of this knowledge is that women have babies and men do not, and pregnancy and birth are topics that stimulate curiosity and questions. Parents may feel embarrassed about giving straightforward descriptions and resort to analogies such as "Daddy plants a seed inside Mommy." Due to their concrete thought processes, children have a tendency to misinterpret fanciful descriptions and analogies (Masters et al., 1992). For example, children may interpret the seed analogy literally, believing that women have a small plot of dirt inside their bodies in which men plant a seed and that one or the other must water and weed it so that the seed will grow into a baby.

The entire story of reproduction may be too complex for preschool children to assimilate, but simple, correct explanations usually satisfy children and avoid confusion. Due to children's tendency to invent and fill in the details of a story they do not fully understand, concealing information will not keep children from "knowing" about sex. But what they "know" may be incorrect. Therefore, formulating appropriate answers to young children's questions about sex and birth requires a delicate balance of providing the correct amount of information without excessive details. Parents' discomfort with the topic of sex complicates these discussions.

"I would love for him to grow up to be a doctor, but I sure wish he'd wait another twenty years to specialize in gynecology," the mother of a 5-year-old told Julius and Zelda Segal (1993, p. 131). This mother humorously expressed her concern over her son and the neighbor's daughter exploring each other's genitals. The Segals explained to the mother that her son's explorations were more curiosity than sexuality and that his behavior was normal. They advised this mother to set limits on her son's sexuality and urged her not to be concerned about her son's curiosity about female genitals.

Punishing children for such explorations can convey the message that something is wrong with the genitals, giving negative messages about sexuality. Masters et al. (1992) warned that sexual explorations during preschool or elementary school are rarely harmful but that parental punishment can be, leaving a permanent impression that something is wrong with such activity. They also argued that the double standard for sexual behavior starts during this age range, with girls warned about sexual exploration and sex play and boys allowed more freedom in their sexuality.

Parents may be unaware that sexual explorations during childhood include same-gender as well as other-gender sexual play (Masters et al., 1992). In addition, parents are not aware of most sexual contact between siblings. The majority of such contact consists of examining the genitals and touching, and a low percentage of sibling sexual activity includes attempted or successful intercourse. Nonetheless, sexual activity between siblings qualifies as **incest,** sexual activity between family members. David Finkelhor (1980) reported that 15% of college women and 10% of college men recalled sexual experiences with a sibling. The majority of these college students did not believe that the experience had harmed them, but an important factor in this evaluation was the age difference between the two siblings; a large age difference was associated with a greater perception of harm.

Age has been a critical factor in defining sexual exploitation of children (Finkelhor, 1984). When sexual contact occurs between children who are close to the same age, this activity falls into the category of *exploration.* When a child has sexual contact with an adult or an adolescent at least five years older than the child, that activity falls into the category of *exploitation* or *sexual abuse.* Also included as abusive are sexual relationships between adolescents and adults whose age exceeds the adolescents' age by at least 10 years.

Incest is one form of sexually abusive relationship, but children can also be sexually abused by nonrelatives, including strangers and adults in positions of authority, such as neighbors, day-care workers, priests, and teachers. Kinsey's (1948, 1953) surveys included questions about childhood sexual experiences with adults, and his results revealed that 25% of girls and 10% of boys reported such contact. In over 50% of the cases, the activity consisted of an adult man exhibiting his genitals to the child. Kinsey also found that over half of the incidents involved adults whom the children did not know. Later research on the sexual abuse of children has confirmed the high percentage of abuse and the gender difference in rates of sexual abuse but has failed to confirm that most abusers are strangers.

Beginning in the 1970s, several groups of researchers attempted to determine the rate of sexual abuse of children. This research is even more difficult than other types of sex surveys. The honesty and memory problems that affect all surveys are more serious when asking adults about sexual abuse during childhood; honesty is a major problem when questioning adults about abuse they may have committed.

Christopher Bagley and Kathleen King (1990) reviewed studies on the prevalence of child sexual abuse, including studies conducted in the United States, Canada, and England; studies that questioned college students and those that attempted to draw representative samples; studies using varying definitions of sexual abuse; and studies employing questions and interview techniques. These variations resulted in different percentages of people who reported being sexually abused as children, with percentages ranging from 11% to 40% for women and from 3% to 8.6% for men. Due to the sampling techniques in the various studies, Bagley and King speculated that these percentages might be underestimates. On the basis of the studies in the review, Bagley and King estimated that at least 15% of girls and 5% of boys are sexually abused during childhood or adolescence.

Despite the differences, the studies reviewed by Bagley and King showed some commonalties: Girls were sexually abused more often than boys, and men were the instigators of abuse far more frequently than women. Both girls and boys are at risk during their entire childhood and adolescence from family members, family friends, adult authority figures, and strangers, but the risk is not equal for all ages or from all adults. Table 11.3 shows the range of estimates and characteristics of sexual abusers and victims for the studies in Bagley and King's review.

Girls are not only more likely to be sexually abused, but they are more likely to be abused at younger ages than boys. The preadolescence years are the riskiest age period for both, with girls between ages 10 and 11 years and boys between age 11 and 12 years at the highest risk. These ages represent the time during which the first victimization is

TABLE 11.3   Summary of Offender and Victim Characteristics for Childhood Sexual Abuse

Characteristic	Range of Estimated Occurrence	
	Lowest	Highest
Girls abused while under age 16 (average age 10.2–10.7 years)	11%	40%
Girls who rated the experience negatively	66	
Girls whose abuser was male	94	100
Boys abused while under age 16 (average age 11.2–12 years)	3	8.6
Boys who rated the experience negatively	38	
Boys whose abuser was male	83	84
Children whose offender was a stranger	11	51
Children whose offender was a friend or an acquaintance	33	49
Children whose offender was a relative	14	50
Girls whose offender was a sibling	15	
Boys whose offender was a sibling	10	
Children whose offender was a biological parent	1	6.8
Girls whose offender was a stepfather	7.6	17
Children who had force or threats used against them	55	
Children whose abuse consisted of exhibition	26	28
Children whose abused consisted of being fondled	26	40
Children whose abuse consisted of forced fondling of offender	10	14
Children whose abuse consisted of intercourse	15	18

SOURCE: Based on *Child sexual abuse: The search for healing* by C. Bagley & K. King, 1990, London: Tavistock.

GENDERED VOICES
My Parents Never Said Anything Until...

"My parents never said anything to us about sexual abuse until my brother was molested," a teenager said. "Then our whole family talked sexual abuse. My brother had to tell us what happened, tell us what the person had done very explicitly. Maybe that wasn't a good thing for him to have to do, because he had to talk about it a lot, but we learned about what to be careful about. And they never said anything before he was molested.

"It was tough on the family, because the person who molested him was a cousin. He was about 4 or 5 years older than my brother, and our families don't speak to each other anymore. It was hard to know what to do, because the cousin had been molested when he was younger, so he was just repeating what happened to him. Should he be punished for doing what he had learned? My brother was still hurt, but it was difficult not to feel sorry for my teenage cousin.

"We went for counseling as a family, and I think it helped. I hear that it can be much worse to ignore it, because it won't go away if you don't talk about it. We talked about it afterward, but not before something happened."

most likely to occur. For many children sexual abuse continues for years, often for as long as they remain in contact with their abusers, who are usually men.

The studies in Bagley and King's review showed that between 94% and 100% of those who abused girls were men, and around 84% of those who abused boys were men. Although abusers are sometimes strangers, more often these men are known to their victims as family members, family acquaintances, or an adult authority figure such as a teacher, scout leader, or priest. Gail Wyatt (1985) compared ethnic differences in sexual abuse for African-American and European-American women, finding that abusers tend to choose victims within their own ethnic group—81% of the cases matched ethnic background of victim and abuser.

Both female and male abusers exist, but the emphasis in research and therapy has been on boys and men as perpetrators and girls and women as victims. This emphasis is not entirely inappropriate; most sexual abuse follows this pattern. The pattern of female-male abuse differs. Whereas male strangers represent approximately one-third of the cases of male abusers, almost all of female abusers are acquaintances of those whom they molest. Toni Johnson (1989) studied female perpetrators and found a common pattern of babysitters molesting the children in their care. In Johnson's study, all of the girls who abused other children had themselves been the victims of abuse, most commonly by a family member.

The scant research on female perpetrators and male victims has demonstrated that many of the instances of such abuse occur in the pattern Johnson (1988, 1989) found—abused girls molesting younger children when in positions of authority over them. But some women victimize boys in the guise of initiating them into sexuality, and according to Scott Sleek (1994), these cases are rarely reported to authorities, making the proportion of male abusers seem higher than it actually is. Another type of female abuser includes those who are coerced by men into committing the abuse, and yet another type includes adolescent girls who commit sexual abuse as part of their initiation into gangs.

The overwhelming focus on female victims and male perpetrators has left sexually abused men and sexually abusive women neglected in both research and treatment. However, this situation is beginning to change.

Incest involving biological fathers and their daughters is not a common type of sexual abuse, but stepfathers are much more likely to force this type of relationship. Diana Russell (1986) found that 17% of stepdaughters were molested by their stepfathers, whereas only 2% of daughters were victims of sexual abuse by their biological fathers. Indeed, having a stepfather is a major risk factor for sexual abuse. David Finkelhor and Larry Baron's (1986) results led to similar conclusions. Although they found no indication of racial or social class differences in child sexual abuse, these researchers also found that living with a stepparent increased the risk for abuse. In addition, living apart from biological parents or having a mother who was unavailable due to illness, handicap, or employment increased the risk for abuse. Children whose parents have a relationship filled with conflict and whose parents use harsh punishment as discipline were also at elevated risk for sexual abuse.

Judith Herman (1981) studied cases of father-daughter incest and concluded that these incestuous relationships have serious, long-term consequences for the daughters, who often have difficulties in school and in their personal relationships, sometimes throughout their adulthood. Later studies have confirmed these contentions of both short-term and long-term damage. Angela Browne and David Finkelhor's review (1986) as well as Finkelhor's (1990) later review concluded that the short-term effects of sexual abuse include fear, anxiety, depression, anger, and sexually inappropriate behavior. The long-term effects include anxiety and depression and also poor self-concept, sexual adjustment problems, and substance abuse disorders. Finkelhor (1990) was able to review studies of sexually abused boys and contended that few gender differences exist between boys and girls who have been the victims of sexual abuse; both suffer similar negative effects from their victimization.

The fathers in Herman's (1981) study who committed incest tended to be traditional men who held unquestioned authority in their families and considered sexual activity with their daughters to be part of their right as the head of the family. Although this pattern of sexual abuse is not the most common, it suggests the underlying commonality in child sexual abuse—power. Adults have social power and power in the family, and this power allows them to abuse children. Family structure usually grants more power to men than women, and this power differential may be an important reason for the gender difference in perpetrators.

In summary, childhood sexuality is more active than most parents imagine, beginning during infancy when children explore and manipulate their genitals. This masturbation continues throughout childhood, which may alarm parents. Other signs of sexuality that parents may find disturbing are children's questions about sex, pregnancy, and birth as well as curiosity about other children's genitals. Such curiosity is normal, and parents' negative reactions can leave children with the belief that there is something wrong with sexual activity.

Sexual explorations during childhood are confined to activities with other children, but when older adolescents or adults initiate sexual activity with children, the activity constitutes abuse. Various surveys have asked adults about their experiences of being molested as children, with the results indicating that at least 15% of women and 5% of men have been sexually abused as children. Girls are much more likely to be abused than boys, and men are much more likely than women to be abusers. There are few gender differences in short-term and long-term effects of childhood sexual abuse, which include anxiety, depression, and anger as well as adult sexual and substance abuse problems.

Heterosexuality

Most people develop erotic or sexual interest that results in attraction to people of the other sex rather than people of the same sex. That is, most people develop a heterosexual rather than a same-gender erotic interest. Signs of heterosexual erotic interest may begin during childhood, but childhood sexuality is difficult to characterize. Sexual activity during childhood is mainly composed of masturbation and exploratory play, which can be directed toward same- or other-gender children. Thus, children's sexuality often is not clearly heterosexual.

During late childhood and preadolescence, children seek the company of same-gender peers and avoid associating with other-gender peers (see Chapter 10). This gender segregation restricts the opportunities for heterosexual activity but does not signal a lack of interest in the other gender. Indeed, children often tease each other by announcing who "likes" whom and by threatening to kiss unwilling others (Thorne, 1986). Such games demonstrate an awareness of heterosexuality and an early knowledge of gender roles in heterosexual interactions.

During Adolescence

John Santrock (1993) listed sexual exploration as one of the functions of dating, and when adolescents start dating, opportunities for sexual activity increase. Bruce Roscoe and his colleagues (Roscoe, Diana, & Brooks, 1987) found that a small percentage (2 to 17%) of adolescents in the study listed sex as the motivation for dating. For the 6th graders, 11th graders, and college students in the study, boys listed sex as a more important reason for dating than did girls, suggesting that boys may be more interested than girls in sexual activity on dates.

First intercourse has been a developmental milestone that traditionally has been associated with marriage. Kinsey's surveys during the 1930s and 1940s revealed that a majority of young men had intercourse before marriage. The substantially smaller percentage of young women who had intercourse before marriage reflected the double standard, but this discrepancy has changed. Jeanne Brooks-Gunn and Frank Furstenberg (1989) traced changes in adolescent sexual behavior over the past 50 years, reporting that in 1938 approximately 7% of European-American girls had intercourse by age 16 years, but during the 1980s the percentage had risen to 44%. Information does not exist to make comparable comparisons for boys, but estimates suggest that boys were more sexually active than girls during the 1940s to the 1960s, with between one-third and two-thirds of boys having intercourse as teenagers. The difference diminished during the 1970s and 1980s. By age 18 years, 60% of young men have had intercourse, and by age 19 years, the percentage is similar for young women. The Janus (1993) survey's age comparison for first intercourse confirmed the diminished gender differences in this indication of sexuality. When comparing adolescents who are currently sexually active, the differences are even smaller—42.5% of boys and 36.4% of girls (Centers for Disease Control, 1992).

The small magnitude of gender differences holds across ethnic backgrounds, but age of first intercourse varies with ethnic background. Randal Day (1992) found a lower age at first intercourse for boys than girls in Chicano (Mexican ethnic background), Latino (Cuban or Puerto Rican ethnic background), African-American, and European-American teens. Black adolescents had first intercourse at a younger age (16.8 years for girls and 14.3 years for boys) than any of the other groups, which did not differ from each other (over age 17 for girls and around age 16 for boys). Despite the small age differences in girls' and boys' initiation of intercourse in Day's study, he contended that each decides to have intercourse for different reasons. He argued that the factors controlling young women's sexual behavior include religion, career goals, and self-esteem, whereas young men are more likely to be controlled by factors in the family and community. For both, having a biological father (but not a stepfather) present in the home raised the age for first intercourse.

Level of acculturation may be a factor in the similarity of Hispanic Americans' and European Americans' sexual attitudes and behavior. Traditional Hispanic cultures prescribe a set of conservative sexual values and behaviors, especially for women, but U.S. culture has become more sexually liberal. Monica Ulibarri and her colleagues (Ulibarri, Wilson, Grijalva, Hunt, & Seligman, 1994) studied Hispanic-American high school students' sexual behavior and found that the factor of acculturation related to sexual behavior: Those students who were more acculturated to U.S. cultural values in general were more likely to engage in a variety of sexual behaviors than the less acculturated students. The factor of acculturation also played a role in the sexual attitudes of Mexican-American college women. Jesse Valdez (1994) found that Mexican-American college women, an acculturated group, did not differ significantly from European-American college women in their sexual attitudes.

Additional confirmation of gender differences in adolescent sexuality comes from a study by Bruce Roscoe, Donna Kennedy, and Tony Pope (1987). They found that female and male adolescents showed a great deal of agreement over what constitutes intimacy in relationships, except on one point: Young men associated intimacy with sex, whereas young women associated intimacy with openness. These different expectancies for intimacy may contribute to relationship problems for adolescent couples and point to the different meanings of sex for young men and women.

These continuing gender differences in adolescent sexuality reflect the double standard of sexual behavior in which boys are allowed, expected, and even encouraged to behave sexually, whereas girls are discouraged and restrained from openly expressing their sexuality. This double standard applies to early sexual experiences and even to the meaning of sex, making sex important for boys' self-concept and status with peers. "For teenage boys, their first sexual experience may be the primary symbol of manhood—a rite of passage" (Stark, 1989, p. 12). Girls are also subject to peer pressure to have sex, but additional pressure comes from boys, who may feel compelled to have sex to prove a point.

On the other hand, young women may need to refuse sex to prove a point, because women who readily consent to sex may be considered promiscuous. This refusal may be social rather than personal; women feel desire, but openly acknowledging that desire may lead to their being unkindly labeled. Charlene Muehlenhard and Lisa Hollabaugh (1988) found that women sometimes showed token resistance to sexual activity—that is, they sometimes said no when they were willing to have intercourse and had every intention of later saying yes. Their reasons for refusal included avoiding the appearance of being "easy" and using refusal as a way of gaining power over their partners. Almost 40% of women sometimes said no for such reasons. This result means that the majority of women who say no mean what they say, but the large minority of women who reported insincere resistance indicates that communication about sex is often not honest. The double standard encourages women to deny their sexuality, and women's refusal provides them with a way to gain power in their relationships.

Muehlenhard and Hollabaugh speculated that such dishonesty might relate to the high incidence of **date rape,** or **acquaintance rape,** forced sexual activity between people who are acquainted. Chapter 9 discussed rape as an aggressive crime disproportionately committed by men. Although most people picture rape as an attack by a stranger, the majority of rapes and other acts involving forced or coerced sex occur

---

✳ GENDERED VOICES
There Were Lots of Rumors

"I grew up in a small town, and I remember that there were *lots* of rumors about people's sex lives. Some of them, you just wouldn't believe, because they seemed too unlikely, and some of them I didn't believe at the time, but now I think they probably *were* true," a woman in her early 20s recounted. "The rumors were entertainment; we didn't even have cable.

"I don't know if they did any harm—maybe so. I remember a rumor about a gym teacher being lesbian, and I don't know if she was or not. She only taught in our school for one year. Maybe the rumors were why she left, so they probably weren't harmless, but they were entertainment. It was a small town.

"When I was in junior high school, the rumors were about how bad the high school students were, how promiscuous, especially the girls. There were rumors about particular girls. In high school there were rumors about homosexuality, but I didn't believe them, because I just couldn't accept that anyone I knew would do something like that. Those rumors may have been true, at least some of them, but I just couldn't believe it.

"There were rumors about sex with animals; it was a rural community with lots of farms. The rumor I didn't believe was about a woman and a cat. I mean, come on, that just doesn't seem possible. The ones I believed were about boys and farm animals, and the reason I believed them was because they had so much detail. Those rumors were a lot more credible than the woman and the cat. How could they have so much detail without being true?"

between acquaintances. Mary Koss and her colleagues (1987) surveyed college students about sexual activities and found that 54% of the young women in the survey claimed to have been the victims of coerced or forced sexual activity at some time during their lives, and over 27% had been raped. Women are less likely to report sexual assaults if they know the perpetrator, especially if the assault occurred during a date, leading to an underrepresentation of the incidence of rape by acquaintances in the crime statistics.

Muehlenhard and her colleagues (Muehlenhard, Friedman, & Thomas, 1985) studied the conditions under which men considered forced sex acceptable. They found that men with more traditional attitudes toward women rated date rape as acceptable under a wider variety of conditions than men with nontraditional attitudes. If the woman asked the man out, the man paid the expenses of the date, and the woman agreed to go to his apartment, men found rape more justifiable than if the date followed another script. Thus, dating partners follow complex and often unexpressed rules about sexual activities on dates. The assumptions about the right to have sex may make men more likely to force sex—that is, to commit date rape. When women offer insincere refusals, they are contributing to men's reluctance to believe that the answer is really no, which may also contribute to date rape.

Concerns about pregnancy play a role in the restraint of sexual behavior in teenage girls, and not without reason; approximately one million teenage girls become pregnant each year (Centers for Disease Control, 1992). Approximately one million teenage boys are also involved in these pregnancies, and condemning girls' sexuality while condoning boys' sexual behavior is the essence of the double standard.

The recent emphasis on condom use as a method of contraception and as a method for controlling sexually transmitted diseases should have changed the balance of responsibility for birth control, stressing male responsibility, but this emphasis may not have prompted the change in responsibility that it might have. Gail Wyatt (1994) described a number of interventions for risky sexual behaviors in which women were the targets for change but men's behaviors were the risk. These programs have often targeted African-American and Hispanic-American women to encourage them to avoid pregnancy or decrease their risk of sexually transmitted diseases. For example, some programs have encouraged women to be responsible for condom use to prevent HIV infection from male partners. Wyatt contended that "Black women have been criticized for their resistance to condom use because they have questioned why they are being singled out when it is men who should actually use them" (p. 752).

Publicity about teen pregnancy, date rape, and sexual exploitation conveys the impression that sexuality is dangerous, especially for young women. Martha Burt and Rhoda Estep (1981) investigated the development of feelings of sexual vulnerability and concluded that this learning occurs during adolescence. The men in the Burt and Estep study expressed few feelings of sexual vulnerability compared to the women, and neither recalled feeling concern or hearing warnings about sexual danger during childhood.

The women in a study by Monique Ward and Gail Wyatt (1994) also recalled more negative (prohibitive) than positive (instructional) verbal messages concerning sexuality from their parents during childhood, especially during adolescence. Their memory of the nonverbal messages concerning sexuality suggested more positive than negative content, which may result in mixed messages about sexuality. In addition, ethnic background was a factor in these women's memory of sexual communications from their parents. Compared to European-American women, African-American women recalled more messages that reinforced nontraditional roles for women but remembered fewer instances of positive nonverbal communication between their parents, such as their parents hugging and kissing.

Both Michelle Fine (1988) and Mariamne Whatley (1990) have criticized the emphasis on sexual victimization and danger in teaching adolescents about sexuality. While acknowledging that dangers exist connected with sexuality, each argued that the emphasis on danger leaves young women with an image of sexuality that omits pleasure and desire.

In summary, adolescent sexuality becomes increasingly heterosexual, and some gender differences appear. Adolescent boys tend to have intercourse in greater numbers and at earlier ages than adolescent girls. These gender differences have diminished over the past 50 years, and now the difference in the percentages of adolescent girls and boys having intercourse at any age are similar, as is the average age of first intercourse. Although these changes signal a decline of the double standard, sex may have a different meaning for boys and girls. Peer pressure is a factor for both, but boys use sex as proof of their masculinity, whereas validation of femininity is not a common reason for girls to have sex.

During Adulthood

Traditionally, marriage has been not only a major transition but also the major context for adult sexuality. The more recent studies of college students and surveys with more representative samples have indicated that the standards for sexual behavior have changed. The decreased age of first intercourse, the increase in sexual activity among female adolescents, and the increased acceptability of a variety of sexual activities suggest an acceptance of more and more varied sexuality for both women and men.

In one specialized survey of Canadian college students, Nancy Netting (1992) found evidence of three styles of sexuality among these young adults—celibacy, monogamy, and free experimentation. Although these styles can apply to same-gender sexuality, Netting concentrated on heterosexual college students. These styles represent very different choices, but Netting found that students who had chosen one style were acceptant of those who had made different choices: "The only value shared almost universally was the right to choose" (p. 970).

Netting found that **celibacy,** refraining from sexual activity, was a fairly popular choice; about a third of the students were in this category. This group included students who had never had intercourse plus those who had had no sexual partner for the previous year. A similar percentage of men and women were celibate, but for different reasons. For the women, celibacy was most often a choice; their most common reason for remaining celibate was that they were waiting for love. For the men, celibacy was often not a matter of choice; their most common reason was that they were waiting for an opportunity to have sex. A similar but smaller percentage of both men and women said that they remained celibate because of moral or religious reasons, but few students said that they were waiting for marriage to have sex.

Monogamy means having only one sexual partner in a committed love relationship. This style of relationship was the ideal alternative for 61% of the women and 37% of the men. These percentages included students who were in a monogamous relationship at the time of the survey and those who were celibate but waiting for such a relationship. A lower percentage of both women and men reported monogamy as their current choice. In addition, many of the students who chose this category described their current behavior rather than their lifetime sexual behavior, and more than half of those who had chosen this style had had more than one sex partner during their lifetimes. Others who were in a supposedly monogamous relationships had had sex with other partners but considered this behavior a violation of their commitment (although they still classified themselves as monogamous). Thus, many of these students subscribed to the ideal of monogamy without adhering to the practice of having one sexual partner for life. The percentage of men who had or wanted this type of relationship was lower than the percentage of women.

The students who chose the style Netting described as free experimentation valued sexual freedom and wanted to participate in a variety of sexual relationships. Counting those who had more than one partner during their lives, about half of the students were in this category. Some of these young adults were in a committed relationship with one partner at the time of the study but believed in having different partners on the way to a monogamous relationship. More students believed in than practiced free sexual expression, but some in this group had many sexual partners and fit the description of experimenting freely with their sexuality. More men than women fit this pattern—28% of men but only 5% of women said that they were sexually active but not monogamous. Table 11.4 summarizes the styles of sexuality Netting found among these college students.

Netting's survey reflected the changes in sexual behavior that have been most prominent among adolescents and young adults—namely, the decreased emphasis on marriage as the only acceptable context for sex, the increased frequency of sexual activity for young women, and some continued gender differences in sexual behavior. These differences may be the result of different desires, but the double standard of sexual behavior is a factor that has shaped both women's and men's sexuality.

Miriam Lewin (1984c) traced this double standard to the Victorian era, especially the last half of the 19th century. The social attitude of the Victorians held women morally superior to men; part of women's purity related to their distaste for sex. In the Victorian family, the husband was the undisputed head of the household, but the wife's power included refusal of sex. The husband was the one who initiated sexual activity, but the wife could decline. Lewin maintained that women's privilege of refusing sex was a form of birth control necessitated by the rising birthrate during the early 19th century. By 1900 the birthrate had fallen, but at the price of societal and individual denial of women's sexuality. Lewin argued that the denial of female sexuality and gender-

TABLE 11.4   **Styles of Sexuality among College Students**

Style	Percentage Choosing		Reason for Choice
	Women	Men	
Celibacy	36%	32%	Women were waiting for love; men were waiting for an opportunity
Monogamy	61	37	Considered monogamy the ideal type of sexuality
	48	34	Were currently monogamous
	25	19	Had had only one partner during their lives
Free Expression	14	33	Valued freedom of expression, including expression of sexuality
	5	28	Sexually active but not currently monogamous

stereotyped sexual behavior persist and affect the behavior of contemporary women and men.

Other researchers have investigated whether gender differences exist or if the double standard of sexual behavior has disappeared. Judith Dilorio (1989) found a great deal of evidence for a double standard of sexual behavior in her study of working-class young adults. Dilorio conducted a study on sexual behavior that differed from most others in that her study used the participant-observer method. Dilorio joined a club centered around vans and participated in this car culture to study the gender roles and sexual attitudes and behavior of the young adults in the club. What Dilorio observed was not so much a repression of female sexuality as a channeling of it into patterns of expression that suited the men in the group. The women were expected to have sex, but they were also expected to be monogamous, whereas the men were not. Any women who sexually pursued a man was considered to be behaving in an unacceptably forward manner, and if that man already had a girlfriend, the other woman was considered a slut or a tramp. Thus, women's sexuality was subject to limits that men's sexuality was not, and the women were the recipients of social censure for their sexuality in ways that the men were not. The results of Netting's survey of college students suggested only the remnants of a double standard, but Dilorio's study showed a strong double standard among working-class young adults.

In addition, the pattern of male initiation and female refusal of sexual activity persists. According to the Janus survey, the majority of men still prefer to initiate sex, but women do not share this opinion; two-thirds of the women in this study replied that men should not always have this role. In their interviews with cohabiting and married couples, Philip Blumstein and Pepper Schwartz (1983) found that initiating and refusing were part of the power dynamics in a couple's relationship. They interpreted women's refusals as a way to exert power in their relationships, much as was the case in the Victorian family. Many of the heterosexual couples in their survey were trying to move away from the traditional male initiation–female refusal pattern, but neither men nor women were finding the changes easy. Older men were more likely than younger men to resent and rebuff their partners' initiation attempts. Women mentioned their hesitation over initiating sex and the care they felt they must exercise in protecting their partners' feelings. Many couples in the survey shared initiation of sexual activity, and these couples were happier than others with the more traditional pattern of male initiation.

Thus, although contemporary couples have tried to overcome this type of gender difference in sexuality, they have only partially succeeded in achieving equality in this area. This traditional pattern of sexual expression may be in the process of disappearing, but it still affects the sexual behavior of women and men.

Another gender difference in sexuality appears in the desire for intercourse. The double standard proposes that women should be less interested in sex because they are less sexual creatures than men. Sarah Blaffer Hrdy (1986) criticized the view that women are less sexual than men, what she called the Myth of the Coy Female, by reporting on females unaffected by the Victorian double standard—nonhuman primates. She argued that male scientists who have seen female reluctance to engage in sex have been influenced by the double standard and have projected these human differences onto nonhuman primates.

According to Hrdy, the sexual behavior of nonhuman animals varies from species to species. The females of some species, such as baboons and chimpanzees, initiate multiple, brief sexual relationships and show no coy reluctance to engage in sex, whereas the females of other species, such as blue monkeys and redtail monkeys, are very selective about their matings and might appear to be coy in their selectivity. Hrdy argued that any tendency to see patterns similar to human sexual behavior in the behavior of other species tells more about the human observer than about the observed species.

If women are less interested in sex than men, then this gender difference might be due to acceptance of the double standard. If women believe that they are or should be less sexual, they may behave accordingly and become less sexual. Oliver and Hyde's (1993) meta-analysis of attitudes toward sexuality—which showed that women accepted the double standard more strongly than men—is consistent with this interpretation. Masters and Johnson's (1966) research suggested that women and men experience similar phases of sexual response, and these researchers maintained that women's sexuality has been constrained. They argued that women could be just as or even more sexual than men if women were free to express their sexuality and to participate in the activities that gave them sexual pleasure. Tavris (1992) contended that rather than loosening the constraints on female sexuality, Masters and Johnson's research had constructed other restrictions by prescribing that women should be as sexual as men and that the sexuality of the two should be similar.

The headline story for this chapter reported on gender differences in motivations for having intercourse and the research of Sprague and Quadagno (1989), who found an age-related change in motivations for having intercourse. As the double standard has it, women have sex for emotional reasons and men for physical pleasure, and Sprague and Quadagno found this stereotype to be true for their younger participants. For older participants, however, women showed more interest in the physical pleasure of sex and men in the emotional intimacy.

In addition to the changing motivations for having sex over the life span, research has indicated that women do not experience orgasm during intercourse as frequently as men (Blumstein & Schwartz, 1983; Janus & Janus, 1993). Nonetheless, the women in Blumstein and Schwartz's survey rated intercourse as a more essential part of lovemaking than did the men. This apparent discrepancy might be the result of women's adherence to a "script" for sexual activity and their belief that intercourse is an essential part of the script (Geer & Broussard, 1990). Alternatively, women might believe that their partners consider intercourse important and behave in ways that they believe will please their partners. Both women and men rate intercourse as an important part of sex, yet women do not experience orgasm from intercourse as reliably as men.

Despite increasing acceptance of oral-genital sex by both men and women, these sexual activities may not be equally important for both. The Janus survey found that over 80% of both women and men found the activities of fellatio and cunnilingus acceptable. Indeed, 18% of women reported that cunnilingus was their preferred way to orgasm, and some women reported that it was the only way they experienced orgasm. The men in Blumstein and Schwartz's survey also valued oral sex. They found that men who received oral sex were happier with their sex lives and with their relationships in general than men who did not, but giving and receiving oral sex was not a factor in women's happiness.

The findings about women's pleasure from oral sex and their lack of emphasis on oral sex are not necessarily contradictory. People may find an activity pleasurable and yet still feel uneasy or hesitant about engaging in that activity. Until recently, oral sex was classified as a deviant sexual behavior, and increasing acceptability does not mean complete acceptance. Blumstein and Schwartz speculated that women's uneasiness about cunnilingus involves embarrassment about their bodies, genitals, and the intimacy of this sexual activity as well as uneasiness about having their partners perform this act. Some of the women in their study had completely overcome negative feelings about oral sex and enthusiastically accepted cunnilingus, but others felt reservations that made them reluctant to receive or give oral sex. Women remain more likely than men to feel such reservations (Wilson & Medora, 1990).

Men are also supposed to be more easily aroused than women and to become aroused to a wider variety to stimuli. Julia Heiman (1975) studied men's and women's sexual responses to erotic stories and found some gender differences, but not the ones she had expected. Heiman tested the hypothesis that women are aroused by romantic fantasy material and men are aroused by explicitly sexual material. She constructed stories of each type and measured the physiological responses of men and women as they listened to these stories.

Heiman found that both men and women experienced sexual arousal when listening to the fantasy stories, but she found no evidence for the expected gender-related differences. Indeed, both women and men were aroused by sexually explicit stories. But

DIVERSITY HIGHLIGHT
The Sexual Buffet

Cultures around the world have chosen a variety of sexual activities for acceptance as "normal" and have designated other choices as abnormal, sinful, or repulsive. Carole Vance (1984, p. 8) described the role of culture in "choosing some sexual acts (by praise, encouragement, or reward) and rejecting others (by scorn, ridicule, or condemnation), as if selecting from a sexual buffet." This selection from the array of available choices has resulted in virtually no universally accepted and no universally rejected set of sexual behaviors. What some cultures have found disgusting, others have found essential.

Forced fellatio performed on adult men by adolescent boys would be the basis for criminal prosecution in many cultures, but Gilbert Herdt (1981) described the acceptability of this practice among the Sambia in New Guinea. According to their beliefs, a preadolescent boy must leave his mother and live with men in order to become a man himself. Part of the process involves swallowing semen, and the Sambia encourage boys to engage in fellatio with unmarried adolescent and adult men. The men must restrict their same-gender sexual activities to these boys, and fellatio with men their own age is strictly forbidden. When these adolescents and young men marry, they are supposed to make the transition to heterosexual behavior and to end all same-gender sexual activities.

In their examination of dozens of cultures, Clellan Ford and Frank Beach (1951) found that kissing was a common activity, but not all cultures had invented kissing. The Balinese do not kiss but bring their faces close together and inhale each other's scent. On the other hand, the Thonga of Africa found the practice of kissing odd and slightly disgusting.

Ford and Beach also found that heterosexual intercourse was a common form of sexual expression, but that it was rarely the only form of sexual expression for any culture. The Lepchas of India engage in only limited sexual activity; they have intercourse, but kissing, breast stimulation, or genital stimulation is almost completely absent. The Trobriand Islanders of the South Pacific include a variety of other types of stimulation with intercourse—kissing, stimulating the breasts, rubbing the skin, biting, pulling hair, as well as manual and oral stimulation of male and female genitals.

Children in some societies are allowed and even expected to experiment with sex, whereas other societies restrict sexuality during childhood (Ford & Beach, 1951). For the societies that allow children to express their sexuality, genital touching and simulated intercourse are more likely to be allowed between peers than between a child and someone older. The Sambia, with their institutionalized adult-adolescent fellatio are an exception, and so are the Lepcha, who believe that girls will not mature unless they engage in early intercourse.

Societies that restrict childhood sexuality tend to do so through restricting not only intercourse but also limiting information about sex, prohibiting masturbation, and enforcing different standards of sexual behavior for men and women. That is, sexually restrictive societies tend to have a double standard and put more restrictions on the sexuality of girls and women than on boys and men.

The variety of selected and rejected options are not equal across cultures. Some activities (kissing, heterosexual intercourse) are a common choice in many societies; other activities are less common but still appear in many societies (intercourse for unmarried adolescents, oral-genital stimulation); still other activities are very uncommon in the world but standard in one society, such as biting off one's partner's eyebrows during intercourse. Although not common, this activity is also one of the choices from the buffet.

Heiman did find a gender difference in recognizing rather than in experiencing the physical signs of sexual arousal. As she pointed out, men have a visible sign of their sexual arousal—an erection—whereas women do not. Women's arousal involves vasocongestion and lubrication in the vagina, all of which are not visibly apparent. Heiman speculated that women lack the feedback that would allow them to know when they are aroused. She also considered the possibility that no difference exists in men's and women's sexual arousal. Rather, the difference may exist in identifying that arousal, with women being less skilled in detecting their sexual arousal than men.

Another area of persistent but declining gender differences in sexuality is extramarital sex; that is, sexual activity by married people with someone other than their spouse. According to Kinsey's surveys (1948, 1953), half of married men but only one-fourth of married women had engaged in extramarital sex. The more recent Janus survey (1993) showed that men are still more likely than women to have affairs outside marriage (one-third of men and one-quarter of women), but the percentages suggest declining gender differences.

Does the research indicate different sexuality for women and men—that the Victorians were correct about men's sexual nature and women's disinterest? Sex surveys as far in the past as Kinsey's have shown that women are indeed interested in sex and experience pleasure from a variety of sexual activities. Sex surveys as recent as the Janus report and the Oliver and Hyde (1993) meta-analysis have shown that women have a higher average age of sexual initiation than men, that fewer women than men masturbate, that women are less likely than men to experience orgasm during intercourse, and that women are slightly less acceptant of oral sex than are men.

These gender differences in sexual behavior have decreased over the time between the older and more recent studies, suggesting that female and male sexuality are subject to change and are influenced by social standards. The Victorian heritage held women as less sexual than men, and so they became. The sexualization of modern culture holds that women should be more sexual than in the past but still less so than men, and so they have become. As Blumstein and Schwartz (1989, p. 122) argued, sexuality is "created by its cultural context." Thus, women and men exhibit a wide variety of sexual behaviors depending on their physiology, culture, personal background, and personal expectations. Tavris (1992, p. 245) summarized heterosexuality by saying, "The question is not whether women are more or less sexual than men. (The answer to that is yes, no, both, and sometimes.) The questions are: What are the conditions that allow women and men to enjoy sex in safety, with self-confidence, and in a spirit of delight? And how do we get there?"

Homosexuality

Some people develop erotic attraction toward people of the same gender. That is, some people experience erotic attraction to and choose to engage in sexual activities with members of their own gender. For years, psychologists failed to make a distinction between *gender role*, the social behaviors associated with one or the other gender, and **sexual orientation,** the erotic attraction to members of one or the other gender (or to both). Psychologists confused gender role and **sexual orientation,** constructing tests that measured masculinity and femininity, aspects of gender role. Men who expressed sexual attraction for other men were assumed to be feminine, and women who were attracted to women were assumed to be masculine, a reversal or inversion of the typical gender role (Constantinople, 1973; Lewin, 1984a, b).

The conceptualization of same-gender sexual orientation as an inversion of gender role was not productive, and these tests generally failed to correctly identify individuals with same-gender erotic interests (Lewin, 1984a). A separation of gender role and sexual orientation has clarified the process of measuring masculinity and femininity and demonstrated that same-gender erotic attraction has little relationship to these traits. That is, men who are erotically attracted to other men are not necessarily feminine in appearance or behavior, and women who find other women sexually attractive are not necessarily more masculine than other women.

The number of people with same-gender sexual interests and behavior constitute a minority, but estimates vary on how small a minority according to the recentness and method of the measurement. Most of the variation in estimates can be explained according to the definition that the researchers have used. For instance, is a person lesbian or gay if she or he has engaged in sexual activity with a person of the same gender at any time during the person's life? With this definition, the percentage of gay men and lesbians is substantial. When Kinsey and his colleagues (1948) obtained this information from men, they found that 37% of the men said that they had engaged in male-male sexual activity at some time during their lives. When asked the equivalent question, 28% of the women surveyed by Kinsey and his colleagues (1953) reported at least one female-female sexual experience during their lifetime. Therefore, a substantial number of both men and women have some sexual experience with a member of their own gender.

Most people who have some sexual experience with members of their own gender do not choose such relationships as their primary form of sexuality throughout their lives. That is, few people have exclusively same-gender sexual relationships. About 4% of the men and about 2% of the women in the Janus report said that their sexuality had been primarily gay or lesbian, and another 5% of men and 1% of women reported exclusively gay or lesbian orientation and experience. Other surveys have obtained different estimates for sexual orientation, but all of the research has found that a substantial minority of people have some sexual experience with members of their own gender, whereas relatively few people adopt this lifestyle as their primary sexuality.

Kinsey believed that the classification of people into homosexual or heterosexual was an inadequate description. Instead, he created a continuum for classifying people's sexual experience and attraction to members of their own and the other gender. This 7-point scale ranged from *strongly heterosexual* to *strongly homosexual,* with gradations in between that indicated sexual activity with and attraction to both same- and other-gender individuals. Those who are sexually attracted to individuals of both genders are sometimes referred to as **bisexuals,** but in the Kinsey continuum, this classification has further gradations to indicate degrees of interest and activity with members of the same and the other gender.

Carmen de Monteflores and Stephen Schultz (1978, p. 59) summarized beliefs about gay and lesbian relationships:

> *Perspectives on homosexuality are diverse. According to many church leaders, homosexuals are sinners; according to the law, they are criminals. Mental health professionals until recently have viewed homosexuality as pathological. . . . Although these perspectives differ and are at points mutually exclusive, the underlying message is clear: Homosexuality is bad and shameful, to be feared and suppressed.*

This statement represents not only the current view in many (but not all) places in the world but also the attitudes from recent history. Homosexual activity has been condemned and suppressed, making the choice to express sexual feelings toward members of one's own sex difficult.

An additional difficulty in adopting the gay lifestyle has been the association of acquired immune deficiency syndrome (AIDS) with gay men. During the early years of the epidemic, the vast majority of those infected with the human immunodeficiency virus (HIV) were gay men and intravenous drug users. A common perception developed that gay men carried AIDS and that any type of association with them was dangerous. This perception was, of course, incorrect. Most gay men are not infected with HIV, and association with infected persons will not transmit the virus. Transmission of the HIV infection requires close contact with bodily fluids, such as blood or semen; casual contact will not transmit this infection.

Although many people already disliked and even feared gays, the association of gay men with HIV infection fueled a growing homophobia, which has led to job and housing discrimination and even physical attacks. The widespread prejudice against gay men and lesbians has implications for many aspects of the lives of those who follow the gay lifestyle. Furthermore, the assumption that adolescents will develop heterosexual interests presents problems for those adolescents who feel attracted to members of their own gender.

During Adolescence

Adolescence is a time of sexual exploration, and adolescent sexual activity has become more common and more accepted over the past 40 years. But the acceptable arrangement for sexual exploration during adolescence includes only heterosexual pairings. Gender segregation during childhood and adolescence for many activities provides many opportunities for contact between same-gender individuals. The great majority of this contact has no sexual connotations, but these opportunities may influence the amount of same-gender sexual activity that occurs among adolescents, meaning that such activity is more common for a wider group of people during adolescence than later in life. Indeed, most of the people who have same-gender sexual experiences do so as part of adolescent experimentation and not as the beginning of a gay lifestyle.

Deborah Zera (1992) reported that almost all gays and lesbians say they have known that they were different even before adolescence, but many of them try to develop heterosexual interests and fit into this accepted pattern of sexuality. Some may succeed, but the changeability of sexual interest has not been established. As de Monteflores and Schultz (1978) pointed out, the basis for the development of sexual orientation—either homosexual or heterosexual—remains elusive. However, some recent research has suggested that sexual orientation may have a biological basis.

Early biological theories of sexual orientation focused on genetics and hormones, but research failed to confirm any simple relationship between sexual orientation and either genetic background or hormonal levels. Both genetics and hormone levels may influence sexual orientation, but in complex ways that involve prenatal hormone levels and their influence on the developing brain (Money, 1987b). The brains of women and men show some differences (see Chapter 4), including a difference in size of the interstitial nuclei of the hypothalamus. This structure is larger in men than in women, and in 1991, Simon LeVay proposed that this structure was smaller in gay men than in heterosexual men.

LeVay studied the brains of three groups: gay men (all of whom had died of AIDS), heterosexual men (less than half of whom had died of AIDS), and heterosexual women (only one of whom had died of AIDS). He found that the third interstitial nucleus of the anterior hypothalamus was twice as large in the heterosexual men as in the gay men. LeVay claimed that he had found a biological basis for male-male sexual interest, but the differences in cause of death for the three groups may have biased the results. That is, the people in LeVay's three groups died of different causes, making them different in a way other than their sexual orientation. This bias weakens the study and casts doubt on his conclusions.

LeVay's evidence produced a great deal of controversy (Gelman, Foote, Barrett, & Talbot, 1992). The notion that sexual orientation might be traced to some biological difference fits into a determinist view of sexual behavior, and determinists hold that a biological basis places behavior beyond personal choice. Many people who want to restrict same-gender sexual activity need to believe that such behavior is a choice so that they can maintain that these individuals must change their sexual behavior to a heterosexual orientation. Members of the gay community viewed LeVay's research with ambivalence, agreeing that they feel as though their sexual orientation is innate but disputing that their sexuality is a problem that should be changed. Rather, they see their sexuality as a difference to be accepted.

Some research (de Monteflores & Schultz, 1978; Zera, 1992) has suggested that social acceptance of sexual orientation may be easier for lesbians than for gay men. Although neither lifestyle is acceptable to most people, the gay male lifestyle is more stigmatized than the lesbian lifestyle. De Monteflores and Schultz discussed a difference between self-acknowledgment of sexual orientation and any specific same-gender sexual activity, noting that men act on their feelings several years sooner than women. However, this difference may not promote acceptance of sexual orientation for men; instead, they may find ways to rationalize their male-male sexual activities rather than accept this behavior as an indication of their sexual orientation. Women too may have trouble accepting their sexual attraction to other women and attribute their feelings to affection rather than sexuality.

The acceptance of same-gender attraction is a major challenge for gay adolescents. They often struggle with the feeling that something is wrong with them, and self-esteem may be a problem. Self-acceptance is a different (and often easier) task than revealing same-gender sexual orientation or behavior to family and friends. **Coming out** is the process of personally recognizing and acknowledging gay or lesbian orientation to others (de Monteflores & Schultz, 1978). The term originated with the phrase "coming out of the closet," referring to the hidden (closeted) nature of sexuality for many gays and lesbians. Thus, coming out is a positive affirmation of sexuality. This process may be part of adolescent development, or it may occur at any time during adulthood.

Coming out may include a public acknowledgment of sexual orientation, or the revelation may be limited to only friends and family. Parents may be acceptant and supportive, or they may be angry and have trouble accommodating the sexual orientation of their child (Zera, 1992). For adults, coming out often includes acceptance into the gay community. For adolescents, such acceptance is not as easy, because activities in

---

✖ GENDERED VOICES
I Never Imagined the Pain

"Lesbians have been telling me about their problems in coming out," a female graduate student in counseling said. "For some reason, two women have confided in me about the problems with staying in the closet and coming out. They are women I knew and they came to trust me, but I'm not their counselor. I never imagined the pain and the problems. I guess I have led a sheltered life. I have known gays and lesbians, but I had never known or imagined the difficulties in essentially leading two lives—one for the public and the real, private one.

"One woman has been in a relationship for 17 years. During those years she and her lover have had to pretend to be 'just roommates' who share a house. She felt that she could never let the people at work know she was lesbian; she thought she would lose her job.

"She said that she felt pressure and tried to be heterosexual. She was even engaged to be married when she was in her early 20s, but her mother sensed something was wrong and told her that she didn't have to get married if she didn't want to. She broke the engagement and stopped trying to be something she wasn't, but she kept her sexual orientation secret for another 20 years.

"This woman has started to come out selectively to people she trusts. Her family still doesn't

know—or at least she hasn't told them. She has found coming out a great relief and would like to be able to be completely out but does not feel comfortable enough to do so.

"The other woman has not yet come out. I guess you would say she is bisexual rather than lesbian; I'm not sure about these classifications. She is married and has a child, but she is attracted to women and has had a number of lesbian affairs, but they upset her. She says that she was 'good' when she went on a shopping trip to a large city and did not pursue a lesbian relationship but 'bad' when she did. She is very unhappy and troubled over whether she should leave her husband and come out as a lesbian. I am really very concerned for her, because she is suicidal, and I am afraid that she might harm herself. This conflict is really a problem for her.

"In listening to these women, I was struck by their pain in essentially living a charade, pretending to be something they know they are not. That must be so difficult and so stressful. Coming out has been like removing a huge burden for the women who have, but I see the problems in that choice, too. Talking to these two women has really been an education for me."

the gay community are oriented toward adults. Charges of seducing adolescents or of promoting same-gender sexual activities present a situation that makes gay adults sensitive about including adolescents in the gay community.

Coming out can be a positive statement of sexuality for adolescents as well as for adults, but adolescents may have more trouble with parental acceptance and, as noted, may not fit into the adult gay community. Zera (1992, p. 854) summarized adolescents' acceptance of gay or lesbian identity by saying, "Despite the pain and confusion in this process of development, it is important to bear in mind that most gay people do successfully resolve these issues and are able to be happy with themselves and participate in healthy relationships."

During Adulthood

Women and men who engage in same-gender sexual activities are often in danger of being arrested if they do so openly because such sexual activities are often illegal. This lack of legal sanction reflects the lack of social acceptability for same-gender sexual activities. Even among college students, a group more accepting of a variety of sexual behaviors than the general population, both young women and men disapproved of same-gender sexual activity (Wilson & Medora, 1990). This lack of acceptance is one reason for the formation of self-contained gay communities. In many large cities, such communities form the context for the lives of many gay people, who may rarely interact with the outside world of heterosexuals. This life is not typical of gays, however, as the vast majority must deal with disapproval and lack of acceptance from the larger society in which they live.

Peter Nardi (1992b) investigated the development of friendships and sexual relationships in gay men and lesbian women and found some gender differences in these relationships. Gay men were much more likely than lesbians to have had sex with both casual and close friends. Indeed, Nardi found evidence of a pattern in which sexual activity forms the basis for later friendship among gay men. He speculated that this pattern represented conformity to the traditional masculine gender role of men using sexual activity as a means to establish intimacy.

Lillian Faderman (1989) asserted that women's romantic friendships have a long history, but until recently these relationships have been presumed to be nonsexual. Perhaps the passionate friendships that were common among women in the 18th and 19th centuries included no sexual activity, but in other respects, these love relationships were similar to today's lesbian relationships, having an emphasis on feelings of closeness and emotional expression (Peplau, Cochran, Rook, & Padesky, 1978).

Lesbians and gay men form love relationships having the elements of intimacy, passion, and commitment, just as in heterosexual couples' relationships. Blumstein and Schwartz (1983) surveyed gay male and lesbian couples as well as heterosexual couples, and their survey revealed similarities as well as differences among these various configurations of couples. The survey included questions about sexual activities and satisfaction with these activities; the results were surprising to those unfamiliar with the gay lifestyle.

In Blumstein and Schwartz's survey, lesbian couples reported a lower level of sexual activity than any other type of couple and some reluctance to perform cunnilingus. Blumstein and Schwartz speculated that lesbians' socialization as women might have an influence on their sexuality, making both partners hesitant about initiating sex and resulting in a lower frequency of sexual activity than in couples that include men, who are socialized to initiate sex. Lesbians who have frequent oral sex were happier with their sex lives and with their relationships than those who had less oral sex. Nevertheless, only 39% of the lesbian couples in the survey reported having oral sex very frequently, and mutual masturbation was the most common sexual activity among these couples. Lesbians also value nongenital physical contact, such as hugging and cuddling, activities that promote intimacy but not orgasm.

Sex is a very important part of life for gay men, and their relationships typically include a lot of sexual activity, especially early in the relationship (Blumstein & Schwartz, 1983). Fellatio is an important activity for gay men, but their sex lives are varied, and mutual masturbation is also a common activity for them. Anal intercourse was never as common an activity as either oral sex or manual stimulation, and its dangers for spreading HIV infection have made it less common than before the appearance of AIDS. Gay men engage in a variety of sexual activities, and their frequency of sexual contact is higher than any other configuration of couples during the early years of their relationships. The frequency of activity with their partners falls sharply after approximately the first two years of the relationship, but this decrease in frequency may be only a decrease in sex with their long-term partners and not in total sexual activity.

Gay men are more acceptant of casual sex than lesbians, and even gay men who are involved in a long-term relationship often have sex with men other than their partners. Indeed, gay men often work out a relationship in which they may have sex with men other than their companions and yet keep their long-term relationship. Affairs can present a problem for any couple, but sex outside the relationship is not as likely to be a factor in the dissolution of gay men's relationships as for other couples.

Gay men and lesbians do not have marriage as a socially accepted context for sexual activity, which gives their love relationships less official sanction than those of heterosexual couples. Perhaps this lack of official acceptance is one factor in the lower level of stability for these couples' relationships than for married couples. Blumstein and Schwartz found that gay men and lesbians were more likely to end their relationships than married couples and that lesbians were even more likely to break up than gay men.

Blumstein and Schwartz also found many similarities among the types of couples they studied, both heterosexual as well as gay and lesbian couples. For example, sex was important to all, and couples that had sex less than once a week were not as happy as couples who had sex more often. Sex formed a physical bond for all types of couples and helped them maintain their relationships, but it was also a common source of problems. Those couples who fought about sex were less stable than those happy with their sexual relationship. For all of the couples, the sexual relationship reflected the problems that happened in other aspects of their relationship: Sex went well when the relationship went well, and unhappiness with the sexual activity in the relationship tended to be associated with unhappiness in the quality of affection in the relationship.

Summary

Gender differences in sexual attitudes and behavior have been the object of speculation and research. Most sex research has used the survey technique, questioning people about their sexual attitudes or behavior. Several problems arise in using this technique. Surveys rely on reports rather than direct observations, and people can misrepresent or misremember, creating accuracy problems. In addition, those people who are willing to answer questions about sex may not be a representative sample of the general population. These drawbacks of sex surveys create doubts about how accurately such surveys reflect people's attitudes and behaviors, but the survey technique is an easier approach than directly observing people having sex.

Although not the first sex survey, Kinsey and his colleagues conducted the most famous sex surveys. Kinsey's survey of male sexuality appeared in 1948, and the survey on female sexuality appeared in 1953. The results about the prevalence of same-gender sexual activity, female orgasm, masturbation during childhood and during marriage, and premarital and extramarital sex diverged from the social norms and shocked many people. Kinsey's results have been disputed, but the importance of his work has not. Kinsey made the study of sexuality a legitimate part of scientific research.

Many other sex surveys have been completed, including the Playboy Foundation survey during the 1970s and the Janus survey during the 1980s. Both of these surveys attempted to obtain a representative sample of U.S. residents and succeeded to a greater degree than Kinsey had. These surveys indicated some changes in sexuality over the intervening years, especially a decrease in the double standard of sexual behavior for men and women, but all of the surveys have shown that people engage in a wide variety of sexual behavior.

Masters and Johnson directly measured sexual response during masturbation and intercourse in an attempt to understand the physiology of sexual response. Their 1966 book detailed the four stages of sexual response—excitation, plateau, orgasm, and resolution. Although the people who are willing to have sex for the sake of science are not representative of the general population, Masters and Johnson believed that sexual response is similar in all people. They found a great deal of commonalty in their four stages of sexual response, including similarities in women and men.

Childhood sexuality includes both exploration and the potential for abuse. Explorations begin very early, with infants manipulating their genitals, young children masturbating to orgasm, and kindergarten children exploring each other's genitals. Parents may find these explorations disturbing, and their condemnation may convey the impression that sexual feelings and activities are unacceptable.

The unequal power between children and adults can create situations for sexual abuse. Sex surveys have revealed that at least 15% of women and 5% of men were sexually abused as children. The large majority of the perpetrators of sexual abuse of children are men, often family members or those in positions of authority, but older girls and women are also perpetrators of abuse. Living with a stepfather dramatically increases a girl's chances of being abused. Abuse has both short-term and long-term negative effects for male and female victims.

Children's sexual explorations involve children of the same as well as the other gender, but most adolescents show increasing heterosexual interest. Sexual activity is now one of the reasons for dating, although boys emphasize sex as a reason for dating more than girls do. Boys also tend to begin intercourse at a younger age than girls, and this difference appears in many ethnic groups. Gender differences in premarital intercourse as well as in other sexual activities have decreased over the past 50 years.

Marriage is no longer the only acceptable context for sexual activity, and a majority of both young men and young women have intercourse before age 25. Celibacy is a choice made by about one-third of both young men and young women, but more women than men choose monogamy as an ideal style of sexual relationship (61% versus 37%), whereas more men than women choose free sexual experimentation (28% versus 5%).

Some research has indicated that motivations for sex change over the life span. Young men's motivations for sex are likely to be for physical pleasure rather than emotional intimacy, and young women's motivations are the opposite. However, older men can develop an interest in the emotional gratification gained from sex, and older women can become more interested in the physical pleasure.

Though decreasing, the persistent gender differences in sexual behavior may be due to the double standard for sexual behavior—the belief that girls and women are less sexual than boys and men. Although differences in attitudes tend to be small, women are less acceptant of and less likely to engage in several sexual behaviors than are men—namely, women are less likely than men to initiate sex, to be enthusiastic about oral-genital stimulation, and to have extramarital affairs. Comparisons of the data from the Kinsey surveys and more recent analyses show that these gender differences have decreased but still exist.

Same-gender sexual activity is not uncommon among children and adolescents, but erotic attraction only to members of the same gender is the orientation for a minority of people. Estimates vary according to the definition, but around 9% of men and 3% of women have primarily or exclusively gay or lesbian erotic interests and sexuality. The underlying reasons for gay or lesbian sexual orientation are not understood, but recent evidence has revealed a difference in the interstitial nucleus of the hypothalamus. This structure seems to be larger in heterosexual men than in homosexual men and heterosexual women, but these conclusions are in question due to bias in the study.

Lesbian and gay lifestyles are not well accepted, and adolescents who are attracted to members of their same gender have trouble accepting themselves and their sexual orientation. The process of coming out, of revealing gay or lesbian interests and behavior, can be a process of positive self-acceptance but can also create family conflict due to parents' difficulty in accepting a child's sexual orientation.

The sexuality of gay men and lesbian women differs, and these couples have both similarities with and differences from heterosexual couples. For instance, both gay men and lesbians value oral sex, but lesbians are more reluctant to perform cunnilingus than gay men are to perform fellatio. Also, lesbian couples have sex less often than other couples. Gay men value and have sex often, especially in the first several years of their relationships. For all types of heterosexual, gay, and lesbian couples, sex provides both a bond of pleasure and a potential for conflict in relationships.

Glossary

Bisexual   a person who is sexually attracted to individuals of the same as well as other gender

Celibacy   refraining from sexual activity

Coming out   the process of recognizing and publicly acknowledging gay or lesbian sexual orientation

Cunnilingus   oral stimulation of the female genitals

Date rape, or **acquaintance rape**   forced sexual activity occurring between people who are acquainted

Double standard for sexual behavior   the social standard that allows men greater freedom of sexual expression than women

Fellatio   oral stimulation of the male genitals

Gay   an alternative for the term *homosexual,* emphasizing the entire lifestyle instead of only the sexual aspects of it; sometimes used to refer to both men and women but more often to men

Incest   sexual activity between family members

Lesbian   a woman who feels sexual attraction for and chooses sexual activity with other women

Masturbation   manipulation of the genitals to produce sexual pleasure

Monogamy   having only one sexual partner

Representative sample   a sample (subset) of the population that reflects the characteristics of the population from which the sample was drawn

Sexual orientation   the erotic attraction to members of the same or the other gender (or to both)

Sexually transmitted diseases   infectious diseases that are spread through sexual activity, including such diseases as syphilis, gonorrhea, herpes, and AIDS

Suggested Readings

Blumstein, Philip; & Schwartz, Pepper. (1983). *American couples.* New York: Pocket Books. This book examines married, cohabiting, gay, and lesbian couples, employing interviews about money and work as well as sex. The chapter about sex is a fascinating examination of what couples do and enjoy as well as what role sex plays in conflict and maintenance of the relationship.

Netting, Nancy S. (1992). Sexuality in youth culture: Identity and change. *Adolescence, 27,* 961–976. This study reports on sexual attitudes of college students in 1980 versus 1990 and analyzes the styles of sexuality in young adults, presenting gender comparisons for those who have chosen celibacy, monogamy, and free experimentation.

Oliver, Mary Beth; & Hyde, Janet Shibley. (1993). Gender differences in sexuality: A meta-analysis. *Psychological Bulletin, 114,* 29–51. This meta-analysis concentrates on sexual attitudes and reports of sexual behaviors. The authors have determined the size of gender differences, finding large differences for a few aspects of sexuality, smaller differences for some attitudes, and no difference for others. Their interpretation is tied to the various theories of sexuality and makes an interesting summary of gender differences in sexuality.

C h a p t e r *12*

Education and Work

HEADLINE

Trouble at the Top: A U.S. Survey Says a "Glass Ceiling"
Blocks Women from Corporate Heights

—*U.S. News & World Report,* June 17, 1991

The trouble at the top that Amy Saltzman (1991) reported was the lack of women in high-level corporate jobs. Despite education and experience, few women or members of ethnic minorities pass from middle-level to upper-level management or government jobs; instead, the vast majority of these positions are occupied by White men. Saltzman reported that only 3 of every 100 top executives are women, with little increase in the past decade.

The story also discussed a government report that surveyed nine major companies and concluded that "women's routes to the top are blocked by a 'glass ceiling' of subtle discrimination that limits their opportunities to participate in everything from overseas assignments to company sponsored training programs" (p. 41). The **glass ceiling** to which she referred is the description for the invisible barrier that seems to prevent women and ethnic minorities from advancing to the highest levels of professional accomplishment.

The glass ceiling describes a barrier to the highest levels of corporate and government jobs, but most women do not even hold the midlevel management jobs that would give them access to such positions—60% of women in the work force have lower-level clerical and sales jobs rather than management or professional positions. "The pay gap between men and women is still yawning. Overall, women now earn just 72 cents for every dollar a man takes home, compared with 64 cents 10 years ago" (p. 42).

The difference in wages extends not only to the overall average but also applies field by field. In the fields in which women occupy most positions, such as nursing and secretarial work, the gap in wages is small, but the relatively few men in these fields still average more money than the women in those same jobs. In careers in which men occupy most positions, such as law and college professorships, the gap in wages is much wider.

Part of the reason for the wage gap between men and women is the concentration of women in low-paying jobs; that is, gender segregation in the workplace. Millions of women work in jobs where they have few male coworkers, and millions of men have few female coworkers as colleagues (although women may be subordinates). The jobs dominated by men, such as machinist and computer programmer, tend to be better paid than those dominated by women, such as elementary school teacher and nursing aide. Even in jobs in which men and women have comparable training and do the same work, the differences in wages favor men.

Saltzman's story also examined the changes in composition of the work force in the United States, noting the shrinking pool of skilled White male workers and the growing ethnic diversity of the work force. Ethnic minorities and women have faced similar discrimination at work and in education. Although the patterns of discrimination based on gender and ethnic background have not been identical, the glass ceiling applies to all workers except White men, who occupy over 90% of the highest-paid and the most prestigious jobs. The basis for this pattern can be found in history, and the foundation for gender and ethnic differences in work can be found in school.

School—Stereotypes and Choices

Even before children go to school, their parents and the society in which they live treat boys and girls differently. Chapter 8 included examples of the process of encouraging gender-stereotypical behavior: dolls for girls but trucks for boys, quiet games for girls but noisy games for boys, frilly dresses for girls but grubby jeans for boys, staying close to home for girls but venturing out for boys.

Not all girls or all boys conform to these stereotypes, but by age 4 or 5 years, children have developed a concept of gender and know what behaviors are expected and approved for each. (See Chapter 7 for a more complete discussion of the development of gender identity.) Thus, when children start kindergarten, they hold beliefs about what clothes, games, and behaviors are appropriate for boys and girls. Their experiences in school often reinforce these stereotypical beliefs, producing differences in attitudes and expectations about careers and resulting in differences in preparation to pursue careers.

Title IX of the Education Amendments of 1972 prohibits gender discrimination in school programs that receive federal funds. With gender discrimination prohibited by law, schools should treat girls and boys equitably, but the study of gender bias in schools sponsored by the American Association of University Women (AAUW) (1992) presented a great deal of evidence concerning continuing lack of gender equity. The sources of problems include unequal attention and access to education materials, promotion of stereotypical gender roles, unequal expectations concerning careers, and increasing sexual harassment in school by classmates and teachers.

One factor in the continuing gender bias in schools is the attitudes of teachers and counselors, and several studies have indicated that educators' attitudes reflect gender and ethnic bias. Prospective teachers explained the differences in educational accomplishment between girls and boys and between Whites and ethnic minorities in a study by Patricia Avery and Constance Walker (1993). Their purpose was to assess the attributions of these future teachers when presented with information about differences in students' accomplishments. The teachers' explanations for gender-related differences in accomplishment tended to revolve around social expectations—that is, prospective teachers explained the greater educational attainment of boys as due to expectations for boys' achievement, discrimination against girls, and lack of encouragement for girls' achievement. Another common attribution was family encouragement and expectations, and a very small percentage of the explanations were in terms of innate differences in ability.

These future teachers exhibited few signs of gender bias, but the attributions of ethnic differences in achievement revealed some bias against ethnic groups that diverge from mainstream culture. Although discrimination was listed as a reason for different educational accomplishments by students from different ethnic backgrounds, the most common explanation was that the students' ethnic culture influenced the students' values, producing differences in attainment. Avery and Walker interpreted their results as indicating that these prospective teachers were more sensitive to gender bias than to ethnic bias.

M. Gail Jones (1989) hypothesized that the recent emphasis on education reform and the increased sensitivity to gender equity in the classroom would lead more recently trained teachers to interact with their students in a more gender-equitable manner than older teachers. Her results failed to confirm this prediction, instead showing that both experienced and new teachers gave boys more attention, feedback, praise, and warnings than they gave girls. Regardless of teaching experience or gender of the teacher, teacher interactions with female students were different and less helpful than were teacher interactions with male students.

Gender equity is not a large part of the curriculum for prospective teachers; neither is it a frequent topic of inservice training for teachers (AAUW, 1992; Sadker & Sadker, 1985). In 1980, Myra and David Sadker examined textbooks used for teacher training and found that these texts devoted very little space to gender equity issues. They concluded that teachers could not be trained to be gender fair when their training focused on these issues so little. In 1993, Jordan Titus completed a similar study, with similar conclusions. Thus, teachers may enter their profession with gender stereotypes that their training as teachers did not address, leaving teachers with a tendency to treat their students in gender-stereotypical ways.

Early School Experience

The problem of teachers promoting stereotypical gender roles may begin very early in the school experience. Jones (1989) suggested that teachers channel children into gender-stereotypical activities, beginning during preschool. She examined evidence that teachers encourage different play activities with boys than with girls and spend the majority of their time—60%—with boys.

Children have the experience of being taught by an overwhelming majority of female kindergarten and elementary school teachers. According to Deborah Cohen (1992), the poor salary, low prestige, and poor image of male elementary school teachers have kept men from teaching these grades. The preponderance of female elementary school teachers has led to the "myth that early-education environments meet the needs of girls better than boys" (AAUW, 1992, p. 18). The AAUW report argued that the opposite is true: Early schooling consists of activities in which girls have more proficiency than boys, giving boys more training in the skills they lack.

Elementary school programs strengthen the skills that boys lack, such as reading, while ignoring those that girls lack, such as science investigation. Girls need practice with large-motor activities, investigatory activities, and experimental activities, but these activities tend to be considered part of "play" rather than part of education. Furthermore, these activities are more likely to result from boys' play than the preferred play of girls. Thus, the activities of the early elementary classroom may strengthen the skills boys lack while failing to provide the same services for girls.

Male elementary school teachers may be rare, but they behave similarly to female elementary school teachers in that both tend to reward children for being compliant (Cohen, 1992). The benefits of having a male elementary teacher come from the decrease in students' gender stereotyping: Those with male teachers make significantly less stereotypical explanations for the behavior of men and women than students who have had only female teachers during the elementary grades (Mancus, 1992). Both boys and girls benefit from seeing men perform the job of teacher during their early years of schooling, but there is no clear evidence that girls benefit and boys are damaged by the gender imbalance of elementary school teachers.

The gender stereotyping in children's books and textbooks has been the subject of extensive research, which has indicated that women and girls are infrequent participants and passive observers in many stories. In her review of this research, Lorrie Hoffman (1982) contended that the portrayals of characters and historical figures in texts reflect the current social expectations for each gender. Children's readers tend to ignore women and girls, containing more boy-centered than girl-centered stories, more adult male than female characters, more biographies of men than women, and even more stories of male than female animals. Even the illustrations in children's books show more boys and men and portray them in more active, powerful ways (Sadker, Sadker, & Steindam, 1989).

In examining the content of the stories available before 1982, Hoffman (1982) concluded that male characters were more likely than female characters to show creativity, bravery, curiosity, and achievement, and female characters were often portrayed as passive, fearful, and incompetent. Adult characters fit the gender stereotypes of female domesticity and male achievement. All these character portrayals give children the message that girls and women have contributed less and do less interesting things than boys and men. When the main characters of stories were women doing nontraditional things, both girls and boys widened their views of what girls could do, indicating a potential for positive change through alterations of story characters.

A later examination of gender role stereotyping in children's books (Kortenhaus & Demarest, 1993) found that the frequency of male and female characters had become more evenly distributed. Unfortunately, male and female characters continued to be portrayed in ways that reflected stereotypical roles. That is, female characters remain passive and dependent in children's picture books, and male characters are only occasionally shown in this way. The portrayal of girls as active has increased, but such portrayals of boys have not decreased, leaving a continuing imbalance in the characterizations of girls and boys in stories for young children. Both girls and boys are disadvantaged by these portrayals, with girls lacking sufficient models for activity and competition and boys lacking models for nurturance and tenderness.

Few gender differences exist in school achievement during the early years of school, yielding no overall picture of advantages for boys or girls. As explored in Chapter 5, some standardized, national tests have shown that girls outscore boys on tests of verbal ability, but other similar tests have shown boys to have a small advantage (AAUW, 1992; Maccoby & Jacklin, 1974). Whatever the direction, the magnitude of the difference is small. Socioeconomic status is a much stronger predictor of elementary school achievement than is gender, with children from the lower socioeconomic levels having consistently poorer school records than children from wealthier families. Even controlling for socioeconomic status, girls tend to make better grades in school, beginning during the elementary grades and persisting through college.

The gender differences in self-perception are also small during elementary school, but these differences reflect the beginnings of gender stereotypes (Eccles, Wigfield, Harold, & Blumenfeld, 1993). As early as first grade, children show differential beliefs in their abilities at various activities. Girls express more positive competency beliefs for reading and music, whereas boys are more positive about their mathematics and sports abilities. No differences exist in these skills at this age, so these differences reflect children's beliefs rather than their abilities.

Changes during Junior High

Gender differences in achievement start to appear during the junior high school years. Girls experience a decreased interest in math and science and a change in career orientation, showing an increased interest in marriage and children and a narrowing of career interests to those careers most commonly occupied by women (Bush & Simmons, 1987). Adolescent girls believe that they will combine a family with paid employment, reflecting the current reality of contemporary family life, but the image of this combination may not correspond to the difficulty of balancing these different roles. Adolescent boys experience a widening of career interests and give less attention to their future family plans, assuming that they are preparing for a career that will be a primary focus of their lives.

During elementary school, girls and boys exhibit few differences in academic ability, and girls make better grades. During junior high school, boys' achievement in math and science begins to exceed that of girls, although the differences are small and vary among different areas within math and science (AAUW, 1992). For example, the male advantage in math problem solving is minimal throughout junior high school but becomes larger during the high school years. The gender difference in science achievement begins during these years and continues throughout all levels of schooling.

The differences in achievement may relate to differences in experience: Girls and boys have different science experiences during junior high school (AAUW, 1992). There are no differences in *interest* in participating in science activities, but boys are more likely to participate in using equipment and performing science activities. For instance, boys are more likely to use science equipment such as microscopes and electricity meters. These differences in experience may be a factor in confidence and possibly in choices for more advanced courses.

Girls start to experience a decline in their confidence in academic ability during junior high school, whereas boys start to feel more confident (Bush & Simmons, 1987). The AAUW report (1992) hypothesized that this diminished confidence might be a reason for girls' tendency to discontinue their studies of math and science, whereas boys who stop studying math and science might do so due to their difficulties in mastering the material. Girls tend to view their mastery problems in math as personal failures, whereas boys explain their decisions to discontinue math courses as lack of interest.

The decrease in academic confidence for girls and the increase for boys may be part of the developmental changes that accompany puberty, forming a complex interaction between school and social structures (Bush & Simmons, 1987). John Hill and Mary Ellen Lynch (1983) proposed that an intensification of gender-related role expectations occurs during puberty for both boys and girls, with each becoming more stereotypical in their interests and achievement-related behavior. Indeed, the timing of puberty affects girls and boys differently (Tobin-Richards, Boxer, & Petersen, 1983). For girls, early puberty presents problems: They must deal with bodies that are more developed than those of their peers, and they must cope with people's reaction to their maturity. For boys, early onset of puberty is an advantage: Their increases in size and strength relative to their peers give them advantages in social dominance and athletic performance, making for welcomed changes.

Therefore, the junior high school years mark the beginning of differences in academic accomplishment for girls and boys. Girls continue to make better grades than boys, but girls become less assertive about classroom activities, such as science demonstrations and equipment use. Their decreased participation may be one reason for their decreased interest in science, but the continued lack of encouragement by their teachers and parents may also contribute to girls' falling interest in science and math during junior high school. Boys also experience a decline of interest in science during this time, but their interest remains higher than that of girls.

High School and Beyond

The differences in academic achievement that begin during junior high school become more pronounced during the high school years, as do differences in confidence and in academic choices. During secondary schooling girls choose to pursue advanced math and science courses less frequently than boys do. The teachers' differential attention to boys and girls remains a factor in the classroom, and counselors' gender stereotypes become a factor in career development. In addition, **sexual harassment,** unwanted sexual attention, from male students and teachers becomes a source of stress for young women at school. Although young men can also experience sexual harassment, few mention being troubled by unwanted sexual attention by female peers or teachers (AAUW, 1992). This reticence may be part of the gender role young men are attempting to fulfill rather than disregard for this type of unwanted attention.

Both girls and boys feel more confident in their abilities at age 9 than at 17 years (Freiberg, 1991). During elementary school 60% of girls and 67% of boys have positive feelings about themselves and their abilities, whereas by high school only 29% of the girls and 46% of the boys still hold these beliefs (see Figure 12.1). Although both experience a decrease, girls report less self-confidence than boys. These feelings also extend to academic subjects. From junior high to high school, girls experience more of a decrease of interest and confidence concerning math and science. This lack of confidence even extends to intellectually gifted young women, who have the ability to succeed at the highest levels but fail to believe that they are academically gifted (Walker, Reis, & Leonard, 1992).

The lack of personal and academic confidence is a factor in the choice of coursework for both boys and girls during high school. The overall gender differences in mathematics course participation are small: Both boys and girls complete an average of around three math courses during high school (AAUW, 1992). Despite the similarity of these averages, boys are more likely to enroll in more advanced math courses and have higher scores on national tests, such as the Scholastic Aptitude Tests. These differences are even more striking for mathematically gifted students: Boys outnumber

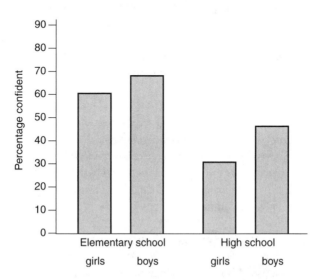

FIGURE 12.1   Self-Confidence of Girls and Boys during Elementary and High School

girls more than 10 to 1 (Benbow & Stanley, 1980, 1983). However, parents' gender stereotyping affects their interactions with their gifted children, possibly discouraging girls with math or science talent from participation in programs that would lead these girls to be identified as gifted or from pursuing careers in these areas (Raymond & Benbow, 1989).

Male and female high school students who pursue science are not equally represented in all types of science courses (AAUW, 1992). Female students are more likely to enroll in advanced biology and social sciences, whereas boys are more likely to take chemistry, physics, and physical sciences. In addition, students enrolled in the same course may have different views of how the course fits into career plans. Even girls with good academic preparation in math and science often fail to choose careers in these areas (AAUW, 1992). For example, young men who enroll in calculus and advanced science in high school are very likely to take these courses in preparation for a career in engineering, whereas very few young women enrolled in the same courses even consider engineering as a career. Therefore, young women not only choose to take fewer advanced math and science courses than boys, but they also fail to develop an interest in science careers, even when they have the ability and preparation to do so.

The differential enrollment of young men and women in advanced math and science courses has been considered a problem for women, because they miss this educational experience and career preparation. Nel Noddings (1991) pointed out that when considering the low enrollment of women in advanced math and science courses, education experts are using male enrollment statistics as the standard to which women are compared and judged. Noddings suggested that educators have given too little consideration to what women are doing and to the reasons behind their choices. She pointed out that stereotypical thinking has imposed limitations on both young women and young men, restricting both from a full range of choices in coursework and careers.

Myra Sadker, David Sadker, and their colleagues (Sadker & Sadker, 1985; Sadker, Sadker, & Klein, 1986; Sadker, Sadker, & Steindam, 1989) have studied teacher-student interactions in the classroom and concluded that boys get much more attention in classroom interactions.

> *Girls and minorities are short-changed in the critical currency of classroom interaction. Teachers from grade school to graduate school ask males more questions, give them more precise feedback, criticize them more, and give them more time to respond. Whether the attention is positive, negative, or neutral, the golden rule of the American classroom is that boys get more. (Sadker, Sadker, & Steindam, 1989, p. 47)*

Counselors' stereotyping of gender-appropriate careers is a factor in the courses that boys and girls take in school as well as in the careers each chooses. Hoffman (1982) discussed how gender bias in counseling may be either overt or covert. Overt bias includes sexist statements, such as telling girls that they are not expected to be good at math or discouraging boys from enrolling in cooking classes. Covert bias includes encouraging girls and boys to behave in stereotypical ways, such as providing

GENDERED VOICES
I Might Have Been an Engineer

"I probably would have been an engineer if I had been given the opportunity. Well, maybe *opportunity* isn't exactly the right word, because nothing really prevented me, but nobody encouraged me, either," a high school science teacher in her early 40s said. "I always liked science and did well in it, but none of my counselors mentioned engineering or being a chemist or any science career except teaching. I think they mentioned those careers to the boys who were good at science but not to the girls. They steered us toward teaching. That's just the way it was, and I'm not sure how much it has changed.

"They just didn't expect girls to be good at science and math, and when we were, they didn't consider science careers, so they didn't tell us about being a scientist. Teaching science, yes, but not being a scientist. If a boy was interested in science, they wouldn't have mentioned teaching, even if that was what he would have been best at. I wonder how many women would have been better scientists and engineers than science teachers and how many men would have been better science teachers."

information concerning traditional but not nontraditional careers and failing to take nontraditional career interests seriously. Hoffman also reviewed research on career education materials and contended that these materials are largely oriented toward boys, leaving girls unrepresented or portrayed in stereotypical ways. Only 3% of the materials contained clear references to both women and men, and 60% made reference to only one gender. Hoffman concluded that the tests and materials used by counselors were biased, presenting barriers to career development, especially for girls.

According to Hoffman, counselors steer adolescents toward traditional careers. They may counsel girls about careers that require education and ability but not careers that lead to high status and prestige. That is, counselors are more likely to recommend that girls become science teachers rather than chemists and that boys become chemists rather than science teachers. Furthermore, girls are increasingly discriminated against as they get older and closer to a career choice.

Vocational education is another area in which girls and boys have not received equal attention. "Vocational education was originally designed to give work skills to high school boys who were not planning to attend college. But research indicates that it may not serve either males or females very well in the current environment" (AAUW, 1992, p. 42). This pessimistic assessment comes from the finding that men who complete vocational educational courses in high school fail to earn more money than those who have not taken these courses. Vocational education does young women a disservice, routing them into office and business occupations that are low-paying and often dead-end jobs. Only around 4% of the students enrolled in construction, mechanics, and machine repair are young women (Burge & Culver, 1990), and the choice to take nontraditional vocational courses places young women at risk for harassment from male classmates and from some teachers.

This harassment may be sexually oriented or not, consisting of unwanted sexual remarks, statements about the unsuitability of women for various types of jobs, or derogatory remarks about women and their abilities. As the AAUW (1992) report pointed out, harassment is about power and authority, and the vast majority of incidents involve boys harassing girls. Although sexual and other harassment that affects the educational process is prohibited by Title IX of the Education Amendments of 1972, those who harass are often allowed to continue. The attitude is often "boys will be boys," with harassment not considered a serious offense. Thus, fear of harassment may make girls reluctant to enroll in courses with a majority of boys or to enroll in nontraditional vocational courses.

In summary, both overt and subtle forces affect adolescents during high school, with both girls and boys making more traditional and stereotypical choices. Although girls' performance in math and science classes equals that of boys, girls enroll in fewer of these classes than boys. Those girls who complete advanced math and science courses tend not to view these courses as part of their career preparation, resulting in a gender imbalance in math and science careers. High school counselors are a major source of gender bias, steering more boys than girls toward prestigious careers. In vocational education, boys are more likely to be guided toward higher-paying skilled craft jobs and girls into low-paying business jobs. However, vocational education may not serve boys well, as those who have and have not completed this coursework earn comparable salaries. Girls who enroll in nontraditional courses face the possibility of sexual or other harassment, and although illegal, this behavior is often not considered a serious infraction of the school's rules.

The effects of stereotypical thinking and gender bias have already influenced young women and men before they enter college, producing differences in expectations and choices. Young men receive the message from their high school counselors and from society that they should prepare for a career that will support a family. Young women get a different message: Their careers will be less important than their husbands' employment, so their college majors need not lead to specific job-related skills.

These differing expectations are consistent with the history of education but not necessarily with contemporary employment patterns. According to Mary Frank Fox (1989), college education for women developed gradually during the 19th century but never approached equal education for men and women, either in numbers or in type of training. Instead, women went to college to find husbands and to prepare for careers that would last only until they married. Thus, higher education for women confined them to careers that would be flexible, but with little chance for advancement. One of the early careers available to women was teaching, and beginning in the 1800s women were in demand as teachers in the growing public school system. One of the reasons for the demand for female teachers was their willingness to work for low salaries.

Throughout most of the 20th century, men attended college in greater numbers than women, but the number of female college students has grown to the point that women now receive more undergraduate degrees than men (Fox, 1989). The pattern of gender-segregated choice of majors has changed to some degree, but women are still more likely to major in education or nursing than men, and men are still more likely to major in engineering, computer science, or physical science than women.

Men have historically received the overwhelming majority of advanced and professional degrees (such as medical, dental, law, veterinary), but that pattern also has changed (Fox, 1989). In the 1960s women earned only about 3% of professional degrees, but by the 1980s the percentage had grown to 33%. This growing number of women in professional fields has changed the composition of most professions, but past differences will take many years to equalize. Women have also begun to receive an increasing proportion of doctoral degrees (Fox, 1989). Like undergraduate and professional degrees, doctoral degrees also show patterns of gender segregation: A greater proportion of doctoral degrees in physical sciences and engineering go to men, whereas a greater proportion of doctoral degrees in education and psychology go to women.

Table 12.1 shows the percent of degrees awarded to women in 1971 compared to 1989 for different majors. Most professions now have a larger proportion of women as a result of the changes in degrees awarded during the past 20 years. Some areas, however, have become even more strongly dominated by women, and few changes have occurred in other areas. In addition, the concentration of doctoral recipients in some

TABLE 12.1   Percentage of Women Earning Degrees in Various Fields, 1971 versus 1989

Field	Bachelor's Degree 1971	1989	Master's Degree 1971	1989	Doctoral Degree 1971	1989
Agriculture	4.2%	31.1%	5.9%	31.2%	2.9%	19.6%
Architecture	11.9	39.3	13.8	35.1	8.3	26.7
Ethnic studies	52.4	59.2	38.3	49.2	16.7	48.2
Business and management	9.1	46.7	3.9	33.6	2.9	26.6
Communications	35.3	60.4	34.6	59.6	13.1	44.8
Computer and information science	13.6	30.7	10.3	27.9	2.3	15.1
Education	74.5	77.7	56.2	75.3	21.2	57.3
Engineering	0.8	13.6	1.1	13.0	0.6	8.8
Foreign language	74.6	73.3	65.5	68.5	38.0	60.0
Health science	77.1	84.9	55.9	78.1	16.3	57.5
Home economics	97.3	90.6	93.9	85.7	61.0	77.6
Law	5.0	60.3	4.8	28.9	0	39.5
Liberal studies	65.5	67.1	44.3	64.8	—	—
Library science	92.0	86.9	81.3	79.3	—	—
Life sciences	29.1	50.2	33.6	49.6	16.3	36.7
Math	38.0	46.0	29.2	39.9	7.8	19.4
Military science	0.3	9.8	—	—	—	—
Philosophy and religion	25.5	29.9	27.1	36.3	5.8	16.3
Physical science	13.8	29.7	13.3	26.7	5.6	19.7
Psychology	44.5	70.8	37.2	67.4	24.0	56.2
Protective services	9.2	38.0	10.3	31.0	—	—
Public affairs	60.2	67.6	49.2	64.3	23.8	50.1
Social sciences	36.8	44.4	28.2	40.2	13.9	32.6
Visual/performing arts	59.7	61.5	47.4	56.3	28.3	35.4

SOURCE: From *Statistical abstracts of the United States, 1992* (112th ed.) (p. 173), U.S. Bureau of the Census, Washington, DC: U.S. Government Printing Office.

areas, such as education and ethnic studies, is even more pronounced for African-American and Hispanic women. Over half of the doctoral degrees earned by these women are in the field of education (Fox, 1989).

Beyond the degree field discrepancies, the treatment of women and men in college differs, mirroring the gender inequities in high school. Men dominate college classroom discussions and ask questions more frequently than women (Pearson & West, 1991). Furthermore, male instructors receive more questions than female instructors, indicating additional gender factors in classroom interactions. Women and men also have different preferences for classroom interactions with teachers and peers (Kramarae & Treichler, 1990). Women feel more comfortable in discussions in which teachers and students collaborate than in situations in which teachers try to impose their views on students. Men feel more comfortable in classrooms with a clear hierarchy and an emphasis on specified goals. Thus, women and men carry their conversational preferences (see Chapter 10) to classroom interactions, and the preferences of each may make the other uncomfortable.

Fox (1989, p. 225) summarized the college classroom situation:

Faculty promote and reinforce the invisibility of women students by subtle practices such as calling directly on men but not on women, addressing men by name more often than they do women, giving men more time to answer a question before going on to another student, interrupting women more frequently or allowing them to be interrupted, and crediting the contributions of men but not those of women.

These subtle differences in interactions extend to professional and doctoral training, and women feel less encouraged and supported than their male colleagues (Fox, 1989). The majority of professors are men, and they tend to choose male students to support, encourage, and assist. These mentoring relationships can be very important to career advancement, not only in academia but also in business (Wilbur, 1987), where young professionals benefit from the guidance and aid of older, more experienced professionals. Mentors tend to choose protégés who reflect themselves, so there is a tendency for men to choose men and women to choose women. With fewer women in high positions in academia and business, young women are thus at a disadvantage in finding mentors.

The close working relationships of mentoring provide situations that can lead to sexual attraction and action. With the imbalance of power in the student-faculty relationship, sexual relationships are almost inevitably exploitative. When those in positions of power exert pressure for sex on those in subordinate positions, sexual harassment occurs. Rey Carr (1991) analyzed the imbalance of power in the university as an arena in which instructors, professors, and administrators addicted to power may sexually harass students, staff, and instructors without much in the way of official objections. Kathy Hotelling's (1991) review of sexual harassment on college campuses acknowledged the lack of concern on the part of university officials as well as the ambiguities involved in identifying sexual harassment and the problems in estimating its prevalence.

Despite a 1980 court interpretation of Title IX of the Education Amendments of 1972 that declared sexual harassment an illegal form of discrimination, unwanted sexual remarks and advances continue on campus. Surveys have revealed that students report behaviors that meet the definition of sexual harassment, although the students may not label them as such (Barak, Fisher, & Houston, 1992). Cheryl Olson (1994) presented college students with scenarios of situations that met the definition of sexual harassment and asked them to evaluate whether they thought the scenarios constituted harassment. She found that both women and men had difficulty in defining these situations as harassment. These college students tended to see the situations as free speech issues and to be hesitant to label even offensive remarks as harassment. In addition, these students tended to see women as responsible for letting men know that their remarks were offensive and to see men as blameless unless they had received a warning about the offensiveness of their behavior.

Perhaps due to the difficulty in defining or identifying the experience of sexual harassment, surveys have obtained different estimates of its prevalence. One survey (Cammaert, 1985) found that 20% of female students in a Canadian university reported inappropriate sexual behavior by someone in a position of authority over them, and another survey (McKinney, Olson, & Satterfield, 1988) found that 9% of men and 35% of women reported that they had been harassed at the university they were attending. Yet another survey (Schneider, 1987) found that 60% of the women who responded to the questionnaire had been exposed to some form of harassment, including being asked on dates or pressured by male faculty to socialize.

When including the behavior of peers, over 80% of both female and male students in a small Canadian university reported at least one incident of sexual harassment, the majority of which occurred in a classroom or with peers (Mazer & Percival, 1989). According to Linda Rubin and Sherry Borgers's review of sexual harassment on campus, the majority of harassers are men in positions of authority who harass younger women in subordinate positions. A survey of male faculty (Fitzgerald, Weitzman, Gold, & Ormerod, 1988) found that 26% admitted sexual involvement with female students.

Hotelling's (1991) review of sexual harassment on college campuses concluded that sexual harassment was a more common experience for women than men, finding that between 20% and 30% of college women are sexually harassed. This estimate means that over one million college students in the United States will experience sexual harassment each year. Due to the close working relationships that form between professors and graduate students, female graduate students are at greatest risk.

Students most often cope with harassment by trying to avoid the harasser and the situation—evading professors, changing majors, and altering examining committees (Hotelling, 1991). Although harassment produces stress for the target, these incidents usually go unreported, as the reporting process causes additional stress. Either reported or unreported, students' careers are affected by harassment from those in positions of power.

Therefore, like high school, college is another school situation in which women and men receive different treatment, which is a factor in their making different choices, including majors and careers. Women and men choose a similar range of majors and careers, but not in equal numbers. Women choose education and social science majors more often than men, who choose engineering and physical science majors more often than women. Although women now receive more undergraduate degrees than men, women do not receive an equal number of professional and doctoral degrees. The number of women in such programs has increased in the past 25 years, and these women have had to contend with less attention and support than their male peers. Despite legal prohibition, sexual harassment is not an uncommon experience on college campuses, and women are more likely than men to be harassed by those in positions of authority as well as by their male peers. The problem is more common for female graduate than undergraduate students, providing an additional barrier to women receiving professional training.

Achievement

Achievement can have many meanings, including success in school. As the previous section showed, girls and women are successful in school, as measured by grades, but men are more successful when the criteria include prominence in prestigious careers and high salaries. What is included in the definition of achievement determines the extent to which women and men are high or low achievers.

Achievement Motivation

Traditionally, researchers have defined job success and recognition as achievement and have not considered personal or family relationships as comparable achievements. Neither women's nor men's roles in homemaking and family care, therefore, have gained the same type of recognition as business, scientific, and political accomplishments. Indeed, women were not a prominent part in psychology's early studies on achievement.

David McClelland and his colleagues (McClelland, Atkinson, Clark, & Lowell, 1953) studied the motivation to achieve, formulating the concept of *need for achievement.* These researchers studied the expression of this need by asking people to interpret ambiguous drawings; that is, to tell a story about a drawing that had many possible interpretations. The rationale behind this technique is that people reveal inner wishes and motivations in interpreting ambiguous situations—by projecting their personal thoughts and feelings into unclear situations.

McClelland and his colleagues used this type of projective technique, reasoning that people would project their need for achievement by including achievement-related imagery in their stories about the pictures. Their results confirmed this prediction, revealing that people varied in the amount of achievement-related imagery in their stories. The need for achievement not only varied among people but was stronger in people who had chosen achievement-oriented careers and in college students who had chosen careers with high risk and high responsibility.

This definition of achievement may be too restrictive (Mook, 1987), ignoring forms of achievement other than business careers. In addition, the need-for-achievement concept was formulated by examining only men, and McClelland et al. found that women did show achievement needs that were important to some men. However, another achievement-related concept has been applied specifically to women—fear of success.

Fear of Success

As McClelland and his colleagues had done, Martina Horner (1969) investigated the imagery associated with achievement and success. When she presented women and men with a description of a successful medical student, the women sometimes imagined negative consequences for the successful female medical student, but the men usually described the successful male medical student in positive terms.

Horner interpreted the women's descriptions of negative consequences accompanying success as a **fear of success,** or a *motive to avoid success.* She reasoned that women equate success with loss of femininity and feel anxious about success, especially when it involves competing with men. Her investigations showed that women often do better when working alone or when in competition with another women than when they must compete against a man. Men, on the other hand, often perform better when they are in competition than when they work alone. Horner concluded that competition is a negative factor in women's achievement and that women do not see achievement situations in the same ways that men do.

Although Horner used the terms *fear of success* and *motive to avoid success,* these labels might be somewhat misleading, as they imply that women do not wish to succeed. What she called fear of success may have been women's acknowledgment that success in male-dominated professions is not socially well accepted for women and that success will have negative as well as positive consequences. What Horner found was that competition may pose problems for women. She did not demonstrate that women try to avoid success but that they attempt to manage some of the negative consequences they believe will accompany success in male-dominated fields. Rather than finding that women fear success, Horner may have demonstrated that women understand the social consequences of competing with men in school and careers.

The social consequences of success in nontraditional careers may be negative for both men and women. Frances Cherry and Kay Deaux (1978) found that men showed fear of success when describing a man in nursing school compared to a man in medical school. Women indicated awareness of negative consequences of success for a woman in medical school but not for a woman in nursing school. That is, fear of success was related to the perceived gender appropriateness of the occupation rather than the gender of the person making the evaluation. Both women and men may have misgivings about violating gender stereotypes related to occupations.

In her review of studies on fear of success, Michele Paludi (1984) found that both men and women exhibited the motive to avoid success at similar rates. After examining 64 studies on the topic, Paludi found that a median of 49% of women and 45% of men exhibited the fear of success. These figures represent a considerable acknowledgment of the negative aspects of success but show no gender differences in this belief.

Examining the dilemma of achievement from both a gender and ethnic point of view, Judith Gonzalez (1988) proposed that achievement for Mexican-American women is a double-bind situation. This dilemma occurs as a result of the desire to form relationships with men from the same ethnic background plus the tendency of Mexican-American men to feel threatened by women's achievements. Gonzalez found that the men in her survey reported that they were not threatened by women's accomplishments but that the women believed otherwise. Gonzalez concluded that these women may experience stress from what they see as conflicting demands for achievement and relationships. Due to their desire to preserve their ethnic heritage, these Mexican-American women may be caught in a more severe version of the dilemma of all women who strive for high achievement in that they "experience conflict as their behavior is changing more rapidly than their sex role attitudes and the attitudes of their male counterparts" (p. 378).

Self-Confidence

Although men and women have a comparable fear of success, their confidence in their own ability differs under some conditions. Ellen Lenny (1977) reviewed studies about confidence in achievement situations and found that the situation is an important factor in confidence. Similar to fear of success, confidence about ability to succeed varies with the gender typing of the activity. Men express more confidence in their abilities than women when they perceive the task as "masculine," but this advantage disappears when the task is perceived as "feminine."

In addition, Lenny's analysis indicated clear information that individuals' ability for specific tasks was another situational factor differentiating the self-confidence of men and women. When such information is available, the ability estimates of men and women are similar, but when this information is absent, men make higher estimates of their ability than women. The same is true for situations in which people expect their performance to be compared to others. Women make lower estimates of their performance than men when they expect their work to be compared to that of others but similar estimates when expecting comparisons on social rather than performance factors. Lenny concluded that situational factors influence self-confidence and that "women do *not* display low self-confidence in *all* achievement situations" (p. 3).

Confidence of managers is one area that shows no gender differences: Both male and female managers exhibit similar levels of confidence in both work and personal situations (Chusmir, Koberg, & Stecher, 1992). Contrary to expectation, these managers showed similar patterns of confidence, with both women and men rating their feelings of confidence higher in work than in personal or family situations. These similarities led Leonard Chusmir and his colleagues to advise that "whatever the cause for the similarities between women and men in management positions, it is clear that commonly accepted 'truths' about gender role behavior may no longer be true" (p. 510).

Tomi-Ann Roberts (1991) considered evidence about how other peoples' evaluations influence men's and women's self-assessments of their performance in achievement situations and concluded that women are more responsive to others' evaluations than are men. That is, women are more likely than men to revise estimates of their performance based on the evaluations they receive from others. This responsiveness might be due to women's greater social responsiveness or less confidence, but Roberts suggested that women accept the feedback from others as more informative than men do. A later study by Roberts and Susan Nolen-Hoeksema (1994) confirmed this interpretation while demonstrating that differences in self-confidence were not the source of women's acceptance of evaluative feedback.

Roberts and Nolen-Hoeksema hypothesized that girls' and boys' experience with evaluative feedback leads to a difference; girls receive less feedback about their classroom performance, so they take what feedback they get quite seriously. Boys, on the other hand, tend to receive not only information about their performance but also about their (mis)behavior, leading them to discount evaluative feedback. These differing experiences lead women to consider the evaluations of others, whereas men tend to reject these evaluations. Both Roberts (1991) and Roberts and Nolen-Hoeksema (1994) argued that either strategy has advantages and disadvantages. Women may be overly responsive and rely too little on their own evaluations, but men may be overly resistant to advice from others and fail to change their behavior when changes would improve their performance.

Confidence and ability are not the same; one may be inappropriately confident or inappropriately unsure of one's abilities. Although Roberts and Nolen-Hoeksema found that low self-confidence was not the source of willingness to accept evaluative feedback, Carol Dweck (1986) discussed the tendency for those with high ability and high achievement to be uncertain about future accomplishments, pointing out that unduly low expectancies are more characteristic of girls and women than of boys and men. The low expectancies for success of girls and women may represent underestimates of their abilities, but the high estimates by men and boys may represent overestimates, indicating that both females and males are somewhat inaccurate in predicting their abilities.

Attributions for Success and Failure

Research has also indicated that gender differences exist in explanations for success and failure. People can attribute their success or failure to either internal factors, such as ability or effort, or external factors, such as luck or the difficulty of the task. Although both ability and effort are factors that come from within each person, ability is a stable factor, whereas effort can vary from situation to situation. A person who believes that she succeeded because she worked hard has no assurance that she will succeed again without additional, similar effort. On the other hand, a person who attributes her success to intelligence should believe that similar success will continue—that is, she will still be intelligent next week and next year. Likewise, the external reasons for success and failure differ in their stability. A person who believes he failed because of bad luck should believe that his luck can change, leading to success on another attempt at the same task. A person who attributes his failure to the difficulty of the task should believe that the task will always be difficult and that he will fail on each attempt. Therefore, people can explain their success or failure in terms of internal or external factors, and they can see each as either stable or unstable. Figure 12.2 shows the possibilities in combining these two dimensions. These explanations, or attributions for success and failure, can affect the amount of effort and the amount of time a person is willing to expend in order to succeed.

Although some research (Deaux, White, & Farris, 1975) showed that women were more likely than men to prefer activities in which luck determined the outcome and to explain their success and failure in terms of luck, other research (Karabenick, Sweeney, & Penrose, 1983; Rosenfield & Stephan, 1978) revealed that the gender typing of the activity was a factor in preferences and attributions for success. Stuart Karabenick and his colleagues (1983) demonstrated that men preferred tasks with a high skill component when the task was "masculine," and women showed the same preference pattern on a "feminine" task. Rather than varying by gender, the preference for a skill- versus a chance-determined task was related to the participants' expectancy of their success on the task, which was influenced by the gender typing of the task.

David Rosenfield and Walter Stephan (1978) also studied the influence of gender typing of task, varying their description of a task to alter beliefs about the gender typing of the task. Although the task was the same for everyone, half of their participants believed the task to be a masculine design coordination task involving geometric shapes and mathematical abstraction, and half believed it to be a feminine design coordination task involving delicate design and sensitivity to subtle cues. The men tended to explain their success on the "masculine" task as due to internal factors and their failure as due to external factors. That is, if they succeeded, they took personal credit, but if they failed, bad luck was to blame. The women showed a similar pattern for the "feminine" task, taking personal credit for success and attributing failure to external factors. Both men and women tended to use different attributions for their performance on the cross-gender task, explaining success or failure in less personal terms and attributing the outcome, either positive or negative, more to external factors, such as luck or task difficulty.

In summary, achievement may consist of a variety of attainments, but studies of achievement have concentrated on career success rather than success in relationships

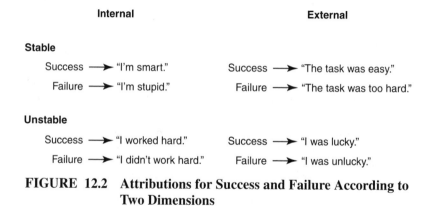

FIGURE 12.2 Attributions for Success and Failure According to Two Dimensions

or families. This emphasis has led to the portrayal of men as having higher achievement motivation than women. In considering women and achievement, the fear of success or motive to avoid success became popular as a way to explain women's lower levels of achievement. Women who exhibited fear of success acknowledged that negative as well as positive consequences accompany success. Further studies have indicated that fear of success may be related to the gender appropriateness of the achievement situation, and men as well as women exhibit misgivings about achievements in gender-inappropriate occupations. The social consequences of achievement are a double bind for all women, but for women from minority ethnic groups, these problems are compounded by their desire to retain their ethnic background.

Studies have shown that women exhibit less confidence in their ability to achieve than do men, but these gender differences in confidence depend on the situation rather than on a general trait. Again, the gender typing of the situation plays a role in the confidence of both men and women, with each having more confidence in gender-appropriate compared to gender-inappropriate situations. The gender typing of the task also influences the attributions that women and men use to explain their performance, with both attributing success to internal, personal sources on gender-typed tasks and resorting to external, situational explanations for failure. Thus, gender role stereotypes are an important factor in achievement, with both men and women being influenced by their perceptions of the characteristics of the achievement situation.

Careers

"Career, in its broadest sense, means 'life path' and thus includes all the roles a person plays throughout life," maintained Helen Farmer and Joan Sidney (1985, p. 338), placing careers in a developmental framework. Their description emphasized the lifelong nature of career development and the many choices and roles that contribute to career development. Farmer and Sidney maintained that ideally, all people should choose a career on the basis of their interest, ability, and potential contribution to society. Farmer and Sidney acknowledged that widespread gender stereotyping provides obstacles to the full development of both men and women.

Despite the encompassing definition of career as the role people play throughout their lives, the study of career development has been limited to the choices and patterns that men have taken, with little study or attention given to women's career development. In examining the study of women's and men's career development, Barbara Gutek and Laurie Larwood (1989) noted: "There was little reason to study the career development of women. It was easily summarized: There was none. Men had careers; women had temporary employment or jobs that took second place to family interest and obligations" (p. 8). This view led to research and theory on men's career development, the neglect of women's career development, and the assumption that the existing research and theories about men would extend to the women who pursued careers.

Women's careers, however, do not easily fit into the same framework as those of men, and Gutek and Larwood argued that men and women are likely to continue to have different career paths in the near future. One reason for this difference is the different expectations about the types of careers each gender will occupy. Although both men and women are now violating these expectations by making gender-atypical choices at higher rates than in the past, most choose gender-traditional occupations. Another expectation is that wives' careers will be secondary to those of their husbands. If someone must stay home with a sick child or if the family must relocate due to job demands, the husband's career will take precedence and the wife will make adaptations in her schedule and employment. These expectations tend to produce interruptions in the careers of women, who may take years away from employment to care for children or to support a husband's career before rejoining the work force.

Women are more likely to hold part-time employment than men—26% versus 11% with part-time jobs (U.S. Department of Labor, 1992). Part-time employment not only leads to lower salaries but also rarely leads to career advancement. Men's careers are more likely to follow a smooth line of development: career choice during schooling, uninterrupted employment, and continuing career advancement throughout adulthood (Larwood & Gutek, 1989).

Helen Astin (1984) formulated a model encompassing gender similarities and differences to explain career development for both women and men. Astin's model includes four components—motivation, expectations, gender role socialization, and opportunity. She assumed that motivation was the same for men and women but that their expectations differ due to their differing gender role socialization. Both the differences in gender role socialization and the differences in opportunities create different outcomes in the work force for men and women. Men have had the opportunity to participate in better-paid and more prestigious as well as a wider variety of work than women. Astin contended that changes have occurred, giving women greater freedom to choose careers dominated by men and equalizing the opportunities in those careers. Lucia Gilbert (1984) questioned the adequacy of Astin's model, especially her optimism about women's greater freedom in career choice and success. Does research on motivation, expectations, gender role socialization, and opportunity support Astin's model? Do women have strong career motivation?

Kristine Baber and Patricia Monaghan (1988) explored the career orientation of college women and found that some were planning careers in areas traditional for women, whereas others were not. They classified some young women as innovators who planned nontraditional careers (such as engineer, regional planner, military officer), whereas some young women fit into the traditional category (teacher, day-care worker, social worker), but all of the young women in their study were planning a work life that fit more closely into the category of career than job. Although this study did not compare women and men, it did demonstrate that young women have strong career motivation, substantiating this factor in Astin's model.

Career Expectations and Gender Role Socialization

Research by Mirra Komarovsky (1982) has confirmed that young women have family- and child-related expectations but also that the career expectations of college women have changed between the 1940s and the 1970s. In the 1940s few college women planned to continue their careers after they married, but in the 1970s very few planned to discontinue their careers after marriage. However, most women, regardless of their career plans, also anticipated marriage and children as part of their life goals.

Baber and Monaghan (1988) also found that college women anticipated combining marriage, motherhood, and career. Their study showed that young women have expanded their career choices so as to include some areas traditionally dominated by men, but the young women in their study anticipated few difficulties in meshing career and family demands. The choices to remain single or to not have children were infrequent, with less than 2% of the young women planning to remain single and less than 3% anticipating a life without children.

These expectations about marriage and motherhood suggest that traditional gender role socialization has affected even college women who plan nontraditional careers. In a study of female and male students from other countries who were pursuing graduate studies in the United States, Nelly Stromquist (1991) discovered that women in nontraditional fields anticipated having more conflict over marriage and career than men in nontraditional fields. Few anticipated serious conflicts with future spouses, but women were more likely to see such possibilities than men. These women indicated that should conflicts arise, their family would take precedence. Stromquist was surprised that these women who had made unconventional choices about their careers would anticipate such a traditional choice of sacrificing career for family.

Ethnicity also plays a role in career expectations. In comparing Mexican-American and European-American high school students, Ellen McWhirter (1994) found both gender and ethnic differences. Female students perceived more barriers to careers than male students, and Mexican-American students saw more barriers and had less confidence in their ability to overcome these barriers than European-American students. For the young women, family-related problems were a more common reason for their lack of confidence than was their ability, and the Mexican-American students were more likely than the European-American students to expect negative attitudes from their families should they attend college. The average ratings for the perception of barriers indicated uncertainty rather than pessimism, but the Mexican-American students and the young women perceived more barriers than the European-American students and the young men.

Gender role expectations also influence the choice of occupations by men and women. Gender segregation of occupations is so prominent that choosing certain occupations places a person in a typical gender role, whereas choosing other careers is a gender-atypical decision. The percentage of the women in U.S. work force has risen to over 45%, with projections for additional increases (Fullerton, 1989), yet during the 1980s over two-thirds of employed women were concentrated in occupations that were over 70% female (Jacobs, 1989). These occupations include a narrow range of clerical, service, or professional positions, such as clerical worker, secretary, child-care worker, teacher, and nurse.

Furthermore, women are moving into male-dominated occupations at a higher rate than men are moving into female-dominated jobs (Gutek, 1985). These choices have perpetuated a gender-segregated work force, with the majority of employed women and men working in jobs occupied by others of the same gender. This gender segregation promotes traditional gender roles and hinders the career development of both women and men, especially those who have an interest in gender-atypical careers.

Career Opportunities

Different education and training create different employment patterns. Table 12.2 shows the gender differences in career choices, presenting the number of men and women in the various occupational categories. Within each category are many different jobs, some of which reflect different levels of prestige and compensation as well as different proportions of men and women. For example, the "professional" category includes jobs such as nursing, teaching, and social work as well as accounting, law, and medicine.

Table 12.3 shows the gender gap in wages. For every occupational category, women earned less than men. For two of the categories, too few people held these occupations to allow a good estimate—that is, too few women were employed in construction and too few men were employed in household service (maids, cooks, child care) for comparisons. Note that for these two categories, the salaries favor men; construction is more lucrative than household service.

TABLE 12.2   Percentage of Women and Men in Occupations, 1992

Occupation	Women	Men
Executive and managerial	47%	53%
Professional	52	47
Technical	49	51
Clerical	79	21
Sales	47	53
Mechanics	3	97
Production and skilled crafts	18	82
Construction	2	98
Manual labor	18	82
Household service	96	4
Protective service (firefighters, police, guards)	13	87
Other service (food, health care, cleaning, personal services)	64	37
Machine operation	40	60
Farming, forestry, and fishing	16	84

Source: From *Statistical abstracts of the United States, 1993* (113th ed.) (pp. 405–407), U.S. Bureau of the Census, Washington, DC: U.S. Government Printing Office.

TABLE 12.3   Weekly Earnings of Men and Women in Various Occupations, 1992

Occupation	Women's Earnings	Men's Earnings
Executive and managerial	$518	$779
Professional	582	760
Technical	449	588
Clerical	363	476
Sales	318	522
Mechanics	496	498
Production and skilled crafts	310	535
Construction	*	499
Manual labor	275	314
Household service	149	*
Protective service (firefighters, police, guards)	399	491
Other service (food, health care, cleaning, and personal services)	245	283
Machine operation	268	410
Farming, forestry, and fishing	240	275

SOURCE: From *Usual weekly earnings of wage and salary workers: First quarter 1992* (table 3), in *Women & Work,* News from the United States Department of Labor, Office of Information and Public Affairs, April 1992, Washington, DC: U.S. Government Printing Office.

*Too few people in these categories for good estimates.

Both gender differences in career choice and gender discrimination in hiring create differences in career opportunities (Gupta, 1993). Discrimination in hiring restricts women's more than men's opportunities for access to careers. Once in a career, discrimination also occurs in promotion, creating gender differences in career advancement and a discrepancy in wages.

Therefore, schooling and gender role expectations create differences in career opportunities for men and women. After entering the job market, women encounter barriers in the form of discrimination in hiring and barriers to career advancement—the glass ceiling mentioned in the headline for this chapter.

Discrimination in Hiring

Discrimination in hiring may be the primary factor in the wage differential between men and women, according to Barry Gerhart (1990), who studied the wage differential between men and women working in a large private firm. He discovered that the women's salaries were 88% of the men's salaries, even after controlling for background, training, length of service with the company, and job title. That is, women seemed to be discriminated against in terms of their wages, as they made less money than men with similar qualifications and experience. Gerhart found that the difference was attributable to initial salaries. When this factor was taken into account, the salary advancements were comparable. The initial salary differences, however, prevented the women's salaries from ever equaling the men's salaries.

In an attempt to understand the factors that affect discrimination in hiring decisions, Peter Glick and his colleagues (Glick, Zion, & Nelson, 1988) submitted fabricated resumés to business professionals for evaluation in a hiring decision. They submitted some resumés with information giving the female or male applicants some characteristics more typical of the other gender, some resumés with information magnifying the stereotypical characteristics of the applicant's gender, and some resumés with neutral personal information. These researchers hypothesized that both men and women would be affected by gender discrimination based on stereotypes but that specific, personal information in the resumés could overcome this bias.

Glick and his colleagues found that the information in the resumés affected the business professionals' ratings of the applicants' personality and suitability for the job but not exactly in the ways they had predicted. Those applicants with "masculine" characteristics were more likely to be rated as worthy of interviews for employment, even when the job's characteristics were "feminine." When the personal information was neutral rather than gender stereotypical, the business professionals were more likely to choose the male rather than the female applicant for interviews, demonstrating the existence of gender discrimination in hiring decisions. Glick and his colleagues concluded that business professionals have strong gender stereotypes for occupations and that these stereotypes are an important factor in gender discrimination in the hiring process.

Additional evidence of gender discrimination in hiring came from a study by Mark Martinko and William Gardner (1983), who studied gender stereotypes in hiring decisions. They concluded that both men and women are subject to positive and negative discrimination on the basis of gender stereotypes. The gender role of the job position is a major factor in discrimination: Men have the advantage in applying for "masculine" jobs, and women have a disadvantage. On the other hand, men can face negative discrimination when they apply for "feminine" jobs, whereas women can have the advantage. Specific, job-related information about an applicant can overcome some gender stereotypes and can thus eliminate some discrimination, but the tendency toward gender stereotyping is a factor in hiring decisions.

Therefore, discrimination based on gender, and especially on the match between gender and gender stereotypes of the job, presents problems for fair hiring decisions. Such discrimination is an important factor in the wage gap between men and women. Providing specific information that shows that an applicant has some characteristics of the other gender can diminish stereotypical perceptions of that applicant and influence hiring. Unfortunately, gender stereotyping is resistant to change, and women experience more disadvantages than men because of such discrimination.

Barriers to Career Advancement

Discrimination occurs not only in hiring but also in career advancement. Whereas women have no advantages in attaining higher positions, even in traditionally female-dominated fields, men seem to have the advantage in all types of jobs. Christine Wil-

GENDERED VOICES
I Never Felt Discriminated Against

A man who had gone to nursing school almost 30 years ago told me about his career decision: "I decided to be a nurse when I was in the 10th grade, after I had surgery. The woman who lived across the street told me about the salaries of nurse-anesthetists, and the work interested me and the money sounded good. I don't remember my parents saying anything. My school counselor got information about nursing, and I didn't discuss it with my friends, so I don't recall any negative comments.

"During a career day at school, we had to choose the areas to attend, and I wrote down that I wanted to be a nurse. Much to my surprise, so did one of my friends, and neither of us knew that the other had thought about becoming a nurse. One other guy wanted to be a surgeon, and we were the only three who had signed up for the health-care option. The guy who wanted to be a surgeon was really mad at us, because he thought we were kidding about being nurses and making fun of him.

"There were only two men in our nursing class. Now many men go into nursing, but then it was uncommon. There had been another guy about 10 years earlier and then the two of us. That's it. I never felt discriminated against by either the teachers or the female students. Everybody was supportive and more than fair. My fraternity brothers were another story. They gave me a lot of static about majoring in nursing. The jokes were pretty good-natured, but there were a lot of them. I joked around a lot, too, so it wasn't really a problem, but it was something that came up a lot.

"The women I have worked with have been great. If anything, I think that being a man has been an advantage to me in my career. Rather than being discriminated against, I think that I was at some advantage. Maybe I got promotions and advancement faster than women, but those who chose me and recommended me were almost always women. I think I was competent and deserved the promotions, so I would have a hard time saying that I advanced in my career because I was a man, but I certainly never felt that it held me back."

I told him about the frequency of sexual harassment in jobs in which the gender ratio is far from equal and asked him if his female-dominated work situation had led to harassment. He replied, "Did I ever feel sexually harassed? That's hard to say. I never was put in the position of 'You do this or it's your job.' Never. But I've had my butt grabbed, and I've gotten a lot of offers. If that's harassment, then I guess I've been harassed, but I can't say that it really bothered me."

liams (1992) labeled the advantages that men have in female-dominated fields the *glass escalator.* She intended for this term to convey that some invisible force was producing an easy ascent to higher positions and to contrast this advantage with the glass ceiling, the invisible barrier that prevents women and minorities from reaching the highest levels of career achievement. Her study revealed that men who choose careers traditionally dominated by women face some discrimination from society in general, but these men have career advantages in terms of rapid promotion. Williams speculated that these advantages come as a result of the perception that men should not be in jobs that women usually perform, and thus men receive promotions to administrative or supervisory positions within that occupation.

For example, Williams included a portion of an interview with a male librarian who had felt happy and confident in his abilities as a children's librarian. Reading stories to children and helping them find books were part of his job, but many people mentioned to him that this was inappropriate for a man to do, and he was transferred to another library and given the position of research librarian. When asked why he did not consider a discrimination lawsuit, the man reported that his new job was really a promotion to a more prestigious position, so he felt that rather than being harmed, he had benefited from these clearly discriminatory actions.

The existence of the glass ceiling seems to be borne out by the research of Catherine Daily (1993). She pointed out that only 3% of senior-level managers in major corporations are women, but about 15% should be, based on the number of women in

---

✪ **DIVERSITY HIGHLIGHT**
At the Bottom of the Work Heap

Disabled women have all of the employment problems that women face plus all of the problems that the disabled face, putting them at the bottom of the work heap, according to Susan McLain and Carol Perkins (1990). These authors explained the problems of disabled women, pointing out that these women must overcome the prejudice against the handicapped as well as gender bias. These two factors result in disabled women's unemployment and underemployment.

McLain and Perkins explained that the unemployment rate among disabled women was 50 to 90%. This high unemployment results in poverty, with the disabled more likely than others to live below the poverty level. Disabled women have disadvantages compared not only to able-bodied women but also to disabled men. Barbara Altman (1985) showed that disabled women have the lowest percentage of employment compared to able-bodied women and to disabled and nondisabled men. Those disabled women who are employed tend to have jobs that rank low in both prestige and salary.

Disabled women earn 64 cents for each dollar an able-bodied woman earns. All women's wages are lower than men's wages, with women earning an average of about 72 cents for each dollar men earn (McLain & Perkins, 1990). Around 67% of able-bodied women are part-time workers, whereas 89% of disabled women work on a part-time basis. These rates compare unfavorably with part-time employment of men. Disabled men are also restricted to part-time employment more often than are able-bodied men, with 26% of able-bodied men being employed part time versus 70% of disabled men.

Disabled men are also at a disadvantage when compared to employed able-bodied men. Disabled men earn 85% of the wages of able-bodied men, a higher percentage than that of disabled versus nondisabled women, which puts disabled women at a greater disadvantage than disabled men. Thus, as McLain and Perkins contended, disabled women have poor work prospects, with the resulting disadvantage for income, standard of living, and feelings of accomplishment.

Disabled women are also at a disadvantage when compared to disabled men in access to rehabilitation services. Altman (1985) compared women and men with several types of disabling conditions and found that men were more likely to receive rehabilitation services, including job counseling and financial assistance. Altman summarized the experience of disability for women and men:

The experience of disability in our social structure is defined differently for men and women. In both rehabilitation and financial assistance areas the disabled male role is associated in one way or another with an active, work related nonstigmatizing philosophy. Rehabilitation for men includes job counseling and job placement.... Women's disabled role on the other hand is a compounding of the dependent identity already associated with the female role.... The financial assistance received by women is primarily in the form of welfare payments, once again a very dependent model without even the redeeming quality of 'having been earned' that the male model provides. Thus disabled women experience more stigma. (pp. 74–75)

management positions 20 years ago. These women should now have the seniority and experience to be senior managers, but they have not attained these positions; they hit the glass ceiling and failed to progress in their careers. As a result, their earnings are lower than those of men.

Several factors contribute to the gender gap in wages—different career choices, different career schedules, and discrimination based on gender stereotypes. Women occupy jobs and pursue careers that are less prestigious and not as well paid as those that men choose. For example, only 27% of lawyers and judges are women compared to 90% of nursing aides, orderlies, and attendants; only 31% of managers in marketing, advertising, and public relations are women compared to 98% of secretaries and stenographers (Saltzman, 1991).

The choice of career is one factor in the wage differential between men and women, but even within each occupation, women's wages lag behind men's in every field (see Table 12.3). As Williams showed, men in female-dominated occupations tend to reach higher-level positions more easily than women in that profession, and this "glass escalator" is a factor in boosting men's salaries in these occupations.

Another factor in career advancement comes from the informal social structure at work and from mentoring relationships, both of which tend to exclude women. Achievement-oriented women who pursue careers in male-dominated fields are in the minority, and Rosabeth Moss Kanter (1977) has discussed the ways in which minority status can handicap career advancement. When a minority member, either a woman or a member of an ethnic minority, enters the corporate world, the person becomes a **token** of the minority group. The token stands out, becoming more visible than other employees, and feels the pressure to succeed and to reflect well on the ability of everyone in the minority group.

As tokens try to fit into the existing corporate and social structure, the dominant group may work toward keeping them on the periphery. Judith Lorber (1989) described the process of the exclusion of women and minorities at work: "The informal norms serve as overt or subtle bases for inclusion of novices in the inner circles of work life or their exclusion. Those who are excluded are felt to be not quite trustworthy—it is felt that they will be unreliable as colleagues or work partners." (p. 348). Such mistrust can isolate tokens and prevent them from joining the interactions of the work group, including forming mentoring relationships.

When a new employee enters an organization, he or she benefits from forming a relationship with someone who has status and an interest in advancing the career of the new employee. This higher-status employee "adopts" the new employee, forming a mentor-protégé relationship. Such relationships tend to form within gender and ethnic lines, and as neither women nor ethnic minorities are common in the upper echelons of organizations, these new employees experience difficulties in finding mentors (Leong, Snodgrass, & Gardner, 1992). Access to mentors can be an advantage for those who find them and an impediment to the career advancement of those who do not (Wilbur, 1987).

The differences in women's and men's career development schedules are also a factor in the gender differences in promotions and wages. Women are more likely than men to take time off from their careers to attend to family, such as staying home with young children. These employment gaps take women out of the workplace and put them off the track to advancement, slowing their progress. Although employment gaps are even more damaging to men's career advancement (Schneer & Reitman, 1990), the fact that women are more likely to interrupt their careers than men means that the overall impact of employment interruption decreases women's wages and advancement more than it does for men.

After studying the career progress of corporate men and women, Linda Stroh and her colleagues (Stroh, Brett, & Reilly, 1992) found that "although the women had done 'all the right stuff'—getting a similar education as the men, maintaining similar levels of family power, working in similar industries, not moving in and out of the work force, not removing their names from consideration for a transfer more often—it was still not enough" (p. 251).

When Stroh and her colleagues used the phrase "all the right stuff," they referred to following a male pattern of career progression and avoiding traditionally feminine career choices and family commitments. "All the right stuff" still left women at a disadvantage in terms of salary progression and geographic mobility. However, both women and men who did not do "all the right stuff" fared more poorly in terms of career progress than women who did. These researchers questioned why the right stuff did not work for women to the same extent that it did for men. If deviating from the pattern does not work and following the pattern does not work, then perhaps no route exists for gender-equal career and salary achievement.

Gender stereotypes not only have an impact on hiring but also on the perception of women in the workplace, affecting colleagues' and supervisors' workplace interactions and their ratings of female workers. In 1975 Kanter described management as a male category, and Madeline Heilman and her colleagues (Heilman, Black, Martell, & Simon, 1989) found evidence that these perceptions continue. Heilman et al. studied the perceptions of male managers concerning the characteristics of men and women (in general), male and female managers, successful male and female managers, and middle managers (gender not specified). They asked the managers to complete an extensive rating of each of these seven categories and found that "men in general still are described as more similar to successful managers than are women in general" (p. 935). These negative stereotypes of women's abilities are important to the perception of competence and suitability for managerial positions. When women were described as "managers" and "successful managers," some of the negative stereotyping disappeared, indicating that specific information about any particular woman can decrease the extent to which the stereotype applies to her. However, this study demonstrated the persistence and general application of gender stereotypes to women in management positions.

Unfortunately, these stereotypes are resistant to change. According to Crystal Owen and William Todor (1993), gender-biased evaluations are likely to persist. They surveyed undergraduate business students and human resources professionals about the suitability of women for management positions and found evidence for stereotypical perceptions of female managers' ability. The negative evaluations were especially strong among the business students, providing a pessimistic note about the future of women in business.

Some researchers have found that there are situations in which gender stereotypes produce more favorable views of women than men. Alice Eagly and her colleagues (Eagly, Mladinic, & Otto, 1991) found that college students rated the social category of women more favorably than the social category of men, but Eagly (1994) contended that this positive evaluation depends on women adhering to their traditional role. When women diverge from their traditional roles, they no longer receive such positive evaluations.

Paul Abramson and his colleagues (Abramson, Goldberg, Greenberg, & Abramson, 1977) asked college students to make an evaluation of the competence of a person. Abramson et al. manipulated the description of the person so that the evaluations were of a male or female attorney or a male or female paralegal worker. Both the male and female participants rated the female attorney as the most vocationally competent due to the barriers to achievement for women. "When an individual achieves a level of success not anticipated, his/her achievement tends to be magnified rather than diminished" (p. 114). These studies demonstrate that women can be perceived as competent and capable of high levels of achievement; that is, some evidence must exist for an exception to gender stereotypes, or else men would always receive higher ratings of competence than do women.

Gender Issues at Work

Stereotypical beliefs about men having greater competence, especially for prestigious occupations, is one factor that perpetuates the gender gap in wages. Although women have entered male-dominated in professions in greater numbers in the past decades than at any previous time, women remain underrepresented in the highest levels of the professions. Even when equating factors such as education, age, type of position, job tenure, and type of job, women earn less money than men (Landau & Arthur, 1992). Jerry Jacobs (1989) contended that about 25% of the wage gap between men and women was the result of gender segregation of occupations.

Gender Segregation on the Job

The gender-typical choices that most men and women make in careers have resulted in gender segregation in most jobs. That is, in most work situations the large majority of jobs are held by either men or women but not by an equal (or nearly equal) mix of both. These associations have created gendered jobs. That is, regardless of the job demands, some jobs have become so associated with either men or women as to be considered male occupations or female occupations.

According to Barbara Gutek (1985), women have a less diversified range of occupations than men. Consequently, women are concentrated in a few occupations, whereas men are employed in a wider variety of jobs. Over two-thirds of women have jobs in clerical or professional fields, but these professional fields are those traditionally dominated by women—nursing and teaching. Gutek pointed out that women are most underrepresented in skilled blue-collar jobs, such as electrician and plumber. (Refer to Table 12.2 for the percentages for the "construction" and "production and skilled crafts" categories.)

In Gutek's study of employment in the Los Angeles area, over 60% of men worked in occupations that were dominated by men (defined as 80% representation by men for that job category). Women are also employed in gender-segregated occupations, but not to the same extent as men. Using the same criterion, Gutek found that over 40% of women worked in jobs that were female dominated. That is, more men work in male-dominated fields than women work in female-dominated fields. Furthermore, more women work in male-dominated occupations than men work in female-dominated jobs; women have entered traditionally male-dominated fields, but men have not entered traditionally female-dominated occupations.

Few people work in gender-integrated fields. Even with the gains for women in traditionally male-dominated occupations, gender segregation at work remains. During the early 1980s, over 60% of employed men and women would have needed to exchange jobs to end gender segregation (McCann & McGinn, 1992). As of 1990, an end to gender segregation would have required a change in jobs for more than half of the men and women in the work force.

When gender integration occurs at work, it may be a source of dissatisfaction, especially for men. According to Amy Wharton and James Baron (1987, 1991), men in mixed-gender work settings were less satisfied and more depressed about their jobs than men in either male-dominated or female-dominated work settings. Men were significantly less satisfied with gender-integrated compared to gender-segregated work situations. Not surprisingly, women were most dissatisfied in work situations in which women were in the majority and the few men received preferential treatment. Women were not as influenced by workplace gender segregation as men, and the differences in satisfaction were small, even for the men.

Gutek suggested that gender segregation may be more extreme in specific work situations than in any occupation as a whole. For example, both men and women wait on tables, but some restaurants hire only waiters, whereas others hire only waitresses. A study by Erica Groshen (1991) confirmed Gutek's contention, finding that within jobs in an establishment, gender segregation is greater than in the occupation. Even people who choose occupations that are not dominated by one gender may work in a company or office in which that occupation is gender segregated and thus spend their time with same-gender colleagues. Groshen maintained that gender segregation tends to raise men's and lower women's salaries. She determined that at least 11% and as much as 26% of the gender wage gap is attributable to gender segregation, with the variation depending on the industry.

Gender segregation declined between 1970 and 1980, and Judith Fields and Edward Wolff (1991) argued that this decrease was related to a decreasing wage gap. Not all occupations showed decreasing gender segregation, and occupations that experienced rapid growth during this time period showed the greatest decline in gender segregation.

Fields and Wolff suggested that rapid growth is associated with lowering of barriers for women entering the field as well as diminishing wage discrimination.

Although jobs are gender segregated for most workers, the workplace is likely to contain both men and women, who, though they may have different jobs, work together in the same setting. For example, most secretaries are women, most managers are men, and most managers have secretaries. Thus, men and women often work together but not at the same job. Indeed, the work situations that produce an interaction between men and women often involve a power differential, with men having the more powerful position and women the more subordinate.

Gender, Communication, and Power in the Workplace

Communication style is one possible explanation for the gender differences in career advancement. Robin Lakoff (1975) contended that "women's language" differs from "men's language," with women using a more tentative and deferent style of communication than men. She hypothesized that this style of speaking fails to convey the assertive, commanding qualities necessary for leadership, making women's speech style a handicap in their careers.

Would women be more successful at work if they talked like men? Mary Glenn Wiley and Arlene Eskilson (1985) investigated this question by presenting two versions of a job interview and asking for evaluations of the applicants. The two versions varied only in speech style, with one version having many pauses, hedges, and questions and the other none of these characteristics. They paired each style with a female and male applicant, for a total of four conditions. Their results indicated a complex pattern, with an interaction of speech style, gender of applicant, and gender of rater. Wiley and Eskilson found a significant effect for speech style, with raters judging applicants with the hesitant style as less likely to be successful. They found no effect for either applicant's or rater's gender, but complex interactions occurred; for instance, speech style made less difference to male raters than to female raters. In addition, male raters liked women who used the hesitant speech style and disliked women whose speech style was more assertive, but women rated women higher if they used the assertive speech style. These results indicated that no simple relationship exists between speech style and ratings of ability.

Elizabeth Aries (1987) reviewed the research on gender and communication and confirmed that the results from Wiley and Eskilson's study were generally true: No distinctive patterns of communication are uniquely associated with success or even with women or men. That is, the hesitant speech style that Lakoff analyzed as "women's language" and the assertive style that she identified as "men's language" are not specific to either. Although women and men may have different goals in speaking, the notion of a male versus a female way of talking is not supported by research. Aries concluded that gender-related differences in communication are complex and that setting and situation are critical factors in men's and women's communication patterns.

One of the situational differences that affects speech is power. Aries reviewed studies suggesting that the power of the speaker influences speech style. That is, those in positions of power tend to use more assertive language. In the workplace, power and gender are related and at least part of the reason for this power differential is the power differential in society. Thus, work roles mirror social roles just as social stereotypes of gender affect behavior and expectations in the workplace. Veronica Nieva and Barbara Gutek (1981) discussed how aspects of the female role carry over into the workplace to produce what they called **sex role spillover.** Gutek (1985) expanded the concept, emphasizing that sex role spillover focuses on gender role behavior that is irrelevant (or even an impediment) to the work role. Spillover can take several different forms, including the expectation that women will be more nurturant or loyal than men, that women will occupy subordinate positions, and that women will be sexual at work.

When men and women are together in the workplace, they may rely on their habitual patterns of interaction, and gender stereotypes may take over. As Gutek pointed out, most men have experience with women as mothers, girlfriends, wives, daughters, and secretaries but possibly not as their professional colleagues. When a man is faced with a woman in the same job, he may rely on one of the other role relationships to guide his interaction with his female colleague. Although treating the new female executive like his mother or his secretary may not be appropriate, these relationships are familiar, and one may be the pattern he chooses. His stereotypes of women will thus inevitably affect his behavior, because he has no experience of an equal relationship with a female colleague.

The new female executive may also fall back on habitual patterns of interacting with men on the job, perpetuating inappropriate work behavior for everyone involved. On the other hand, her behavior may be shaped by the executives she has known, most of whom were men, as well as her conception of how an executive should act. Thus, she may act like a male executive, enacting a version of the role with which she is most familiar. Some evidence exists that women who occupy jobs most commonly filled by men adopt a male style of work-related behavior, demonstrating how powerful situational demands can be. In a review of the research on gender and leadership roles, Alice Eagly and Blair Johnson (1990) concluded that both women and men who have attained managerial status in organizations tend to be similar in leadership style. Job requirements and the selection of people for the job make managers more alike than different, regardless of gender.

When women adopt the same power styles as men, they may not be evaluated equally positively. Although an authoritative and even autocratic style of management is common for men, women are expected to be more "people oriented" and interpersonally sensitive. When managers exhibit different styles, the choice of autocratic versus democratic often corresponds to the male versus the female style (Eagly & Johnson, 1990). The choice of democratic style is a wise one on the part of female leaders (Eagly, Makhijani, & Klonsky, 1992), and women who use the directive male power style of leading are devalued relative to the men who choose this style.

The story of Ann Hopkins provides a dramatic example of what can happen when women violate gender stereotypical expectations on the job (Fiske, Bersoff, Borgida, Deaux, & Heilman, 1991). Ann Hopkins was an employee of Price Waterhouse, and she was so successful as to be nominated for partner in that company, the only woman nominated that year. She was not chosen to be a partner, and she became the object of criticism for being too aggressive and "macho" as well as for not being sufficiently feminine in her behavior and appearance. Hopkins sued the company for applying different criteria to its male and female employees, contending that gender stereotyping was a factor in their decision. Eventually, the U.S. Supreme Court agreed with these arguments, condemning the double bind that women face when penalized for using an aggressive, powerful style when only such a style can lead to success.

If women are penalized for using the same methods to gain power that men use, how do women get power at work? Belle Rose Ragins and Eric Sundstrom (1989) reviewed the development of power in organizations and concluded that women have many obstacles to accumulating power. They acknowledged that the social system and most organizational systems work to prevent women from gaining power. Different career expectations, entry-level jobs, assignments within the company, and promotion rates all favor the accumulation of power by men rather than women. One method open to women is the use of expert power—that is, specific expertise to accomplish a task. Ragins and Sundstrom found that studies of successful female executives have shown that these women tended to accumulate power from being expert in performing their jobs and that such power was especially important early in their careers. After they had a power base, these women were more likely to turn their attention to gaining power through interpersonal skills and influence.

A laboratory study by John Dovidio and his colleagues (Dovidio, Ellyson, Keating, Heltman, & Brown, 1988) demonstrated how effective expert power can be in determining social dominance. These researchers manipulated who had expert power and observed the effects on the nature of the social interaction, finding an interaction between gender and expert power. When women had expert power, they behaved in a dominant way, and their male partners acknowledged this dominance by their reactions. When the women received no power in the situation, the nature of the male-female interactions fell into more gender-stereotypical patterns: The men showed signs of social dominance and the women of social submission. Thus, expert power can change the power dynamics away from the gender-stereotypical pattern, giving women a way to assert and accumulate power at work.

In summary, although research has failed to support the notion of different communication styles that are unique to women or men, it has shown that communication styles relate to the power of the speaker and the communication situation. The issues of gender, communication, and power also relate to adherence to stereotypical gender roles in the workplace, giving power to men and placing obstacles in the way of women's career advancement. The extension of habitual patterns of interaction between men and women to the workplace produces a power differential, with men having the advantage. When women use the same behaviors as men to exert power, they are often perceived as behaving inappropriately and are penalized. Women have the option of relying on expert power to gain a power base and working from it to attain power at work, but the spillover of gender roles to work situations gives men an advantage in the accumulation and use of power.

The power difference between men's and women's positions offers not only the opportunity for men to be more successful at work but also the opportunity for men to sexually exploit the women who work for them. Although sexuality at work can also be interpreted as a power issue, the term *sexual harassment* has become the label for sexual exploitation in the workplace.

Sexual Harassment at Work

Gutek (1985) contended that "sex role spillover facilitates the expression of sexuality at work to the extent that the sex object aspect of the female sex role and the sexual aggressor aspect of the male sex role carry over into the work setting" (p. 18); that is, sexual harassment is a function of sex role spillover. Mutually entered sexual relationships also occur in the workplace, and sometimes the distinction between this type of sexuality and harassment is difficult to define.

In 1976 sexual harassment became illegal as a form of gender discrimination (Dworkin, 1993). The first recognized form of sexual harassment was the **quid pro quo form** in which employers or supervisors demand sexual favors as a condition of employment or as a condition for promotion. As this form of harassment involves a supervisor and a subordinate, it is a clear abuse of power. For the same reason, women are the more common targets of this form of harassment.

The other legally recognized form of sexual harassment was not recognized until 1986 and involves **hostile environment sexual harassment.** This concept of harassment

> is based on the idea that the employer should use its power to control its workplace so that employees are not forced to tolerate abusive conditions to earn a living. Failure to use this power to control employees' verbal or physical conduct (usually of a sexual nature) that unreasonably interferes with an employee's work, or that creates an intimidating hostile, or offensive working environment, will subject the employer to liability. (Dworkin, 1993, p. 53)

Table 12.4 gives examples of each type of harassment.

In addition, the standards for what constitutes a harassing environment have changed. Prior to 1991, what a "reasonable man" would consider objectionable was the criterion, but now the **"reasonable woman" standard** applies. This change in the standard may be a factor in the increased number of lawsuits over inappropriate sexuality in the workplace. As Nancy Dodd McCann and Thomas McGinn (1992, p. 3) said in defending this standard, "What may not seem offensive to a man can traumatize a woman."

The two forms of sexual harassment are not equal in frequency or in perceived severity; the hostile environment form is more common, but the quid pro quo form is perceived as more serious (Riger, 1991). Despite the perceived lack of severity of hostile environment sexual harassment, Louise Fitzgerald (1994) found that workplaces that have this type of harassment tend to also have the quid pro quo type. Fitzgerald emphasized environmental rather than personal factors in sexual harassment. She reported that environments that allow insulting remarks and unwanted sexual attention also tend to permit sexual coercion. Despite the separate legal standards for these two types of

TABLE 12.4   Examples of the Two Types of Sexual Harassment

Quid Pro Quo Type

Demands for sex in exchange for hiring

Demands for sex in exchange for promotion or favorable job evaluation

Demands for sex to keep a job

Demands for sex to avoid being put into an undesirable job

Hostile Environment Type

Sexual touching

Sexual comments and jokes

Degrading comments about women's (or men's) ability or behavior as a group, not confined to sexual comments

Displays of sexual material, such as drawings or photographs

Nonverbal sexual posturing, including sexual gestures

Personal remarks about sexuality

Sexually oriented comments about appearance

Discussions about a person in sexual terms in the person's presence but phrased as though the person was not present

---

sexual harassment and the differences in frequency and perceived severity, the two often coexist.

Women are the more frequent targets of all sexual harassment, when defined in terms of *unwanted* sexual attention. In Gutek's (1985) study, men reported a comparable number of sexual overtures as did women and as many instances of sexual touching, but men were less likely than women to find sexual attention unwanted and thus to label their experience as harassment. These different standards may contribute to miscommunication and exacerbate harassment.

As Frank Saal and his colleagues (Saal, Johnson, & Weber, 1989) discovered, gender differences exist in what counts as sexual signals. When they asked people to observe social interactions between men and women, the male participants saw less friendliness and more sexiness in the women's behavior than the female observers saw. These findings suggested that men and women may not have the same interpretation of sexual intention, even when they observe the same behavior. These differences may lead to misunderstandings about sexual intentions, with men believing that women are *sending* signals of interest when men *perceive* such signals.

Gender-related differences in perception of sexuality are also a factor in defining sexual harassment. Gutek (1985) found that the biggest gender difference concerning sexuality at work had to do with attitudes about sexual propositions. She found that two-thirds of the men in her study said that they felt flattered by such propositions, but only 17% of women felt the same way. Indeed, over 60% of the women said that they would feel insulted by a sexual proposition at work. The main problem, however, comes from the perceptions of both; neither the men nor the women in Gutek's study

GENDERED VOICES
Hardly a Day Went By

In two stories I heard about sexual harassment, the behaviors of the harrassors and the targets were amazingly similar. One story was about a woman and the other about a man who harassed a coworker.

A man told me, "I worked in a car dealership selling cars after I graduated, and one of the other salespeople was a woman—the only woman who was in sales. She sexually harassed the finance manager. It was blatant. She propositioned him in front of everybody, saying things like 'Let's go in the back room now,' and things much more vulgar.

"He seemed embarrassed and usually didn't reply; he tried to ignore her. He was married, and he never gave her any encouragement at all. She would go over and stand very close to him, never touching him but standing close and making him uncomfortable. And she would proposition him; rarely a day went by when she didn't. The guy was clearly uncomfortable, but nobody ever did anything."

A young woman said, "I worked as a cashier in a discount store, and one of the department manag-ers sexually harassed me. He would come over to the cash register where I was working, and he would proposition me. He made reasons to be close to me, and he kept saying what a good idea it would be for us to have sex. I didn't think it was such a good idea. I always said no, and I asked him to stop asking. His offers embarrassed me. Hardly a day went by without some sexual offer from him or some remark with sexual connotations. He never touched me or fondled me, but he made my job harder, and he embarrassed me.

"I complained to my supervisor, but she told me to just ignore him. He wasn't my boss, and he never made any threats or attacked me or anything. But I think that he shouldn't have been allowed to harass me the way he did. Nobody did one thing to stop him. I don't think that the store manager ever said a word."

were aware of the perception of the other. The men believed that the women felt flattered by sexual attention when in actuality the women felt insulted or angered.

Although women often feel insulted and angered by sexual comments and propositions from supervisors and coworkers, they may have problems in labeling these behaviors as harassment (Gutek, 1985). Therefore, the estimates about rates for harassment may be low if the figures are based on personal reports. Gutek estimated that 21% of women had definitely been the targets of sexual harassment at some time during their work lives and that up to 53% were probable victims. For men, at least 9% and up to 37% have experienced sexual harassment. Thus, sexuality at work is common, but women are more likely than men to label sexual experiences at work as harassment.

According to Gutek's study, men who sexually harass women do not differ from employed men in general, but women who are targets of harassment differ in some ways; they are more likely to be unmarried, younger than the average employed woman, and attractive. Women who initiate sexual relationships at work are much less likely to be perceived as harassers than are men, and like the women who are the targets of harassment, they are younger and more likely to be unmarried than the average employed woman. In cases of men who reported they were sexually harassed, their harassers were similar to the women who initiated sex at work—young, unmarried, and attractive.

Another difference between male and female harassers is their status. Male harassers are likely to be in supervisory positions and thus have power over the women whom they harass, but female harassers are not, giving them no power to demand or coerce sexual favors from men with whom they work. Gutek hypothesized that the small percentage of men (as few as 9%) who describe incidents of being sexually harassed may feel harassed by the seductive behavior of their coworkers or subordinates, but the men's careers are not at risk from the sexual behavior of women at work.

Women's careers, on the other hand, are often endangered by sexual harassment. Gutek found that over 30% of employed women had experienced some negative job consequences as a result of sexual harassment, compared to around 10% of men. These problems included quitting a job, asking for a transfer, or losing a job for refusing to have sex with an employer or supervisor.

Perhaps these differences in consequences of sexuality at work explain the differences in perceptions of harassment: Why should men feel harassed by sex at work when they are very unlikely to experience negative consequences? Why should women welcome sexual attention at work when their careers are so much more likely to be harmed? Given an equal interest in sexual relationships with people at work, the unequal consequences of sexual behavior on careers suggests that men and women should have different views of sexuality at work—and they do.

Summary

Men and women have different experiences in education, and thus their employment differs. Although Title IX of the Education Amendments of 1972 prohibits discrimination based on gender in schools that receive federal funds, girls and boys do not receive the same treatment in school. Teachers treat boys and girls differently, beginning during the earliest school years and continuing throughout college. Boys receive more attention and feedback about their performance in classroom work. Textbooks present stereotypical images of male and female characters, reinforcing gender-typical behavior. Despite different treatment, girls and boys have similar levels of achievement during elementary school. During junior high school, however, girls become less confident of their academic abilities, and their achievement in math and science begins to lag.

During high school, girls' and boys' choices of coursework differ, with girls failing to pursue advanced courses in math and science as frequently as boys. These choices affect career options. In addition, counselors convey higher career expectations to boys and fail to present the full range of career options to girls. Boys who enter vocational education programs are more likely to be steered toward lucrative skilled trades, whereas women in vocational education learn low-paying clerical skills. Sexual harassment, especially from peers, becomes a problem for girls during high school and continues to be a problem during the college years.

Although women have not traditionally attended college in numbers comparable to men, that pattern has changed. Women now receive more undergraduate degrees than men, but gender differences in choice of major persist, with a small percentage of the science and engineering degrees and a large percentage of the education and liberal arts degrees going to women. An increasing number of women are receiving advanced and professional degrees, but again, the choices are disproportionately stereotypical.

Early research in achievement suggested that women had a lower need for achievement than men, but these researchers defined achievement in terms of career success rather than the family or personal relationships to which women have devoted their energies. Women were believed to have a fear of success, a reluctance to compete with men to achieve success, but later research demonstrated that misgivings about the consequences of success appear as often in men as in women. Neither are women always less confident about their abilities than men. Although some studies have found a gender difference in confidence about success, a review of the studies indicated that situational factors influence confidence. Both women and men tend to feel more confident of their abilities when they believe the task is one on which their gender does better. Beliefs about gender appropriateness also influence people's explanations for success or failure on a task, and there is a tendency to make internal attributions for gender-appropriate success and external attributions for failure.

Theories of career development have concentrated on men, because women's careers have traditionally revolved around their family rather than their employment. Although career motivation is similar for men and women, social expectations still hold that women will place a higher priority on family than career. Research indicates that college women expect to combine both, but employment statistics indicate that women have fewer career opportunities than men.

The limitations on women's careers come from their career choices, interruptions in their employment, and discrimination in hiring and promotion. Career choices and preparation lead men into a wider variety of occupations than women, and men's jobs typically pay better. Interruptions in employment affect both men's and women's careers negatively, but women more often interrupt their careers to devote time to family. Discrimination in hiring is a major factor in the wage gap between men and women. Specific, personal information about a job applicant can partially overcome the gender stereotyping that affects hiring decisions, but employers have a tendency to try to match the gender of the applicant to the gender stereotype of the job, discriminating against both women and men who apply for gender-atypical jobs.

Women occupy a very small percentage of executive positions, being blocked in their career progress by an invisible barrier called the glass ceiling. Many factors have contributed to the formation of barriers to the advancement of women and ethnic minorities. The informal social structure in corporations excludes newcomers who differ from the majority. Thus, token women or minorities have difficulty being trusted and

in forming important mentoring relationships. Gender stereotypes influence the perception of female managers' performance, making their competence difficult to acknowledge. Gender stereotypes can boost men in gender-typical careers, providing them with easier access to promotions. Even women who have comparable training, personal background, and performance do not advance in their careers as rapidly as men, providing evidence of discrimination in career advancement.

Gender-based interactions at work obstruct women from gaining power and demonstrating their competence, since these characteristics are not part of the feminine stereotype. Women who fail to adhere to traditional standards of femininity can be penalized, but those who follow these standards cannot succeed in the corporate world. Women can accumulate power through the use of their expertise, but women have to overcome many barriers to gain power at work.

The work force is gender segregated: Most men and women work with colleagues of the same gender, and few occupations have an equal proportion of men and women. Even in occupations that are not gender segregated, jobs situations may be. This segregation is more pronounced for men than women, as women have moved into traditionally male-dominated fields more rapidly than men have moved into female-dominated jobs. Gender segregation on the job has resulted in the association of jobs with gender and the spillover of male and female characteristics to the work environment. This gender role spillover tends to produce patterns of interaction between men and women rather than between coworkers, bringing sexuality into the workplace.

Another consequence of sexuality at work is sexual harassment. Although illegal, both women and men are pressured for sexual favors from employees and supervisors and subjected to unwanted sexual attention at work. Women are more likely to find sexual attention unwanted than men, possibly because they are more likely to be harmed by sexual relationships with coworkers. Men are likely to find sexual attention flattering, but women are likely to find such attention insulting. Although there is little difference in the amount of sexual attention men and women receive at work, women are more likely to label their experiences as sexual harassment than are men.

Glossary

Fear of success   the term applied to negative consequences associated with success

Glass ceiling   the invisible barrier that seems to prevent women and ethnic minorities from reaching the highest levels of business success

Hostile environment sexual harassment   the type of sexual harassment that occurs when employers allow offensive elements in the work environment

Quid pro quo form   sexual harassment in the form of demands for sexual favors in exchange for employment or promotion

"Reasonable woman" standard   the standard that defines a sexually harassing environment in terms of what a reasonable woman would find offensive

Sexual harassment   unwanted sexual attention

Sex role spillover   the hypothesis that gender role characteristics spill over into the workplace, creating stereotyping and a sexualized atmosphere

Title IX of the Education Amendments of 1972   the federal act that prohibits educational institutions that receive federal funds from discriminating against women

Token   a symbol or example, in this case, of a minority group

Suggested Readings

Dworkin, Terry Morehead. (1993). Harassment in the 1990s. *Business Horizons, 36*(2), 52–58. This brief, approachable article examines the recent changes in attitudes and laws concerning sexual harassment.

Fox, Mary Frank. (1989). Women and higher education: Gender differences in the status of students and scholars. In Jo Freeman (Ed.), *Women: A feminist perspective* (4th ed.) (pp. 217–235). Mountain View, CA: Mayfield. Fox reviews the history of education for women, examining the changes in attitudes, increases in number of women as students and educators, and problems that women face in both roles.

Lopata, Helena Znaniecka. (1993). The interweave of public and private: Women's challenge to American society. *Journal of Marriage and the Family, 55,* 176–190. Lopata examines the history of women's work and employment, using the Doctrine of the Two Spheres as her theoretical basis. She contends that the increase in women's employment has posed challenges not only to women but to society.

Saltzman, Amy. (1991, June 17). Trouble at the top. *U.S. News & World Report,* pp. 40–48. The article that furnished the headline for this chapter discusses many aspects of gender and employment, providing details on the gender gap in wages and stories of women who have made various choices about their employment and families.

Chapter *13*

Health and Fitness

HEADLINE

Women and Survival

—*New York Times* Science Watch, November 12, 1991

The Science Watch column of the *New York Times* on November 12, 1991, presented a brief report about women's survival advantages. Rather than citing contemporary figures about the gender differences in heart disease or cancer, this report focused on anthropologist Donald Grayson's (1990) analysis of deaths during the Donner party expedition of 1846 to 1847. As Grayson pointed out, the story of the Donner party's hardships and their resort to cannibalism has become a well-known footnote in U.S. history, but information about who survived and the circumstances of their survival is less familiar. Grayson analyzed the demographic characteristics of the survivors and fatalities in the group, and his findings confirm information about health that exists today as it did over 100 years ago.

Of the 87 members of the Donner group who were emigrating from Illinois to California, 40 died. Most of these deaths resulted from starvation and exposure. Early snows in the Sierra Nevada mountains prevented the party from reaching Sacramento, and a harsh winter trapped the group without adequate shelter or food. Although the circumstances of the deaths differed from most deaths then and now, the demographics were similar in many ways: The youngest and oldest members of the group were at higher risk than others, the women were more likely to survive than the men, the men were more likely to die as a result of violence, and size of family was a factor in survival. Each of these findings reflects not only the forces that affected survival for the Donner party but also current figures about **mortality** (death) rates and **morbidity** (illness) rates.

Children younger than 5 years old are more vulnerable to illness and death than older children and young adults. Children in the Donner party showed this pattern of greater mortality than adults—62.5% of the children under age 5 years died compared with 45.9% of all people in the group. Although death rates are lower now than in the mid 1800s, the patterns remain similar (U.S. Bureau of the Census [USBC], 1975, 1992). Infants were especially vulnerable to fatal diseases during the 1800s and early 1900s, even under normal circumstances, with death rates over 10 times higher than those of adults. Under normal circumstances, the death rate for children was nowhere near 62%, but young children in the 19th century were at elevated risk of death compared with older children and young adults. The decrease in infant mortality has been one of the most dramatic changes in patterns of health during the middle to late 20th century, but even now, infants are about twice as likely to die as older children and young adults.

Death rates for those between ages 5 and 40 are comparatively low, but starting around age 40, death rates begin to increase (USBC, 1992). This disadvantage for older people was dramatic in the Donner party—100% of those over age 49 died. Grayson's analysis indicated that those who survived were, on the average, younger than those who died, showing the advantage of young adulthood for survival under the harsh conditions of starvation and cold exposure. Aging is, of course, still strongly related to mortality, and older adults begin to show sharply increased mortality after age 55.

The female members of the Donner expedition were also more likely to survive than the male emigrants—56.6% of the boys and men died versus 29.4% of the girls and women. Furthermore, the men who died did so earlier in the expedition than the women. Grayson discussed the possible biological basis of women's advantage, including a lower basal metabolism rate and more subcutaneous fat. Both of these factors would lead women to be more resistant to starvation and cold, giving them a survival advantage in circumstances such as the Donner expedition endured. Such hardships are not a factor in many deaths, either in the 19th century or today, but the female advantage remains. Current life expectancy in the United States is not equal for women and men: Women's life expectancy is over six years longer than men's expected life span (USBC, 1992). For all causes of death and for all ethnic backgrounds, women have a lower mortality rate than men.

In addition to age and gender as factors in survival for members of the Donner expedition, family size was related to survival. Grayson examined size of the kin group for each person and discovered that those who survived were from larger family groups than those who died. Grayson attributed this survival advantage to social support, a factor that researchers Lisa Berkman and Lester Syme (1979) related to health and longevity. Berkman and Syme found that people who were part of families and other social networks were less likely to be seriously ill or to die than those with less social support. Grayson contended that social support in the form of a large kin group acted as a survival advantage in the Donner party. Grayson pointed out that many of the young adults who died had small kin groups; some were traveling without any family. This disadvantage appeared in Grayson's analysis for the men but not for the women in the group. That is, being part of a large family group was a survival advantage for the men but not for the women in the Donner party.

Of those in the Donner party who died from causes other than starvation and cold exposure, all were men. Before the expedition encountered weather problems, five men had died, four as a result of violence. None of the women died as a result of violence. This prevalence of men who die violently is similar to today's figures: Men are two to four times more likely than women to die of accidents, homicide, or suicide (USBC, 1992).

Therefore, the story of the Donner party is not only of historical interest but also provides a good illustration of demographic factors in mortality. For this group of emigrants in the 19th century as for the men and women of the late 20th century, gender is a factor in mortality. The women in the Donner party had a substantial survival advantage under conditions of starvation and cold exposure. Those conditions were unusual, but women of that time normally outlived men. Although mortality has decreased for both men and women, women of today have a greater survival advantage than during the 1800s—that is, women's survival advantage has increased rather than decreased during the past 100 years. However, women are more frequently patients in the health care system than are men. Neither mortality nor morbidity treats women and men equally, but rather treats each differently.

Mortality: No Equal Opportunity

"At every moment across the lifespan, from conception to death, girls and women are, on the average, biologically more advantaged and live longer than boys and men" (Strickland, 1988, p. 381). The life expectancy for men is currently shorter than for women, and this difference exists in all economically developed countries. Women's advantage in life expectancy is not a recent development but has existed for over 100 years, persisting over time and in many cultures. (See Diversity Highlight: "Life Expectancy around the World.") Figure 13.1 shows the advantage in life expectancy for women over the past 90 years in the United States. Notice the increase of the discrepancy during the first half of the 20th century and the recent narrowing of women's survival advantage. Also notice the difference between life expectancy for Whites and nonwhites, including the small discrepancy between men and women in the early 1900s, the advantage for Whites, and the increasing discrepancy in life expectancy for nonwhite women and men.

In addition, these gender differences hold in economically developed countries for the leading causes of death—cardiovascular disease, cancer, and accidents. These three causes of death account for about 70% of all deaths in the United States. For cardiovascular disease and cancer, men tend to die at younger ages than women, resulting in not only an excess of overall deaths of men but death at younger ages.

Cardiovascular Disease

Cardiovascular disease (CVD) includes a group of disorders involving the heart and circulatory system, some of which are life threatening and some of which are not. For example, angina pectoris is one of the disorders in this category, causing shortness of breath, difficulty in performing physical activities, and chest pain, but it poses no immediate threat to life. On the other hand, myocardial infarction (heart attack) and stroke

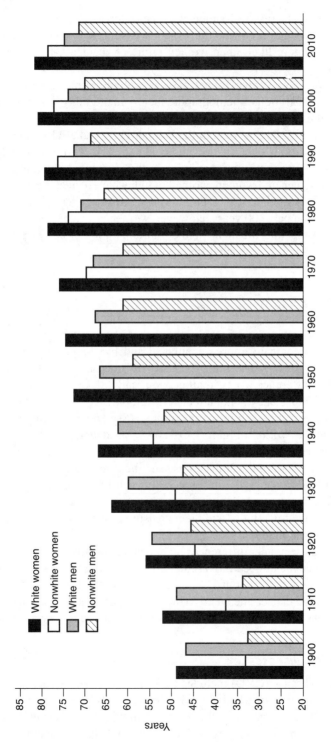

FIGURE 13.1 Life Expectancy for U.S. Women Men, 1900 to 2010 (1990 to 2010 projected)

SOURCE: From *Historical statistics of the United States, colonial times to 1970* (p. 55), U.S. Bureau of the Census, 1975, Washington, DC: U.S. Government Printing Office; and *Statistical abstract of the United States, 1992* (112th ed.) (p. 76), U.S. Bureau of the Census, 1992, Washington, DC: U.S. Government Printing Office.

DIVERSITY HIGHLIGHT
Life Expectancy around the World

The pattern of leading causes of death in the United States—cardiovascular disease, cancers, and accidents—also appears in other developed, industrialized countries. Cardiovascular disease and cancers are also the leading causes of death in other countries, including Australia, Canada, Finland, Israel, Italy, Japan, the Netherlands, Norway, Sweden, Switzerland, and the United Kingdom, but violent death is not as common in many of these countries as in the United States (Britannica Book of the Year, 1992). A different pattern appears in developing countries, and a third pattern occurs in undeveloped countries.

These three patterns can be seen in the table below. Notice the high rate of cardiovascular disease and cancer deaths in the developed countries compared to the developing countries. Countries such as Brazil and Egypt have lower death rates for cardiovascular disease and cancer but higher rates for infectious diseases. Infectious diseases tend to be fatal for infants and children more often than for adults, so the life expectancy in these countries is lower than that in developed countries.

Undeveloped countries such as Angola, Chad, Bangladesh, and Laos have lower life expectancies than developing countries and a higher rate of death due to infectious disease. Undeveloped countries also have poorer reporting concerning causes of death, so the figures from these countries may not be as accurate as in more developed countries, which keep better health records (Kane, 1991). The picture, however, is clear: A higher incidence of infectious illness decreases life expectancy, and countries with longer life expectancies show higher death rates for cardiovascular disease and cancer.

Cardiovascular disease and cancer are diseases that occur much more frequently in old age than in childhood or young adulthood, and countries with high rates of death from these causes tend to have a longer life expectancy than countries with lower CVD and cancer rates. Some developed countries, however, have much higher CVD and cancer rates than others, contributing to their relatively high death rates.

The survival advantage for women is larger in developed than in developing and undeveloped countries, and this difference is mainly attributable to the high death rate due to complications from pregnancy and childbirth (Kane, 1991). Poor health care services for pregnant women increase the

Average Life Expectancies, Death Rates, and Causes of Death for Developed, Developing, and Undeveloped Countries

Life Expectancy		Death Rate	Causes (per 100,000 population)			
Male	Female		CVD	Cancer	Accident	Infectious Disease
Developed Countries (Australia, Bulgaria, Canada, Finland, France, Germany, Israel, Italy, Japan, Sweden, Switzerland, USSR, United Kingdom, and United States; also Hong Kong)						
73.3	80	9	396.6	203.9	50.2	37+
Developing Countries (Brazil, India, Iran, Mexico, Peru, Thailand)						
63.3	67.8	7.3	147.7	68.52	84.5	55.7
Undeveloped Countries (Angola, Bangladesh, Chad, Laos)*						
46.5	48.5	17.3				

SOURCES: Causes of death from *Britannica book of the year, 1992* (pp. 538–741), 1992, Chicago: Encyclopedia Britannica; life expectancies from *The world factbook 1992,* Central Intelligence Agency, 1992, Washington, DC: U.S. Government Printing Office.
*Leading causes of death include bronchitis, influenza, pneumonia, sleeping sickness, malaria.

Continued

DIVERSITY HIGHLIGHT *Continued*

chances of maternal mortality as well as infant mortality due to complications during delivery. In some countries, complications during pregnancy and childbirth are the leading cause of death for women during their reproductive years.

Another practice that can decrease the survival advantage for girls and women is son preference—that is, the preference for sons over daughters (Kane, 1991). Son preference can lead to the murder of infant girls but is more often expressed through preferential treatment for sons—better feeding and medical attention. These advantages increase male chances for survival. Son preference is common in

south Asia and, combined with these countries' high rates of death during pregnancy and childbirth, results in close to equal life expectancies for men and women.

In countries where girls and boys receive more equal treatment during infancy and childhood, girls have a survival advantage over boys, as women do when compared to men. Thus, the female survival advantage holds across many cultures. Furthermore, women benefit more from the better health services that accompany economic prosperity and thus show more of a survival advantage in developed countries.

---

can be immediately fatal. Heart disease and stroke account for 45% of deaths in the United States (USBC, 1992). Although this rate is high, deaths from heart disease and stroke have decreased over the past 15 years, with stroke decreasing more rapidly than heart disease.

As Table 13.1 shows, heart disease mortality for women and men does not differ greatly over the life span, and women have more fatal strokes than men, but men die from CVD at younger ages than women. The discrepancy in heart disease deaths for men and women between ages 35 and 74 is especially dramatic, showing how much men are affected by premature death from this cause. In addition, deaths due to stroke have decreased 48% in the past two decades (Strickland, 1988).

Cardiovascular disease is one of the **chronic diseases**—health problems that develop over a period of time, often without noticeable symptoms, and persist over time without a complete cure. Such diseases differ from acute conditions such as infectious diseases or accidents. Acute conditions have a rapid onset with specific symptoms, and people can recover completely. CVD develops over years but exhibits few symptoms until the condition is serious. For many people, heart attack is the first symptom of cardiovascular disease, and almost half of those who have a heart attack die as a result (Ellestad, 1986). Thus, for many people, death is the first symptom of CVD.

About half of the people who have a heart attack survive, and that percentage has grown over the past two decades (Cohn, Kaplan, & Cohen, 1988). Improved hospital treatment and greater availability of paramedic care have contributed to the improvement in survival rates, and several options exist for diagnosis and treatment. Some of these diagnostic techniques are relatively simple and painless, but unfortunately, they tend to be less accurate in diagnosing CVD. The more accurate techniques tend to be more involved and invasive.

A gender difference exists in the rate at which physicians refer people who report symptoms of CVD for further testing and treatment, with women being treated less aggressively than men (Ayanian & Epstein, 1991; Steingart et al., 1991). Women are less likely than men to receive further diagnostic testing and treatment for cardiovascular disease when they report the same symptoms as men. Richard Steingart and his colleagues (1991) found that men were twice as likely to be recommended for extensive cardiac testing or for coronary bypass surgery than women. John Ayanian and Arnold Epstein (1991) found a similar pattern, with women receiving treatment at later stages of the disease than men. Such neglect could be a negative factor in the outcome of treatment (or alternatively, men might be overtreated for possible CVD).

These differences in treatment indicate either overt or covert bias on the part of health care professionals, who may choose to ignore women's complaints, dismissing their reports of symptoms as inaccurate or overstated. Alternatively, these professionals may succumb to the stereotypical belief that women do not experience CVD as frequently as men and thus discount the likelihood that women's symptoms indicate CVD. Either or some combination of these two approaches in dealing with women's reports of symptoms might account for the less aggressive treatment of CVD in women.

As with other chronic diseases, the causes of cardiovascular disease are not well understood. No infection or other specific agent appears to be responsible, but instead, several physical conditions and behaviors are risk factors in the development of CVD. A **risk factor** is associated with an increased probability that a condition will develop. For example, high blood pressure is a risk factor for CVD in that people with elevated blood pressure have an increased risk of heart attack and stroke.

Gender is a risk factor for CVD, with men at elevated risk compared to women. Karen Matthews (1989) hypothesized that biological sex might not be as much of a risk factor in disease as gender role and the behaviors related to these roles. That is, male physiology might not be the primary risk factor, but risky behaviors that are more typical of men might be. For example, smoking and eating a high-fat diet are risk factors for cardiovascular disease, and more men than women smoke and eat a diet high in fat. Thus, behaviors that increase risk are part of gender roles. James Harrison (1978) may

TABLE 13.1   U.S. Death Rates for Cardiovascular Disease in Men and Women, 1989 (in thousands)

Age	Women Stroke	Women Heart Disease	Men Stroke	Men Heart Disease
<15	0.1	0.6	0.1	0.7
15–24	0.1	0.3	0.1	0.6
25–34	0.5	1.1	0.5	2.4
35–44	1.1	2.9	1.3	8.8
45–54	2.2	7.9	2.4	23.1
55–64	4.8	25.1	5.7	56.2
65–74	13.0	64.2	13.3	101.6
75–84	29.9	122.0	20.8	112.3
85+	36.5	141.5	13.1	62.4
Total	88.2	365.7	57.3	368.2

SOURCE: From *Statistical abstracts of the United States, 1992* (112th ed.) (p. 83), U.S. Bureau of the Census, 1992, Washington, DC: U.S. Government Printing Office.

have been correct when he wrote his article titled "Warning: The Male Sex Role May Be Dangerous to Your Health."

Vicki Helgeson (1990) confirmed Harrison's assertion, finding that some aspects of the male role were predictive of heart attack severity. She surveyed male and female heart attack patients to determine their gender roles, using a questionnaire that separated the positive aspects of masculinity and femininity from the negative aspects. For example, aggression, hostility, and not needing others are negative aspects of the masculine gender role—that is, characteristics associated with men that are not positive—whereas decisiveness is also stereotypically masculine but is a positive characteristic. Men were more likely to have high scores on negative masculinity than women, and high scores on the index of negative masculinity were related to heart attack severity for both men and women. This research demonstrated that the association between sex and health risk may be mediated by gender role factors.

Marianne Frankenhaeuser (1991) has investigated gender differences in physiological responses to stress, attempting to find a link between stress and the physical responses to stress that might be a clue in the development of cardiovascular disease. She found a number of gender-related differences in the release of epinephrine as a response to stress, and because epinephrine elevates heart rate and blood pressure, increases in its release could relate to cardiovascular problems.

Frankenhaeuser found that boys and men reacted more strongly and their bodies released more epinephrine than girls and women under conditions of performance stress. These gender-related differences were greatest when the stress was less severe and decreased under conditions of more severe stress, although even under extreme performance stress, men showed higher epinephrine release than women. However, women and men who held similar management positions and experienced similar stresses showed similar levels of epinephrine release. That is, this gender-related difference in reactivity to stressful situations may relate more strongly to the positions that men and women typically occupy than to biological sex. Nonetheless, these differences may account for some of the gender differences in the development of CVD.

In summary, cardiovascular disease, including heart disease and stroke, is the leading cause of death in the United States, accounting for about 45% of deaths. Men die of heart disease at younger ages than women, but the overall death rates are similar. Stroke is a more common cause of death in women than men, but women die of stroke at older ages. The death rates from both heart disease and stroke have fallen in the past 15 years, with strokes decreasing at a more rapid rate than heart disease. These gender differences in risk may be related to physiological differences, but they may also be a facet of gender-related behaviors. Research has indicated that negative aspects of the masculine role are related to heart attack severity, demonstrating that the masculine role may be a factor in the leading cause of death.

Cancer

Cancer is the term applied to a variety of malignant neoplasms, the uncontrolled growth of tissue that may form a tumor as well as spread to other areas of the body.

Most types of tissue can develop cancers, and these growths are not restricted to human or even to animal tissues. That is, plants and all types of animals develop malignancies. Such uncontrolled growths can be life threatening, and cancer is the second leading cause of death in the United States, accounting for about 23% of deaths.

Men have a higher overall death rate from cancer than women, including the totals for all cancer types and at all ages. Table 13.2 presents the mortality rates for women and men for various ages and types of cancer. As the table shows, some gender differ-

TABLE 13.2   U.S. Death Rates for Cancer in Women and Men by Age, 1989 (per 100,000)

Women

Age	Lung	Breast	Digestive System	Genital	Lymphatic (excluding leukemia)	Leukemia	Urinary
35–44	5.5	17.7	5.4	6.9	2.3	2.0	0.7
45–54	34.2	44.7	22.0	18.5	6.1	3.9	3.1
55–64	104.3	78.6	68.2	39.5	17.5	9.1	8.9
65–74	175.9	111.1	154.5	70.1	39.2	19.1	19.4
75–84	187.7	147.5	301.2	93.6	72.5	37.2	38.1
85+	128.1	185.8	485.4	109.7	82.8	63.5	63.3

Total: 183.0 per 100,000*

Men

Age	Lung	Breast	Digestive System	Genital	Lymphatic (excluding leukemia)	Leukemia	Urinary
35–44	9.0	0.1	8.4	0.7	4.7	2.7	1.4
45–54	64.1	0.2	38.9	2.9	10.5	5.3	7.0
55–64	227.1	0.6	124.5	27.0	26.2	14.6	22.7
65–74	425.5	1.1	261.8	113.7	53.4	35.1	50.1
75–84	581.3	2.2	458.9	340.5	101.0	71.9	106.6
85+	500.7	4.1	670.1	698.0	128.8	100.0	174.1

Total: 217.6 per 100,000*

SOURCE: From *Statistical abstracts of the United States, 1992* (112th ed.) (p. 89), U.S. Bureau of the Census, Washington, DC: U.S. Government Printing Office.

*All ages, including individuals under age 35 and cancers of other sites.

ences exist according to site and age of death. For example, women are much more likely to develop breast cancer than are men (although men do get breast cancer), and women have earlier mortality rates for cancers of the genitals and reproductive organs than men. Lung cancer is the leading site of fatal cancer for both men and women, but more men die of lung cancer than women.

Cigarette smoking is a major factor in lung cancer death. The gender difference from this cause of death reflects the past difference in smoking rates for men and women—that is, until recently more men than women have been smokers. Smoking takes time to produce health problems, so past smoking differences continue to appear in current health statistics (USDHHS, 1989). However, the increase in women's rates of smoking and the decrease in men's rates of smoking will produce changes in the future: Women will develop lung cancer more, and men will develop it less often. This pattern has already started to appear. In 1986 lung cancer passed breast cancer as the leading cause of cancer deaths among women. However, the overall lung cancer death rate has started to level off.

According to Richard Doll and Richard Peto (1981), use of tobacco products accounts for about 30% of cancers and diet for another 35%. In addition to foods that contain known or suspected carcinogens, dietary components have been implicated in the development of cancer, especially a high-fat diet. A substantial amount of evidence indicates that people who eat a high-fat diet are at increased risk for cancers of the digestive tract. In addition, a high-fat diet for women can increase their chance of breast cancer (Travis, 1988a). On the average, women eat a lower-fat diet than men, so this behavioral difference may explain some of the discrepancy in cancer death rate.

Another dietary difference that may relate to cancer comes from intake of foods high in beta carotene, vitamins C and E, and selenium. Mounting evidence indicates that these nutrients may offer some protection against cancer, putting "meat and potatoes" men at a disadvantage. Beta-carotene is abundant in carrots, sweet potatoes, and other yellow vegetables. Vitamin C comes from many types of fruits and vegetables and is high in citrus fruits. Vitamin E and selenium occur in grain products. In addition, the fiber in fruits and vegetables provide dietary benefits that may include protection against cancer.

Occupational exposure accounts for another 4% of cancer deaths (Doll & Peto, 1981). Men are at increased risk for cancers due to their exposure to workplace hazards (Waldron, 1991). Men are more likely than women to hold jobs that bring them into contact with carcinogens such as asbestos, benzene, and various petroleum products. Exposure to such substances may also be a factor in the difference in cancer deaths between women and men.

Sexual behavior and reproduction also contribute to the development of cancer, and Doll and Peto (1981) estimated that about 7% of cancers are attributable to these factors. Women who have sexual intercourse at an early age and have many sexual partners are at elevated risk for cancers of the reproductive tract (Levy, 1985). These cancers constitute less of a risk than breast cancer, and women who complete a pregnancy before age 20 are at decreased risk for breast cancer compared to women with later pregnancies and to women who do not bear children. Thus, early intercourse presents a risk and early pregnancy a protection against cancer.

Men's sexual behavior can place them at risk for cancer, but their behavior can also be a risk for their female sex partners (Levy, 1985). Men who are the receptive partner in unprotected anal intercourse are at increased risk for anal cancer as well as for infection with human immunodeficiency virus (HIV) which is related to the development of acquired immune deficiency syndrome (AIDS). One of the diseases associated with AIDS is a form of cancer, Kaposi's sarcoma. Thus, receptive anal intercourse is a direct risk for anal cancer and an indirect risk for Kaposi's sarcoma. Men who have many sexual partners, especially those who have sex with prostitutes, endanger their partners by elevating the women's risk for cervical cancer. In addition, men's poor genital hygiene is associated with increased risk of cervical cancer in their female sexual partners.

As Table 13.2 shows, women experience a higher mortality rate from cancers of the genitals than men until after age 65 years. Mortality from cancers of the genitals and reproductive tract plus breast cancer deaths account for much of women's cancer deaths during early and middle adulthood. Indeed, cancer is responsible for a greater proportion of women's deaths than cardiovascular disease until after age 65. The opposite pattern occurs for cardiovascular deaths, with men vulnerable to premature death from CVD. Although men have a higher mortality from cancer, women are vulnerable to premature death due to cancer.

Violent Deaths

Violent deaths account for about 4% of deaths in the United States (USBC, 1992), reflecting a relatively high rate of violence compared to other industrialized, economically developed countries. Violent death rates are lower in Australia, Canada, Japan, most of the countries in Western Europe, Scandinavia, and other countries scattered throughout the world (Britannica Book of the Year, 1992). Men are about three times more likely than women to die of accidents, suicide, and homicide. This discrepancy holds for all ages, from birth until old age, and the differences are most pronounced early in life. Violent deaths are the leading cause of death for adolescents and were the leading cause of death for young adults until 1993, when AIDS took that place (CDC: News..., 1995). Men are at least three times more likely to die violently than are women (Waldron, 1991).

People from different ethnic backgrounds are not equally likely to die of violence. As Table 13.3 shows, African Americans in the United States are much more likely than European Americans to die from accidents and homicide, but European Americans are more likely to die from motor vehicle accidents and suicide. The ethnic and age differences in violent deaths are reflected in Table 13.3, revealing that young men are at much greater risk than young women and that African-American men are disproportionately vulnerable, especially to death due to homicide.

**TABLE 13.3   U.S. Death Rates from Accidents and Violence, 1989
(per 100,000 population)**

Cause	European Americans		African Americans	
	Women	Men	Women	Men
Motor vehicle	12.1	27.0	9.3	28.3
Other accidents	12.7	24.5	15.0	37.0
Suicide	5.2	21.4	2.4	12.2
Homicide	2.8	8.2	12.9	61.1
All Accidents and Violent Deaths				
Ages				
15–24	32.7	107.1	33.9	188.0
25–34	26.6	96.0	47.4	205.9
35–44	24.7	80.4	40.8	184.9
45–54	25.5	73.8	30.8	144.0
55–64	28.7	80.1	37.3	130.6
65+	81.4	122.4	87.8	187.1
Average*	32.8	81.1	39.4	138.6

SOURCE: From *Statistical abstracts of the United States, 1992* (112th ed.) (p. 88), U.S. Bureau of the Census, Washington, DC: U.S. Government Printing Office.
*Includes individuals under 15 years old.

The gender differences in risky behaviors account for the differences in risk of violent death. Men tend to behave in ways that increase their risks, such as heavy alcohol use, low seat belt use, occupational risks, and illegal activities. Alcohol use increases the chances of accidents, suicide, and homicide (Eckhardt et al., 1981). By slowing responses and altering judgment, alcohol contributes to traffic accidents. People who have been drinking (even those who are not legally intoxicated) are more likely to be involved in fatal traffic accidents; about half of all traffic fatalities are related to alcohol. Seat belt use is an important factor in traffic fatalities, and women are more likely to use seat belts than men (Tipton, Camp, & Hsu, 1990). For the same reasons that alcohol use increases the chances of traffic accidents, alcohol use is also related to death from falls, fires, and drownings as well as to boating, airplane, and industrial accidents. Intoxication also increases the chances of being a pedestrian victim of an auto accident (U.S. Department of Health and Human Services [USDHHS], 1990).

About 70% of adults in the United States drink alcohol, but only about 9 to 10% are heavy drinkers (USDHHS, 1990). This 10% of the population accounts for about half of all alcohol consumed. Any amount of alcohol consumption can increase the risk of accidents, but heavy drinking is especially risky. Men are more likely to be heavy drinkers than women; about 14% of men but only 4% of women are heavy drinkers (Travis, 1988a). In addition, drinking varies by age group, with younger adults being heavier drinkers. These gender and age differences in drinking patterns correspond to the differential risks of violent death. The gender differences in alcohol consumption may be decreasing, as more women have begun drinking at light and moderate levels, and a significant increase has taken place in problem drinking among women (Rodin & Ickovics, 1990). These changes have the potential to decrease the current female advantage in avoiding violent death.

Men are also more likely to hold risky jobs than women (Waldron, 1991). In addition to exposure to hazardous materials, which increases the chances of cancer, men are more likely than women to have jobs that involve working around or operating dangerous machinery. Around 95% of the fatal accidents at work involve men, and Ingrid Waldron (1991) estimated that gender differences in workplace accidents account for between 2 and 3% of the total gender difference in mortality in the United States. Therefore, occupational accidents are a substantial factor in the gender difference of accidental deaths.

Men are more likely to be the victims of suicide, but women make more suicide attempts (Kessler & McRae, 1983). This difference has not always existed but began to appear during the 1950s, increased during the 1960s, and began to decrease during the 1970s. The ratio of attempted to completed suicides is about 10 to 1 (Travis, 1988a). The main reason for the higher rate of suicide completion among men is that they choose more lethal methods, such as guns and jumping from high places, whereas women more often attempt suicide by taking drugs. (No method is certain to be successful or to be nonlethal, so any suicide attempt is serious.) The lethality of the chosen method produces a higher suicide rate among men, despite women's more frequent attempts.

Chapter 9 described the gender difference in crime rate, explaining that men are more likely than women to commit crimes. This discrepancy is even greater for crimes involving violence, with men being the more likely perpetrators and victims (U.S. Department of Justice, 1990). The increase in lawbreaking among women in the past decades has not changed these figures, as the increasing number of women who commit crimes are more likely to be involved in nonviolent crimes. Thus, homicide affects men to a larger degree than women, with an especially disproportional impact on young African-American men.

In summary, men die in accidents, by suicide, and by homicide at a higher rate than women. Alcohol use contributes to all of these causes of violent deaths, and men are more likely to be heavy users of alcohol than women. In addition, women are more likely to use automobile seat belts, protecting them in case of crashes. Men are more likely to have jobs that subject them to workplace accidents, placing them at higher risk than women at work. Although women make more attempts, men complete suicide more often. Men are more likely to be involved in violent illegal activities and are the more frequent perpetrators and victims of homicide. This difference is especially prominent for African-American men. All of these causes of violent deaths put men at a survival disadvantage and account for some of women's survival advantage. Women, however, do not experience the same advantages when seeking health care; women experience greater morbidity than men.

The Health Care System

Although women live longer than men, they are sick more often. Defining what constitutes being sick is not simple, but using hospital admissions, restriction of activities, or self-description as indicators, women meet any of these definitions of illness more often than men (Travis, 1988a). The combination of greater morbidity with lower mortality seems a contradiction, but several possibilities exist to reconcile these two findings. The first possibility involves the difference in gender roles related to seeking and receiving health care. Another possibility is that women's reproduction and its medicalization account for their increased use of medical services; pregnancy and childbirth are functions that now receive medical attention. A third possibility is that women are not as healthy as men but that their health problems are less often life-threatening, producing the combination of poorer health but longer life.

Gender Roles and Health Care

People seek and receive health care from a variety of formal and informal sources, and gender roles are a factor in receiving help from both types of sources. Traditional male and female gender roles differ in amount of vulnerability and the permissibility of seeking help. One facet of the masculine role, the Sturdy Oak, holds that men are strong and invulnerable; this aspect of the role would restrain men from showing signs of physical illness or seeking medical care (Brannon, 1976). The traditional feminine role, on the other hand, allows and even encourages weakness and vulnerability to emotional and physical problems (Lorber, 1975).

Elizabeth Klonoff and Hope Landrine (1992) confirmed that feminine gender role orientation was related to reporting symptoms of illness. These researchers also found that unemployment was a significant factor in symptom reporting and that women were more likely than men to have no employment outside their homes. Thus, adherence to traditional gender roles may hinder men from seeking help for their symptoms, but elements of the traditional feminine gender role relate positively to women's seeking medical care.

These traditional roles are not the only determinant in health-related behaviors. Klonoff and Landrine found that feminine gender role and unemployment account for only part of the gender-related variations in seeking medical care; the expectations generated by these roles influence both people who seek and those who provide such care. That is, women and men may behave differently in seeking medical care, but the health care professionals who provide care tend to treat men and women differently.

Gender and Seeking Health Care

The decision to seek medical care is influenced by many factors, including the perception of symptoms and beliefs about the consequences of seeking or failing to seek treatment. People who feel healthy may enter the medical care system when they receive routine exams, but many skip such screening procedures, finding it easy to ignore their health as long as they feel well. Charlotte Muller (1990) pointed out that men are more likely to avoid regular health care than women. Men are less likely than women to have a regular physician, sometimes avoiding checkups for years. Men explain these omissions in terms consistent with the masculine gender role, saying that they feel fine and thus do not need to consult a physician. This belief can be fatal, as cardiovascular disease often develops with few symptoms, and the first sign of heart disease can be a fatal heart attack. Nonetheless, the belief that a lack of symptoms equals good health can lead men to avoid regular contacts with the health care system.

Women, on the other hand, find it more difficult to avoid the health care system, regardless of how well they may feel. Penny Kane (1991) explained that young women must seek medical advice to obtain many forms of contraception, especially birth control pills. These young women count in the statistics as women who have consulted a physician, but no illness is involved in their medical care. Furthermore, such medical consultations often include physical examinations that may reveal health problems that require additional treatment. For example, blood tests may reveal anemia, and blood pressure readings may show hypertension. Each of these conditions merits further treatment, involving these women in additional physician visits and medication. Young men receive no comparable medical attention during young adulthood to reveal physical problems, and these differences in treatment for healthy young men and women contribute to the statistics concerning gender differences in seeking health care.

The personal perception of symptoms is an important factor in seeking medical care. People who sense that their body is not working correctly are more likely to seek medical advice than those who sense no problem. Perceiving a symptom, however, is not sufficient to lead people to make an appointment with their physician. Although some people readily seek professional medical advice and care, most people experience some degree of reluctance to become part of the health care system.

This reluctance has many origins, including financial resources, convenience and accessibility of medical care, and personal considerations. Health care costs have risen faster than personal income, making them an increasing problem for many people. Scheduling of appointments and changing of one's daily routine to keep a medical appointment are problems that contribute to personal reluctance. In addition, anxiety about the diagnosis or treatment may keep people from seeking professional care; the diagnosis may be threatening, or the treatment may be painful or expensive, or both.

These factors that influence reluctance to seek medical care may not affect men and women equally. Gender can be a factor in the financial considerations involved in seeking health care. Women are more likely than men to be outside the paid work force and to be employed on a part-time basis, whereas men are more likely to have the types of jobs that offer health insurance benefits. Muller (1990) pointed out that their employment situations can put women at a disadvantage in seeking health care, leaving them with less money to pay for health care and without the health insurance that might cover their expenses.

Women can be included in these health insurance benefits if they are married to men who have good insurance plans. For both men and women in this situation, continued health insurance depends on the continued employment of the men and the continuation of the marriage. Not only can women lose their health insurance through divorce, but children can also lose insurance coverage due to their parents' divorce. Mothers are most often granted custody, and children may lose their coverage unless their mothers have employment that includes these benefits. Thus, women and children are less likely to have health insurance than men, making health care less accessible for these individuals.

The male gender role, with its emphasis on physical invulnerability, influences men, making them less willing to seek medical care. Research by Lois Verbrugge (1986) offered confirmation that gender roles affect likelihood of seeking care. She reported that men and women have similar experiences of daily symptoms, but women are more likely to seek medical care for these symptoms. James Pennebaker (1982) studied factors involved in the perception of physical symptoms—how people interpret their body's signals. His research suggested that women are more sensitive to their body's signals than men, making women more capable of reporting a physical symptom, and their traditional gender role allows them to do so more readily than men.

Men and women also seek health care from different types of providers (Kane, 1991). Both women and men are more likely to consult a pharmacist than any other type of health care professional, and women make more inquiries than men. Kane suggested that women may ask pharmacists for advice about over-the-counter remedies for their entire family, so the number of consultations may not reflect any gender difference in personal need. Men experience more injuries due to accidents and sports participation, so they are more likely to seek the services of a physiotherapist than are women. Women, on the other hand, are more likely to seek the services of a chiropractor or a nutritionist. Women are also more likely to use alternative health care services, such as herbal medicine and acupuncture. None of these differences is large; thus, the types of health care professionals that men and women seek vary to a small extent.

The difference in seeking medical care may be partly attributable to access to medical care, with women at a disadvantage due to their financial resources and poorer insurance coverage. Another difference may lie in women's greater sensitivity to symptoms, but a difference also exists in the willingness to report symptoms. These differences are consistent with the gender roles with men denying and women accepting help.

Gender and Receiving Health Care

After a person has contacted a health care professional and becomes part of the health care system, gender becomes a factor in treatment. Again, gender roles influence the behavior of both patient and practitioner. Although some patients and practitioners are coming to view their relationship as a collaboration, the traditional conceptualization of the patient-practitioner relationship has included the subordinate patient and the controlling practitioner. The patient role is thus more compatible with the stereotypically feminine than the stereotypically masculine role, whereas the practitioner role is more consistent with traditional masculinity. The combination of gender roles and patient-provider roles puts women at a disadvantage in receiving equitable medical care.

Both women and men may have trouble adopting the patient role. Being a patient requires a person to relinquish control and follow the advice or orders of the practitioner.

Gender is not a reliable predictor of patient compliance (Brannon & Feist, 1992), but the combination of the demographic factors of gender, age, ethnic background, cultural norms, religion, and educational level relate to patients' compliance with physicians' treatment advice. For example, people who are part of a culture that trusts physicians and accepts their advice as the best way to get well are more likely to follow physicians' advice than people from cultures that accept herbalists as the preferred health care professionals. Therefore, gender is only one factor in a configuration of variables that relate to compliance with medical advice. Indeed, the interaction between patient and practitioner is more important in following health advice than patients' personal characteristics, and gender is often a factor in that interaction.

The medical profession has been the target of criticism for its treatment of female patients, and this criticism has taken several forms. The most radical form of criticism holds that women were healers throughout history but have been replaced by a technological, male-dominated form of healing, with female nurses and male physicians (Ehrenreich & English, 1973). Other critics, such as Cheryl Travis (1988a), have protested that negative stereotypes of female patients have led to a poorer level of medical care for them than for men. Yet other critics, such as Carol Tavris (1992), have protested the use of men as the medical standard against which women are compared, claiming that omitting women from medical training and research leaves physicians ill prepared to treat women.

Travis (1988a) argued that physicians often have stereotypical views of women, and these views influence their treatment of female patients. She further contended that medical school promotes the view that women are emotional and incapable of providing accurate information about their bodies. This view leads physicians to discount the information provided by female patients and to believe that women cannot participate in decisions concerning their own health and treatment. Such physicians may reveal too little information to female patients to allow them to make informed choices about options concerning their care.

Evidence supporting Travis's view comes from the treatment women receive when they have heart disease. Women are less likely than men to receive additional testing and treatment when they report symptoms of heart disease (Steingart et al., 1991). Instead, women are more likely to be referred for psychiatric treatment. This failure to take symptom reports as a serious indication of heart disease and the tendency to refer women for psychiatric services demonstrate that women do not have the credibility that men have when they report symptoms of heart disease. Only after women have experienced a heart attack is their treatment comparable to men's treatment.

Tavris's (1992) criticism was aimed toward a more subtle type of discrimination in medicine. She contended that medical training represents men as the standard. Physicians receive instruction about how to dissect and prescribe drugs for a standard patient, a 154-pound man. With men as the standard, women become exceptions. Thus, any condition that men do not develop comes to be considered as deviant, including even the normal conditions associated with women's physiology—menstruation, pregnancy, and childbirth.

In addition to holding men as the standard in medicine, a great deal of medical research has omitted women entirely; that is, many studies have failed to include women as research subjects. The rationale for such omissions have included both women's low rate of developing certain diseases and women's hormonal variations. For example, women develop cardiovascular disease at a lower rate than men, so studies that follow healthy people until they show signs of cardiovascular disease would have to include many more women than men to obtain a group of women with this disorder. Using only male subjects results in studies that are easier to complete but reveal nothing about cardiovascular disease in women. Assuming that women are similar to men in their development of CVD is unwarranted, because their differences are the motivation for excluding women from these studies.

Medical researchers have also excluded women from studies that test the safety and effectiveness of new drugs because women experience cyclic variations in their hormonal levels. The researchers have feared that hormonal variations may interact with medication, making the task of assessing drug effects more difficult. As Tavris pointed out, omitting women from such studies may be convenient for researchers but dangerous for women. If women have not participated in the testing, then the drug's safety and effectiveness have not been established for them.

During the 1980s, the practice of excluding women from medical research was the target of increasing criticism, and pressure mounted to give additional emphasis to women's health. That pressure resulted in the creation of the Office of Research on Women's Health, a part of the National Institutes of Health (Kirschstein, 1991). This office's mission is to improve the prevention and treatment of diseases in women, and one of its first steps was to attempt to end the exclusion of women from medical research studies with U.S. government sponsorship.

Some of the participants at a 1992 conference on women's health proposed the creation of a new medical specialty on women's health (Skolnick, 1992). Those who advocate such a specialty claim that the medical specialties of obstetrics and gynecology emphasize surgery rather than the primary care of women. These advocates believe that all medical students should receive education and training concerning women's health.

No comparable movement has proposed a medical specialty on men's health. Although medicine is male dominated, men may not receive optimum or even appropriate care. During childhood, parents are somewhat more likely to take their sons to the doctor than their daughters (Kane, 1991), but once men are responsible for seeking their own medical care, they tend to avoid regular medical care. Men seek care for their injuries but not for regular exams and screening tests. Kane reported a survey in which men were more likely than women to say that they had been ill within the past two weeks but had failed to seek medical care. Men are less likely to have a regular physician than women, so getting an appointment to see a physician is a greater inconvenience in that they must first find a physician. However, when they become involved in the health care system, they are more likely to be taken seriously in their reports of symptoms and more likely to receive aggressive treatment, as in the case of heart disease.

In summary, the Sturdy Oak component of the male gender role may be a factor in men's avoiding health care; feelings of invulnerability and the belief that illness represents weakness lead men to ignore their health. Such avoidance can result in serious health problems that might have been prevented or detected through routine physical exams. Men can avoid regular physical exams more easily than women, as they typically require no medical assistance connected with reproduction or contraception, the primary contacts that women of reproductive age have with the health care system. Thus, men seldom use the health care system until they become ill, perhaps to the detriment of their health. Not only do reproduction and contraception prompt women and not men to seek medical care during the reproductive years, the differences in their reproductive systems account for a large proportion of the gender difference in seeking and receiving health care.

Reproductive Health

Many of women's encounters with the health care system do not involve illness but occur as a result of contraception, pregnancy, childbirth, and menopause. Although these functions were accomplished throughout history with little medical assistance, they became increasingly "medicalized" during the 19th and 20th centuries (Ehrenreich & English, 1973). Knowledge of physiology increased dramatically during the 19th century, with resulting changes in medicine, including growth and increase of educational requirements for medical practice. During this time, college education was restricted largely to men, and they came to dominate the growing profession of medicine.

This expansion of medicine included attending women during childbirth, a role that had been performed by midwives. Childbirth was not the only function to gain medical attention; pregnancy came to be considered an appropriate area for regular medical care. The increasing number of contraceptive technologies during the 20th century almost exclusively depended on controlling women's rather than men's fertility, and physicians gained control over access to contraception techniques such as birth control pills. During the middle of the 20th century, even menopause became a "disease" that could be "cured" by hormone replacement (Wilson, 1966). Thus, medicine has become involved in all facets of women's reproductive health, from contraception during adolescence to hormone replacement after menopause.

Some critics have argued that medicine has burdened women by forcing them to give birth in sterile, impersonal surroundings and subjecting them to increasingly large hospital bills for these services. According to this argument, birth is a natural process requiring no medical intervention. However, as statistics from the time before routine medical care during pregnancy and delivery suggest, death is also a natural process. There is no question that technological medicine has dramatically cut both maternal and infant mortality (Kane, 1991). Nonetheless, women may receive treatment that is inappropriate. As Muller (1990) suggested, women may be overtreated in some ways (such as too many hysterectomies or Cesarean section deliveries) and undertreated in other respects (such as too little testing or surgery for symptoms of heart disease).

Kane (1991) argued that women's more numerous consultations with health care professionals are due largely to their more complex reproductive system. Not only do women get pregnant and bear children, but the organs of their reproductive system are subject to a greater variety of problems than the male system. Figure 13.2 shows the female and Figure 13.3 the male reproductive system. Except for children under age 15 years, girls and women receive more treatment for problems related to their reproductive system than boys and men.

Both systems can have problems in prenatal development, producing individuals with a mismatch between internal and external reproductive organs (refer to Chapter 3 for a more complete discussion of such cases). Some of the problems in the reproductive organs that appear during early childhood begin prenatally and result in congenital conditions that are more common in boys than girls. During infancy and early childhood, boys have more problems with their genitourinary system than girls, requiring more hospital stays and physician consultations for these problems (Kane, 1991). Beginning at age 15 years, girls make more visits to health care professionals regarding their reproductive systems and require more hospitalizations.

The majority of the physician visits and hospitalizations for women during their reproductive years involve contraception, pregnancy, and childbirth, and most of these contacts with the health care system are not due to illness or problems but because women's reproductive functions have come under medical supervision. Although over 80% of pregnancies and deliveries proceed without any problem, most women in industrialized countries receive medical care during their pregnancies, and the majority of deliveries take place in a hospital (Hyde, 1990). This system has unquestionably

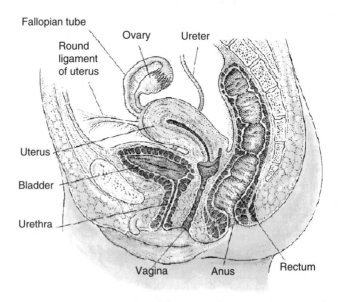

FIGURE 13.2 Female Reproductive System

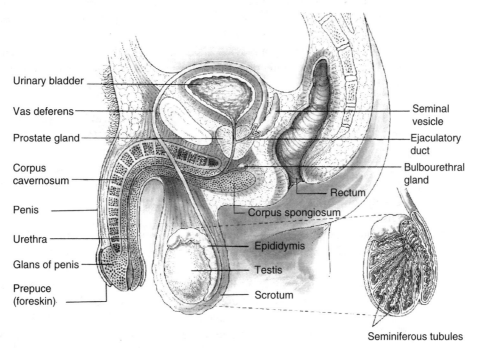

Urinary bladder

Vas deferens

Prostate gland

Corpus
cavernosum

Penis

Urethra

Glans of penis

Prepuce
(foreskin)

Seminal
vesicle

Ejaculatory
duct

Bulbourethral
gland

Rectum

Corpus spongiosum

Epididymis

Testis

Scrotum

Seminiferous tubules

FIGURE 13.3   Male Reproductive System

decreased mortality during pregnancy and delivery, but these visits count toward the statistics showing women's greater use of health care.

Many of the methods of contraception for women—birth control pills, intrauterine devices (IUDs), diaphragms, sterilization, abortion—not only require medical supervision but also increase health risks. For example, birth control pills provide very effective contraception, but women over age 35 years who take contraceptive pills have significantly increased risk of stroke, and smoking multiplies this risk (Rodin & Ickovics, 1990). Therefore, contraception is not only more often a woman's responsibility but also more of a health threat to women.

Both men and women are subject to **sexually transmitted diseases (STDs)**, infectious diseases that are spread through sexual contact. The infectious agents can be bacterial, viral, fungal, or parasitic, and many can be transmitted by vaginal, oral, or anal sexual activity. These bacterial infections include gonorrhea, syphilis, and chlamydia and do not always produce symptoms; women especially are likely to be symptom free until advanced stages of the diseases. Although bacterial infections can be cured by antibiotics, people without symptoms may not receive treatment until their disease is serious. Furthermore, delays in treatment allow infected persons to transmit the disease to others.

Delays in treatment are also a problem for the fungal and parasitic STDs. *Candidiasis albicans,* a yeastlike fungus, produces itching and swelling of the genitals. It can be transmitted through sexual intercourse, but this infection is not always an STD, being more common in women who take contraceptive pills or who are pregnant or diabetic. These conditions alter the chemistry of the vagina, allowing this fungus to grow at a rapid rate, producing annoying and painful symptoms. Chemical treatments exist to control this type of infection. Trichomoniasis is a one-celled animal that can infect the vagina in women and the urethra in men. It is almost always sexually transmitted, and an effective drug treatment exists.

No drugs exist to cure viral diseases, and thus the viral STDs pose an even more serious problem than other types of STDs. The human immunodeficiency virus (HIV) is the virus that produces acquired immune deficiency syndrome (AIDS), and this virus can be sexually transmitted. The virus damages the immune system, leaving the body open to a variety of diseases. Years may pass between infection and the development of symptoms, allowing an infected person to be unaware of his or her condition and to transmit the infection to others.

Genital herpes, viral hepatitis, and genital warts are also viral STDs. Genital warts sometimes can be surgically removed, and several medications exist to manage the symptoms of herpes infections. Like other viral infections, these STDs are difficult to manage and presently without a cure. Herpes infections are especially problematic, producing chronic problems with painful blisters on the genitals.

Not all problems of the reproductive organs are related to reproduction; these organs can be the site of diseases and cancers. Again, women are more likely than men to seek health care concerning problems with their reproductive organs. Although women are at greater risk for cancers of organs in the reproductive system than men throughout young and middle adulthood, men are most likely to develop testicular cancer at a young age, between ages 20 and 35 years (Hyde, 1990). This form of cancer is quite rare, affecting only 2 of 100,000 men, but men are most likely to develop this form of cancer during the years when they tend to avoid regular physical checkups. They may have no regular physician to tell about the lump they have detected on a testicle, and the tumor may go untreated for a dangerously long period. This form of cancer is rarely fatal if treated early, but fatality rates rise sharply with delays in treatment, going from a 90% survival rate to only a 25% survival rate. Thus, this rare form of cancer that affects men in their 20s may be more often fatal than it would be if men gave more attention to their health.

Prostate cancer is much more common than testicular cancer, but prostate cancer tends to develop in older men. This form of cancer is not common until after age 75 years, when it increases sharply (USBC, 1992). Malignant tumors of the prostate typically are small and grow slowly, making this form of cancer less life threatening than many other forms (Hyde, 1990). Even without malignancy, the prostate enlarges, beginning during puberty, which can cause problems, such as difficulty during urination, and require surgery.

Cervical cancer is the most common cancer of the genitals in women, accounting for 13% of cancers in women (Travis, 1988a). Women can also develop cancer of the uterine lining (endometrium), ovaries, vulva, vagina, and fallopian tubes, but these cancers together account for only 18% of cancers in women (Levy, Ewing, & Lippman,

1988). None of these sites is the most common for cancer—the breast is. About 1 in 9 women will develop breast cancer. (But lung cancer, due to its high fatality rate, is the leading cause of cancer death for both men and women.) From ages 15 until 45 years, cancers of the reproductive system are a major cause of mortality for women but not for men.

During menopause women lose their fertility; they cease ovulation and menstruation, and their production of estrogen and progesterone declines. Some women experience uncomfortable symptoms associated with menopause, the most common of which is the "hot flash," a sudden feeling of heat and skin flushing. These feelings may be uncomfortable and embarrassing but are not health threatening, and only 10% of menopausal women experience serious problems with hot flashes (Hyde, 1990). Estrogen replacement therapy can alleviate this symptom, but this medical intervention remains controversial. Some contend that hormone replacement is an example of overtreatment of women, that menopause is not a disease. In addition, this treatment can increase the risk for breast cancer (Steinberg et al., 1991).

Men's hormone production also drops with aging, but they undergo no symptoms as visible as women do during menopause. The decrease in hormone production in men results in the decrease but not the end of their fertility. Men who lose the ability to get an erection may receive hormone replacements, but many fewer men than women receive analogous hormone replacement therapy.

Thus, malignancies of the reproductive system account for a small portion of the reproductive health care received by women but a larger portion for men. Women not only get pregnant and bear children, but they also have the majority of responsibility for contraception. In addition, menstruation is often painful, and some women experience pain sufficiently serious to prompt them to consult a health care professional. The decline in hormone production associated with menopause also brings medical treatment to some women. Therefore, a great deal of the excess of health care received by women is due to their reproductive system needs, but this is only part of the reason for women's greater number of contacts with the health care system.

Gender, Lifestyle, and Health

Men have a shorter average life span than women in all developed and most undeveloped countries, now and in the past, yet women make more use of health care. Both men's shorter lives and women's poorer health may be related to their lifestyles. That is, men may decrease their life span by their behaviors, and factors in women's lives may increase their morbidity. Karen Matthews (1989) hypothesized that women's healthier lifestyle is a factor in their longer lives and that men's lifestyle choices and occupational health risks place men in greater danger than women for life-threatening diseases and accidents. These risky behaviors are associated with the male gender role. As Harrison (1978) suggested, the male gender role may be dangerous to health.

An alternative view has come from Walter Gove and Michael Hughes (1979), who suggested that the female gender role has elements that endanger health. They postulated that the nurturant role that many women fulfill places them in the position of taking care of everyone except themselves. Women are in the position of providing social support and nurturant care for their families and friends, but these demands can be emotionally and physically draining. In addition, women may not receive the same quality of care that they give, leaving them without the support they offer to others. A dramatic example of such support occurred in the Donner expedition, when Tamsen Donner refused to leave her ill husband (Grayson, 1990). The support she gave him cost her life. More commonplace examples abound, as when women reported to Gove and Hughes that they were too busy to take care of themselves when they felt unwell, that chores still needed to be done when they were sick, and that family members interrupted their rest when they were unwell.

More recent research by Verbrugge (1989) confirmed Gove and Hughes's contention that the female role may offer risks for morbidity. Verbrugge (1989, p. 294) argued that "contemporary life puts women, not men, at greater risk of daily symptoms and longer-run health troubles." Her study showed that women are more vulnerable to stress and feel more vulnerable to illness than men.

Ravenna Helson and James Picano (1990) provided additional evidence of the dangers of the female gender role. These researchers measured gender roles for young women and related this measurement to adjustment and health for these women more than 20 years later. Their results indicated that the young women who fulfilled the traditional female gender role were well-adjusted, but during middle age, traditionally feminine women were more poorly adjusted and less healthy than more nontraditional women.

Therefore, both traditional gender roles carry health risks. Robert Kaplan and his colleagues (Kaplan, Anderson, & Wingard, 1991) contended that women's morbidity is a factor that significantly decreases their quality of life. Even after adjusting for this factor, women still had a greater life expectancy of years during which they were well compared to men. Therefore, women's greater illness is a factor in their lives, but women still have a health advantage over men. As Verbrugge (1985, pp. 162–163) concluded:

> *Women have more frequent illness and disability, but the problems are typically not serious (life threatening) ones. In contrast, men suffer more from life threatening diseases, and these cause more permanent disability and earlier death for them. One sex is "sicker" in the short run, and the other in the long run. There is no contradiction between the health and mortality statistics since both point to more serious health problems for men.*

Verbrugge also noted that the causes of death for both men and women are the same. Although women die at lower rates, they die from the same causes as men. The sources of disease and disability are also similar. "What differs most is the rates, not the ranks" (Verbrugge, 1985, p. 163).

Two behaviors that relate to health and longevity are eating and exercising, and these behaviors show gender-related differences.

Eating

Everyone eats, but not everyone shares the same eating pattern, and eating does not have the same meaning to everyone (Belasco, 1989). Women show more concern with eating to control weight, and women are more likely to diet than men. This concern with weight and their attempts to restrict food intake lead women to hold different attitudes toward eating than men do.

Gender differences in eating patterns do not appear during childhood but start during adolescence (Rolls, Fedoroff, & Guthrie, 1991). Adolescent boys, on the average, eat sufficient food to obtain the required calories, but adolescent girls do not. This food restriction puts adolescent girls at risk for nutritional inadequacies. Adult women also eat less than adult men, but the discrepancy is not as great as during adolescence. Nonetheless, women may eat too little to receive adequate nutrients.

Not only do men eat more than women, but they have somewhat different patterns of food consumption. Judith Green (1987) examined the eating patterns of men and women by observing them for over six hours in a laboratory setting. Although both showed similar patterns of food consumption, men ate more calories because they took bigger bites. DeAnna Mori and her colleagues (Mori, Chaiken, & Pliner, 1987) found that eating less and taking smaller bites may relate to efforts to appear feminine. These researchers observed male and female participants as they snacked and talked with a same-gender or other-gender partner. The female participants ate less when they were paired with an attractive male partner than with an unattractive man or with another woman.

The men in the Mori et al. study did not alter their eating patterns in response to the characteristics of their partners as much as women did, but the men showed a tendency to eat less when paired with a female partner. A later study (Pliner & Chaiken, 1990) demonstrated that men too are affected by the desire to present themselves in a socially desirable way by eating less. Both the men and women in this study ate less when paired with an attractive other-gender partner. This study also revealed that women's eating is motivated by the desire to appear feminine as well as the desire to give a good social impression. Thus, women have two constraints on their social eating, whereas men have only one.

Additional research by Shelly Chaiken and Patricia Pliner (1987) demonstrated that eating style can affect social perception; people form an impression of others based on how much they see them eating. Participants in this study described women who eat small meals as more feminine, more concerned about appearance, and better looking than women who eat larger meals. Therefore, women and men eat somewhat differently, partly due to men's greater caloric requirements and partly due to the impression that women may wish to convey through their eating style.

Differences in eating styles may be more than a way to give an impression; the thinner ideal body image for women mandates differences in eating for men and women. Women have more body fat than men, but the ideal body image for women demands thinness. Thus, women may believe that they must diet to achieve their desired weight. Extreme concerns with weight and dieting can produce abnormal eating habits and severe eating disorders. A growing consensus holds that body image and eating disorders are linked; an unattainably thin body image can prompt these unhealthy eating patterns.

Body Image

The image of what constitutes an attractive female or male body currently emphasizes thinness for women and muscularity for men. Kim Chernin (1978) discussed the development of the contemporary ideal body image for women, pointing out that the current emphasis on thinness has developed within the past 100 years. In the past plumpness has been the ideal for women, signifying their health and wealth, but that ideal faded. The thin image arose during the early part of the 20th century, signifying a departure from the plump image of traditional femininity. Janet Polivy and Linda Thomsen (1988) discussed the social class basis for the thin ideal, saying that when rich women began to have a preference for thinness, this preference began to spread throughout all social classes in emulation of the rich.

The ideal body image for men does not emphasize thinness as much as muscularity, and men are also under pressure to conform to this ideal body image (Mishkind, Rodin, Silberstein, & Striegel-Moore, 1986). Men who are overweight are not as socially censured as overweight women (Stake & Lauer, 1987), but being overweight has become a stigma for both men and women.

Although body image and weight concerns affect men as well as women, men and women are not equally affected by the changed standards for weight. The changes in ideal body image have been more extreme for women than for men. David Garner and his colleagues (Garner, Garfinkel, Schwartz, & Thompson, 1980) demonstrated the degree of change in the ideal body for women by examining two images—*Playboy* centerfolds and Miss America contestants—from 1959 until 1978. They found that women in both categories had become thinner over the 20-year period.

Claire Wiseman and her colleagues (Wiseman, Gray, Mosimann, & Ahrens, 1992) updated the research on ideal body images, extending the examination of *Playboy* centerfolds and Miss America contestants from 1979 through 1988. During that decade, Miss America contestants became significantly thinner, and both images were significantly thinner than average women of comparable age. The actual average weight for women did not decrease over the time period of these two studies, but the image of the ideal weight did. What women saw as their ideal became thinner and thus more difficult to attain.

Judith Rodin and her colleagues (Rodin, Silberstein, & Striegel-Moore, 1985) explored the pressures on women to be thin and how women feel about their bodies. They contended that women develop an image of their own bodies and the ideal body. A comparison of the two leads almost all women to be discontent; no matter how attractive, every person's body has flaws. Rodin et al. maintained that so many women are dissatisfied with their bodies that weight concerns have become a normative discontent.

This discontent is not limited to adults or even adolescents. Elizabeth Collins (1991) found evidence of body image discontentment in preadolescent children. As young as age 6 or 7 years, both girls and boys chose an ideal body thinner than their own, but boys' choices were less extreme than girls' choices. The girls also chose ideal adult bodies that were significantly thinner than the boys' choices. This study indicates that the thin ideal affects girls more than boys, but both genders experience self-criticism concerning weight, and this tendency begins before adolescence.

Research indicates that the concern with weight and appearance not only starts early but persists throughout life. Patricia Pliner and her colleagues (Pliner, Chaiken, & Flett, 1990) studied concerns with eating, body weight, and physical appearance in individuals as young as 10 and as old as 79 years old. The greater concern with weight and appearance among women was apparent at all ages, but a similar degree of concern did not appear in the men in this study.

Adam Drewnowski and Doris Yee (1987) found evidence of dissatisfaction with weight among college men. Indeed, these researchers found comparable rates but different patterns of dissatisfaction with weight and body image in college men and women. The 85% of women who were dissatisfied with their weight wanted to lose weight, expressing discontentment similar to that found by other investigators. A comparable percentage of men expressed dissatisfaction with their weight, but 40% of the men wanted to lose and 45% wanted to gain weight. The men and women who felt overweight had similar negative feelings about their bodies, but the men were more likely to use exercise as a way to control weight, whereas the women were more likely to diet. This study suggests that discontentment with weight and body image is widespread among both men and women, but the behavioral strategies for dealing with these discontents might show gender differences.

Ironically, both women and men misestimate what body type the other finds most attractive. April Fallon and Paul Rozin (1985) asked male and female college students to indicate their current body size, their ideal body, and the body that would be most attractive to the other gender. For men, the differences among these three body images were small, but for women, the three differed. Women rated their current body as heavier than the one most attractive to men, which was heavier than the women's ideal body. In addition, women believed that men would like a thinner body than the men actually rated most attractive, and men believed that women would like a heavier body than women rated most attractive. These findings suggest that both women and men are striving for ideal bodies that are not ideal to the other gender, but men tend to see their bodies as closer to the ideal than do women.

Heterosexual attraction may not be the only factor involved in weight concerns for either women or men. As Fallon and Rozin discovered, women seem to want bodies that are thinner than they believe men would like, indicating that some other factor is operating in their choice of ideal body type. Susan Brownmiller (1984) suggested that competition may be that factor. Women compare themselves to each other according to weight, with the woman who is thin gaining a feeling of competitive superiority. Thinness is a visible sign that she has won the battle to achieve the ideal, whereas other, heavier women have not been as successful.

In examining the sources of pressure to achieve these different ideal bodies, Arnold Andersen and Lisa DiDomenico (1992) examined magazines popular with young adults. They found that women's magazines contained over 10 times as many advertisements and articles oriented toward weight loss compared to men's magazines. The magazines for men contained messages to change body shape rather than to lose weight. Therefore, both women and men are subjected to pressures to change their bodies, but the methods for achieving these changes differ. If these messages are effective, men and women should take different strategies to achieve their ideal bodies: Women should be more likely to experience eating disorders, whereas men would be more likely to encounter exercise-related problems.

Eating Disorders

Anorexia nervosa and bulimia are two eating disorders that have received a great deal of publicity, but Polivy and Thomsen (1988) contended that dieting is also an eating disorder. Indeed, they argued that dieting is related to the development of the more serious eating disorders of anorexia and bulimia. **Anorexia nervosa** is a disorder consisting of self-starvation in pursuit of thinness, and **bulimia** consists of binge eating followed by some method of purging (induced vomiting or excessive laxative use).

Dieting, anorexia, and bulimia are all more common among women than men; around 90% of people treated for eating disorders are women (Rolls et al., 1991). Beginning during the early years of adolescence, girls express greater dissatisfaction with their bodies and diet to lose weight more frequently than boys. This dissatisfaction continues into late adolescence and adulthood, and the gender differences persist. Dieting has become more common for both men and women over the past 25 years, but more women than men attempt to control their body weight and body shape through food restriction. Ironically, the majority of dieters are within the normal weight range and thus have no health-related reasons to diet. Their perceptions of overweight are body image problems rather than body fat problems.

Polivy and Thomsen (1988) argued that dieting itself is an eating disorder with physical and psychological effects. They cited evidence that dieting can produce a variety of symptoms and conditions, including fatigue, low blood pressure, anemia, headaches, cardiac problems, and other physical problems. In addition, food restriction prompts a lowering of the metabolic rate, and chronic dieting may produce a permanently lowered metabolism, which makes weight loss even more difficult (Brownell & Stein, 1989). The psychological problems associated with dieting include irritability, anxiety, poor concentration, and depression. The relationship between dieting and depression exists in both women and men, but the relationship is stronger for men (Zimmer-Schur & Newcomb, 1994). Thus, dieting is not the answer to the problem of overweight, and the risks of dieting outweigh the benefits.

Dieting has become increasingly common among both men and women. In a survey of employed women and men in the midwestern United States, Robert Jeffery and his colleagues (Jeffery, Adlis, & Forster, 1991) found that at any one point in time, 13% of the men and 25% of the women were dieting. Throughout their lives a total of 47% of the men and 75% of the women had dieted to lose weight. In addition to finding more female dieters, these researchers found that more women than men who were near ideal weight were dieting—30% of women versus 10% of men.

Dieting is very common, but anorexia and bulimia are much less frequent. Anorexia is most common among young women, but Barbara Rolls and her colleagues (1991) estimated that only around 1% of adolescent girls have this disorder, and its appearance in the general population is even lower. They estimated that bulimia is more common, occurring in about 2% of the general population. Again, young women are most likely to be bulimic, and some estimates of the frequency of bulimia on college campuses run as high as 4%. Although these percentages are low, these disorders affect thousands of people, so the problem is not minor.

Several factors relate to the development of eating disorders. As the rates of anorexia and bulimia suggest, both gender and age are factors, with women more at risk than men and young women more subject to eating problems than older women (Hsu, 1990). Social class has been a factor, but pressures for thinness now occur in all social classes, and this factor no longer differentiates risk for eating disorders. Occupation is also a factor, with young women who are in modeling or dance school more likely to have eating disorders than comparable young women whose careers do not demand thinness (Garner & Garfinkel, 1980).

Attitudes concerning gender roles may relate to the development of eating disorders in women. Brett Silverstein and his colleagues (Silverstein, Carpman, Perlick, & Perdue, 1990; Silverstein, Perdue, Wolk, & Pizzolo, 1988) found that women who felt conflicts between their own achievement orientation and their family's attitudes were at risk for eating disorders. College women who were concerned with achievement in nontraditional fields and whose families held traditional beliefs were more likely to show signs of eating disorders than women without such conflicts.

About 10% of people with eating disorders are male (Rolls et al., 1991). Some of these men have occupations that require thinness, such as jockeys or dancers, and would be subject to pressures for slimness similar to women who are dancers or models. Other men who develop weight concerns so serious as to change their eating to a pathological pattern are involved in athletics. High mileage runners have a greater chance of showing symptoms of eating disorders than those who run less (Kiernan, Rodin, Brownell, Wilmore, & Crandall, 1992). Sexual orientation may also relate to disordered eating in men. David Herzog and his colleagues (Herzog, Newman, & Warshaw, 1991) found that men with a homosexual preference chose a thinner ideal body than men with a heterosexual preference. This body preference puts such men at risk for eating disorders. Therefore, the men who develop anorexic or bulimic eating patterns share the abnormal eating patterns and body concerns exhibited by women with such disorders, but generally men do not express their body concerns through disordered eating as frequently as women.

Both anorexia and bulimia are serious disorders, but anorexia is more serious, as it is more often life threatening. That is, between 5% and 15% of anorexics starve themselves to death (Hsu, 1990). Furthermore, treatment for anorexia is difficult. Anorexics do not cooperate with their treatment and persist in their desire to lose weight—even at the risk of their lives. Bulimia is more easily treated, as bulimics typically feel guilty about their binge eating and purging and have a desire to change their behavior.

✛ GENDERED VOICES
I'm Afraid Some of Them Are Not Going to Be Around

"I'm afraid some of them are not going to be around," a 14-year-old dancer told her mother concerning other dancers who showed symptoms of anorexia. The dancers in her classes were encouraged to be thin, and the girl believed that several were in danger; they were so thin that she considered them in danger of dying. Her mother was angry because she believed that the instructor was encouraging unhealthy eating in her students, telling her normal-weight daughter that she needed to lose weight. The girl knew that she was heavier than many of the other dancers, but she believed that they had the problem, not her.

She had begun to hear criticisms about her weight when she was 12, and she started to become self-conscious about it, but resisted dieting, partly because she thought the other girls were too thin and partly because she didn't want to change her eating habits. She had also received conflicting messages about her weight, with her mother and others telling her that she wasn't too heavy, her dance teacher telling her that she needed to be thinner, and her classmates dieting to the point of anorexia.

Another girl's story confirmed the prevalence of weight consciousness among early adolescents. This 12-year-old came home from school one day and told her mother that they had gone swimming for gym class, and most of the girls had gone into the pool with their T-shirts over their bathing suits. She didn't understand why they had done so; a wet T-shirt made swimming more difficult. When she asked one why she had kept her shirt on, the other girl said, "Because I'm so fat. I don't want anyone to see me in a bathing suit." The 12-year-old told her mother, "But they're not fat." She considered her classmates' perceptions of their bodies very odd. Judging from the number of girls who had been reluctant to be seen in a bathing suit, her classmates' distorted perception was more common than her accurate assessment of what was normal and overweight.

Therapy can be unsuccessful with both disorders, resulting in persistent eating problems and permanent damage to health.

Eating disorders, then, may be the result of concerns with body image and the exaggerated attempt to attain thinness. Because the ideal body image for women is thin, they are more likely than men to develop eating disorders. Over the past several decades, both men and women have begun to feel increased pressure to attain and maintain an attractive body, and women tend to try to achieve this goal through dieting and exercise, whereas men use exercise as a primary means and dieting as a secondary means of shaping their body.

Exercising

Exercise is a factor in the weight maintenance equation. To maintain a steady body weight, the energy (calories) from food consumed must equal the body energy expenditures. Such expenditures come from the energy required to maintain basal metabolism and from the energy required for physical activity. Increases in physical activity require more calories, or weight loss occurs. Thus, increases in physical activity can produce weight loss.

As noted earlier, men are more likely to exercise and women are more likely to diet as their main strategy to lose weight, although dieting is not always effective in producing weight loss (Polivy & Herman, 1983). When dieters eat less, their basal metabolism slows, and their bodies require fewer calories. This mechanism protects against starvation but makes weight loss difficult. To overcome this problem, the dieter must eat even less, increasing the chances of nutritional deficits and difficulties in maintaining the diet. Thus, dieting is not only difficult, it also is not as effective for weight control as dieting plus exercise.

Increased concern with body image and the increasing evidence that dieting may not be a good weight control strategy has led to an increased emphasis on exercise, but weight control is a minor factor in considering the benefits of exercise; physical activity is a basic part of life. The amount of physical activity varies from person to person and from time to time, but people are physically active creatures.

Some people enjoy exercise and participate in various types of activities that require a great deal of physical effort, whereas others prefer a more sedentary life. Some people have jobs that require a great deal of physical effort, but most jobs in technological societies are sedentary. The choice of leisure activities is another factor that influences exercise, with some people preferring active sports and others choosing television or other sedentary activities as a way to spend their leisure time. Therefore, physical activity is variable; some people choose to participate in and others to avoid strenuous exercise.

Even during the preschool years, gender differences exist in levels of physical activity, with boys more active than girls. Catherine Poest and her colleagues (Poest, Williams, Witt, & Atwood, 1989) found not only a gender difference in the activity level of young children but also a deficiency of physical activity among some young children. These researchers found that the family's attitude toward exercise and their exercise habits influenced the activity level of preschool children. They also determined that nursery school and day-care workers can influence the activity level of their pupils, either promoting a more active or a more sedentary orientation.

Throughout childhood boys are more likely to engage in physical activities requiring gross motor skills that use the large muscles of the body. Games that include running, jumping, throwing, and kicking—namely, baseball, football, soccer, and basketball—are preferred by boys more than by girls. Girls are not sedentary, but their childhood activities are less likely to involve gross motor activity. Girls and boys do not play together often during childhood, segregating themselves according to gender. This segregation decreases the chances that boys and girls will share the same physical activities. Middle childhood is a time during which "that's a game for girls" is an insult to boys. (See Chapter 10 for a discussion of gender segregation and friendships during childhood.)

Watching television and playing computer games have become popular recreational activities for children, taking the place of more active games and decreasing the physical activity of both boys and girls. Although children with athletic talent are encouraged to participate in sports, the emphasis on sports may leave the majority of children without adequate encouragement to participate in exercise. Many children of both genders may therefore avoid physical activity. Not having the ability to excel, they shun exercise, resulting in poor fitness and an increased probability of obesity.

Gender differences in exercising increase during adolescence, with girls decreasing and boys increasing their participation in athletics. The traditional gender roles hold that women should look slender and dainty and should feel reluctant to compete. Men, on the other hand, should look muscular and strong and should feel excited to compete. Athletic participation, with its emphasis on size, strength, and competition, is more compatible with the male than the female gender role. Adolescents feel the pressures to adopt these gender roles; thus, boys are urged to "try out" for sports while girls are urged to give up their athletic activities.

Athletics

The social forces that push boys toward and girls away from athletics still exist, but young women now participate in organized sports at a higher rate than in the past. Title IX of the Education Amendments of 1972 mandated that school programs receiving federal funds support athletic programs for women. Given this mandate, both secondary schools and higher education have increased funding for women's athletics, and women have increased their participation in competitive athletics. Laura Mansnerus (1992) noted the dramatic changes that Title IX brought about. In 1971, girls constituted only 7% of the athletic participants in high schools, but in 1991, the percentage was 36%. Women now constitute about one-third of the participants in college athletics.

This increase has not resulted in equal participation, equal funding, or equal acceptance for women in athletics. Title IX required comparable—not equal—opportunities for training, competition, locker rooms, medical services, and scholarships (Dubbert & Martin, 1988). The sports that are the most popular for spectators—football, baseball, and basketball—are dominated or exclusively played by men. Volleyball and softball, the sports added as part of the Title IX mandate, are not equally popular among spectators or as well funded in terms of training facilities and scholarships. Despite the dramatic changes in the availability of sports to high school and college women, their participation is not equal, and even the extraordinarily talented do not have an equal chance for public adulation and lucrative professional careers in sports.

Mansnerus discussed the increased acceptability of women's participation in athletics, but she also acknowledged that women athletes still have image problems in that there still exists the traditional association between men and athletic competition. The image of female athletes was the subject of Nancy Theberge's (1991) research investigating newspaper coverage of gender and physical activity. She found that stereotypical images of female athletes and women's participation in fitness activities are still the norm. These stereotypes have resulted in the perception of female athletes as masculine (and possibly lesbian) as well as unattractive. These perceptions have changed to some extent, partly due to Title IX and the increased number of women who participate in athletics (and perhaps due to the realization that *all* those women cannot be lesbians). In addition, the media coverage of beautiful female athletes, such as Florence Griffith-Joyner, Nancy Kerrigan, Gabriella Sabatini, and Summer Sanders, has demonstrated that world-class female athletes are not necessarily masculine in appearance.

Regardless of the appearance of female athletes, their performance is measured in terms of speed, strength, agility, and endurance—the same criteria as for male athletes.

As Jerry Thomas and Karen French (1985) pointed out, men and women are not equal in speed and strength, and this inequality has a major impact on athletic performance. Female and male athletes do not compete against each other, because women's performance does not match that of men. In some cases, women's athletic performance surpasses the records for men in the past. For example, women's finish times for the marathon have fallen more rapidly than men's times, and current women's records are better than men's records of 40 years ago. However, the current times for men and women are not equal; men's times are faster.

Perhaps the continued participation of women in sports and access to excellent training will result in parity, but men on average are larger and stronger than women on average. Some women are taller and stronger than some men; that is, the height distributions for women and men overlap, but the physical gender differences in size and in strength are two of the more dramatic differences between men and women. These differences are minimal before puberty but increase during adolescence, producing a physical basis for differences in motor performance. Thomas and French (1985) examined the development of such differences for a variety of physical tasks (such as throwing, balance, dash, grip strength) and concluded that the male advantage in most motor tasks is due to differences in expectations and practice opportunities. Other differences are due to men's greater average height, upper body strength, greater muscle mass, and longer limb length. For most sports, adolescent and adult men have the advantage that comes from greater physical ability and more practice.

Their advantages do not make all boys and men athletic; many people of both genders avoid physical activity. Children and adolescents have many entertainment options that do not include physical activity. As society has become more technological and service oriented, a greater proportion of people hold sedentary jobs, and if they wish to be physically fit, they must choose leisure activities that promote fitness.

GENDERED VOICES
I Didn't Get to Play

"When I was a teenager, I was interested in sports, and I was good, especially at baseball," a woman in her 40s told me. "That was before Title IX, and there was no effort at all to allow women access to athletics, so I didn't get to play. It was partly social censure. Girls weren't supposed to be athletic, except for acceptable athletics. Dancing and cheerleading were acceptable for girls, but not baseball, which was the sport I liked.

"My mother didn't like my athletic inclinations and tried to urge me away from baseball and volleyball. I think I could have made the boys' baseball team, but of course, that was out of the question. No more. The changes are amazing. Girls play on boys' teams in baseball and even football in junior high and high school. Of course I regret not being able to play the sports I liked, but the changes in access to sports for women and even in attitudes toward athletic women are substantial.

"Rather than being discouraged from pursuing sports, my cousin got a volleyball scholarship that paid for her college education. I saw a news story about a girl who played linebacker on her junior high school football team. Those changes have not come easily, but I can remember when things were much different for athletic women. There has definitely been improvement."

Fitness

Several different types of fitness exist, including strength, endurance, flexibility, and cardiorespiratory (aerobic) fitness (Kuntzleman, 1978). Different types of activity are required to achieve and maintain each of these different types of fitness, and people who participate in only one type of exercise lack some types of fitness. For example, jogging promotes aerobic fitness but not flexibility, and weight training produces muscle strength but not aerobic fitness. Thus, people who are interested in comprehensive physical fitness must engage in several different types of exercise.

A growing body of research evidence indicates that exercise provides physical and psychological benefits to both men and women. Patricia Dubbert and John Martin (1988) reviewed the research that shows cardiovascular benefits, especially for men. As most of the studies on cardiovascular disease have excluded women, the exercise benefits for women concerning CVD are not as well established as those benefits for men. Women, however, benefit from exercise in connection with **osteoporosis,** the process of bone demineralization, which is more common among women than men and more common among postmenopausal women than any other group. This problem can lead to orthopedic problems such as fractures. Exercise slows and may reverse this process.

In addition to the physical benefits, exercise promotes psychological benefits (Dubbert & Martin, 1988; Plante & Rodin, 1990). Exercise is related to improvements in mood and to feelings of psychological well-being and self-esteem. The efficacy of exercise to counter depression is particularly notable. Thus, people who exercise experience improvements in psychological and physical health, but these benefits accrue to relatively few people; most children and adults lead sedentary lives (Dubbert, 1992).

Men's greater sports participation during adolescence makes them more likely than women to continue this athletic activity throughout their lives, but this background is no guarantee of an active lifestyle (Verbrugge, 1989). After they leave school, men become less likely to continue their physical activity, resulting in adult men who lead sedentary lives, with desk jobs and sedentary hobbies.

Until women started to participate in sports during their school years, they did not have physical activity background comparable to that of men. The traditional feminine gender role holds that women are less physically fit, active, and competitive than men. The changes in school athletics programs have influenced the number of young women who participate in athletics, giving more women background experience in physical activity. In addition, recent pressures on women to be thin have extended to fitness, with an increasing number of articles in women's magazines urging women to achieve thinness through not only diet but also exercise (Wiseman et al., 1992). Although they may or may not have a history of participation in activities that promote physical fitness, women are subject to increasing pressure to exercise.

Women feel the pressure to pursue physical fitness as a way to achieve their weight goals rather than fitness goals. Karen McDonald and J. Kevin Thompson (1992) studied physically active men and women to investigate their motivations for exercise, their eating habits, and their satisfaction with their body. They found that women were more likely than men to exercise to achieve good body tone and weight loss rather than for fitness. In this study, both the women and men who exercised for reasons of health and fitness were less likely to show symptoms of eating disorders than those who exercised for weight control and to improve appearance.

People who exercise may not have fitness as a goal, and their exercise may symptomize problems with eating and body image rather than a healthy lifestyle. Exercise may allow both women and men to achieve fitness, but exercise may also provide a format for enacting body image dissatisfaction and unrealistic weight concerns. Research has indicated that exercise can be pathological and that addicted exercisers are more likely than more moderate exercisers to have psychological problems and eating disorders (Ashel, 1991; Davis, Elliott, Dionne, & Mitchell, 1991; Pasman & Thompson, 1988). Addicted exercisers seem similar to anorexics; they share an obsession with a thin body image and a fanatical pursuit of the ideal body.

In summary, exercise can be a healthy habit, providing a number of physical and psychological benefits. Although men are more likely to have a background in sports, both women and men may pursue exercise for a variety of reasons. Men are more likely to use exercise as a way to shape their body, and women are more likely to use exercise as an adjunct to dieting to lose weight. Both of these goals may be the basis for pathological exercising, but moderate exercise is a factor in a healthy lifestyle, and men are more likely to be physically active than women.

Summary

Women live longer than men. This gender difference has existed in most countries and in most times. In economically developed countries, such as the United States, Canada, Australia, and the countries of Scandinavia and Western Europe, cardiovascular disease, cancer, and violent deaths account for the majority of deaths. These causes of death do not affect men and women equally; women have lower rates of mortality from all these causes.

Cardiovascular disease (CVD) includes diseases of the heart and circulatory system. Although not all CVD is life threatening, heart attack and stroke account for almost half of the deaths in the United States, and men are more likely to die of CVD than women, especially before the age of 65 years. Women do develop CVD, however, and their reports of symptoms are not taken as seriously or treated as aggressively as the same symptoms reported by men. This differential treatment suggests bias on the part of physicians.

Cancer is the second most common cause of death, and men are more likely than women to die from this cause. Lung cancer is the deadliest form of cancer for both men and women, and this form of cancer is related to cigarette smoking. Until recently men have smoked at a higher rate than women, and this habit is reflected in their higher incidence of lung cancer. With the rise in women's smoking, their lung cancer rates have and will continue to increase. Both women and men develop cancer of the reproductive organs, but women are more likely to die of such cancers, especially before age 65 years.

The gender difference in violent deaths is large, with men dying of accidents, suicide, and homicide at higher rates than women. The male gender role, which holds that men are supposed to be reckless and aggressive, may play a part in the high death rates from these causes. Men's greater prevalence of heavy alcohol use increases their chances of dying of any violent cause. Violent deaths also vary from country to country, with the United States having a high rate of violent deaths. Within the United States, different ethnic groups are unequally affected, and African Americans are especially vulnerable to violent death.

Although women live longer than men, women seek health care more often. Gender and gender roles influence seeking health care. The female gender role allows and even encourages vulnerability to illness, but the male gender role discourages the acceptance of any weakness, including illness. Although women may be more sensitive to symptoms, they may be less financially able to seek health care. Their lower rate of employment, lower salaries, and lower insurance coverage affect their access to medical care.

The interaction of gender roles for the patient and health care provider have an impact on receiving health care. Physicians have been the target of criticism concerning their treatment of female patients, including being reluctant to believe female patients, using men as a standard against which all patients are judged, and omitting women from medical research. These biases in medicine against women do not necessarily mean that men receive the best health care, but they do result in women's treatment being less than optimum. Concern over these problems may result in the creation of a medical specialty oriented toward treating women.

Reproductive health is a major source of the gender difference in receiving health care. Women not only become involved in the health care system due to pregnancy and childbirth, but contraception and menopause have become reasons for consulting a physician. Both women and men are affected by sexually transmitted diseases and disorders of the reproductive organs. Both develop cancers of the genitals, with breast cancer being the most frequent cancer among women.

Lifestyle differences may account for some of the gender differences in morbidity and mortality. The thin body ideal has become so widespread among women that dieting is a way of life for millions of women. Because they cannot be as thin as the ideal, women develop body image problems and are more prone to the eating disorders such as anorexia nervosa and bulimia. Men also experience body image dissatisfaction, but they are more likely to attempt to alter their bodies through exercise rather than through dieting.

Exercise can be a positive factor for fitness and weight control, and men are more likely to participate in sports and physical activity than women. The passage of Title IX of the Education Amendments of 1972 removed some barriers that prevented women from participating in athletics, but the negative image of female athletes continues to be a factor in preventing women from sports participation. In an increasingly technological and sedentary society, most men and women must use their leisure time to pursue fitness. Athletic activities can build fitness and contribute to health, but excessive exercise can also be symptomatic of body image problems.

Glossary

Anorexia nervosa   an eating disorder consisting of self-starvation in pursuit of thinness

Bulimia   an eating disorder consisting of binge eating, followed by some method of purging, either by induced vomiting or excessive laxative use

Cardiovascular disease   a group of diseases involving the heart and circulatory system, with heart attack and stroke the most common

Chronic diseases   health problems that persist over time without a complete cure

Morbidity   illness

Mortality   death

Osteoporosis   the process of bone demineralization, resulting in greater likelihood of orthopedic problems and injuries

Risk factor   any condition or factor that increases the probability that an illness will develop

Sexually transmitted diseases (STDs)   infectious diseases that are spread through sexual contact, including bacterial infections, viral infections, fungal infections, and parasitic infections

Suggested Readings

Kane, Penny. (1991). *Women's health: From womb to tomb*. New York: St. Martin's Press. This book offers an interesting look at gender differences in health from a cross-cultural and developmental perspective. Kane draws information from cultures throughout the world, offering not only information on these various cultures but also an opportunity to see the differences among economically developed, developing, and undeveloped countries.

Polivy, Janet; & Thomsen, Linda. (1988). Dieting and other eating disorders. In Elaine A. Blechman & Kelly D. Brownell (Eds.), *Handbook of behavioral medicine for women* (pp. 345–355). New York:

Pergamon Press. These researchers review the evidence on eating disorders and argue that dieting should be added to the list of these disorders.

Strickland, Bonnie R. (1988). Sex-related differences in health and illness. *Psychology of Women Quarterly, 12,* 381–399. Strickland's article concentrates on figures from the United States, but this review of gender differences in health provides a brief summary of the physical and behavioral differences that may relate to these gender differences.

Verbrugge, Lois M. (1989). The twain meet: Empirical explanations of sex differences in health and mortality. *Journal of Health and Social Behavior, 30,* 282–304. Verbrugge explains the apparent contradiction between women's lower mortality and higher morbidity by relying on behavioral and social factors for the differences.

Chapter *14*

Stress, Coping, and Psychopathology

Is It Sadness or Madness?

—*Newsweek,* March 15, 1993

The subtitle of Jean Seligmann and David Gelman's (1993) *Newsweek* story was "Psychiatrists Clash Over How to Classify PMS." The classification of a behavioral syndrome related to the menstrual cycle is one of the controversies raised in connection with the *Diagnostic and Statistical Manual of Mental Disorders* (DSM), the system constructed by the American Psychiatric Association and used by most professions involved in the diagnosis of people's behavior problems. As Chapter 3 detailed, premenstrual syndrome (PMS) is well accepted, despite sparse research support, and the process of its classification as a mental disorder by the American Psychiatric Association (ApA) has sparked great controversy.

The American Psychiatric Association and its manual are at the center of this controversy, which began in 1987 with the inclusion of **late luteal phase dysphoric disorder (LLPDD)** as a classification in the appendix of the revised third edition of the *Diagnostic and Statistical Manual of Mental Disorders* (DSM-III-R). Although the placement in the appendix of "disorders needing further study" should have qualified the use of this diagnostic category, LLPDD came to be used much as any of the other diagnostic classifications and prompted an outpouring of criticism from those both inside and outside the psychiatric community who believed that the classification put millions of women at risk for psychiatric diagnosis

The controversy over the LLPDD diagnosis and the vote to include a similar diagnosis, **premenstrual dysphoric disorder (PMDD),** in the fourth edition of the DSM

379

(DSM-IV) has continued the controversy. Seligmann and Gelman's article reported that the ApA's task force on the topic recommended that PMDD should be included in the main body of the DSM-IV as one of the mood disorders, in the same category as depression. The proponents argued that the inclusion of PMDD would allow women with this diagnosis more credibility when reporting their symptoms and increase the chances for insurance reimbursement for their treatment. The critics claimed that a psychiatric diagnosis only for women stigmatizes the entire gender and opens millions of women to such diagnosis and labeling.

Paula Caplan (1993), a vocal critic of the diagnosis, argued, "There is a danger that real causes of women's depression or other problems will be ignored. Attributing symptoms to hormones also increases the risk of overlooking serious medical problems." Caplan also cited a lack of research support for this diagnosis as well as the lack of evidence that such a diagnosis would be helpful to women who present the symptoms. Those who oppose this diagnosis "are saying that the physical premenstrual symptoms some women experience are not signs of mental illness" (p. 13) and thus do not belong in a system to diagnose mental disorders.

Despite her public objections, Caplan was involved as an advisor and consultant to the subcommittees on late luteal phase dysphoric disorder, which became premenstrual dysphoric disorder in DSM-IV. Caplan (1991) reported on her experiences with the DSM development and revision, leveling charges of political expediency and gender bias in the acceptance of DSM categories.

Premenstrual dysphoric disorder was not included as a mood disorder in DSM-IV. When the new edition of the *Diagnostic and Statistical Manual of Mental Disorders* appeared in 1994, PMDD was in an appendix rather than in the manual itself, still with the disorders requiring further study. This continued controversy highlights the political nature of the process of diagnosing problem behavior and suggests that women and men may receive different diagnoses based not only on their behavior but also on the characteristics of the diagnostic system.

These controversies continue as a result of the discrepancy in diagnosis of mental disorders for women and men—women have a higher rate of diagnosis and treatment for psychological problems than men. Does this higher rate of diagnosis of

---

✣ GENDERED VOICES
I Think I Have It

Male psychologist Have you read the new description of PMS that will appear in the fourth edition of the DSM? I'm really very concerned.

Female psychologist Yes, I have. Premenstrual dysphoric disorder, which will replace late luteal phase dysphoric disorder. I'm concerned, too. It's supposed to appear in the main body of the classifica-

tion under mood disorders, and I understand that the treatment will be antidepressant drugs. It's been very controversial, and I think that this move will keep it that way. What bothers you?

Male psychologist According to my reading of the diagnostic criteria, I think I have it.

psychopathology mean that women are at a disadvantage in the diagnosis process? Is their disproportionate representation among psychiatric patients a reflection of differences in stress, different coping resources or strategies, biases in the diagnostic criteria, biases in the diagnostic process, or some combination of these factors?

Stress and Coping

The explanations for psychological problems have ranged from possession by demons to genetic vulnerability. The belief that madness results from demonic possession has faded, but many authorities accept that some mental disorders have a genetic component, including depression and schizophrenia. The gender differences in distribution of diagnoses, however, are too large to be accounted for by genetics (Cleary, 1987). Therefore, the search for risk factors for mental disorders has focused on life circumstances and stresses.

Stress is an inevitable part of life, making the search for the stresses that relate to the development of mental disorders a complex task. Researchers cannot simply identify sources of stress but must investigate how people perceive various stressors and how they cope with the stress in their lives.

Sources of Stress for Men and Women

The stresses that relate to the development of behavioral problems show some differences for women and men. As Chapter 10 explored, the many combinations of marriage, parenthood, and employment provide women with complex roles within the family. Men have traditionally occupied the breadwinner role and have not been involved with providing the majority of housekeeping or child-care functions within their family, making their roles more straightforward and their stress related to occupation. Both women's and men's roles may be stressful, but the research emphasis has been on women's multiple roles. Fulfilling these roles may be stressful and thus related to the development of some mental disorders.

An additional possibility for gender differences in life experience concerns violence. As Chapter 9 presented, men are more likely to commit and to be the victims of violence. However, women are much more likely to be the targets of sexual abuse and violence in families, placing them at risk for the aftermath of such violence. Poverty is yet another possibility for prompting stress and producing mental problems. Do these life experiences relate to the development of mental disorders? And are the gender differences in mental disorders related to these life experiences?

Family Roles

Elaine Wethington and her colleagues (Wethington, McLeod, & Kessler, 1987) reviewed evidence about gender differences in life events and psychological distress and concluded that no inherent gender differences exist. Women are not more prone to stress-related psychological disorders, but they argued that the roles women occupy are inherently stressful. These researchers noted that women's roles obligate them to respond to others, and they contended that these demands are an important source of gender differences in mental health.

The gender differences in family roles revolve around marriage, parenthood, and employment. Jessie Bernard (1972) contended that all marriages consists of "his" and "hers" and that men benefit more from marriage than women. This contention holds for mental health, with married men showing better mental health than married women (Fowers, 1991). Indeed, the differences in mental health are greatest among married people (Rosenfield, 1989). For married people, the greatest difference is between employed men and women who are homemakers (Cleary & Mechanic, 1983). Thus, both marriage and employment are factors in the mental health of men and women, with men having the advantage when they are married and employed.

Walter Gove's (1980, 1984) position concerning gender differences in mental health is similar to the one taken by Wethington and her colleagues, emphasizing the stress of the social roles typically occupied by men and women. Gove argued that women's roles are less structured than men's roles but demand them to supply more nurturance. Women usually perform the majority of family work, but their duties have more flexibility and thus less structure. On the other hand, men's roles tend to be structured, with many fixed components typically furnished by occupations and limited family work. In addition, family members often rely on women to provide nurturance, which can be draining for the women who provide emotional and physical nurturance to husbands, children, and sometimes aging parents as well.

In support of the notion that family roles are associated with depression, married women with children and single parents show a higher rate of depression than married men and unmarried women (Aneshensel, Frerichs, & Clark, 1981). Sarah Rosenfield (1989) attempted to explain the lifestyles that lead to depression and anxiety by proposing that both low power and role overload can lead to these problems—that is, both factors are mediated through a lack of control. She gave the occupation of housewife as an example of a position with low power, and she discussed full-time employment plus caring for children as an example of role overload. In support of her position, research has found that housewives and those who are responsible for the care of young children are especially vulnerable to depression (Cleary & Mechanic, 1983).

Rosalind Barnett and Grace Baruch (1987) contended that women do not need to fulfill the role of wife and mother to be psychologically healthy. Women who are mothers may benefit from that role, depending on their other roles and the assistance they receive in fulfilling their family and workplace obligations. Unmarried mothers with many young children are at a disadvantage in maintaining both physical and mental health, and married women's advantage disappears when their husbands do not help with family work. (See Chapter 10 for more information about gender-related division of labor in marriage relationships.) Aneshensel et al. (1981) found that parents with children living in the household were more likely to be depressed than people without children or whose children lived elsewhere. This effect was stronger for women than men, and single mothers and married women with children at home showed the highest rate of depression. Therefore, under some circumstances, multiple roles can be a disadvantage for women.

Multiple roles do not inevitably lead to stress and stress-related problems; the amount of strain from each role is an important factor (Aneshensel & Pearlin, 1987). When employed mothers experience little strain in either role, they are at low risk for depression. When married, employed mothers experience strain in each role, they are at high risk for depression—a level of risk comparable to housewives. As Rosenfield pointed out, when family demands are equal, employed men and women have comparable rates of depression and anxiety disorders, but the burdens of family care fall disproportionately on women. Therefore, the social circumstances of some women are risks for the development of depression.

Although women's mental health benefits from employment, their husbands' may not. Rosenfield (1992) described the shift in power that accompanies wives' employment, arguing that when the wife's employment decreases the husband's relative contribution to family income and increases his share of domestic duties, the husband's mental health suffers. Thus, men are also subject to role overload and the negative effects of loss of power and diminished personal control.

The research on stresses in men's lives has concentrated on job-related stress and its effects, but some investigators have explored men's multiple roles in the workplace and family. Recent research by Rosalind Barnett, Nancy Marshall, and Joseph Pleck (1992) investigated the importance of family roles to men's psychological health. These researchers found that work roles and family roles contribute equally to men's feelings of distress and well-being. The quality of men's marital relationships and the quality of their parental relationships were important factors in their lives, and Barnett and her colleagues concluded that researchers have neglected the importance of family roles in men's lives. Satisfaction with family roles can buffer men against the stresses of the workplace: "Men operate in two areas—home and work—and the quality of their experiences in each area contribute equally to their psychological health" (Barnett et al., 1992, p. 366).

High commitment to the breadwinner role can be a source of strain for men, especially those who do not perceive their wives as supportive in their attempts to fulfill work and parenting roles (Greenberger & O'Neil, 1993). Women also experience strain when they spend many hours on their jobs and feel a lack of support from their husbands and neighbors for their employment and parenting efforts. Thus, both husbands and wives can experience role strain when they believe that their efforts are not supported by their partners, but men tend to feel more strain and anxiety over their work roles than do women.

Therefore, both men and women experience distress or satisfaction from occupying the roles that come with marriage, parenthood, and employment. Whether these roles result in satisfaction or distress depends on the combination and quality of each. Women and men who have good marriage relationships are less likely to experience psychological problems than those who have problems in their marriage. Indeed, divorced men and women are at heightened risk for psychological problems.

Parenthood is more likely to be a risk for distress in women than in men. For men, pleasure in parenting can buffer against other stresses, but women who care for small children are more likely to experience psychological problems than women who do not have child-care responsibilities. This stress is ameliorated by sharing the responsibility for child care. Employment is related to positive mental health for both women and men, but women may experience stress and psychological problems from the overload of family and work responsibilities.

Violence

As discussed earlier, men are more likely than women to be both the perpetrators and the victims of violence, but women's victimization may be especially traumatic, because women are more likely to be the victims of violence by family and friends than by strangers (Russo, 1990; Walker, 1989). A growing body of research has implicated violence as a risk to mental health, and this research has concentrated on intimate violence in families—childhood sexual abuse, rape, and marital violence.

Mary Koss (1990, p. 374) conceptualized the relationship between violence and mental problems by saying that "experiencing violence transforms people into victims and changes their lives forever. Once victimized one can never feel quite as invulnerable." Koss (1993) reviewed the evidence that a history of violence is related to the development of a wide variety of psychological problems, including posttraumatic stress disorder, depression, substance abuse, obsessive-compulsive disorder, eating disorders, and suicide attempts. She proposed that violence is a factor that psychology has largely overlooked in explanations of the development of mental disorders.

The American Psychological Association established a Task Force on Male Violence Against Women in 1991 (Goodman, Koss, Fitzgerald, Russo, & Keita, 1993). This task force estimated that between 21 and 34% of women in the United States are physically assaulted by a man who has a close relationship with them, and between 14 and 25% of adult women will be raped at some time during their lives. These figures demonstrate the prevalence of male violence toward women.

Despite the widespread publicity of male violence toward women, Clifton Flynn (1990) contended that the attention to domestic violence has been selective and that the rate of female violence toward men is nearly as high as male violence toward women. He examined evidence from many studies and concluded that the rates of violence toward intimate partners are similar for women and men, but the patterns differ. Women are most likely to be violent in protecting themselves from and retaliating for violent attacks by men, whereas men are more likely to initiate such attacks. A growing body of research indicates that the aftermath of victimization has implications, especially for the mental health of women.

The risk of depression and anxiety disorders rises in rape victims. Comparing rape victims to a group of women who had not been the victims of rape, assault, or robbery, Dean Kilpatrick and his colleagues (Kilpatrick, Best, Saunders, & Veronen, 1988) found that boyfriends and husbands were twice as likely to be the rapists as strangers. Also, the aftermath of women's rape experience was costly in mental health terms. Compared to the women who had not been raped, the victimized women were 11 times more likely to be clinically depressed and six times more likely to be fearful in social situations.

Susan Cutler and Susan Nolen-Hoeksema (1991) hypothesized that violence is a significant contributor to the prevalence of depression among women and might be the factor that accounts for the gender difference in this disorder. These researchers pointed out that childhood sexual abuse is more common for girls than boys and that evidence exists linking childhood sexual abuse and anxiety, depression, and low self-esteem. Support for this relationship came from a study by Mark Yama and his colleagues (Yama, Tovey, & Fogas, 1993), who studied a group of women who were sexually abused as children and compared them to women with no history of sexual abuse. These researchers demonstrated the lasting effects of this type of childhood abuse for the development of anxiety and depression.

Other research has shown that sexual abuse at any age increases the risk for a variety of mental disorders in both men and women (Burnam et al., 1988). This research revealed that being a victim of sexual abuse increases the chances of depression, substance abuse or dependence, phobia, panic disorder, and obsessive-compulsive disorder, with a magnitude of increase between two and four times. The effects were especially dramatic for those who had been abused during childhood. Women are much more likely to be the victims of sexual abuse than men, but this study found no gender difference in likelihood of developing psychological problems among those who had experienced abuse. The form of subsequent problems differed somewhat for men and women, with men more likely to experience drug and alcohol problems than women, but sexual victimization clearly increased the risk for a variety of problems.

Violence in the form of criminal victimization also relates to the development of psychological disorders, especially posttraumatic stress disorder (PTSD) (Resnick, Kilpatrick, Best, & Kramer, 1992). Those women who were victims of crimes involving violence or the threat of extreme violence were much more likely to develop symptoms of PTSD than women who were the victims of less violent crimes. However, all crime victims had an elevated risk of PTSD, demonstrating the psychological risks of crime.

The evidence concerning family roles and mental health is complex, with many different configurations and effects. The evidence for the relationship between violence and mental disorders is much more straightforward. Violence increases the risk for several mental disorders, and childhood victimization is especially harmful. Women are more likely to be the targets of childhood sexual abuse and rape, two types of violence that research has related to the development of disorders, but men who are victimized are also at elevated risk.

Poverty

Poverty presents a risk for mental disorders for both women and men (Neugebauer, Dohrenwend, & Dohrenwend, 1980). Those who live in poverty are at least two and a half times as likely to receive a diagnosis of mental disorder compared to those who are not poor. Not only are poor people more likely to receive a diagnosis of some type of mental disorder, but a community study (Holzer et al., 1986) indicated that mental disorders are almost three times more common among those who are in the lowest as compared to those in the highest socioeconomic class.

Deborah Belle (1990) pointed out that the life circumstances associated with poverty are also associated with poor mental health. That is, not only is low income itself a problem, creating many stresses, but unemployment or underemployment, divorce, and single parenthood are all sources of stress and are all associated with poverty. In addition, low income can lead to poor housing in neighborhoods that have higher crime rates, subjecting poor people to higher risk of violence and its psychological effects. Poverty may be an independent risk factor for mental disorder, but it is associated with other risks that increase the chances for problems.

Belle's (1990) assessment of poverty in the United States indicated that poverty affects women and ethnic minority families more than others. Single mothers are more likely to be poor than any other demographic group, affecting not only their mental and physical health but also placing their children at risk for the stress associated with poverty. The National Institute of Mental Health has recognized the negative impact of poverty on women's mental health and has made the topic a priority for the Women's Research Agenda, but poverty is also a risk to men's mental health.

Poverty has a negative impact on the ability to cope. Financial limitations deprive people of the ability to deal with other problems that can produce stress. Lack of money limits opportunities and choices, putting people in a position of dependency on government bureaucracy for housing, health care, food, and other essentials. As Belle (1990) pointed out, the economically advantaged may be able to extricate themselves from problem situations and relationships that poor people cannot avoid. Both the situation and the lack of control can produce stress.

Coping Resources and Strategies

The number and intensity of stresses are important factors in any resulting problems, but resources and strategies for coping are even more important. Those who have resources to cope with the stresses in their lives may not perceive the situations as stressful. Richard Lazarus and Susan Folkman (1984) proposed that each person's appraisal of a potentially stressful situation varies according to his or her perception of the personal importance of the situation plus personal resources to deal with the situation. Those who do not have or believe that they do not have the resources to cope with events in their lives are vulnerable to stress, whereas others who experience the same events but have the resources to cope do not experience stress from the events. Thus, stress varies according to perception, and that perception depends on the evaluation of resources for coping.

The resources for coping may differ for women and men, as men often have more power and greater financial resources than women. Power and money offer advantages for avoiding many of life's problems and for dealing with others. For example, the loss of a job may be more stressful for a single mother of two with only a high school education and job skills as a sales clerk than for a married male engineer with an employed wife and a sizable savings account. Not that both of these jobless people will avoid stress; losing a job is stressful for almost everyone. However, the engineer has resources for dealing with his situation that the sales clerk lacks.

One of the most important differences between the male engineer and the female sales clerk is the social support the engineer has in the form of his family. The sales clerk may receive support from her children, but she must also offer them nurturance. As Gove (1980, 1984) contended, women's roles carry obligations for providing nurturance, whereas men's roles offer them the provision of emotional support. Providing nurturance can be stressful, whereas receiving social support is more likely to relieve stress. On the other hand, the possibility exists that involvement in social relationships offers more advantages than costs in coping with stress.

Social Support

Social support is more than a matter of social relationships or social contacts; support implies providing emotional and material resources. Therefore, the number of acquaintances a person has or the number of people with which she or he associates is not a good measure of social support. James House (1984) discussed four elements of social support, including emotional concern, instrumental aid (such as money or other assistance), information and advice, and feedback. If a person has few contacts with other people, then that person is more likely to be socially isolated than the person with many contacts. Social support requires more than contact or acquaintanceship, and friends and family are the usual sources of social support. People who have a high amount of social support have a wide network of people on whom they can count for emotional and material support.

As the "Friendships" section of Chapter 10 covered, women are more likely than men to form friendships that include emotional intimacy, which may give them the advantage in acquiring a network that provides them with social support. Men's friendships tend to be activity oriented, which may offer them the material support but not the emotional intimacy that is important for social support. Men's advantage in social support probably comes from their relationships with women, on whom men tend to rely for emotional support as well as many aspects of physical care.

As Wethington et al. (1987) explained, women's roles obligate them to provide support for their families and friends, and husbands are major recipients of this support. Women often provide more support than they receive in marriage, giving them a disadvantage and their husbands an advantage. This difference may contribute to the gender difference in mental health between married men and women.

Single, childless women have some advantage in mental health compared to married women and compared to single women with children, especially women who have no employment outside their homes. Employment can enhance social support by increasing the number of friends. Single and divorced men are at greater risk than married men, again indicating that social support is a factor in mental health. Those at greater risk typically have less social support, and those at lesser risk typically have more sources of social support.

The breadth and strength of social networks vary with ethnicity as well as with gender (Renzetti & Curran, 1992). Some ethnic groups maintain close family relationships, whereas in other ethnic groups increased mobility and small families decrease the chances of having close friends as well as complicate family contact. The isolated nuclear family consisting of father, mother, and children has become the image of family life in the Western world, but many people live in extended families in close contact with other relatives.

Hispanic-, African-, and Asian-American families tend to form extended family groupings—grandparents, parents, children, and other relatives who live in close proximity. This pattern differs from the isolated nuclear family typical of many (but by no means all) European Americans, with resulting advantages and disadvantages. The advantages of an extended family include a wider range of people and their emotional and material support and advice. The disadvantages may include many demands for emotional and material support. If these other family members are poor (and members of ethnic minorities are more likely to be poor than members of the dominant ethnic group), then being part of a support network can lead to many demands and obligations to fulfill those demands. Thus, being part of an extended family network can not only provide social support but also impose social costs, and these networks are more common among some ethnic groups than among others.

Coping Strategies

How people deal with the events in their lives makes a critical difference in the amount of stress they experience, making coping strategies an essential part of the stress process. Coping is the process of changing thoughts and behaviors to manage the situation that involves a potential stressor (Lazarus & Folkman, 1984). These management strategies vary among people and situations, and these differences may distinguish among people who feel more or less stress.

Researchers have considered gender-related factors involved in coping with stress. J. T. Ptacek, Ronald Smith, and John Zanas (1992) discussed the differences between two views of gender and coping. One view of gender differences in coping strategies concerns the socialization of men and women. This *socialization view* holds that the expectations for women and men differ, with women expected to react to stress emotionally and men expected to react with active, problem-solving strategies. This view predicts that men and women will react differently in similar situations, whereas the *structural view* holds that the major differences between men and women come from the different stressful situations the two encounter.

Susan Folkman and Richard Lazarus (1980) found evidence for gender differences in the experience of stress but few differences in coping strategies in a community sample of adults. Their results showed that women were more likely to report stress from health-related concerns and men were more likely to report stressful situations at work. More of the men than the women in their study were employed, so their results may have reflected situation rather than strategy differences.

The men in Folkman and Lazarus's study were likely to use problem-focused coping strategies to deal with their workplace stress, being more likely to employ cognitive efforts or take action to solve the problem that produced the stress. This tendency for men to use action-oriented techniques is consistent with the stereotypical view of men as taking action to solve problems. But Folkman and Lazarus found no difference in the frequency of emotion-focused coping efforts—cognitive and behavioral efforts that are directed at managing or reducing emotional distress. The stereotypical view holds that women should be more likely than men to use this type of strategy, but this study failed to confirm these stereotypes. Indeed, it found that both men and women tended to use both types of strategies to manage any particular stress. Folkman and Lazarus acknowledged that the gender difference they found might not reflect a difference in strategies but a difference in situations; that is, the women and men in their study did not have comparable lives.

Several studies have attempted to assess coping strategies for men and women in comparable situations. Sandra Hamilton and Beverly Fagot (1988) interviewed male and female college students over a two-month period to test for frequency and perception of stressors and use of coping strategies. Women reported more stressors, but few other gender differences emerged. Both women and men reported the same types of events as stressful and not stressful and the same strategies for dealing with each. Interestingly, the situations each judged as not stressful may have been rendered so by the use of direct, problem-focused coping techniques, which both women and men said they used in these situations. Both reported that negative interpersonal interactions were sources of stress, and both said that they did not often approach these situations with problem-solving strategies. This study showed few gender differences but did demonstrate that both men and women use similar coping strategies in similar situations.

Another study that compared men's and women's coping in similar situations measured coping strategies on the job. Kathleen Fontenot and Linda Brannon (1991) matched women and men for job experience and pay and asked them to report on stressful situations and how they coped with these situations. These researchers found few gender differences but significant situational differences. Both women and men said that personal conflict situations were more likely to prompt emotion-focused coping and that task-related stress situations were more likely to elicit problem-focused coping strategies. This study also demonstrated that situations were more likely than gender to be the source of differences in coping efforts.

Ptacek et al. (1992) studied college students and also found that women reported that they found more events stressful than did men, but women and men both tended to use a variety of coping methods and to use problem-focused coping more often than other strategies. Women, however, made greater use of social support as an aid to coping than did men. As detailed earlier, women are likely to be part of a network of people who provide social support for each other, so it is not surprising that they use these resources to help them deal with stress. The women in the Ptacek et al. study tended to use social support as a coping strategy for relationship stresses, but both men and women were similar in their approach to coping with school-related stress.

Both men and women evaluated problem-focused coping as most effective and emotion-focused coping strategies as least effective, with seeking of social support ranked between the other two strategies in effectiveness. Although few gender differences appeared in the results from the Ptacek et al. study, their results indicated that women reported more stress and less control over stress than did the men in the study. Both tended to use coping strategies that could be classified as problem focused, but women used a greater variety of coping strategies, including seeking social support. This and other studies indicated few gender differences in coping with stress but larger differences in coping related to the types of stressful situations.

Overall, these studies failed to confirm the stereotypical view of men as problem focused and women as emotion focused in their coping efforts. Instead, both women and men show a variety of coping techniques that they use to help them deal with the stresses of their lives. This body of research reiterated the greater stress felt by women but did not reveal great gender differences in coping.

Thus, gender differences in coping with stress are not the source of gender differences in stress; those differences seem to be more easily attributable to lifestyle and social circumstances. The magnitude of the gender differences in stress and coping does not account for the preponderance of women in treatment for behavior problems. Possibilities for the source of these differences lie in the criteria used and in the process of diagnosis.

Diagnosis of Mental Disorders

Before someone with an illness can receive appropriate treatment, the person must receive a **diagnosis,** a statement of the classification of the problem. Without a diagnosis, treatment would be haphazard and unconnected to the problem. Thus, classification of both physical and mental problems is an essential step in receiving proper care. Irwin and Barbara Sarason (1993) proposed several characteristics for a good clinical classification system. Specifically, such a system should provide information about the cause of the condition, enable clinicians to make predictions about the course of the disorder, and suggest a course of treatment as well as methods of prevention. In addition, a system of classification should provide a set of common terminology for professionals to communicate among themselves. No system of diagnosis meets these goals perfectly, but these goals are common to the diagnosis of physical and mental problems.

Diagnosis is not a simple task; it consists of matching information about what constitutes a disorder against a description of symptoms. Because any person's symptoms will not match the textbook description of a disorder, the clinician must use personal judgment in the diagnostic process. This judgment provides for the possibility that personal bias and subjective attitudes can enter the diagnostic process.

Although diagnosis according to a system of classification is a necessary part of treatment, diagnosis has disadvantages as well as advantages (Sarason & Sarason, 1993). The advantages include providing an accepted standard that allows reliable diagnosis of the same problem by different clinicians. One of the problems involves labeling—applying a label to the diagnosis. With mental disorders, many labels carry a stigma, and people who have been labeled with a diagnosis of mental disorder may be the targets of discrimination. Furthermore, labeling also puts people into categories, and grouping people tends to magnify the similarities and obscure the individual differences of those within a category.

The diagnosis of mental disorders in the United States dates back to 1840, when the single term *idiocy* was applied to all mental illness (Sarason & Sarason, 1993). The classification of mental disorders expanded, and by 1880 the diagnoses included eight terms. Currently, two systems exist for the classification of mental disorders, the International Classification of Diseases (ICD) of the World Health Organization and the *Diagnostic and Statistical Manual of Mental Disorders* (DSM) of the American Psychiatric Association, the controversial system that was the subject of this chapter's headline story.

The two systems are not entirely separate, and both organizations have cooperated in the development of their respective systems. The American Psychiatric Association, however, wanted a system specifically suited to psychiatric diagnosis in the United States. Until the fourth edition of the DSM, the two systems coexisted but were not very compatible, but greater compatibility was one of the goals for this latest edition.

The DSM Classification System

The *Diagnostic and Statistical Manual of Mental Disorders* (DSM) of the American Psychiatric Association (ApA) has become the standard for professionals who provide mental health care, especially in North America. The first version of the manual appeared in 1952, with a second edition in 1968 (Sarason & Sarason, 1993). These two editions were relatively brief, strongly influenced by psychoanalytic theory, and heavily weighted with psychoanalytic terminology. To make a diagnosis using the system of classification described in the DSM-I or -II, the clinician needed to understand internal, unobservable psychological processes. Understandably, these schemes of classification led to a great deal of variation in diagnoses.

The third edition of the DSM appeared in 1980 and represented a substantial revision. The goal was to create a description-based system of classification for mental disorders, a set of unambiguous descriptions of mental disorders that would lead clinicians to make reliable judgments. A revision of the DSM-III appeared in 1987. This revision, termed DSM-III-R, consisted of relatively minor changes in the existent system. The DSM-IV, which appeared in 1994, contained no major changes but allowed for greater compatibility with the ICD.

The system of the DSM consists of five dimensions, or *axes,* providing for comprehensive physical, psychological, and social diagnosis. The first three axes provide the diagnosis, and the two other axes provide an evaluation of stressors and overall functioning. The manual contains over 240 different diagnoses along with descriptions of the symptoms that characterize the disorders. Information also appears concerning typical age of onset, course of the disorder, and the gender ratio of the disorder; that is, how common the problem appears in men compared to women. In addition, the manual also contains information concerning the similarities among each diagnosis and other similar disorders so that clinicians can distinguish among disorders that have similar symptoms.

Axis I describes the major clinical disorders, such as schizophrenia, depression, and anxiety disorders, among many others. Axis II includes mental retardation and personality disorders, such as antisocial personality, histrionic personality, and dependent personality. Axis III contains a classification for physical disorders and is compatible with the ICD diagnosis system. Axis IV allows reporting of psychosocial and environmental problems related to the diagnosis of psychopathology, including events such as death of a loved one, problems in school, homelessness, or loss of a job. Axis V allows for an overall rating of functioning on the Global Assessment of Functioning Scale, which takes psychological, social, and occupational functioning into account. Diagnosis includes a rating on each of the five axes.

For example, a diagnosis on Axis I might be **posttraumatic stress disorder (PTSD),** a subclassification of anxiety disorders. The DSM-IV describes the diagnosis for this disorder as composed of several criteria. To be diagnosed with posttraumatic stress disorder, the person must meet five criteria: (a) "the person experienced, witnessed, or was confronted with an event or events that involved actual or threatened death or serious injury, or a threat to the physical integrity of self or others" and "the person's response involved intense fear, helplessness, or horror" (ApA, 1994, pp. 427–428), (b) reexperience of the event in some form, (c) avoidance of stimuli associated with the traumatic event or numbing of responsiveness, (d) increased arousal, such as irritability, difficulty concentrating, or hypervigilance, and (e) duration of at least one month.

The combination of these criteria must be present and must produce "clinically significant distress or impairment in social, occupational, or other important areas of functioning" (ApA, 1994, p. 429) before a diagnosis of PTSD can be made. The DSM-IV offers guidelines to the clinician for the different forms of reexperiencing the event, the types of avoidance and numbing that might occur, and the symptoms of increased arousal that accompany PTSD.

In addition, the manual includes examples of the types of unusual events that might precipitate PTSD, examples of the behaviors of affected individuals, and suggestions for disorders that often accompany PTSD. Depression and substance-related disorders often coincide with PTSD, sometimes preceding and sometimes developing after the traumatic stress. If evidence of these disorders exists, the clinician should diagnose all of the conditions. Although the DSM provides the gender ratio for many diagnoses, no such information appears for PTSD.

For a person with a diagnosis of PTSD on Axis I, the Axis II diagnosis might or might not indicate pathology. That is, an Axis I diagnosis of some clinical disorder does not mandate a problem in the developmental and personality disorders described on Axis II. Nor does one prohibit the other. The clinical disorders on Axis I and the personality disorders on Axis II can be related, but the diagnoses are made according to separate criteria. Thus many people who receive a diagnosis of PTSD have no other condition that predisposes them to the disorder and might receive a diagnosis of "no problem" on Axis II (Sarason & Sarason, 1993). Alternatively, people with PTSD might have some separate developmental or personality disorder, and that problem might relate to the PTSD. Some personality disorders, such as paranoid personality disorder would tend to worsen PTSD.

If the person with a diagnosis of PTSD has developed the disorder as a result of battle experiences or rape, then the person may also have physical injuries that stem from the same situation. Indeed, some evidence exists indicating a much greater likelihood of PTSD in soldiers (Helzer, Robins, & McEvoy, 1987) and in crime victims (Resnick et al., 1992) who have been injured. The Axis III diagnosis would note these or other physical conditions that would affect the person's psychological functioning.

Axis IV includes an opportunity for the clinician to note the social and environmental problems that might affect the development, recurrence, or exacerbation of mental disorders. The DSM-IV instructs clinicians to note as many of these problems as are relevant and have occurred within the prior year. PTSD is an exception; these events may have occurred more than a year before diagnosis and still be relevant to the problem.

Axis V allows a rating of the global functioning of the person on the Global Assessment of Functioning Scale based on the person's overall psychological, social, and occupational functioning (excluding physical and environmental limitations). This scale ranges from 1 to 100, with low numbers indicating a low level of functioning and high numbers indicating fewer impairments. A person with PTSD resulting from battle experiences might also show some problem drinking, sleep problems, sensitivity to loud noises, and outbursts of violence with little provocation. Such a person would probably receive a global assessment between 50 and 60, indicating moderate difficulty in social and occupational functioning, but PTSD can produce symptoms that result in either more or less impairment.

The DSM-III, DSM-III-R, and DSM-IV represent improvements over the earlier versions of the *Diagnostic and Statistical Manual.* The extensive descriptions of problem behavior allow clinicians to match patients' symptoms to the description without relying on unobservable, internal psychological processes. The descriptive nature of the DSM makes diagnosis more reliable, but as the headline story for this chapter suggested, the system has sparked controversy. One criticism has concerned the DSM's inclusiveness; some of the diagnostic categories describe behaviors that are arguably within the normal range. For example, nicotine dependence and nicotine withdrawal are diagnoses applied to smokers and smokers who have quit, respectively. Applying a diagnosis in such cases implies that these behaviors represent mental disorders and should be labeled. Many people, including mental health care professionals, disagree with the extension of diagnostic classifications to behaviors that fall within the range of normal for many people.

Gender Inequity in the Diagnosis of Mental Disorders

Criticisms of the multiaxial system of DSM appeared immediately on its release in 1980, and some of these criticisms concerned gender bias in this diagnostic system. That is, some critics, such as Marcie Kaplan (1983a, b) and Carol Tavris (1992), have asserted that the DSM system includes descriptions of disorders that make the diagnosis of problem behavior in women likely, even when the behavior is not due to any pathology. Ellen Piel Cook and her colleagues (Cook, Warnke, & Dupuy, 1993, pp. 312–313) described the situation:

> *Diagnostic categories represent professional assumptions about the nature of psychological dysfunction and are influenced by widespread societal values concerning desirable behavior. Traditionally, professionals have used male-based norms to define healthy versus pathological behavior. That is, masculine qualities such as independence, interpersonal assertion, and goal-directed activity mirroring the qualities most rewarded in our society have been considered fundamental to mental health. In contrast, qualities traditionally associated with women such as interdependence, a concern with nurturing others, and emotional expression have been viewed, at best, as secondary to mental health and, at worst, as signs of emotional immaturity and dysfunction.*

Cook et al. also criticized the DSM system for its failure to consider the life circumstances of those receiving a diagnosis. The DSM system focuses on personal behavior, assuming that disorders are personal problems and not attributable to the circumstances or situational context of behavior. A DSM diagnosis implies that the person creates the mental disorder and that the person's circumstances, although possibly relevant, are not the source of the problem. Thus, if a battered woman experiences distress or depression, she will still be diagnosed according to her symptoms as having depression or one of the anxiety disorders. The violence of her home life may be taken into account, but when the symptoms warrant a diagnosis of mental disorder, that diagnosis is given. Thus, people may receive a diagnosis and then treatment for depression or substance abuse disorder without addressing the social context of the problem and without the clinician considering it appropriate to do so. A recent survey of clinical psychology interns (Middaugh, 1994) showed that 19% of male (but only 5% of female) interns believed that female clients must learn to adjust to their circumstances. Although these percentages indicate that a minority of clinicians hold such attitudes, the criticism is that such attitudes make women responsible for the behavior of others. For example, women could receive psychiatric diagnosis and treatment for their abusive husbands' problems (Stephenson & Walker, 1979).

The accusation of "medicalizing" normal female behavior is an extension of the criticism of diagnosing other problems that should fall within the range of normal. This criticism applies to premenstrual dysphoric disorder (PMDD), the diagnosis applied to symptoms very similar to premenstrual syndrome (PMS), which is the topic of the headline story for this chapter. As Seligmann and Gelman's (1993) headline story suggests, a diagnostic category limited only to women is destined to provoke controversy, and such controversy continued with the publication of the DSM-IV and its inclusion of PMDD.

The Axis II personality disorders have also been the target of criticism and the source of controversy. Laura Brown (1992) argued that the diagnostic categories on this axis have much poorer research support than necessary for their acceptance and allow for gender, ethnic, and social class biases. She concluded that "the claims to a scientific basis for these diagnoses hang upon an extremely slender thread" (p. 215). The DSM-IV warned clinicians that they "must be cautious not to overdiagnose or underdiagnose certain Personality Disorders in females or in males because of social stereotypes about typical gender roles and behaviors" (p. 632), but research has suggested that such bias occurs and affects diagnoses.

Gender biases are not limited to stereotypes of the feminine role. Some of the DSM diagnostic categories seem to draw heavily from elements of the traditional female gender role, but as Janet Williams and Robert Spitzer (1983) pointed out, other categories seem to be exaggerations of the traditional male gender role. For example, **schizoid personality disorder** is characterized by "detachment from social relationships and a restricted range of expression of emotions in interpersonal settings" (ApA, 1994, p. 638). **Antisocial personality disorder** appears as a "pervasive pattern of disregard for, and violation of, the rights of others" (p. 645) including lying, fighting, stealing, and physical cruelty. Both of these personality disorders include exaggerations of the traditional male gender role as described by Robert Brannon (1976). Indifference to social relationships resembles the Sturdy Oak facet of the male role, with its emphasis on self-reliance and lack of emotion. Elements of antisocial personality disorder resemble the Give 'Em Hell facet, with its emphasis on dominance and aggression. Not surprisingly, men receive these two diagnoses more often than women (ApA, 1994; Kass, Spitzer, & Williams, 1983). Table 14.1 shows the personality disorders, along with their prevalence and the gender-related differences in their diagnosis.

If some DSM diagnostic categories are biased against men, then why is there no protest from men against this categorization? The charges of gender bias in the DSM have come mostly from women who have contended that the system is unfair to them. Although some diagnostic categories are exaggerations of the male gender role and

TABLE 14.1   Prevalence and Gender-Related Differences in Personality Disorders

Disorder	Estimated Rate in General Population	Gender Difference
Paranoid	0.5–2.5%	More common among men in clinical populations
Antisocial	3% men, 1% women	More common among men in both general and clinical populations
Borderline	2%	More common in women—75% of those diagnosed are women
Histrionic	2–3%	More commonly diagnosed in women
Narcissistic	<1%	More common among men
Dependent	Most common of personality disorders	More commonly diagnosed in women
Schizoid	Uncommon	More common among men

SOURCE: Based on *Diagnostic and statistical manual of mental disorders* (4th ed.), American Psychiatric Association, 1994, Washington, DC: Author.

men receive these diagnoses more often than women, no analogous criticisms have come from men about gender bias in the DSM. Perhaps this silence is related to the overall lower rate of psychiatric diagnosis for men. The protests of gender bias coming from women apply not only to the DSM but also to diagnosis of mental disorder according to any system. That is, some critics have expressed concern that women will be considered less psychologically healthy than men because men constitute the standard for what is mentally healthy.

An early study that laid the foundation for the concerns over gender bias in clinical diagnosis of mental disorders was the influential study by Inge Broverman and her colleagues (Broverman, Broverman, Clarkson, Rosenkrantz, & Vogel, 1970). These researchers investigated what constitutes a well-adjusted, healthy adult and found that the description significantly differed from what constitutes a well-adjusted, healthy woman. Broverman et al. noted that the gender role for socially desirable behavior in women was not consistent with the psychological standards for a well-adjusted adult. For example, such stereotypically feminine traits as dependence and emotionality are not part of the concept for adult mental health. These researchers contended that the discrepancy between the ideal of mental health for women and for an adult reflects a double standard.

Broverman et al. tested their hypothesis concerning a double standard for mental health by asking clinically trained psychologists, psychiatrists, and social workers to rate either a normal adult, a normal adult man, or a normal adult woman on a lengthy questionnaire. These professionals' ratings showed that their concept of a healthy adult and a healthy man were similar, whereas their views of a healthy adult and a healthy woman differed. Broverman and her colleagues interpreted these results as support for a double standard of mental health, pointing out that the standard for mental health is male and that feminine traits are viewed as detracting from health.

This study has been influential and widely cited, but Thomas Widiger and Shirley Settle (1987) contended that the results were biased by the questions. They argued that Broverman et al. included a higher proportion of male-valued than female-valued items on their questionnaire, resulting in a bias for the male-valued questions. By altering the proportion of male-valued or female-valued items, Widiger and Settle produced findings that were biased in favor of men or women or not biased. They thus concluded that the bias in the Broverman et al. study was in the questions and not necessarily in the professionals' judgments.

Perhaps the methodology of the Broverman et al. (1970) study was biased, but it is also possible that current mental health professionals have less bias than those studied more than 25 years ago. A study by Roger Phillips and Faith Gilroy (1985) suggested that mental health professionals do not exhibit a great deal of sexism in their diagnoses. Using a method comparable to that of the Broverman et al. study, they failed to find significant gender-related differences for standards of mental health. Phillips and Gilroy questioned whether these nonsexist attitudes are translated into practice.

Other research, however, has suggested that gender bias in the diagnosis of behavior problems does exist and is not only a facet of measurement. David Adler and his colleagues (Adler, Drake, & Teague, 1990) presented clinicians with descriptions of patients designed to meet the criteria for several different personality disorders; the two versions of these descriptions differed only in the gender of the patients. These researchers found that the patient's gender affected the clinicians' views in stereotypical directions.

In 1972 Phyllis Chesler proposed that diagnosis of mental disorders is fundamentally gender biased. Chesler contended that women who overconform or underconform to the traditional feminine gender role are subject to diagnosis; if they are either too aggressive or too submissive, they are deviant. Although Chesler's argument centered on the diagnosis of women's problems, the rationale can also extend to men. Those men who fail to conform to the male gender role may be at increased risk for diagnosis. This early critique of the diagnosis of psychological disorders created interest in gender bias, and subsequent research has confirmed Chesler's contention that adherence to and deviation from traditional gender roles are factors in the diagnosis of mental disorders.

A study by Sandra Hamilton and her colleagues (Hamilton, Rothbart, & Dawes, 1986) showed that clinicians exhibit some bias in diagnosing personality disorders. The study included descriptions of histrionic personality disorder and antisocial personality disorder. Histrionic personality disorder is characterized by excessive emotionality and attention-seeking in a variety of situations. Antisocial personality disorder is characterized by a persistent disregard for and violation of the rights of others. The former is more often diagnosed in women, and the latter more often diagnosed in men. When the case studies were equated for severity of pathology, case descriptions of women were found to receive more extreme ratings for histrionic personality disorder than case descriptions portraying men, even when the symptoms were identical. No comparable bias appeared for antisocial personality disorder, demonstrating a tendency to maximize female but not male pathology.

Hope Landrine (1987, 1989) explored the differential diagnosis for mental disorders by conceptualizing personality disorders as extensions of gender role stereotypes. That is, she argued that gender bias in diagnosis is not the reason for the distribution of women into certain classifications of personality disorders and men into other categories. Rather, she proposed that the degree of overlap between several personality disorders and gender role stereotypes accounts for women predominating in some categories and men predominating in others. She substantiated this view by asking people to match descriptions of various cases with diagnoses.

In one study Landrine (1987) presented clinical psychologists and psychiatrists with stereotypical descriptions of lower-class men, single middle-class women, married middle-class women, and married upper-class men and asked for a diagnosis of these cases. Although she warned the clinicians that the cases might be normal, the clinicians tended to label the lower-class man as antisocial personality, the single middle-class woman as histrionic personality, the married middle-class woman as dependent personality, and only the married upper-class man as normal.

Approaching the same problem in another way, Landrine (1987, 1989) presented university students with DSM-III descriptions of various personality disorders and asked them to guess the gender, race, social class, age, and marital status of the person described. The students labeled the description of antisocial personality as a lower-class man; histrionic personality as a single upper-class or middle-class woman; dependent personality as a married middle-class woman; and paranoid, compulsive, and narcissistic personality disorders as middle-class men. The borderline and schizoid personality disorders did not receive consistently different gender labels. Thus, both professionals and university students perceive consistent gender and social class patterns associated with the personality disorders, and these patterns correspond to the frequency of the diagnoses.

Landrine's studies included only the personality disorders that appear on Axis II (and the appendix categories labeled "needing further study" of DSM-III-R), but gender differences appear in several diagnoses for Axis I, such as anxiety disorders, depression, and substance abuse disorders. Rosenfield (1982) studied gender role stereotyping related to these categories of psychiatric diagnosis. Her research indicated that women and men who showed signs of the types of psychopathology more typical of the other gender were more likely to be judged as candidates for hospitalization than those who showed gender-typical disorders. Men with depression or anxiety disorders and women with personality disorders or substance abuse problems—patients displaying "deviant" deviance—were judged more likely to be candidates for hospitalization than were men who showed substance abuse disorders or women who showed depression—their "normal" disorders.

The research by Landrine and by Rosenfield has confirmed and extended Chesler's conceptualization of the relationship between deviance and gender role behaviors, suggesting not only that gender differences exist in diagnoses but also that gender roles and stereotyping play a part in the process of arriving at the diagnoses of mental disorders.

Steven Regeser López (1989) considered the process of diagnosis and in doing so revised the definition of clinical bias and provided a conceptual framework for bias in diagnostic judgments. López maintained that the most commonly studied form of diagnostic bias has been *overdiagnosis,* identifying people as having a disorder when they do not. López, however, expanded diagnostic bias by including *underdiagnosis,* the mistake of failing to identify problems by overlooking symptoms. By using this expansion, he found that diagnostic bias was twice as common as previously estimated.

López conceptualized the clinical diagnostic process as complex decision making, complete with the strategies and mistakes that occur in such situations. Rather than presenting the clinician as a biased individual, López explained that the clinician is "like any other information processor who has to synthesize much complex information to make decisions regarding diagnosis and treatment" (López, 1989, p. 192). He contended that bias in clinical diagnosis is not a matter of the clinician reacting to some single patient characteristic, such as gender or ethnic background. Rather, López asserted that gender and ethnic background are pieces of information that a clinician considers in making a diagnosis.

Clinical diagnosis can be biased, either by over- or underdiagnosing behavior problems, but López maintained that prejudice is rarely a part of the process. "Although there may be some therapists practicing today who fit that rather extreme model of bias, it is unlikely that many therapists do" (p. 192). Instead, bias becomes part of the process by the use of all available information in making a diagnosis. This process can result in a more common diagnosis of alcohol abuse among poor African Americans than among middle-income European-American patients, even when the symptoms are identical, because the clinician incorporates information about ethnic background, income, age, and gender into the process of classifying the problem.

Research from Selina Redman and her colleagues (Redman, Webb, Hennrikus, Gordon, & Sanson-Fisher, 1991) confirmed the tendency toward under- and overdiagnosis, but they found a pattern of gender bias in these decisions showing that overdiagnosis was more common for female patients, and underdiagnosis was more common for male patients. Contrasting the diagnoses of men and women on a questionnaire measuring psychological disturbance with physicians' ratings of the degree of disturbance, these researchers found that the questionnaire assessed a similar number of men and women as psychologically disturbed, though the physicians did not. Instead they showed a tendency to underrate the psychological disturbance of men and overrate that of women. Furthermore, Redman et al. found no difference between interns and practicing physicians, indicating that no recent changes in medical training have altered the gender stereotyping in physicians' diagnoses of psychological problems.

If López is correct concerning bias in clinical diagnosis, then the over- and underdiagnosing of behavior problems are not part of overt prejudice on the part of clinicians. His explanation does not reduce the amount of bias in diagnosis, however, or change the outcome of the biased decisions. Even without simple prejudice or malice, both identifying problems in certain groups of patients who have no pathology and failing to diagnose problems in other types of patients who have mental disorders present problems for those who are over- and underdiagnosed. With the evidence from Redman et al. that overdiagnosis is more common in female patients and underdiagnosis is more common in male patients, the picture is one of systematic gender bias.

Gender Comparisons in Psychopathology

"A survey of the recent literature shows that there is a general consensus among social scientists that women experience more psychological distress than men and that this is largely due to aspects of their societal roles," proclaimed Gove in 1984 (p. 77). Gove's statement asserted that women experience higher rates of psychological disorder than men, and Gove (1980) had earlier proposed that these differences are real and not attributable to greater willingness to seek help or to biased judgments on the part of clinicians.

Chapter 13 presented information about gender differences in seeking health care, showing that women are more likely to seek health care than men. This tendency also applies to psychological problems. Ronald Kessler and his colleagues (Kessler, Brown, & Broman, 1981) studied data from four large-scale surveys of mental health problems

✿ DIVERSITY HIGHLIGHT
Ethnic Diversity and Psychiatric Diagnosis

Gender stereotypes are not the only possibility for biased diagnosis with the DSM system; ethnic stereotypes can also influence the labeling of mental disorders. The DSM system represents the summary of the American Psychiatric Association's evaluation of mental disorders, and the psychiatrists who compose this organization are mostly male and mostly White. The descriptions of categories within the DSM system may themselves include gender and ethnically based components. Alison Solomon (1992) contended that the DSM system contains a Western bias and that this bias may be a problem for people from different cultures who live in a Western country. These people are judged by standards that they may not understand or accept. Alternatively, the application of the system may be biased by practitioners, as Hope Landrine (1987) found. Or both biases may occur in the process of psychiatric diagnosis.

In a study of clinician bias, Marti Loring and Brian Powell (1988) presented psychiatrists with case studies for diagnosis. These researchers manipulated the gender and ethnic background of the cases to determine the effect on the psychiatrists' diagnosis. They found that, even with clear-cut diagnostic criteria, the psychiatrists were influenced in the stereotypical direction by gender and ethnic information.

Jacquelyn Flaskerud (1986) failed to find the expected differences among ethnic groups in psychiatric diagnoses. She compared the diagnosis and treatment of African-American, Mexican-American, Vietnamese-American, Philippino-American, and European-American clients in a mental health agency. Some differences existed among these groups, but not of the magnitude she had expected. Flaskerud speculated that this failure related to the low economic status of all these clients.

In a similar study, Flaskerud and Li-tze Hu (1992) examined the relationship between ethnic background and psychiatric diagnosis for over 26,000 clients of a county mental health system. They found differences in ethnic background for several categories of diagnosis. These categories included a greater proportion of African-American and Asian-American clients who received diagnoses

of serious mental disorders compared to European-American clients, who in turn, received more of these diagnoses than Latino clients. Asian-American clients were less likely than any other ethnic group to receive diagnoses involving substance abuse. Surprisingly, these researchers failed to find any difference in diagnosis relating to social class.

Other researchers have found that both ethnicity and social class relate to psychiatric disorders. Charles Holzer and his colleagues (1986) confirmed previous findings about an inverse relationship between socioeconomic status (SES) and psychiatric disorder; that is, as SES decreases, psychiatric disorders increase. David Williams and his colleagues (Williams, Takeuchi, & Adair, 1992) studied diagnosis and social class in African Americans and European Americans, finding a strong inverse relationship for both ethnic groups. The strongest relationship was for alcohol abuse, but other disorders showed some relationship. For European Americans, depression increased as SES decreased; for African Americans, no relationship appeared. White men with lower SES had a higher rate of mental disorders than their African-American counterparts. Gender differences also appeared, forming complex patterns of gender, ethnicity, and socioeconomic class.

To eliminate diagnostic bias, the criteria and the clinicians using them should be sensitive to the cultural background of the individual who is receiving the diagnosis, and that diagnosis should be more than an expression of the dominant culture. Alison Solomon (1992) cautioned against misdiagnosis based on judgments of what is "dysfunctional or abnormal in the dominant culture" (p. 371) but functional and normal in another.

The fourth edition of the DSM addressed these problems by including information about various ethnic and cultural groups in each diagnosis to allow clinicians to take this information into account. Perhaps the professionals who use the DSM will be able to include this information to attain a cultural sensitivity in their diagnoses that has been lacking, but the listing of symptoms inherent in the multiaxial DSM system does not easily lend itself to the type of flexibility Solomon thought necessary.

and concluded that women have a greater tendency than men to interpret nonspecific problems and distress as mentally related and thus to seek mental health care. These researchers did not contend that all gender differences in mental health treatment were due to women's help seeking, but they did contended that between 10 and 28% of the excess in treatment of women for mental health problems is due to their greater tendency to seek such care.

Women, however, are not more likely to be patients under all circumstances. Philip Leaf and Martha Bruce (1987) studied the use of mental health care services in men and women. They found that women were more likely than men to consult a general physician about mental health problems, but no gender difference appeared in the use of mental health specialty services. Cheryl Travis (1988b) explained this situation by saying that the context of a general health visit can open the possibility for mental health consultation. As men do not make as many physician visits as women (see Chapter 13), a comparable number of opportunities do not arise for them. Thus, men who seek mental health consultations are likely to seek that service directly, whereas women are more likely to receive such care in the context of regular health visits. The overall rate for hospitalization for mental disorders is somewhat higher for women (Kane, 1991), but the difference is limited to the elderly. For men and women in other age groups, men have a higher hospitalization rate than women, suggesting that men's mental health problems may be more severe or that men's symptom reports may be taken more seriously.

Not all disorders show gender differences, but several do. Anxiety disorders, depression, and substance abuse disorders are among those problems that show marked gender differences, whereas other diagnoses are evenly distributed between women and men.

Depression

As Ivan Miller and his colleagues commented: "The term *depression* has been used to describe a wide variety of human experiences, ranging from mild, transient dysphoria experienced by everyone to a severe, completely disabling, and life-threatening disorder which requires intensive intervention" (Miller, Norman, & Dow, 1988, p. 399). Although depression is a common experience, the severe, debilitating problems of severe depression lie outside the range of normal experience. In the DSM system, depression is classified as a type of mood disorder and appears as a diagnosis on Axis I. Two subclassifications of depressive disorder exist—**major depression** and **dysthymia.** Table 14.2 shows the prevalence and gender-related differences for mood disorders.

Symptoms of major depression include dissatisfaction and anxiety, loss of interest and loss of pleasure, feelings of helplessness and hopelessness, changes in sleep or eating habits, and difficulty in concentrating. These symptoms must persist for at least two weeks to warrant a diagnosis of major depression. Dysthymia is milder than major depression and tends to be a chronic condition that may last for years. This diagnosis applies to people who chronically experience depressed mood, loss of interest, or other

TABLE 14.2   Prevalence and Gender-Related Differences in Mood Disorders

Disorder	Estimated Rate in General Population	Gender Difference
Major depression	2–9%	More common in women, with a ratio of 2:1
Dysthymic disorder	3%	More common in women, with a ratio of 2–3:1
Bipolar disorder	0.4–1.6%	No difference

SOURCE: Based on *Diagnostic and statistical manual of mental disorders* (4th ed.), American Psychiatric Association, 1994, Washington, DC: Author.

symptoms of depression, almost like a personality trait. Major depression and dysthymia can co-occur or exist separately.

The ratio of depression in women compared to men is about 2 to 1, considering either the figures obtained from treatment or those from community surveys (ApA, 1994; Nolen-Hoeksema, 1987). These numbers apply to many (but not all) societies around the world, and the explanations for these figures have included biological as well as social theories. The biological theories rely on the differences in reproductive hormones to account for gender differences in depression, but Susan Nolen-Hoeksema (1987) contended that these theories have very little clear support. Studies have failed to consistently demonstrate a link between hormonal fluctuations and mood, and in addition, the differences in depression are not found in all cultures.

The exceptions to the greater prevalence of depression among women provide evidence that gender differences are not biologically based. If reproductive hormones were responsible for the greater prevalence of depression in women, then these differences would appear in all cultures. Although most societies show a ratio of female to male depression similar to that of the United States, several rural nonmodern cultures have similar rates of depression in women and men. Among these cultures are the old order Amish, a rural farming society in the United States. In addition, university students, the elderly, and the bereaved show no gender differences in rates of depression. These exceptions suggest that the gender difference in depression has a social basis, and a number of researchers have concentrated on social and family roles as the source of this difference. (See the "Family Roles" section earlier in this chapter for a review of this research.)

Nolen-Hoeksema (1987) proposed an alternative explanation for gender differences in depression, concentrating on cognitive strategies for dealing with distressing events. She contended that women tend to ruminate on their feelings, whereas men tend to deal with negative feelings by taking action. Dwelling on problems and negative feelings, she maintained, tends to amplify the feelings that lead to depression. Although action may not solve problems, activity is at least a distraction, preventing people from focusing on their problems. Nolen-Hoeksema argued that the "sex differences in rates of depression arise because women's ruminative response styles amplify and prolong their depressive episodes...whereas men's active response styles dampen their depressive episodes" (p. 276). In a program of laboratory experimental research and naturalistic studies on depression, Nolen-Hoeksema (1994) demonstrated that the rumination style of dealing with negative events magnifies depression, whereas the action-oriented style minimizes negative affect.

Another possible explanation for the gender differences in depression is that they do not really exist (Nolen-Hoeksema, 1987; Tavris, 1992). That is, women and men experience the negative feelings that underlie depression at similar rates, but they express their feelings differently. Women tend to turn their negative feelings inward, whereas men tend to express their negative feelings in action. In women, the feelings produce symptoms consistent with the female gender role and hence with the DSM diagnostic criteria for depression. In men, the feelings produce symptoms such as substance abuse, risk taking, and violence. Therefore, this view holds that the symptoms of depression are an expression of gender role socialization for women, and men exhibit different symptoms that receive other diagnoses.

In summary, two types of depression appear in the DSM classification—major depression and dysthymia. Women from many cultures are more likely than men to report symptoms of and receive treatment for depressive disorders at an approximately 2 to 1 ratio. The exceptions to this rule suggest that gender differences in depression are not biologically based. Several socially based explanations for the gender differences in depression exist, including family role differences, personal control differences, and cognitive differences in coping with negative events. Another view holds that the gender differences in depression are a product of the ways in which women and men deal with distress. Women become passive, expressing symptoms of depression, and men become active, expressing symptoms of risk taking, violence, or drug use.

Substance-Related Disorders

Substance-related disorders involve the use of **psychoactive substances,** drugs that affect thoughts, emotions, and behavior. Examples include alcohol, amphetamines, marijuana (cannabis), cocaine, hallucinogens, opiates, and sedatives and hypnotics. In order to receive a diagnosis of one of the types of substance-related disorders, the person must not only use the drug but must also exhibit a strong desire to use the substance and experience problems in social or occupational functioning due to drug use.

Alcohol is the most frequently used and abused substance, and men drink more than women in all categories of drinking (Biener, 1987). That is, more men than women fall into the categories of light, moderate, and heavy drinking. As Landrine and her colleagues (Landrine, Bardwell, & Dean, 1988) demonstrated, drinking and drunkenness are associated with the male, and not the female, gender role. People expect men to drink beer and to get drunk, but the same expectation does not apply to women. Indeed, women (and especially feminine women) are not expected to drink beer (but are expected to drink wine) and should *not* get drunk.

Alcohol is not equally intoxicating for men and women. Women tend to weigh less than men, and body weight affects intoxication, meaning that each drink has a greater effect for smaller people. In addition, some research has indicated that women's alcohol metabolism produces higher alcohol concentration in the blood compared to men, even with the body weight factor taken into account (Frezza et al., 1990). Both these factors result in greater risks to women who drink heavily. Because fewer women than men are heavy drinkers, men are more likely to experience the problems associated with heavy drinking, including the health risks and social problems associated with alcohol abuse.

A variety of evidence suggests that drinking is related to depression, both in men and in women. Bertrand Berger and Vincent Adesso (1991) studied gender differences in alcohol consumption and expectancies for mood changes related to drinking. They tested depressed and nondepressed men and women who showed moderate levels of depression, all of whom were nonproblem drinkers. Men expected more positive effects from drinking, and the men in this study drank more than the women. Berger and Adesso found that depressed men consumed more alcohol than any other group, and they found that drinking decreased these men's perception of depression. This study demonstrated the relationship between negative mood and drinking, especially for men. Perhaps these men are at risk for developing problem drinking, but their strategy of drinking to manage depression showed some signs of being effective.

Victor Hesselbrock and his colleagues (Hesselbrock, Hesselbrock, & Workman-Daniels, 1986) studied depression among alcoholic men and women who were in treatment for their drinking problems. These researchers found that depression did not alter the course of alcoholism for either male or female alcoholics, but those problem drinkers with a history of depression reported that they drank to relieve their depressive symptoms.

Another study that showed a relationship between depression and problem alcohol use tested the relationship over a 3-year time span. Allan Horowitz and Helene White (1991) found a significant relationship between depression at age 21 years and alcohol problems at age 24 years for men, but no such relationship appeared for women. These results demonstrated that the link between depression and problem drinking is stronger in men than in women.

Illegal drug use is also higher among men than women, with men's use and abuse of drugs such as heroin, amphetamines, cocaine, and marijuana paralleling their alcohol use (Biener, 1987). On the other hand, women are more likely to use prescription tranquilizers and sedatives. That is, women are more likely to describe symptoms to physicians that lead to diagnosis of a mental disorder treatable by drugs. The higher rate of prescription drug use by women and the greater use of illegal drugs by men result in similar rates but different patterns of substance use. Table 14.3 summarizes the prevalence and gender-related differences in substance use.

Men's drug use is more apt to be illegal, making them more likely to receive diagnoses of disorder because of their drug use. This difference in diagnosis may not reflect much of a differential tendency in substance use. Perhaps women too might resort to illegal drug use if physicians were less willing to prescribe drugs for them. As Lois Biener (1987, p. 336) concluded, "The sex differences in the use of alcohol and prescription psychotropics are not inconsistent with the hypothesis that men and women

TABLE 14.3   Prevalence and Gender-Related Differences in Substance-Related Disorders

Disorder	Estimated Rate in General Population	Gender Difference
Alcohol	5–8%	More common in men, with a ratio as high as 5:1, varying with age and cultural background
Amphetamine	Possibly as high as 2%	More common in men, with a 3:1 ratio
Cannabis	4%	More common in men
Cocaine	0.2%	No difference
Hallucinogen	0.3%	More common in men, with a 3:1 ratio
Opiates	0.7%	More common in men, with a ratio of 3–4:1
Sedatives, hypnotics, or anxiolytics	1.1%	Women are at higher risk

SOURCE: Based on *Diagnostic and statistical manual of mental disorders* (4th ed.), American Psychiatric Association, 1994, Washington, DC: Author.

are equally likely to resort to substance use for coping, and that the sex difference is merely in the choice of substances."

The research indicates that a relationship exists between depression and drinking; depressed people drink more than the nondepressed and even attribute their drinking to depression. The tendency to drink more heavily when depressed is stronger among men but not exclusive to them. Perhaps men choose this strategy for dealing with negative feelings more often than women and, as Tavris (1992) and Nolen-Hoeksema (1987) suggested, this difference in dealing with negative feelings may account for some of the gender differences in depression and substance abuse disorders. The overall pattern of drug use for men and women probably differs little, but women tend to use legal prescription drugs, whereas men's drug use is more likely to come in the form of alcohol and illegal drugs.

Anxiety Disorders

The group of disorders labeled anxiety disorders includes panic attack, phobias, obsessive-compulsive disorder, and posttraumatic stress disorder, all involving features of anxiety and avoidance of problem situations. A survey of over 18,000 people indicated that anxiety disorders affect more than 7% of adults in the United States (Regier, Narrow, & Rae, 1990). No gender differences exist for some anxiety disorders, but others appear much more often in women than in men.

Panic attack is characterized by periods of intense fear that occur without any fear-provoking situation. These attacks are typically accompanied by physical symptoms of distress, such as sweating, dizziness, and shortness of breath. This disorder is about equally common in women and men, but panic disorder with **agoraphobia** is about twice as common in women. "The essential feature of Agoraphobia is anxiety about being in places or situations from which escape might be difficult (or embarrassing) or in which help may not be available in the event of having a Panic Attack . . . or panic-like symptoms" (ApA, 1994, p. 396). These feelings of anxiety lead people to avoid the situations that might provoke such feelings.

Agoraphobia can also occur without panic disorder, and women are also more likely to have this disorder (ApA, 1994; Cameron & Hill, 1989). Other phobias, unreasonable fear concerning some object or situation, constitute another category of anxiety disorder. *Social phobias* appear as persistent fears of a social situation, such as speaking in public, in which the person is judged by others or in which the person may do something embarrassing. The American Psychiatric Association (1994) stated that women in the general population are more likely to have social phobias, but in clinical populations, the gender ratio is closer to equal or men predominate. *Specific phobias,* fears of some object or situation other than the anticipation of a panic attack or some social situation, are more common among women.

Obsessive-compulsive disorder is the combination of obsession—recurrent, intrusive thoughts about something the person would prefer to ignore—and compulsion—repetitive behaviors intended to prevent anxiety. To receive this diagnosis, a person must be distressed by the obsessive thoughts and must spend over one hour per day on the compulsive behaviors. According to the DSM-IV (ApA, 1994) and Oliver Cameron and Elizabeth Hill (1989), this pattern of behavior is equally common in women and men, but Paul Cleary (1987) found it more common among women.

Posttraumatic stress disorder (PTSD), defined and discussed earlier, was originally applied to men who experienced lasting effects from war experiences. As research accumulated on PTSD, its wider application became evident. Now the diagnosis is given to people experiencing the prolonged aftereffects of many different types of trauma, including natural disasters, accidents, and violent crime as well as military combat. There is no information about gender differences for PTSD, but a random sample of women revealed that over 12% met the criteria for PTSD, a much higher percentage than previous estimates (Resnick, Kilpatrick, Dansky, Saunders, & Best, 1993).

Although gender differences may exist for anxiety disorders, no coherent pattern has appeared. Table 14.4 summarizes the prevalence figures presented in DSM-IV and gender-related differences for these disorders. Research has shown a consistent pattern of higher prevalence for women for agoraphobia (with and without panic disorder) and for specific phobias. Contradictory findings exist concerning gender differences for social phobias and obsessive-compulsive disorder. Overall, more women than men receive the diagnosis of some type of anxiety disorder, indicating that agoraphobia and specific phobias are sufficently common to cause women to dominate this diagnosis.

Gabriele Scheibe and Margot Albus (1992) found that women with anxiety disorders experienced more severe symptoms than men with anxiety disorders and that stress within their marriage was the most frequent event that preceded the development of the disorder. Anxiety and fear are more characteristic of the feminine stereotype than

TABLE 14.4   Prevalence and Gender-Related Differences in Anxiety Disorders

Disorder	Estimated Rate in General Population	Gender Difference
Panic attack with and without agoraphobia	1.5–3.5%	More common in women, with a ratio of 2–3:1
Agoraphobia	More common than with panic attack	Much more common in women
Specific phobias	9–11.3%	Women have 55 to 95% of specific phobias
Social phobias	2–13%	More common in women in general population; more common in men in clinical settings
Obsessive-compulsive disorder	1.5–2.1%	No difference
Posttraumatic stress disorder	1–14%	Not specified in DSM-IV

SOURCE: Based on *Diagnostic and statistical manual of mental disorders* (4th ed.), American Psychiatric Association, 1994, Washington, DC: Author.

of stereotypical male characteristics. The match between gender role traits and mental disorders that Landrine (1987, 1989) found for personality disorders may also apply to anxiety disorders and may constitute an explanation for the higher overall rate of anxiety disorders among women. The gender differences among the different anxiety disorders suggest varying gender-related ways of expressing anxiety.

Other Disorders

Several important classifications of mental disorders show few or no gender differences in prevalence, but men and women with these disorders may not exhibit identical symptoms or the same time course of the disorder. For example, **schizophrenia**—a serious and complex disorder involving thought disturbances, problems in personal relationships, and possibly hallucinations—has been diagnosed equally often in women and men. This equal prevalence does not require that men and women have identical experiences with the disorder, and they do not.

Chung-Chou Chu and colleagues (Chu, Abi-Dargham, Ackerman, Cetingök, & Klein, 1989) studied gender differences in schizophrenics and found that male schizophrenics were younger than female schizophrenics at the time of their diagnosis and that the men were less likely to be married than the women. In terms of symptoms, female schizophrenics tended to be talkative, agitated, irrelevant, and silly, whereas male schizophrenics were less active than normal, grandiose, withdrawn, and more likely to have auditory hallucinations.

Shon Lewis (1992) found gender differences similar to those from the Chu et al. study, but he also found that male schizophrenics tended to have poorer functioning before the onset of their disorder and that they were more likely to be involved in substance abuse than female schizophrenics. In addition, Lewis found that women were more likely to show favorable responses to treatment. Despite the differences, Lewis emphasized the similarities between male and female schizophrenics.

Bipolar disorder is one of the mood disorders, along with major depression and dysthymia (see Table 14.2). Bipolar disorder is a disorder characterized by periods of mania, high activity, and elevated mood combined with periods of depression. These drastically different mood states change in a cyclic fashion such that the affected person experiences both mania and depression over a period of weeks or months, interspersed with periods of normal moods. Unlike the other two mood disorders, bipolar disorder shows no gender differences in prevalence (ApA, 1987; Cleary, 1987).

Based on an examination of individuals with bipolar disorder in the United Kingdom, Charles Sibisi (1990) concluded that the time course of the disorder was somewhat different for men and women. Although Sibisi found no overall gender differences in prevalence, he noted that women were more likely than men to receive a diagnosis during their middle years. As with schizophrenia, men are more likely than women to be diagnosed with bipolar disorder at younger ages.

The **somatoform disorders** show some gender differences. This classification of disorders includes problems for which physical symptoms but no physical basis for disease exist. As a group, women are more likely to receive the diagnosis of somatoform disorder but some of these disorders show no gender differences. *Conversion disorder,* the loss of physical function without any physical basis for the disability, was originally called *hysteria.* In the late 1800s, this disorder was so strongly associated with women that the extension of the label to men was controversial. The DSM-IV (ApA, 1994) stated that this disorder occurs rarely in men, and Kristinn Tomasson and her colleagues (Tomasson, Kent, & Coryell, 1991) found that the diagnosis of conversion disorder was three times more common in women than men.

Another of the somatoform disorders is *somatization disorder,* the recurrence of physical complaints and the seeking of medical attention without receiving any diagnosis for a physical problem. These complaints are often dramatic or exaggerated, and the affected person seeks care from many medical professionals. The Tomasson et al. study found that 95% of somatization disorder patients were women. The diagnosis is so rare for men that Jacqueline Golding and her colleagues (Golding, Smith, & Kashner, 1991) questioned its existence in men, but their investigation revealed that this disorder does occur in men. In addition, the symptoms and the course of the disorder are similar for men and women.

The DSM-IV cautions that physical disorders that involve many variable symptoms can erroneously lead to the diagnosis of somatization disorder. Given physicians' tendency to dismiss the physical complaints of women and attribute those complaints to emotional problems (see Chapter 13), this diagnosis may be erroneously applied to women with physical rather than mental problems.

Sexual disorders consist of two groups of disorders, paraphilias and sexual dysfunctions. **Paraphilias** are characterized by intense sexual feelings in response to objects or situations such as nonhuman objects, children, or nonconsenting persons or to the suffering of self or others. These nonhuman objects include items of clothing or animals, and the situations include exposing one's genitals to strangers, fondling strangers in public places, observing sexual activity, or dressing in gender-inappropriate clothing. Sexual masochism—experiencing pleasure from pain or humiliation—and sexual sadism—experiencing pleasure from hurting one's sexual partner—are also among the paraphilias. About 20% of sexual masochists are women, and this disorder is the most common paraphilia among women. That is, women are rarely diagnosed as having any of the paraphilias.

Sexual dysfunctions, the other subcategory of sexual disorders, consist of low levels of sexual desire or difficulty in arousal or orgasm. Women are more likely to receive a diagnosis indicating an abnormally low level of sexual desire or inhibited orgasm, but men also experience these sexual problems. A summary of the prevalence and gender-related differences in schizophrenia, somatoform, and sexual disorders appears in Table 14.5.

When a person receives a diagnosis of abnormally low (or high) sexual interest or activity, that diagnosis requires a standard of comparison. That standard may be the

---

GENDERED VOICES
When the Doctor Won't Listen

The case of a young woman who was in one of my classes is a good example of a woman whose physician failed to take her complaints seriously. This young woman felt unwell, experiencing a variety of symptoms including chest pain, abdominal pain, and lack of energy. She consulted her physician, who had been her family's doctor since she was a child. He asked her about her symptoms and about her life. She described how she felt and where it hurt, along with the stresses and problems she had recently experienced: Her parents were getting divorced, and she felt so tired that school was difficult to manage. The physician said that she was experiencing stress and told her to relax, assuring her that she would feel better.

She tried but felt no better. After several visits, the woman was convinced that she had a problem that the physician was missing, and he was equally convinced that she had a mental problem that she failed to acknowledge. She consulted another physician, who might have behaved much as the first did, but in this case, the physician did a series of tests that revealed a kidney tumor, which required immediate surgery. Her many symptoms and the stresses in her life were consistent with a number of diagnoses, but her family physician failed to take her physical complaints seriously, insisting that she was experiencing psychological distress rather than organically based physical problems. This woman's experience is by no means unique. Men also may be erroneously diagnosed in a medical examination, but the overwhelming majority of horror stories of physical problems diagnosed as psychological disorders come from women who have experienced biased diagnosis and treatment. Therefore, biased diagnosis may be the source of some of the gender differences in somatization disorder.

TABLE 14.5   **Prevalence and Gender-Related Differences in Rate of Selected Axis I Disorders**

Disorder	Estimated Rate in General Population	Gender Difference
Schizophrenia	0.2–2%	No difference in prevalence
Somatoform disorders		
Conversion disorder	11–300 per 100,000	More common in women, with a ratio of 2–10:1
Somatization disorder	0.2–2% in women, less than 0.2% in men	Rarely diagnosed in men
Sexual disorders		
Paraphilias	No estimate	Rarely diagnosed in women, with the ratio of men to women at 20:1
Sexual dysfunctions	No estimate	More common in women

SOURCE: Based on *Diagnostic and statistical manual of mental disorders* (4th ed.), American Psychiatric Association, 1994, Washington, DC: Author.

person's previous behavior, as compared with their currently lowered (or raised) interest. The standard can also be the clinician's judgment about what is normal, and this standard may be biased or arbitrary. Despite warnings in the DSM concerning other physical or behavioral problems that can produce sexual dysfunctions, the possibility exists that patients may be held to some arbitrary standard of what constitutes normal levels of sexual activity and diagnosed on the basis of behavior that is deviant according to definition.

In summary, several mental disorders show patterns of gender differences, and some disorders that have no difference in prevalence show gender differences in onset or experience. The most dramatic gender differences occur for anxiety and somatoform disorders, diagnoses overwhelmingly given to women, and sexual paraphilias, diagnoses overwhelmingly given to men. Schizophrenia and bipolar disorder show no gender difference in prevalence, but male schizophrenics show some behavioral differences compared to female schizophrenics. The gender differences in bipolar disorder relate to age of onset, with women receiving more diagnoses in middle age than men, who tend to be diagnosed at younger ages.

Although psychopathology is more than exaggerated gender role behavior, all of the gender differences in mental disorders lend themselves to an interpretation relating to gender roles. People tend to exhibit pathology related to their gender roles; that is, women show signs of weakness and physical complaints, whereas men show violence and unusual sexuality. Male schizophrenics are more violent and socially withdrawn, whereas female schizophrenics are more talkative and silly; both behaviors are consistent with traditional gender roles.

The patterns of mental disorders reflect the power of male and female gender roles. The most common patterns of disorder for both men and women show consistencies with what is considered to be appropriate gender-related behaviors. When violations of gender roles occur, clinicians are likely to perceive that these patients have more severe problems than patients who exhibit psychopathology consistent with their gender roles.

Summary

Gender differences in patterns of psychopathology have been the source of accusations of gender bias. The patterns of gender difference in mental disorders may also relate to differences in stress and coping strategies. Research indicates that women experience more stress than men, and women's roles are the most probable sources of these differences. Women's roles obligate them to provide nurturance for their families, but they may not receive as much social support as they give. The stress of women's role obligations and their more extensive involvement with social support networks provide a basis for the difference in perceived stress between women and men.

Although men are the more common targets of violence, women are more commonly the victims of intimate violence, including childhood sexual abuse, rape, and spouse battering. Both women and men become the victims of violent crime, and both are subject to the resulting effects. An increasing body of evidence has implicated violence as a factor in a variety of mental disorders. Poverty is also a source of stress that disproportionately affects women and ethnic minorities, both of which have higher rates of mental disorders than White men.

The stereotypical view holds that women tend to cope with stress by using emotion-focused techniques and men tend to use problem-focused coping, but research has not confirmed these gender differences. Instead, research on gender and coping has revealed that both men and women use a variety of coping strategies and that the situation is a more important factor in the choice of coping strategy than gender.

Accusations of gender bias in psychiatric diagnosis have centered around the *Diagnostic and Statistical Manual of Mental Disorders* (DSM) of the American Psychiatric Association (ApA). This publication contains a system for assigning diagnoses to people's behavioral problems, and the third edition of the DSM (ApA, 1980) proposes a descriptive, multiaxial system of classification. Revisions appeared in 1987 (DSM-III-R) and 1994 (DSM-IV), and these revisions refine but do not make basic changes in the system of classification.

Using the DSM system, clinicians match each patient's symptoms against a description and make diagnoses on each of five axes. Axis I contains descriptions of the major clinical disorders, Axis II describes mental retardation and personality disorders, and Axis III provides a diagnosis of physical conditions. Axis IV contains a listing for the stressors in the patient's life, and Axis V allows for an overall rating of level of functioning.

Women's higher rate of treatment and the gender differences in some categories of disorders have led some researchers to argue that there is gender bias in the DSM, especially in the personality disorder diagnoses that appear on Axis II. Some personality disorder diagnoses are more common in women, whereas others are much more common in men. Indeed, the descriptions of these disorders seem like exaggerations of the female and male gender roles.

In addition to the possibility that the DSM classification system is biased, the clinicians who apply the criteria may also be biased, holding men as the standard for mental health. Early research indicated that clinicians value masculine traits above feminine ones, but later research has indicated that these biases may be weakening. However, physicians are more likely to overdiagnose women's and underdiagnose men's mental disorders. Although clinicians may not be personally prejudiced, their attention to gender and ethnic information can lead them to use this information in their diagnoses, creating a difference in the numbers of women and men who receive various diagnoses.

In addition to the personality disorders that show gender differences, the statistics concerning some Axis I diagnoses reflect different rates for women and men. Many categories of mental disorders show few gender differences, but major depression and substance-related disorders show marked gender differences, with women being more often diagnosed with depression and men with substance abuse problems. Various explanations for these differences exist, including biological, social role, and cognitive theories. An alternative explanation holds that the gender differences in these two behavior problems reflect differences in expressing similar underlying negative feelings: Women express their negative feelings in the form of depression, and men express their negative feelings in the form of alcohol and drug abuse.

Other mental disorders show some differences in women and men. Some anxiety disorders, such as phobias, are more common among women, but others, such as obsessive-compulsive disorder, show little gender difference in prevalence. Likewise, bipolar disorder and schizophrenia are about equally common in men and women, but the paraphilias are very rare in women. Therefore, the pattern of mental disorders seems to reflect the gender roles appropriate to men and women; that is, the patterns of abnormal behavior reflect aspects of the gender role of each. Research indicates that when people deviate from their gender-typical patterns of disordered behavior, their problems are judged to be more severe than those who conform to the pattern of disorders typical of their gender.

Glossary

Agoraphobia a phobic disorder characterized by anxiety about being in places or situations in which escape would be difficult or embarrassing

Antisocial personality disorder a personality disorder in DSM-IV that is characterized by irresponsible and antisocial behavior such as lying, fighting, stealing, and physical cruelty

Bipolar disorder one of the mood disorders characterized by periods of mania, high activity and elevated mood, alternating with depression

Diagnosis a statement of the classification of the problem

Dysthymia diagnosis within the category of mood disorders that is applied to those who experience depressed mood, loss of interest and pleasure, or other symptoms over an extended period, often for months or years

Late luteal phase dysphoric disorder (LLPDD) a diagnosis with symptoms that resemble premenstrual syndrome; this controversial category appeared in the appendix rather than the body of DSM-III-R, along with other personality disorders that require more study

Major depression diagnosis within the category of mood disorders that is applied to severe symptoms of depression, such as loss of interest and pleasure, feelings of helpless and hopelessness, and changes in eating and sleep habits

Panic attack one of the anxiety disorders characterized by periods of intense fear that occur without any fear-provoking situation and accompanied by physical signals of distress

Paraphilias a type of sexual disorder characterized by intense sexual feelings in response to objects or situations that are unusual

Posttraumatic stress disorder (PTSD) one type of anxiety disorder that includes the experience of some distressing event outside the range of normal human experience, the reexperience of the event, avoidance of stimuli associated with the event, and increased sensitivity to associated experiences; these symptoms must persist for at least one month

Premenstrual dysphoric disorder (PMDD) a controversial diagnostic category that appears in an appendix of DSM-IV; its symptoms are those of premenstrual syndrome, and the broad description of these symptoms presents the possibility that vast numbers of women could be diagnosed as mentally ill

Psychoactive substances drugs that affect thoughts, emotions, and behavior

Schizoid personality disorder a personality disorder on Axis II of DSM-IV that is characterized by lack of concern about personal and social relationships as well as a restricted range of emotional experience and expression

Schizophrenia a serious and complex disorder involving thought disturbances, problems in personal relationships, and possibly hallucinations

Sexual dysfunctions a subcategory of the sexual disorders that includes problems with low level of sexual desire or difficulty in arousal or orgasm

Social support receipt of emotional and material resources from friends and family members

Somatoform disorders a classification of disorders that includes problems with physical symptoms of disease but with no physical basis for these symptoms

Suggested Readings

Cook, Ellen Piel; Warnke, Melanie; & Dupuy, Paula. (1993). Gender bias and the DSM-III-R. *Counselor Education and Supervision, 32,* 311–322. This recent article presents a thoughtful summary of bias in the DSM as well as its application by clinicians and the potential for gender bias in counseling.

Landrine, Hope. (1989). The politics of personality disorder. *Psychology of Women Quarterly, 13,* 325–339. Landrine demonstrated the congruence between social stereotypes and various descriptions of personality disorders. She argues that by incorporating these ethnic and gender stereotypes, the diagnosis of personality disorders becomes politicized.

Nolen-Hoeksema, Susan. (1987). Sex differences in unipolar depression: Evidence and theory. *Psychological Bulletin, 101,* 259–282. An excellent review of the gender differences in depression, including some interesting exceptions to the higher prevalence of this disorder in women and a proposal for cognitive strategies that might underlie the gender differences in depression.

Wethington, Elaine; McLeod, Jane D.; & Kessler, Ronald C. (1987). The importance of life events for explaining sex differences in psychological distress. In Rosalind C. Barnett, Lois Biener, & Grace K. Baruch (Eds.), *Gender and stress* (pp. 144–156). New York: Free Press. These authors take a social role point of view in examining the gender differences in stress that relate to mental distress. They propose that women's roles carry obligations for nurturance that men's roles do not and that these differences are important for mental health.

Treatment for Mental Disorders

Stereotypes of the Sexes Persisting in Therapy

—*New York Times,* April 10, 1990

Psychotherapy and psychiatric diagnosis are still often used to enforce conventional standards of masculinity and femininity and sometimes to brand as mentally ill people who depart from the norm," according to Daniel Goleman's (1990a, p. C1) *New York Times* story. Goleman contended that men as well as women could be the victims of stereotyping by mental health workers, particularly to those who depart from conventional gender roles. In support, Goleman discussed research by John Robertson and Louise Fitzgerald (1990), who found evidence of gender stereotyping by counselors.

These researchers studied counselors and therapists assessing a male "client," who was a trained actor. Robertson and Fitzgerald made two versions of a videotape—one in which the man led a traditional life and another in which he violated the traditional gender role for men. In the traditional version, the man portrayed himself as an engineer with a wife who was a homemaker. In the nontraditional version, the man was responsible for household and child-care duties, while his wife was the engineer and primary breadwinner of the family. The man described his problems in the same terms in both versions of the videotapes, and the researchers arranged the experiment such that the therapists made comments at specified pauses during the tape as though they were counseling with the man on the videotape.

Robertson and Fitzgerald hypothesized that the therapists would react to the man's home situation as well as to his symptoms, and their results largely supported their predictions. For the man taking the nontraditional role, the therapists directed 10% of their responses to the man's home situation, whereas no counselor made comments about the home situation of the man who took the traditional breadwinner role. The comments to the man who was a homemaker included "What messages do you have from your childhood about what a man is?" and "You probably need to renegotiate this contract that (you've) got at home" (Robertson & Fitzgerald, 1990, p. 5). These comments suggest that the therapists interpreted the man's nontraditional family choices as a source of his problems and behaved differently with the client whose choices violated traditional gender roles.

In addition, the therapists' diagnosis of the client indicated more severe pathology for the man who had made nontraditional choices. Some of the therapists even suggested that the man's family choices were an appropriate target for therapeutic intervention. These results indicate not only that men who have made nontraditional choices have difficulties getting others to accept the validity of their choices but also that therapy can be used to enforce traditional values.

Approaches to Therapy

Formal psychological treatment for mental disorders or behavior problems has a relatively short history, and throughout that history, the approach to treatment has been related to the conceptualization of the source of these problems. Until the middle of the 19th century, little treatment existed for people with mental disorders, and the dominant belief was that abnormal and socially unacceptable behavior was a moral or spiritual problem (Schultz & Schultz, 1992). Several changes brought about treatment for psychological problems, including a reconceptualization of the source of mental disorders and the growth of medical knowledge. The reconceptualization of mental disorders from possession by demons or moral deficiencies to problems in mental functioning came about during the 19th and early 20th centuries, and medicine became the model for understanding these problems. With the growing acceptance of mental illness as a counterpart to physical illness, medical researchers began to seek methods of treatment for abnormal behavior.

Therapies for the treatment of mental disorders arose and became part of psychiatry and psychology. The earliest modern therapy was **psychoanalysis,** Freud's version of treatment for psychological problems, but some therapists who were dissatisfied with psychoanalysis devised other talk-based therapies. In addition, psychological research on operant conditioning was applied to changing undesirable behavior, resulting in the therapy called **behavior modification.** Psychiatrists also use psychoactive drugs in the treatment of behavior problems, sometimes instead of and sometimes in addition to psychotherapy. Therefore, several professions provide a variety of treatments for people with mental disorders.

Psychoanalysis

Sigmund Freud was among the early researchers who investigated causes and sought cures for mental disorders, and he developed a system of therapy that has influenced treatment as well as contemporary thought about mental disorders. Freud's system of therapy was psychoanalysis, a talk-based approach toward understanding and alleviating psychological problems. Psychoanalysis was part of Freud's comprehensive theory of personality development and functioning. (Chapter 6 presented the Freudian approach to personality development.) Freud believed that psychological problems develop when people are incapable of dealing with problems and use **repression** to push problematic material into the region of the unconscious. The unconscious does not function rationally, so repressed material has the potential to remain in the unconscious throughout childhood and adulthood and can produce problems at any time.

Problems typically result from conflict during childhood, when the ego is not sufficiently well developed to deal with the many difficulties of early childhood. Adult problems represent childhood traumas that have been repressed, leaving the troubled person with mental conflict, distress, or problems in functioning. Psychoanalysts attempt to help patients resolve their problems by bringing unconscious material to consciousness so that patients may deal with these problems rationally. Once patients gain insight into the source of their conflicts, Freud believed that their conscious mind could deal with the problems, thus alleviating them. Therefore, bringing repressed material to consciousness was a goal of psychoanalysis. Table 15.1 summarizes the elements of psychoanalytic therapy.

Although Freud and his colleagues were physicians, psychoanalysis developed as a psychological treatment for mental disorders. That is, the source of mental disorders was psychological, and the treatment was accomplished through talking about the source of the problem. This approach influenced popular thought and prompted the development of other talk-based treatments. Although medically based treatments for mental disorders also developed, talked-based psychotherapy remains a prominent approach to the treatment of mental disorders.

Some talk-based therapies arose in a direct opposition to the Freudian system. Karen Horney (1939) was one of the psychoanalysts who protested the Freudian view of women and offered alternative approaches to dealing with psychological problems. (See Chapter 6 for more about Freud's theory and Horney's alternatives to it.) Other

TABLE 15.1 Elements of Psychoanalytic Therapy

Category	Description
Underlying source of problems	Childhood trauma and insufficient ego to deal with trauma
Cause of problems	Repression of unconscious conflict
Immediate cause of problems	Repressed material escapes from unconscious
Goal of therapy	To bring repressed material to consciousness
Techniques	Talking, free association, dream analysis
Practitioners	Psychoanalysts (who are usually psychiatrists)

alternative therapies originated with Carl Rogers (1951), who developed a humanistic therapy called client-centered therapy, and Albert Ellis (1962), who developed a cognitive therapy called rational-emotive therapy. These therapists objected to the emphasis on the unconscious in psychoanalysis and offered therapies that emphasized coping with current life problems rather than exploring developmental trauma from childhood.

Humanistic Therapies

The psychoanalytic view of human nature is rather pessimistic, holding that psychological development is filled with potentially debilitating problems and that few people develop into healthy adults. Psychoanalysis can help people resolve the problems that result from unconscious conflicts and trauma, but the maintenance of a healthy, functioning personality is always a delicate balancing act. The humanistic theories of personality hold the more optimistic view that people are innately drawn toward fulfilling their human potential. If they fail, the reasons lie in their circumstances and in their environment, which somehow prevent complete development. This optimistic view of humanity is reflected in humanistic psychotherapy, for example in Rogers's client-centered therapy and Fritz Perls's Gestalt therapy.

Rogers (1951, 1961, 1980) proposed that human development follows a natural course toward health unless some event impedes this development. Rogers believed that problems originate from distortions in self-concept, and these distortions arise due to a lack of acceptance of true feelings. When children get messages that the feelings they experience are unacceptable, they begin to deny these feelings. Lack of acceptance of feelings leads to an inaccurate self-concept and interferes with many facets of development.

Rogers's system of client-centered therapy seeks to help people solve problems and restore their development toward attaining their full potential. Client-centered therapy holds that troubled people have within themselves the capacity to understand and solve their own problems with the help of an acceptant, empathic counselor (Kaplan & Yasinski, 1980).

The relationship with this counselor is of primary importance. Client-centered counselors offer three conditions—unconditional acceptance, empathy, and congruence to their clients—and the most important of these is congruence. "To be congruent means to be real or genuine, to be whole or integrated, to be what one truly is" (Feist, 1994, p. 650). These three conditions are essential for clients to experience growth, and all come from clients' relationship with the counselor. Given these three conditions, the process of therapy can take place.

A major goal of client-centered therapy is the elimination of the discrepancy between clients' actual feelings and their recognized feelings. By coming to recognize their true feelings—including negative feelings—clients can accept themselves. That is, clients develop congruence during the course of successful client-centered therapy. In addition, they become open to change and new experiences, develop a freshness of attitude, and come to trust in themselves.

The counselor's job is to provide clients with a therapeutic relationship so that clients can reclaim their ability to move toward personal growth and development. The counselor does not work directly on changing clients; they must do that for themselves. This approach focuses on allowing clients to think in undistorted ways, assuming that behavior change will follow.

Gestalt therapy is another humanistic therapy, and it has similarities to client-centered therapy. The word *gestalt* means "whole" in German, and Perls (1969), the originator of this therapy, believed that the basis of psychological problems comes from a feeling of not being whole. The failure to acknowledge their emotions leads people to this feeling of not being whole; they have a sense that parts of themselves are psychologically disowned. Gestalt therapy seeks to help clients to become whole again by allowing them to recognize and express their emotions, and Gestalt therapists use a variety of techniques oriented around understanding and integrating emotions to further this goal.

The humanistic therapies all share the view that fulfillment is a natural goal that people can reach, but impediments produce barriers that block psychological growth. Humanistic therapists attempt to provide an atmosphere that permits clients to move in the direction of self-enhancement. Table 15.2 summarizes the elements of humanistic therapy.

Humanistic therapy typically involves individual and group counseling for 10 to 30 sessions, with counselors helping clients to achieve the goals clients set for themselves. The goals of this type of therapy may not be very specific, and therapy can be lengthy. Nonetheless, this approach to counseling has been enormously influential, with many therapists taking a humanistic approach.

Cognitive Therapy

Clients' thoughts are important in humanistic therapy, but thought processes are the major focus in cognitive therapy. Cognitive therapists believe that thought processes

TABLE 15.2   Elements of Humanistic Therapy

Category	Description
Underlying source of problems	Discrepancy between genuine feelings and acknowledged emotions; feelings of not being whole
Cause of problems	Blockage of development toward full potential
Immediate source of problems	The problem that prompts a client to seek therapy
Goal of therapy	To provide an atmosphere that allows clients to move toward personal growth
Techniques	Empathic listening, providing unconditional positive regard, showing congruence
Practitioners	Psychologists, social workers, counselors

are the basis of feelings and behavior, creating psychological problems and providing the potential for alleviating those problems. Behavior and emotions follow from cognition, so a change in cognition provides the foundation for changing behavior.

Ellis (1962) developed rational-emotive therapy, one of the earliest cognitive therapies, in response to what he saw as the failure of psychoanalysis to solve people's problems. Ellis objected to both the length and nondirective nature of psychoanalysis, instead insisting that therapists should set goals and that therapy should be brief and problem oriented.

Rational-emotive therapy views psychological problems as a result of people's irrational beliefs. Such beliefs lead people to unrealistic views of themselves and the world, and when these expectations go unmet, people are miserable. Rational-emotive therapy attempts to change these irrational cognitions and assumes that a change in cognitions will produce changes in behavior. Correcting these irrational beliefs is the basic goal of rational-emotive therapy.

Aaron Beck (1985) developed a cognitive therapy specifically for depression, concentrating on the distorted, self-defeating thoughts that accompany depression. Beck contended that depressed people overgeneralize personal failures into the belief that they are worthless and explain positive occurrences as an exception to the general rule of failure. Depressed people also magnify the enormity of negative events, seeing these events as catastrophic and unchangeable. Selective perception is another cognition that adds to depression, causing depressed people to notice the negative elements of their surroundings and ignore the positive ones. These distortions of thinking magnify and maintain negative cognitions and thus perpetuate depression.

Beck's cognitive therapy attempts to help clients change their negative cognitions by testing the cognitions and evaluating their validity. Rational-emotive therapy attempts to confront irrational beliefs with logic, but Beck's cognitive therapy is less directive and more experiential. Rather than arguing against such cognitions, Beck might formulate ways for clients to evaluate their cognitions and test their validity. Lack of pleasure is often a prominent component of depression, and Beck's cognitive therapy urges depressed people to introduce pleasurable experiences into lives.

Table 15.3 summarizes cognitive therapies. These therapies, such as rational-emotive therapy and Beck's cognitive therapy, assume that cognitions underlie psychological problems and that changing cognitions will change behavior. Rather than concentrating on behavior itself, these therapies concentrate on thoughts. Another therapeutic orientation takes an alternative approach; behavior modification emphasizes behavior rather than cognitions.

Behavior Modification

Behavior modification arose from laboratory research in psychology on the process of learning (Kantrowitz & Ballou, 1992). In exploring learning principles, researchers discovered that the principles of operant conditioning—reinforcement and punishment—are powerful forces in determining behavior. Not only do these principles apply to the nonhuman animals commonly used in laboratories but also to humans and their

TABLE 15.3   Elements of Cognitive Therapy

Category	Description
Underlying source of problems	Irrational beliefs
Cause of problems	Application of irrational beliefs to personal circumstances
Immediate source of problems	The problem that brings a person to therapy
Goal of therapy	To change irrational to more rational beliefs
Techniques	Confronting and disputing irrational beliefs, testing the validity of negative cognitions
Practitioners	Psychologists, social workers, counselors

complex behaviors. Applying these principles to problem behavior results in the view that such behaviors are learned and maintained by reinforcement and punishment, and these principles can change unacceptable behavior to more acceptable alternatives.

Behavior modification strives to replace inappropriate or deviant behaviors with other, healthier behavior patterns through the application of operant conditioning. Although both have been used in behavior modification programs, reinforcement for desirable behavior is more common than punishment for undesirable behavior.

Behavior modification is more specific and task-oriented than talk-based psychotherapies. For example, behavior modification is often used for various skills training, such as developing assertiveness skills, dealing with phobias, or changing eating patterns. In such programs, a client "learns a repertoire of behavior likely to produce desirable consequences in specific situations" (Blechman, 1980, p. 225). Women are major consumers of behavior modification, as they most often seek treatment for assertiveness problems, eating disorders, depression, and phobias.

Cognitive behavior modification is a variation that incorporates the concept that cognition is an important factor in behavior with the application of principles of reinforcement to bring about behavior change (Fodor, 1988). As with behavior modification, this therapeutic approach assumes that problems are the result of learned patterns of maladaptive behavior.

The process of cognitive behavior therapy typically differs from behavior modification in several ways. Rather than concentrating on behavior and ignoring internal cognitive processes, cognitive behavior modification attempts to change cognitions and thereby change behavior. This therapy tends to be more collaborative than behavior modification, with the client playing an active role. Client and therapist cooperate to establish goals, and the client rather than the therapist may monitor and reward the desired behavior. Table 15.4 summarizes behavior modification and cognitive behavior modification therapy.

Behavior modification and cognitive behavior modification have provided alternatives to more traditional therapy, differing from the psychoanalytic and humanistic

TABLE 15.4   Elements of Behavior Modification and Cognitive Behavior Modification Therapy

Category	Description
Underlying source of problems	None
Cause of problems	Behavior that is not adaptive or successful in specific situations
Immediate source of problems	The problem that brings a person to therapy
Goal of therapy	To change behavior (or cognitions that underlie behavior) to more acceptable alternative behaviors
Techniques	Reinforcement for acceptable behaviors, desensitization for phobias, assertiveness training
Practitioners	Psychologists, social workers, counselors

approaches. The behavior modification approach emphasizes specific problems and the analysis of behavior that contributes to the problem. This behavior-oriented emphasis is also important in the application of reinforcement to change maladaptive to more adaptive behaviors. Therefore, behavior modification and cognitive behavior modification represent a different approach to understanding and treating problem behavior.

Some therapists use behavior modification and cognitive behavior modification with all clients and for all problems. Many therapists, however, take a more eclectic approach, using a variety of techniques rather than adhering to a single therapy orientation. These therapists argue that an eclectic approach offers them the opportunity to choose from a variety of approaches, fitting the problem and the client to the approach.

Medical Therapies

Talk-based psychotherapies and behavior modification are practiced by psychologists, social workers, counselors, and psychiatrists, but psychiatrists and other physicians can also use medical therapies for behavior problems. Psychoactive drugs are the most common of the medical therapies, but **electroconvulsive therapy** is also a medical approach to behavior problems. These medical therapies take the approach of altering brain function in order to change thought and behavior, but the exact mechanisms of the therapeutic benefits for both psychoactive drugs and electroconvulsive therapy are not completely understood. Nonetheless, physicians may use these therapies alone or in conjunction with psychotherapy.

Since the 1950s, the use of psychoactive drugs has escalated, and the number of such drugs has grown. Psychiatrists use psychoactive drugs to treat schizophrenia, depression, and anxiety disorders. Women receive more drug prescriptions than men, and this difference is higher for psychoactive than for other types of drugs. Ruth Cooperstock (1970) reviewed the patterns of prescription psychoactive drug use in Canada, the United States, and the United Kingdom, finding a consistently higher rate of use for women.

In addition, she found some evidence for both differences and similarities in patterns of drug use for men and women. The similarities included a higher rate of use for those not in the work force. The differences included a greater use of tranquilizers by women during early adulthood and middle age, whereas men's use peaked at older ages.

Since Cooperstock's review, the prescription of psychoactive drugs has increased for both men and women, but the pattern is similar (Ashton, 1991). New drugs have appeared for the treatment of schizophrenia, anxiety disorders, and depression, but women in North America and Europe are prescribed psychoactive drugs twice as often as men. The trend in psychiatry is toward a greater use of drug therapy and a decline in talk-based therapy.

Arthur Nikelly (1994) examined one possible source of overprescription of drugs—the advertising of pharmaceuticals. His analysis showed that the advertising of drugs for depression tended to depict women far more often than men, to show women in stereotypical ways, to present depression as a medical problem, and to ignore the social context of depression. For example, one advertisement showed a color photograph of a well-ordered kitchen superimposed over a black-and-white photograph of a disorderly kitchen, with the message that the drug allowed patients to get back to their normal activities. Nikelly suggested that such drug advertisements convey not only the impression that female patients should receive such drugs but also that these drugs are the best approach to treating depression, despite the evidence that occupational, marital, economic, and social factors contribute to the problem (see Chapter 14).

The use of electrical shock to alter behavior became common during the 1940s and remains in use today. This therapy involves delivering electric shock to the brain, and the resulting convulsions have a therapeutic effect. Although the reasons for the beneficial effects remain unclear and there can be serious side effects, electroconvulsive therapy is now used almost exclusively for depression that has failed to respond to antidepressant drugs (Sarason & Sarason, 1993). Because a majority of the cases of depression occur in women, they are the most frequent recipients of this therapy.

Table 15.5 summarizes medical therapies. Despite the growth of medically based treatment for behavior problems, this approach is controversial. Drugs and

TABLE 15.5   Elements of Medical Therapy

Category	Description
Underlying source of problems	Biological or biochemical abnormalities
Cause of problems	Chemical or biological malfunction in brain
Immediate source of problems	The problem that brings a person to therapy
Goal of therapy	To change biological functioning
Techniques	Psychoactive drugs, surgery, electroconvulsive therapy
Practitioners	Psychiatrists and other physicians

electroconvulsive shock alter behavior, sometimes bringing about substantial improvements. These therapies do not cure mental disorders but rather decrease or diminish the severity of symptoms. These effects can be beneficial but are not permanent; the symptoms reappear when patients stop taking the drugs, and the therapeutic effects of electroconvulsive therapy rarely last for more than a few months (Sarason & Sarason, 1993). Psychoactive drugs, like other drugs, can cause serious side effects, and electroconvulsive therapy typically produces memory loss. The benefits of medical treatments outweigh the risks for some people, but the risks exist.

Accusations of Gender Bias in Therapy

As discussed in Chapter 6, Freudian theory has come under heavy criticism for its sexism, and psychoanalytic therapy is no exception. As Ronald Levant (1990) observed, traditional therapy was designed primarily by men to treat women. The cultural views of gender roles accepted during the late 1800s became incorporated into psychoanalysis, and the cases treated by Freud and his colleagues reflect those men's views of women and their problems. Rachel Hare-Mustin (1983) contended that Freud's behavior in treating Dora, one of his famous case studies, exemplified his mistreatment of female patients and the sexism of his system; he refused to listen to or believe her and treated her as a child. Hare-Mustin argued that psychotherapy in general and psychoanalysis in particular have failed to meet the needs of female patients.

The American Psychological Association's Task Force on Sex Bias and Sex-Role Stereotyping in Psychotherapeutic Practice (Brodsky & Holroyd, 1975) listed the sexist use of psychoanalytic concepts as one of the four main causes of gender bias in therapy. The gender bias in psychoanalysis comes from the notion that female development is a variation of male development and that girls' perception of their inadequacy is a critical element in personality development. Freud and his followers accepted men as the standard and women as a deviation of normal psychological development—a deviation that could never meet the male standard. Thus, critics have argued that psychoanalysis is inherently gender biased. This bias extends not only to psychoanalytic therapy but also to all of the other therapies that have accepted Freudian concepts, which includes some (but not all) of the other talk-based psychotherapies.

Neither humanistic nor cognitive therapy is inherently gender biased in the way that psychoanalysis is, but both emphasize personal rather than social and environmental factors in functioning (Lerman, 1992). Ruth Waterhouse (1993) argued that such neglect will make client-centered counseling inadequate for women due to its emphasis on the individual and its failure to take the social and political aspects of personal problems into account. By stressing the individual and orienting counseling toward the "here and now," Waterhouse contended that women can be made to accept responsibility for the problem behavior of others, intensifying rather than diminishing their problems.

The practice of humanistic and cognitive therapies can be gender-biased through the application of the therapists' personal values to the therapy situation. Although not part of the therapy process, these approaches allow for therapists to impose their personal values, including any gender biases they might have. Therapists may encourage their clients to adhere to traditional gender roles as a way to handle their problems, as the therapists in Robertson and Fitzgerald's (1990) study did, attributing adjustment problems to the choice of nontraditional gender role. Such therapists may encourage clients to adopt more traditional gender roles, making the practice of these therapies sexist.

Behavior modification is value free, having no theoretical component related to gender. Any behavior can be the target for modification, however, and the choice of which behaviors to encourage or discourage can express traditional or nontraditional values. Although behavior modification is not inherently gender biased, its practice can also be sexist (Blechman, 1980). As Ricki Kantrowitz and Mary Ballou (1992, pp. 79–80) asked, "Are cognitive-behavioral techniques being used to encourage clients to conform to normative standards?" The normative standard enforces traditional gender roles, and these critics fear that behavior modification is used to enforce women's conformity rather than their personal development.

Medical therapies have also been the target of criticisms of sexist bias. As Chapter 13 detailed, women and men receive different treatment in the health care system. Physicians tend to take men's symptom reports more seriously than similar reports from women and to attribute women's complaints to psychological rather than physical causes. This tendency toward overdiagnosis for women and underdiagnosis for men results in inappropriate psychological treatment for women and a lack of appropriate psychological treatment for men.

Women are more likely to receive prescriptions for psychoactive drugs than men, a pattern that has persisted since the 1960s (Ashton, 1991; Cooperstock, 1970). Heather Ashton (1991) contended that some of these prescriptions are unnecessary and that both women and men may be overmedicated with psychoactive drugs. Table 15.6 summarizes the potential sources of bias in the various types of therapy.

TABLE 15.6   Sources of Gender Bias in Therapies for Behavior Problems

Type of Therapy	Source of Potential Gender Bias
Psychoanalysis	Psychoanalytic theory assumes that women are inferior.
Humanistic	Therapists may apply personal standards that are sexist; therapy focuses on the individual and ignores the social context of personal problems.
Cognitive	Therapists may apply personal standards that are sexist; therapy fails to address the social context of personal problems.
Behavior modification	Therapists may choose to reinforce traditional, gender-related behaviors.
Medical	Women and men are diagnosed and treated according to stereotypical and traditional values.

In an early and vehement indictment of gender bias in diagnosis and therapy, Phyllis Chesler (1972) argued that diagnosis has been used to identify women who deviate from their traditional gender roles and that therapy has been used to restore women to those roles. Chesler contended that women experience problems when they either underconform or overconform to traditional gender roles and that therapy is a process to reimpose the traditional feminine role. Women may behave in many deviant ways, but when they fail to be subservient and domestic, they are labeled as needing therapy.

This therapy may be of any variety, but according to Chesler, all therapies seek to restore women to the traditional feminine gender role. One of the respondents to a survey by the American Psychological Association (APA Task Force on Sex Bias, 1978) confirmed Chesler's contention by saying, "I have had women report to me that they could not continue in therapy because the objective seemed to be for them to learn to adjust better to their roles as wives, mothers, daughters (underlings of one kind or another), and they needed to become free persons" (p. 1122).

By surveying female psychologists, the APA Task Force (Brodsky & Holroyd, 1975) determined that four main areas of sexist bias exist in the practice of psychotherapy. As mentioned previously, the sexist use of psychoanalytic concepts was one of the four. The other areas included fostering traditional sex roles, having biased expectations concerning women, devaluing of women's potential, and responding to women as sex objects, including therapists' sexual exploitation of clients.

As Robertson and Fitzgerald's (1990) research showed, men are also subject to gender bias in therapy. A substantial proportion of therapists in this study commented on the lifestyle of the man who had chosen a nontraditional role and urged him to consider a change to more traditional masculine behavior. Therefore, evidence exists that the practice of therapy is not value-free and that therapy tends to work toward preserving traditional values for both men and women.

Gender Issues in Therapy

One gender issue in therapy relates to gender preferences for counselors. In one study the most common preference was no preference (Bernstein, Hofmann, & Wade, 1987). That is, between 30 and 50% of college students expressed no preference for either a male or a female counselor. Of those who had a preference, male counselors were more often chosen, especially for vocational-educational or social-personal concerns. For sexual concerns or problems, people showed some tendency to prefer same-gender counselors. Those people who expressed a preference for a male counselor tended to be traditional in their gender roles; both traditional men and women preferred a male counselor. People with less traditional gender role attitudes showed no preference concerning counselor gender.

The results of another study (Blier, Atkinson, & Greer, 1987) suggested that gender role rather than gender may be the source of the gender preference for counselors. This study varied the descriptions of counselors to determine the effect on willingness to see a counselor. No difference for counselor gender appeared, but gender role produced a significant difference. Prospective clients were more willing to see a feminine rather than a masculine counselor for personal concerns but preferred a masculine counselor for assertiveness and academic concerns. These results demonstrated the power of gender role stereotyping in influencing expectations about counselors' behavior and thus on clients' preferences.

Do preferences for male or female counselors supersede the desire for an effective counselor? N. Dean DeHeer and his colleagues (DeHeer, Wampold, & Freund, 1992) varied descriptions of counselors both in their gender and in their competence. These researchers hypothesized that people who were strongly gender typed would use gender as a factor in choosing a counselor, whereas people who were more androgynous would use information concerning competence. Their results indicated that competence, not gender, was a factor for all types of participants. Therefore, under some circumstances, some people prefer male or female counselors, but the effectiveness of the counselor is more important than gender in clients' choices.

Another gender issue in therapy is the suitability of various types of therapy for women or men. Although women more often seek counseling and psychotherapy and tend to be better at the therapy tasks involved, their needs may not be met by the process. The gender bias in psychoanalysis and the potential for gender bias in other therapies have presented important issues for therapy, and several alternative approaches have endeavored to correct these biases.

The 1975 report from the APA's Task Force on Sex Bias and Sex-Role Stereotyping in Psychotherapeutic Practice (Brodsky & Holroyd, 1975) sensitized psychologists to the need for attention to gender-related issues in therapy, and a second report from the task force (APA Task Force on Sex Bias..., 1978) issued guidelines for therapy with women. Although these guidelines were written with women in mind, the task force mentioned that other groups have been subject to prejudice and mistreatment in therapy, and these guidelines set forth ways to avoid bias.

Recognizing the potential for bias in therapy has led to the notion that good therapy should be nonsexist, and professionals have worked toward the principles underlying nonsexist therapy. Feminist alternatives to therapy arose from the belief that ignoring gender issues does not make therapy gender fair. The contention that nonsexist therapy is not an adequate answer to the gender bias in therapy prompted the development of therapies that are specifically feminist, oriented toward women's problems, and practiced exclusively by women. As Edna Rawlings (1993) declared, "The sexism in so-called nonsexist brands of psychotherapy may be less blatant, but any approach to psychotherapy that conceptualizes women's social problems as personal pathology and promotes 'cures' for women's distress primarily through individual personal change strengthens the patriarchal status quo" (p. 90).

Feminist Therapy

In her review of the history of feminist therapy, Carolyn Enns (1993) traced feminist therapy to the early 1970s and the women's rights movement. Women, both inside and outside the mental health care professions, began to criticize therapy for its traditional goals and for its power in maintaining the status quo for women. Some women in professions that provide mental health care responded by attempting to combine feminist goals with therapy, and the results diverge from traditional therapy in several ways.

According to Lucia Gilbert (1980), two important principles underlie the practice of feminist therapy. The first principle is one borrowed from the feminist movement—"the personal is political." That is, personal experience recapitulates the social and political structure of the society, making the problems of any individual woman a reflection of the society.

Feminist therapy strives to enact this principle in several ways. Clients explore the influence of social roles on their individual behavior, examining the difference between what they have been taught about appropriate behavior and what is actually appropriate. During feminist therapy women have a forum for validating their experiences as women, including the situations and problems that are unique to women. "Feminist therapists help clients see that their problems have social as well as personal causes" (Cammaert & Larsen, 1988, p. 15).

Feminist therapy is political, striving to bring about change in society. The early feminist therapists were politically active in the women's movement, and indeed, such activity was a requirement for declaring oneself a feminist therapist. These therapists sought to bring about changes in the status of women and advocated political activism for their clients. Their position was that significant change was not possible in women's lives through personal changes in psychological adjustment; only change in society and in women's roles would lead to beneficial changes for women.

The second principle of feminist therapy states that therapists and clients should form an egalitarian relationship rather than the traditional therapeutic relationship in which therapists are powerful and dominant and clients are subordinate. This principle ensures that clients understand the type of therapy that they will receive and that they know about the options for other sources of assistance (Hare-Mustin, Marecek, Kaplan, & Liss-Levinson, 1979). This level of informed consent represents a consumer orientation to therapy, and feminist therapy intends to promote such an orientation.

The equal relationship between client and therapist also aims to "demystify" the therapist as a person who has special knowledge and power (Gilbert, 1980). The rationale for this position lies in the attempt to counter the typical subordinate position that women occupy and to promote the belief that feminist therapy is an appropriate place for women to begin to feel a sense of personal power.

Feminist therapists participate in therapy by modeling appropriate behaviors for their female clients and by sharing personal experiences with their clients. This degree of personal openness and the advocacy of political activity on the part of the therapist differentiates the role of feminist therapists from therapists in most traditional therapies. Feminist therapists consider these differences essential to their approach.

Theoretical Orientations of Feminist Therapy

Feminist therapists hold a variety of theoretical orientations. Indeed, feminist therapists have followed theories as diverse as psychoanalysis and behavior modification and all varieties of humanistic and cognitive therapies. The goals of feminist therapy differ somewhat, depending on the orientation of the therapist, but the feminist component has produced similarities in the goals of all feminist therapy. "The emphasis becomes growth rather than adjustment or remediation, development rather than blame or illness" (Cammaert & Larsen, 1988, p. 23).

Considering that psychoanalysis has been criticized for its sexism, it is ironic that psychoanalytic therapy is the orientation adopted by many feminist therapists. Cynthia Daugherty and Marty Lees (1988) presented revisions to traditional psychoanalytic theory that have made it an appropriate basis for feminist therapy, including the work of revisionists such as Nancy Chodorow (1978) and Dorothy Dinnerstein (1976). These revised psychoanalytic theories retain the emphasis on early childhood development and the importance of unconscious forces in personality development and functioning.

The feminist psychoanalytic approach rejects the notion that women's personality is a variation on the male pattern, instead attempting to explain both. These theorists have rejected the notion that women are developmentally inferior to men, including the beliefs that anatomy is destiny, that women unconsciously desire a penis, that female sexuality is oriented toward bearing a son, and that normal women are masochistic, dependent, narcissistic, and passive.

Feminist psychoanalytic therapy uses many of the techniques of traditional psychoanalysis, including "uncovering and exploring the traumatic memories and painful affects associated with childhood that develop into symptoms and psychological conflicts" (Daugherty & Lees, 1988, p. 78). Both versions of psychoanalysis have as their goal the uncovering of unconscious conflicts, bringing this material to consciousness so that "the client could then choose more satisfying behaviors for conflict resolution" (Daugherty & Lees, 1988, p. 80). Feminist psychoanalytic therapists share the principles of feminist therapy, conveying their feminist values to their clients and attempting to build an egalitarian counseling relationship.

Cognitive, behavioral, and cognitive behavioral therapy lend themselves more easily to feminist adaptations than does psychoanalysis. Iris Goldstein Fodor (1988) traced the development of behavior therapy and the inclusion of feminist goals in cognitive and behavioral therapies. She mentioned the behavioral treatment for phobias as one of the earliest of these therapies and noted that women are the most common clients for such treatment.

Fodor described cognitive behavioral therapy as the integration of behavioral and cognitive therapy with research from cognitive and social psychology. During the 1970s, when feminist therapy arose, cognitive behavioral therapy gained prominence, and the integration of this therapy with feminist goals occurred. The cognitive component of this therapy was especially compatible with feminist therapy; analyzing the social system and restructuring thought processes are consistent with understanding that the personal is political. For example, a woman who is stressed by her work situation might be urged to consider her supervisor's sexism rather than blaming herself for her difficulties in obtaining promotions. Cognitive behavioral therapy has social learning theory as its basis, with its view that the environment shapes behavior. This position is compatible with feminist therapy's view that the social context of behavior is essential to understanding the behavior.

Although behavioral and cognitive behavioral therapies are often the choice for assertiveness and other skills training, Fodor acknowledged that these therapies, are not the ideal feminist therapy. Both of these approaches to therapy view change as the responsibility of clients, and therapists must be vigilant to maintain a cooperative rather than dominant relationship with clients. Furthermore, these therapies originated and are most successful with White, middle-class clients.

Clients of Feminist Therapy

During the early years of feminist therapy, the majority of clients were White middle-class women—demographic descriptions that match many of the clients who seek therapy. Questions arose over the suitability of feminist therapy for all women. After all, some women who seek therapy do not endorse feminist goals, and many are not White or middle-class. Is feminist therapy appropriate for all women? And is it ever appropriate for men?

Jeanne Marecek and her colleagues (Marecek, Kravetz, & Finn, 1979) studied women in feminist and traditional therapy to evaluate the relative effectiveness of each therapy. They found that the women who identified themselves as members of the women's movement evaluated feminist therapy as more helpful than traditional therapy, but women who did not identify themselves as part of the women's movement found the two types of therapy to be equally helpful. Moderate and conservative women were equally benefited by traditional and feminist therapy, but feminists did not find traditional therapy as helpful as feminist therapy. These results suggest that feminist therapy has the possibility for a wider appeal than traditional therapy.

Enns and her colleagues (Enns & Hackett, 1990; Hackett, Enns, & Zetzer, 1992) also found that college women expressed a preference for feminist counselors, especially for career counseling or sexual assault concerns. These studies showed that women had some reluctance to see a radical feminist therapist and that more moderate feminist therapists were generally preferred over traditional or nonsexist therapists, even among women with traditional gender role values.

As feminist therapy expanded, its clients became more diversified. Vickie Mays and Lillian Comas-Diaz (1988) discussed the advantages of feminist therapy for ethnic minority clients. They argued that the sensitivity to environmental factors and the acknowledgment of the impact of social reality on psychological functioning make feminist therapy better suited to ethnic minority clients than therapies that conceptualize problems as personal and internal.

Feminist therapy offers both African-American and Hispanic-American clients a method to help them feel empowered, to give them skills to solve their problems, and to furnish opportunities to change society. By allowing these clients to center on family and community, feminist therapy can be useful to both minority men and women.

The emphasis on the social environment as a factor in psychological problems makes feminist therapy "one of few models of behavior change that intentionally perceives the variability of sexual orientations in human beings as a simple fact, rather than a matter for concern and intervention" (Brown, 1988, p. 206). Thus, Laura Brown (1988) argued that feminist therapy is an obvious choice for helping lesbians and gay men. Due to internalized homophobia in society, gaining acceptance of their sexual orientation is a problem for many lesbians and gays, and dealing with homophobia can also create adjustment problems that are unique to lesbians and gay men. Feminist therapy offers these clients acceptance of their sexual orientation so that they may proceed to deal with problems related to sexual orientation as well as other personal concerns.

Although men may seem to be unlikely clients for feminist therapy, Anne Ganley (1988) suggested that male clients can also benefit from this approach. She argued that feminist therapy may be the best approach for dealing with the problems of the masculine gender role. Traditional therapy holds a male model of mental health, viewing women as deficient for their femininity and attempting to reconcile men with their role as breadwinners and competitors. Many feminist therapists adhere to a different model of mental health, an androgynous model. This view holds that both masculine and feminine characteristics are beneficial to mental health and that individuals who can combine these characteristics have many advantages.

By taking this approach with male clients, feminist therapists attempt to develop relationship skills, appropriate emotionality, empathy, and communication skills—skills that men often lack due to their masculine socialization. Feminist therapy with men also works toward altering views of gender roles, changing men's attitudes concerning what is appropriate for both women and men. By examining and questioning traditional gender roles, feminist therapy with men upholds the principle that the personal is political, one of the basic principles of feminist therapy.

Ganley described several ways in which feminist therapy with men differs from its practice with women. Traditional gender roles may make the attainment of an egalitarian relationship between therapist and client more difficult with male clients and female therapists. The attempts to give clients power in the therapeutic relationship may make men willing to take the dominant position, which is consistent with their traditional gender role but not with the goals of feminist therapy.

Feminist therapists should be models for the behavior their clients need to develop, but this aspect of feminist therapy is difficult when men are the clients. Men need to develop communication, nurturing, and nonviolent problem-solving skills (Ganley, 1988), but because these skills are stereotypically associated with women, observing a female therapist model these skills only reinforces the gender-traditional view. The obvious answer is for male therapists to practice feminist therapy and serve as role models for their male clients. Most feminist therapists, however, believe that the practice of feminist therapy is restricted to women. When male therapists adopt the principles of feminist therapy, they are labeled "profeminist." With either male of female therapists, men as clients in feminist therapy can find appropriate models as well as support through participation in group therapy.

Therefore, feminist therapy is appropriate for a wide range of people. From its beginnings as a radical therapy for women discontent with traditional therapy (both as therapists and as clients), feminist therapy has broadened its scope and clientele. Studies have shown that women with both traditional and feminist beliefs can profit from feminist therapy, but feminists have problems with traditional therapy. Its emphasis on the political and social aspects of mental health makes feminist therapy well-suited for people from other minority groups—ethnic minorities, lesbians, and gay men. In addition, men can benefit from feminist therapy, learning to develop communication and nurturing skills not associated with the masculine gender role. By adopting more androgynous behavior, both men and women can overcome gender role stereotyping and can gain greater flexibility in their lives.

Therapy with Men

Feminist therapy may be appropriate for men, but men rarely seek this type of therapy. Indeed, men are reluctant to seek even traditional types of psychotherapy. Of those who seek therapy, women outnumber men by a margin of two to one (Good, Dell, & Mintz, 1989). Murray Scher (1981) discussed the difficulties that men encounter in counseling. Although therapy tends to uphold traditional gender roles, the format of therapy emphasizes behaviors associated with the feminine rather than the masculine role, and both clients and counselors experience difficulties in the counseling process due to male clients' stereotypically masculine behavior.

James O'Neil (1981) and Joseph Pleck (1981a, b) have proposed that men experience conflict and strain due to their gender role expectations, which hold that they should strive for power, control, and achievement. Men thus can become obsessed with competition and success. These strivings require that men reject all aspects of femininity, resulting in their restricted emotionality and distrust and fear of women. These attitudes create problems for men in forming intimate relationships and in fulfilling their full potential as humans and, in addition, present special problems in counseling men.

Investigations into the relationship between masculine gender role and attitudes toward seeking psychological counseling have revealed that stereotypical masculine beliefs negatively relate to willingness to seek help. Glen Good, Don Dell, and Laurie Mintz (1989) measured attitudes toward help seeking and elements of the traditional masculine gender role in college men. These investigators found that men with more traditional gender role attitudes—men who restricted their display of emotion and who were reluctant to express affection toward other men—also felt less willing to seek psychological help.

Robertson and Fitzgerald (1992) contended that masculine socialization keeps men away from therapy. Men who show emotion, express their vulnerability, and seek help from others fail to fit the masculine gender role, and all of these elements are part of psychotherapy. As Robertson and Fitzgerald (1992, p. 240) explained, "Many approaches to personal counseling require that clients bring a sense of self-awareness to the counseling room; yet men appear to be socialized away from self-awareness and encouraged to control (or hide) their feelings." Furthermore, the masculine gender role demands that men hide their vulnerabilities, whereas counseling calls for disclosing them. Counseling urges clients to share their problems with another person, and men have been socialized to hide their problems and approach problem solving in an intellectual rather than an emotional way.

Thus, counseling is a process that men might avoid. Both Good and his colleagues (1989) and Robertson and Fitzgerald (1992) found that traditionally masculine attitudes were negatively related to the willingness to seek psychological counseling. That is, men with stereotypically masculine values expressed less favorable attitudes about psychological counseling than men with less stereotypical values.

Aaron Kipnis (1991) maintained that one reason for men's reluctance to seek therapy comes from bias against men by mental health care professionals. Kipnis contended that psychology has responded to women's needs by addressing women's problems, but no such changes have taken place for men. He cited several examples of men who, along with their wives, had sought therapy and who had felt that the female therapists had aligned themselves with the wives but had failed to see the men's point of view. These comments substantiate Carol Tavris's (1992) contention that women's communication style has become the language of psychotherapy, and this situation may alienate some men. Table 15.7 presents some of the barriers that can deter men from seeking and succeeding in counseling.

Robertson and Fitzgerald (1992) found that psychological services can be made more approachable for men through changing the description of those services. When traditionally oriented men read a brochure describing psychological services in terms of classes, workshops, seminars, and videotapes, they rated these services as more attractive than when the services were presented as those of a college counseling center. This study demonstrated that masculine values may be a barrier to seeking counseling and that traditional men may be more willing to seek counseling services that are presented in a way that is compatible with their masculine values.

Scher (1981, p. 199) advocated the advantages of counseling for men, discussing the harm that their masculine gender roles convey: "Men need counseling because many of them are unhappy, dissatisfied with their lives, and damaged by their roles." Scher, along with others such as O'Neil (1981) and Pleck (1981a, b), proposed that men need help in relinquishing some of the toxic elements of their masculine role, so that they can learn to understand the value of being in touch with their emotions, ask for assistance when they need it, and encourage freedom from constraining gender roles in themselves and in others.

TABLE 15.7   Barriers to Counseling Men

Help seeking is discouraged by elements of the masculine gender role:

- Men should not require help.
- Men should deny and suppress their emotion.
- Men should not express their vulnerability.

Therapy often takes a talk-based rather than action-based or intellectual approach to problem solution.

Emotional sharing is difficult for many men.

Men may believe that counselors are biased against men's needs.

Psychology has responded by addressing women's, not men's, needs.

Presentation of psychological services may be in a format that does not appeal to men.

Gender Aware Therapy

Can therapy meet the needs of both women and men while not discriminating against either? Glenn Good, Lucia Gilbert, and Murray Scher (1990) sought to integrate conceptions of male and female gender development with the revisions to psychotherapy proposed by feminist therapists. Their proposal was gender aware therapy (GAT), a therapy approach that has both similarities to and differences with nonsexist and feminist therapy. These theorists acknowledged that society's conception of mental health is changing to a more androgynous standard and that conforming to traditional standards is not a desirable goal for either gender.

Good and his colleagues presented five principles that they claimed should be part of all types of therapy. Gender aware therapy has its foundation in feminist therapy, and its five principles incorporate the basis of feminist therapy but also attempt to extend and enlarge that approach. The first of these principles urges therapists to consider gender an integral aspect of counseling and mental health. They argued that gender aware therapy "incorporates an understanding of gender effects and sexism in its therapeutic strategies and goals" (p. 377). They claimed that nonsexist therapy strives for equal treatment of men and women by ignoring gender. However, the differences in women's and men's lives make ignoring gender unrealistic, and many issues raised in therapy relate to gender and gender roles.

The second principle of gender aware therapy echoes "the personal is political" basis of feminist therapy in holding that consideration of the societal context of problems is essential. The third principle also incorporates the political activism of feminist therapy by urging therapists to question traditional gender roles, both for themselves and for their clients. The fourth principle urges gender aware therapists to form a collaborative relationship with their clients, and the fifth principle directs therapists to respect their clients' freedom to choose. Table 15.8 presents these five points.

This freedom to choose includes the adoption or rejection of traditional gender roles. Good and his colleagues recognized that both traditional and nontraditional gender roles can be rigid and confining, and they advocated that therapists allow their clients to find a combination that will enhance their full development. Gender aware therapy "eschews notions of political correctness" (p. 377), urging clients to explore, find, and choose what is right for them. "In summary, GAT supports the notion that particular behaviors, preferences, and attributes need not be categorized as falling into the domain of traditional or nontraditional, male or female, gender roles. Rather, what GAT advocates is simply choice, despite gender conceptions or political correctness" (p. 377).

Research with counselors in training (Brems & Schlottmann, 1988) indicated that the aims of gender aware therapy may be feasible. By studying graduate students in counseling and clinical psychology (who would soon be therapists), these researchers found that gender-bound definitions of mental health have decreased; gender role stereotyping was almost entirely absent in the counselors in training. These findings present an optimistic picture that therapists are now being trained who are less bound by gender stereotypes, for both themselves and their clients. Such therapists are necessary for gender aware therapy.

TABLE 15.8   Five Principles of Gender Aware Therapy

1. Regard the conception of gender as an integral aspect of counseling and mental health.

2. Consider problems within their societal context.

3. Actively seek to change gender injustice experienced by women and men.

4. Emphasize development of collaborative therapeutic relationships.

5. Respect clients' freedom to choose.

SOURCE: Based on Gender aware therapy: A synthesis of feminist therapy and knowledge about gender (p. 377) by G.E. Good, L.A. Gilbert, & M. Scher, 1990, *Journal of Counseling & Development, 68.*

Therefore, gender aware therapy is an extension of feminist therapy, which attempts to incorporate the awareness of gender and its far-reaching implications for people's lives with an emphasis on individual needs. Many therapists have acknowledged that gender-fair counseling and therapy are imperative, and this approach may fulfill those needs.

Sexual Exploitation in Therapy

The preponderance of women as clients and men as therapists poses a situation in which gender is always either an overt or covert issue in the therapy process. One of the ways identified by the APA Task Force on Sex Bias and Sex-Role Stereotyping in Psychotherapeutic Practice (Brodsky & Holroyd, 1975) that gender can be a problem is when therapists treat clients as sex objects, including erotic or sexual behavior with clients.

Most female clients consider sexual behavior on the part of therapists to be exploitation, but when professionals began to recognize this problem, they found that not all of their colleagues considered erotic contact and sexual relationships with their clients completely unacceptable. Jean Holroyd and Annette Brodsky (1977) surveyed licensed psychologists in clinical practice to determine their attitudes toward sexual and nonsexual physical contact with their clients.

Nonsexual physical contact was acceptable under some circumstances to 27% of the therapists in Holroyd and Brodsky's survey, but a large majority of the therapists reported that erotic contact between clients and therapists would not be beneficial to clients. Significantly more female than male therapists (88% versus 70%) believed that such contact would not be beneficial during therapy. A significant gender difference also appeared in the percentage of therapists who reported any type of sexual contact with clients—10.9% of male and 1.9% of female therapists. When considering only those therapists who admitted having intercourse with past or present clients, the survey found that 8.1% of the male and 1% of the female therapists acknowledged this behavior.

Both a counseling intern and a counselor with 30 years of experience told me, "Of course I've felt attracted to some of my clients. I think it's almost inevitable." Both reported that the attraction made them very aware of the nature of the counseling relationship and how inappropriate these feelings were. Both also became very conscious of behaving so as to conceal signs of their attraction, because it was considered professionally unacceptable.

"Part of our training includes the ethical unacceptability of any type of personal relationship with clients, especially any sexual relationship. It's completely unacceptable," the counseling intern said. "So feeling attracted to a client raised flags and made me aware that I needed to be very careful about what I did. I didn't want to convey my feelings to my client, and I didn't want to let my feelings affect my counseling. It's a difficult situation and an inevitable conflict, I think."

The veteran counselor agreed. "It's practically inevitable, although I have been sexually attracted to very few of my clients. When I felt attracted, those feelings made counseling more difficult. I tried to conceal how I felt, which is dishonest, while remaining honest in all other aspects. And I tried very hard to do a good job in counseling the client. It made the counseling relationship more difficult.

"Nothing in our training taught me how to deal with these feelings," the intern said. "A great deal was oriented toward the ethics of counseling but not how to handle my feelings or situations in which clients express some attraction for me. It was all 'Don't do that,' but nothing about what to do.

"I wouldn't feel comfortable talking to my supervisor about my feelings because of the ethical prohibition. I know it's unreasonable to imagine that counselors won't feel attracted to clients, but it's so forbidden that I feel I shouldn't have or admit to the attraction. I know that I will think about how to avoid letting any client know about my attraction, but teaching me how to deal with such feelings and what to do—no, that was lacking in my training."

The experienced counselor said that his training included how to deal with clients' attraction to him but not his toward clients. "The whole issue of sexual exploitation of clients hadn't been publicized or addressed in counselor training, so those issues were not part of my training."

Of those therapists who admitted at least one sexual relationship with a patient, 80% acknowledged more than one such relationship. This figure suggests that some therapists have formed a pattern of habitual sexual exploitation of their patients. Indeed, a small minority of therapists reported to Holroyd and Brodsky that they believed sexual contact between therapist and client to be beneficial to the client.

Subsequent research has investigated the effects of sexual intimacy between therapists and clients. Kenneth Pope (1988) detailed the factors that make such contact more likely on the part of professionals and the ways in which clients are harmed by sexual contact with their counselors. Among the factors that contribute to therapists' willingness to enter into sexual relationships with their clients are a lack of preparation for sexual attraction to clients and denial of the harm that such relationships can exert.

The possibility of sexual attraction on the part of clients toward therapists and for therapists toward clients underlies the theory of psychoanalytically oriented therapies, but other theoretical orientations have no reason to include this possibility in the training process. Pope (1988) contended that the failure to acknowledge this possibility produced a gap in the training of counselors, leaving them unprepared to deal with the possibility that they may develop sexual feelings for their clients. Therapists receive training concerning ethics and the unacceptability of sexual contact with their clients, but most training programs devote very little time to discussions about what to do when therapists feel sexually attracted to clients, and Pope's review indicated that a large majority of therapists experience such attraction. Without preparation, therapists are left with no strategies for dealing with the feelings that many of them develop for their clients.

Denial of the existence of therapist-client sex has been a substantial problem. Pope discussed the initial reluctance of journals to publish articles and conventions to feature presentations on the topic. Widespread denial of the existence of this problem prevents therapists from having colleagues to consult when they feel sexually attracted to clients and brings forth a censorious attitude (but possibly no constructive action) from colleagues when they discover that counselors have exploited clients. In addition, the discovery of a sexual relationship typically leads to the dissolution of the therapy relationship, and thus, few therapists become aware of the lasting harm that their clients experience as a result of the sexual relationship.

Pope's review also detailed the variety of negative effects that occur in clients who have participated in sexual relationships with their therapists. Clients may not exhibit any immediate negative effects of sexual intimacy with their therapists, but evidence indicates that at least 90% eventually experience negative effects. The effects are stronger when the relationship occurs concurrently with therapy, but clients who begin a relationship with their therapists after the termination of therapy are still at risk.

The therapist-client relationship is one of trust and intimacy, but when sexual intimacy becomes part of the relationship, a betrayal of clients' trust has occurred. Thus, impaired ability to trust is a potential lifelong problem (Pope, 1988). This situation often leaves clients feeling ambivalent, experiencing rage and a longing to escape combined with a fear of separation from the therapist. Sexually exploited clients may also feel guilt, isolation, emptiness, and sexual confusion. Some evidence also exists that sexually exploited clients are at heightened risk for emotional instability and suicide. Therefore, clients often experience a variety of serious problems after sexual involvement with their therapists.

The growing awareness of the sexual exploitation of clients by therapists has produced changes in the codes of ethics for all of the professions that provide mental health care (Vasquez & Kitchener, 1988). The ethical codes that govern psychiatrists, psychologists, social workers, and marriage and family therapists all specifically prohibit sexual activity between therapists and clients. In an attempt to inform the public, the Committee on Women in Psychology (1989) published a brochure with information about the harmful effects of client-therapist sexual relationships and about clients' rights to refuse such overtures.

Pope's (1988) review included an evaluation of several studies that had questioned psychologists, psychiatrists, and social workers about their sexual intimacies with clients, and different professions show similar rates of sexual exploitation of clients. Studies completed during the 1970s indicated that over 10% of male therapists and between 2 and 3% of female therapists reported sexual intimacy with their clients.

Later studies have shown lower rates of sexual exploitation of clients, suggesting that the increased attention to this problem may be having positive effects. On the other hand, in a national survey of psychiatrists, 65% reported that they had treated patients who had been previously sexually involved with their therapists (Gartrell, Herman, Olarte, Feldstein, & Localio, 1987). This figure suggests that a great majority of cases of sexual exploitation by therapists go unreported. through the patients experience problems. Even though decreasing, sexual exploitation of clients remains the most common of reported ethical violations by therapists, accounting for half of the complaints to state licensing boards (Marecek & Hare-Mustin, 1991).

The Self-Help Movement

A growing lack of confidence in psychotherapy and mounting awareness of sexual exploitation of clients have led to increased reluctance to seek therapy on the part of thousands of troubled people. A vast (and growing) number of such people have dealt with a variety of personal problems without the assistance of mental health care professionals. These people have joined self-help groups, and the self-help movement constitutes a growing force in people's attempts to deal with personal problems. These people meet to share similar problems, and in the process, they receive emotional support as well as information that can assist in helping them cope with their problems.

Marion Jacobs and Gerald Goodman (1989, p. 537) described the characteristics of self-help groups, saying that "the typical self-help group is like a miniature mental health democracy." Self-help groups typically do not have professional therapists and often have no one designated as leader. The philosophy of the self-help approach is that other people with similar problems can offer social support and information, and both can be helpful and beneficial.

"Member-governed self-help groups vary widely from tiny, freestanding gatherings to large, nationally networked assemblies and from formats that are laissez-faire to those that are thoroughly programmed by members or audiotape" (Jacobs & Goodman, 1989, p. 537). Although the concerns of people in these groups vary, the underlying philosophy is similar.

According to Susan Baxter (1993), self-help groups proliferated during the 1980s. In 1963, around 300 self-help groups existed, but in 1992, the number had grown to more than 500,000. Jacobs and Goodman (1989) estimated that 6.25 million people were involved in self-help groups in 1987 and that the numbers would grow to approximately 7 million people in 1990 and 10 million by 1999. These numbers equal or exceed those receiving therapy from a professional, and the variety of problems that form the basis for these groups is large. Jacobs and Goodman reported that self-help groups were formed around nearly 200 different topics in the state of California alone. Table 15.9 presents examples of the problems served by self-help groups.

One of the reasons for the rapid gain in the self-help movement "lies in our stars—namely Oprah, Geraldo, Phil, and Ann Landers; also *New Woman, Cosmopolitan,* and other magazines; plus prime-time TV dramas, which refer, with increasing frequency, to self-help groups" (Baxter, 1993, p. 74). People who have experienced personal problems and who have found help from these groups have presented their stories on

TABLE 15.9   Examples of Self-Help Groups and Problems Served

Problem	Group	Problem	Group
Alcoholism	Alcoholics Anonymous	Gambling	Gamblers Anonymous
Breast cancer survivors	Bosom Buddies	Alcoholic parent	Ala-Teen
Gambling	Gamblers Anonymous	Overeating	Overeaters Anonymous
Substance abuse	Narcotics Anonymous	Divorced parents	Parents without Partners
Parental bereavement	Compassionate Friends	Heart attack survivors	Mended Hearts
Love addiction	Women Who Love Too Much	Down syndrome	Parents of Children with Down Syndrome

Other Problems Served by Groups

Cancer survivors	Caretakers of Alzheimer's patients
Persons with AIDS	Incest survivors
Partners of persons with AIDS	Adult children of alcoholics
Former dieters	Rape victims
Parents of children with diabetes	Parents of children with cancer
Heart transplant patients	Parents of children with attention deficit hyperactive disorder
Anorexics	Persons with multiple sclerosis
Parents and families of anorexics	Persons with arthritis
People with disfigurements, including specific types such as burn victims, neurofibromatosis	Medical and psychological problems associated with gays
Chronic money management problems	Impotence
Psychological problems associated with retirement	Parents of children with schizophrenia
Alopecia (radical hair loss)	Sexual addiction
Couples with fertility problems	Narcolepsy (sleep disorder)
Agoraphobia	Codependency

television talk shows; magazines have featured their stories; TV dramatizations have shown the positive effects of self-help.

This publicity has come at a time when traditional sources of help have disappeared or were the targets of growing mistrust (Baxter, 1993; Jacobs & Goodman, 1989). Smaller families and increasing mobility have reduced the availability of social support to family members. In addition, families are often the *source* of problems for which people seek help. Many people have come to mistrust psychotherapy, partly as a result of the growing lack of confidence in public institutions and partly due to the negative publicity regarding sexual exploitation of clients.

"Self-help groups flourish because people find solace and strength in being with others who share a common experience" (Jacobs & Goodman, 1989, p. 538). The similarity of the individuals involved provides an automatic empathy. People in self-help groups find that discussing their problems is easier because the other members of the group share important elements of their experience.

The financial advantages of self-help groups are another factor in the growth of this approach. These groups may charge participants a minimal fee, and many of them charge nothing. With the growing emphasis on cost containment, authorities (including former Surgeon General C. Everett Koop) have promoted cooperation between medicine and self-help groups (Baxter, 1993).

Free therapy is certainly cost-effective, but the therapeutic benefits of self-help groups have not been established (Baxter, 1993; Jacobs & Goodman, 1989). Psychologists have a bias against self-help groups, and Jacobs and Goodman proposed that this bias has prevented psychologists from conducting research on the effectiveness of self-help groups. Such research would be difficult, as members of self-help groups may concurrently be involved in individual therapy. This concurrent participation, combined with the lack of control over who participates in what type and how many groups, makes research in this area difficult.

Baxter maintained that people with serious psychological problems can become involved with self-help groups and that these groups fail to provide the professional supervision that such people need. Thus, members with serious problems may endanger their own mental health and possibly that of the other members.

Jacobs and Goodman, on the other hand, expressed optimism about the potential for self-help groups. They called on psychologists to become involved in the self-help movement by lending their professional assistance but not by taking over the groups. Jacobs and Goodman predicted a revolution in health care, including mental health care, and saw the potential for prevention through self-help groups.

Self-help groups share a common philosophy that rests on the power of social support from people with similar problems. The variety of problems having a corresponding support group has expanded to a figure in the hundreds, and one variety of support group, consciousness raising, specifically addresses problems related to gender roles.

Support Groups

People who have friends and family on whom they can depend for emotional and material help are healthier and better adjusted than people who are more socially isolated. That is, social support is a factor in both mental and physical health (Gartner, Gartner, & Ouellette Kobasa, 1988). Self-help groups allow people to form relationships with others with similar problems and to receive and give support. This format for increasing social support may be effective in helping people deal with problems.

The prototype for the self-help movement is Alcoholics Anonymous (AA). Founded in 1935 by two alcoholics who had stopped drinking, AA proclaimed that people with drinking problems could stay sober through the social support of others with similar problems (Robinson, 1979). The format is a meeting in which people acknowledge their alcoholism and their powerlessness over alcohol. To change their behavior, AA members seek the assistance of "a higher power" and attempt to abstain from drinking for a lifetime, one day at a time. The AA philosophy holds that alcoholics never recover, but instead spend their lives in recovery. AA meetings and the support of other recovering alcoholics are part of this process. This approach to dealing with problem drinking has been enormously influential and is included in most treatment programs for problem drinking, especially in the United States.

The format for AA has prompted the formation of other support groups for different problems. Addictions and other compulsive disorders were the concerns of the early support groups, such as Narcotics Anonymous, Gamblers Anonymous, and Overeaters Anonymous, but support groups now exist for a wide variety of problems. "There are groups for almost every serious medical problem and almost every presenting problem that clinicians confront, plus groups for dozens of conditions virtually unserved by therapists" (Jacobs & Goodman, 1989, p. 537). In addition, support groups have formed for problems in dealing with life transitions, such as menopause, and for people who care for others with problems, such as parents of children with mental disorders and caregivers for those with Alzheimer's disease.

Many support groups perform a valuable function for participants, but other groups have been the focus of a great deal of criticism, much of which centers on groups oriented around the concept of codependency. This concept originated with treatment involving the families of alcoholics and describes a pattern of pathological dependency among family members combined with behaviors that allow the alcoholic to continue with problem drinking. This notion of codependency spread to people other than families with an alcoholic member and expanded "to denote any person who is either product of or a participant in a dysfunctional relationship involving abuse of any kind" (Lyons & Greenberg, 1991, p. 436). This definition includes a great many people, the majority of whom are women concerned about their relationships with men.

The topic of codependency has not been the subject of much research, but Deborah Lyons and Jeff Greenberg (1991) investigated the validity of the concept. In their study they portrayed male experimenters as either exploitive or nurturant and gave female subjects the opportunity to offer assistance. Half the female subjects came from families with an alcoholic father and met the definition of codependency, whereas the other half did not. Lyons and Greenberg found that the women with alcoholic fathers assisted the exploitive experimenter significantly longer than the nurturant one and that the women without alcoholic fathers showed the opposite pattern, assisting the nurturant experimenter longer than the exploitive one. These results confirmed the notion of codependency, but Lyons and Greenberg explained that this concept is not new. Karen Horney (1942) proposed the existence of morbid dependency in terms that were very similar to current descriptions of codependency. Thus, codependency has some experimental confirmation, but the concept is not original to the self-help movement.

Patricia Roehling, Nikole Koelbel, and Christina Rutgers (1994) argued that the concept of codependency has no place in mental health treatment. These researchers found little support for the validity of the codependency concept, and their research showed that codependency was only marginally related to parental alcoholism. Instead, codependency showed a stronger relationship to the negative aspects of femininity (such as subservience, dependency, and complaining). Roehling et al. argued that the concept of codependency is a way to "pathologize" femininity, blaming women for the problems within families.

The center and possible origin for the criticism of support groups involving the concept of codependency has been Robin Norwood's (1985) bestselling book, *Women Who Love Too Much*. In this book Norwood described women's "addiction" to relationships, borrowing the addiction framework from Alcoholics Anonymous as a model for providing advice to these women. Support groups have formed for these "women who love too much" and are similar to AA meetings, complete with a reliance on assistance from a "higher power" and an acceptance that complete recovery is not possible but the process of recovering lasts a lifetime.

Although Norwood's book promised to offer solutions for these women's relationship difficulties, Tavris (1989, p. 220) maintained that it delivered less than promised, providing only "friendly sermons that emphasize the healing power of love" rather than giving specific advice on how to produce changes. Tavris criticized Norwood's advice to accept the blame for all negative aspects of one's life, arguing that this advice creates helplessness. By taking the blame for the behavior of others, people believe that they are the ones who must change. This view leaves the women in these groups passively accepting rather than actively challenging the men with whom they have bad relationships. The assumptions of this approach are very similar to the gender bias in traditional psychotherapies—the notion that change is up to the individual and that women are to blame for the negative aspects of their lives. Critics believe that this form of support group repeats some of the most undesirable elements of traditional therapy for women.

Support groups offer emotional support and information to help people cope with a wide variety of problems. Some support groups, especially the ones for people with medical problems and for those who care for family members with medical problems, offer a way for people to help themselves without relying on professional assistance. Other support groups, especially the ones that promote codependency as the source of women's relationship problems, may harm their members by urging them to be passive and to accept the blame for others' behavior.

Consciousness-Raising Groups

Consciousness-raising groups originated as a way for women to share their unique experiences, explore the similarities of their lives, and increase interaction with other women (Morgan, 1970). These groups began to form in the mid 1960s as part of the women's movement, and as part of this movement, the aims were political as well as personal. The early consciousness-raising groups consisted "primarily of radical feminists, and group discussions focused on political analyses and the development of feminist ideology" (Kravetz, 1980, p. 268).

An essential part of that ideology was the oppression of women as a class (Travis, 1988b). To recognize that their problems come from the shared experiences of being part of a group, women must accept that they are part of a class, and many women find this acceptance difficult. Humans tend to see themselves as unique and exceptions to

GENDERED VOICES
What Are These Groups Doing to You?

During one lecture on the tendency for bystanders to stand by rather than assist in emergency situations, I asked my class, "What would you do if someone fell out of his or her chair, unconscious? Would you wait for someone else to help, or would you feel comfortable in giving assistance, even to someone whom you might not know all that well?"

Most of my students expressed the indecision that is typical of such a question. After thinking for a moment, one middle-aged woman said, "I'm so codependent that I would probably help the person." I was shocked. I knew that she had been part of a self-help group for her drinking problems and possibly other groups as well, but I was stunned at her belief that rendering help to an unconscious person would be considered codependent. I told her, "Helping in a medical emergency isn't a sign of codependency. In my opinion, it's a sign of being a decent human. What are these groups doing to you?"

the rule, so women often find it difficult to acknowledge that they have been the targets of discrimination or exploitation. Instead, they see their problems as personal instead of social. Consciousness raising aims to lead women to see their membership in the class of women and to see their similarities to other women's situations and problems.

The early emphasis on political ideology shifted to personal development, and research by Diane Kravetz (1978) indicated that increasing political activity was not among the goals for most women who joined consciousness-raising groups. Instead, Kravetz found that the most important goals were to share thoughts and feeling about being a woman, to learn about other women's experiences, to increase self-awareness, to get emotional support, and to examine the traditional gender role for women. Participants rated the groups as very successful in helping them to attain these goals, and the majority of participants encouraged other women to join a group.

Enns (1992) contended that the personal changes experienced by women during consciousness-raising groups were therapeutic, leading to these groups becoming a substitute for or an adjunct to therapy. Although consciousness-raising groups may have therapeutic effects, these groups differ from group therapy sessions in several ways (Kravetz, 1980). First, these groups seek to help women understand that their problems are not personal but social, whereas psychotherapy places the source of problems and potential for change within each individual. Second, the groups are explicitly political, whereas therapy is exclusively personal. Third, consciousness-raising groups have no designated leader and emphasize the equality of their members, whereas traditional therapists are the experts and clients seek their advice and direction. Fourth, consciousness-raising groups take place in homes, churches, libraries, schools, and community centers rather than in therapists' offices or mental health centers.

The benefits of consciousness raising coupled with its differences from traditional therapy highlighted the need for an examination of therapy. Indeed, consciousness-raising groups formed the basis for feminist therapy, which kept elements of these groups—the political orientation and the concept of egalitarian relationships between therapists and clients.

The men's movement has also devised group meetings for the purpose of making members more sensitive to the politics and the disadvantages of their gender role. Although the men's movement began later than the women's movement, the early men's consciousness-raising groups were similar to women's groups; both concentrated on the social inequities women had experienced and how rigid gender roles had harmed men as well as women. Men sought to understand how they had participated in and had been harmed by society's mandates for their behavior.

The men who adopted feminist goals followed androgyny as a model for men's behavior, a counterpart to the androgyny that early women's groups advocated. Androgyny seeks to allow an incorporation of the positive elements of traditionally masculine and feminine behaviors, increasing positive masculine behaviors for women and positive feminine behaviors for men. Women's groups worked toward increasing assertiveness and allowing for the expression of anger. Men's groups worked toward increasing sensitivity and allowing for the appropriate display of a range of emotions.

In the 1980s the goals of the men's movement began to diverge from those of the women's movement (Faludi, 1991). For example, Warren Farrell was among the early feminists in the men's movement who advocated changes in the behavior of both men and women toward a more androgynous goal. He changed his mind during the 1980s and began to highlight the oppression of men. This theme became the focus of many men's groups during that decade. These groups concentrated on the gender inequity of divorce and custody laws as well as the emphasis on men's breadwinner role and the pressures on men to earn money and attain success. Similar to the political focus of women's consciousness-raising groups, these men's groups tend to strive for political and legal changes to allow men more rights in divorce and custody cases. This variation of men's groups often has become antifeminist, proclaiming that society has oppressed men and benefited women.

Kipnis (1991) proposed a male counterpart to codependency—"men who give too much." He contended that men have experienced economic exploitation in their relationships with women. Kipnis discussed men's feelings of being incomplete without a woman. Men feel that they must take care of women and that they are loved for this care rather than for themselves. This situation results in strivings for career, success, and money rather than attention to personal or relationship needs. The belief that they are needed for what they can provide rather than for who they are can lead men to give too much.

Another variety of men's consciousness-raising group came from the publication of Robert Bly's (1990) *Iron John.* This book remained on the *New York Times* bestseller list for weeks and captured the imagination of thousands of men. These men sought out experiences that would allow them to understand masculinity and how they could attain it by banding together with other men. Termed *mythopoetic,* these groups focus on the anthropological, mythic, and poetic images of men in order to guide participants to positive images of masculinity.

Proponents of this approach (Kipnis, 1991; Moore & Gillette, 1990) have contended that men need to discover alternative styles of masculinity, as the current masculine gender role is immature as well as destructive to both society and to individual men.

The mature masculinity they seek is not exploitive, violent, or lacking in emotion. They do not attempt to integrate feminine characteristics; rather, they consider these positive characteristics undiscovered masculine attributes.

Men's groups have a greater diversity than women's consciousness-raising groups, but fewer men's groups exist. Women's groups tend to be oriented toward sensitizing women to the political goals of feminism, but men's groups have a variety of possible goals. Some of these groups have political goals, such as groups organized around gay rights, divorce, or custody rights; others supplement therapy for substance abuse; still others explore social conceptions of masculinity and ways to bring about positive changes.

These varieties of men's groups all share the social support and focus on gender roles that characterize consciousness raising. Both types of groups also have indulged in fixing blame; men's groups have blamed women for their problems, and women's groups have blamed men for the oppression of women. Some consciousness-raising groups have tried to move beyond recrimination toward discovering how to enact greater flexibility of gender roles, but the focus on gender-specific inequities and support from others for expressing feelings make blaming easy. As yet, men's consciousness-raising groups have not produced a radical therapy based on men's needs, as women's consciousness-raising groups have produced feminist therapy.

Although men's groups have a shorter history and a greater diversity than women's groups, both types of consciousness-raising groups share the goals of reexamining gender roles and seeking possible avenues of change, unlike traditional psychotherapy. The women and men who join such groups may do so out of a need to explore their gender roles or to bond with others. Many women and men prefer the self-help approach to formal therapy due to prior negative experiences with therapy.

Summary

Charges of gender bias extend not only to the diagnosis of mental disorders but also to treatment for such disorders. Research indicates that departures from traditional gender roles are the focus of recommendations for treatment. Therapy can enforce traditional gender roles.

Psychoanalysis was an early form of treatment for mental disorders. Based on Freud's conceptualization of personality development and functioning, this therapy uses talk to help people bring unconscious material to consciousness. The pessimism of this view of humanity, combined with the length and expense of psychoanalysis, prompted others to develop alternative talk-based therapies. The humanistic approach to therapy includes client-centered and Gestalt therapies. Humanistic therapy attempts to help people accept their emotions and feelings, allowing them to progress toward fulfilling their potential.

Cognitive therapy focuses on thoughts as the basis for behavior, assuming that thoughts underlie behavior. The theory holds that irrational and self-defeating thoughts form the basis for psychological problems and that changes in behavior follow from changes in cognition. Behavior modification centers on overt behavior rather than cognitive processes, applying the principles of operant conditioning to alter undesirable behaviors. Cognitive behavior modification is a blending of cognitive therapy and behavior modification, attempting to alter cognitions and establish different behaviors.

Medical therapies are also used to treat behavior problems. Psychoactive drugs have increased in use since the 1950s, and psychiatrists and other physicians prescribe a variety of such drugs for depression, anxiety disorders, and schizophrenia. Women receive more prescriptions for psychoactive drugs than men. The use of electroconvulsive therapy decreased during the 1970s but began to increase during the 1980s. Once used for many mental disorders, electroconvulsive therapy is now used largely for depression that has not responded to antidepressant drugs.

All therapies have been criticized for gender bias. Psychoanalysis holds men as the standard for psychological development, a standard that women can never attain. Humanistic, cognitive, behavior modification, and cognitive behavior modification therapies are not inherently gender biased, but each offers a format in which therapists can impose their values, and all concentrate on the individual and ignore the social and political aspects of problems.

Nonsexist therapy was an attempt to remove the gender bias in therapy, but many female therapists believed that therapy should go further, and propose and promote feminist goals. Feminist therapists hold that personal problems are a reflection of social problems and that the relationship between client and therapist must be equal. From its initial political activism, feminist therapy has expanded. Its emphasis on social context makes feminist therapy appropriate for gays and lesbians as well as people from a variety of ethnic backgrounds.

Men are also clients of feminist therapists, but men are less often the clients of any type of therapist than are women. Men's reluctance to seek therapy relates to the masculine gender role, and men with more traditional values are less willing to seek help than men with less traditional values. Men might be unwilling to discuss emotions or acknowledge their vulnerability, but they might also feel discriminated against in therapy. Research indicates that therapy tends to encourage men to adopt the traditional breadwinner role.

Gender aware therapy is an attempt to extend feminist therapy to a form that is applicable to the full range of clients. By integrating an awareness of the impact of gender with encouragement to men and women to find what is right for them, gender aware therapy concentrates on individual needs rather than political correctness.

A growing attention to complaints of gender bias in therapy led the American Psychological Association to survey female psychologists about their experiences, and the results of this survey revealed four areas of concern: (1) sexist use of psychoanalytic concepts, (2) fostering traditional gender roles, (3) diminished expectations for female clients, and (4) treating women as sex objects, including having sex with clients.

Surveys of therapists have revealed that the sexual exploitation of clients by therapists occurs with between 9 and 12% of male therapists and between 2 and 3% of female therapists. The prevalence of this problem led professional associations to include prohibitions against sexual relationships with clients, but this section remains the most commonly violated of the ethical codes. A growing body of evidence indicates that intimate relationships with therapists do long-lasting harm to clients.

Rather than seeking therapy from professionals, a growing number of people join self-help groups. These groups mushroomed during the 1980s, and now over 7 million people in the United States participate in at least one self-help group. These groups offer emotional support and information from others who share the same type of problem. The low cost of self-help groups is attractive, but the lack of professional involvement can be risky for those with serious psychological problems.

Substantial evidence exists concerning the benefits of social support, and groups that enlarge people's support networks can be helpful. Alcoholics Anonymous has provided a model for many support groups, and a common theme that has recently become the focus of support groups is the concept of codependency. Initially applied to children of alcoholics, the concept has expanded to apply to anyone with a dysfunctional family background who becomes involved in a dependent relationship. Critics have accused groups organized around women's codependency ("women who love too much") of blaming women for the behavior of others and of endorsing traditional feminine behavior.

Consciousness-raising groups are a type of support group, but these groups are oriented toward understanding how the personal is political—how each person's experience reflects social and not personal circumstances. Although the focus of women's consciousness-raising groups is political rather than therapeutic, research has indicated that women experience positive psychological changes from these groups. Feminist therapy derived its philosophy from women's consciousness-raising groups. Men's consciousness-raising groups have a shorter history but greater variety. These groups may have a feminist orientation but tend to concentrate on the social inequities of the male gender role. Other men's groups have attempted to redefine masculinity, searching for alternative means to achieve personal growth by seeking a way to attain genuine masculinity.

Glossary

Behavior modification   the application of principles of conditioning to behavior, with the goal of changing undesirable behavior to more acceptable alternatives

Electroconvulsive therapy   the application to the brain of electric current sufficient to induce a convulsion, which, for unknown reasons, produces therapeutic effects

Psychoanalysis   Freud's talk-based treatment for psychological problems that consists of attempts to bring unconscious material to consciousness

Repression   a defense mechanism used to push troubling material from the conscious into the unconscious

Suggested Readings

Baxter, Susan. (1993, March/April). The last self-help article you'll ever need. *Psychology Today,* pp. 70–71, 74–77, 94. This popular article goes beyond criticism into satire but presents the range of activities included in the self-help movement along with the opinions of experts in the area.

Enns, Carolyn Zerbe. (1993). Twenty years of feminist counseling and therapy: From naming biases to implementing multifaceted practice. *Counseling Psychologist, 21,* 3–87. For those who are interested in feminist therapy, this comprehensive article details the history and current status of the field.

Marecek, Jeanne; & Hare-Mustin, Rachel T. (1991). A short history of the future: Feminism and clinical psychology. *Psychology of Women Quarterly, 15,* 521–536. For those who think that Enns's article is too long, this brief history of feminist criticism in clinical psychology will be easier to read. Marecek and Hare-Mustin review the history of clinical psychology and discuss the actual and potential contributions of feminist thought.

O'Neil, James M. (1981). Patterns of gender role conflict and strain: Sexism and fear of femininity in men's lives. *Personnel and Guidance Journal, 60,* 203–210. O'Neil's article is not new, but it summarizes the problems that men may feel in seeking counseling and the problems that the masculine gender role may create so that men need counseling.

Pope, Kenneth S. (1988). How clients are harmed by sexual contact with mental health professionals: The syndrome and its prevalence. *Journal of Counseling and Development, 67,* 222–226. Pope summarizes the statistics on prevalence of sexual contact among therapists and clients and details the evidence concerning the damage done to clients.

How Different?

You New Women Want It All!

—*Essence,* July 1985

Donald Singletary's (1985, p. 114) story described the changes in gender roles for women and men:

> *It happened so suddenly. Things hadn't changed very much for decades. Then came the middle sixties, while the Black movement was in full fury, and eventually people began questioning, challenging, their sexual roles. Age-old ideas about love, marriage, sex, family and children began to change for women— and for men as well.*

Singletary focused on the problems of new gender roles and complained about men's difficulties in understanding what women want. As the title of his story suggests, Singletary contended that women now want it all, including goals that he considered contradictory. "New women" want to be independent and dependent, to act assertively and passively, to enter into casual affairs and to have committed relationships. Furthermore, Singletary argued, women want men to do it all, too—to be businesslike and romantic, sensitive and aggressive, supportive of women's achievement and achieving for themselves.

Singletary did not advocate a return to traditional roles, but he maintained that neither women nor men have adapted to the gender role changes. He blamed women, whom he characterized as arbitrary, unreasonable, and contradictory in what they want from men. The women he described were all successful professional women who had taken advantage of the wider choices available to them for education and careers.

Singletary alleged that these women wanted two sets of rules—one that applied to their professional life and the other for their personal relationships. When seeking relationships with men, Singletary argued, these women want to be courted in a traditional way, which forces men to keep their traditional gender role. "During the day he holds the door at work and she's furious. At night she stands in place until he opens it" (Singletary, 1985, p. 115).

Singletary complained not only about the difficulty of following two sets of rules for relating to women but also about the pressure that the traditional gender role places on men. He maintained that men experience the stress of taking the initiative in relationships, asking women for dates, and paying the tab. He and his friends had imagined that when women gained access to education, careers, and salaries similar to men's, then women and men would have similar attitudes, thus relieving men of some of the stress in forming and maintaining relationships. Singletary complained that this similarity had failed to materialize.

The "new women" acted like men in some ways but not in the ways that Singletary and his friends had wanted. These women were career-oriented and achieving, standing "pinstripe to pinstripe, Gucci to Gucci, M.B.A. to M.B.A." with men (Singletary, 1985, p. 115). But these career women did not automatically assume that they should pay for a date when they initiated the invitation, they were not as aggressive in pursuing men as men felt they needed to be in attracting women, and they were not necessarily serious about developing a permanent relationship when men were. That is, these "new women" suited themselves rather than relying on men to set the pace for their lives. Singletary's complaint about women failing to follow the rules may have emerged because the rules were not the ones he and his friends originated.

The women about whom Singletary complained were not interviewed for his article, so their views and complaints about men were not included. But many other articles and books have examined women's problems in trying to "have it all"—careers, relationships (usually marriage), and children. These multiple roles have created changes in both women's and men's lives.

Multiple Roles Have Become the Rule

The traditional assumptions about women's lives hold that they will choose a job to support themselves until they marry but that marriage will be their primary career. If they continue employment after marriage, the birth of children will interrupt and most likely end their employment. Men's lives are supposed to follow a pattern that prepares them for a career that will last throughout their lives and will provide support for them and their families.

The stereotypical assumptions about women's and men's careers no longer hold for many women and men. A growing number of women pursue careers on a full-time, uninterrupted basis. As a result, men no longer provide the sole support for their family. This situation has produced changes in family life, but comparable changes in attitudes about careers and roles have not occurred. Despite joining the work force of paid employment, women still are expected (and expect themselves) to occupy the role of wife and mother, including performing a majority of family work.

Men have experienced few changes in their roles; the majority of husbands have not assumed equal responsibility for family work. As Carol Tittle (1986, p. 1165) explained, "Although there have been some changes in attitudes toward a wife's roles there has been little or no change in preferences regarding the husband's roles." The increasing number of employed women has led to increased acceptance of women in the work force in addition to their role in the family, but men's roles have not undergone comparable changes and remain centered on their role as breadwinner.

The movement of women into the work force has not produced an equitable distribution of household work, and men's reluctance to participate in the work of the household is another source of women's complaints. Rather than sharing household work, employed women have added the demands of employment to those of caring for a house, husband, and family. This distribution of labor sounds unfair, but ironically, many women do not feel disadvantaged. Brenda Major (1993) concluded that men feel entitled to the care they receive from their wives. Furthermore, Major examined the cognitive processes of wives and determined that they cannot compare themselves to their husbands and remain content with their share of household work. Instead, they must compare their contributions to those of other women to avoid a feeling of disadvantage.

All employment creates additional demands on women's time and energy, but some high-level managerial and professional careers require long hours and extraordinary dedication. The corporate, male-dominated careers that women began entering in somewhat larger numbers in the 1970s did not change to accommodate women's family duties. Men provided the model for these careers, men who had wives to provide a support system for husbands' careers. These wives offer not only emotional support at home but also social support in the public functions of the organization (Lopata, 1993). That is, the "corporate wife" joins auxiliaries, organizes social functions, and boosts her husband's career. Women need "wives" to provide this support, but few husbands are willing to be the homemaker who offers support to a successful female breadwinner. Bebe Moore Campbell (1986) contended that job demands in two-career families frequently have led to either divorce or to women dropping off the track to success in high-prestige careers.

Some evidence exists to indicate that both men and women are dissatisfied with the inequity in household work. Francine Deutsch and her colleagues (Deutsch, Lussier, & Servis, 1993) studied couples, both before and after the arrival of their first child, to compare the couples' expectation of participation with their actual behavior. These researchers found that husbands participated very little in child care—to the disappointment of both husbands and wives. Wives' work load from outside employment was a significant factor in the amount of child care their husbands performed, as were husbands' gender role attitudes. Not surprisingly, men with nontraditional gender role attitudes were more likely to participate in child care than men with more traditional attitudes. These results show that gender roles are a powerful force in determining who performs which tasks. Even when partners plan an equitable sharing of household work, they have a difficult time implementing these plans.

Employed women must fulfill at least two roles, whereas men's role demands revolve around their paid employment. Women who are employed outside their homes work the "second shift," according to sociologist Arlie Hochschild (1989), using this term to refer to the time that employed women spent on family work in addition to their paid employment. She calculated that the average employed woman works an extra month of 24-hour days per year at home on family work.

The second shift is not a recent development, but during the past 40 years an increasing proportion of women have joined or remained in the labor force after having children. In 1950, 30% of women were in the labor force, but in 1993, around 57% of women were in the labor force, and only 23% of women were keeping house as their primary career (U.S. Department of Labor, 1993). In about 57% of marriages, both partners are employed. Multiple roles have implications for careers, life satisfaction, and even health.

What are the consequences of role restriction or role expansion? Judith Rodin (1991) discussed three models that hypothesize different consequences of multiple roles. The *job stress model* holds that multiple roles lead to role conflict, because people who try to fulfill many roles experience conflict when the multiple roles produce stress in their lives. This model proposes that role restriction would be healthier. An alternative model, the *health benefits model,* holds that employment offers direct benefits, such a feelings of control and self-esteem, social support from colleagues in the workplace, and financial gain. This model proposes that multiple roles are beneficial. The *role expansion model* emphasizes the indirect benefits of employment, proposing that the satisfaction of fulfilling several roles and the protection of occupying several different roles will be beneficial. Table 16.1 shows these models and their position on the benefits of multiple roles.

Research tends to support the advantages of multiple roles, especially the benefits that come from employment. Furthermore, a meta-analysis of job-related stress revealed no gender differences in experienced or perceived stress on the job (Martocchio & O'Leary, 1989). Employment may cause stress, but its impact is similar for men and women and does not adversely affect women more than men. Indeed, a study by Leslie Abrams and Russell Jones (1994) showed that multiple roles *decreased* psychological

TABLE 16.1   Three Models of Multiple Roles

Model	Results of Multiple Roles	Benefits
Job stress model	Role conflict	None
Health benefits model	Feelings of control, increased self-esteem, social support from coworkers, financial benefit	Direct
Role expansion model	Feelings of success at several roles and of protection of occupying several roles	Indirect

distress in business women, suggesting that the benefits of paid employment outweigh the stresses of fulfilling multiple roles. Considering the economic and power benefits, women gain many advantages from paid employment. As John Archer and Barbara Lloyd (1982, p. 194) explained, "Being at work protects women from the full impact of marriage."

Lois Verbrugge (1983) found that married parents have the best health profiles, and Walter Gove and Carol Zeiss (1987) found a positive relationship between multiple roles and happiness. These advantages extended to both men and women, demonstrating that multiple roles can be beneficial to both. In analyzing the contribution of employment, marriage, and parenthood on health, Verbrugge's study showed employment to be the strongest and parenthood the weakest effects. In the Gove and Zeiss study, the multiple roles of marriage, employment, and children were more positive for women than men. Thus, multiple roles offer health and happiness benefits for women and men, and employment is an important contributor to the benefits.

Less research exists on the effects of multiple roles in men's lives, and much of the existing research has focused on jobs and the breadwinner role. Rosalind Barnett and Grace Baruch (1987) reviewed the evidence that marriage benefits men more than women, demonstrating the advantage of the husband's role. Their study of fathers indicated that participation in child care and family chores increased fathers' feelings of competence as parents, but these men were likely to feel that family responsibilities interfered with their careers. The men in this study saw their job as their core role and believed that their family enriched that role and made it meaningful, but they also believed that their family should not interfere with their core role.

Although the research on multiple roles has concentrated on women and has focused on assessing the impact of employment and family roles on women's well-being, men also fulfill multiple roles. The research on the effects of combining employment, marriage, and parenting generally indicates advantages for both women and men in fulfilling these multiple roles. Both can experience stress in trying to fulfill work and family roles, and the extent of support spouses receive from each other influences the strain they feel.

Although multiple roles have become the rule and evidence exists of the benefits of multiple roles, these changes may not be what women and men want. Singletary's (1985) article stated that women have changed, now wanting "it all"—both the traditional benefits of the female role and the benefits of recent changes. Singletary was clearly unhappy with some of the changes in the "new women," but are his feelings representative of most men's? What do women and men want from each other?

What Do Women Want? What Do Men Want?

Questioning what women want became popular after Sigmund Freud asked the question of Marie Bonaparte in the 1930s (Jones, 1955). His version of the question, as many others have been, was an exasperated plea prompted by a genuine lack of understanding of women's motivation (Feist, 1994). Other men, like Singletary, have contended that women's goals are unreasonable rather than mysterious. Are women's motives so troublesome and difficult to understand? And how different are the things that women and men want?

Men's motives have not been subject to the same degree of scrutiny, but the changes in women's roles have forced men to examine their own lives to consider what they want. Much of this examination has centered on what men want from women and the difficulties that changes in women's lives have created for men. Do men want traditional women, "new" women, or some combination?

Have Women Become More Like Men?

"Why Can't a Woman Be More Like a Man?" was the title of a song in the musical play *My Fair Lady* (Lerner & Loewe, 1956). Henry Higgins sang about how unreasonable women were in comparison to men and longed for women and men to be more similar, voicing the stereotypical belief that women and men differ in many ways. Although this view was common at the time the musical appeared (and for some people even now), the differences may have been exaggerations. Gender differences may not have been as large as people believed, but these beliefs have continued through focusing on the differences and maintaining the dichotomy of the concept of the "opposite" sex.

Women have begun to take the opportunity to pursue some of the goals that were reserved for men. If large differences existed between men and women, perhaps the intervening years have allowed Higgins's wish to come true. Have women become more like men? And if this wish has come true, what do men think of these changes?

Higgins's wishes centered around emotionality; he listed negative characteristics for women and positive ones for men. Of course, Higgins himself deviated from this ideal quite a bit, but his beliefs about differing emotionality in men and women may be partially correct concerning emotion. Frank Fujita and his colleagues (Fujita, Diener, & Sandvik, 1991) found that women reported a greater emotional intensity than men, experiencing more positive as well as negative moods. This evidence suggests some confirmation for the stereotype of emotional women, but other evidence produces a more complex picture.

People may not express the emotions that they feel, either exaggerating or diminishing their feelings in the reports. Gender roles influence these processes. For example, girls and women report more positive feelings for infants than do boys and men, but these self-reports allow participants to conform to expectations about what they should feel (Berman, 1980). When using physiological measurements of responses during emotion, few gender differences appear.

Their gender role allows women to be more expressive of some emotions than men's gender role permits them. The difference in display holds true for many emotions, making women and men more different in the display than in their experience of emotion. For example, surveys (Averill, 1982) have indicated few differences in the experience of anger for men and women, but the expression of this emotion differs. Indeed, men express many emotions as anger, and women sometimes have trouble expressing anger at all. Henry Higgins probably was not thinking about anger when he pleaded for women to be more like men, but the reviews of research on anger and aggression suggest that the two are quite similar.

Increasing evidence indicates that women and men may be comparably aggressive and that the apparent differences in expression relate to efforts to maintain gender roles (Eagly & Steffen, 1986). Laboratory studies on willingness to harm another person sometimes find women less willing than men to enact this form of aggression, but women's reluctance reflects concerns over retaliation and guilt. Under circumstances of anonymity, no differences appear.

Women's willingness to behave aggressively extends to interpersonal violence, including battering their children and their husbands. The acceptance of violence as a way to resolve conflicts leads to incidents of violence between couples and battering incidents with children. Clifton Flynn (1990) found comparable rates of courtship and marital violence for women and men, but he also found that women's violence was likely to be retaliation to aggression initiated by their male partners. Relationship violence by men may be a more serious social problem than the violence committed by women, but women do perform harmful acts of aggression toward their families.

Rather than women becoming more like men, the opposite trend has appeared in relationships; the typical feminine style of intimacy has become the standard for both men and women (Cancian, 1986). Although men often feel uncomfortable in sharing emotions with others, especially with other men, a growing number of men are seeking

---

✖ GENDERED VOICES
I've Had This Conversation Before

Melinda was a single mother with a 2-year-old son who told me about her experiences with the woman she had hired to care for her son. She considered herself and her son extremely fortunate; the nanny was a retired pediatric nurse, ideally qualified to be a nanny, and a wonderful person. Like many mothers with careers, Melinda felt less than enthusiastic at the thought of leaving her son in the care of someone else, and she felt fortunate not only to be able to afford a full-time, live-in nanny but also to have found a great person. Indeed, they had become like a family.

Melinda's business career was demanding but fulfilling. She had worked as a secretary during the time that she was married, but she had divorced and pursued a sales and management career and had become successful. Like other women with demanding and fulfilling careers, she worked long and sometimes irregular hours. Her son's nanny took

care of him and the house, cooking dinner for herself and the child. She said that she could easily cook for Melinda as well; she would be glad to do so, but Melinda needed to be home to eat with them.

Melinda explained that she didn't always know when she would need to work late, and she couldn't be sure about being home in time for dinner every night. "But that doesn't matter. If I'm late, just leave my dinner. It's no big deal." The nanny said that it was a big deal; she didn't want to cook dinner and have her be late and have cold food. It just wasn't right. Melinda thought, "I've had this conversation before—when I was married. Only this time I'm being the 'husband,' and last time I was the wife. My husband said all the things I'm saying and gave all the excuses I'm giving, and I said the words I'm hearing from my nanny.' Melinda got to see how flexible gender roles can be because she had played both the husband and the wife.

this style of friendship. Pressure for men to become more emotionally intimate has also occurred in marriages and committed love relationships. Thus, women have not become more like men in this respect, but instead, men have become more like women.

Sexual behavior continues to show some gender differences, but those differences have decreased. When Alfred Kinsey and his colleagues (Kinsey et al., 1948; Kinsey et al., 1953) conducted their surveys in the 1930s and 1940s, women reported more sexual activity and enjoyment than the popular image of women portrayed, but the double standard for sexual behavior constrained women's sexuality. Women were less likely to masturbate and to have intercourse outside marriage than men. Later surveys, such as the Janus's report (Janus & Janus, 1993), have shown a decrease in the differences, with women becoming more like men.

Women now endorse a greater variety of sexual behaviors and have sexual intercourse for the first time at younger ages than in previous decades, but gender differences in sexual behavior remain. Mary Beth Oliver and Janet Shibley Hyde's (1993) meta-analysis of studies on sexual attitudes and reported behavior showed persistent differences in the percentages of men and women who masturbate and in attitudes toward casual premarital sex, with men masturbating more and favoring casual sex more than women.

The failure for women to become like men in their sexuality was one of Singletary's (1985) complaints. Singletary and his friends felt disappointed that women did not pursue them as aggressively as they pursued women. That is, the sexual revolution had not turned out to be as much of a revolution as they had wanted, and women's sexuality had not changed in the ways that men wanted. According to one of Singletary's friends, a similar style of sexual behavior for men and women was his criterion for assessing the success of the women's movement: "I'll believe women are liberated when one walks up to me, says, 'Hey good lookin',' buys me dinner and pats me on the cakes" (Singletary, 1985, p. 68).

Barbara Ehrenreich and her colleagues (Ehrenreich, Hess, & Jacobs, 1986) argued that a sexual revolution has occurred, with women making radical changes in their sexual attitudes and behavior between the 1930s and the 1970s. The conservatism of the 1980s and the growing fear of AIDS produced some decrease in the willingness for sexual exploration in both men and women, but Ehrenreich and her colleagues made a case for the reality of a sexual revolution for women. They also argued that increased sexual freedom has allowed women to explore their sexuality, which has taken them in directions that were not necessarily compatible with men's sexual preferences. Indeed, increased acceptance of sexuality other than intercourse led women to be less sexually dependent on men. Ehrenreich et al. contended that this decreased dependence became a source of men's discontent. Women became more sexual, but not like men and not necessarily to men's liking.

Women have become more like men in terms of their achievements, and educational differences between men and women have decreased, with women and men receiving comparable numbers of college degrees. Differences still persist in several areas of training and in the advanced and professional degrees awarded, with men receiving more training for prestigious careers such as law, business, and medicine. Women have made gains, but men still dominate high-status, high-salary professions.

Employment gives women more economic advantages but also produces greater demands. Some women have sought employment out of a desire for personal fulfillment, whereas economic necessity is the reason for most women's employment. The degree to which women are satisfied with their employment varies according to the support they receive from their families. Women whose husbands provide little assistance and emotional support for their employment are less satisfied than women with more supportive families.

In needing and providing support, women and men are now similar, but these similarities represent changes in their traditional roles. Female homemakers were the traditional caregivers, but employed women need to receive support from as well as provide support to their families. In the past, male breadwinners could expect the support of their wives, but they are now expected to provide their wives with emotional support and also help with household work. Through these changes women and men have become more alike, but this change was probably not what men had in mind, having in the past enjoyed the support of women without having to provide emotional support or share household chores.

Both women and men need the support of the other to be able to fulfill their dependency needs, according to Luise Eichenbaum and Susie Orbach (1983). These authors inspected dependency in the lives of men and women and concluded that the needs are similar but the chances of fulfillment may not be. Eichenbaum and Orbach argued that despite the helplessness and passivity some women may display, they do not have someone on whom they can rely for emotional support, leaving dependency needs unmet. The lack of compatibility between dependency and the male gender role can make men feel ashamed of their dependency needs. Whereas men have been able to rely on women for emotional support, women's increasing requests for emotional support from men can be an unwelcome change for many men.

Life expectancy for both men and women has increased in all industrialized countries. Although women still have the advantage, life expectancy has not increased as rapidly for women as for men. Health habits are not equal for women and men, and some of the differences have shown changes. For example, women have started to smoke at higher rates than in the past and have begun to experience greater smoking-related health problems. Their illness and death rates for smoking-related disorders have not reached the level for men, but the discrepancy has decreased. Despite predictions that women would experience increases in heart disease when they moved into prestigious corporate jobs, both men and women in the United States have experienced a decrease in heart disease during the past 20 years.

The differences in weight concerns have decreased, but not because women have decreased their dieting. Indeed, men have become more like women in their concern with weight. Although the percentages are not close to identical, an increasing number of men are dieting and also developing eating disorders. Many people feel the pressure to have an attractive body, but standards for women focus on thinness, whereas those for men emphasize athletic muscularity. Thus, women and men are alike in their body image concerns but differ in the expression of these concerns.

The current physical differences in speed and strength virtually guarantee that women will not soon become like men in athletics, but women have become more like men in terms of their athletic competition. Women now participate in a greater variety of sports than in the past, and the world records have been bettered faster for women than for men. Girls and women have made headlines by playing along with men on various sports teams, but these coeducational football and baseball teams remain novelties rather than the rule for sports participation.

These decreases in gender differences support the notion that women and men have become more similar in education, employment, sexual attitudes and behavior, smoking rate, and athletic competition. The changes have occurred mostly in women. However, whereas women have become more like men, men generally have not begun to adopt the positive aspects of women's behavior. This one-way change is not surprising when considering the situations that have produced the changes. Women have moved into the educational and employment worlds formerly occupied by men, but for the most part men have not made corresponding moves into women's worlds. Thus, men encounter few and women encounter many situations that encourage the adoption of a more flexible style.

Despite superficial endorsement of the virtues of the traditional feminine role of homemaker and mother, society has accorded little value to nurturing skills or other traditional feminine behaviors. Men's traditional masculine style of assertive, independent, agentic behavior has set the mold for behavior in a variety of situations. Women who enter these situations tend to adopt the style of the situation, which is usually agentic rather than communal. Society's value of masculine over feminine traits results in women receiving rewards for adopting such active, instrumental behaviors and men receiving little encouragement for becoming more expressive or communal in their behavior. Thus, women have more freedom to become androgynous by combining the positive aspects of masculinity with expressive, communal behaviors, but men have little encouragement to become more androgynous.

Confirmation for the value of masculine over feminine traits comes from a study by Jennifer Aube and Richard Koestner (1992), who investigated the long-term developmental implications of masculine and feminine interests and traits. They studied men who at age 12 years had expressed interests and traits more commonly associated with women. The results showed that these men exhibited poorer personal adjustment at ages 31 and 41 years of age than men who had more traditionally masculine interests as children. These researchers failed to find similar negative effects for women who endorsed nontraditional interests and traits. Indeed, they found that masculine instrumental traits were positively related to adjustment during adulthood for both women and men. That is, an androgynous combination of interests was a negative factor for men's but not for women's adjustment.

Jacob Orlofsky and Connie O'Heron (1987) obtained similar results in their study of gender-stereotypical traits and personal adjustment. Their results also indicated that both women and men show better adjustment when they endorsed masculine instrumental traits than when they endorsed feminine expressive traits. Both of these studies demonstrated society's emphasis on masculine values and suggested that women have found it easier to become more like men because they receive social rewards for these behaviors.

How do women feel about these changes? According to Susan Faludi (1991), a great deal of media attention has focused on the negative effects of the changes in women's lives. Faludi contended that the negative publicity about women's increased economic and sexual independence represents a reaction against these changes but that the stories misrepresent women's feelings; women would like more opportunities rather than a return to traditional gender roles. These media reports tend to focus on interviews with selected discontented women rather than present studies with more representative samples. Faludi reviewed opinion polls that showed women's approval of the changes in the opportunities available to them and portrayed the majority of women as anxious for more.

Has Henry Higgins's wish come true? Have women become more like men? And are the changes all that he (and men like him) had hoped for? Men and women may have not been as different as Henry imagined, but women and men are more alike than they have been. As women have entered male domains, their behavior has changed to accommodate the situation. Although some men have sought to adopt positive feminine behaviors, such as emotional expressiveness, men have not entered female domains to the same extent that women have entered the domain of men. Men are not encouraged or rewarded for feminine behavior, thus the changes have altered women's more than men's behavior.

These changes may not be what either women or men had in mind. Most people find change difficult and anxiety provoking, and as Singletary (1985) expressed, changes in expectations for men and women have come about very rapidly. Indeed, the changes have occurred faster than social institutions have changed to accommodate them. People have few models to emulate in adopting new gender roles and live in a society that pressures them to be more traditional. When gender roles were narrowly defined, everyone knew what to do. Although the rules were unquestionably restrictive, preventing people from doing gender-inappropriate activities, the roles were clear. Greater flexibility has produced uncertainty as well as options.

The power and privilege of men's role put them in a position to have more to lose through change, and men are less content than women with the changes that have occurred. Although some men have welcomed the opportunities to form more intimate relationships with friends and partners and to be involved in their children's lives, many others have resisted making changes or have found themselves not knowing how to enact the changes they want to make. The increased options have created opportunities for men that few of them want, such as careers as elementary school teachers or secretaries. Employed wives' income may be very attractive, but no one welcomes the prospect of more household chores. Therefore, many men have not gotten what they wanted as women have become more like men.

Women too may not be entirely satisfied with the changes in their lives. As the many polls indicate, the majority of women favor more equal treatment in politics and jobs, but they too may be resistant to making other changes in the roles and underlying assumptions about their relationships with men, their sexuality, and their children. As Wendy Kaminer (1993, p. 51) explained, women become less interested in change when "it requires profound individual change as well, posing an unsettling challenge that well-adjusted people instinctively avoid. Why question norms of sex and character to which you've more or less successfully adapted?" Women do not want to lose their femininity in gaining equal rights.

Some women long for a return to traditionalism, but that longing is stronger in men, who believe that changes in gender roles have caused them to lose more and gain less than women. Women tend to complain not about what they have lost but about what they have gained—the equivalent of two full-time jobs. Men tend to complain about what they have lost—services and subservience. "New" women are more independent and more difficult for men to control (Campbell, 1986; Gallagher, 1987).

Why Can't a Man Be More Like a Woman?

Thomas Skovholt (1978) discussed the status of styles of masculinity, naming three categories of men and their reactions to the changes in women's roles. *Traditional men* regret the changes that have occurred, seeing no advantages for them in greater freedom for women. Indeed, these men feel the competition for grades and jobs and resent the presence of women in the workplace. Traditional men have stereotypical attitudes toward their own gender role and prefer women to adhere to traditional femininity. These men do not feel the appeal of expanding their gender role to include behaviors traditionally reserved for women, so they see nothing but disadvantages connected with changing gender roles.

The men whom Skovholt called *men in transition* are able to accomplish the task Singletary (1985) was not—to interact with women as people as well as with women as romantic partners. Men in transition have the "cognitive capacity, to turn on and off the person-woman light bulb when interacting with a female" (Skovholt, 1978, p. 5). These men are not necessarily sympathetic with the goals of the feminist movement, but they are attempting to integrate the changes in women's role by changing their attitudes and behavior.

The *male liberationists* embrace the feminist movement and extend the notion that gender roles are oppressive to men, highlighting the stresses of the male gender role and calling for changes for everyone. Table 16.2 summarizes these three categories of men.

Women have become more like men, but men have declined more often than taken opportunities to become more like women. That is, women have developed a more instrumental orientation, but men have failed to develop their expressive skills. The asymmetry of these changes may have created a situation in which women want men to change. Women are asking Henry Higgins's question from their point of view: "Why can't a man be more like a woman?"

This question exists in two versions, one social and one personal. The first version applies to the question on a social level, challenging the wisdom of continuing to use men and masculine values as the preferred style. For example, what makes the hierarchical, directive (sometimes autocratic) style of leadership that men typically use preferable to the cooperative, democratic style women typically use? If differences in moral reasoning exist, why should the style dominant among women be considered in-

TABLE 16.2   Three Categories of Contemporary Men

Approach	Characteristics	See Women As
Traditional	Wish to return to traditional gender roles for men and women	Subordinate
Men in transition	Attempt to adapt to the changes in gender roles	People as well as romantic partners
Male liberationists	See dangers of male gender role; embrace feminism	Equals

ferior? Why can't men accept the value of the feminine style? The second version of the question is more personal, challenging men to include more expressiveness in personal relationships and to participate more fully in "women's work," that is, household work and child care. Women contend that society as well as their individual lives would profit from men accepting the value of expressive behaviors.

Carol Johmann (1985) discussed the advantages of women's typical style of moral reasoning, which focuses on preserving relationships and avoiding injury to any party. She pointed out that this style might have advantages in corporate business, creating loyalty and emulating elements of the Japanese management style. In fact, women's democratic style may suit many business situations better than the more autocratic management and leadership style typical of men (Eagly & Johnson, 1990). Johmann concluded that the feminine style has much to offer.

Some evidence exists to indicate that people have no problem accepting the value of the communal qualities associated with women. Alice Eagly and her colleagues (Eagly, 1994; Eagly, Mladinic, & Otto, 1991) investigated evaluations of men and women, finding that women received more positive personal evaluations than men. People think of women as a social category in very positive terms, a finding Eagly (1994) called the "Women are Wonderful" effect. These positive evaluations may signal a change in the social evaluation of women, allowing for a greater acceptance of feminine values.

However, these positive evaluations from Eagly and her colleagues seem in contradiction with the disadvantage that women experience in so many realms. Eagly (1994) found that these positive evaluations applied to women in traditional roles and failed to carry over to women who diverged from those traditional roles; that is, women are wonderful as mothers but not as business executives. Eagly et al. (1991) suggested that "although people evidently think that these qualities are wonderful human attributes, they may value them more in close relationships than in highly paid sectors of the work force" (p. 213). Thus, the evidence concerning positive attitudes about women does not ensure the social acceptance of their style in roles other than traditional ones.

Personality theories that emphasize the development of gender differences, such as Freud's theory, use men as the standard for development. These theorists would see little motivation for men to become more feminine. Indeed, cross-gender identification is a problem in these theories. In addition, if men are the standard, then the acceptance of feminine values might be a problem. Feminist personality theories also predict that men will have difficulty in adopting a more feminine style. According to Nancy Chodorow (1978), boys exert a great deal of psychological effort to separate themselves from their mother, becoming as unlike her as they can in order to establish a separate identity. According to Ellyn Kaschak (1992), men's proprietary views of women do not provide anything men want to emulate. Therefore, theories of personality predict that men may be unwilling or find it difficult to become more like women, and some personality theories predict that men will have trouble accepting the value of women or their characteristics.

Not only would women like for men to consider feminine behaviors as acceptable and appropriate, they would like for men to behave more expressively in their personal relationships (Tavris, 1992). This wish has been the subject of a number of popular books oriented around communication between women and men. The places that books such as Deborah Tannen's *You Just Don't Understand* (1990) and John Gray's *Men Are from Mars, Women Are from Venus* (1992) have occupied on the bestseller lists speak to the strength of women's wish to have more expressive partners.

Some men have recognized the value of developing greater emotional expressiveness and have attempted to make changes in their behavior. Although these men believe that women and men should have equal power in relationships and equal access to education and careers, they may find these principles difficult to incorporate into their lives. Society offers few models for couples with equal relationships and many examples of traditional couples.

Campbell (1986) detailed how marriages between feminist men and women do not always work as the partners envisioned. The lack of social support for equitable marriages pushes men and women toward traditional gender roles. Even men who have agreed to share in household work and child care find these promises difficult to keep, and Campbell contended that women's success can leave men feeling neglected and jealous of the time their wives spend on work. Pursuing demanding careers, the wives do not have time to do household work and child care without their husbands' help. When their husbands refuse to help, their marriages experience trouble. Campbell described the disintegration of marriages that began with the men being liberationists but ended with both partners realizing that the men were more traditional than either had believed.

The motivation to make personal changes in ways of dealing with partners and children has been a focus in many of the men's movement groups, as men attempt to feel comfortable with emotional sharing and intimate disclosure. A growing number of men have accepted that the male gender role constrains their emotional expressiveness in ways that have harmed their relationships and possibly their well-being. This attitude has encouraged men to change.

What are the prospects for men becoming more like women? And how would women feel if they did? Currently, the rewards for men who adopt more expressive behaviors are not as great as for women who become more instrumental, which leads to the prediction that men may not change as much as women have. If the men who are involved in the men's movement provide any omen of changes to come, then men have little interest in adopting very many feminine qualities. Leaders in the men's movement, such as Sam Keen (1991) and Robert Bly (1990, 1994), have urged men to explore their masculinity and make changes in their attitudes and behavior, but their recommendations do not include listening to women to know what changes to make. The men's movement concept of authentic masculinity includes increased expressiveness and responsibility, making this view of what men should become correspond to the changes that many women want.

Will these views of masculinity influence men's attitudes and behavior? Although the vast majority of men are not involved in the men's movement, social changes become personal and affect people's lives. The women's movement produced changes in the society, for women's lives, and for men's lives. The men's movement may have a parallel effect, and the discomfort may be similar, with women disliking some of the choices for change that men make in their lives.

Men and women may both want too much from each other, including things that appear to be contradictory. Each may want to be both independent and dependent, aggressive and passive, businesslike and romantic. These behaviors are not necessarily contradictory, but the rules that allow the display of both are more complex than the rules that allowed each gender only one pattern. Flexibility and acceptance of individual choices are goals for both the women's and men's movement, but both men and women are struggling with these new, more complicated rules.

Where Are the Differences?

One of the places where differences exist between the genders is in the theories that have attempted to explain psychological factors related to gender. The traditional dichotomy for theories of gender is the biological versus environmental view—attributing differences to nature or nurture. Although these opposing points of view have influenced research in gender, another approach overrides the nature-nurture debate in gender—the maximalist versus the minimalist position.

The maximalist view holds that men and women have large, essential differences, whereas the minimalist view holds that the differences between men and women are small compared to their similarities. The older versions of maximalist theory are biologically based, emphasizing gender differences and offering genetic or hormonal explanations of behavior as well as anatomy. These theorists tend to accept biological explanations as evidence of unchanging, fixed patterns of behavior. Thus, offering a biological explanation means accepting inevitable differences. These theorists tend to rationalize the disadvantaged social position of women (and often of ethnic minorities) by citing biological programming as the source of differences. Naomi Weisstein (1982, p. 41) summarized this position by saying, "Men are biologically suited to their life of power, pleasure, and privilege, and women must accept subordination, sacrifice, and submission. It's in the genes. Go fight city hall."

Not surprisingly, feminist scholars have disputed the biological basis of behavioral differences between men and women, proposing that social experiences produce differences in learning and thus in behavior. According to this view, social learning, not biology, forms the basis for psychological gender differences. This approach holds that behavior varies according to circumstances and surroundings, and these theorists attribute gender differences to the different situations that women and men typically encounter. Those who hold this view tend to be minimalists, accepting few essential differences between men and women.

Newer versions of the maximalist position also rely on social learning to explain gender differences. Although these theorists see the differences between women's and men's behavior as learned, they believe that the differences are large and persistent. Many of these maximalist theorists are also feminists, advocating the superiority of women's style and characteristics. Rather than accepting the differences as deficiencies, they promote the female version as the better alternative.

Katha Pollitt (1992, p. 802) argued that the ideas of these theorists (including Gilligan, Chodorow, and Tannen) are appealing to some women because "they offer a flattering account of traits for which they have historically been castigated." She also contended that this view is a modernized version of the Doctrine of the Two Spheres, the Victorian view that women were moral, pure, spiritual, emotional, and intellectually inferior. It is not possible to separate the positive from the negative characteristics of this view. The virtues that these maximalists idealize are among the characteristics that rationalize the continued subordination of women. Pollitt considered the popularity of this view ironic, given that the roles of women and men are more similar than they have been during the history of the West.

Both maximalists and minimalists look at the same research and find evidence to support their positions. The ability to maintain different interpretations of the same information highlights the constructed nature of theories; that is, those who support one view or the other have constructed their position in accordance with their beliefs about gender. Building and maintaining a theoretical position requires an examination of the research evidence, but theory goes beyond evidence. Therefore, theorists can maintain discrepant positions with regard to gender differences, with some theorists holding a maximalist and others a minimalist position.

Theories are not the only place that gender differences exist; gender-related differences also exist in behavior. The extent of gender-related differences, however, depends on the type of study considered. In considering studies on ability, few gender differences have appeared. In considering the choices that men and women have made about what to do in their lives, the gender differences are larger.

Differences in Ability

Considering the many comparisons of abilities of women and men, the gender differences are largest for physical strength. This difference relates to size and muscle mass, with men being significantly larger and stronger than women. The differences among people are also large; some women are stronger than other women, and some men stronger than other men. However, gender differences are larger than individual differences, making gender a good predictor of strength. Despite the magnitude of these gender differences, their existence does not have the same implications it once did. As Thomas Skovholt (1978) pointed out, strength is not as important as it has been in the past, and few positions of prestige and power require strength.

Gender is a very poor predictor of mental abilities. In both verbal abilities and mathematical abilities, only small gender differences exist. Despite the widespread belief that men have superior mathematical and women superior verbal abilities, the technique of meta-analysis has revealed that the gender differences are small (Hyde, Fennema, & Lamon, 1990; Hyde & Linn, 1988). In addition, the differences have decreased over the past several decades, with larger differences appearing in studies conducted before the mid 1970s and small or no differences in more recent studies.

Spatial abilities and gender have a complex relationship. Researchers have used many tasks to study spatial ability, resulting in many definitions of these abilities. On some tasks involving spatial abilities, men have done better, but women have performed better on others. (See Chapter 5 for examples of each.) Furthermore, training and experience improve performance on tasks of spatial ability for both women and men, showing that performance is more than the expression of innate ability (Baenninger & Newcombe, 1989). Research on spatial ability has failed to demonstrate a consistent pattern of gender differences.

Research conducted in laboratory settings tends to show few if any gender differences. When men and women are put into situations without gender-related cues, their behavior tends to be quite similar. For example, a literature review (Frodi, Macaulay, & Thome, 1977) and a meta-analysis (Eagly & Steffen, 1986) of aggression have shown that women and men show similar willingness to behave aggressively in laboratory situations, but outside the laboratory, gender differences appear.

Perhaps the laboratory setting minimizes behavioral differences, making this approach unsuited to demonstrating gender-related differences. The laboratory setting has demonstrated gender similarities, and to find differences, researchers may have to look at behavior in social settings. When examining the behavioral choices that men and women make, gender differences appear larger than when considering abilities.

Differences in Choices

Women and men make different choices about important facets of their lives, and these choices reflect encouragement for these alternatives. Although many barriers that prevented women and men from attempting some activities seem to have fallen, constraints remain in the form of expectations. Social expectations push each toward different options and thus toward different lives. These choices are more important than ability in determining what happens in people's lives. The gender differences that exist in education, employment, family life, relationships, sexuality, emotionality, health-related behaviors, body image, and behavior problems reflect these different choices and the expectations that foster them.

Although men and women have similar mathematical ability, young men choose to take more math courses during high school and college than young women. The choice not to take advanced math courses eliminates many career options, highlighting the effect of choice on people's subsequent lives. Unlike the men enrolled in these courses, the women who enroll in advanced math courses tend not make this choice as an avenue to science careers. Even women who complete the background do not choose science and engineering careers as often as men (AAUW, 1992).

The expectation that men will pursue careers consistent with the breadwinner role and that women will seek careers compatible with family duties eliminates many choices for each. Men are limited in their family involvement by careers that require dedication and long hours. Men do not receive encouragement when they make different choices, such as allotting time to family by choosing part-time employment or by choosing to be a homemaker. Indeed, this choice is considered deviant, and men who have made such a decision are encouraged to reconsider (Robertson & Fitzgerald, 1990).

The movement of women into the paid work force has increased their options in some ways but not in others. Rather than giving women a choice concerning employment or homemaking, women now expect to be employed in addition to having a husband and children (Baber & Monaghan, 1988). Women who have chosen to be homemakers feel that their choice is not as well accepted or respected as the choice of pursuing paid employment. Thus, the change in patterns of employment for women has resulted in an additional role rather than an additional option.

Men and women tend to choose different styles of friendships, and this difference is clearly a choice. That is, most women and men are capable to adopting the style of friendship more common in the other. A woman can be "one of the boys," and a man can adopt the emotionally intimate friendship pattern more common among women, but each chooses a gender-typical style of relating to others. This choice gives women more intimate friendships with other women than with men and prevents men from forming intimate friendships with other men (and possibly with women). Friendships are one source of social support, which has advantages for physical and mental health. Women's style of friendship tends to provide more emotional support, whereas men's style of friendship tends to offer more material support. The advantages of social support come from both types of support and extend to both women and men.

Women's choice of achieving intimacy through emotional sharing and talk has become the accepted style for love relationships (Cancian, 1986), and men have started to feel deficient if they are not adept at this type of relating. Men's attempts to establish intimacy through sexual activity are not entirely compatible with women's strategy to create intimacy through talk and sharing feelings. Thus, sexuality may have different meanings for women and men. Even with comparable levels of desire, men and women make different choices concerning the expression of their sexuality.

Different choices also appear to be related to the varying life expectancies of men and women, with women choosing a healthier and safer lifestyle in terms of their use of health care services, diet, limitation of alcohol intake, and seat-belt use. On the other hand, men tend to make better choices concerning exercise and avoidance of unhealthy dieting. Both patterns of choices fit well with the interpretation that men's and women's health-related behaviors are oriented toward maintaining their gender roles. Women behave in healthy ways not because of their health concerns but due to their concerns

GENDERED VOICES
How Can I Do That to the Women?

Toni had been the auditor for the bank in the small town where she grew up, and she was the first woman to be promoted to vice-president of the bank. After three years as vice-president, she had a talk with the president of the bank.

She knew that she had made some big mistakes, and she was afraid that she might lose her job. He assured her that she was in no danger of losing her job, but he agreed that she had made some pretty serious mistakes and couldn't expect the bonuses she had gotten last year.

In their conversation, Toni told the president of the bank that she didn't really like being a vice-president as much as she had liked her auditing job, and he mentioned that it might be possible for her to have that job again if she wanted. She said, "Oh no, I couldn't do that to the women." She felt that her promotion was so visible and her performance so crucial to other women in business in the town that she couldn't leave the job she disliked; it would be an admission of failure not only on a personal level but for all women. She couldn't consider the possibility.

over thinness, and men's exercise and risky health-related behaviors maintain their muscular appearance and their Give 'Em Hell masculine gender role behaviors.

Men's and women's strategies for handing negative feelings can lead them to appear different in their experience of emotion. These differences appear both in statistics on violence and rates of various types of psychopathology. The display rules for emotion allow (and perhaps even encourage) men to openly express anger, leading to more acts of violence and crime committed by men. Women are encouraged to restrict their displays of anger, leading not to a decrease in the experience but to a difference in the expression of anger. One difference is that women often cry when they are angry, whereas men rarely do.

Different choices for dealing with negative feelings may be reflected in the statistics on psychiatric diagnosis. Women are more likely to receive the diagnosis of depression than men, but men are more likely to drink alcohol and use other psychoactive substances than women. Some evidence exists that men use alcohol to cope with negative feelings (Berger & Adesso, 1991), whereas women ruminate over negative events and become depressed (Nolen-Hoeksema, 1987). These different choices produce an apparent difference in psychopathology that may not indicate a difference in the experience of negative emotions.

The expression of psychopathology tends to fall along gender-stereotypical lines (Chesler, 1972; Rosenfield, 1982). The categories of psychopathology more common among women are an exaggeration of the elements of the feminine gender role—dependent (dependent personality disorder), passive (major depression), self-sacrificing (self-defeating personality disorder), fearful (agoraphobia), and emotional (histrionic personality disorder). Men experience psychopathology that seems to be an exaggeration of the elements of the masculine gender role—irresponsible, untruthful, and violent (antisocial personality disorders), recklessness (psychoactive substance abuse disorder), and inappropriately sexual (paraphilias). Although these patterns may not represent intentional choices, the reflection of gender-typical differences is clear.

The choices that men and women make tend to fall along the lines sanctioned by tradition. Women's choices and men's choices tend to keep men and women in their own category, creating a male domain and a female domain, with limited "visitation privileges" of one to the other. Yet these two domains are not different planets, as the bestselling book *Men Are from Mars, Women Are from Venus* (Gray, 1992) suggested. "The truth is, there is only one culture, and it shapes each sex in distinct but mutually dependent ways in order to reproduce itself" (Pollitt, 1992, p. 806).

The freedom to make cross-gender choices is still limited. An argument has been made that there are benefits in perpetuating gender categories. Although categorization may be convenient, limiting options to two well-defined choices ignores the inherent complexity of individual differences and fails to allow for a wide range of individual choices. The abilities of men and women demand a wider range of choices than the bipolar classification of the traditional dichotomy.

Summary

The roles that men and women occupy have undergone changes in the past three decades, allowing women to move into careers that have formerly been the province of men. As women acquired careers and salaries comparable with men's, some men imagined that women would become more like men, making relationships easier. Some of these men have been disappointed, because women often have made changes in their lives that are not what many men had in mind.

The changes in women's employment were additive rather than substitutive; that is, most women who are employed outside their home also have family work to do at home. Thus, most women are now employees, wives, and mothers. These multiple roles present stress in women's lives but also offer rewards. Research indicates that the rewards outweigh the stresses for most women. Men also occupy the multiple roles of employee, husband, and father, but men do a minority of family work at home, making the breadwinner role their core role. Research indicates that men find multiple roles rewarding, but they are less eager than women to allow family work to intrude on their employment obligations.

Men have wondered what women want and have expressed the desire for women to behave in ways more similar to men. Gender differences may have never been as large as many people imagined, but men have gotten their wish in several respects: Women's behavior has changed to become more like men's behavior. These changes, however, have not resulted in the transformations that some men imagined. Men did not envision competition from women at work as a desirable similarity, but women have moved into the world of paid employment, assuming roles and behaviors required by these situations. Men and women have become more alike in terms of their education, employment, sexual attitudes and behavior, athletic competition, and smoking rate. Few gender differences exist in the experience of emotion, but differences remain in the display of emotion. Men have become more like women in their style of forming close personal relationships, and are beginning to explore the rewards of emotional sharing and talk.

Although the changes in women's lives have prompted men to change, these alterations have not been equal to the ones that women have experienced. The devaluation of traditionally feminine behaviors and the value placed on the activities that men perform have pushed women toward change. Some men dislike these changes, longing for traditional roles for both; some men are trying to make the transition; and some men have welcomed the increasing similarities. Women, however, are more pleased with the changes in their lives than are men.

Women also wish for changes in men, wanting men to accept and adopt some of the characteristics typical of women. Women would like for men to accept the validity of the feminine approach and to feel comfortable in adopting positive behaviors traditionally associated with women. One of these desired changes has occurred to some extent—the change in communication in intimate relationships. Women would like men to be more emotionally expressive and to communicate intimate thoughts and feelings to their partners. Women would also like men to become more active with their families, sharing household work and child care. These changes may be difficult to accomplish. The devaluation of women's characteristics and work means that men have few incentives for becoming more like women.

If women have become more like men in a number of ways and men have become more like women in some ways, how many gender differences remain? Differences continue in theories, with maximalist theories promoting the difference between the genders and minimalist theories arguing for more similarities than differences.

Research on gender and ability has revealed relatively few differences. The largest of these differences in ability lies in men's strength advantage, but few differences exist when measuring other abilities in laboratory situations. When examining the choices that men and women make concerning how to live their lives, larger gender differences appear. Indeed, the difference in choices may promote the idea that greater differences

exist than research has confirmed. Women choose different educational experiences and careers than men. Women are more likely to put their family before their career, whereas careers are the primary focus of many men's lives. Men tend to choose an activity-based style of forming close relationships, whereas women choose to establish intimacy through emotional sharing. Men also choose a riskier lifestyle than women, and their decreased life expectancy reflects these choices. Men's abuse of alcohol and psychoactive drugs accounts for a gender difference in diagnosis of psychopathology, whereas women are more likely to be depressed, dependent, and phobic. Indeed, patterns of psychopathology reflect exaggerations of traditional gender roles.

The choices that women and men make tend to preserve well-defined gender roles rather than allowing people to make freer choices and develop the most satisfying lives. Strict enforcement of gender-related behaviors may simplify rules of conduct, but preserving this dichotomy extracts a high price for individual women and men.

Suggested Readings

Kaminer, Wendy. (1993, October). Feminism's identity crisis. *Atlantic Monthly,* pp. 51–53, 56, 58–59, 62, 64, 66–68. Kaminer discusses the failure of most women to embrace feminism, despite their agreement with many of its goals, and she examines the implications of the maximalist and minimalist positions.

Linn, Marcia C. (1986). Meta-analysis of studies of gender differences: Implications and future directions. In Janet Shibley Hyde & Marcia C. Linn (Eds.), *The psychology of gender: Advances through meta-analysis* (pp. 210–231). Baltimore: Johns Hopkins University Press. Linn's summary chapter examines the results of the meta-analyses reported in this volume and fits these results in historical context. Her examination considers the various mental abilities and social factors that have generally shown minimal gender differences, and she discusses the implications for these findings, giving an excellent and thoughtful summary.

References

Abrams, Leslie R.; & Jones, Russell W. (1994, August). *The contribution of social roles to psychological distress in businesswomen*. Paper presented at the 102nd annual convention of the American Psychological Association, Los Angeles, CA.

Abramson, Paul R.; Goldberg, Philip A.; Greenberg, Judith H.; & Abramson, Linda M. (1977). The talking platypus phenomenon: Competency ratings as a function of sex and professional status. *Psychology of Women Quarterly, 2,* 114–124.

Adler, David A.; Drake, Robert E.; & Teague, Gregory B. (1990). Clinicians' practices in personality assessment: Does gender influence the use of DSM-III axis II? *Comprehensive Psychiatry, 31,* 125–133.

Ahrentzen, Sherry; Levine, Douglas; W., & Michelson, William. (1989). Space, time, and activity in the home: A gender analysis. *Journal of Environmental Psychology, 9,* 89–101.

Alda, Alan. (1975, October). What every woman should know about men. *Ms.,* pp. 15–16.

Altman, Barbara Mandell. (1985). Disabled women in the social structure. In Susan E. Browne, Debra Connors, & Nanci Stern (Eds.), *With the power of each breath: A disabled women's anthology* (pp. 69–76). San Francisco: Cleis Press.

American Association of University Women (AAUW). (1992). *The AAUW report: How schools shortchange girls*. Washington, DC: AAUW Education Foundation and National Educational Association.

American Psychiatric Association. (1980). *Diagnostic and statistical manual of mental disorders* (3rd ed.). Washington, DC: American Psychiatric Association.

American Psychiatric Association. (1987). *Diagnostic and statistical manual of mental disorders* (3rd ed. rev.). Washington, DC: American Psychiatric Association.

American Psychiatric Association. (1994). *Diagnostic and statistical manual of mental disorders* (4th ed.). Washington, DC: American Psychiatric Association.

American Psychological Association Task Force on Sex Bias and Sex-Role Stereotyping in Psychotherapeutic Practice. (1978). Guidelines for therapy with women. *American Psychologist, 33,* 1122–1123.

Andersen, Arnold E.; & DiDomenico, Lisa. (1992). Diet vs. shape content of popular male and female magazines: A dose-response relationship to the incidence of eating disorders? *International Journal of Eating Disorders, 11,* 283–287.

Aneshensel, Carol S.; Frerichs, Ralph R.; & Clark, Virginia A. (1981). Family roles and sex differences in depression. *Journal of Health and Social Behavior, 22,* 379–393.

Aneshensel, Carol S.; & Pearlin, Leonard I. (1987). Structural contexts of sex differences in stress. In Rosalind C. Barnett, Lois Biener, & Grace K. Baruch (Eds.), *Gender and stress* (pp. 75–95). New York: Free Press.

Antill, John K. (1983). Sex role complementarity versus similarity in married couples. *Journal of Personality and Social Psychology, 45,* 145–155.

Archer, John; & Lloyd, Barbara (1982). *Sex and gender.* Cambridge, England: Cambridge University Press.

Aries, Elizabeth. (1987). Gender and communication. In Phillip Shaver & Clyde Hendrick (Eds)., *Sex and gender* (pp. 149–176). Newbury Park, CA: Sage.

Ashel, Mark H. (1991). A psycho-behavioral analysis of addicted versus non-addicted male and female exercisers. *Journal of Sport Behavior, 14,* 145–154.

Ashton, Heather. (1991). Psychotropic-drug prescribing for women. *British Journal of Psychiatry, 158*(Suppl. 10), 30–35.

Astin, Helen S. (1984). The meaning of work in women's lives: A sociopsychological model of career choice and work behavior. *Counseling Psychologist, 12,* 117–126.

Astrachan, Anthony. (1986). *How men feel: Their response to women's demands for equality and power.* Garden City, NY: Anchor Press.

Aube, Jennifer; & Koestner, Richard. (1992). Gender characteristics and adjustment: A longitudinal study. *Journal of Personality and Social Psychology, 63,* 485–493.

Averill, James R. (1982). *Anger and aggression: An essay on emotion.* New York: Springer-Verlag.

Avery, Patricia G; & Walker, Constance. (1993). Prospective teachers' perceptions of ethnic and gender differences in academic achievement. *Journal of Teacher Education, 44,* 27–37.

Ayanian, John Z.; & Epstein, Arnold M. (1991). Differences in the use of procedures between women and men hospitalized for coronary heart disease. *New England Journal of Medicine, 325,* 221–225.

Baber, Kristine M.; & Monaghan, Patricia. (1988). College women's career and motherhood expectations: New options, old dilemmas. *Sex Roles, 19,* 189–203.

Baenninger, Maryann; & Newcombe, Nora. (1989). A role of experience in spatial test performance: A meta-analysis. *Sex Roles, 20,* 327–343.

Bagley, Christopher; & King, Kathleen. (1990). *Child sexual abuse: The search for healing.* London: Tavistock/Routledge.

Bailey, William T.; Silver, N. Clayton; & Oliver, Kathleen A. (1990). Women's rights and roles: Attitudes among Black and White students. *Psychological Reports, 66,* 1143–1146.

Bakan, David. (1966). *The duality of human existence.* Chicago: Rand McNally.

Ball, Richard E.; & Robbins, Lynn. (1986). Marital status and life satisfaction among Black Americans. *Journal of Marriage and the Family, 48,* 389–394.

Balmary, Marie. (1982). *Psychoanalyzing psychoanalysis: Freud and the hidden fault of the father* (Ned Lukacher, Trans.). Baltimore: Johns Hopkins University Press. (Original work published 1979)

Bandura, Albert. (1986). *Social foundations of thought and action: A social cognitive theory.* Englewood Cliffs, NJ: Prentice-Hall.

Barak, Azy; Fisher, William A.; & Houston, Sandra. (1992). Individual difference correlates of the experience of sexual harassment. *Journal of Applied Social Psychology, 22,* 17–37.

Barnett, Rosalind C.; & Baruch, Grace K. (1987). Social roles, gender, and psychological distress. In Rosalind C. Barnett, Lois Biener, & Grace K. Baruch (Eds.), *Gender and stress* (pp. 122–143). New York: Free Press.

Barnett, Rosalind C.; Marshall, Nancy L.; & Pleck, Joseph H. (1992). Men's multiple roles and their relationship to men's psychological distress. *Journal of Marriage and the Family, 54,* 358–367.

Baron, Larry; & Straus, Murray A. (1989). *Four theories of rape in American society: A state-level analysis.* New Haven, CT: Yale University Press.

Baumeister, Roy F. (1988). Should we stop studying sex differences altogether? *American Psychologist, 43,* 1092–1095.

Baxter, Susan. (1993, March/April). The last self-help article you'll ever need. *Psychology Today,* pp. 70–71, 74–77, 94.

Beal, Carole R.; & Lockhart, Maria E. (1989). The effect of proper name and appearance changes on children's reasoning about gender constancy. *International Journal of Behavioral Development, 12,* 195–205.

Beck, Aaron T. (1985). *Anxiety disorders and phobias: A cognitive perspective.* New York: Basic Books.

Beckwith, Barbara. (1984, July/August). How magazines cover sex difference research. *Science for the People,* pp. 18–23.

Belasco, Warren J. (1989, December). The two taste cultures. *Psychology Today,* pp. 29–36.

Belenky, Mary Field; Clinchy, Blythe McVicker, Goldberger, Nancy Rule; & Tarule, Jill Mattuck. (1986). *Women's ways of knowing: The development of self, voice, and mind.* New York: Basic Books.

Belle, Deborah. (1990). Poverty and women's mental health. *American Psychologist, 45,* 385–389.

Bem, Sandra Lipsitz. (1974). The measurement of psychological androgyny. *Journal of Consulting and Clinical Psychology, 42,* 155–162.

Bem, Sandra Lipsitz. (1981). Gender schema theory: A cognitive account of sex-typing. *Psychological Review, 88,* 354–364.

Bem, Sandra Lipsitz. (1985). Androgyny and gender schema theory: A conceptual and empirical integration. In Theo B. Sonderegger (Ed.), *Nebraska symposium on motivation, 1984: Psychology and gender* (pp. 179–226). Lincoln: University of Nebraska Press.

Bem, Sandra Lipsitz. (1987). Gender schema theory and its implications for child development: Raising gender-aschematic children in a gender-schematic society. In Mary Roth Walsh (Ed.), *The psychology of women: Ongoing debates* (pp. 226–245). New Haven, CT: Yale University Press.

Bem, Sandra Lipsitz. (1989). Genital knowledge and gender constancy in preschool children. *Child Development, 60,* 649–662.

Bem, Sandra Lipsitz. (1993). Is there a place in psychology for a feminist analysis of the social context? *Feminism & Psychology, 3,* 230–234.

Benbow, Camilla Persson; & Stanley, Julian C. (1980). Sex differences in mathematical ability: Fact or artifact? *Science, 210,* 1262–1264.

Benbow, Camilla Persson; & Stanley, Julian C. (1983). Sex differences in mathematical reasoning ability: More facts. *Science, 222,* 1029–1031.

Benderly, Beryl Lieff. (1987). *The myth of two minds.* New York: Doubleday.

Benderly, Beryl Lieff. (1989, November). Don't believe everything you read... *Psychology Today,* pp. 67–69.

Benin, Mary Holland; & Angostinelli, Joan. (1988). Husbands' and wives' satisfaction with the division of labor. *Journal of Marriage and the Family, 50,* 349–361.

Berger, Bertrand D.; & Adesso, Vincent J. (1991). Gender differences in using alcohol to cope with depression. *Addictive Behaviors, 16,* 315–327.

Berkman, Lisa F.; & Syme, S. Leonard (1979). Social networks, host resistance, and mortality: A nine-year follow-up study of Alameda County residents. *American Journal of Epidemiology, 109,* 186–204.

Berman, Phyllis W. (1980). Are women more responsive than men to the young? A review of developmental and situational variables. *Psychological Bulletin, 88,* 668–695.

Bernard, Jessie. (1972). *The future of marriage.* New York: World Publishing.

Bernard, Jessie. (1981). The good-provider role: Its rise and fall. *American Psychologist, 36,* 1–12.

Bernardo, Donna Hodgkins; Shehan, Constance L.; & Leslie, Gerald R. (1987). A residue of tradition: Jobs, careers, and spouses' time in housework. *Journal of Marriage and the Family, 49,* 381–390.

Berndt, Thomas J. (1982). The features and effects of friendship in early adolescence. *Child Development, 53,* 1447–1460.

Berndt, Thomas J.; & Perry, T. Bridgett. (1986). Children's perceptions of friendships as supportive relationships. *Developmental Psychology, 22,* 640–648.

Bernstein, Bianca L.; Hofmann, Barbara; & Wade, Priscilla. (1987). Preferences for counselor gender: Students' sex role, other characteristics, and type of problem. *Journal of Counseling Psychology, 34,* 20–26.

Biener, Lois. (1987). Gender differences in the use of substances for coping. In Rosalind C. Barnett, Lois Biener, & Grace. K. Baruch (Eds.), *Gender and stress* (pp. 330–349). New York: Free Press.

Biernat, Monica. (1991). Gender stereotypes and the relationship between masculinity and femininity: A developmental analysis. *Journal of Personality and Social Psychology, 61,* 351–365.

Bigler, Rebecca S.; & Liben, Lynn S. (1993). A cognitive-developmental approach to racial stereotyping and reconstructive memory in Euro-American children. *Child Development, 64,* 1507–1518.

Bjorklund, David F. (1987, February). What are little boys (and girls) made of? *Parents Magazine,* pp. 88–91.

Blair, Sampson Lee; & Lichter, Daniel T. (1991). Measuring the division of household labor: Gender segregation of housework among American couples. *Journal of Family Issues, 12,* 91–113.

Blakeslee, Sandra. (1988, November 18). Female sex hormone is tied to ability to perform tasks. *New York Times,* pp. A1, D20.

Blakeslee, Sandra. (1991, November 14). Men's test scores linked to hormone. *New York Times,* p. B14.

Blechman, Elaine A. (1980). Behavior therapies. In Annette M. Brodsky & Rachel Hare-Mustin (Eds.), *Women and psychotherapy* (pp. 217–244). New York: Guilford Press.

Blechman, Elaine A.; Clay, Connie J.; Kipke, Michele D.; & Bickel, Warren K. (1988). The premenstrual experience. In Elaine A. Blechman & Kelly D. Brownell (Eds.), *Handbook of behavioral medicine for women* (pp. 80–91). New York: Pergamon Press.

Blier, Michael J.; Atkinson, Donald R.; & Greer, Carol A. (1987). Effect of client gender and counselor gender and sex roles on willingness to see the counselor. *Journal of Counseling Psychology, 34,* 27–30.

Block, Jeanne H. (1976). Debatable conclusions about sex differences [book review of *The psychology of sex differences*]. *Contemporary Psychology, 21,* 517–522.

Blumstein, Philip; & Schwartz, Pepper. (1983). *American couples.* New York: Pocket Books.

Blumstein, Philip; & Schwartz, Pepper. (1989). Intimate relationships and the creation of sexuality. In Barbara J. Risman & Pepper Schwartz (Eds.), *Gender in intimate relationships* (pp. 120–129). Belmont, CA: Wadsworth.

Bly, Robert. (1990). *Iron John.* Reading, MA: Addison-Wesley.

Bly, Robert. (1994, August). *Where are men now?* Paper presented at the 102nd annual convention of the American Psychological Association, Los Angeles, CA.

Booth, Alan: Shelley, Greg; Mazur, Allan; Tharp, Gerry; & Kittok, Roger. (1989). Testosterone, and winning and losing in human competition. *Hormones and Behavior, 23,* 556–571.

Brannon, Linda. (1994). *No name required: Gender stereotyping based on passage content.* Paper presented at the 102nd annual convention of the American Psychological Association, Los Angeles, CA.

Brannon, Linda; & Feist, Jess. (1992). *Health psychology: An introduction to behavior and health* (2nd ed.). Belmont, CA: Wadsworth.

Brannon, Robert. (1976). The male sex role: Our culture's blueprint of manhood and what it's done for us lately. In Deborah S. David & Robert Brannon (Eds.), *The forty-nine percent majority* (pp. 1–45). Reading, MA: Addison-Wesley.

Brecher, Edward M. (1969). *The sex researchers.* Boston: Little, Brown.

Brems, Christiane; & Schlottmann, Robert S. (1988). Gender-bound definitions of mental health. *Journal of Psychology, 122,* 5–14.

Britannica Book of the Year, 1992. (1992). Chicago: Encyclopedia Britannica.

Brodsky, Annette; & Holroyd, Jean. (1975). Report of the Task Force on Sex Bias and Sex-Role Stereotyping in ₁sychotherapeutic Practice. *American Psychologist, 30,* 1169–1175.

Brooks-Gunn, Jeanne; & Furstenberg, Frank F., Jr. (1989). Adolescent sexual behavior. *American Psychologist, 44,* 249–257.

Broverman, Inge K.; Broverman, Donald M.; Clarkson, Frank E.; Rosenkrantz, Paul S.; & Vogel, Susan R. (1970). Sex-role stereotypes and clinical judgments of mental health. *Journal of Consulting and Clinical Psychology, 34,* 1–7.

Broverman, Inge K.; Vogel, Susan Raymond; Broverman, Donald M.; Clarkson, Frank E.; & Rosenkrantz, Paul S. (1972). Sex-role stereotypes: A current appraisal. *Journal of Social Issues, 28*(2), 59–78.

Brown, Laura S. (1988). Feminist therapy with lesbians and gay men. In Mary Ann Dutton Douglas & Lenore E. A. Walker (Eds.), *Feminist psychotherapies: Integration of therapeutic and feminist systems* (pp. 206–227). Norwod, NJ: Ablex.

Brown, Laura S. (1992). A feminist critique of personality disorders. In Laura S. Brown & Mary Ballou (Eds.), *Personality and psychopathlogy: Feminist reappraisals* (pp. 206–228). New York: Guilford Press.

Browne, Angela; & Finkelhor, David. (1986). Impact of child sexual abuse: A review of the research. *Psychological Bulletin, 99,* 66–77.

Brownell, Kelly D.; & Stein, L. J. (1989). Metabolic and behavioral effects of weight loss and regain: A review of the animal and human literature. In Albert J. Stunkard & Andrew Baum (Eds.), *Perspectives in behavioral medicine: Eating, sleeping, and sex* (pp. 39–52). Hillsdale, NJ: Erlbaum.

Brownmiller, Susan. (1975). *Against our will: Men, women and rape.* New York: Simon & Schuster.

Brownmiller, Susan. (1984). *Femininity.* New York: Simon & Schuster.

Buhrmester, Duane; & Furman, Wyndol. (1987). The development of companionship and intimacy. *Child Development, 58,* 1101–1113.

Bukowski, William M.; Gauze, Cyma; Hoza, Betsy; & Newcomb, Andrew F. (1993). Differences and consistency between same-sex and other-sex peer relationships during early adolescence. *Developmental Psychology, 29,* 255–263.

Burge, Penny L.; & Culver, Steven M. (1990). Sexism, legislative power, and vocational education. In Susan L. Gabriel & Isaiah Smithson (Eds.), *Gender in the classroom: Power and pedagogy* (pp. 160–175). Urbana: University of Illinois Press.

Burnam, M. Audrey; Stein, Judith A.; Golding, Jacqueline M; Siegel, Judith M.; Sorenson, Susan B.; Forsythe, Alan B.; & Telles, Cynthia A. (1988). Sexual assault and mental disorders in a community population. *Journal of Consulting and Clinical Psychology, 56,* 843–850.

Burt, Martha R.; & Estep, Rhoda E. (1981). Apprehension and fear: Learning a sense of sexual vulnerability. *Sex Roles, 7,* 511–522.

Bush, Diane M.; & Simmons, R. G. (1987). Gender and coping with the entry into early adolescence. In Rosalind C. Barnett, Lois Biener, & Grace K. Baruch (Eds.), *Gender and stress* (pp. 185–217). New York: Free Press.

Buss, David M. (1991). Conflict in married couples: Personality predictors of anger and upset. *Journal of Personality, 59,* 663–688.

Buss, David M.; & Barnes, Michael. (1986). Preferences in human mate selection. *Journal of Personality and Social Psychology, 50,* 559–570.

Bussey, Kay; & Bandura, Albert. (1984). Influence of gender constancy and social power on sex-linked modeling. *Journal of Personality and Social Psychology, 47,* 1292–1302.

Bussey, Kay; & Bandura, Albert. (1992). Self-regulatory mechanisms governing gender development. *Child Development, 63,* 1236–1250.

Byne, William; Bleier, Ruth; & Houston, Lanning. (1988). Variations in human corpus callosum do not predict gender: A study using magnetic resonance imaging. *Behavioral Neuroscience, 102,* 222–227.

Byrnes, James P.; & Takahira, Sayuri. (1993). Explaining gender differences on SAT-math items. *Developmental Psychology, 29,* 805–810.

Cairns, Robert B. (1986). An evolutionary and developmental perspective on aggressive patterns. In Carolyn Zahn-Waxler, E. Mark Cummings, & Ronald Iannotti (Eds), *Altruism and aggression: Biological and social origins* (pp. 58–87). Cambridge, England: Cambridge University Press.

Cairns, Robert B.; Cairns, Beverley D.; Neckerman, Holly J.; Ferguson, Lynda L.; & Gariépy, Jean-Louis. (1989). Growth and aggression: 1. Childhood to early adolescence. *Developmental Psychology, 25,* 320–330.

Caldwell, Mayta A.; & Peplau, Letitia Anne. (1982). Sex differences in same-sex friendship. *Sex Roles, 8,* 721–732.

Cameron, Oliver G.; & Hill, Elizabeth M. (1989). Women and anxiety. *Psychiatric Clinics of North America, 12,* 175–186.

Cammaert, Lorna P. (1985). How widespread is sexual harassment on campus? Special Issue: Women in groups and aggression against women. *International Journal of Women's Studies, 8,* 388–397.

Cammaert, Lorna P.; & Larsen, Carolyn C. (1988). Feminist frameworks of psychotherapy. In Mary Ann Dutton Douglas & Lenore E. A. Walker (Eds.), *Feminist psychotherapies: Integration of therapeutic and feminist systems* (pp. 12–36). Norwod, NJ: Ablex.

Campbell, Bebe Moore. (1986). *Successful women, angry men: Backlash in the two-career marriage.* New York: Random House.

Cancian, Francesca M. (1986). The feminization of love. *Signs, 11,* 692–709.

Cancian, Francesca M. (1987). *Love in America: Gender and self-development.* Cambridge, England: Cambridge University Press.

Cannon, Walter B. (1927). The James-Lange theory of emotions: A critical examination and an alternative theory. *American Journal of Psychology, 39,* 106–124.

Caplan, Paula J. (1991). How *do* they decide who is normal? The bizarre, but true, tale of the DSM process. *Canadian Psychology, 32,* 162–170.

Caplan, Paula J. (1993). Premenstrual syndrome DSM-IV diagnosis: The coalition for a scientific and responsible DSM-IV. *Psychology of Women: Newsletter of Division 35, American Psychological Association, 20*(3), 4–5, 13.

Caplan, Paula J.; MacPherson, Gael M.; & Tobin, Patricia. (1985). Do sex-related differences in spatial abilities exist? A multilevel critique with new data. *American Psychologist, 40,* 786–799.

Carr, Rey A. (1991). Addicted to power: Sexual harassment and the unethical behavior of university faculty. *Canadian Journal of Counselling, 25,* 447–461.

CDC: News AIDS is top youth killer may prompt changes. (1995, February 4). *Lake Charles American Press,* p. 20.

Centers for Disease Control. (1992). Sexual behavior among high school students. *Journal of the American Medical Association, 267,* 628.

Central Intelligence Agency. (1992). *The world factbook 1992.* Washington, DC: U.S. Government Printing Office.

Chafetz, Janet Saltzman. (1989). Marital intimacy and conflict: The irony of spousal equality. In Jo Freeman (Ed.), *Women: A feminist perspective* (pp. 149–156). Mountain View, CA: Mayfield.

Chaiken, Shelly; & Pliner, Patricia. (1987). Women, but not men, are what they eat: The effect of meal size and gender on perceived femininity and masculinity. *Personality and Social Psychology Bulletin, 13,* 166–176.

Chehrazi, Shahla. (1986). Female psychology: A review. *Journal of the American Psychoanalytic Association, 34,* 111–162. Also in Mary Roth Walsh (Ed). (1987). *The psychology of women: Ongoing debates* (pp. 22–38). New Haven: Yale University Press.

Chernin, Kim. (1978). *The obsession: Reflections on the tyranny of slenderness.* New York: Harper & Row.

Cherry, Frances; & Deaux, Kay. (1978). Fear of success versus fear of gender-inappropriate behavior. *Sex Roles, 4,* 97–101.

Chesler, Phyllis. (1972). *Women and madness.* New York: Avon.

Chess, Stella; & Thomas, Alexander. (1982). Infant bonding: Mystique and reality. *American Journal of Orthopsychiatry, 52,* 213–222.

Chodorow, Nancy. (1978). *The reproduction of mothering: Psychoanalysis and the sociology of gender.* Berkeley, CA: University of California Press.

Chodorow, Nancy. (1979). Feminism and difference: Gender, relation, and difference in psychoanalytic perspective. *Socialist Review, 46,* 42–64. Also in Mary Roth Walsh (Ed.) (1987). *The psychology of women: Ongoing debates* (pp. 249–264). New Haven: Yale University Press.

Christensen, Larry B. (1991). *Experimental methodology* (5th ed.). Boston: Allyn and Bacon.

Chu, Chung-Chou; Abi-Dargham, Annissé; Ackerman, Bette; Cetingök, Maummer; & Klein, Helen E. (1989). Sex differences in schizophrenia. *International Journal of Social Psychiatry, 35,* 237–244.

Chusmir, Leonard H.; Koberg, Christine S.; & Stecher, Mary D. (1992). Self-confidence of managers in work and social situations: A look at gender differences. *Sex Roles, 26,* 497–512.

Cicone, Michael V.; & Ruble, Diane N. (1978). Beliefs about males. *Journal of Social Issues, 34*(1), 1–15.

Cleary, Paul D. (1987). Gender differences in stress-related disorders. In Rosalind C. Barnett, Lois Biener, & Gracᴇ K. Baruch (Eds.), *Gender and stress* (pp. 39–72). New York: Free Press.

Cleary, Paul D.; & Mechanic, David. (1983). Sex differences in psychological distress among married people. *Journal of Health and Social Behavior, 24,* 111–121.

Cohen, Deborah. (1992). Why there are so few male teachers in early grades. *Education Digest, 57*(6), 11–13.

Cohen, Theodore F. (1992). Men's families, men's friends: A structural analysis of constraints on men's social ties. In Peter M. Nardi (Ed.), *Men's friendships* (pp. 115–131). Newbury Park, CA: Sage.

Cohn, Barbara A.; Kaplan, George A.; & Cohen, Richard D. (1988). Did early detection and treatment contribute to the decline in ischemic heart disease mortality? Prospective evidence from the Alameda County Study. *American Journal of Epidemiology, 127,* 1143–1154.

Colby, Anne; & Damon, William. (1983). Listening to a different voice: A review of Gilligan's *A Different Voice. Merrill-Palmer Quarterly, 29,* 473–481. Also in Mary Roth Walsh (Ed.) (1987), *The psychology of women: Ongoing debates* (pp. 321–329). New Haven: Yale University Press.

Collins, M. Elizabeth. (1991). Body figure perceptions and preferences among preadolescent children. *International Journal of Eating Disorders, 10,* 199–208.

Coltrane, Scott; & Valdez, Elsa O. (1993). Reluctant compliance: Work-family role allocation in dual-earner Chicano families. In Jane C. Hood (Ed.), *Men, work, and family* (pp. 151–175). Newbury Park, CA: Sage.

Committee on Women in Psychology. (1989). If sex enters into the psychotherapy relationships. *Professional Psychology: Research and Practice, 20,* 112–115.

Condry, John; & Condry, Sandra. (1976). Sex differences: A study in the eye of the beholder. *Child Development, 47,* 812–818.

Constantinople, Anne. (1973). Masculinity-femininity: An exception to a famous dictum. *Psychological Bulletin, 80,* 389–407.

Cook, Ellen Piel; Warnke, Melanie; & Dupuy, Paula. (1993). Gender bias and the DSM-III-R. *Counselor Education and Supervision, 32,* 311–322.

Cooperstock, Ruth. (1970). A review of women's psychotropic drug use. *Canadian Journal of Psychiatry, 24,* 29–34.

Crawford, June; Kippax, Susan; Onxy, Jenny; Gault, Una; & Benton, Pam. (1992). *Emotion and gender: Constructing meaning from memory.* London: Sage.

Crawford, Mary. (1989). Agreeing to differ: Feminist epistemologies and women's ways of knowing. In Mary Crawford & Margaret Gentry (Eds.), *Gender and thought: Psychological perspectives* (pp. 128–145). New York: Springer-Verlag.

Crawford, Mary; & Gressley, Diane. (1991). Creativity, caring, and context: Women's and men's accounts of humor preferences and practices. *Psychology of Women Quarterly, 15,* 217–231.

Crawford, Mary; & Marecek, Jeanne. (1989). Psychology reconstructs the female: 1968–1988. *Psychology of Women Quarterly, 13,* 147–165.

Crook, Thomas H.; Youngjohn, James R.; & Larrabee, Glenn J. (1993). The influence of age, gender, and cues on computer-simulated topographic memory. *Developmental Neuropsychology, 9,* 41–53.

Cutler, Susan E.; & Nolen-Hoeksema, Susan. (1991). Accounting for sex differences in depression through female victimization: Childhood sexual abuse. *Sex Roles, 24,* 425–438.

Dabbs, James M., Jr. (1992). Testosterone and occupational achievement. *Social Forces, 70,* 813–824.

Dabbs, James M. Jr.; de la Rue, Denise; & Williams, Paula M. (1990). Testosterone and occupational choice: Actors, ministers, and other men. *Journal of Personality and Social Psychology, 59,* 1261–1265.

Dabbs, James M. Jr.; Hopper, Charles H.; & Jurkovic, Gregory J. (1990). Testosterone and personality among college students and military veterans. *Personality and Individual Differences, 11,* 1263–1269.

Dabbs, James M. Jr.; & Morris, Robin. (1990). Testosterone, social class, and antisocial behavior in a sample of 4,462 men. *Psychological Science, 1,* 209–211.

Dabbs, James M. Jr.; Ruback, R. Barry; Frady, Robert L.; Hopper, Charles H.; & Sgoutas, Demetrios S. (1988). Saliva testosterone and criminal violence among women. *Personality and Individual Differences, 9,* 269–275.

Daily, Catherine M. (1993). The (R)Evolution of the American woman. *Business Horizons, 36*(2), 1–5.

Darwin, Charles. (1872). *The expression of emotions in man and animals.* New York: Philosophical Library.

Daugherty, Cynthia; & Lees, Marty. (1988). Feminist psychodynamic therapies. In Mary Ann Dutton Douglas & Lenore E. A. Walker (Eds.), *Feminist psychotherapies: Integration of therapeutic and feminist systems* (pp. 68–90). Norwod, NJ: Ablex.

Davenport, Donna S.; & Yurich, John M. (1991). Multicultural gender issues. *Journal of Counseling and Development, 70,* 64–71.

Davis, Caroline; Elliott, Stuart; Dionne, Michelle; & Mitchell, Ian. (1991). The relationship of personality factors and physical activity to body satisfaction in men. *Personality and Individual Differences, 12,* 89–694.

Day, Randal D. (1992). The transition to first intercourse among racially and culturally diverse youth. *Journal of Marriage and the Family, 54,* 749–762.

Dean, Karol E.; & Malamuth, Neil M. (1994, August). *Predictors of appeal of sexual aggression.* Paper presented at the 102nd annual convention of the American Psychological Association, Los Angeles, CA.

Deaux, Kay. (1984). From individual differences to social categories: Analysis of a decade's research on gender. *American Psychologist, 39,* 105–116.

Deaux, Kay. (1987). Psychological constructions of masculinity and femininity. In June Machover Reinisch, Leonard A. Rosenblum, & Stephanie A. Sanders (Eds.), *Masculinity/femininity: Basic perspectives* (pp. 289–303). New York: Oxford University Press.

Deaux, Kay; & Lewis, Laurie. (1984). The structure of gender stereotypes: Interrelationships among components and gender label. *Journal of Personality and Social Psychology, 46,* 991–1004.

Deaux, Kay; White, Leonard; & Farris, Elizabeth. (1975). Skill versus luck: Field and laboratory studies of male and female preferences. *Journal of Personality and Social Psychology, 32,* 629–636.

Degler, Carl N. (1974). What ought to be and what was: Women's sexuality in the nineteenth century. *American Historical Review, 79,* 1467–1490.

DeHeer, N. Dean; Wampold, Bruce E.; & Freund, Richard D. (1992). Do sex-typed and androgynous subjects prefer counselors on the basis of gender or effectiveness? They prefer the best. *Journal of Counseling Psychology, 39,* 175–184.

de Lacoste-Utamsing, Christine; & Holloway, Ralph L. (1982). Sexual dimorphism in the human corpus callosum. *Science, 216,* 1431–1432.

de Monteflores, Carmen; & Schultz, Stephen J. (1978). Coming out: Similarities and differences for lesbians and gay men. *Journal of Social Issues, 34*(3), 59–72.

Denmark, Florence L. (1994). Engendering psychology. *American Psychologist, 49,* 329–334.

Denworth, Lydia. (1989, December). Why we want sex: The difference between men and women. *Psychology Today,* p. 12.

Deutsch, Francine M.; Lussier, Julianne B.; & Servis, Laura J. (1993). Husbands at home: Predictors of paternal participation in childcare and housework. *Journal of Personality and Social Psychology, 65,* 1154–1166.

Dilorio, Judith A. (1989). Being and becoming coupled: The emergence of female subordination in heterosexual relationships. In Barbara J. Risman & Pepper Schwartz (Eds.), *Gender in intimate relationships* (pp. 94–107). Belmont, CA: Wadsworth.

Dinnerstein, Dorothy. (1976). *The mermaid and the minotaur: Sexual arrangements and the human malaise.* New York: Harper & Row.

Doll, Richard; & Peto, Richard. (1981). *The causes of cancer.* New York: Oxford University Press.

Dollard, John; Doob, Leonard; Miller, Neal; Mowrer, O. Hobart; & Sears, Robert. (1939). *Frustration and aggression.* New Haven, CT: Yale University Press.

Dovidio, John F.; Ellyson, Steve L.; Keating, Caroline F.; Heltman, Karen; & Brown, Clifford E. (1988). The relationship of social power to visual displays of dominance between men and women. *Journal of Personality and Social Psychology, 54,* 233–242.

Drewnowski, Adam; & Yee, Doris K. (1987). Men and body image: Are males satisfied with their body weight? *Psychosomatic Medicine, 49,* 626–634.

Dreyfus, Colleen K. (1994, August). *Stigmatizing attitudes toward male victims.* Paper presented at the 102nd annual convention of the American Psychological Association, Los Angeles, CA.

Dubbert, Patricia M. (1992). Exercise in behavioral medicine. *Journal of Consulting and Clinical Psychology, 60,* 613–618.

Dubbert, Patricia M.; & Martin, John E. (1988). Exercise. In Elaine A. Blechman & Kelly D. Brownell (Eds.), *Handbook of behavioral medicine for women* (pp. 291–304). New York: Pergamon Press.

DuBois, David L.; & Hirsch, Barton J. (1990). School and neighborhood friendship patterns of Blacks and Whites in early adolescence. *Child Development, 61,* 524–536.

Duck, Steve. (1991). *Understanding relationships.* New York: Guilford Press.

Dweck, Carol S. (1986). Motivational processes affecting learning. *American Psychologist, 41,* 1040–1048.

Dworkin, Terry Morehead. (1993). Harassment in the 1990s. *Business Horizons, 36*(2), 52–58.

Eagly, Alice H. (1987a). Reporting sex differences. *American Psychologist, 42,* 756–757.

Eagly, Alice H. (1987b). *Sex differences in social behavior: A social-role interpretation.* Hillsdale, NJ: Erbaum.

Eagly, Alice H. (1994, August). *Are people prejudiced against women?* Paper presented at the 102nd annual convention of the American Psychological Association, Los Angeles, CA.

Eagly, Alice H.; & Johnson, Blair T. (1990). Gender and leadership style: A meta-analysis. *Psychological Bulletin, 108,* 233–256.

Eagly, Alice H.; & Kite, Mary E. (1987). Are stereotypes of nationalities applied to both women and men? *Journal of Personality and Social Psychology, 53,* 451–462.

Eagly, Alice H.; Makhijani, Mona G.; & Klonsky, Bruce G. (1992). Gender and the evaluation of leaders: A meta-analysis. *Psychological Bulletin, 111,* 3–22.

Eagly, Alice H.; Mladinic, Antonio; & Otto, Stacey. (1991). Are women evaluated more favorably than men? An analysis of attitudes, beliefs, and emotions. *Psychology of Women Quarterly, 15,* 203–216.

Eagly, Alice H.; & Steffen, Valerie J. (1986). Gender and aggressive behavior: A meta-analytic review of the social psychological literature. *Psychological Bulletin, 100,* 309–330.

Eagly, Alice H.; & Wood, Wendy. (1985). Gender and influenceability: Stereotype versus behavior. In Virginia E. O'Leary, Rhoda Kesler Unger, & Barbara Strudler Wallston (Eds.), *Women, gender, and social psychology* (pp. 225–256). Hillsdale, NJ: Erlbaum.

Eccles, Jacquelynne S. (1987). Gender roles and achievement patterns: An expectancy value perspective. In June Machover Reinisch, Leonard A. Rosenblum,

& Stephanie A. Sanders (Eds.), *Masculinity/femininity: Basic perspectives* (pp. 240–280). New York: Oxford University Press.

Eccles, Jacquelynne S. (1989). Bringing young women to math and sceince. In Mary Crawford & Margaret Gentry (Eds.), *Gender and thought: Psychological perspectives* (pp. 36–58). New York: Springer-Verlag.

Eccles, Jacquelynne S.; & Jacobs, Janis E. (1986). Social forces shape math attitudes and performance. *Signs, 11,* 367–380.

Eccles, Jacquelynne; Wigfield, Allan; Harold, Rena D.; & Blumenfeld, Phyllis. (1993). Age and gender differences in children's self- and task perceptions during elementary school. *Child Development, 64,* 830–845.

Eckhardt, Michael J.; Harford, Thomas C.; Kaelber, Charles T.; Parker, Elizabeth S.; Rosenthal, Laura S.; Ryback, Ralph S.; Salmoiraghi, Gian C.; Vanderveen, Ernestine; & Warren, Kenneth R. (1981). Health hazards associated with alcohol consumption. *Journal of the American Medical Association, 246,* 648–666.

Ehrenreich, Barbara; & English, Deirdre. (1973). *Witches, midwives, and nurses: A history of women healers.* New York: Feminist Press.

Ehrenreich, Barbara; Hess, Elizabeth; & Jacobs, Gloria. (1986). *Re-making love: The feminization of sex.* Garden City, NY: Anchor Press.

Eichenbaum, Luise; & Orbach, Susie. (1983). *What do women want: Exploding the myth of dependency.* New York: Coward-McCann.

Eisenberg, Nancy; & Lennon, Randy. (1983). Sex differences in empathy and related capacities. *Psychological Bulletin, 94,* 100–131.

Ekman, Paul. (1984). Expression and the nature of emotion. In Klaus R. Scherer & Paul Ekman (Eds.), *Approaches to emotion* (pp. 319–343). Hillsdale, NJ: Erlbaum.

Ekman, Paul; Levenson, Robert W.; & Friesen, Wallace V. (1983). Autonomic nervous activity distinguishes among emotions. *Science, 221,* 1208–1210.

Ellenberger, Henri F. (1970). *The discovery of the unconscious.* New York: Basic Books.

Ellestad, Myrvin H. (1986). *Stress testing* (3rd ed.). Philadelphia: Davis.

Ellis, Albert. (1962). *Reason and emotion in psychotherapy.* New York: Stuart.

Enns, Carolyn Zerbe. (1992). Self-esteem groups: A synthesis of consciousness-raising and assertiveness training. *Journal of Counseling and Development, 71,* 7–13.

Enns, Carolyn Zerbe. (1993). Twenty years of feminist counseling and therapy: From naming biases to implementing multifaceted practice. *Counseling Psychologist, 21,* 3–87.

Enns, Carolyn Z.; & Hackett, Gail. (1990). Comparison of feminist and nonfeminist women's reactions to variants of nonsexist and feminist counseling. *Journal of Counseling Psychology, 37,* 33–40.

Epstein, Cynthia Fuchs. (1988). *Deceptive distinctions: Sex, gender and the social order.* New Haven, CT: Yale University Press.

Eron, Leonard D. (1987). The development of aggressive behavior from the perspective of a developing behaviorism. *American Psychologist, 42,* 435–442.

Eron, Leonard D.; Huesmann, L. Rowell; Brice, Patrick; Fischer, Paulette; & Mermelstein, Rebecca. (1983). Age trends in the development of aggression, sex typing, and related television habits. *Developmental Psychology, 19,* 71–77.

Faderman, Lillian. (1989). A history of romantic friendship and lesbian love. In Barbara J. Risman & Pepper Schwartz (Eds.), *Gender in intimate relationships* (pp. 26–31). Belmont, CA: Wadsworth.

Fagot, Beverly I.; & Hagan, Richard. (1991). Observations of parent reactions to sex-stereotyped behaviors: Age and sex effects. *Child Development, 62,* 617–628.

Fagot, Beverly I.; & Leinbach, Mary D. (1989). The young child's gender schema: Environmental input, internal organization. *Child Development, 60,* 663–672.

Fagot, Beverly I.; & Leinbach, Mary D. (1993). Gender-role development in young children: From discrimination to labeling. *Developmental Review, 13,* 205–224.

Fagot, Beverly I.; Leinbach, Mary D.; & O'Boyle, Cherie. (1992). Gender labeling, gender stereotyping, and parenting behaviors. *Developmental Psychology, 28,* 225–230.

Fallon, April E.; & Rozin, Paul. (1985). Sex differences in perceptions of desirable body shape. *Journal of Abnormal Psychology, 94,* 102–105.

Faludi, Susan. (1991). *Backlash: The undeclared war against American women.* New York: Crown.

Farmer, Helen S.; & Sidney, Joan Seliger. (1985). Sex equity in career and vocational eduction. In Susan S. Klein (Ed.), *Handbook for achieving sex equity through education* (pp. 338–359). Baltimore: Johns Hopkins University Press.

Fausto-Sterling, Anne. (1985). *Myths of gender: Biological theories about women and men.* New York: Basic Books.

Fee, Elizabeth. (1986). Critiques of modern science: The relationship of feminism to other radical epistemologies. In Ruth Bleier (Ed.), *Feminist approaches to science* (pp. 42–56). New York: Pergamon Press.

Feingold, Alan. (1988). Cognitive gender differences are disappearing. *American Psychologist, 43,* 95–103.

Feist, Jess. (1994). *Theories of personality* (3rd ed.). Fort Worth: Harcourt Brace Jovanovich.

Feld, Scott L.; & Straus, Murray A. (1989). Escalation and desistance of wife assault in marriage. *Criminology, 27,* 141–161.

Fennema, Elizabeth. (1980). Sex-related differences in mathematics achievement: Where and why. In Lynn H. Fox, Linda Brody, & Dianne Tobin (Eds.), *Women and the mathematical mystique* (pp. 76–93). Baltimore: Johns Hopkins University Press.

Ferree, Myra Marx; & Hess, Beth B. (1985). *Controversy and coalition: The new feminist movement.* Boston: Twayne

Feyerherm, William. (1981). Measuring gender differences in delinquency: Self-reports versus police contact. In Marguerite O. Warren (Ed.), *Comparing female and male offenders* (pp. 46–54). Beverly Hills. CA: Sage.

Fields, Judith; & Wolff, Edward N. (1991). The decline of sex segregation and the wage gap, 1970–80. *Journal of Human Resources, 26,* 608–622.

Fine, Michelle. (1988). Sexuality, schooling, and adolescent females: The missing discourse of desire. *Harvard Educational Review, 58,* 29–53.

Finkelhor, David. (1980). Sex among siblings: A survey on prevalence, variety, and effects. *Archives of Sexual Behavior, 9,* 171–193.

Finkelhor, David. (1984). *Child sexual abuse: New theory and research.* New York: Free Press.

Finkelhor, David (1990). Early and long-term effects of child sexual abuse: An update. *Professional Psychology Research and Practice, 21,* 325–330.

Finkelhor, David; & Baron, Larry. (1986). Risk factors for child sexual abuse. *Journal of Interpersonal Violence, 1,* 43–71.

Fischer, Agneta H. (1993). Sex differences in emotionality: Fact or stereotype? *Feminism & Psychology, 3,* 303–318.

Fiske, Susan T. (1993). Controlling other people: The impact of power on stereotyping. *American Psychologist, 48,* 621–628.

Fiske, Susan T.; Bersoff, Donald N.; Borgida, Eugene; Deaux, Kay; & Heilman, Madeline E. (1991). Social science research on trial: Use of sex stereotyping research in *Price Waterhouse v. Hopkins. American Psychologist, 46,* 1049–1060.

Fitzgerald, Louise F. (1994, August). *Sexual harassment—A feminist perspective on the prevention of violence against women in the workplace.* Paper presented at the 102nd annual convention of the American Psychological Association, Los Angeles, CA.

Fitzgerald, Louise F.; Weitzman, Lauren M.; Gold, Yael; & Ormerod, Mimi. (1988). Academic harassment: Sex and denial in scholarly garb. *Psychology of Women Quarterly, 12,* 329–340.

Flaskerud, Jacquelyn H. (1986). Diagnostic and treatment differences among five ethnic groups. *Psychological Reports, 58,* 219–235.

Flaskerud, Jacquelyn H.; & Hu, Li-tze. (1992). Relationship of ethnicity to psychiatric diagnosis. *Journal of Nervous and Mental Disease, 180,* 296–303.

Flynn, Clifton P. (1990). Relationship violence by women: Issues and implications. *Family Relations, 39,* 194–198.

Fodor, Iris Goldstein. (1988). Cognitive behavior therapy: Evaluation of theory and practice for addressing women's issues. In Mary Ann Dutton Douglas & Lenore E. A. Walker (Eds.), *Feminist psychotherapies: Integration of therapeutic and feminist systems* (pp. 91–117). Norwood, NJ: Ablex.

Folkman, Susan; & Lazarus, Richard S. (1980). An analysis of coping in middle-aged community sample. *Journal of Health and Social Behavior, 21,* 219–239.

Fontenot, Kathleen; & Brannon, Linda. (1991, August). *Gender differences in coping with workplace stress.* Paper presented at the 99th convention of the American Psychological Association, San Francisco, CA.

Ford, Clellan S.; & Beach, Frank A. (1951). *Patterns of sexual behavior.* New York: Harper.

Fowers, Blaine J. (1991). His and her marriage: A multivariate study of gender and marital satisfaction. *Sex Roles, 24,* 209–221.

Fox, Mary Frank. (1989). Women and higher education: Gender differences in the status of students and scholars. In Jo Freeman (Ed.), *Women: A feminist perspective* (4th ed.) (pp. 217–235). Mountain View, CA: Mayfield.

Frable, Deborrah E. S. (1989). Sex typing and gender ideology: Two facets of the individual's gender psychology that go together. *Journal of Personality and Social Psychology, 56,* 95–108.

Frankenhaeuser, Marianne. (1991). Psychophysiology of sex differences as related to occupational stress. In Marianne Frankenhaeuser, Ulf Lundberg, & Margaret Chesney (Eds.), *Women, work, and health: Stress and opportunities* (pp. 39–61). New York: Plenum Press.

Freiberg, Peter. (1991). Self-esteem gender gap widens in adolescence. *APA Monitor, 22*(4), 29.

Freud, Sigmund. (1925/1989). Some psychical consequences of the anatomical distinction between the sexes. In Peter Gay (Ed.), *The Freud reader* (pp. 670–678). New York: Norton.

Freud, Sigmund. (1933/1964). Femininity. In James Strachey (Ed. and Trans.), *New introductory lectures on psychoanalysis* (p. 112–135). New York: Norton.

Frezza, Mario; di Padova, Carlo; Pozzato, Gabriele; Terpin, Maddalena; Baraona, Enrique; & Lieber, Charles S. (1990). High blood alcohol levels in women: The role of decreased gastric alcohol dehydrogenase activity and first-pass metabolism. *New England Journal of Medicine, 322,* 95–99.

Frodi, Ann M.; & Lamb, Michael E. (1978). Sex differences in responsiveness to infants; A developmental study of psychophysiological and behavioral resonses. *Child Devleopment, 49,* 1182–1188.

Frodi, Ann M.; Macaulay, Jacqueline; & Thome, Pauline R. (1977). Are women always less aggressive than men? A review of the experimental literature. *Psychological Bulletin, 84,* 634–660.

Fujita, Frank; Diener, Ed; & Sandvik, Ed. (1991). Gender differences in negative affect and well-being: The case for emotional intensity. *Journal of Personality and Social Psychology, 61,* 427–434.

Fullerton, Howard N., Jr. (1989). New labor force projections spanning 1988 to 2000. *Monthly Labor Review, 112*(11), 3–12.

Furman, Wyndol; & Bierman, Karen Linn. (1984). Children's conceptions of friendship: A multimethod study of developmental changes. *Developmental Psychology, 20,* 925–931.

Furstenberg, Frank F.; & Spanier, Graham B. (1984). *Recycling the family: Remarriage after divorce.* Beverly Hills, CA: Sage.

Galea, Liisa A.; & Kimura, Doreen. (1993). Sex differences in route-learning. *Personality and Individual Differences, 14,* 53–65.

Gallagher, Maggie. (1987, May 22). What men really want. *National Review,* pp. 39–40.

Ganley, Anne L. (1988). Feminist therapy with male clients. In Mary Ann Dutton Douglas & Lenore E. A. Walker (Eds.), *Feminist psychotherapies: Integration of therapeutic and feminist systems* (pp. 186–205). Norwod, NJ: Ablex.

Garner, David M.; & Garfinkel, Paul E. (1980). Sociocultural factors in the development of anorexia nervosa. *Psychological Medicine, 10,* 647–656.

Garner, David M.; Garfinkel, Paul E.; Schwartz, Donald M.; & Thompson, Michael G. (1980). Cultural expectations of thinness in women. *Psychological Reports, 47,* 483–491.

Gartner, Alan; Gartner, Audrey J.; & Ouellette Kobasa, Suzanne C. (1988). Self-help. In Elaine A. Blechman & Kelly D. Brownell (Eds.), *Handbook of behavioral medicine for women* (pp. 330–342). New York: Pergamon Press.

Gartrell, Nanette; Herman, Judith L.; Olarte, Silvia; Feldstein, Michael; & Localio, Russell. (1987). Reporting practices of psychiatrists who knew of sexual misconduct by colleagues. *American Journal of Orthopsychiatry, 57,* 287–295.

Gay, Peter. (1988). *Freud: A life for our time.* New York: Norton.

Geer, James H.; & Broussard, Deborah Bice. (1990). Scaling heterosexual behavior and arousal: Consistency and sex differences. *Journal of Personality and Social Psychology, 58,* 664–671.

Gelles, Richard J. (1979). *Family violence.* Beverly Hills, CA: Sage.

Gelles, Richard J.; & Cornell, Claire Pedrick. (1990). *Intimate violence in families* (2nd ed.). Newbury Park, CA: Sage.

Gelman, David; Foote, Donna; Barrett, Todd; & Talbot, Mary. (1992, February 24). Born or bred? *Newsweek,* pp. 46–53.

Gergen, Kenneth J. (1985). The social constructionist movement in modern psychology. *American Psychologist, 40,* 266–275.

Gerhart, Barry. (1990). Gender differences in current and starting salaries: The role of performance, college major, and job title. *Industrial and Labor Relations Review, 43,* 418–433.

Geschwind, Norman; & Galaburda, Albert S. (1987). *Cerebral lateralization.* Cambridge, MA: MIT Press.

Gibbons, Ann. (1991). The brain as "sexual organ." *Science, 253,* 957–959.

Gilbert, Lucia A. (1980). Feminist therapy. In Annette M. Brodsky & Rachel Hare-Mustin (Eds.), *Women and psychotherapy* (pp. 245–265). New York: Guilford Press.

Gilbert, Lucia A. (1984). Comments on the meaning of work in women's lives. *Counseling Psychology, 12,* 129–130.

Gilligan, Carol. (1982). *In a different voice: Psychological theory and women's development.* Cambridge, MA: Harvard University Press.

Gilligan, Carol; & Attanucci, Jane. (1988). Two moral orientations. In Carol Gilligan, Janie Victoria Ward, & Jill McLean Taylor, with Betty Bardige (Eds.), *Mapping the moral domain: A contribution of women's thinking to psychological theory and education* (pp. 73–86). Cambridge, MA: Harvard University Press.

Gilligan, Carol; Ward, Janie Victoria; & Taylor, Jill McLean; with Bardige, Betty (Eds.). (1988). *Mapping the moral domain: A contribution of women's thinking to psychological theory and education.* Cambridge, MA: Harvard University Press.

Ginsburg, Herbert; & Opper, Sylvia. (1969). *Piaget's theory of intellectual development: An introduction.* Englewood Cliffs, NJ: Prentice-Hall.

Glick, Peter; Zion, Cari; & Nelson, Cynthia. (1988). What mediates sex discrimination in hiring decisions? *Journal of Personality and Social Psychology, 55,* 178–186.

Golding, Jacqueline M.; Smith, G. Richard; & Kashner, T. Michael. (1991). Does somatization disorder occur in men? Clinical characteristics of women and men with multiple unexplained somatic symptoms. *Archives of General Psychiatry, 48,* 231–235.

Goldsmith, Ronald E.; & Matherly, Timothy A. (1988). Creativity and self-esteem: A multiple operationalization validity study. *Journal of Psychology, 122,* 47–56.

Goleman, Daniel. (1988, August 23). Sex roles reign powerful as ever in the emotions. *New York Times,* pp. C1, 13.

Goleman, Daniel. (1990a, April 10). Stereotypes of the sexes persisting in therapy. *New York Times,* Sec. C, pp. 1, 10.

Goleman, Daniel. (1990b, July 17). Aggression in men: Hormone levels are a key. *New York Times,* sec. C, p. 1.

Gonzalez, Judith Teresa. (1988). Dilemmas of the high-achieving Chicana: The double-bind factor in male/female relationships. *Sex Roles, 18,* 367–380.

Good, Glenn E.; Dell, Don M.; & Mintz, Laurie B. (1989). Male role and gender role conflict: Relations to help seeking in men. *Journal of Counseling Psychology, 36,* 295–300.

Good, Glenn E.; Gilbert, Lucia A.; & Scher, Murray. (1990). Gender aware therapy: A synthesis of feminist therapy and knowledge about gender. *Journal of Counseling & Development, 68,* 376–380.

Goodman, Lisa A.; Koss, Mary P.; Fitzgerald, Louise F.; Russo, Nancy Felipe; & Keita, Gwendolyn Puryear. (1993). Male violence against women: Current research and future directions. *American Psychologist, 48,* 1054–1058.

Gorman, Christine. (1992, January 20). Sizing up the sexes. *Time,* pp. 42–51.

Gorski, Roger A. (1987). Sex differences in the rodent brain: Their nature and origin. In June M. Reinisch, Leonard A. Rosenblum, & Stephanie A. Sanders (Eds.), *Masculinity/femininity: Basic perspectives* (pp. 37–67). New York: Oxford University Press.

Gottman, John M. (1991). Predicting the longitudinal course of marriages. *Journal of Marriage and Family Therapy, 17,* 3–7.

Gould, Stephen Jay. (1981). *The mismeasure of man.* New York: Norton.

Gove, Walter R. (1980). Mental illness and psychiatric treatment among women. *Psychology of Women Quarterly, 4,* 345–362.

Gove, Walter R. (1984). Gender differences in mental and physical illness: The effects of fixed roles and nurturant roles. *Social Science and Medicine, 19*(2), 77–84.

Gove, Walter R.; & Hughes, Michael. (1979). Possible causes of the apparent sex differences in physical health: An empirical investigation. *American Sociological Review, 44,* 126–146.

Gove, Walter R.; & Zeiss, Carol. (1987). Multiple roles and happiness. In Faye J. Crosby (Ed.), *Spouse, parent, worker: On gender and multiple roles* (pp. 125–137). New Haven: Yale University Press.

Graham, Sandra; Hudley, Cynthia; & Williams, Estella. (1992). Attributional and emotional determinants of aggression among African-American and Latino young adolescents. *Developmental Psychology, 28,* 731–740.

Gray, John. (1992). *Men are from Mars, women are from Venus.* New York: HarperCollins.

Grayson, Donald K. (1990). Donner party deaths: A demographic assessment. *Journal of Anthropological Research, 46,* 223–242.

Green, Judith. (1987). Patterns of eating in normal men and women. *Psychology—A Quarterly Journal of Human Behavior, 24*(4), 1–14.

Greenberger, Ellen; & O'Neil, Robin. (1993). Spouse, parent, worker: Role commitments and role-related experiences in the construction of adults' well-being. *Developmental Psychology, 29,* 181–197.

Greeno, Catherine G.; & Maccoby, Eleanor E. (1986). How different is the "different voice"? *Signs, 11*(2), 310–312.

Greenwald, Anthony G. (1975). Consequences of prejudice against the null hypothesis. *Psychological Bulletin, 82,* 1–20.

Gregory, Robert J. (1987). *Adult intellectual assessment.* Boston: Allyn and Bacon.

Groshen, Erica L. (1991). The structure of the female/male wage differential: Is it who you are, what you do, or where you work? *Journal of Human Resources, 26,* 457–472.

Grossman, Michele; & Wood, Wendy. (1993). Sex differences in intensity of emotional experience: A social role interpretation. *Journal of Personality and Social Psychology, 65,* 1010–1022.

Gupta, Nabanita Datta. (1993). Probabilities of job choice and employer selection and male-female occupational differences. *American Economic Review, 83*(2), 57–62.

Gutek, Barbara A. (1985). *Sex and the workplace.* San Francisco: Jossey-Bass.

Gutek, Barbara A.; & Larwood, Laurie. (1989). Introduction: Women's careers are important and different. In Barbara A. Gutek & Laurie Larwood (Eds.), *Women's career development* (pp. 7–14). Newbury Park, CA: Sage.

Hackett, Gail; Enns, Carolyn Z.; & Zetzer, Heidi A. (1992). Reactions of women to nonsexist and feminist counseling: Effects of counselor orientation and mode of information delivery. *Journal of Counseling Psychology, 39,* 321–330.

Hahn, William Kerr. (1987). Cerebral lateralization of function: From infancy through childhood. *Psychological Bulletin, 101,* 376–392.

Haidt, Jonathan; Koller, Silvia Helena; & Dias, Maria G. (1993). Affect, culture, and morality, or is it wrong to eat your dog? *Journal of Personality and Social Psychology, 65,* 613–628.

Halpern, Diane F. (1985). The influence of sex-role stereotypes on prose recall. *Sex Roles, 12,* 363–375.

Halpern, Diane F. (1989). The disappearance of cognitive gender differences: What you see depends on where you look. *American Psychologist, 44,* 1156–1158.

Halpern, Diane F. (1992). *Sex differences in cognitive abilities* (2nd ed.). Hillsdale, NJ: Erlbaum.

Hamilton, Sandra; & Fagot, Beverly I. (1988). Chronic stress and coping styles: A comparison of male and female undergraduates. *Journal of Personality and Social Psychology, 55,* 819–823.

Hamilton, Sandra; Rothbart, Myron; & Dawes, Robyn M. (1986). Sex bias, diagnosis, and DSM-III. *Sex Roles, 15,* 269–274.

Harding, Sandra. (1986). *The science question in feminism.* Ithaca: Cornell University Press.

Hare-Mustin, Rachel T. (1983). An appraisal of the relationship between women and psychotherapy: 80 years after the case of Dora. *American Psychologist, 38,* 593–601.

Hare-Mustin, Rachel T.; & Marecek, Jeanne. (1988). The meaning of difference: Gender theory, postmodernism, and psychology. *American Psychologist, 43,* 455–464.

Hare-Mustin, Rachel T.; Marecek, Jeanne; Kaplan, Alexandra G.; & Liss-Levinson, Nechama. (1979). Rights of clients, responsibilities of therapists. *American Psychologist, 34,* 3–16.

Harlow, Harry F. (1959). Love in infant monkeys. *Scientific American, 200*(6), 68–74.

Harlow, Harry F. (1971). *Learning to love.* San Francisco: Albion.

Harlow, Harry F.; & Harlow, Margaret Kuenne. (1962). Social deprivation in monkeys. *Scientific American, 207,* 136–146.

Harrison, James. (1978). Warning: The male sex role may be dangerous to your health. *Journal of Social Issues, 34*(1), 65–86.

Heilman, Madeline E.; Black, Caryn J.; Martell, Richard F.; & Simon, Michael C. (1989). Has anything changed? Current characterizations of men, women, and managers. *Journal of Applied Psychology, 74,* 935–942.

Heiman, Julia. (1975, April). Women's sexual arousal. *Psychology Today,* pp. 90–94.

Helgeson, Vicki S. (1990). The role of masculinity in a prognostic predictor of heart attack severity. *Sex Roles, 22,* 755–776.

Helson, Ravenna; & Picano, James. (1990). Is the traditional role bad for women? *Journal of Personality and Social Psychology, 59,* 311–320.

Helzer, John E.; Robins, Lee N.; & McEvoy, Larry. (1987). Post-traumatic stress disorder in the general population: Findings of the Epidemiologic Catchment Area survey. *New England Journal of Medicine, 317,* 1630–1634.

Hendrick, Susan S.; Hendrick, Clyde. (1992). *Liking, loving, and relating* (2nd ed.) Pacific Grove, CA: Brooks/Cole.

Hendrick, Susan S.; Hendrick, Clyde; & Adler, Nancy L. (1988). Romantic relationships: Love, satisfaction, and staying together. *Journal of Personality and Social Psychology, 54,* 980–988.

Herdt, Gilbert H. (1981). *Guardians of the flutes: Idioms of masculinity.* New York: McGraw-Hill.

Herdt, Gilbert. (1990). Mistaken gender: 5-alpha reductase hermaphorditism and biological reductionism in sexual identity reconsidered. *American Anthropologist, 92,* 433–446.

Hergenhahn, B. R. (1988). *An introduction to theories of learning* (3rd ed.). Englewood Cliffs, NJ: Prentice Hall.

Herman, Dianne F. (1989). The rape culture. In Jo Freeman (Ed.), *Women: A feminist perspective* (pp. 20–44). Mountain View, CA: Mayfield.

Herman, Judith Lewis. (1981). *Father-daughter incest.* Cambridge, MA: Harvard University Press.

Herrmann, Douglas J.; Crawford, Mary; & Holdsworth, Michelle. (1992). Gender-linked differences in everyday memory performance. *British Journal of Psychology, 83,* 221–231.

Herzog, David B.; Newman, Kerry L.; & Warshaw, Meredith. (1991). Body image and dissatisfaction in homosexual and heterosexual males. *Journal of Nervous and Mental Diseases, 179,* 356–359.

Hesselbrock, Victor M.; Hesselbrock, Michie N.; & Workman-Daniels, Kathryn L. (1986). Effect of major depression and antisocial personality on alcoholism: Course and motivational patterns. *Journal of Studies on Alcohol, 47,* 207–212.

Hilgard, Ernest R. (1987). *Psychology in America: A historical survey.* San Diego: Harcourt Brace Jovanovich.

Hill, John P.; & Lynch, Mary Ellen. (1983). The intensification of gender-related role expectations during early adolescence. In Jeanne Brooks-Gunn & Anne C. Petersen (Eds.), *Girls at puberty: Biological and psychosocial perspectives* (pp. 201–228). New York: Plenum Press.

Hinde, Robert A.; Titmus, Graham; Easton, Douglas; & Tamplin, Alison. (1985). Incidence of "friendship" and behavior toward strong associates versus non-

associates in preschoolers. *Child Development, 56,* 234–245.

Hochschild, Arlie; with Machung, Anne. (1989). *The second shift: Working parents and the revolution at home.* New York: Viking.

Hoffman, Curt; & Hurst, Nancy. (1990). Gender stereotypes: Perception or rationalization? *Journal of Personality and Social Psychology, 58,* 197–208.

Hoffman, Lorrie. (1982). Empirical findings concerning sexism in our schools. *Corrective and Social Psychiatry and Journal of Behavior Technology, Methods and Therapy, 28,* 100–108.

Hoffman, Valerie; & Bolton, Ralph. (1994, August). *Gender differences in sexual motivations.* Paper presented at the 102nd annual convention of the American Psychological Association, Los Angeles, CA.

Holroyd, Jean Corey; & Brodsky, Annette M. (1977). Psychologists' attitudes and practices regarding erotic and noneroitc physical contact with patients. *American Psychologist, 32,* 843–849.

Holzer, Charles E.; Shea, Brent M.; Swanson, Jeffrey W.; Leaf, Philip J.; Myers, J.; George, L.; Weissman, M.; & Bednarski, P. (1986). The increased risk for specific psychiatric disorders among persons of low socioeconomic status. *American Journal of Social Psychiatry, 6,* 259–271.

Horner, Martina. (1969, November). Fail: Bright women. *Psychology Today,* pp. 36–38, 62.

Horney, Karen. (1926/1967). The flight from womanhood: The masculinity complex in women as viewed by men and by women. In Harold Kelman (Ed.), *Feminine psychology* (pp. 54–70). New York: Norton.

Horney, Karen. (1932/1967). The dread of women: Observations on a specific difference in the dread felt by men and by women respectively for the opposite sex. In Harold Kelmen (Ed.), *Feminine Psychology* (pp. 133–146). New York: Norton.

Horney, Karen. (1937). *The neurotic personality of our time.* New York: Norton.

Horney, Karen. (1939). *New ways in psychoanalysis.* New York: Norton.

Horney, Karen. (1942). *Self-analysis.* New York: Norton.

Horowitz, Allan V.; & White, Helene R. (1991). Becoming married, depression, and alcohol problems among young adults. *Journal of Health and Social Behavior, 32,* 221–237.

Hort, Barbara E.; Fagot, Beverly I.; & Leinbach, Mary D. (1990). Are people's notions of maleness more stereotypically framed than their notions of femaleness? *Sex Roles, 23,* 197–212.

Hort, Barbara E.; Leinbach, Mary D.; & Fagot, Beverly I. (1991). Is there coherence among the cognitive components of gender acquisition? *Sex Roles, 24,* 195–207.

Hotelling, Kathy. (1991). Sexual harassment: A problem shielded by silence. *Journal of Counseling & Development, 69,* 497–501.

House, James S. (1984). Barriers to work stress: I. Social support. In W. Doyle Gentry, Herbert Benson, & Charles deWolff (Eds.), *Behavioral medicine: Work, stress, and health.* The Hague, Netherlands: Nijhoff.

Howard, Judith A.; Blumstein, Philip; & Schwartz, Pepper. (1987). Social or evolutionary theories? Some observations on preferences in human mate selection. *Journal of Personality and Social Psychology, 53,* 194–200.

Hoyenga, Katharine Blick; & Hoyenga, Kermit T. (1993). *Gender-related differences: Origins and outcomes.* Boston: Allyn and Bacon.

Hrdy, Sarah Blaffer. (1986). Empathy, polyandry, and the myth of the coy female. In Ruth Bleier (Ed.), *Feminist approaches to science* (pp. 119–146). New York: Pergamon Press.

Hsu, L. K. G. (1990). *Eating disorders.* New York: Guilford Press.

Hubbard, Ruth. (1990). *The politics of women's biology.* New Brunswick: Rutgers University Press.

Hudak, Mary A. (1993). Gender schema theory revisited: Men's stereotypes of American women. *Sex Roles, 28,* 279–293.

Hudley, Cynthia; & Graham, Sandra. (1993). An attributional intervention to reduce peer-directed aggression among African-American boys. *Child Development, 64,* 124–138.

Huesmann, L. Rowell; Eron, Leonard D.; Lefkowitz, Monroe M.; & Walder, Leopold O. (1984). Stability of aggression over time and generations. *Developmental Psychology, 20,* 1120–1134.

Humphreys, Ann P.; & Smith, Peter K. (1987). Rough and tumble friendship and dominancy in school children: Evidence for continuity and change with age in middle childhood. *Child Development, 58,* 201–212.

Hunt, Morton. (1974). *Sexual behavior in the 1970s.* Chicago: Playboy Press.

Hyde, Janet Shibley. (1981). How large are cognitive gender differences? A meta-analysis using ω^2 and d. *American Psychologist, 36,* 892–901.

Hyde, Janet Shibley. (1984). How large are gender differences in aggression? A developmental meta-analysis. *Developmental Psychology, 20,* 722–736.

Hyde, Janet Shibley. (1986). Introduction: Meta-analysis and the psychology of gender. In Janet Shibley Hyde & Marcia C. Linn (Eds.), *The psychology of gender: Advances through meta-analysis* (pp. 1–13). Baltimore: Johns Hopkins University Press.

Hyde, Janet Shibley. (1990). *Understanding human sexuality* (4th ed.). New York: McGraw-Hill.

Hyde, Janet Shibley; Fennema, Elizabeth; & Lamon, Susan J. (1990). Gender differences in mathematics performance: A meta-analysis. *Psychological Bulletin, 107,* 139–155.

Hyde, Janet S.; Fennema, Elizabeth; Ryan, Marilyn; Frost, Laurie A.; & Hopp, Carolyn. (1990). Gender comparisons of mathematics attitudes and affect: A meta-analysis. *Psychology of Women Quarterly, 14,* 299–324.

Hyde, Janet Shibley; & Linn, Marcia C. (Eds.). (1986). *The psychology of gender: Advances through meta-analysis.* Baltimore: John Hopkins University Press.

Hyde, Janet Shibley; & Linn, Marcia C. (1988). Gender differences in verbal ability: A meta-analysis. *Psychological Bulletin, 104,* 53–69.

Ickes, William. (1993). Traditional gender roles: Do they make, and then break, our relatonships? *Journal of Social Issues, 49*(3), 71–85.

Idle, Tracey; Wood, Eileen; & Desmarais, Serge. (1993). Gender role socialization in toy play situations: Mothers and fathers with their sons and daughters. *Sex Roles, 28,* 679–691.

Imperato-McGinley, Julianne; Guerrero, Luis; Gautier, Teofilo; & Peterson, Ralph E. (1974). Steroid 5-α-reductase deficiency in man: An inherited form of male pseudohermaphroditism. *Science, 186,* 1213–1215.

Jacklin, Carol Nagy. (1989). Female and male: Issues of gender. *American Psychologist, 44,* 127–133.

Jacklin, Carol Nagy; & Maccoby, Eleanor E. (1978). Social behavior at thirty-three months in same-sex and mixed-sex dyads. *Child Development, 49,* 557–569.

Jacobs, Janis E.; & Eccles, Jacquelynne S. (1992). The impact of mothers' gender-role stereotypic beliefs on mothers' and children's ability perceptions. *Journal of Personality and Social Psychology, 63,* 932–944.

Jacobs, Jerry A. (1989). Long-term trends in occupational segregation by sex. *American Journal of Sociology, 95,* 160–173.

Jacobs, Marion K.; & Goodman, Gerald. (1989). Psychology and self-help groups: Predictions on a partnership. *American Psychologist, 44,* 536–545.

Jacobs, Michael. (1992). *Sigmund Freud.* London: Sage.

James, William. (1890). *Principles of psychology* (Vols. 1–2). New York: Holt.

Janoff-Bulman, Ronnie; & Frieze, Irene H. (1987). The role of gender in reactions to criminal victimization. In Rosalind C. Barnett, Lois Biener, & Grace K. Baruch (Eds.), *Gender and stress* (pp. 159–184). New York: Free Press.

Janus, Samuel S.; & Janus, Cynthia L. (1993). *The Janus report on sexual behavior.* New York: Wiley.

Jeffery, Robert W.; Adlis, Susan A.; & Forster, Jean L. (1991). Prevalence of dieting among working men and women: The healthy worker project. *Health Psychology, 10,* 274–281.

Johmann, Carol. (1985, May). Sex and morality. *Omni,* pp. 20, 80.

Johnson, D. Kay. (1988). Adolescents' solutions to dilemmas in fables: Two moral orientations—Two problem solving strategies. In Carol Gilligan, Janie Victoria Ward, & Jill McLean Taylor, with Betty Bardige (Eds.), *Mapping the moral domain: A contribution of women's thinking to psychological theory and education* (pp. 49–71). Cambridge, MA: Harvard University Press.

Johnson, Toni C. (1988). Child perpetrators—Children who molest other children: Preliminary findings. *Child Abuse and Neglect, 12,* 219–229.

Johnson, Toni C. (1989). Female child perpetrators: Children who molest other children. *Child Abuse and Neglect, 13,* 571–585.

Jones, Ernest. (1955). *The life and work of Sigmund Freud.* (Vol. 2). New York: Basic Books.

Jones, M. Gail. (1989). Gender issues in teacher education. *Journal of Teacher Education, 40,* 33–38.

Jussim, Lee; & Eccles, Jacquelynne S. (1992). Teacher expectations: II. Construction and reflection of student achievement. *Journal of Personality and Social Psychology, 63,* 947–961.

Kalat, James W. (1992). *Biological psychology* (4th ed.). Belmont, CA: Wadsworth.

Kaminer, Wendy. (1993, October). Feminism's identity crisis. *Atlantic Monthly,* pp. 51–53, 56, 58–59, 62, 64, 66–68.

Kane, Penny. (1991). *Women's health: From womb to tomb.* New York: St. Martin's Press.

Kanter, Rosabeth Moss. (1975). Women and the structure of organizations: Explorations in theory and behavior. In Marcia Millman & Rosabeth M. Kanter (Eds.), *Another voice* (pp. 34–74). Garden City, NY: Anchor/Doubleday.

Kanter, Rosabeth Moss. (1977). *Men and women of the corporation.* New York: Basic Books.

Kantrowitz, Ricki E.; & Ballou, Mary. (1992). A feminist critique of cognitive-behavioral therapy. In Laura S. Brown & Mary Ballou (Eds.), *Personality and psychopathology: Feminist reappraisals* (pp. 70–87). New York: Guilford Press.

Kaplan, Alexandra G. (1980). Human sex-hormone abnormalities viewed from an androgynous perspective: A reconsideration of the work of John Money. In Jacquelynne E. Parsons (Ed.), *The psychobiology of sex differences and sex roles* (pp. 81–91). Washington, DC: Hemisphere.

Kaplan, Alexandra G.; & Yasinski, Lorraine. (1980). Psychodynamic perspectives. In Annette M. Brodsky & Rachel Hare-Mustin (Eds.), *Women and pschotherapy* (pp. 191–216). New York: Guilford Press.

Kaplan, Marcie. (1983a). The issue of sex bias in DSM-III: Comments on the articles by Spitzer, Williams, and Kass. *American Psychologist, 38,* 802–803.

Kaplan, Marcie. (1983b). A woman's view of the DSM-III. *American Psychologist, 38,* 786–792.

Kaplan, Robert M.; Anderson, John P.; & Wingard, Deborah L. (1991). Gender differences in health-related quality of life. *Health Psychology, 10,* 86–93.

Karabenick, Stuart A.; Sweeney, Catherine; & Penrose, Gary. (1983). Preferences for skill versus change-determined activities: The influence of gender and task sex-typing. *Journal of Research in Personality, 17,* 125–142.

Karlen, Amy; Hagin, Rosa A.; & Beecher, Ronnie. (1985). Are boys really more vulerable to learning disability than girls? *Academic Psychology Bulletin, 7,* 317–325.

Kaschak, Ellyn. (1992). *Engendered lives.* New York: Basic Books.

Kass, Frederic; Spitzer, Robert L.; & Williams, Janet B. W. (1983). An empirical study of the issue of sex bias in the diagnostic criteria of DSM-III axis II personality disorders. *American Psychologist, 38,* 799–801.

Katz, Phyllis A.; & Ksansnak, Keith R. (1994). Developmental aspects of gender role flexibility and traditionality in middle childhood and adolescence. *Developmental Psychology, 30,* 272–282.

Keen, Sam. (1991). *A fire in the belly: On being a man.* New York: Bantam.

Keller, Evelyn Fox. (1985). *Reflections on gender and science.* New Haven: Yale University Press.

Kessler, Ronald C.; Brown, Roger L.; & Broman, Clifford L. (1981). Sex differences in psychiatric help-seeking: Evidence from four large-scale surveys. *Journal of Health and Social Behavior, 22,* 49–64.

Kessler, Ronald C.; & McRae, James A., Jr. (1983). Trends in the relationship between sex and attempted suicide. *Journal of Health and Social Behavior, 24,* 98–110.

Kidder, Louise. (1994, August). *Al pores open.* Paper presented at the 102nd annual convention of the American Psychological Association, Los Angeles, CA.

Kiernan, Michaela; Rodin, Judith; Brownell, Kelly D.; Wilmore, Jack H.; & Crandall, Christian. (1992). Relation of level of exercise, age, and weight cycling history to weight and eating concerns in male and female runners. *Health Psychology, 11,* 418–421.

Kilpatrick, Dean G.; Best, Connie L.; Saunders, Benjamin E.; & Veronen, Lois J. (1988). Rape in marriage and in dating relationships: How bad is it for mental health? *Annals of the New York Academy of Sciences, 528,* 335–344.

Kimura, Doreen. (1989, November). How sex hormones boost—or cut—intellectual ability. *Psychology Today,* pp. 62–66.

Kimura, Doreen. (1992, September). Sex differences in the brain. *Scientific American,* pp. 119–125.

Kinsey, Alfred C.; Pomeroy, Wardell B.; & Martin, Clyde E. (1948). *Sexual behavior in the human male.* Philadelphia: Saunders.

Kinsey, Alfred C.; Pomeroy, Wardell B.; Martin, Clyde E.; & Gebhard, Paul H. (1953). *Sexual behavior in the human female.* Philadelphia: Saunders.

Kipnis, Aaron R. (1991). *Knights without armor: A practical guide for men in quest of masculine soul.* Los Angeles: Jeremy P. Tarcher.

Kirschstein, Ruth L. (1991). Research on women's health. *American Journal of Public Health, 81,* 291–293.

Klaus, Marshall H.; & Kennell, John H. (1976). *Maternal infant bonding.* St. Louis: Mosby.

Klonoff, Elizabeth A.; Landrine, Hope. (1992). Sex-roles, occupational roles, and symptom-reporting: A test of competing hypotheses of sex differences. *Journal of Behavioral Medicine, 15,* 355–364.

Koehler, Mary Schatz. (1990). Classrooms, teachers, and gender differences in mathematics. In Elizabeth Fennema & Gilah C. Leder (Eds.)., *Mathematics and gender* (pp. 128–148). New York: Teachers College Press.

Koeske, Randi K.; & Koeske, Gary F. (1975). An attributional approach to moods and the menstrual cycle. *Journal of Personality and Social Psychology, 31,* 473–478.

Kohlberg, Lawrence. (1966). A cognitive-developmental analysis of children's sex-role concepts and attitudes. In Eleanor E. Maccoby (Ed.), *The development of sex differences* (pp. 52–173). Stanford, CA: Stanford University Press.

Kohlberg, Lawrence. (1981). *The philosophy of moral development.* San Francisco: Harper & Row.

Komarovsky, Mirra. (1982). Female freshmen view their future: Career salience and its correlates. *Sex Roles, 8,* 299–313.

Kopper, Beverly A.; & Epperson, Douglas L. (1991). Women and anger: Sex and sex-role comparisons in the expression of anger. *Psychology of Women Quarterly, 15,* 7–14.

Kortenhaus, Carole M.; & Demarest, Jack. (1993). Gender role stereotyping in children's literature: An update. *Sex Roles, 28,* 219–232.

Koss, Mary P. (1990). The women's mental health research agenda: Violence against women. *American Psychologist, 45,* 374–380.

Koss, Mary P. (1992). The underdetection of rape: Methodological choices influence incidence estimates. *Journal of Social Issues, 48*(1), 61–75.

Koss, Mary P. (1993). Rape: Scope, impact, interventions, and public policy responses. *American Psychologist, 48,* 1062–1069.

Koss, Mary P.; Gidycz, Christine A.; & Wisniewski, Nadine. (1987). The scope of rape: Incidence and prevalence of sexual aggression and victimization in a national sample of higher education students. *Journal of Consulting and Clinical Psychology, 55,* 162–170.

Kramarae, Cheris; & Treichler, Paula A. (1990). Power relationships in the classroom. In Susan L. Gabriel & Isaiah Smithson (Eds.), *Gender in the classroom: Power and pedagogy* (pp. 41–59). Urbana: University of Illinois Press.

Kravetz, Diane. (1978). Consciousness-raising groups of the 1970s. *Psychology of Women Quarterly, 3,* 168–186.

Kravetz, Diane. (1980). Consciousness-raising and self-help. In Annette M. Brodsky & Rachel Hare-Mustin (Eds.), *Women and psychotherapy* (pp. 267–283). New York: Guilford Press.

Kuhn, Deanna; Nash, Sharon C.; & Brucken, Laura. (1978). Sex role concepts of two- and three-year-olds. *Child Development, 49,* 445–451.

Kuhn, Thomas S. (1962). *The structure of scientific revolutions.* Chicago: University of Chicago Press.

Kuntzleman, Charles T. (1978). *Rating the exercises.* New York: Morrow.

Kurdek, Lawrence A. (1993). The allocation of household labor in gay, lesbian, and heterosexual married couples. *Journal of Social Issues, 49*(3), 127–139.

Lakoff, Robin. (1975). *Language and woman's place.* New York: Harper & Row.

Landau, Jacqueline; & Arthur, Michael B. (1992). The relationship of marital status, spouse's career status, and gender to salary level. *Sex Roles, 27,* 665–681.

Landrine, Hope. (1987). On the politics of madness: A preliminary analysis of the relationship between social roles and psychopathology. *Psychology Monographs, 113,* 341–406.

Landrine, Hope. (1989). The politics of personality disorder. *Psychology of Women Quarterly, 13,* 325–339.

Landrine, Hope; Bardwell, Stephen; & Dean, Tina. (1988). Gender expectations for alcohol use: A study of the significance of the masculine role. *Sex Roles, 19,* 703–712.

Landrine, Hope; Klonoff, Elizabeth A.; & Brown-Collins, Alice. (1992). Cultural diversity and methodology in feminist psychology: Critique, proposal, empirical example. *Psychology of Women Quarterly, 16,* 145–163.

Larwood, Laurie; & Gutek, Barbara A. (1989). Working toward a theory of women's career development. In Barbara A. Gutek & Laurie Larwood (Eds.), *Women's career development* (pp. 170–183). Newbury Park, CA: Sage.

Lavallee, Marguerite; & Pelletier, Rene. (1992). Ecological value of Bem's gender schema theory explored through females' traditional and nontraditional occupational contexts. *Psychological Reports, 70,* 79–82.

Lavin, Thomas J., III. (1987). Divergence and convergence in the causal attributions of married couples. *Journal of Marriage and the Family, 49,* 71–80.

Law, David J.; Pellegrino, James W.; & Hunt, Earl B. (1993). Comparing the tortoise and the hare: Gender differences and experience in dynamic spatial reasoning tasks. *Psychological Science, 4,* 35–40.

Lazarus, Richard S. (1984). On the primacy of cognition. *American Psychologist, 39,* 124–129.

Lazarus, Richard S.; & Folkman, Susan. (1984). *Stress, appraisal, and coping.* New York: Springer.

Leaf, Philip J.; & Bruce, Martha L. (1987). Gender differences in the use of mental health-related services: A re-examination. *Journal of Health and Social Behavior, 28,* 171–183.

Leder, Gilah C. (1990). Gender differences in mathematics: An overview. In Elizabeth Fennema & Gilah C. Leder (Eds.)., *Mathematics and gender* (pp. 10–26). New York: Teachers College Press.

Lefkowitz, Monroe M.; Eron, Leonard D.; Walder, Leopold O.; & Huesmann, L. Rowell. (1977). *Growing up to be violent: A longitudinal study of the development of aggression.* New York: Pergamon.

Leinbach, Mary D.; & Fagot, Beverly I. (1993). Categorical habituation to male and female faces: Gender schematic processing in infancy. *Infant Behavior and Development, 16,* 317–332.

Lenny, Ellen (1977). Women's self-confidence in achievement settings. *Psychological Bulletin, 84,* 1–13.

Leong, Frederick T. L.; Snodgrass, Coral R.; & Gardner, William L., III. (1992). Management education: Creating a gender-positive environment. In Uma Sekaran & Leong Frederick T. L. (Eds.), *Womanpower: Managing in times of demographic turbulence* (pp. 192–220). Newbury Park, CA: Sage.

Lerman, Hannah. (1992). The limits of phenomenology: A feminist critique of the humanistic personality theories. In Laura S. Brown & Mary Ballou (Eds.), *Personality and psychopathology: Feminist reappraisals* (pp. 8–19). New York: Guilford Press.

Lerner, Alan Jay; & Loewe, Frederick. (1956). *My fair lady: A musical play in two acts.* Based on *Pygmalion* by Bernard Shaw. New York: Coward-McCann.

Leslie, Leigh A.; Huston, Ted L.; & Johnson, Michael P. (1986). Parental reactions to dating relationships: Do they make a difference? *Journal of Marriage and the Family, 48,* 57–66.

Levant, Ronald F. (1990). Psychological services designed for men: A psychoeducational approach. *Psychotherapy, 27,* 309–315.

LeVay, Simon. (1991). A difference in hypothalamic structure between heterosexual and homosexual men. *Science, 253,* 1034–1037.

Levy, Gary D. (1989). Relations among aspects of children's social environments, gender schematization, gender role knowledge, and flexibility. *Sex Roles, 21,* 803–823.

Levy, Gary D.; & Fivush, Robyn. (1993). Scripts and gender: A new approach for examining gender-role development. *Developmental Review, 13,* 126–146.

Levy, Jerre. (1969). Possible basis for the evolution of lateral specialization of the human brain. *Nature, 224,* 614–625.

Levy, Sandra M. (1985). *Behavior and cancer: Lifestyle and psychosocial factors in the initiation and progression of cancer.* San Francisco: Jossey-Bass.

Levy, Sandra M.; Ewing, Linda J.; & Lippman, Marc E. (1988). Gynecological cancers. In Elaine A. Blechman & Kelly D. Brownell (Eds.), *Handbook of behavioral medicine for women* (pp. 126–139). New York: Pergamon Press.

Lewin, Miriam. (1984a). "Rather worse than folly?" Psychology measures femininity and masculinity: 1. From Terman and Miles to the Guilfords. In Miriam Lewin (Ed.), *In the shadow of the past: Psychology portrays the sexes* (pp. 155–178). New York: Columbia University Press.

Lewin, Miriam. (1984b). Psychology measures femininity and masculinity: 2. From "13 gay men" to the instrumental-expressive distinction. In Miriam Lewin (Ed.), *In the shadow of the past: Psychology portrays the sexes* (pp. 179–204). New York: Columbia University Press.

Lewin, Miriam. (1984c). The Victorians, the psychologists, and psychic birth control. In Miriam Lewin (Ed.), *In the shadow of the past: Psychology portrays the sexes* (pp. 39–76). New York: Columbia University Press.

Lewis, Carol D.; & Houtz, John C. (1986). Sex-role stereotyping and young children's divergent thinking. *Psychological Reports, 59,* 1027–1033.

Lewis, Shon. (1992). Sex and schizophrenia: Vive la difference. *British Journal of Psychiatry, 161,* 445–450.

Lewontin, R. C.; Rose, Steven; & Kamin, Leon J. (1984). *Not in our genes.* New York: Pantheon.

Liben, Lynn S.; & Golbeck, Susan L. (1984). Performance on Piagetian horizontality and verticality tasks: Sex-related differences in knowledge of relevant physical phenomena. *Developmental Psychology, 20,* 595–606.

Linn, Marcia C.; & Petersen, Anne C. (1986). A meta-analysis of gender differences in spatial ability: Implications for mathematics and science achievement. In Janet Shibley Hyde & Maricia C. Linn (Eds.), *The psychology of gender: Advances through meta-analysis* (pp. 67–101). Baltimore: Johns Hopkins University Press.

Lips, Hilary M. (1989). Gender-role socialization: Lessons in femininity. In Jo Freeman (Ed.), *Women: A feminist perspective* (pp. 197–216). Mountain View, CA: Mayfield.

Lloyd, Barbara; Duveen, Gerard; & Smith, Caroline. (1988). Social representation of gender and young children's play: A replication. *British Journal of Developmental Psychology, 6,* 83–88.

Lobel, Thalma E.; Bempechat, Janine; Gewritz, Jonathan C.; Shoken-Topaz, Tamar; & Bashe, Elinor. (1993). The role of gender-related information and self-endorsement of traits in preadolescents' inferences and judgments. *Child Development, 64,* 1285–1294.

Locksley, Anne; Borgida, Eugene; Brekke, Nancy; & Hepburn, Christine. (1980). Sex stereotypes and social judgments. *Journal of Personality and Social Psychology, 39,* 821–831.

Lopata, Helena Znaniecka. (1993). The interweave of public and private: Women's challenge to American society. *Journal of Marriage and the Family, 55,* 176–190.

López, Steven Regeser. (1989). Patient variable biases in clinical judgment: Conceptual overview and methodological considerations. *Psychological Bulletin, 106,* 184–203.

Lorber, Judith. (1975). Women and medical sociology: Invisible professionals and ubiquitous patients. In Marcia Millman & Rosabeth M. Kanter (Eds.), *Another voice* (pp. 75–105). Garden City, NY: Anchor/Doubleday.

Lorber, Judith. (1989). Trust, loyalty, and the place for women in the informal organization of work. In J. Freeman (Ed.), *Women: A feminist perspective* (pp. 347–355). Mountain View, CA: Mayfield.

Loring, Marti; & Powell, Brian. (1988). Gender, race, and DSM-III: A study of the objectivity of psychiatric diagnostic behavior. *Journal of Health and Social Behavior, 29,* 1–22.

Lueptow, Lloyd B. (1985). Conceptions of femininity and masculinity: 1974–1983. *Psychological Reports, 57,* 859–862.

Lyons, Deborah; & Greenberg, Jeff. (1991). Evidence of codependency in women with an alcoholic parent: Helping out Mr. Wrong. *Journal of Personality and Social Psychology, 61,* 435–439.

Lyons, Nona Plessner. (1988). Two perspectives: On self, relationships, and morality. In Carol Gilligan, Janie Victoria Ward, & Jill McLean Taylor with Betty Bardige (Eds.), *Mapping the moral domain: A contribution of women's thinking to psychological theory and education* (pp. 21–48). Cambridge, MA: Harvard University Press.

Maccoby, Eleanor E. (1988). Gender as a social category. *Developmental Psychology, 24,* 755–765.

Maccoby, Eleanor E. (1990). Gender and relationships. *American Psychologist, 45,* 513–520.

Maccoby, Eleanor Emmons; & Jacklin, Carol Nagy. (1974). *The psychology of sex differences.* Stanford, CA: Stanford University Press.

MacLusky, Neil J.; & Naftolin, Frederick. (1981). Sexual differentiation of the central nervous system. *Science, 211,* 1294–1303.

Major, Brenda. (1993). Gender, entitlement, and the distribution of family labor. *Journal of Social Issues, 49*(3), 141–159.

Mancus, Dianne Sirna. (1992). Influence of male teachers on elementary school children's stereotyping of teacher competence. *Sex Roles, 26,* 109–128.

Mansnerus, Laura. (1992, January 5). Women take to the field. *New York Times,* Sec. 4A, pp. 40–41.

Marecek, Jeanne; & Hare-Mustin, Rachel. (1991). A short history of the future: Feminism and clinical psychology. *Psychology of Women Quarterly, 15,* 521–536.

Marecek, Jeanne; Kravetz, Diane; & Finn, Stephen. (1979). Comparison of women who enter feminist therapy and women who enter traditional therapy. *Journal of Consulting and Clinical Psychology, 47,* 734–742.

Martin, Carol Lynn. (1987). A ratio measure of sex stereotyping. *Journal of Personality and Social Psychology, 52,* 489–499.

Martin, Carol Lynn. (1989). Children's use of gender-related information in making social judgments. *Developmental Psychology, 25,* 80–88.

Martin, Carol Lynn; & Halverson, Charles. F., Jr. (1981). A schematic processing model of sex-typing and stereotyping in children. *Child Development, 52,* 1119–1134.

Martin, Carol Lynn; & Little, Jane K. (1990). The relation of gender understanding to children's sex-typed preferences and gender stereotypes. *Child Development, 61,* 1427–1439.

Martin, Carol Lynn; Wood, Carolyn H.; & Little, Jane K. (1990). The development of gender stereotype components. *Child Development, 61,* 1891–1904.

Martinko, Mark L; & Gardner, William L. (1983). A methodological review of sex-related access discrimination problems. *Sex Roles, 9,* 825–839.

Martocchio, Joseph J.; & O'Leary, Anne M. (1989). Sex differences in occupational stress: A meta-analytic review. *Journal of Applied Psychology, 74,* 495–501.

Masson, Jeffrey Moussaieff. (1984). *The assault on truth: Freud's suppression of the seduction theory.* New York: Farrar, Straus and Giroux.

Masters, William H.; & Johnson, Virginia E. (1966). *Human sexual response.* Boston: Little, Brown.

Masters, William H.; Johnson, Virginia E.; & Kolodny, Robert C. (1992). *Human sexuality* (4th ed.). New York: HarperCollins.

Matthews, Karen A. (1989). Are sociodemographic variables markers for psychological determinants of health? *Health Psychology, 8,* 641–648.

Mays, Vickie M.; & Comas-Diaz, Lillian. (1988). Feminist therapy with ethnic minority populations: A closer look at Blacks and Hispanics. In Mary Ann Dutton Douglas & Lenore E. A. Walker (Eds.), *Feminist psychotherapies: Integration of therapeutic and feminist systems* (pp. 228–251). Norwod, NJ: Ablex.

Mazer, Donald B.; & Percival, Elizabeth F. (1989). Students' experiences of sexual harassment at a small university. *Sex Roles, 20,* 1–22.

Mazur, Allan. (1985). A biosocial model of status in face-to-face primate groups. *Social Forces, 64,* 377–402.

McCann, Nancy Dodd; & McGinn, Thomas A. (1992). *Harassed: 100 women define inappropriate behavior in the workplace.* Homewood, IL: Business One Irwin.

McClelland, David C.; Atkinson, J. W.; Clark, R. W.; & Lowell, E. L. (1953). *The achievement motive.* New York: Appleton.

McDonald, Karen; & Thompson, J. Kevin. (1992). Eating disturbance, body image dissatisfaction, and reasons for exercising: Gender differences and correlational findings. *International Journal of Eating Disorders, 11,* 289–292.

McDougall, William. (1923). *Outline of psychology.* New York: Scribners.

McFarlane, Jessica; Martin, Carol Lynn; & Williams, Tannis MacBeth. (1988). Mood fluctuations: Women versus men and menstrual versus other cycles. *Psychology of Women Quarterly, 12,* 201– 223.

McGuiness, Diane; Olson, Amy; & Chapman, Julia. (1990). Sex differences in incidental recall ofr words and pictures. *Learning and Individual Differences, 2,* 263–285.

McHale, Susan M.; & Crouter, Ann C. (1992). You can't always get what you want: Incongruence between sex-role attitudes and family work roles and its implications for marriage. *Journal of Marriage and the Family, 54,* 537–547.

McHugh, Maureen C.; Koeske, Randi D.; & Frieze, Irene H. (1986). Issues to consider in conducting nonsexist psychological research: A guide for researchers. *American Psychologist, 41,* 879–890.

McKinney, Kathleen; Olson, Carol V.; & Satterfield, Arthur. (1988). Graduate students' experiences with and responses to sexual harassment: A research note. *Journal of Interpersonal Violence, 3,* 319–328.

McLain, Susan June; & Perkins, Carol O. (1990). Disabled women: At the bottom of the work heap. *Vocational Educational Journal, 65*(2), 54–53.

McManus, I. C.; & Bryden, M. P. (1991). Geschwind's theory of cerebral lateralization: Developing a formal, causal model. *Psychological Bulletin, 110,* 237–253.

McWhirter, Ellen Hawley. (1994, August). *Perceived barriers to education and career: Ethnic and gender differences.* Paper presented at the 102nd annual convention of the American Psychological Association, Los Angeles, CA.

Meehan, Anita M.; & Janik, Leann M. (1990). Illusory correlation and the maintenance of sex role stereotypes in children. *Sex Roles, 22,* 83–95.

Melson, Gail F.; & Fogel, Alan. (1988a). The development of nurturance in young children. *Young Children, 43,* 57–65.

Melson, Gail F.; & Fogel, Alan. (1988b, January). Learning to care: Boys are as nurturant as girls, but in different ways. *Psychology Today,* pp. 39–45.

Mesquita, Batja; & Frijda, Nico H. (1992). Cultural variations in emotions: A review. *Psychological Bulletin, 112,* 179–204.

Meyer-Bahlburg, Heino F. L. (1980). Sexuality in early adolescence. In Benjamin B. Wolman & John Money (Eds.), *Handbook of human sexuality* (pp. 61–82). Englewood Cliffs, NJ: Prentice-Hall.

Middaugh, Anne. (1994, August). *Clinical psychology interns' attitudes and information about women,* Paper presented at the 102nd annual convention of the American Psychological Association, Los Angeles, CA.

Miller, Ivan W.; Norman, William H.; & Dow, Michael G. (1988). Depression. In Elaine A. Blechman & Kelly D. Brownell (Eds.), *Handbook of behavioral medicine for women* (pp. 399–418). New York: Pergamon Press.

Miller, Randi L.; & Gordon, Michael. (1986). The decline in formal dating: A study in six Connecticut high schools. *Marriage and Family Review, 10,* 139–156.

Mirowsky, John; & Ross, Catherine E. (1987). Belief in innate sex roles: Sex stratification versus interpersonal influence in marriage. *Journal of Marriage and the Family, 49,* 527–540.

Mischel, Walter. (1966). A social-learning view of sex differences in behavior. In Eleanor E. Maccoby (Ed.), *The development of sex differences* (pp. 56–81). Stanford, CA: Stanford University Press.

Mischel, Walter. (1993). *Introduction to personality* (5th ed.). Fort Worth: Harcourt Brace Jovanovich.

Mishkind, Marc E.; Rodin, Judith; Silberstein, Lisa R.; & Striegel-Moore, Ruth H. (1986). The embodiment of masculinity: Cultural, psychological, and behavioral dimensions. *American Behavioral Scientist, 29,* 545–562.

Mittwoch, Ursula. (1973). *Genetics of sex differentiation.* New York: Academic Press.

Money, John. (1986). *Venuses penuses: Sexology, sexosophy, and exigency theory.* Buffalo, NY: Prometheus Books.

Money, John. (1987a). Propaedeutics of diecious G-I/R: Theoretical foundations for understanding dimorphic gender-identity/role. In June Machover Reinisch, Leonard A. Rosenblum, & Stephanie A. Sanders (Eds.), *Masculinity/femininity: Basic perspectives* (pp. 13–28). New York: Oxford University Press.

Money, John. (1987b). Sin, sickness, or status? Homosexual gender identity and psychoneuroendocrinology. *American Psychologist, 42,* 384–399.

Mook, Douglas G. (1987). *Motivation: The organization of action.* New York: Norton.

Moore, Robert; & Gillette, Douglas. (1990). *King warrior magician lover: Rediscovering the archetypes of the mature masculine.* San Francisco: HarperSanFrancisco.

Morgan, Robin. (1970). Introduction: The women's revolution. In Robin Morgan (Ed.), *Sisterhood is powerful: An anthology of writings from the women's liberation movement* (pp. xv–xivi). New York: Vintage Books.

Mori, DeAnna; Chaiken, Shelly; & Pliner, Patricia. (1987). "Eating lightly" and the self-presentation of femininity. *Journal of Personality and Social Psychology, 53,* 693–702.

Mori, Lisa; Selle, Lynn L.; Zarate, Mylene G.; & Bernat, Jeffrey. (1994). *Asian American and Caucasian college students' attitudes towards rape.* Paper presented at the 102nd annual convention of the American Psychological Association, Los Angeles, CA.

Muehlenhard, Charlene L.; Friedman, Debra E.; & Thomas, Celeste M. (1985). Is date rape justifiable? The effects of dating activity, who initiated, who paid, and men's attitudes toward women. *Psychology of Women Quarterly, 9,* 297–309.

Muehlenhard, Charlene L.; & Hollabaugh, Lisa C. (1988). Do women sometimes say no when they mean yes: The prevalence and correlates of women's token resistance to sex. *Journal of Personality and Social Psychology, 54,* 872–879.

Muller, Charlotte F. (1990). *Health care and gender.* New York: Russell Sage Foundation.

Nardi, Peter M. (1992a). "Seamless souls": An introduction to men's friendships. In Peter M. Nardi (Ed.), *Men's friendships* (pp. 1–14). Newbury Park, CA: Sage.

Nardi, Peter M. (1992b). Sex, friendship, and gender roles among gay men. In Peter M. Nardi (Ed.), *Men's friendships* (pp. 173–185). Newbury Park, CA: Sage.

Netting, Nancy S. (1992). Sexuality in youth culture: Identity and change. *Adolescence, 27,* 961–976.

Neugebauer, D. D.; Dohrenwend, Bruce P.; & Dohrenwend, Barbara S. (1980). The formulation of hypotheses about the true prevalence of functional psychiatric disorders among adults in the United States. In Bruce P. Dohrenwend, Barbara S. Dohrenwend, M. S. Gould, B. Link, R. Neugebauer, & R. Wunsch-Hitzig (Eds.), *Mental illness in the United States* (pp. 45–94). New York: Praeger.

New York Times (1991, November 12). Science Watch: Women and survival. Author, Sec. C, p. 5.

Nicholas, Karen B.; & McGinley, Hugh. (1986). Preschool children's selective imitation of adults: Implication for sex role development. *Journal of Genetic Psychology, 146,* 143–144.

Nieva, Veronica F.; & Gutek, Barbara A. (1981). *Women and work: A psychological perspective.* New York: Praeger.

Nikelly, Arthur G. (1994, August). *Drug advertisements and the medicalization of unipolar depression in women.* Paper presented at the 102nd annual convention of the American Psychological Association, Los Angeles, CA.

Noddings, Nel. (1991/1992, December/January). The gender issue. *Educational Leadership, 49*(4), 65–70.

Nolen-Hoeksema, Susan. (1987). Sex differences in unipolar depression: Evidence and theory. *Psychological Bulletin, 101,* 259–282.

Nolen-Hoeksema, Susan. (1994). *Rumination in response to depression.* Paper presented at the 102nd annual convention of the American Psychological Association, Los Angeles, CA.

Nordheimer, Jon. (1991, August 14). When a fellow needs a friend, not just a buddy. *New York Times,* pp. C1, C8.

Norwood, Robin. (1985). *Women who love too much: When you keep wishing and hoping he'll change.* New York: Pocket Books.

Oliver, Mary Beth; & Hyde, Janet Shibley. (1993). Gender differences in sexuality: A meta-analysis. *Psychological Bulletin, 114,* 29–51.

Olson, Cheryl B. (1994, August). *Hostile environment: Gender, self-esteem and perception of sexual harassment.* Paper presented at the 102nd annual convention of the American Psychological Association, Los Angeles, CA.

O'Neil, James M. (1981). Patterns of gender role conflict and strain: Sexism and fear of femininity in men's lives. *Personnel and Guidance Journal, 60,* 203–210.

Orlofsky, Jacob L.; & O'Heron, Connie A. (1987). Stereotypic and nonstereotypic sex role trait and behavior orientations: Implications for personal adjustment. *Journal of Personality and Social Psychology, 52,* 1034–1042.

Ornstein, Robert. (1972). *The psychology of consciousness.* San Francisco: Freeman.

Osgood, D. Wayne; O'Malley, Patrick M.; Bachman, Jerald G.; Johnston, Lloyd D. (1989). Time trends and age trends in arrests and self-reported illegal behavior. *Criminology, 27,* 389–417.

Owen, Crystal L.; & Todor, William D. (1993). Attitudes toward women as managers: Still the same. *Business Horizons, 36*(2), 12–16.

Paludi, Michele A. (1984). Psychometric properties and underlying assumptions of four objective measures of fear of success. *Sex Roles, 10,* 765–781.

Parish, Thomas S.; & Powell, Merton E. (1980). A comparison of adult women's and men's ascriptions of negative traits to the same and opposite sex. *Sex Roles, 6,* 457–462.

Parlee, Mary Brown. (1973). The premenstrual syndrome. *Psychological Bulletin, 83,* 454–465.

Pasman, Larry; & Thompson, J. Kevin. (1988). Body image and eating disturbances in obligatory runners, obligatory weightlifters, and sedentary individuals. *International Journal of Eating Disorders, 7,* 759–769.

Pearson, Judy C.; & West, Richard. (1991). An initial investigation of the effects of gender on student questions in the classroom: Developing a descriptive base. *Communication Education, 40,* 22–32.

Pennebaker, James W. (1982). *The psychology of physical symptoms.* New York: Springer-Verlag.

Peplau, Letitia Anne; & Campbell, Susan Miller. (1989). The balance of power in dating and marriage. In Jo Freeman (Ed.), *Women: A feminist perspective* (4th ed.) (pp. 121–137). Mountain View, CA: Mayfield.

Peplau, Letitia Anne; Cochran, Susan; Rook, Karen; & Padesky, Christine. (1978). Loving women: Attachment and autonomy in lesbian relationships. *Journal of Social Issues, 34*(3), 7–27.

Peplau, Letitia Anne; & Conrad, Eva. (1989). Beyond nonsexist research: The perils of feminist methods in psychology. *Psychology of Women Quarterly, 13,* 379–400.

Peplau, Letitia Anne; & Gordon, Steven L. (1985). Women and men in love: Gender differences in close heterosexual relationships. In Virginia E. O'Leary, Rhoda Kesler Unger, & Barbara Strudler Wallston (Eds.), *Women, gender, and social psychology* (pp. 257–291). Hillsdale, NJ: Erlbaum.

Peplau, Letitia Anne; Hill, Charles T.; & Rubin, Zick. (1993). Sex role attitudes in dating and marriage: A 15-year follow-up of the Boston couples study. *Journal of Social Issues, 49*(3), 31–52.

Perls, Fritz S. (1969). *Gestalt therapy verbatim.* Lafayette, CA: Real People Press.

Perry, David G.; Perry, Louise C.; & Weiss, Robert J. (1989). Sex differences in the consequences that children anticipate for aggression. *Developmental Psychology, 25,* 312–319.

Phillips, Roger D.; & Gilroy, Faith D. (1985). Sex-role stereotypes and clinical judgments of mental health: The Brovermans' findings reexamined. *Sex Roles, 12,* 179–193.

Pickhardt, Irene. (1983, December). Sexist piglets: Studies show that sex-stereotyping is part of childhood. *Parents' Magazine,* pp. 32–37.

Piirto, Jane. (1991). Why are there so few? (Creative women: Visual artists, mathematicians, musicians). *Roeper Review, 13,* 142–147.

Pinel, John P. J. (1993). *Biopsychology* (2nd ed.). Boston: Allyn and Bacon.

Pittman, Frank. (1992, January/February). Why the men's movement isn't so funny. *Psychology Today,* p. 84.

Plante, Thomas G.; & Rodin, Judith. (1990). Physical fitness and enhanced psychological health. *Current Psychology Research and Reviews, 9,* 3–24.

Pleck, Joseph H. (1981a). *The myth of masculinity.* Cambridge, MA: MIT Press.

Pleck, Joseph H. (1981b, September). Prisoners of manliness. *Psychology Today,* pp. 68–79.

Pleck, Joseph H. (1984). The theory of male sex role identity: Its rise and fall, 1936 to the present. In Miriam Lewin (Ed.), *In the shadow of the past: Psychology portrays the sexes* (pp. 205–225). New York: Columbia University Press.

Pleck, Joseph H.; Sonenstein, Freya L.; & Ku, Leighton C. (1993). Masculinity ideology: Its impact on adolescent males' heterosexual relationships. *Journal of Social Issues, 49*(3), 11–29.

Pliner, Patricia; & Chaiken, Shelly. (1990). Eating, social motives, and self-presentation in women and men. *Journal of Experimental Social Psychology, 26,* 240–254.

Pliner, Patricia; Chaiken, Shelly; & Flett, Gordon L. (1990). Gender differences in concern with body weight and physical appearance over the life span. *Personality and Social Psychology Bulletin, 16,* 263–273.

Plutchik, Robert. (1984). Emotions: A general psychoevolutionary theory. In Klaus R. Scherer & Paul Ekman (Eds.), *Approaches to emotion* (pp. 197–219). Hillsdale, NJ: Erlbaum.

Poest, Catherine A.; Williams, Jean R.; Witt, David D.; & Atwood, Mary E. (1989). Physical activity patterns of preschool children. *Early Childhood Research Quarterly, 4,* 367–376.

Polivy, Janet; & Herman, C. Peter. (1983). *Breaking the diet habit: The natural weight alternative.* New York: Basic Books.

Polivy, Janet; & Herman, C. Peter. (1985). Dieting and binging: A causal analysis. *American Psychologist, 40,* 193–201.

Polivy, Janet; & Thomsen, Linda. (1988). Dieting and other eating disorders. In Elaine A. Blechman & Kelly D. Brownell (Eds.), *Handbook of behavioral medicine for women* (pp. 345–355). New York: Pergamon Press.

Pollitt, Katha. (1992, December 28). Are women morally superior to men? *Nation,* pp. 799–807.

Pope, Kenneth S. (1988). How clients are harmed by sexual contact with mental health profesionals: The syndrome and its prevalence. *Journal of Counseling and Development, 67,* 222–226.

Ptacek, J. T.; Smith, Ronald E.; & Zanas, John. (1992). Gender, appraisal, and coping: A longitudinal analysis. *Journal of Personality, 60,* 747–770.

Purifoy, Frances E.; & Koopmans, Lambert H. (1979). Androstenedione, testosterone, and free testosterone concentration in women of various occupations. *Social Biology, 26,* 179–188.

Quinn, Susan. (1987). *A mind of her own: The life of Karen Horney.* New York: Summit Books.

Ragins, Belle Rose; & Sundstrom, Eric. (1989). Gender and power in organizations: A longitudinal perspective. *Psychological Bulletin, 105,* 51–88.

Raisman, Geoffrey; & Field, Pauline M. (1971). Sexual dimorphism in the preoptic area of the rat. *Science, 173,* 731–733.

Rawlings, Edna I. (1993). Reflections on "Twenty years of feminist counseling and therapy." *Counseling Psychologist, 21,* 88–91.

Ray, William J. (1993). *Methods toward a science of behavior and experience* (4th ed.). Belmont, CA: Wadsworth.

Raymond, Cindy L.; & Benbow, Camilla Persson. (1989). Educational encouragement by parents: Its relationship to precocity and gender. *Gifted Child Quarterly, 33,* 144–151.

Redman, Selina; Webb, Gloria R.; Hennrikus, Deborah J.; Gordon, Jill J.; & Sanson-Fisher, Robert W. (1991). The effects of gender upon diagnosis of psychological disturbance. *Journal of Behavioral Medicine, 14,* 527–540.

Regier, Darrel A.; Narrow, William E.; & Rae, Donald S. (1990). The epidemiology of anxiety disorders: The Epidemiologic Catchment Area (ECA) experience. *Journal of Psychiatric Research, 24* (Suppl. 2), 3–14.

Reid, Helen M.; & Fine, Gary Alan. (1992). Self-disclosure in men's friendships: Variations associated with intimate relations. In Peter M. Nardi (Ed.), *Men's friendships* (pp. 132–152). Newbury Park, CA: Sage.

Rejskind, F. Gillian; Rapagna, Socrates O.; & Gold, Dolores. (1992). Gender differences in children's divergent thinking. *Creativity Research Journal, 5,* 165–174.

Renzetti, Claire M.; & Curran, Daniel J. (1992). *Women, men, and society* (2nd ed.). Boston: Allyn and Bacon.

Resnick, Heidi S.; Kilpatrick, Dean G.; Best, Connie L.; & Kramer, Teresa L. (1992). Vulnerability-stress factors in development of posttraumatic stress disorder. *Journal of Nervous and Mental Disease, 180,* 424–430.

Resnick, Heidi S.; Kilpatrick, Dean G.; Dansky, Bonnie S.; Saunders, Benjamin E.; & Best, Connie L. (1993). Prevalence of victim trauma and posttraumatic stress disorder in a representative national sample of women, *Journal of Consulting and Clinical Psychology, 61,* 984–991.

Riessman, Catherine Kohler. (1990). *Divorce talk: Women and men make sense of personal relationships.* New Brunswick: Rutgers University Press.

Riger, Stephanie. (1991). Gender dilemmas in sexual harassment policies and procedures. *American Psychologist, 46,* 497–505.

Riger, Stephanie. (1992). Epistemological debates, feminist voices: Science, social values, and the study of women. *American Psychologist, 47,* 730–740.

Risman, Barbara J. (1989). Can men "mother"? Life as a single father. In Barbara J. Risman & Pepper Schwartz (Eds.), *Gender in intimate relationships: A microstructural approach* (pp. 155–164). Belmont, CA: Wadsworth.

Roberts, Tomi-Ann. (1991). Gender and the influence of evaluations on self-assessments in achievement settings. *Psychological Bulletin, 109,* 297–308.

Roberts, Tomi-Ann; & Nolen-Hoeksema, Susan. (1994). Gender comparisons in responsiveness to others' evelutions in achievement settings. *Psychology of Women Quarterly, 18,* 221–240.

Robertson, John; & Fitzgerald, Louise F. (1990). The (mis)treatment of men: Effects of client gender role and life-style on diagnosis and attribution of pathology. *Journal of Counseling Psychology, 37,* 3–9.

Robertson, John; & Fitzgerald, Louise F. (1992). Overcoming the masculine mystique: Preferences for alternative form of assistance among men who avoid counseling. *Journal of Counseling Psychology, 39,* 240–246.

Robinson, David. (1979). *Talking out of alcoholism: The self-help process of Alcoholics Anonymous.* Baltimore: University Park Press.

Rodin, Judith. (1991). Foreword. In Marianne Frankenhaeuser, Ulf Lundberg, & Margaret Chesney (Eds.), *Women, work, and health: Stress and opportunities* (pp. vii-xi). New York: Plenum Press.

Rodin, Judith; & Ickovics, Jeannette R. (1990). Women's health: Review and research agenda as we approach the 21st century. *American Psychologist, 45,* 1018–1034.

Rodin, Judith; Silberstein, Lisa; & Striegel-Moore, Ruth. (1985). Women and weight: A normative discontent. In Theo B. Sonderegger (Ed.), *Nebraska symposium on motivation 1984: Psychology and gender* (Vol. 32) (pp. 267–307). Lincoln: University of Nebraska Press.

Roehling, Patricia V.; Koelbel, Nikole; & Rutgers, Christina. (1994, August). *Codependence: Pathologizing femininity?* Paper presented at the 102nd annual convention of the American Psychological Association, Los Angeles, CA.

Rogers, Carl R. (1951). *Client-centered therapy: Its current practice, implications, and theory.* Boston: Houghton Mifflin.

Rogers, Carl R. (1961). *On becoming a person: A therapist's view of psychotherapy.* Boston: Houghton Mifflin.

Rogers, Carl R. (1980). *A way of being.* Boston: Houghton Mifflin.

Rolls, Barbara J.; Fedoroff, Ingrid C.; & Guthrie, Joanne F. (1991). Gender differences in eating behavior and body weight regulation. *Health Psychology, 10,* 133–142.

Ronan, Colin A. (1982). *Science: Its history and development among the world's cultures.* New York: Facts On File Publications.

Roscoe, Bruce; Diana, Mark S.; & Brooks, Richard H., II. (1987). Early, middle, and late adolescents' views on dating and factors influencing partner selection. *Adolescence, 22,* 59–68.

Roscoe, Bruce; Kennedy, Donna; & Pope, Tony. (1987). Adolescents' views of intimacy: Distinguishing intimate from nonintimate relationships. *Adolescence, 22,* 511–516.

Rose, Suzanna; & Frieze, Irene Hanson. (1993). Young singles' contemporary dating scripts. *Sex Roles, 28,* 499–509.

Rosenfield, David; & Stephan, Walter G. (1978). Sex differences in attributions for sex-typed tasks. *Journal of Personality, 46,* 244–259.

Rosenfield, Sarah. (1982). Sex roles and societal reactions to mental illness: The labeling of "deviant deviance." *Journal of Health and Social Behavior, 23,* 18–24.

Rosenfield, Sarah. (1989). The effects of women's employment: Personal control and sex differences in mental health. *Journal of Health and Social Behavior, 30,* 77–91.

Rosenfield, Sarah. (1992). The costs of sharing: Wives' employment and husbands' mental health. *Journal of Health and Social Behavior, 33,* 213–225.

Rosenkrantz, Paul; Vogel, Susan; Bee, Helen; Broverman, Inge; & Broverman, Donald M. (1968). Sex-role stereotypes and self-concepts in college students. *Journal of Consulting and Clinical Psychology, 32,* 287–295.

Rossi, Alice. (1977). A biosocial perspective on parenting. *Daedalus, 106*(2), 1–31.

Rozen, Leah. (1990, May 28). Raging hormones: The unofficial PMS survival guide. *People Weekly,* pp. 29–30.

Rubin, Linda J.; & Borgers, Sherry B. (1990). Sexual harassment in universities during the 1980s. *Sex Roles, 23,* 397–411.

Rubin, Robert T.; Reinisch, June M.; & Haskett, Roger F. (1981). Postnatal gonadal steroid effects on human behavior. *Science, 211,* 1318–1324.

Russell, Diana E. H. (1986). *The secret trauma: Incest in the lives of girls and women.* New York: Basic Books.

Russell, James A. (1991). Culture and the categorization of emotions. *Psychological Bulletin, 110,* 426–450.

Russell, James A. (1994). Is there universal recognition of emotion from facial expression: A review of the cross-cultural studies. *Psychological Bulletin, 115,* 102–141.

Russo, Nancy Felipe. (1990). Overview: Forging research priorities for women's mental health. *American Psychologist, 45,* 368–373.

Saal, Frank E.; Johnson, Catherine B.; & Weber, Nancy. (1989). Friendly or sexy? It may depend on whom you ask. *Psychology of Women Quarterly, 13,* 263–276.

Sadker, David; & Sadker, Myra. (1985). The treatment of sex equity in teacher education. In Susan S. Klein (Ed.), *Handbook for achieving sex equity through education* (pp. 145–161). Baltimore: Johns Hopkins University Press.

Sadker, Myra P.; & Sadker, David M. (1980). Sexism in teacher-education texts. *Harvard Educational Review, 50,* 36–46.

Sadker, Myra; Sadker, David; & Klein, Susan S. (1986). Abolishing misperceptions about sex equity in education. *Theory into Practice, 25,* 219–226.

Sadker, Myra; Sadker, David; & Steindam, Sharon. (1989). Gender equity and educational reform. *Educational Leadership, 46,* 44–47.

Saltzman, Amy. (1991, June 17). Trouble at the top. *U.S. News & World Report,* pp. 40–48.

Santrock, John W. (1993). *Adolescence: An introduction* (5th ed.). Madison, WI: Brown & Benchmark.

Sarason, Irwin G.; & Sarason, Barbara R. (1993). *Abnormal psychology: The problem of maladaptive behavior* (7th ed.). Englewood Cliffs, NJ: Prentice Hall.

Savage, Robert M.; & Gouvier, W. Drew. (1992). Rey Auditory-Verbal Learning Test: The efects of age and gender, and norms for delayed recall and story recognition trials. *Archives of Clinical Neuropsychology, 7,* 407–414.

Schachter, Stanley; & Singer, Jerome E. (1962). Cognitive, social, and psychological determinants of emotional state. *Psychological Review, 69,* 379–399.

Scheibe, Gabriele; & Albus, Margot. (1992). Age at onset, precipitating events, sex distribution, and co-occurrence of anxiety disorders. *Psychopathology, 25,* 11–18.

Scher, Murray. (1981). Men in hiding: A challenge for the counselor. *Personnel and Guidance Journal, 60,* 199–202.

Scherer, Klaus R.; Wallbott, Harald G.; & Summerfield, Angela B. (Eds.). (1986). *Experiencing emotion: A cross-cultural study.* Cambridge, England: Cambridge University Press.

Schneer, Joy A.; & Reitman, Freida. (1990). Effects of employment gaps on the careers of M.B.A.'s: More damaging for men than for women? *Academy of Management Journal, 33,* 391–406.

Schneider, Beth F. (1987). Graduate women, sexual harassment, and university policy. *Journal of Higher Education, 58,* 46–65.

Schofield, Janet Ward. (1981). Complementary and conflicting identities: Images and interaction in an interracial school. In Steven R. Asher & John M. Gottman (Eds.), *The development of children's friendships* (pp. 53–90). Cambridge, England: Cambridge University Press.

Schratz, Marjorie M. (1978). A developmental investigation of sex differences in spatial (visual-analytic) and mathematical skills in three ethnic groups. *Development Psychology, 14,* 263–267.

Schultz, Duane P.; & Schultz, Sidney Ellen. (1992). *A history of modern psychology* (5th ed.). Fort Worth: Harcourt Brace Jovanovich.

Schwartz, Steven. (1986). *Classic studies in psychology.* Palo Alto, CA: Mayfield.

Scully, Diana. (1990). *Understanding sexual violence: A study of convicted rapists.* London: HarperCollins Academic.

Sedney, Mary A. (1987). Development of androgyny: Parental influences. *Psychology of Women Quarterly, 11,* 311–326.

Segal, Julius; & Segal, Zelda. (1993, May). What five-year-olds think about sex: And when and how to give them the answers that they need to hear. *Parents' Magazine,* pp. 130–132.

Segal, Naomi. (1988). Freud and the question of women. In Edward Timms & Naomi Segal (Eds.), *Freud in exile: Psychoanalysis and its vicissitudes* (pp. 241–253). New Haven, CT: Yale University Press.

Seligmann, Jean; & Gelman, David. (1993, March 15). Is it sadness or madness? Psychiatrists clash over how to classify PMS. *Newsweek,* p. 66.

Sells, Lucy W. (1980). The mathematics filter and the education of women and minorities. In Lynn H. Fox, Linda Brody, & Dianne Tobin (Eds.), *Women and the mathematical mystique* (pp. 66–75). Baltimore: Johns Hopkins University Press.

Sharabany, Ruth; Gershoni, Ruth; & Hofman, John E. (1981). Girlfriend, boyfriend: Age and sex differences in intimate friendship. *Developmental Psychology, 17,* 800–808.

Sharps, Matthew J.; Welton, Angela L.; & Price, Jana L. (1993). Gender and task in the determination of spatial cognitive performance. *Psychology of Women Quarterly, 17,* 71–83.

Shaywitz, Sally E.; Shaywitz, Bennett A.; Fletcher, Jack M.; & Escobar, Michael D. (1990, August

22–29). Prevalence of reading disability in boys and girls. Results of the Connecticut Longitudinal Study. *Journal of the American Medical Association, 264,* 998–1002.

Sherif, Carolyn W. (1982). Needed concepts in the study of gender identity. *Psychology of Women Quarterly, 6,* 375–398.

Sherman, Julia. (1971). *On the psychology of women: A survey of empirical studies.* Springfield, IL: Charles C. Thomas.

Sherman, Julia. (1978). *Sex-related cognitive differences: An essay on theory and evidence.* Springfield, IL: Charles C. Thomas.

Shields, Stephanie A. (1975a). Functionalism, Darwinism, and the psychology of women: A study in social myth. *American Psychologist, 30,* 739–754.

Shields, Stephanie A. (1975b). Ms. Pilgrim's progress: The contributions of Leta Stetter Hollingworth to the psychology of women. *American Psychologist, 30,* 852–857.

Shields, Stephanie A. (1984). "To pet, coddle, and 'do for'": Caretaking and the concept of maternal instinct. In Miriam Lewin (Ed.), *In the shadow of the past: Psychology portrays the sexes* (pp. 256–273). New York: Columbia University Press.

Shields, Stephanie A. (1987). Women, men, and the dilemma of emotion. In Phillip Shaver & Clyde Hendrick (Eds.), *Sex and gender* (p. 229–250). Newbury Park, CA: Sage.

Shields, Stephanie A. (1994, August). *Practicing social constructionism—Confessions of a feminist empiricist.* Paper presented at the 102nd annual convention of the American Psychological Association, Los Angeles, CA.

Shields, Stephanie A.; & Cooper, Pamela E. (1983). Stereotypes of traditional and nontraditional childbearing roles. *Sex Roles, 9,* 363–376.

Sibisi, Charles D. (1990). Sex differences in the age of onset of bipolar affective illness. *British Journal of Psychiatry, 156,* 842–845.

Silverstein, Brett; Carpman, Shari; Perlick, Deborah; & Perdue, Lauren. (1990). Nontraditional sex role aspriations, gender identity conflict, and disordered eating among college women. *Sex Roles, 23,* 687–695.

Silverstein, Brett; Perdue, Lauren; Wolk, Cordulla; & Pizzolo, Cecelia. (1988). Bingeing, purging, and estimates of parental attitudes regarding female achievement. *Sex Roles, 19,* 723–733.

Silverstein, Louise B. (1993). Primate research, family politics, and social policy: Transforming "cads" into "dads." *Journal of Family Psychology, 7,* 267–282.

Singletary, Donald. (1985, May). You new women want it all! *Essence,* pp. 67–68, 114–115.

Skolnick, Andrew A. (1992). Women's health specialty, other issues on agenda of "Reframing" conference. *Journal of the American Medical Association, 268,* 1813–1814.

Skovholt, Thomas M. (1978). Feminism and men's lives. *Counseling Psychologist, 7*(4), 3–10.

Slade, Pauline. (1984). Premenstrual emotional changes in normal women: Fact or fiction? *Journal of Psychosomatic Research, 28,* 1–7.

Sleek, Scott. (1994, January). Girls who've been molested can later become molesters. *APA Monitor,* pp. 34–35.

Snodgrass, Sara E. (1985). Women's intuition: The effect of subordinate role on interpersonal sensitivity. *Journal of Personality and Social Psychology, 49,* 146–155.

Snodgrass, Sara E. (1992). Further effects of role versus gender on interpersonal sensitivity. *Journal of Personality and Social Psychology, 62,* 154–158.

Solomon, Alison. (1992). Clinical diagnosis among diverse populations: A multicultural perspective. *Families in Society, 73,* 371–377.

Spence, Janet T. (1985). Gender identity and its implications for the concepts of masculinity and femininity. In Theo B. Sonderegger (Ed.), *Nebraska symposium on motivation, 1984: Psychology and gender* (Vol. 32) (pp. 59–95). Lincoln: University of Nebraska Press.

Spence, Janet T.; & Helmreich, Robert. (1978). *Masculinity and femininity: The psychological dimensions, correlates, and antecedents.* Austin: University of Texas Press.

Spence, Janet T.; Helmreich, Robert; & Stapp, Joy. (1974). The Personal Attributes Questionnaire: A measure of sex-role stereotypes and masculinity-femininity. *JSAS Catalog of Selected Documents in Psychology, 4,* 43 (Ms. no. 617).

Sprague, Joey; & Quadagno, David. (1989). Gender and sexual motivation; An exploration of two assumptions. *Journal of Psychology and Human Sexuality, 2,* 57–76.

Springer, Sally P.; & Deutsch, Georg. (1989). *Left brain, right brain* (3rd ed.). New York: Freeman.

Sroufe, L. Alan; Bennett, Christopher; Englund, Michelle; & Urban, Joan. (1993). The significance of gender boundaries in preadolescence: Contemporary correlates and antecedents of boundary violation and maintenance. *Child Development, 64,* 455–466.

Stake, Jayne E.; & Lauer, Monica L. (1987). The consequences of being overweight: A controlled study of gender differences. *Sex Roles, 17,* 31–47.

Stangor, Charles; & Ruble, Diane N. (1987). Development of gender role knowledge and gender constancy. In Lynn S. Liben & Margaret L. Signorella (Eds.), *Children's gender schemata* (pp. 5–22). San Francisco: Jossey-Bass.

Stark, Ellen. (1989, May). Teen sex: Not for love. *Psychology Today,* pp. 10–12.

Steil, Janice M. (1989). Marital relationships and mental health: The psychic costs of equality. In Jo Freeman (Ed.), *Women: A feminist perspective* (pp. 138–148). Mountain View, CA: Mayfield.

Steinberg, Karen K., Thacker, Stephen B., Smith, Jay, Stroup, Donna F.; Zack, Matthew M.; Flanders, Dana; & Berkelmen, Ruth L. (1991). A meta-analysis of the effect of estrogen replacement therapy on the risk of breast cancer. *Journal of the American Medical Association, 265,* 1985–1990.

Steingart, Richard M.; Packer, Milton; Hamm, Peggy; Coglianese, Mary Ellen; Gersh, Bernard; Geltman, Edward M.; Sollano, Josephie; Katz, Stanley; Moyé, Lem; Basta, Lofty L.; Lewis, Sandra J.; Gottlieb, Stephen S.; Bernstein, Victoria; McEwan, Patricia; Jacobson, Kirk, Brown, Edward J.; Kukin, Marrick L.; Kantrowitz, Niki E.; & Pfeffer, Marc A. (1991). Sex differences in the management of coronary artery disease. *New England Journal of Medicine, 325,* 226–230.

Stephenson, P. Susan; & Walker, Gillian A. (1979). The psychiatrist-woman patient relationship. *Canadian Journal of Psychiatry, 24,* 5–16.

Sternberg, Robert J. (1986). A triangular theory of love. *Psychological Review, 93,* 119–135.

Sternberg, Robert J. (1987). Liking versus loving: A comparative evaluation of theories. *Psychological Bulletin, 102,* 331–345.

Straus, Murray A.; & Gelles, Richard J. (1986). Societal change and change in family violence from 1975 to 1985 as revealed by two national surveys. *Journal of Marriage and the Family, 48,* 465–479.

Straus, Murray A.; Gelles, Richard J.; & Steinmetz, Suzanne K. (1980). *Behind closed doors: Violence in the American family.* Garden City, NY: Anchor.

Strickland, Bonnie R. (1988). Sex-related differences in health and illness. *Psychology of Women Quarterly, 12,* 381–399.

Stroh, Linda K.; Brett, Jeanne M.; & Reilly, Anne H. (1992). All the right stuff: A comparison of female and male managers' career progression. *Journal of Applied Psychology, 77,* 251–260.

Stromquist, Nelly P. (1991). *Daring to be different: The choice of nonconventional fields of study by international women students.* New York: Institute of International Education.

Stumpf, Heinrich. (1993). Performance factors and gender-related differences in spatial ability: Another assessment. *Memory & Cognition, 21,* 828–836.

Swaab, D. F.; & Fliers, E. (1985). A sexually dimorphic nucleus in the human brain. *Science, 228,* 1112–1115.

Swain, Scott O. (1992). Men's friendships with women: Intimacy, sexual boundaries, and the informant role. In Peter M. Nardi (Ed.), *Men's friendships* (pp. 153–171). Newbury Park, CA: Sage.

Swim, Janet K. (1994). Perceived versus meta-analytic effect sizes: An assessment of the accuracy of gender sterotypes. *Journal of Personality and Social Psychology, 66,* 21–36.

Swim, Janet; Borgida, Eugene; Maruyama, Geoffrey; & Myers, David G. (1989). Joan McKay versus John McKay: Do gender stereotypes bias evaluations? *Psychological Bulletin, 105,* 409–429.

Tannen, Deborah. (1990). *You just don't understand: Women and men in conversation.* New York: William Morrow.

Tavris, Carol. (1982). *Anger: The misunderstood emotion.* New York: Touchstone.

Tavris, Carol. (1989, December). Do codependency theories explain women's unhappiness—or exploit their insecurities? *Vogue,* pp. 220, 224–226.

Tavris, Carol. (1992). *The mismeasure of woman.* New York: Simon and Schuster.

Tavris, Carol; & Wade, Carole. (1984). *The longest war: Sex differences in perspective* (2nd ed.). New York: Harcourt Brace Jovanovich.

Terman, Lewis M.; & Merrill, Maud A. (1937). *Measuring intelligence.* Boston: Houghton Mifflin.

Theberge, Nancy. (1991). A content analysis of print media coverage of gender, women, and physical activity. *Journal of Applied Sport Psychology, 3,* 36–48.

Thomas, Jerry R.; & French, Karen E. (1985). Gender differences across age in motor performance: A meta-analysis. *Psychological Bulletin, 98,* 260–282.

Thompson, Linda; & Walker, Alexis J. (1989). Gender in families: Women and men in marriage, work, and parenthood. *Journal of Marriage and the Family, 51,* 845–871.

Thorne, Barrie. (1986). Girls and boys together. . .but mostly apart: Gender arrangements in elementary school. In Willard W. Hartup & Zick Rubin (Eds.), *Relationships and development* (pp. 167–184). Hillsdale, NJ: Erlbaum.

Tieger, Todd. (1980). On the biological basis of sex differences in aggression. *Child Development, 51,* 943–963.

Tipton, Robert M.; Camp, Charissa C.; & Hsu, Katharine. (1990). The effects of mandatory seat belt legislation on self-reported seat belt use among male and female college students. *Accident Analysis and Prevention, 22,* 543–548.

Tittle, Carol Kehr. (1986). Gender research and education. *American Psychologist, 41,* 1161–1168.

Titus, Jordan J. (1993). Gender messages in education foundations textbooks. *Journal of Teacher Education, 44,* 38–43.

Tjaden, Patricia Godeke; & Tjaden, Claus D. (1981). Differential treatment of the female felon: Myth or reality? In Marguerite O. Warren (Ed.), *Comparing female and male offenders* (pp. 73–88). Beverly Hills, CA: Sage.

Tobin-Richards, Maryse H.; Boxer, Andrew M.; & Petersen, Anne C. (1983). The psychological significance of pubertal change sex differences in perceptions of self during early adolescence. In Jeanne Brooks-Gunn & Anne C. Petersen (Eds.), *Girls at puberty: Biological and psychosocial perspectives* (pp. 127–154). New York: Plenum Press.

Tomasson, Kristinn; Kent, D.; & Coryell, W. (1991). Somatization and conversion disorders: Comorbidity and demographics at presentation. *Acta Psychiatrica Scandinavica, 84,* 288–293.

Travis, Cheryl Brown. (1988a). *Women and health psychology: Biomedical issues.* Hillsdale, NJ: Erlbaum.

Travis, Cheryl Brown. (1988b). *Women and health psychology: Mental health issues.* Hillsdale, NJ: Erlbaum.

Tucker, Don M. (1981). Lateral brain function, emotion, and conceptualization. *Psychological Bulletin, 89,* 19–46.

Ulibarri, Monica D.; Wilson, Cynthia; Grijalva, Annette; Hunt, William K.; & Seligman, Ross. (1994, August). *Acculturation and sexual behavior of Mexican-American adolescents.* Paper presented at the 102nd annual convention of the American Psychological Association, Los Angeles, CA.

Unger, Rhoda K. (1979). Toward a redefinition of sex and gender. *American Psychologist, 34,* 1085–1094.

Urberg, Katheryn A. (1979). Sex role conceptualizations in adolescents and adults. *Developmental Psychology, 15,* 90–92.

U.S. Bureau of the Census. (1975). *Historical Statistics of the United States, Colonial Times to 1970.* Washington, DC: U.S. Government Printing Office.

U.S. Bureau of the Census. (1992). *Statistical abstracts of the United States, 1992* (112th ed.). Washington, DC: U.S. Government Printing Office.

U.S. Bureau of the Census. (1993). *Statistical abstracts of the United States, 1993* (113th ed.). U.S. Department of Commerce, Bureau of the Census. Washington, DC: U.S. Government Printing Office.

U.S. Department of Health and Human Services. (1989). *Reducing the health consequences of smoking: Nicotine addiction.* A report of the Surgeon General, 1988 (DHHS Publication no. DC 88–8406). Washington, DC: U.S. Government Printing Office.

U.S. Department of Health and Human Services. (1990). *Alcohol and health: Seventh special report to the U.S. Congress* (DHHS Publication no. ADM 90–1656). Washington, DC: U.S. Government Printing Office.

U.S. Department of Justice. (1990). *Sourcebook of criminal justice statistics, 1989.* Washington, DC: U.S. Government Printing Office.

U.S. Department of Justice. (1993). *Uniform crime reports for the United States, 1992.* Washington, DC: U.S. Government Printing Office.

U.S. Department of Labor, Bureau of Labor Statistics. (1993). *Employment and earnings* (Vol. 40, no. 5). Washington, DC: U.S. Government Printing Office.

U.S. Department of Labor, Office of Information and Public Affairs. (1992, April). *Women & work.* Washington, DC: U.S. Government Printing Office.

Valdez, Jesse N. (1994, August). *Ethnic identity, sex roles, and sexual attitudes.* Paper presented ath the 102nd annual convention of the American Psychological Association, Los Angeles, CA.

Vance, Carole S. (1984). Pleasure and danger: Toward a politics of sexuality. In Carole S. Vance (Ed.), *Pleasure and danger: Exploring female sexuality* (pp. 1–27). Boston: Routledge & Kegan Paul.

Vasquez, Melba J. T.; & Kitchener, Karen Strohm. (1988). Introduction to special feature: Ethics in counseling: Sexual intimacy between counselor and client. *Journal of Counseling and Development, 67,* 214–217.

Vazquez-Nuttall, Ena; Romero-Garcia, Ivonne; & De Leon, Brunilda. (1987). Sex roles and perceptions of femininity and masculinity of Hispanic women. *Psychology of Women Quarterly, 11,* 409–425.

Verbrugge, Lois M. (1983). Multiple roles and physical health of women and men. *Journal of Health and Social Behavior, 24,* 16–30.

Verbrugge, Lois M. (1985). Gender and health: An update on hypotheses and evidence. *Journal of Health and Social Behavior, 26,* 156–182.

Verbrugge, Lois M. (1986). From sneeze to adieu: Stages of health for American men and women. *Social Science Medicine, 22,* 1195–1212.

Verbrugge, Lois M. (1989). The twain meet: Empirical explanations of sex differences in health and mortality. *Journal of Health and Social Behavior, 30,* 282–304.

Veroff, Joseph; Reuman, David; & Feld, Sheila. (1984). Motives in American men and women across the adult life span. *Developmental Psychology, 20,* 1142–1158.

Vetter, Betty. (1992). Ferment: yes; Progress: maybe; Change: slow. *Mosaic, 23*(3), 34–41.

Waber, Deborah. (1976). Sex differences in cognition: A function of maturation rate? *Science, 192,* 572–573.

Wainryb, Cecilia. (1993). The application of moral judgments to other cultures: Relativism and universality. *Child Development, 64,* 924–933.

Waldron, Ingrid. (1991). Effects of labor force participation on sex differences in mortality and morbidity. In Marianne Frankenhaeuser, Ulf Lundberg, & Margaret Chesney (Eds.), *Women, work, and health: Stress and opportunities* (pp. 17–38). New York: Plenum Press.

Walker, Betty A.; Reis, Sally M.; & Leonard, Janet S. (1992). A developmental investigation of the lives of gifted women. *Gifted Child Quarterly, 36,* 201–206.

Walker, Lenore E. A. (1989). Psychology and violence against women. *American Psychologist, 44,* 695–702.

Walker, William D.; Rowe, Robert C.; & Quinsey, Vernon L. (1993). Authoritarianism and sexual aggression. *Journal of Personality and Social Psychology, 65,* 1036–1045.

Wallston, Barbara Strudler. (1981). What are the questions in psychology of women? A feminist approach to research. *Psychology of Women Quarterly, 5,* 597–617.

Walsh, Mary Roth. (1985). Academic professional women organizing for change: The struggle in psychology. *Journal of Social Issues, 41*(4), 17–28.

Ward, L. Monique; & Wyatt, Gail Elizabeth. (1994). The effects of childhood sexual messages on African-American and White women's adolescent sexual behavior. *Psychology of Women Quarterly, 18,* 183–201.

Warr, Mark. (1985). Fear of rape among urban women. *Social Problems, 32,* 238–250.

Warren, Marguerite O. (1981). Gender comparisons in crime and delinquency. In Marguerite O. Warren (Ed.), *Comparing female and male offenders* (pp. 7–16). Beverly Hills, CA: Sage.

Waterhouse, Ruth L. (1993). "Wild women don't have the blues": A feminist critique of "person-centered" counseling and therapy. *Feminism & Psychology, 3,* 55–71.

Weisner, Thomas S.; & Wilson-Mitchell, Jane E. (1990). Nonconventional family life-styles and sex typing in six-year-olds. *Child Development, 61,* 1915–1933.

Weisstein, Naomi. (1970). "Kinde, küche, kirche" as scientific law: Psychology constructs the female. In Robin Morgan (Ed.), *Sisterhood is powerful: An anthology of writings from the women's liberation movement* (pp. 228–245). New York: Vintage Books.

Weisstein, Naomi. (1982, November). Tired of arguing about biological inferiority? *Ms.* pp. 41–46, 85.

Weitzman, Lenore. (1985). *The divorce revolution: The unexpected social and economic consequences for women and children in America.* New York: Free Press.

Wellman, Barry. (1992). Men in networks: Private communities, domestic friendships. In Peter M. Nardi (Ed.), *Men's friendships* (pp. 74–114). Newbury Park, CA: Sage.

Welter, Barbara. (1978). The cult of true womanhood: 1820–1860. In Michael Gordon (Ed.), *The American family in social-historical perspective* (2nd ed.) (pp. 313–333). New York: St. Martin's Press.

Wethington, Elaine; McLeod, Jane D.; & Kessler, Ronald C. (1987). The importance of life events for explaining sex differences in psychological distress. In Rosalind C. Barnett, Lois Biener, & Grace K. Baruch (Eds.), *Gender and stress* (pp. 144–156). New York: Free Press.

Wharton, Amy S.; & Baron, James N. (1987). So happy together? The impact of gender segregation on men at work. *American Sociological Review, 52,* 574–587.

Wharton, Amy S.; & Baron, James N. (1991). Satisfaction? The psychological impact of gender segregation on women at work. *Sociological Quarterly, 32,* 365–387.

Whatley, Mariamne H. (1990). Sex equity in sex education. *Education Digest, 55*(5), 46–49.

Wheeler, Ladd; Reis, Harry; & Nezlek, John. (1983). Loneliness, social interaction, and sex roles. *Journal of Personality and Social Psychology, 45,* 943–953.

Whiting, Beatrice Blyth; & Edwards, Carolyn Pope. (1988). *Children of different worlds: The formation of social behavior.* Cambridge, MA: Harvard University Press.

Whitley, Bernard E., Jr. (1988). Masculinity, femininity, and self-esteem: A multitrait-multimethod analysis. *Sex Roles, 7/8,* 419–431.

Widiger, Thomas A.; & Settle, Shirley A. (1987). Broverman et al. revisited: An artifactual sex bias. *Journal of Personality and Social Psychology, 53,* 463–469.

Wilbur, Jerry. (1987). Does mentoring breed success? *Training & Development Journal, 41*(11), 38–41.

Wiley, Mary Glenn; & Eskilson, Arlene. (1985). Speech style, gender stereotypes, and corporate success: What if women talk more like men? *Sex Roles, 12,* 993–1007.

Williams, Christine L. (1992). The glass escalator: Hidden advantages for men in the "female" professions. *Social Problems, 39,* 253–267.

Williams, David R.; Takeuchi, David T.; & Adair, Russell K. (1992). Socioeconomic status and psychiatric disorder among Blacks and Whites. *Social Forces, 71,* 179–194.

Williams, Janet B. W.; & Spitzer, Robert L. (1983). The issue of sex bias in DSM-III: A critique of "A woman's view of DSM-III" by Marcie Kaplan. *American Psychologist, 38,* 793–801.

Williams, John E.; & Best, Deborah L. (1990). *Measuring sex stereotypes: A multination study* (rev. ed.). Newbury Park, CA: Sage.

Williams, Juanita H. (1983). *Psychology of women: Behavior in a biosocial context* (2nd ed.). New York: Norton.

Wilson, Robert A. (1966). *Feminine forever.* New York: M. Evans.

Wilson, Stephan M.; & Medora, Nilufer P. (1990). Gender comparisons of college students' attitudes toward sexual behavior. *Adolescence, 25,* 615–628.

Wiseman, Claire V.; Gray, James J.; Mosimann, James E.; & Ahrens, Anthony H. (1992). Cultural expectations of thinness in women: An update. *International Journal of Eating Disorders, 11,* 85–89.

Witelson, Sandra F. (1985). The brain connection: The corpus callosum is larger in left-handers. *Science, 224,* 665–668.

Witelson, Sandra F. (1991). Sex differences in neuroanatomical changes with aging. *New England Journal of Medicine, 325,* 211–212.

Witkin, Herman A.; Mednick, Sarnoff A.; Schulsinger, Fini; Bakkestrìm, Eskild; Christiansen, Karlo O.; Goodenough, Donald. R.; Hirschhorn, Kurt, Lundesteen, Claes, Owen, David R.; Philip, John; Rubin, Donald B.; & Stocking, Martha. (1976). Criminality in XYY and XXY men. *Science, 193,* 547–555.

Wyatt, Gail E. (1985). The sexual abuse of Afro-American and White-American women in childhood. *Child Abuse and Neglect, 9,* 507–519.

Wyatt, Gail Elizabeth. (1992). The sociocultural context of African American and White American women's rape. *Journal of Social Issues, 48*(1), 77–91.

Wyatt, Gail Elizabeth. (1994). The sociocultural relevance of sex research: Challenges for the 1990s and beyond. *American Psychologist, 49,* 748–754.

Yama, Mark F.; Tovey, Stephanie L.; & Fogas, Bruce S. (1993). Childhood family environment and sexual abuse as predictors of anxiety and depression in adult women. *American Journal of Orthopsychiatry, 63,* 136–141.

Yee, Doris K.; & Eccles, Jacquelynne S. (1988). Parent perceptions and attributions for children's math achievement. *Sex Roles, 19,* 317–333.

Yoder, Janice D.; & Kahn, Arnold S. (1993). Working toward an inclusive psychology of women. *American Psychologist, 48,* 846–850.

Zajonc, R. C. (1984). On the primacy of affect. *American Psychologist, 39,* 117–123.

Zera, Deborah. (1992). Coming of age in a heterosexist world: The development of gay and lesbian adolescents. *Adolescence, 27,* 849–854.

Zimmer-Schur, Lori A.; & Newcomb, Michael D. (1994, August). *Dieting and exercise behaviors: Subscale development gender differences and depression.* Paper presented at the 102nd annual convention of the American Psychological Association, Los Angeles, CA.

Name Index

Subject Index

AA. *See* Alcoholics Anonymous
Abuse. *See* Domestic violence; Sexual molestation
Accidents, as cause of death, 345–346, 351–353
Achievement, 314–319
  definitions of, 314–315
  educational, gender differences in, 305–312
  fear of success and, 315–316, 319
  gender role changes and, 456–457
  internal vs. external explanations for, 317–319
  in Male Sex Role Identity, 171, 172
  need for, 314–315
  self-confidence and, 316–317, 319
  See also Educational achievement
Acquaintance or date rape, 219, 283–284
Acquired immunodeficiency syndrome (AIDS), 362
  homophobia and, 293
  impact on behavior of, 269–270, 456
  risk factors for, 351
Addiction to exercise, 375
Addictions, support groups for, 440–442. *See also* Substance abuse
Adolescents
  dating by, 239–241
  eating disorders in, 370
  eating patterns in, 365
  educational issues for, 305–314
  exercise patterns in, 372
  friendships among, 230, 233–234
  gender development in, 160–161
  gender stereotyping by, 160–161, 187
  health services use by, 360
  heterosexual behavior among, 281–285
  homosexual behavior among, 293–296
  physiological changes in, 50–53
  pregnancy concerns of, 284
  sexual activity by, 266, 281–285

  See also College students
Adrenal gland, in endocrine system, 44
Adrenogenital syndrome, 55
Adulthood
  gender development in, 161–162
  gender stereotyping role in, 187–188
African-Americans
  childhood aggression among, 214
  doctoral degree fields of, 312–313
  gender stereotyping and, 181–182
  marital power among, 249
  marital satisfaction among, 244
  psychiatric diagnoses and, 400, 401
  rape reporting and, 218
  risk of violence among, 351, 352
  sexuality and, 282, 284, 285
African culture
  science and, 20
  Thonga sexual practices, 290
Age
  body image concerns and, 366–367
  eating disorders and, 369
  mortality and, 341–342
Agency, as nongendered term, 35
Agentic traits, masculinity and, 191
Aggression, 208–223
  anger and, 209–211, 214, 221, 222
  cognitive intervention for, 214
  definition of, 209
  developmental differences and, 211–215, 221, 222
  display rules and, 223–224
  in Freudian theory, 115
  frustration and, 209
  gender stereotypes and, 221–222
  hormones and, 41, 63–68, 221
  as instinctive behavior, 208
  in laboratory vs. social settings, 465
  longitudinal study of, 211–213
  in Male Sex Role Identity, 172
  physical vs. social, 208–209, 214–215
  power and, 215–216
  sexual, 217–221

  social expressions of, 213–214, 215, 221
  worldview and, 214
Agoraphobia, 406, 407, 439
AIDS. *See* Acquired immunodeficiency syndrome
Alcoholics Anonymous (AA), 439, 440–441
Alcohol use
  depression and, 404
  experience of violence and, 384, 385
  gender and, 352–353, 403–404
  marital relationship and, 251
  mental disorders and, 403–404, 405
  mortality and, 352, 353
  self-help groups for, 439, 440–441
Alpha-fetoprotein, 49
Alternative medicine, gender and use of, 356
Alzheimer's patients, support groups for caretakers of, 439, 441
American Psychiatric Association
  diagnostic category controversy in, 379–381, 394
  DSM classification system, 391–393
American Psychological Association (APA), women's studies division,
Anal stage, in Freudian theory, 115, 117
Androgen insensitivity syndrome, 55–56
Androgens, 42–43, 50
Androgyny, 188, 190–191, 192
  as feminist therapy model, 431, 444
  as gender aware therapy model, 434
  as men's movement model, 444
  societal values and, 458
Anger
  aggression and, 209–211, 214, 221, 222
  differences in expression of, 195–196, 210, 221, 454–455, 467
  gender and, 210–211
  gender role and, 221
Anorexia nervosa, 368–370